art:21

Marina Abramović

Ai Weiwei

David Altmejd

El Anatsui

assume vivid astro focus

Lynda Benglis

Rackstraw Downes

Glenn Ligon

Robert Mangold

Catherine Opie

Mary Reid Kelley

Sarah Sze

Tabaimo

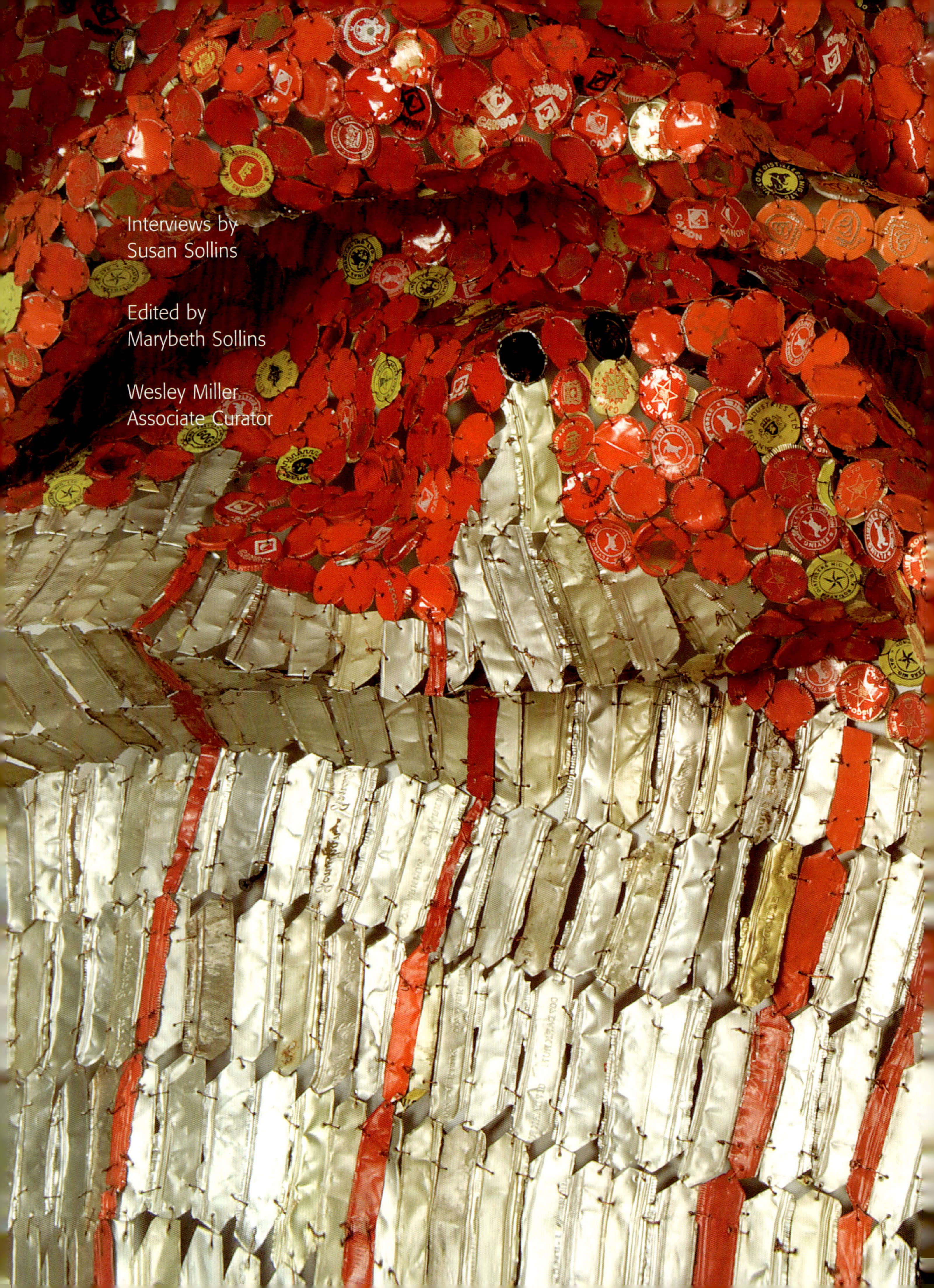

Interviews by
Susan Sollins

Edited by
Marybeth Sollins

Wesley Miller
Associate Curator

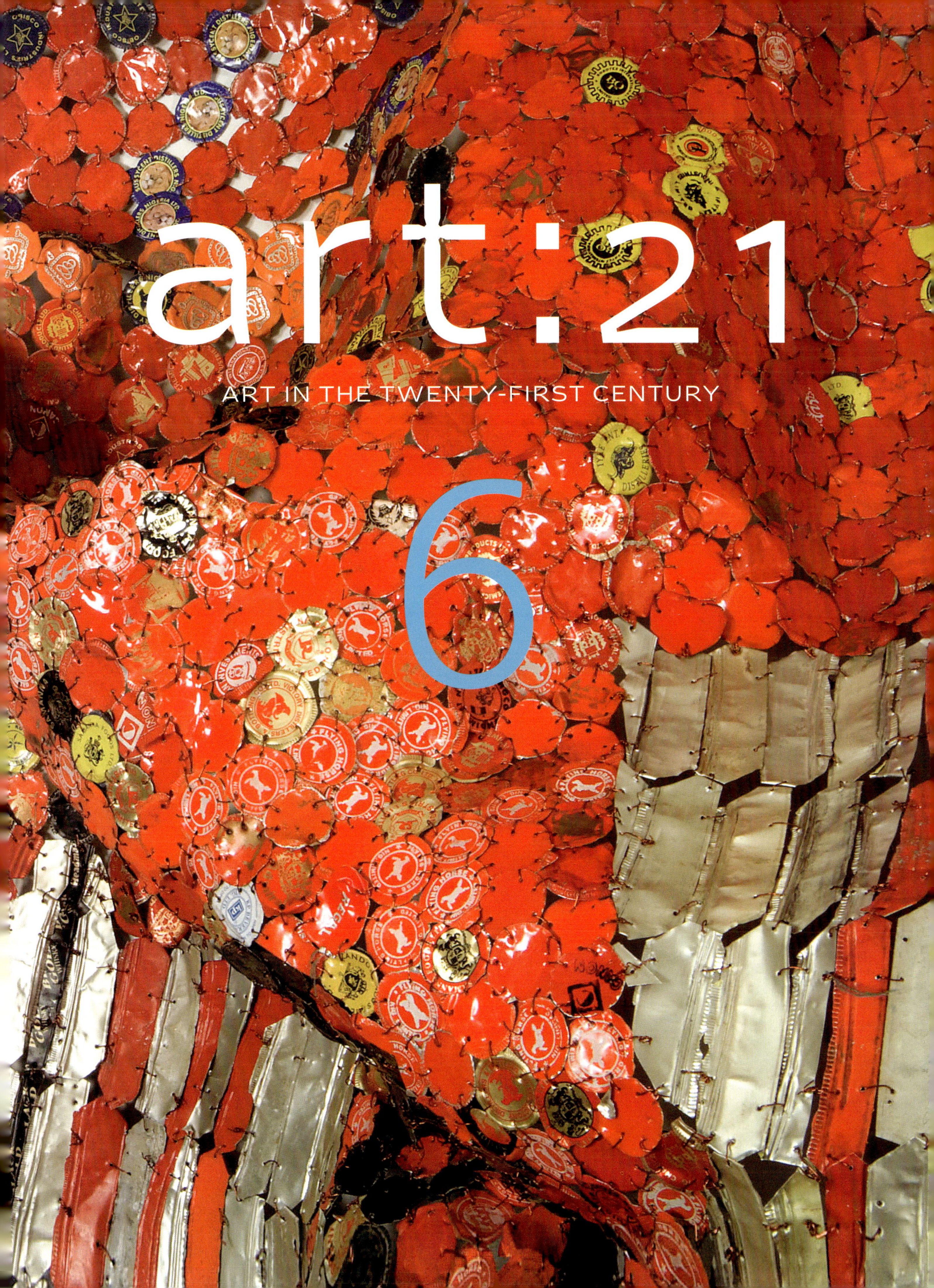
art:21
ART IN THE TWENTY-FIRST CENTURY
6

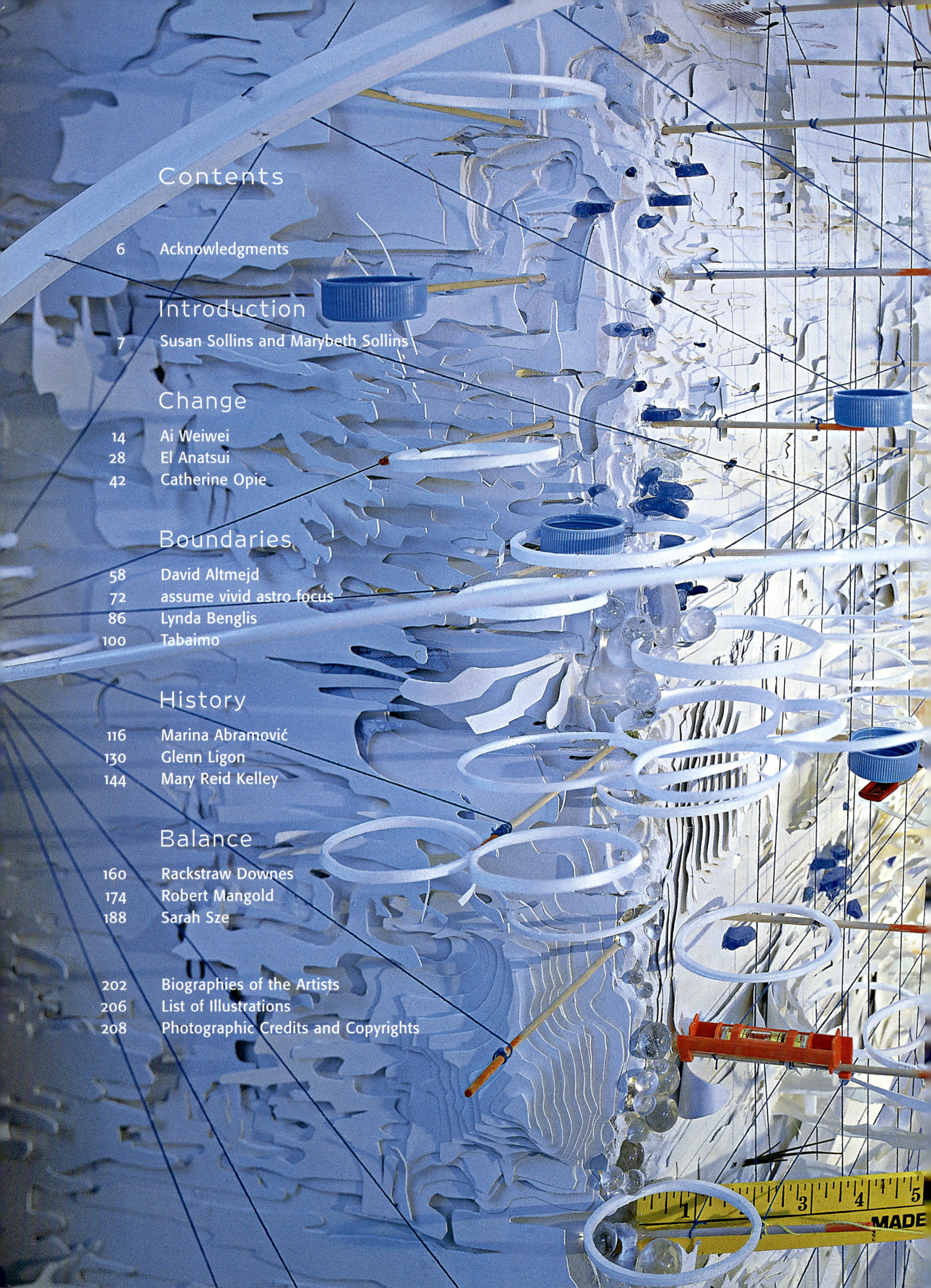

Contents

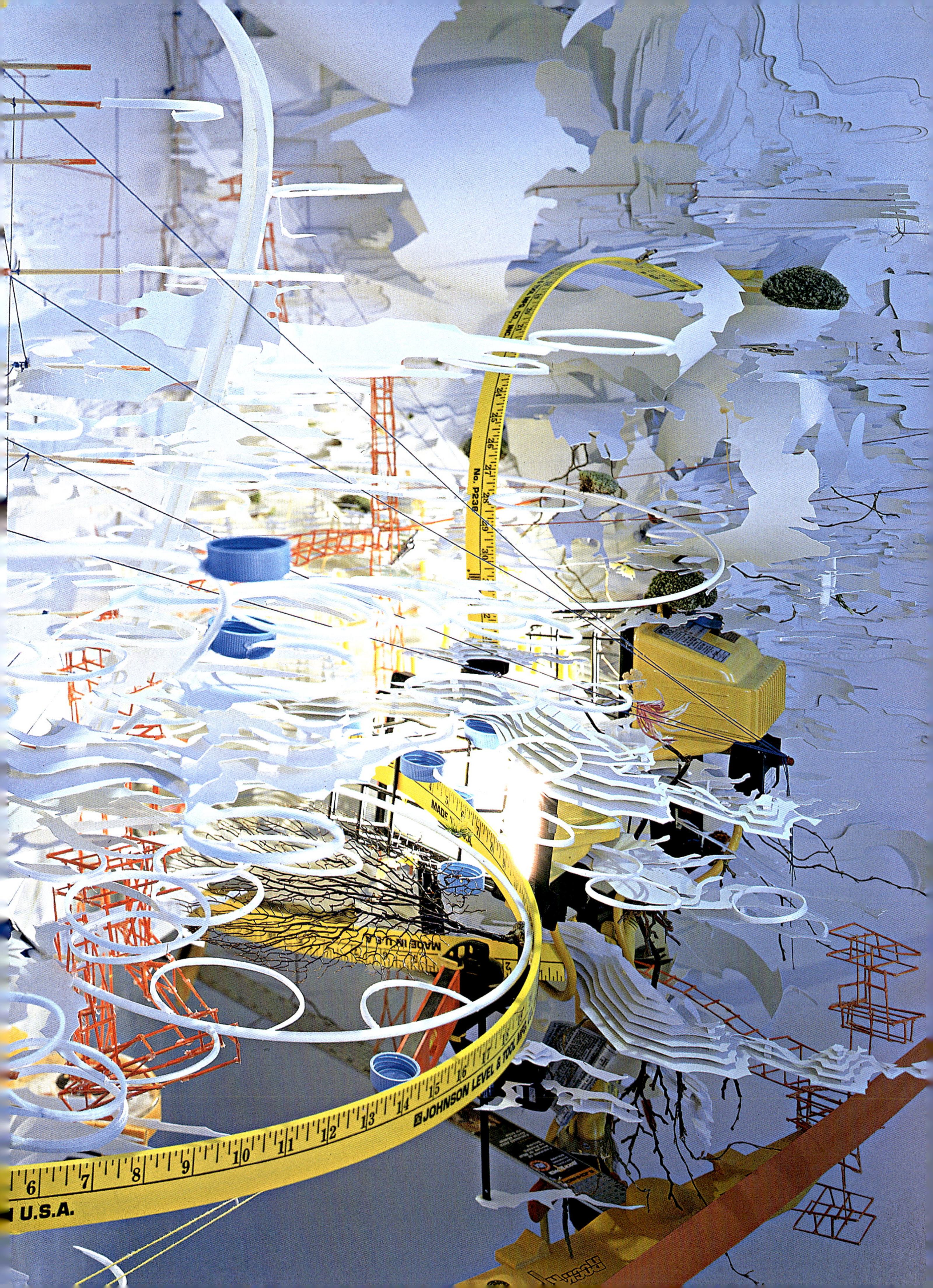
JOHNSON LEVEL & TOOL
U.S.A.

Acknowledgments

I prepare these acknowledgments with pleasure, in anticipation of this volume's publication and the broadcast of Season Six of *Art:21—Art in the Twenty-First Century*. I am grateful to Art21's extraordinary staff—Eve Moros Ortega, Wesley Miller, Nick Ravich, Diane Vivona, Jessica Hamlin, Jonathan Munar, Joe Fusaro, Ian Forster, Kaitlin Clifton Forcier, Claudine Isé, Heather Reyes, and Carrie Caroselli, along with former staff members Daniel Barrett, Marc Mayer, Kelly Shindler, and Sara Simonson—for all their contributions to Season Six. I also owe special thanks to our colleagues at PBS; consulting directors Charles Atlas and Catherine Tatge; and all who worked with Art21 in the filming, editing, and production of Season Six, including Lizzie Donahue and Mark Sutton.

For the provision of images reproduced in this volume, I thank the Marina Abramović Archives; Asia Society; AW Asia; Tanya Bonakdar Gallery; Chambers Fine Art; Cheim & Read; James Cohan Gallery; Pilar Corrias Gallery; Betty Cuningham Gallery; Fredericks & Freiser Gallery; Sean Kelly Gallery; Lisson Gallery; Museum for African Art; Pace Gallery; Parrish Art Museum; Peres Projects; Regen Projects; Andrea Rosen Gallery; Jack Shainman Gallery; Three Shadows Photography Art Centre; Susanne Vielmetter Los Angeles Projects; and the Whitney Museum of American Art. I especially acknowledge Marco Anelli, Katie Bachner, Nash Baker, Tanya Brodsky, Jessica Lin Cox, Philip Ennik, Tamsen Greene, Teneille Haggard, Jon Mason, Allison Peller, Renee Reyes, Ellen Robinson, Emily Ruotolo, Sidney Russell, Elena Soboleva, Lauren Staub, Jacqueline Tarquinio, and Art21 interns Paulina V. Ahlstrom, Don Edler, and Maren Miller, all of whom assisted in compiling information for this volume. I wish to extend special thanks to Charles Atlas for the creation of Marina Abramović's segment in New York; Wesley Miller for his work with Catherine Opie in Ohio; and Phil Tinari for his interview with Ai Weiwei in China. In addition, I thank Dahlia Fischbein, Bahron Thomas, and Alex Zustra for capturing the production stills from Art21 footage. Interview translation was provided by Hitomi Iwasaki, Justin Jesty, Keiko Koshihara, Manami Beer, Manami Fujimori, Ashley Rawlings, and Reiko Tomii; transcription was provided by Pat Casteel Transcripts and Transcript Associates, Inc. Wesley Miller worked diligently with artists and galleries to select the images for the book and, with the assistance of Kelly Shindler, attended to the many details required in a project of this magnitude.

The support and involvement of Marybeth Sollins, who created the text from my interviews with the artists, assisted me with the introduction, and edited this volume, have been invaluable. Her editorial skills, wisdom, and calm have made this book possible. To Marybeth and to Russell Hassell, the designer who has applied his magical touch and talent to create this sixth splendid Art21 publication, I extend affectionate gratitude and admiration. Once again, Russell has designed a book that mirrors Art21's spirit and philosophy.

To the artists in the series, I extend my grateful appreciation for their generous and open participation in the series and its ancillary education projects. To the entire Art21 Board of Trustees, I send heartfelt thanks for support and belief in this endeavor. In closing, I wish to acknowledge the extraordinary generosity of the individuals, foundations, corporations, and other funders of Season Six and this volume.

Susan Sollins
Executive Director & Curator
Art21, Inc.

Art21 Funders

National Endowment for the Arts
PBS
Agnes Gund
Bloomberg
The Andy Warhol Foundation for the Visual Arts
Horace W. Goldsmith Foundation
The Broad Art Foundation
Japan Foundation
Toby Devan Lewis

Introduction

Whenever I do new paintings, I think of connections—with my own work of the past and sometimes with other people's work. . . . There are always cultural connections in the work. I don't paint from subject matter. I live in the country, and I see wonderful sunlight and great cloud formations . . . but I'm never aware of any of that coming into my art in any direct way. So rather than the influence coming from nature, it comes from culture . . . from the history of art and the culture of our times.

Robert Mangold

As the premiere of another season of *Art:21—Art in the Twenty-First Century* draws near, there is a moment for reflection on the myriad words and images that comprise the vast corpus of material from which the broadcast series and this companion volume have been created. Questions abound. Will Art21's sixth season tell a new story, or will it be viewed as a thought-provoking chapter in the narrative of the preceding seasons? Do the profiles of the hundred artists and the themes under which they have been presented since 2001 unify our understanding of the decade in art? Or do they reveal the impossibility of such categorization? Inevitably, the replies to these queries—whether yes or no—demand more questions: why? why not? in what ways? Each season has certainly brought something quite new and difficult to synthesize or categorize. The answers to almost any question about Art21's investigations of contemporary art will be as varied and diverse as its worldwide audience—and yet all will hinge on viewers' experiences and perceptions of the present and its relation to the past. All of us—whether creators or viewers of art—exist within the contexts of far-reaching histories, cultures, and physical environments that stimulate, channel, and connect our creative impulses to our ways of seeing, understanding, and communicating.

Change, *Boundaries*, *History, Balance:* these words serve as chapter headings for this volume and as programmatic divisions for the broadcast series. As thematic terms they are porous and interchangeable—intended as broad signifiers of meanings that can be derived from the work of the artists treated here. As with any definitions, one can explore them in positive as well as negative terms. Change turns our thoughts to stasis; history implies both knowledge and ignorance of the past; boundaries can hold us in or keep us out; balance needs imbalance to find equilibrium, whether perfect or uneasy. These themes are intended to be expansive, not limiting—and they point towards the plurality of artists' ideas and investigations of the culture of our time.

The essence of Robert Mangold's statement, cited above, holds true for all the artists in this series. Knowledge of art history and Culture (here, perhaps, best given a capital C to denote tradition and the long view) provides food for thought for each of them, albeit in strikingly different ways. And the culture of *this* particular time—complex, replete with contradiction, conflict, a multitude of information and stimuli, and rapid change—offers a repast that cannot be rejected or denied. It simply *is* the nourishment of daily life, time, and place, of which all partake. Among the artists presented here it is perhaps Ai Weiwei who must come to mind first, as he exemplifies full engagement and active immersion in the tumult of time and place, against a cultural backdrop that has survived millennia despite countless political upheavals. On 3 April 2011, Chinese state security officials detained him in Beijing, prevented him from leaving China, and made it impossible for him to participate in already scheduled activities abroad, including the interview for this volume. Ai, an outspoken critic of Chinese political and social restrictions, was arrested, held for three months, and later charged with tax evasion. Upon release, he was prohibited from engaging in public speech. The blank space in lieu of text on pages 16 through 27 of this volume reflects the silencing of his voice. Ai makes work that speaks of immediacy, using materials of the moment—like the children's backpacks in his poignant but imperative citizen-artist's retort to the Chinese government in the aftermath of the Sichuan earthquake and deaths of thousands of school children (*Remembering*, 2009). But in *Dropping a Han Dynasty Urn* (1995), *Colored Vases* (2006), and *Template* (2007), Ai also draws upon the very long history of Chinese art for allusions, materials and actual artifacts, which he does not hesitate to bury, destroy, or recycle. He drops a Han Dynasty urn on the floor, transforms Neolithic vases with bright industrial paint, and reuses discarded doors of Ming and Qing Dynasty houses in works that comment metaphorically on the present.

For Robert Mangold, thoughtful musings on art history also trace back across centuries and cultures—from Native American ceramics and weavings displayed in his studio, to paintings by Giotto or Piero della Francesca, to references from de Chirico through Jackson Pollock, to the 'art of the moment' of his student years and, perhaps most important for him, the works of Barnett Newman. It seems that Mangold ponders and synthesizes the "very interesting stuff" that most captivates him—whether the allure of a painted image on the sculptural form of a Native American pot, the architectural space and "sense of the viewer in relation to the *zip*" of a Newman painting, or the questions and problems he continues to address in his examinations of form, as in *Ring Image C* (2008) and *Split Ring Image I* (2009). With a singularity of vision and discipline, he finds endless combinatorial and provocative potential for the expression of complex ideas in the simplest of abstract forms and lines, and the subtle uses of color.

Allusions to art of the past are abundant in the work of Marina Abramović, some of whose performance pieces resonate with imagery that stems from her experience of the Orthodox Church's traditions of ritual and iconography. "Coming from former Yugoslavia and an 'interesting' family background," she says, "in which mother and father were Communist atheists, grandmother a religious fanatic, and grandfather a saint of the Orthodox Church, was a kind of unbeatable combination, full of contradictions, from which to grow as an artist." Only look to her use of ritual objects and symbols—bones, skulls, and pentagrams in *Balkan Baroque* (1997) and *Count on Us* (2003), respectively—and to Abramović herself, suspended above the altar-like table laden with ceremonially arranged vessels in *The Kitchen I—Homage to Saint Therese* (2009). But look again and discover evidence of other aspects of Abramović's personal history, imbued with cultural referents and allusions to past and present politics and struggles, set within the frame of her quest for endurance and self-transformation.

Explore this volume and you will come to Catherine Opie's photographs, which document lives, communities, queer subculture, and the landscape of our time in America. But what are the origins of her vision? Think about painting and art history. "I have vivid memories of going to the National Portrait Gallery," says Opie. "I was probably eight or nine. . . . I really felt very good about seeing those paintings, and that's one of the reasons why I've always been in love with a kind of rich light. I think that's why people often call my work painting." To the core, Opie has formal ideas of "the way things should look," which go back to seeing those paintings early in childhood—the age at which she first picked up a camera. She speaks about her comfort in controlling framing in her photographs, the resonance of space and shapes, and her use of the tropes of a formal language in the construction of images. There is an undeniable interplay between her early and lasting responses to art history and what she looks at, thinks about, and works on every day. Think about Hans Holbein portraits; seventeenth-century Dutch landscape painting; Norman Rockwell; American genre painting; and the works of an array of FSA photographers of the 1930s and '40s. As Opie puts it, one "innately learns things" early, by looking, and that becomes one's language. Although an artist's language can change with different bodies of work, the structure remains somewhat the same. One particular body of work or another—Opie's *Portraits* series, from the early 1990s, and *Self-Portrait/Pervert* (1994)—must not limit our understanding. "I want work to be talked about in relationship to a history of American genre painting," she says. "Guess what? It looks this way because I'm creating a conversation in relationship to that history. And if you only define it by portraits that were taken early on, then you're missing the whole point of how to expand the language."

While David Altmejd also speaks about art as language, he thinks about it as process and invention rather than as conversation that builds from formal tropes. Instead, art evolves from an almost childlike fascination with objects that grow, transform, and reshape themselves, which Altmejd relates to his early interest in science and biology. Lacking the rigorous approach required to 'learn the language of science', he did not pursue its study. "I wasn't interested," he says, "in *learning a language*, but in *inventing languages*. . . . To make something new . . . and have people react to it—that's what I found fascinating." Altmejd's comments about influences on his work take us in a singularly different direction from other artists discussed here. "What has influenced me? A total atmosphere, but not necessarily something that one would be able to describe. Just a brief moment connected to a very specific sensibility: a light, a sound, random films in which there were certain very short scenes where a certain light is combined with a certain music and a certain texture. I guess something would touch me from that combination, and those were the most defining moments because they described. . . something that I connected to—and I thought, 'Oh wow, that's me.' " And, though Altmejd reveals that it is painting that he "likes best" in contemporary art, he says that it is Louise Bourgeois who "has sculpture" as he understands it today. "She was not really interested in representing the body," he says. "She was more interested in making her sculpture function like the body. Everything I do is based on that idea." Altmejd's interest lies in the *making*—concentrating every gesture in building an object that will generate meaning—as seen in *The Swarm* (2011) and *The Vessel* (2011). New work evolves from old. "I don't feel like I need to look at other people's work as much as I used to," he says. "I still do—I'm not disconnected—but I just get a lot from my own work. Every time I make a new piece, I get new ideas. I make new mistakes; I solve them."

Although Robert Mangold is emphatic that surroundings or 'nature' do not influence his work, we must acknowledge the natural world as an influential component of culture for others. There can be no doubt that Lynda Benglis's early experience of the watery world of Louisiana's bayous and marshes, and the lush Mississippi Delta region that teemed with snakes, birds, and fish during her childhood, has had significant bearing on the extraordinary energy and 'flow' of her work. Likewise, the effect of her early travels to spend long periods of time with her family in the Greek islands, surrounded by relics of ancient Greece and immersed in a sensorium of sea, sunlight, wind, sea creatures, and insect-life. "All artists," says Benglis, "are in a situation that patterns their early memories." Describing her discovery of scuba diving, she speaks of feeling "boundless energy, without gravity, floating, where there was no up and down, no edge." Using similar language, she describes her work. "There's a body feeling about one's energy . . . a contained nutshell of a painting that becomes a kind of flowering or a bursting of energy that implodes or explodes," that relates to "an architecture of gestures, how to make a painting physically, how to present it so that they're coming together." When creating *Phantom* (1971), she says, she thought about the phosphorescence of seaweed and fireflies, about spirits, light, and volumes, and the momentary flicker of light in darkness. In the context of other works, she speaks of creating arrays of sparkles—reminiscent of phosphorescent images of carnival lights on Lake Pontchartrain that have lasted a lifetime. "When you focus on something, what are you focusing on?" she asks. "What are you feeling? You're feeling the texture, the dimension, the gestalt . . . freely associating everything." Look at *Contraband* (1969). Consider what Benglis says about her work in the context of the culture of her time: "Brice Marden has referred to it as *facts*: you make these *facts*. In other words, they're like statements of a reality that you feel in the context of the conversations that artists have with each other, with the world, and with their times." Perhaps these words will refresh your understanding of the work of this pioneer of a form of abstraction that continues to express boundless innovative energy.

As a young art student in New York, Glenn Ligon immersed himself in the collections of the Metropolitan Museum and absorbed a broad knowledge of the history of art. His early work reflected the influence of what he saw in the New York galleries—first, the paintings of the Abstract Expressionists Willem de Kooning, Franz Kline, and Jackson Pollock. But then he became interested in Robert Rauschenberg and Jasper Johns, who brought letters, numbers, and images into their play with abstraction—and then Joseph Kosuth, Barbara Kruger, and Jenny Holzer, who brought social and political contexts to the fore. Deciding to incorporate into his work the things about which he was thinking and reading, Ligon began developing his own visual language and subject matter, in particular the use of texts—from sources in American literature (Walt Whitman, Zora Neale Huston, Gertrude Stein, James Baldwin) and culture (the jokes of comedian Richard Pryor)—and images of historic American figures such as Malcolm X. Not interested in telling his own stories, Ligon distanced himself from the notion of self-expression implied by using his own handwriting and began instead to use letter stencils. The instability of his medium—oil crayon—transformed the texts he quoted by making them almost abstract, difficult to read, and layered in meaning, much like the difficult subject matter that he had appropriated. The transitions between legible and illegible words rendered in paint, combined with line breaks and the progression of words from top to bottom, further transformed the texts, teasing out new meanings. (See the paintings of the early 1990s, and those from 2009 in which Ligon employs acrylic, silkscreen, and coal dust.) "Artworks are ideas," says Ligon. "My work is always about quotation. If there are things that are shocking or transgressive in the work they come from a source that is already in the world. . . . While the work in some cases might touch on the notion of identity in general, it's never about my identity. If it's about identity, it's about American identity. The work starts from me because that's where any artist's work starts, but . . . it's quickly about the way one is placed in the culture, in society. It's not about *me*. It's about *we*."

For Rackstraw Downes, subject matter lies in his environment or surroundings. Both words imply that the world curves around us (see *The Pulaski Skyway, Crossing the Hackensack River* (2007) or *The Sandhills, Presidio . . .* (2010)), and both simply reject the idea of a flat-plane worldview, which—as Downes says—comes from looking at flat paintings on a flat wall. He takes issue with the terms 'realist' and 'landscape', both of which have been used frequently to describe his work. "There is no solution to the representation of the world," he says. "As soon as you take a three-dimensional world . . . and place it on a two-dimensional surface, you move into the world of metaphor. The idea that there could be such a thing as *real* realism, *final* realism, seems to me to be nonsense." And so, Downes prefers not to use the term 'realism'. Seeing and the art of representation are culturally taught, he says, and perspective is an attempt to standardize the metaphor of the depiction of space. Why does one culture accept one delineation of the world and not another as realistic? Why do the Japanese see things isometrically, while we see them with a vanishing point? As for landscape painting, Downes thinks that the image interferes with and intrudes on the painting process, and that 'received' notions of landscape and the picturesque turn the genre into an exercise in flat-plane depiction. Instead he suggests the notion (based in American abstract painting of the 1940s and '50s) that one can paint directly, putting paint down on canvas, looking at it. "It's got to be alive," he says. "Then, in order to make it evolve. . . you introduce the image because the image makes certain demands on you. . . . But, finally, it's a blob of paint." Not a surprise from someone who started out as an abstract painter. Downes—like the other artists presented here—encourages us to consider far more than what meets the eye. Not only must we reflect on what he does—but on what he doesn't do. Once we comprehend the distinctions he makes with respect to the terms 'realism' and 'landscape', we want to look across the spectrum of art history—and cultures—to augment our understanding of a genre so often considered simple and without challenges.

Just as Downes makes us think about the culturally determined approaches to looking at, being in, and representing our surroundings, so does Tabaimo. We cannot view her video installations without considering their cultural sources, and she states that viewpoint clearly. "I create from the place where I myself stand, and I think of that as a kind of method. . . . I don't set out to create from within the Western context and, if you try to interpret my work from that context, it might lead you in a slightly different direction—which might in itself lead to an interesting interpretation. But I'm expressing the world I'm looking at, and I'm seeing the way I see it." The connections she cites between Japanese culture and art (and contemporary art) are "novels, films, and maybe ukiyo-e," commenting that art has not particularly influenced her and that, in fact, she has not seen very much of it. Influences she counts as important, even in advance of working on a project, are specific: horror mangas by Umezu Kazuo and Itō Junji; Terayama Shōji's film, *Pastoral: To Die in the Country*; and the work of Tanaami Keiichi, her teacher. Tabaimo's understanding of cultural dislocation—experienced while living in England and on her return to Japan—resounds in her statement, "I create from the place where I myself stand," and in recent works in which there is an element of unsteadiness or disequilibrium. Whether part of a work "shifts and sways and isn't firmly grounded . . . or there are bubbles coming up from below," Tabaimo is reflecting on the unsteadiness of her generation. But might that unsteadiness be viewed as openness to possibility, with disequilibrium being a sign of cultural transition and change—a looking backward, forward, and all around? "My generation," she says, "seems to stand on unstable ground." Loss of balance implies the need to concentrate, focus, and perhaps take action to determine where one actually stands. Tabaimo wants viewers to complete her work. "I see the work succeeding when the viewer engages with it actively—so I don't much endorse the idea of viewing things to try to discover the artist's message. Rather, I think that when the viewer takes on the work of . . . setting out to discover something, that will really bring the work together. I'm really happy when people can look at a work without being sidetracked by everyday ways of accounting for things. I want the viewer to think, 'what does this work mean to me?' Then the work will become complete in a very positive way. I don't want my viewers to be affected by established or commonsensical ideas. I want them to be free from those ideas and then look at my work. . . . Unless you have an idea of where you stand and what world you're looking at, it's almost impossible to say what's correct." Consider the word 'correct' as relative, differing according to where one stands. "Difference itself," says Tabaimo, "is an interesting thing."

Like Tabaimo, Mary Reid Kelley is primarily a video artist. Drawing and storytelling play key roles for both of them. But Reid Kelley creates performances and directs productions with live actors for the camera, writes scripts, and designs and makes costumes for her characters. She describes her work variously—as videos, films, texts, and moving paintings. As a painter, Reid Kelley found particular interest in the works of Kara Walker and Jenny Holzer, as well as Adrian Piper, Hannah Wilke, and other women artists of the 1960s and '70s. She was drawn to language and the many possibilities of interpretation in its layered meanings. "Either I was going to make paintings that were just giant blocks of text," says Reid Kelley, "or I could do what I really wanted to do—spend time writing." She realized that the visual works that interested her—even if static—were cumulative and narrative, or had a text component. Looking at paintings, she recognized the pleasure and value of repeated viewings, and realized the possibilities inherent in making her own work time-based. History—and what people want from it (authoritative, literal truth, among other things)—fascinates Reid Kelley. But she wants to imagine for it an "artistic language and context" and to use history to create metaphors. Her work synthesizes artistic process, imagination, and research with influences ranging from Enlightenment and Romantic philosophy and literature to Daumier, to Dada and the Surrealists, the architecture of nineteenth-century Paris, and the role of women in history.

Look at the "to do" lists posted on assume vivid astro focus's website. You will find hundreds of influences—contemporary and past—that permeate the work of this collective, also known as avaf. If there were a time and place to which its founding member relates most strongly it might be 1980s' New York, but the key to understanding avaf's work is to experience it in the moment of an exhibition opening. Perhaps one of avaf's most pointed statements about its work is that critics should stop trying to relate it to the past and simply discuss what they experience and see. And what they see is an enormous opening-night party, something like a happening on a grand scale beyond the wildest imaginings of anyone who ever attended one, staged by a community of avaf's core members and friends—a multinational mix of visual artists, musicians, performance artists of all sorts, and other collaborators. An avaf installation is unlike any other: it's a given that it will be a large-scale hedonistic spectacle of flamboyant color, sound, and light effects, in which subjects, performers, and viewers relinquish identities and merge into a community of celebrants and a mash-up of extraordinarily vivid associations and references to pop culture *now*. There may be references to history and the past in this work (or is it play?), but don't spend time being too serious about teasing out a deep art-world interpretation. Do, however, be aware of the works' messages on social and political issues. And look at the profusion of images and objects in avaf's mixed-media installations. The intention is to create energy and a sense of freedom. "We see the installation as a space of diversity and multiplicity," says avaf's founder. "The dialogue with a particular place's architecture is the first guideline we follow, either by enhancing, contradicting, or challenging it. The next step is to blow it. It's like being inside the shell of an exploding bomb; the space fixes your presence like a comfortable amicable trap but then the contents burst you in a million tiny pieces."

As a student in Ghana in the 1960s, El Anatsui studied at an offshoot of Goldsmith's College, London. The faculty, a mix of Europeans and Africans, had not trained in African art or the art of other cultures. In his penultimate year of study, Anatsui began to visit the cultural center in Kumasi, Ghana, where he discovered "something known as art that belongs to the place," quite unlike what he was exposed to in school. That discovery set his direction. He started to look inward, to consider African traditions, augmenting what he learned about European art. That experience only enriched him further. "With hindsight, I can say that . . . we weren't exposed to what was happening in Europe in the 1960s. In art history it was the Modern—say, the Impressionists, Expressionists—and that was about it. But I knew that at that time conceptual and other forms of art were already in Europe." It was only later, when he was teaching art in Nigeria, that Anatsui began to make use of the rich history and traditions of African art and language. Separated from immediate family in early childhood and brought up by an uncle in a missionary compound, Anatsui had been fascinated by signs, symbols, shape, and form well before being able to read—and it is that visual, conceptual language that underpins his sculpture even in early works that contain elements of figuration. His frequent use of found materials—clay or wood in earlier work, and the brightly colored liquor-bottle caps that have become a basic, modular material in his most recent sculptures, such as *Dusasa II* (2007)—echoes the prevalent respect in African societies for the cycle of destruction, regeneration, and re-use and the "positive affirmation," as Anatsui puts it, "of destruction as a prerequisite for new ideas or for new growth."

Sarah Sze also uses accumulations of found materials (though store-bought, and never "trash") in her architectonic sculptural environments. For Sze, formal qualities (color, light, edge, texture, weight, gravity) are as essential as any particular object in the work—but improvisation is crucial. Like Tabaimo, she plays with an idea of unsteadiness or teetering, as in *360 (Portable Planetarium)* (2010), with the result that the structure of her pieces seems to be in a state of constant flux. If you think you've located the end of a piece, you discover there's more or, as Sze expresses it, "the idea of complexity where there is no center that's stable." She works the edge between life and art, juxtaposing the familiar and the unfamiliar, keeping the viewer moving between the two, and blurring the distinction between what is seen in the work and in the real world. Once you are drawn into looking at the birds that perch in her High Line piece, you will begin to notice birds elsewhere. Like Rackstraw Downes, Sze thinks about how we experience the world, space, and information culturally, and the representation of three-dimensional and two-dimensional space (what you can do with a drawing that you can't do with a sculpture, and vice versa). Perhaps because she began as a painter and architect, she ponders what's essential to one medium or another, trying to make things that sit 'in between'. Again, like Downes, she reflects on the culturally perpetuated traditions of perspective—isometric versus one-point—and how one can play with them. It seems that for artists there is a constant flow of connections between experiences in and of culture and art. For Sze, an experience of living in Japan was revelatory because it showed her how aesthetics and art, and the way they can be integrated into life, could be entirely different in another culture.

Looking, seeing, and making art. The more you look, the more you'll see—and, if you're an artist, the actions of looking and making are linked. "Most artists," says Sarah Sze, "are addicted to looking as much as they are to making art. It was only when I tried to stop making art, and had a profound sense of loss and disorientation, that I knew that looking at art had been such a sustenance for me and began to realize that looking and making are married so closely. That's when I really started to become an artist, knowing that I wouldn't be able *not* to. But I think my work became interesting when it began to relate more to thinking about experiences I had in the world that were completely unrelated to art." *Experiences* in the world. Each level of the dictionary definition of the word seems to echo and expand on the quotation from Robert Mangold that begins this essay. Experience is "the direct observation of or participation in events as a basis for knowledge; the conscious events that make up an individual life; the events that make up the conscious past of a community, nation, or humankind," in other words, the apprehension of culture—and Culture. To this, add the transformative magic that creates art.

Ai Weiwei

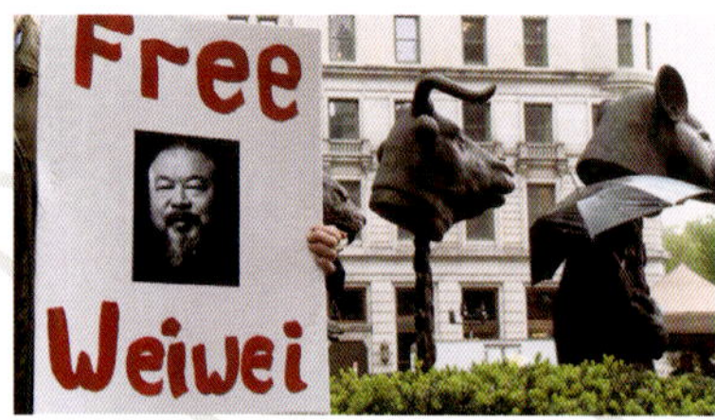

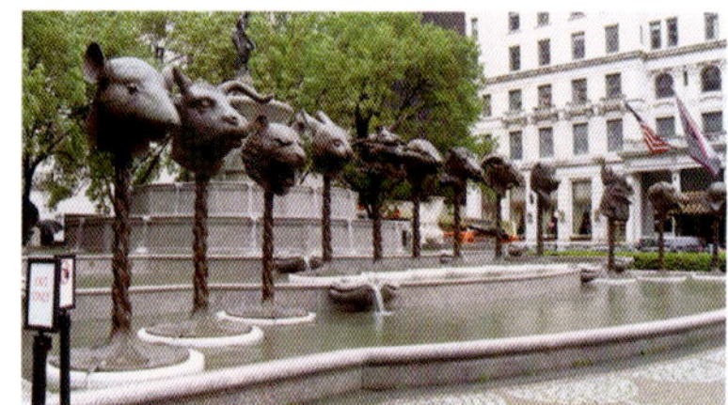
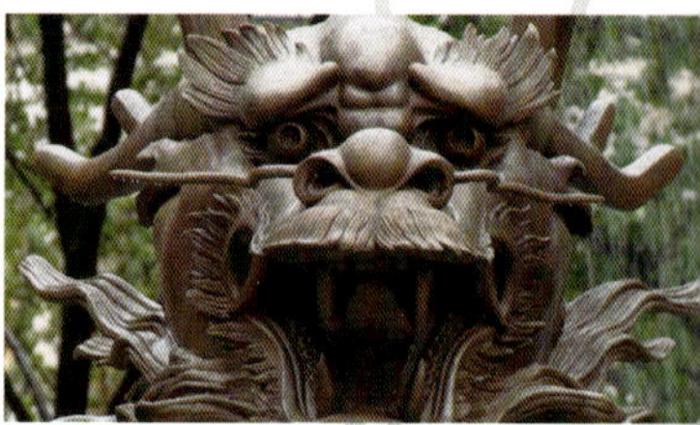

El Anatsui

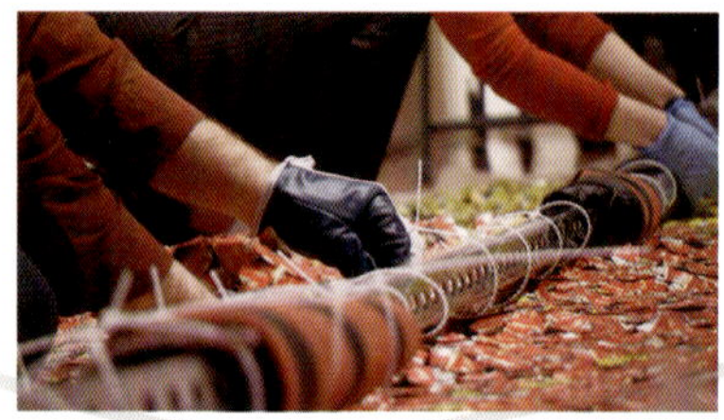
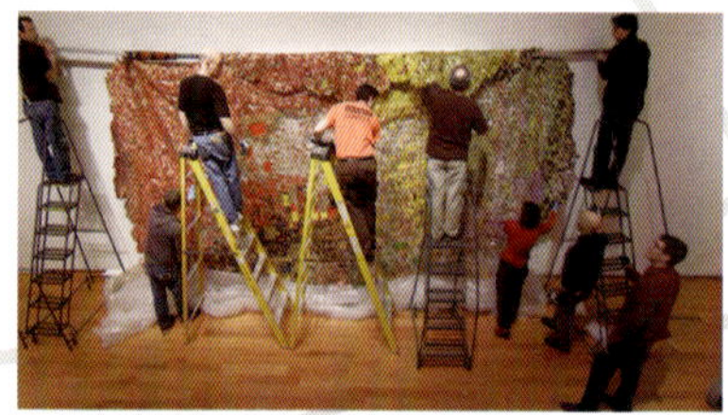
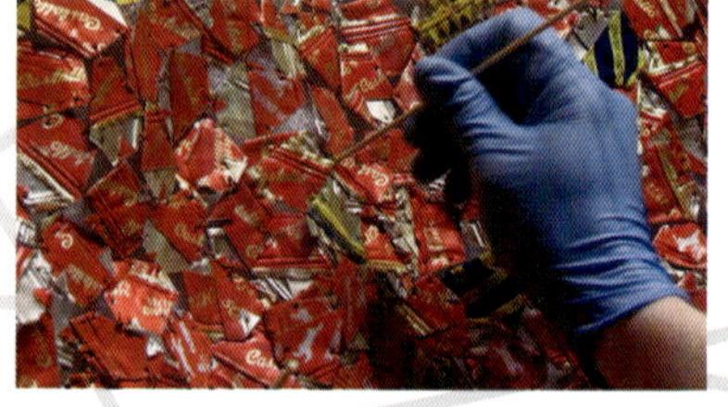

Catherine Opie

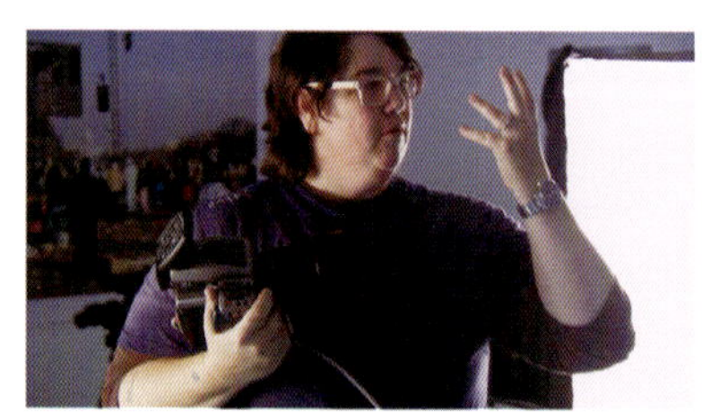
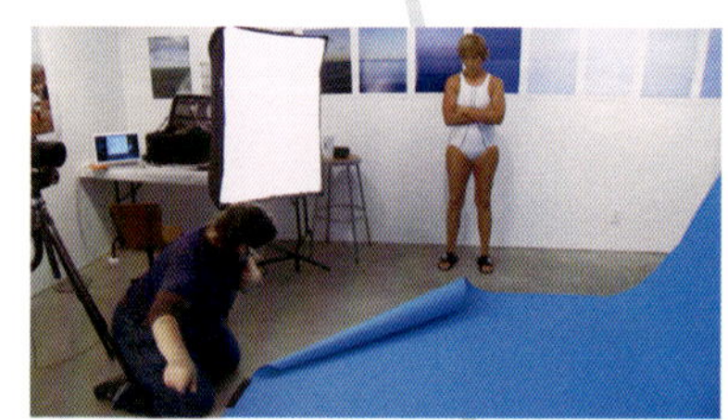

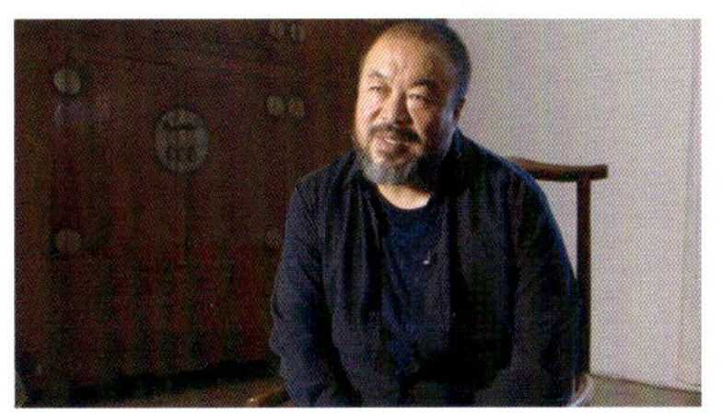
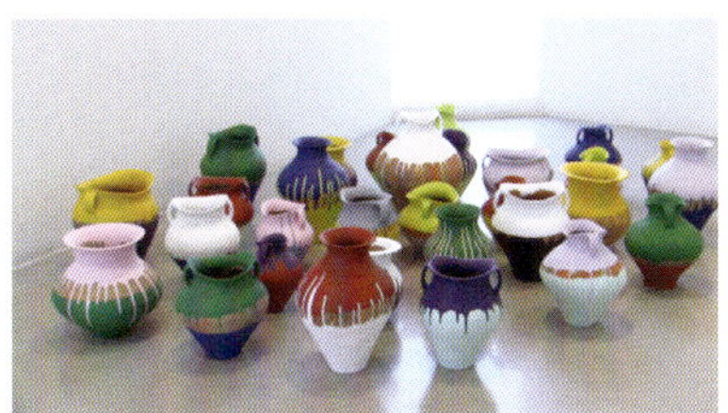
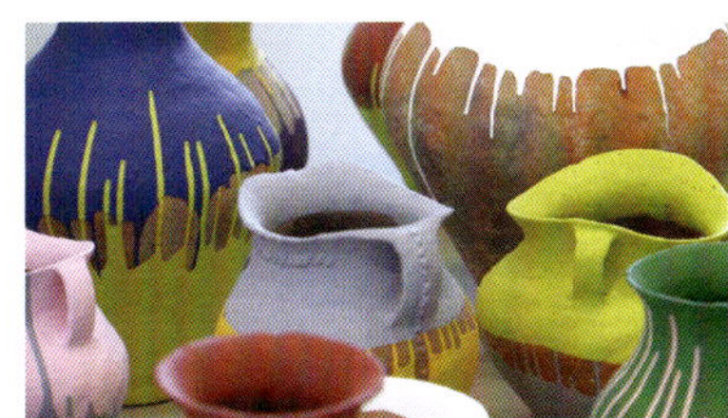

Change

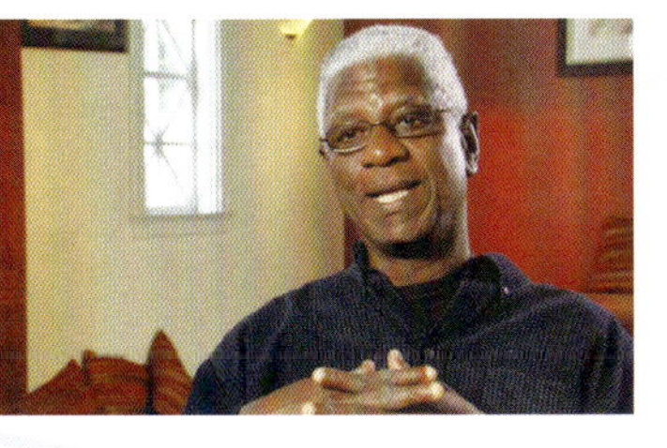
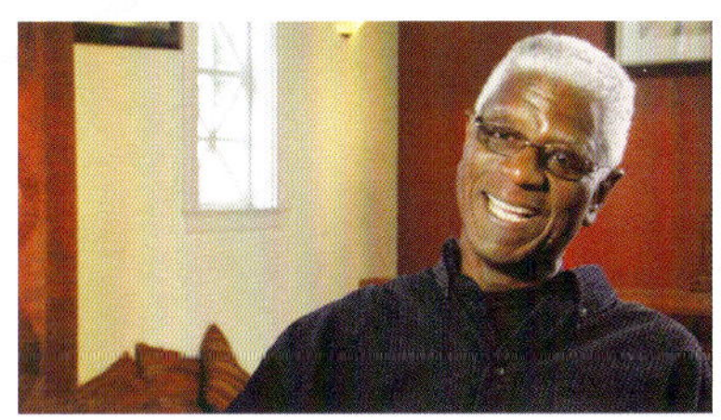
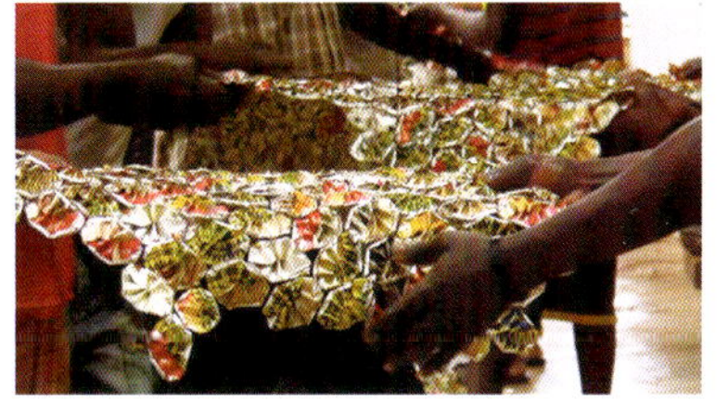

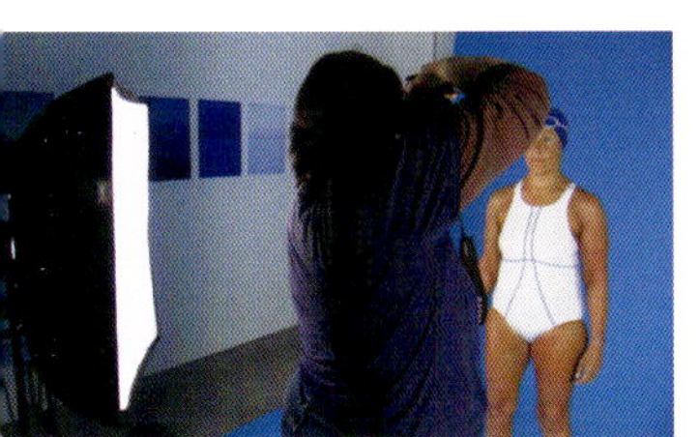
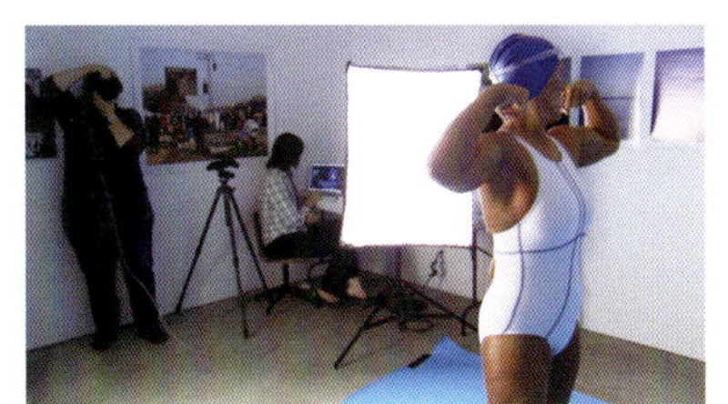
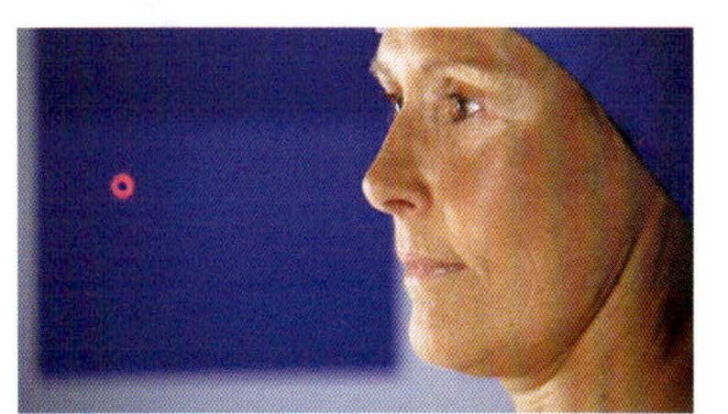
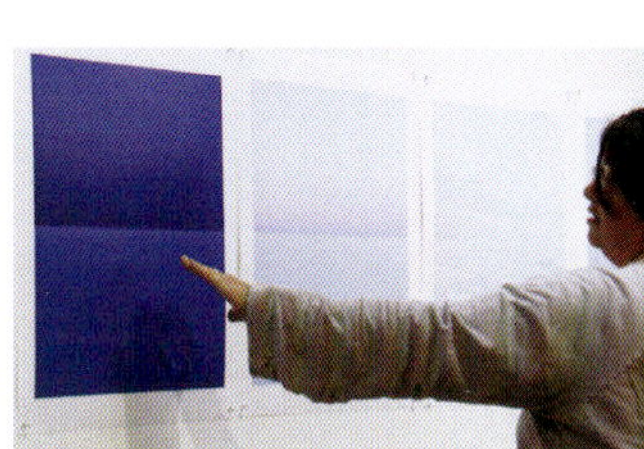

Ai Weiwei

On 3 April 2011, Chinese state security officials detained Ai Weiwei in Beijing as he was about to board a flight to Hong Kong, prevented him from leaving China, and made it impossible for him to participate in exhibition openings and other scheduled activities abroad, including the interview for this volume. Ai, an outspoken critic of Chinese political and social restrictions, was arrested, held for three months, and later charged with tax evasion. Upon his release, he was prohibited from engaging in public speech. The blank space in lieu of text in the following pages reflects the silencing of his voice.

Ai Weiwei

TOP
AIDS protest, 1989
Inkjet on Fantac Innova Ultra Smooth Gloss, 20 x 24 inches

BOTTOM
Bill Clinton at his last campaign stop in New York, 1992
Inkjet on Fantac Innova Ultra Smooth Gloss, 20 x 24 inches

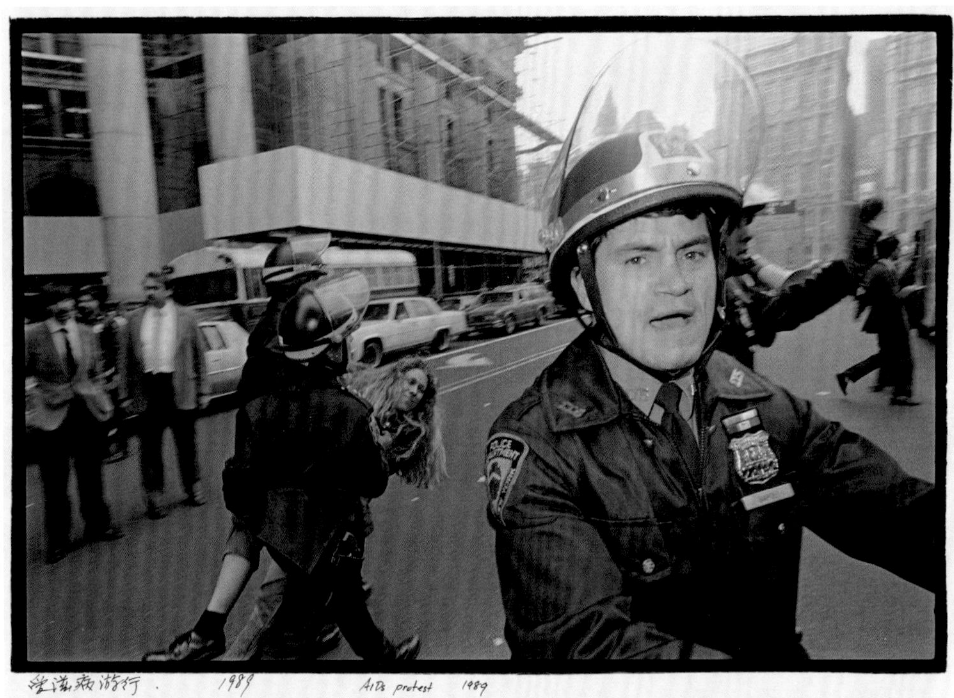

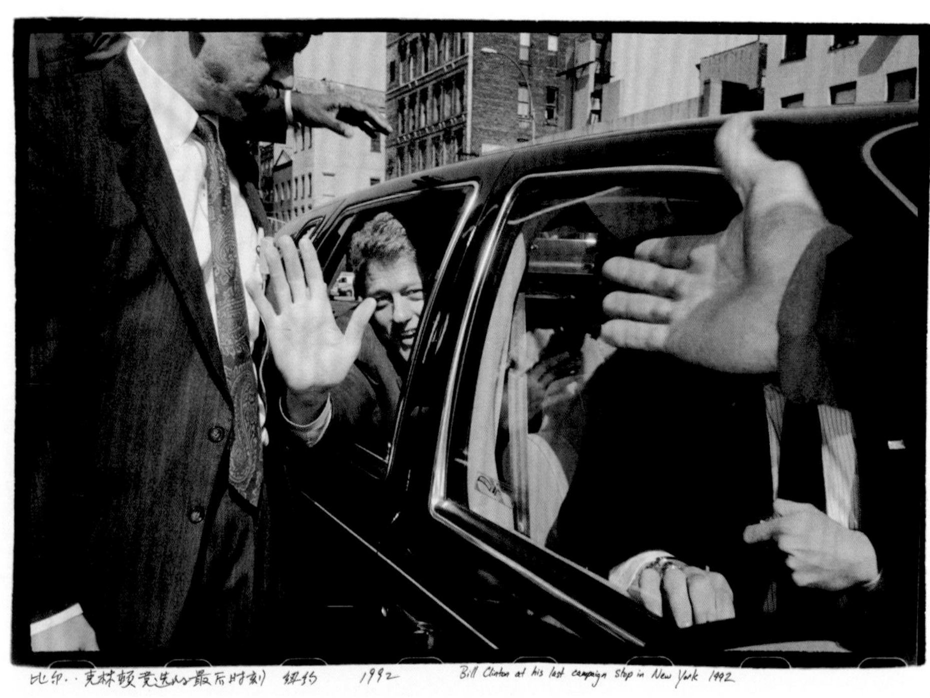

Ai Weiwei

TOP
Study of Perspective–Tiananmen, 1995–2003
Black-and-white print, 35 x 50 inches

CENTER
Study of Perspective–Eiffel Tower, 1995–2003
Color print, 35 x 50 inches

BOTTOM
Study of Perspective–The White House, 1995–2003
Color print, 35 x 50 inches

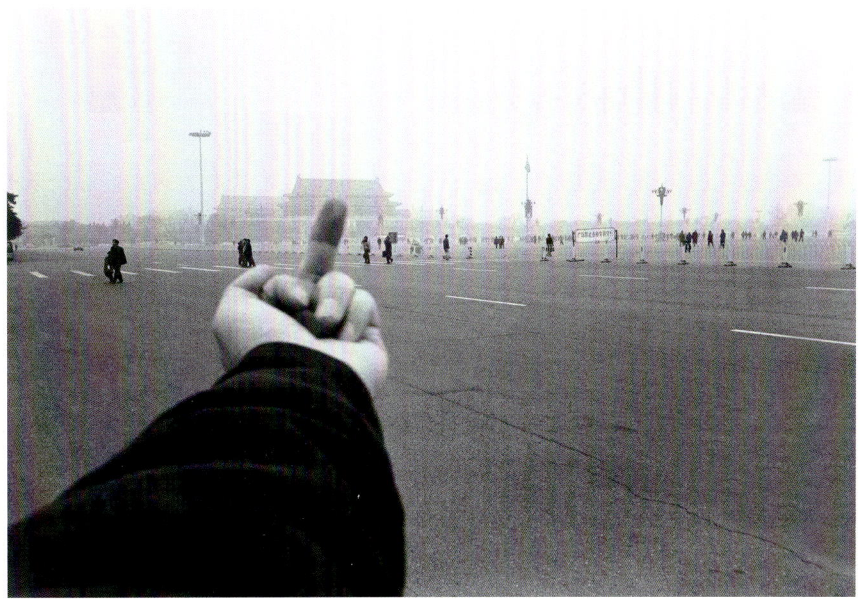

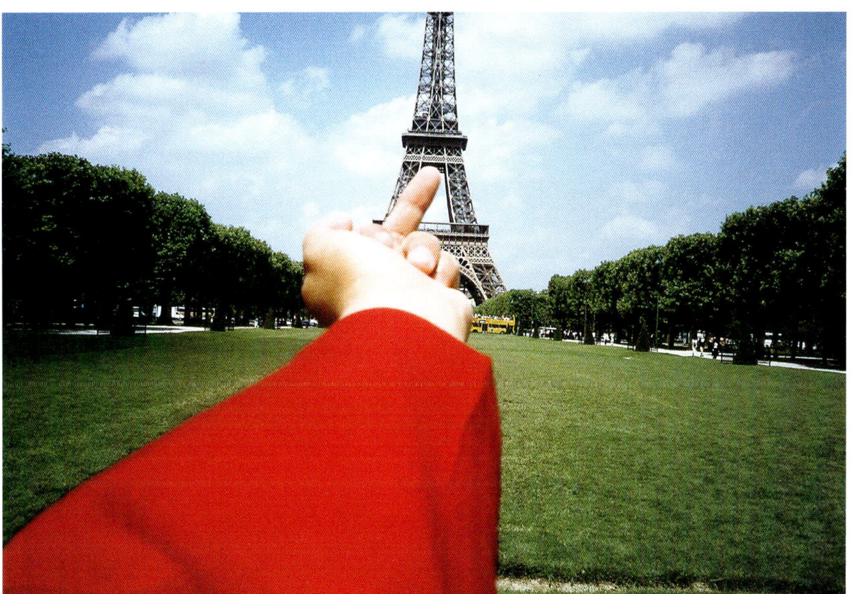

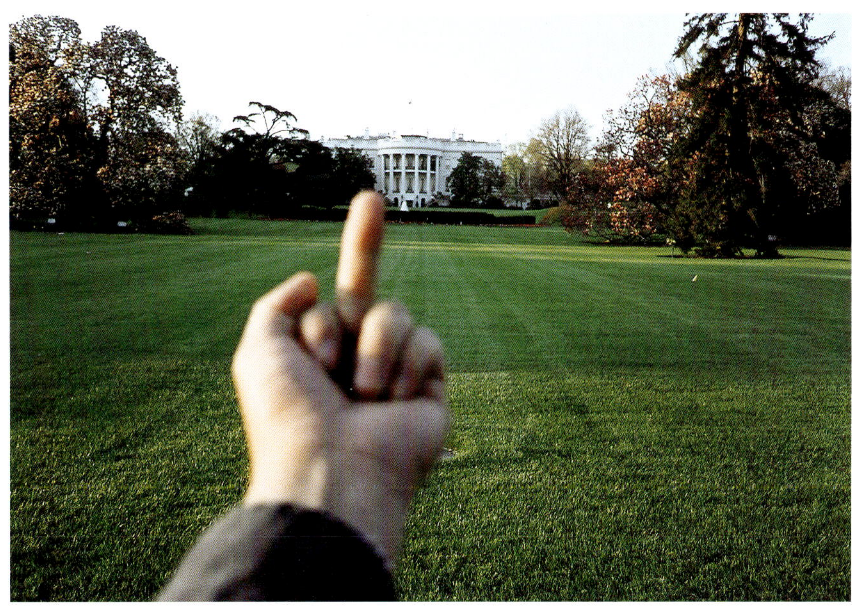

Ai Weiwei

RIGHT
Dropping a Han Dynasty Urn, 1995
Three black-and-white photographs,
58 x 48 inches each

OPPOSITE, TOP AND BOTTOM
Colored Vases, 2006
51 Neolithic vases (5000–3000 BCE), industrial paint, height varies from 8–16 inches

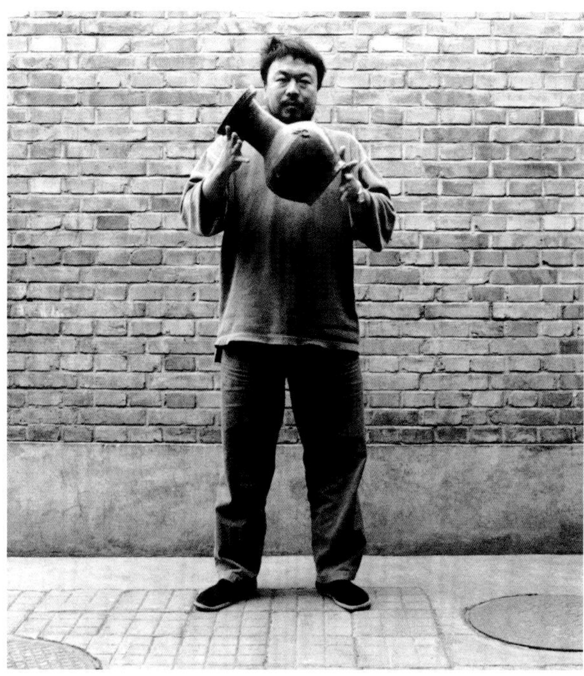

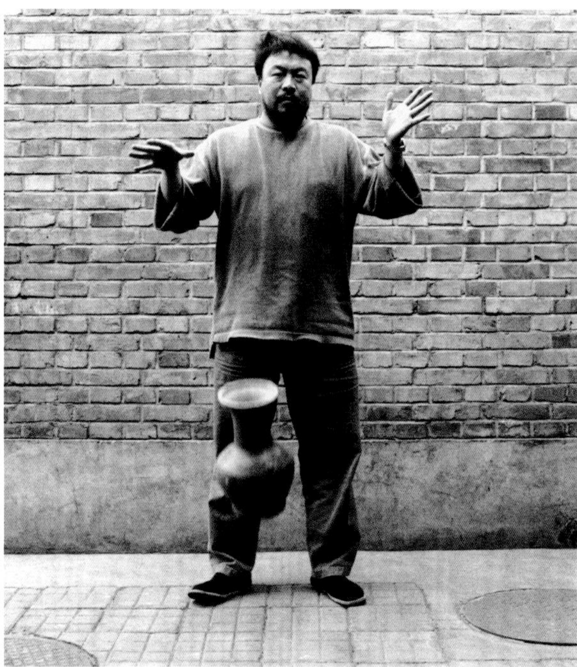

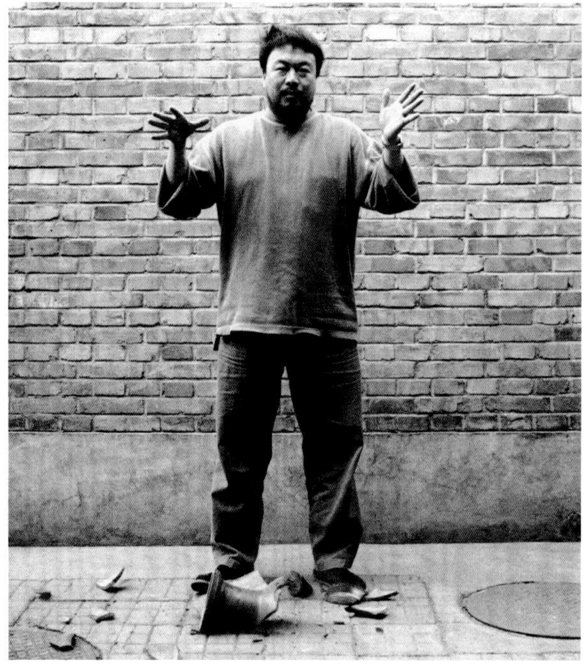

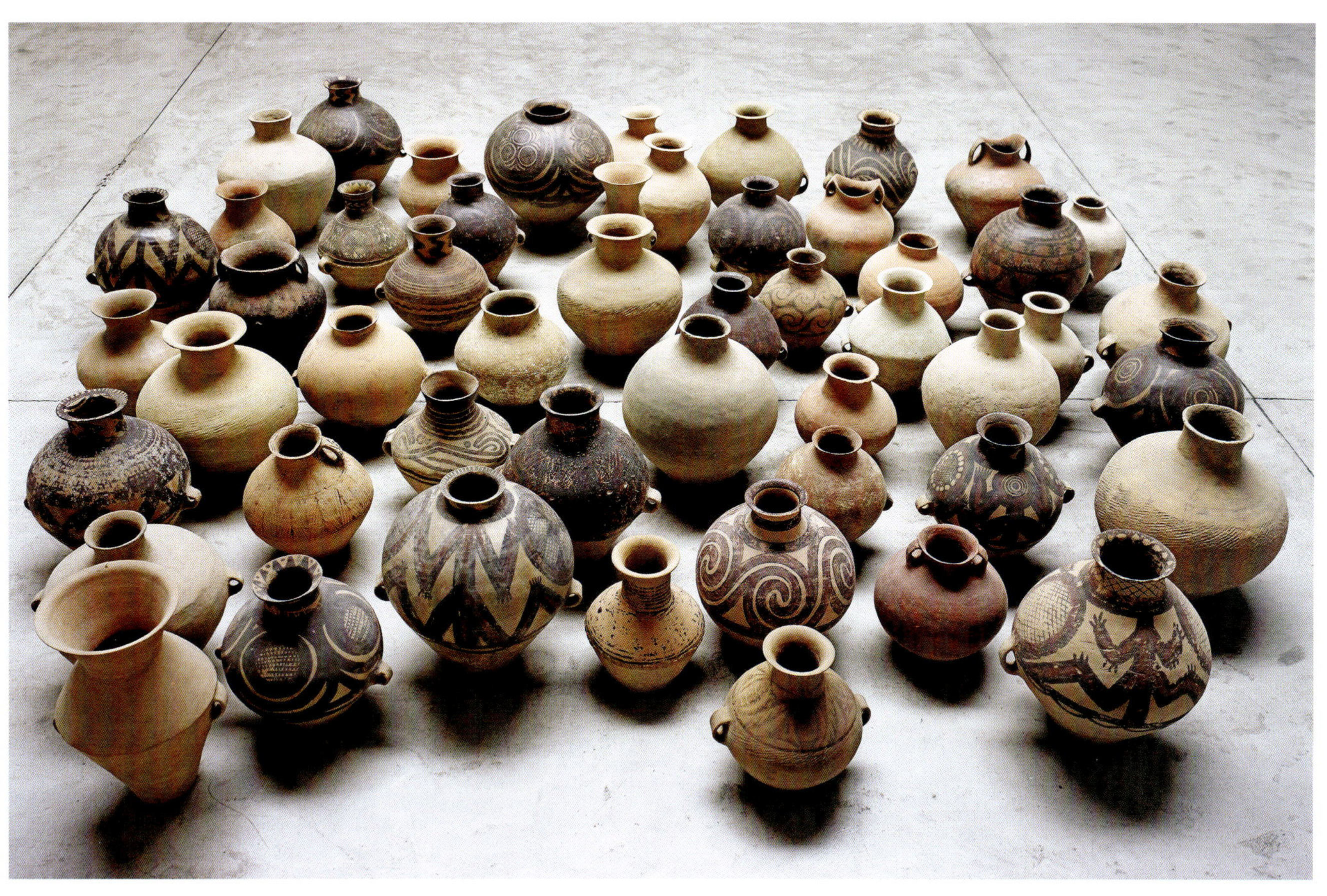

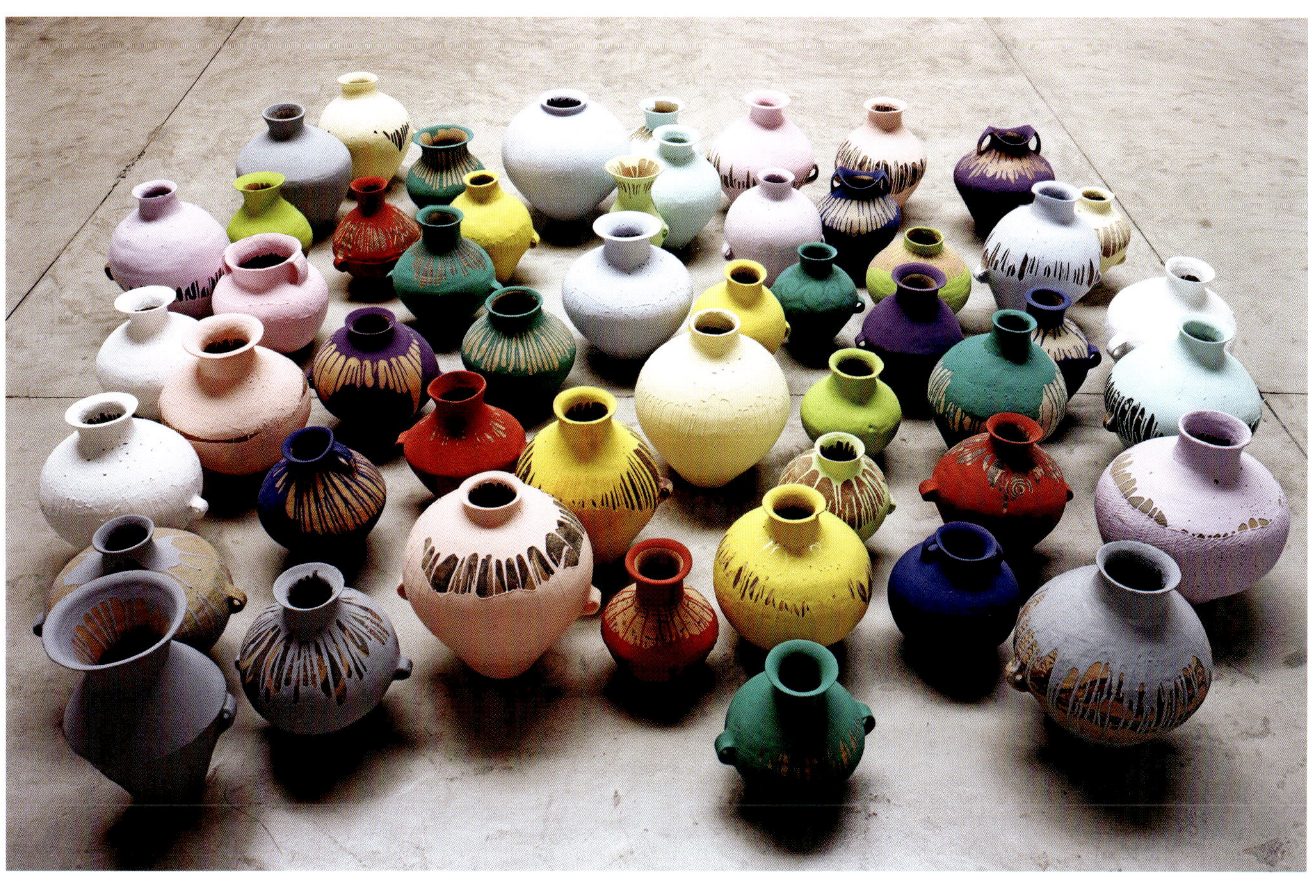

Ai Weiwei

Remembering, 2009
Backpacks and metal structure, approximately 30 x 348 feet
Haus der Kunst, Munich

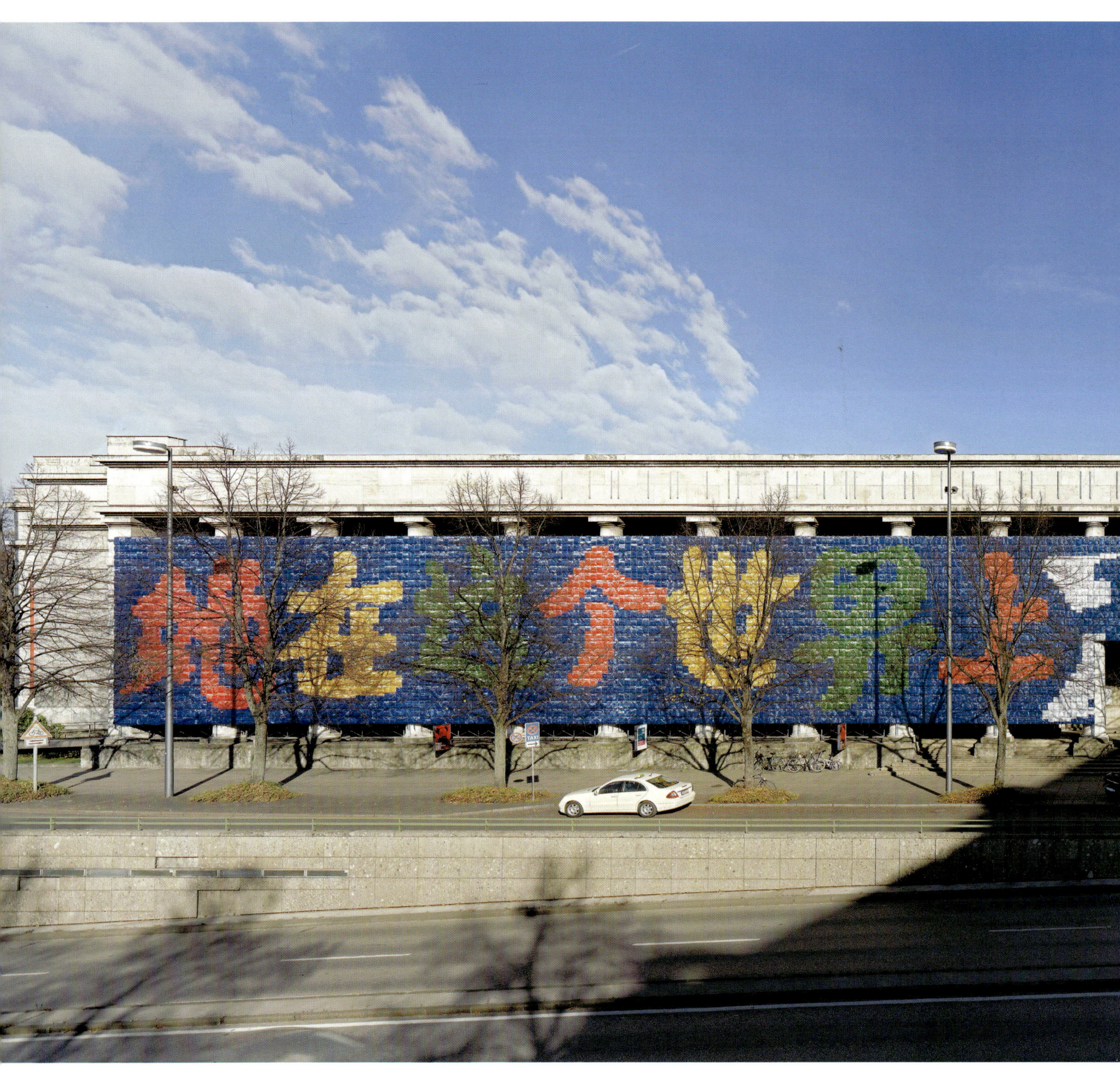

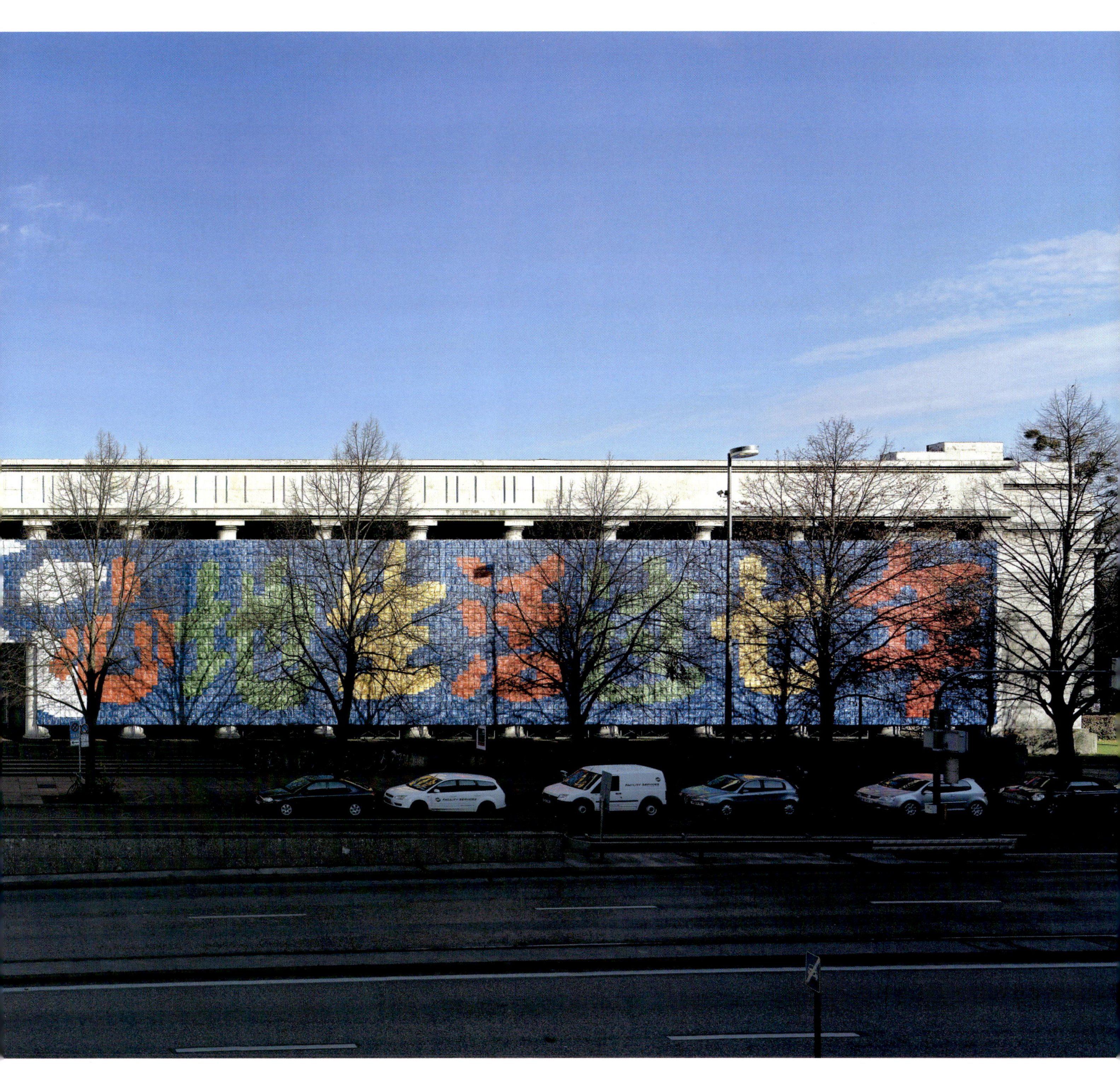

Ai Weiwei

BELOW, LEFT AND RIGHT
Sunflower Seeds, 2010
Porcelain, paint, 100 million sunflower seeds, dimensions variable
The Unilever Series, Tate Modern, London

OPPOSITE, TOP AND BOTTOM
Template, 2007
Wood doors and windows from destroyed Ming and Qing Dynasty houses (1368–1911), Wooden base, 24 x 39 x 28 feet (before colllapsing); 14 x 36 x 29 feet (after collapsing)
Documenta 12, Kassel

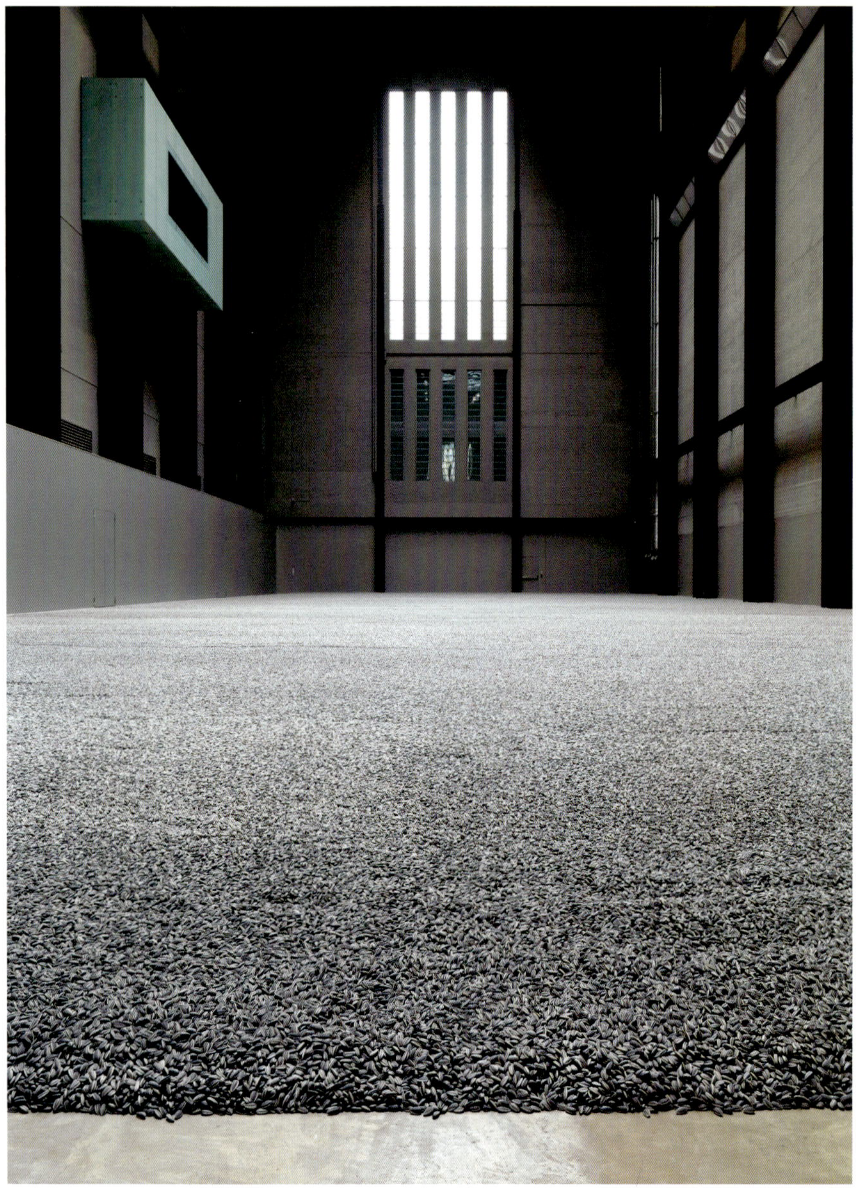

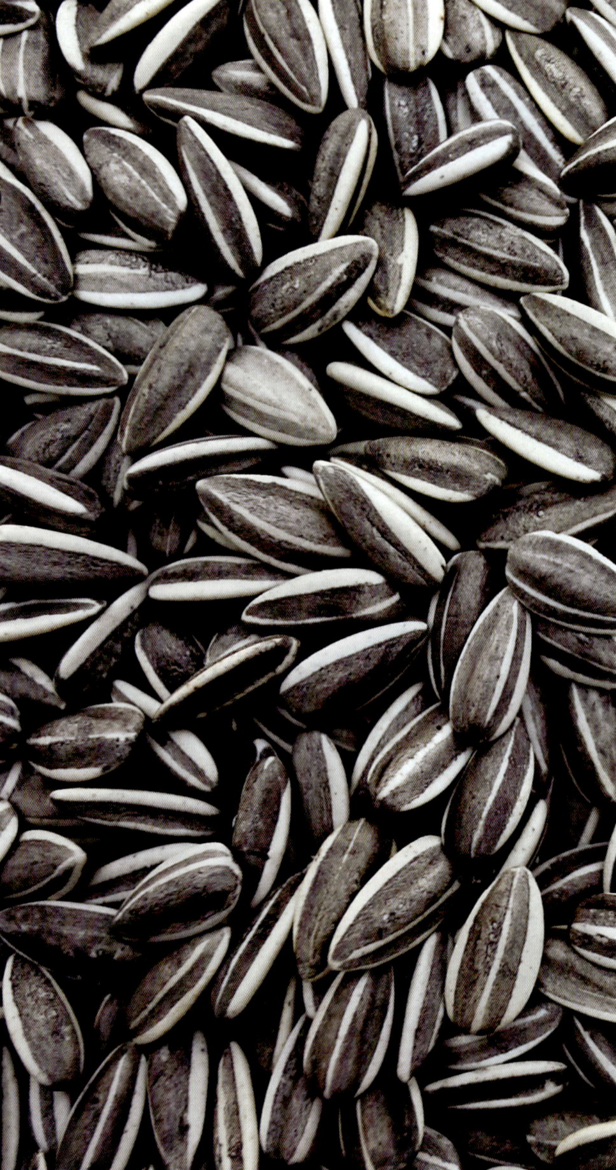

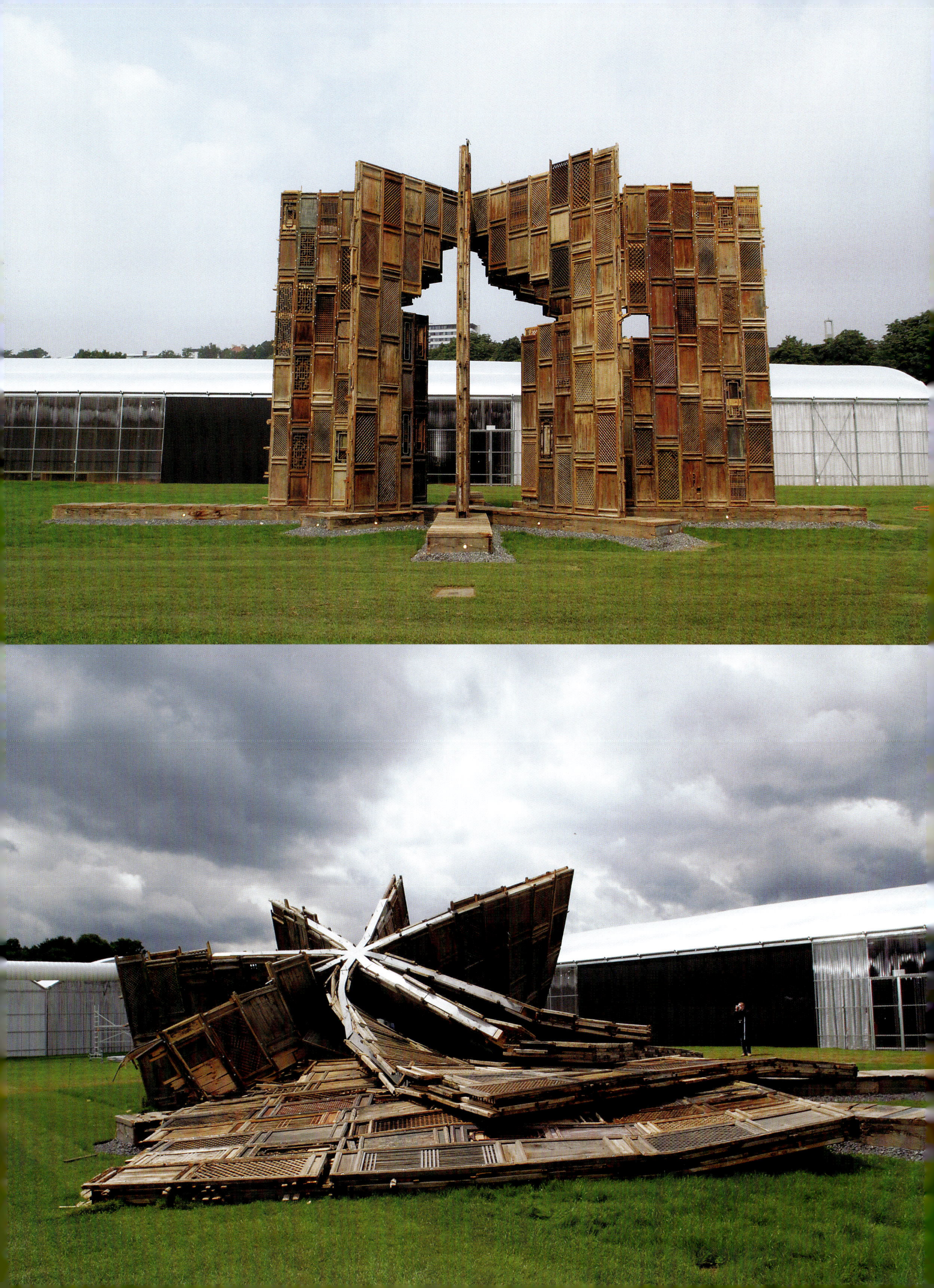

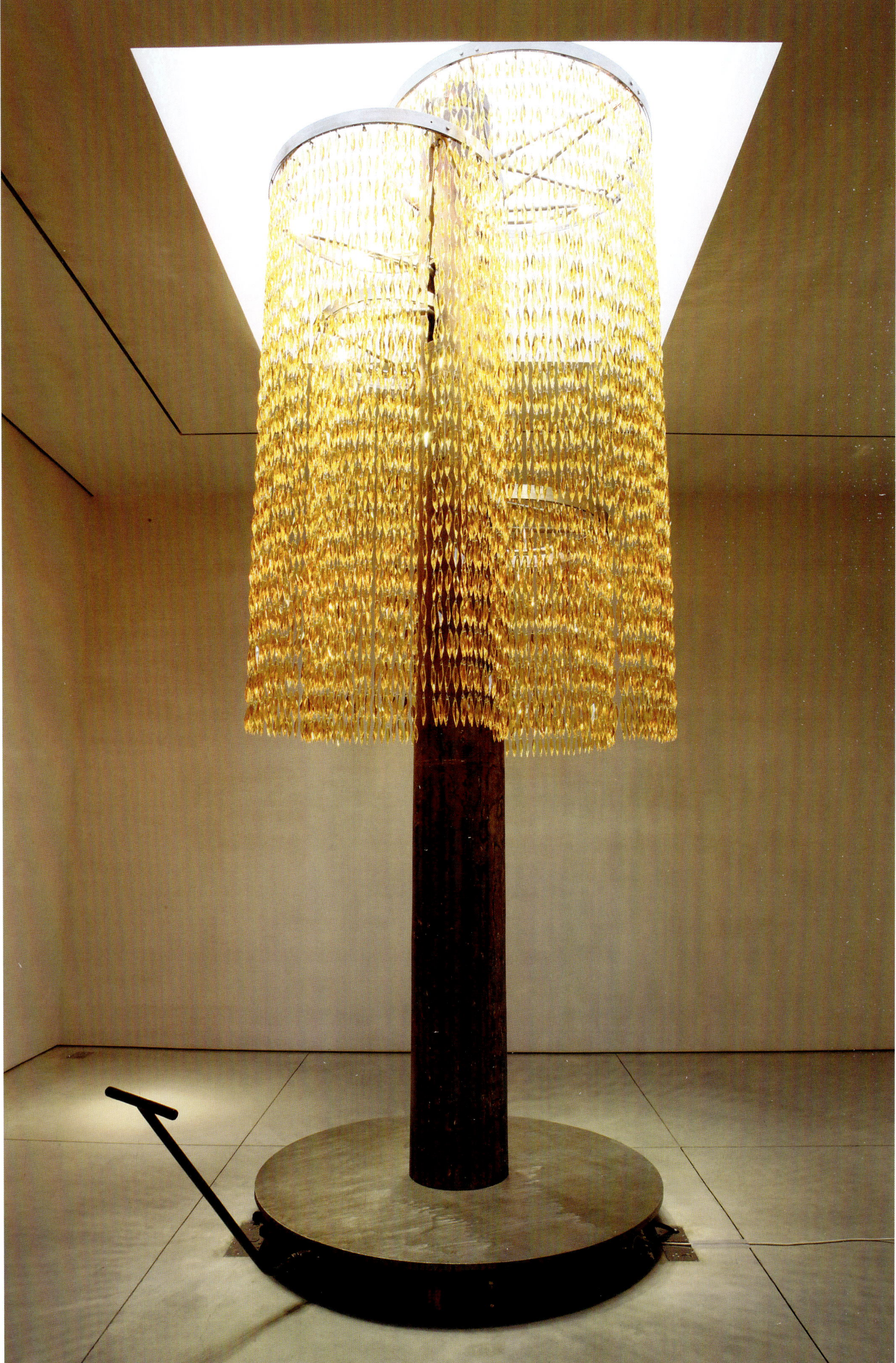

Ai Weiwei

OPPOSITE
Traveling Light, 2007
Tieli wood, glass crystal, lights, metal, 16 x 8 x 6 feet
Mary Boone Gallery, New York

BELOW
Descending Light, 2007
Glass crystal, lights, metal, 13 x 22 x 15 feet
Mary Boone Gallery, New York

FOLLOWING PAGES
Circle of Animals/Zodiac Heads, 2010
12 pieces, bronze
Height: approximately 10 feet; diameter: 3 feet
Pulitzer Fountain, New York

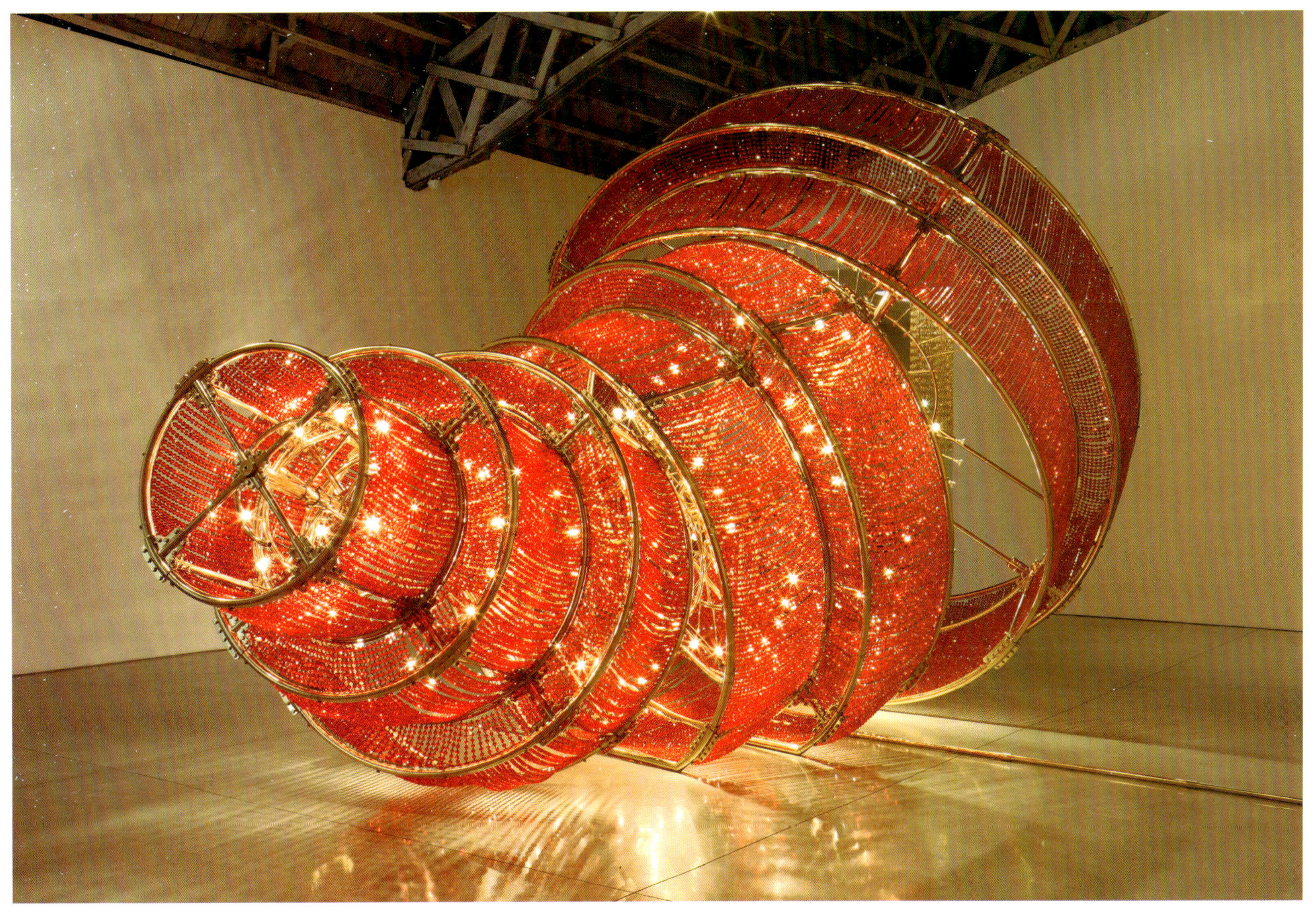

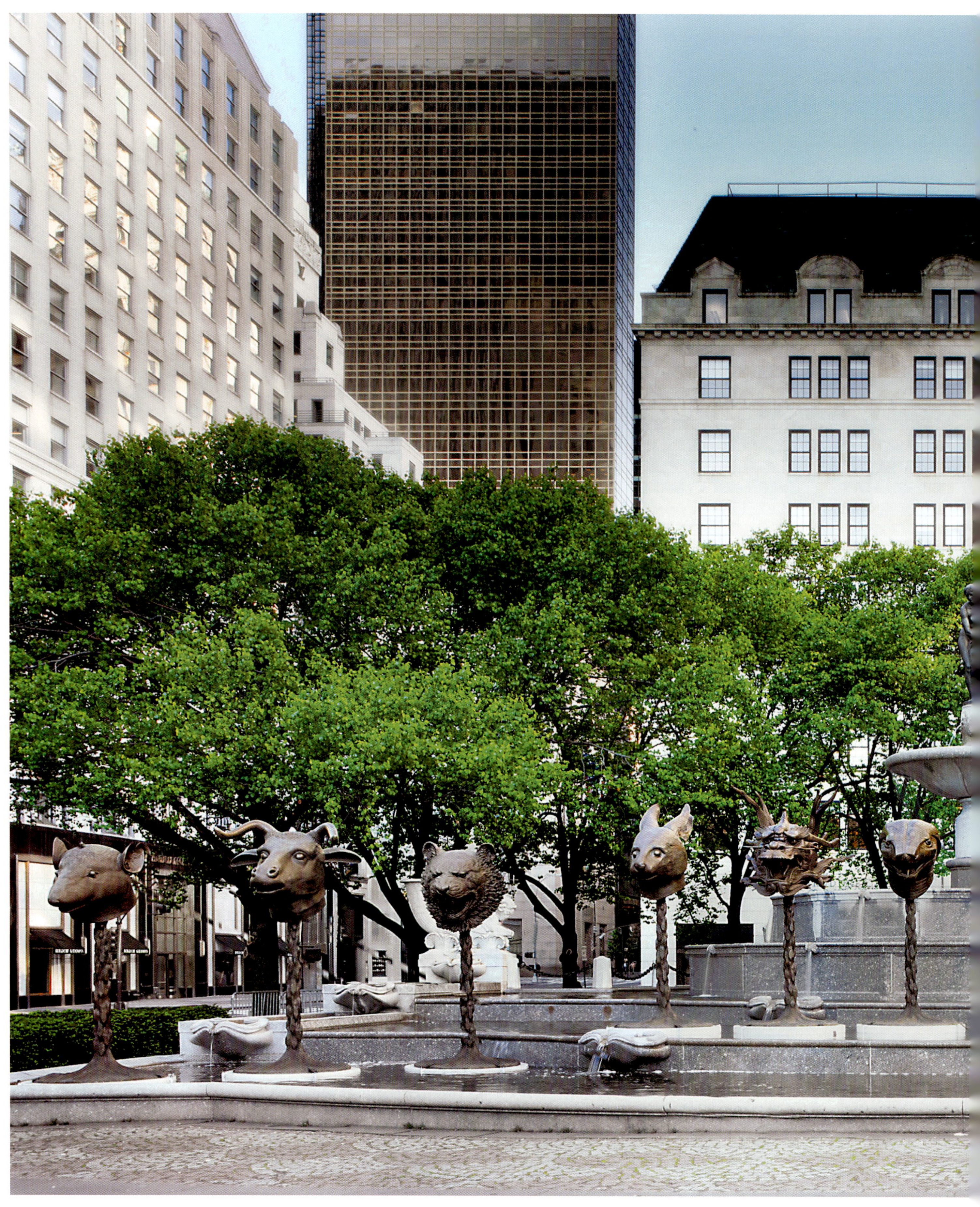

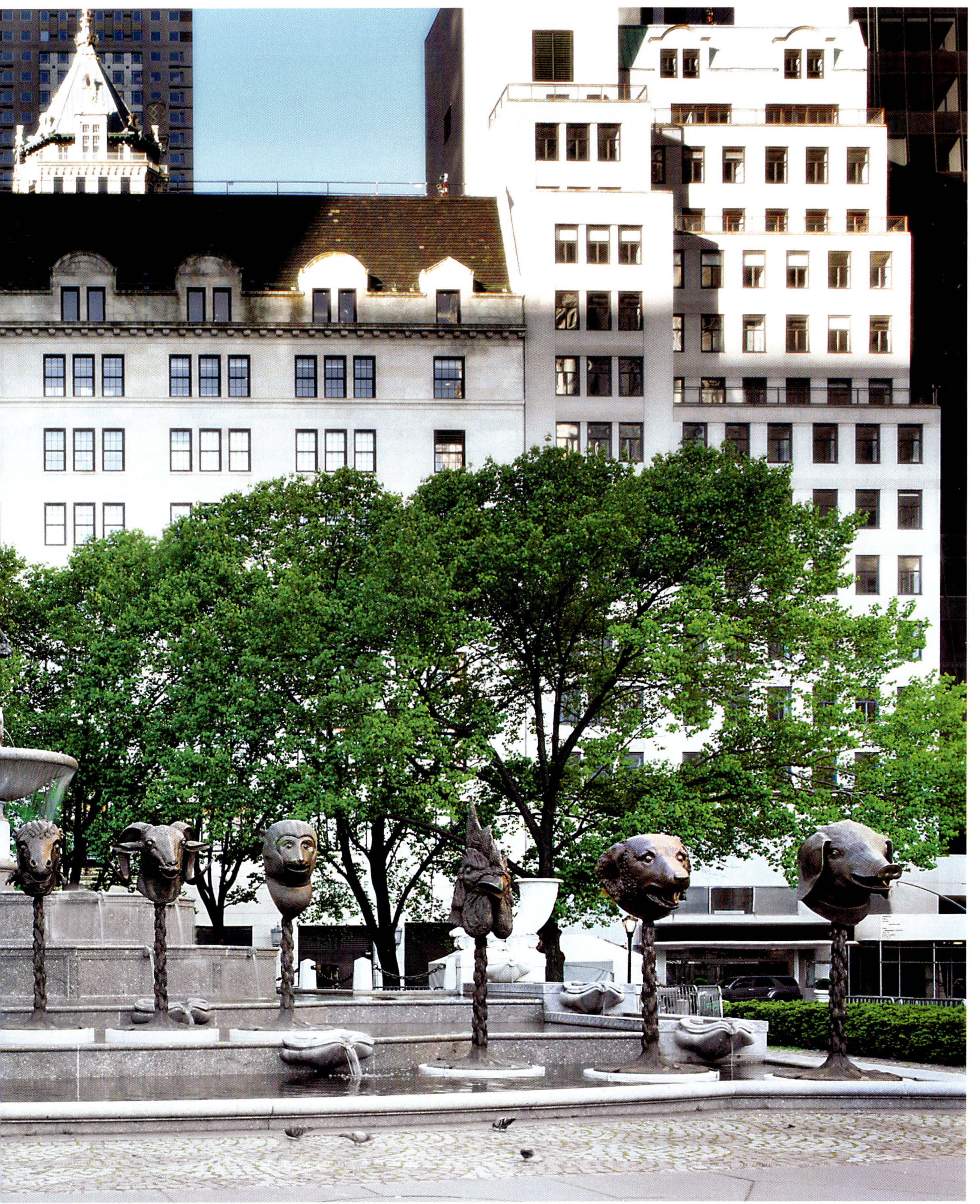

El Anatsui

When I started working on pieces with bottle caps everybody seized upon the idea of kente cloth as the aim of my work. The fact was that, when I started with these, I was thinking about sculpture. But somehow, uncannily, the colors of the bottle caps seemed to have replicated those of kente cloth. I was thinking about a form so free and flexible that you could shape it any way and still have it doing something that—every time you touch it—changes. I was thinking like a sculptor, not like a weaver or a textile designer. But I was intrigued by kente, and so I called the first two pieces that I made *Man's Cloth* and *Woman's Cloth*. I didn't help matters by giving these names, and it became difficult for me to really get people to think of these works as sculptures and not textiles. A lot of people even called them tapestries. Not that there's anything wrong with tapestries or textiles, but the tendency is that once people say, "Textiles," they stop at that. They are only looking for something visual, and nothing beyond that. Kente is a very rich visual form, but that wasn't what I was aiming at doing. It was sculpture.

This idea of looking for a free form, a form which is not cut-and-dried, not a definite thing, had not only been with me with these works, but when I was working with wood strips. That idea was behind it all—having wood strips all laid next to each other. (I put numbers on them, but the numbers were just an initial proposal for their arrangement. Anybody else arranging them was free to change sequences and create something new.) So when I started with these bottle-cap things I saw that here is a form made of metal but pliant enough to answer the kind of yearning that I have been looking for.

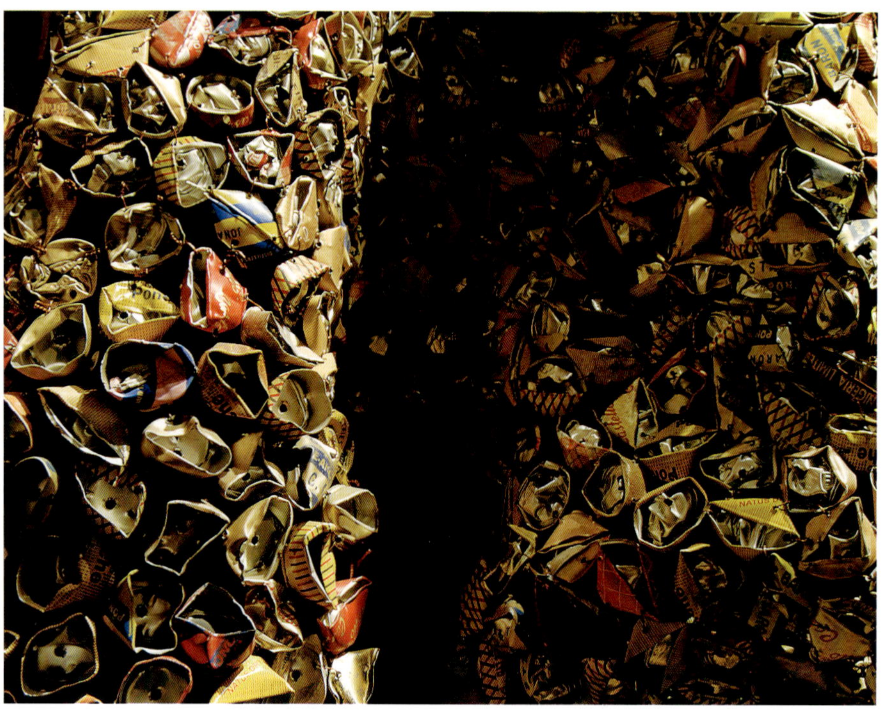

RIGHT AND OPPOSITE
Dusasa II, 2007
Aluminum liquor bottle caps and copper wire, 240 x 240 x 6 inches
Installation view of *Think with the Senses, Feel with the Mind: Art in the Present Tense*, 52nd Venice Biennale, June 10–November 21, 2007

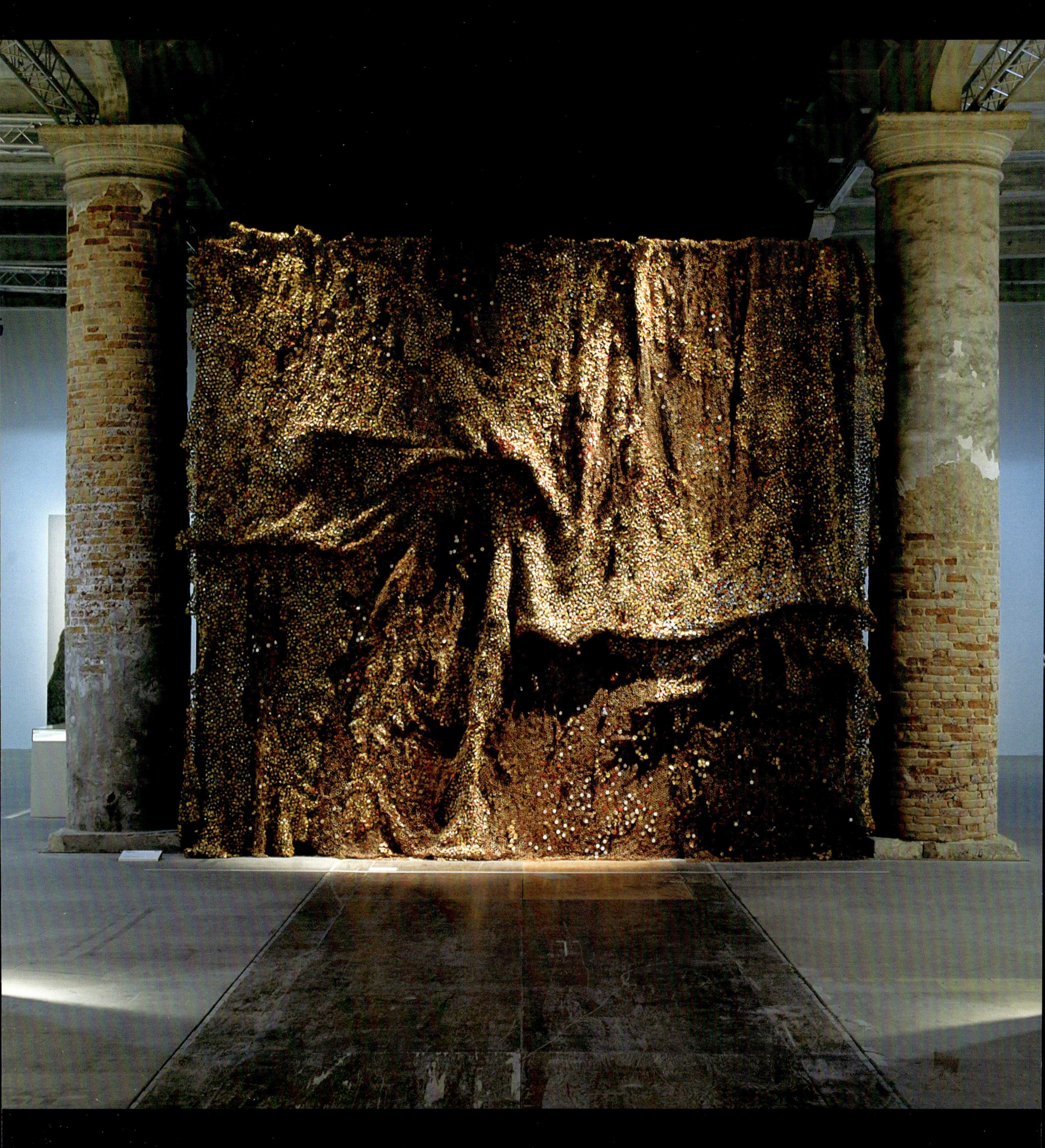

El Anatsui

RIGHT
Gbeze, 1979
Ceramic and manganese,
$14\frac{3}{4}$ x 15 inches
Collection of the artist

BELOW
Akua's Surviving Children, 1996
Wood and metal, installation dimensions variable; height of tallest individual piece: 65 inches
Collection of the artist and October Gallery, London

OPPOSITE
Wonder Masquerade, 1990
Wood and iron, 67 x $14\frac{1}{2}$ inches
Collection of Wole Soyinka, ESSAY Foundation for Humanities

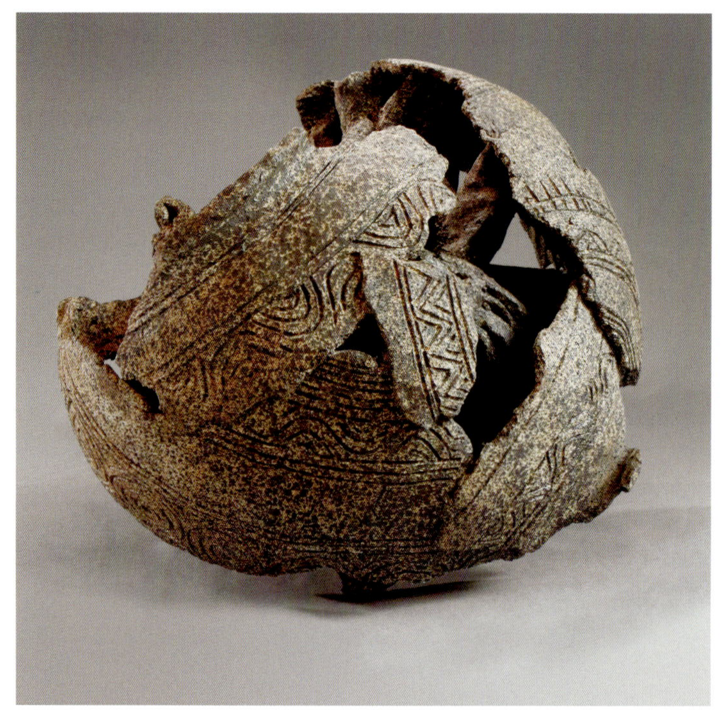

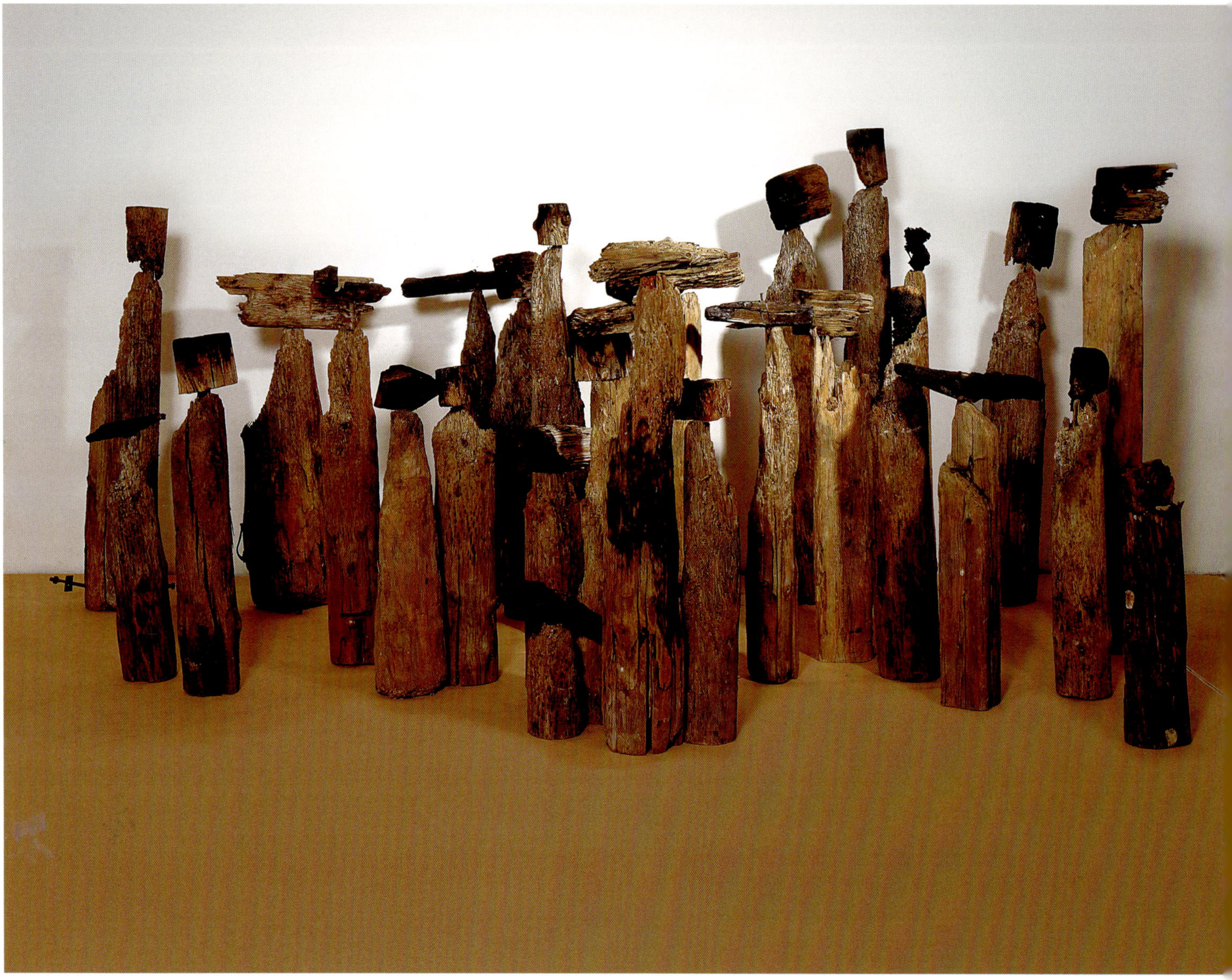

The ceramic pieces? You know, in most parts of Africa when a pot is broken, it's not the end of its life. It's a kind of stage in which it passes into even better—and more—uses than if it was whole. A water pot, when it's whole, is used for water only. But when it's broken, I use the potshard for so many things. Sacrifices are normally offered in broken pots, not in whole pots. It's like the pot has died and therefore it's fit to serve the spirits. And the idea of the broken pot is a kind of positive affirmation of destruction as a prerequisite for new ideas or for new growth. In ceramics, you find that a broken pot is ground and mixed back into fresh clay and, because it's been through fire before, it lends fresh clay more strength. All these ideas are behind the theme of broken pots—the need for things to break in order to pass into more uses, in order to come back to fresh life as a strengthening force. Clay is probably one of the best materials that any sculptor can handle. It yields to the touch and can take any shape that you want it to take. The pot is one of the best forms that clay can make because of its round nature. There's a lot of support built into the round shape.

What I do mostly is concentrate on a medium and go at it for a long, long time, until such time that maybe a new medium or a new process or a new idea is strong enough to take over. If you go through my career so far you would see that I don't take a medium and go at it for one or two weeks and leave it. I go for years. Like clay. I worked at the ceramic pieces for well over five years and only stopped when the facilities broke down. Then came wood—the wood strips and the chainsaw—fourteen or fifteen years. Then wood was supplanted by the metals, and the metals have been with me well over eleven years and they're not exhausted yet. So I'm someone who believes not only in change or variety, but in having to delve for a long time, to explore that thing for a long time, to make sure that I have extracted something substantial out of it before shifting attention to another one. But I'm sure, if I sit down and go through most of the works I've done, one might be able to find links—harbingers—within them.

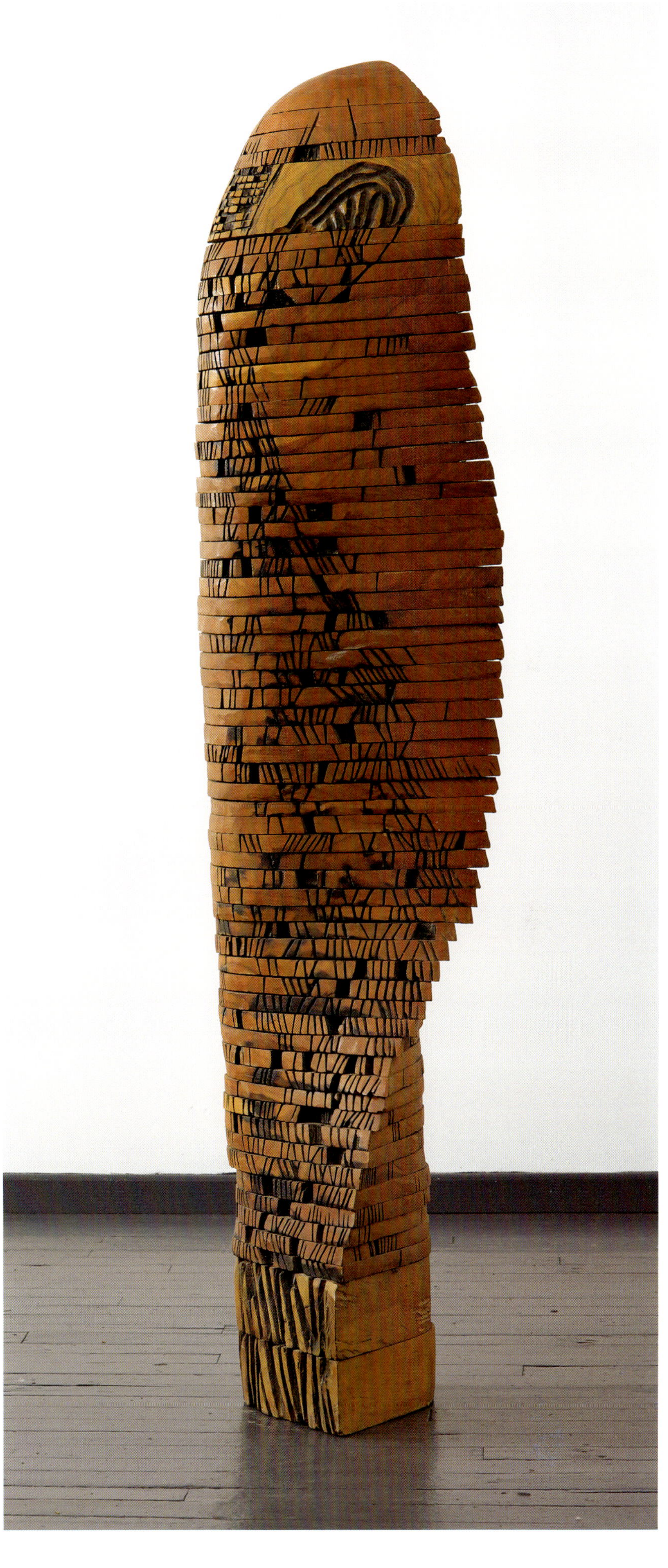

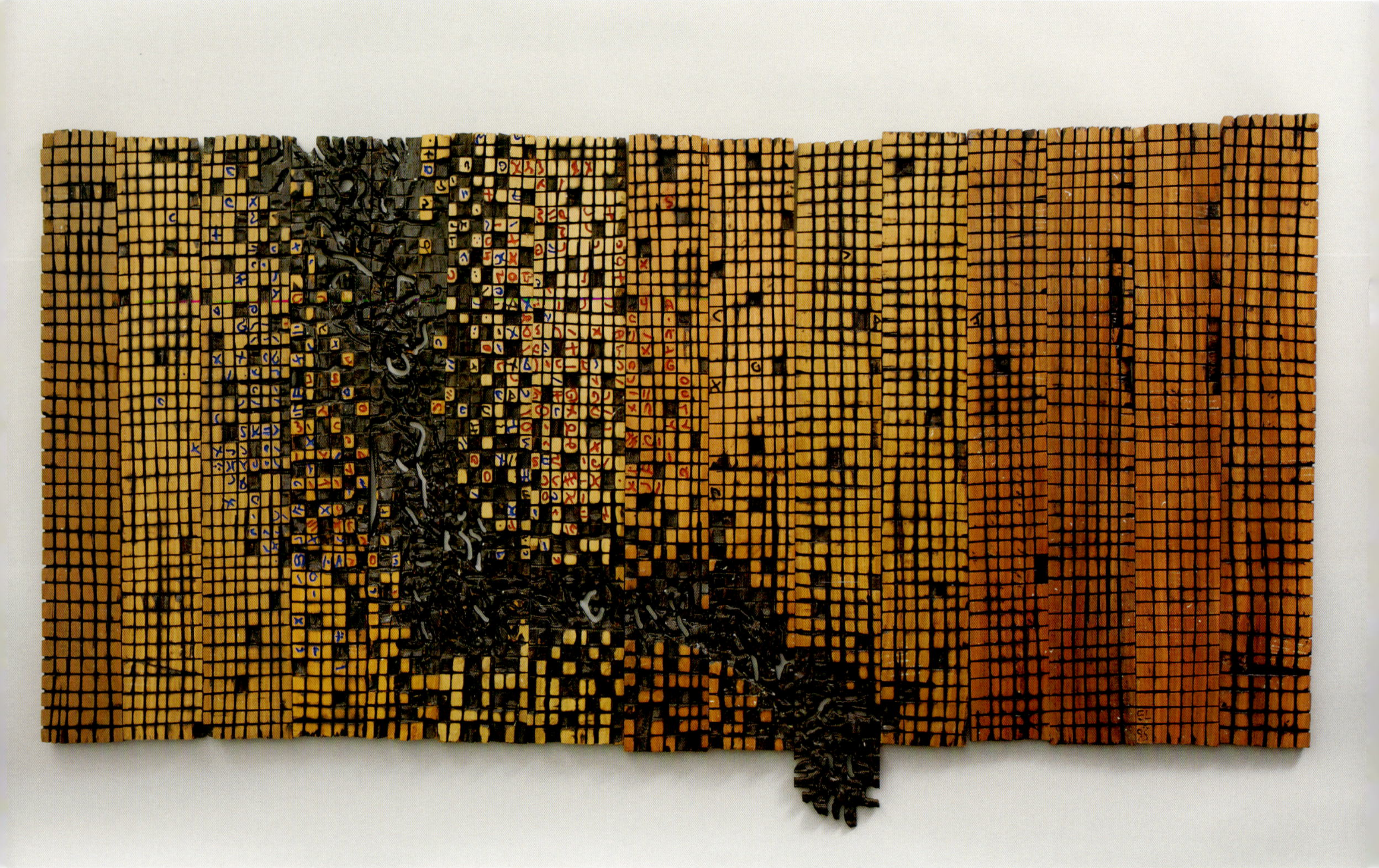

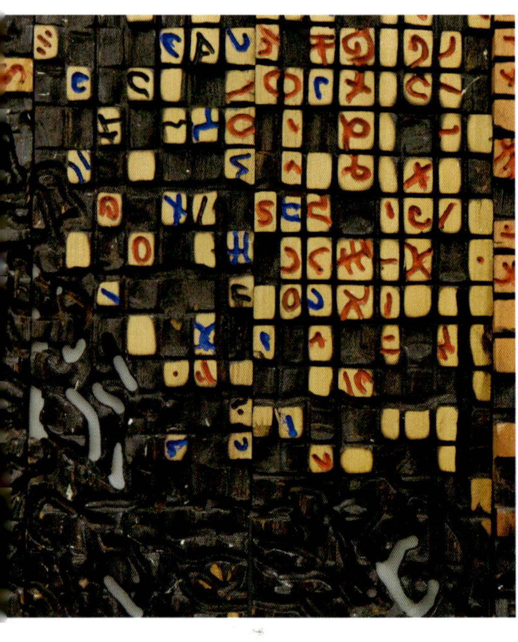

A tradition that actually started me off in my profession was a collection of *Adinkra* symbols. Adinkra means 'saying goodbye'. It's actually a series of signs and symbols that are printed on textiles. When I saw them for the first time, I remember, I had read a couple of books in which there were claims that Africa didn't have art, or that African art is not abstract. Then I saw these signs, in which you clearly see people making attempts to encapsulate abstract ideas, like the oneness of God, or unity, with very intriguing forms. That really opened my eyes and I stayed with those signs for well over five years after I finished school, working with them, exploring them, in order to educate my ethos and make it start to work like that of my forebears. Just as in Europe, where you go to the museum to see the artworks of your forebears, this was *my* museum that I discovered. And that was what started me off. When I came to Nigeria I saw that they also had some very intriguing graphic sign systems and, later on, I think I discovered a book in which somebody was talking about Africa and the written word. And it showed samples of many forms of writing that way in Africa, long before Europeans came there.

All this gave me the impetus to really study about my place in order to have a kind of foundation, which I added to the exposure I had to European art. With hindsight, I can say that what was taught to us was probably not what was being taught in Europe at the time. It was a watered-down

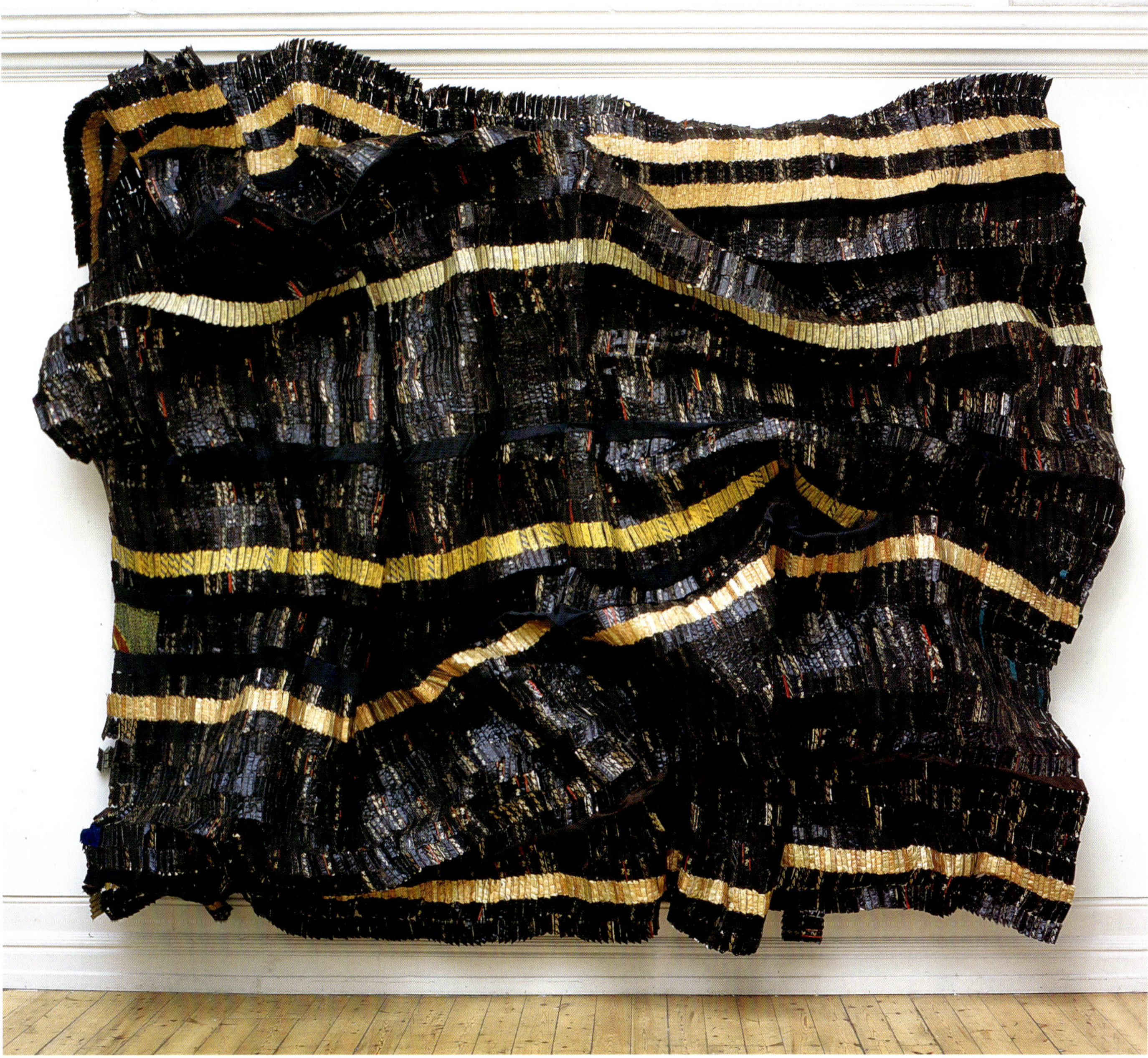

version—because later on, reading books, I saw that we weren't exposed to what was happening in Europe in the '60s (I went to university in the '60s). In art history for instance it was the Modern—say, the Impressionists, Expressionists—and that was about it. But I knew that at that time conceptual and other forms of art were already in Europe. I was reading a book about a founder of the ancient kingdom of Mali and saw an episode in it in which this chap did a conceptual presentation in the year 1230! Then I said, "This idea of the conceptual is not even European; it's a world thing—because at that time Europe was not even in the Renaissance yet." And I thought, "Okay, these ideas are cyclic and don't belong to any particular culture."

Adinsibuli is a word that I made up myself—an acronym made up of *adinkra*, *nsibidi*, and *uli*. These are three sign traditions, sign-writing or symbol traditions, that I have worked with—one from Ghana and two from Nigeria. I worked with adinkra from 1970 to '75 or thereabouts. Then, when I went to Nigeria, I encountered nsibidi, which is a sign system used by a secret society in some part of southeastern Nigeria. And then uli is a very poignant painting tradition of the Igbos. So I coined the name Adinsibuli from these three traditions because the work that I did had a lot of signs and symbols, and I think that they derived from those traditions.

El Anatsui

OPPOSITE, TOP AND BOTTOM
Old Cloth Series (with detail), 1993
Wood and paint, 31½ x 60¼ inches
Collection of Neil Coventry

ABOVE
Adinkra Sasa, 2003
Aluminum and copper wire,
192 x 216 inches
Collection of Mr. and Mrs. Guido Roberto Vitale

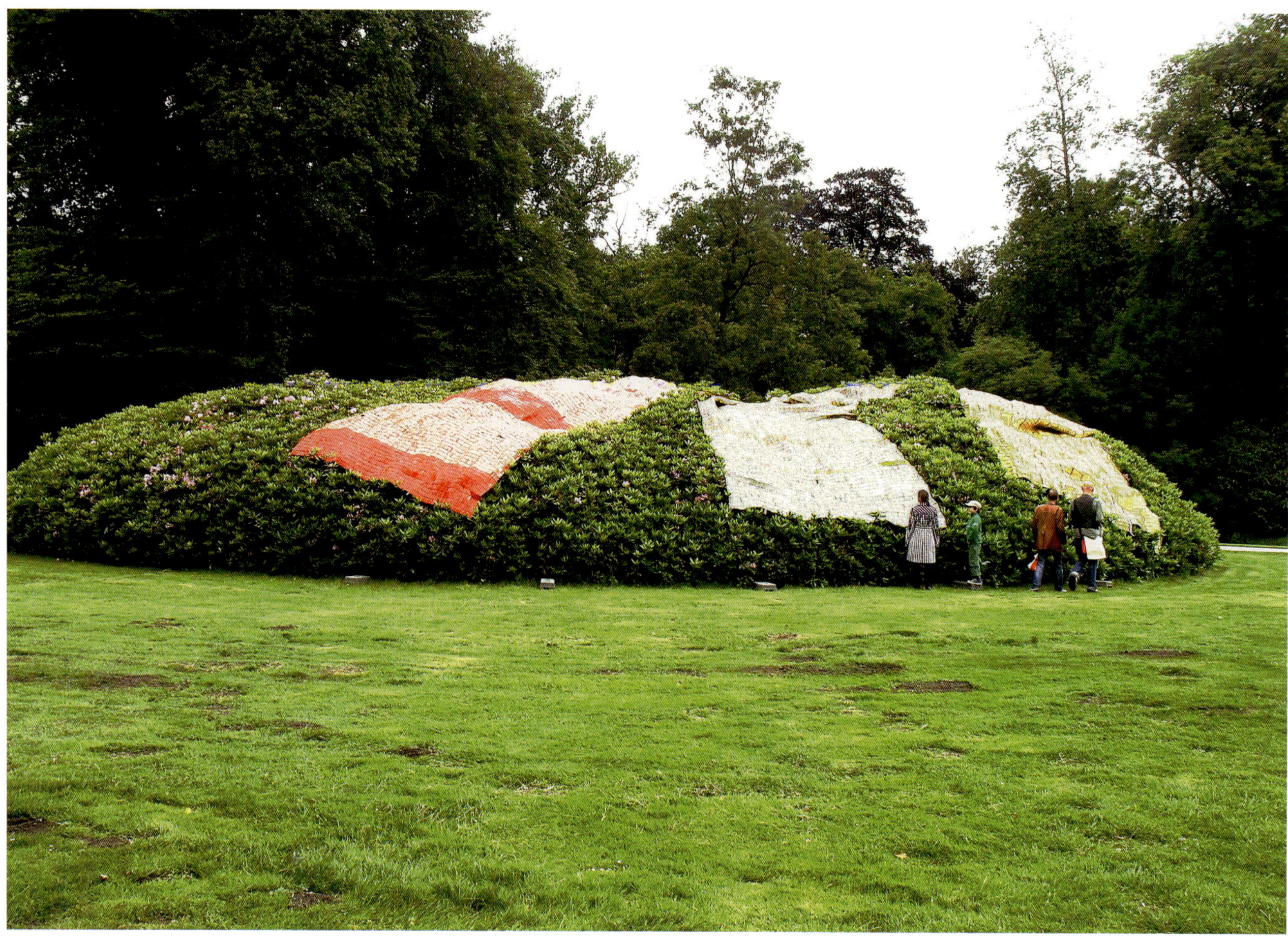

El Anatsui

ABOVE
Drying Towels, 2008
Aluminum and copper wire, 3 elements, 157 x 472 inches each
Installation view, *Grandeur,* 10th Sonsbeek International Sculpture Exhibition, Sonsbeek Park, Arnhem, The Netherlands, June 13–September 21, 2008

OPPOSITE, ABOVE
Sacred Moon, 2007
Aluminum and copper wire, 103 x 141 inches
Mott-Warsh Collection, Flint, Michigan

OPPOSITE, BELOW
River Crossing, 2007
Aluminum and copper wire, 103 x 141 inches

Later on, I got interested in the idea of cloth itself because I come from a family (not only a family but a town) that had a lot to do with cloth. The men—most of them fishermen—would weave during off-season, and I remember that as a kid when I visited home I would see almost everybody going around spinning thread for weaving. I think that must have become a part of me. But I haven't been interested in textiles as a form of art, or craft, or whatever you call it. Yeah, my family wove—and in art school we were introduced to all the areas of art and the one that least attracted me was textiles. But then, I find it intriguing that what I do now is very much like trying to get away from textiles, but textiles are following me.

When I started working with bottle caps, I thought it was going to be a very short run. Then, as time went on, I saw that the possibilities are just endless. There have been so many revelations. So many works are revelations. Initially I wasn't concerned with color; my attention was on the structure as a sculpture. Now I'm concerned with color, like a painter. I saw that I could organize the colors as very strong elements. I'm combining sculpture and painting. The concerns of the sculptor and the painter are inherent in each of the works that I do with these bottle caps. And I see that even the modes of display are beginning to expand—not only on the wall but on hedges, on trees, on just anything, on the floor. And the textures are getting more and more with each time.

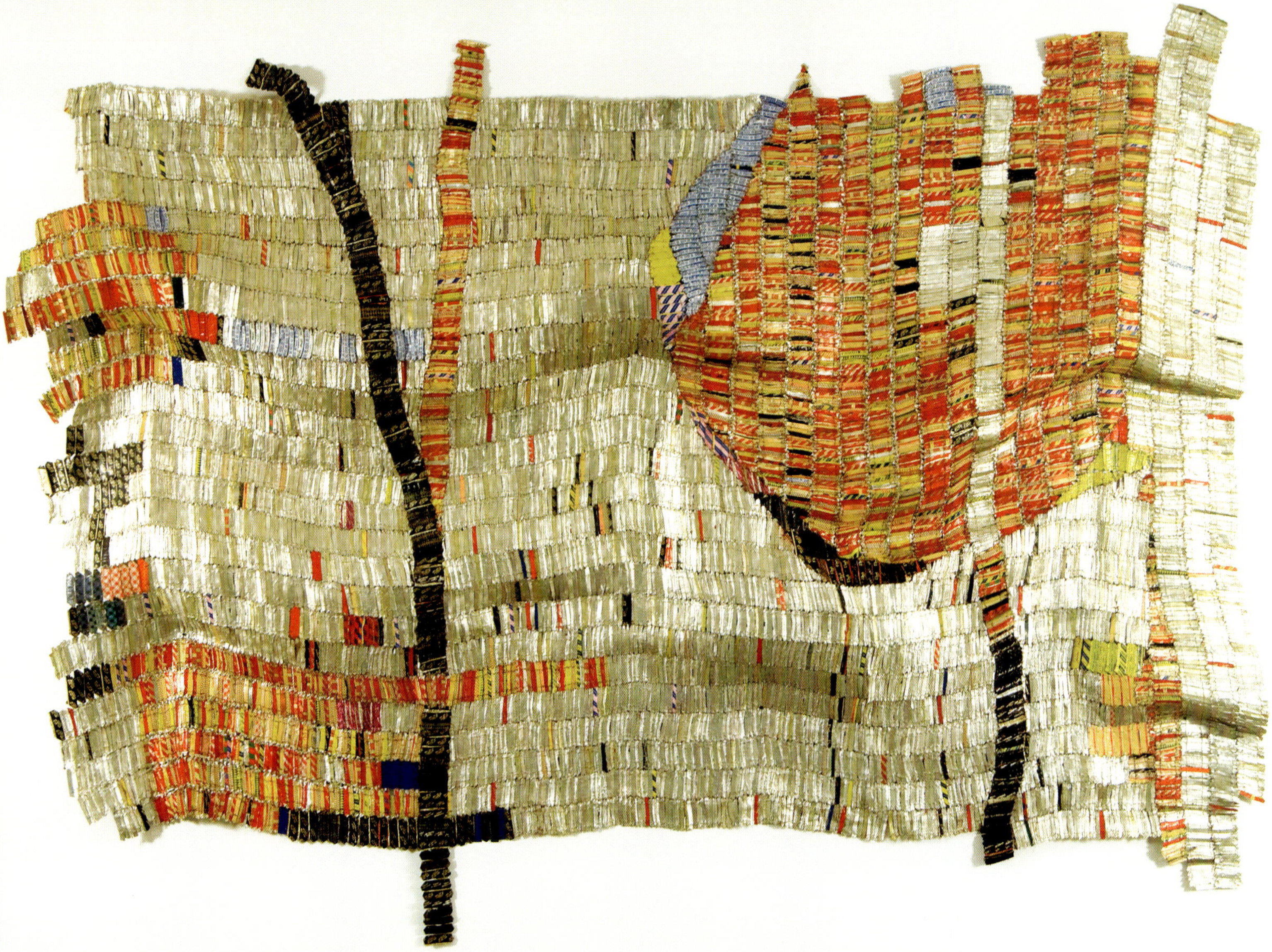

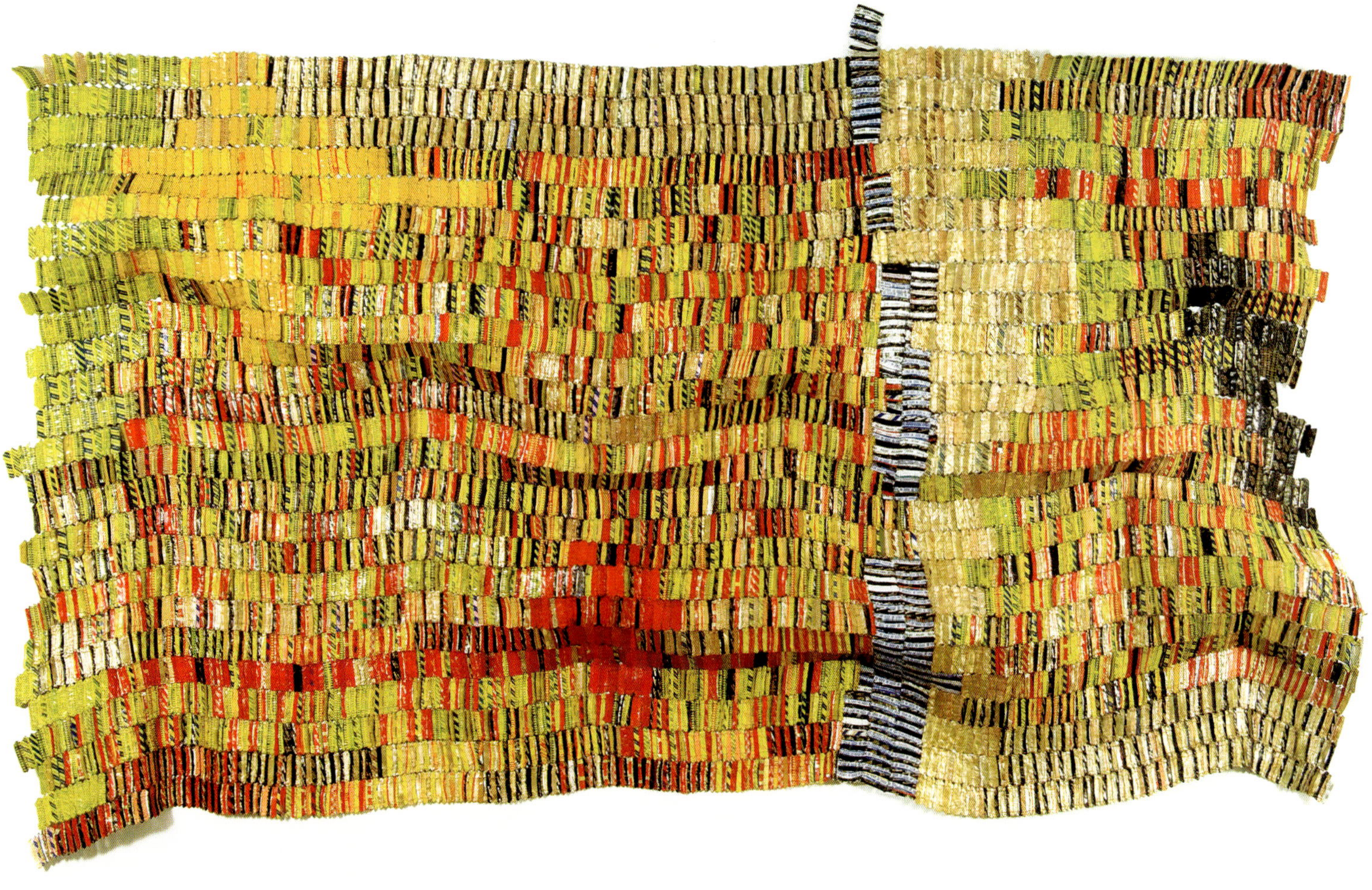

El Anatsui

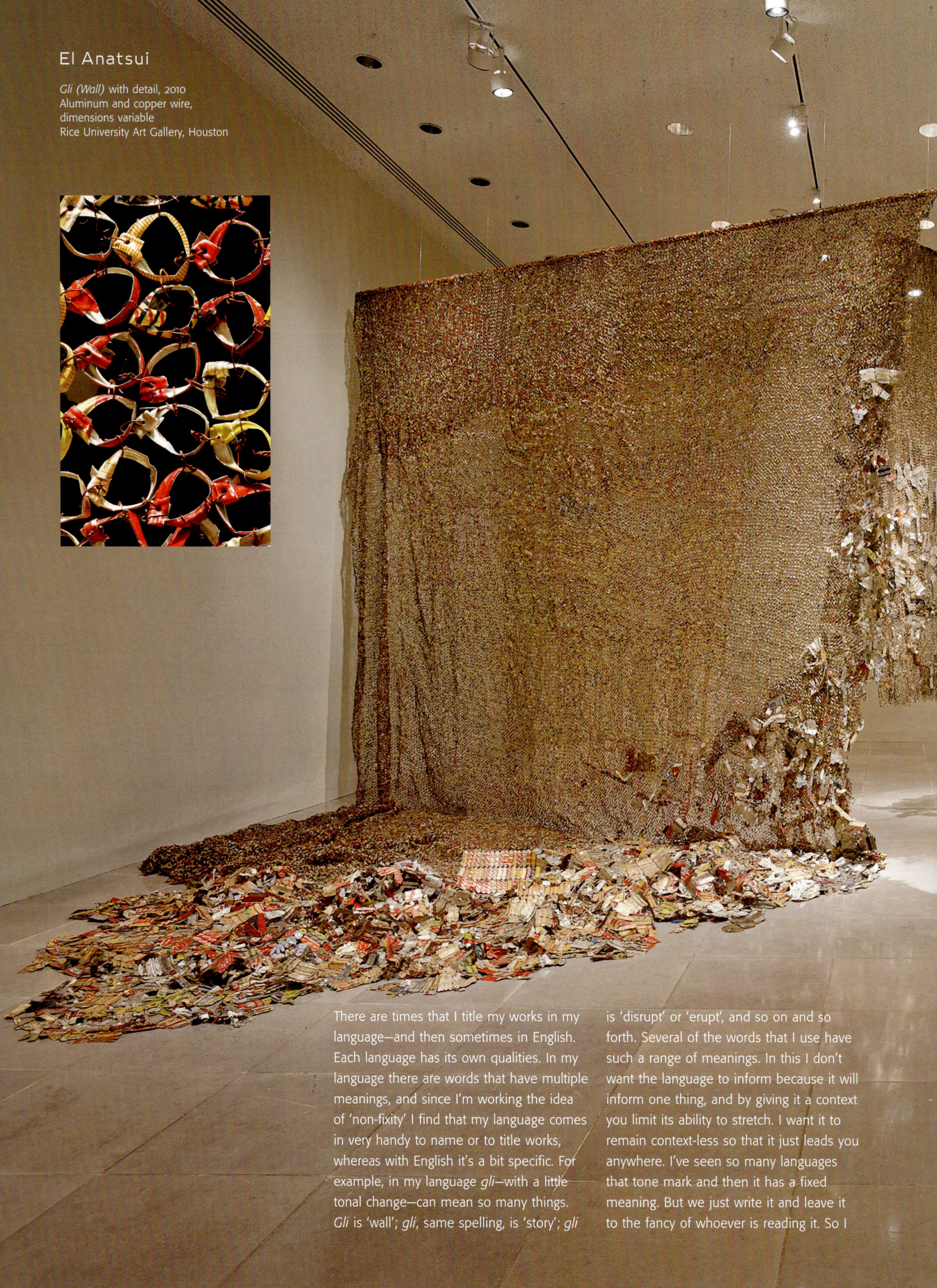

Gli (Wall) with detail, 2010
Aluminum and copper wire,
dimensions variable
Rice University Art Gallery, Houston

There are times that I title my works in my language—and then sometimes in English. Each language has its own qualities. In my language there are words that have multiple meanings, and since I'm working the idea of 'non-fixity' I find that my language comes in very handy to name or to title works, whereas with English it's a bit specific. For example, in my language *gli*—with a little tonal change—can mean so many things. *Gli* is 'wall'; *gli*, same spelling, is 'story'; *gli* is 'disrupt' or 'erupt', and so on and so forth. Several of the words that I use have such a range of meanings. In this I don't want the language to inform because it will inform one thing, and by giving it a context you limit its ability to stretch. I want it to remain context-less so that it just leads you anywhere. I've seen so many languages that tone mark and then it has a fixed meaning. But we just write it and leave it to the fancy of whoever is reading it. So I

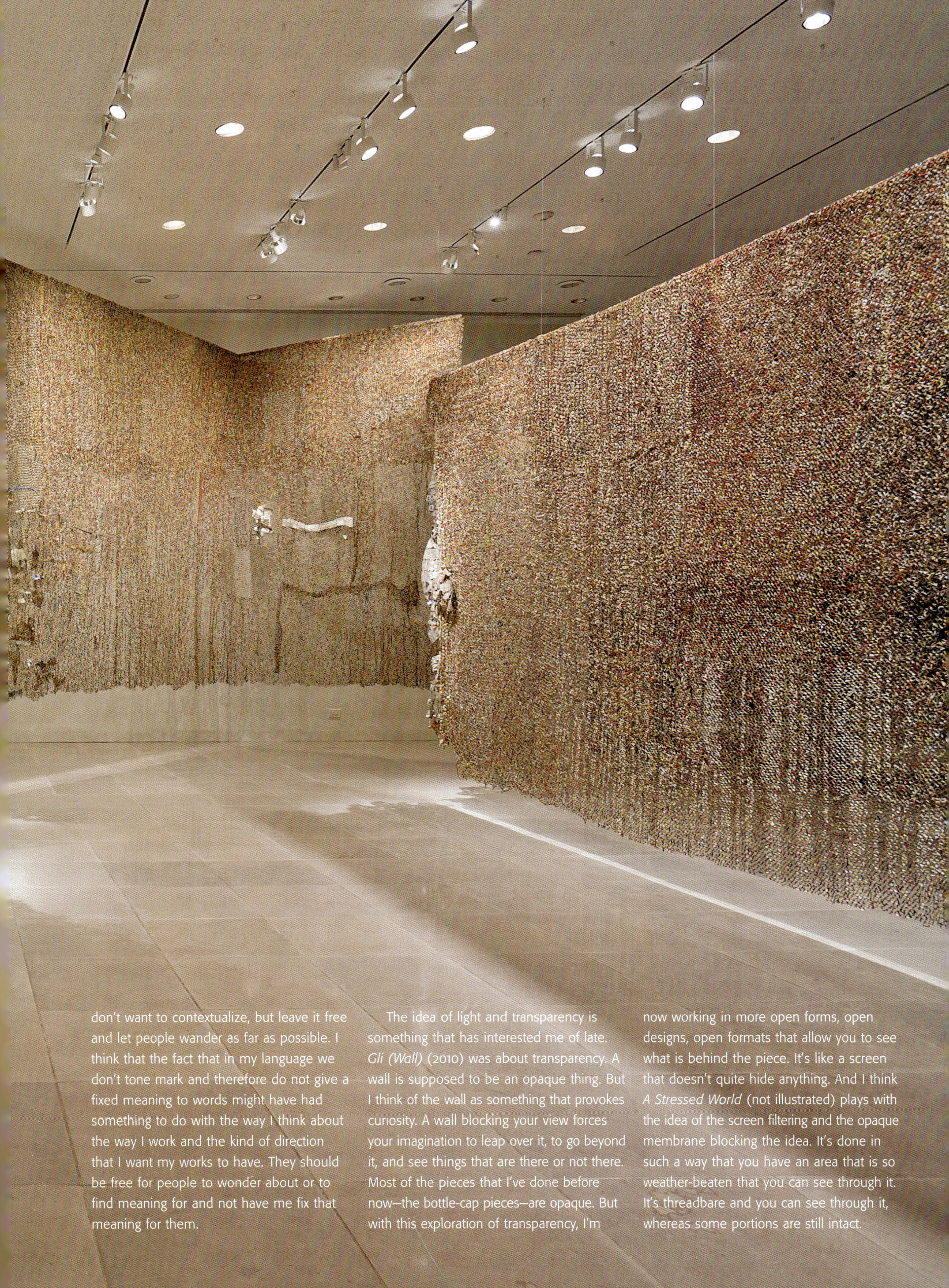

don't want to contextualize, but leave it free and let people wander as far as possible. I think that the fact that in my language we don't tone mark and therefore do not give a fixed meaning to words might have had something to do with the way I think about the way I work and the kind of direction that I want my works to have. They should be free for people to wonder about or to find meaning for and not have me fix that meaning for them.

The idea of light and transparency is something that has interested me of late. *Gli (Wall)* (2010) was about transparency. A wall is supposed to be an opaque thing. But I think of the wall as something that provokes curiosity. A wall blocking your view forces your imagination to leap over it, to go beyond it, and see things that are there or not there. Most of the pieces that I've done before now—the bottle-cap pieces—are opaque. But with this exploration of transparency, I'm now working in more open forms, open designs, open formats that allow you to see what is behind the piece. It's like a screen that doesn't quite hide anything. And I think *A Stressed World* (not illustrated) plays with the idea of the screen filtering and the opaque membrane blocking the idea. It's done in such a way that you have an area that is so weather-beaten that you can see through it. It's threadbare and you can see through it, whereas some portions are still intact.

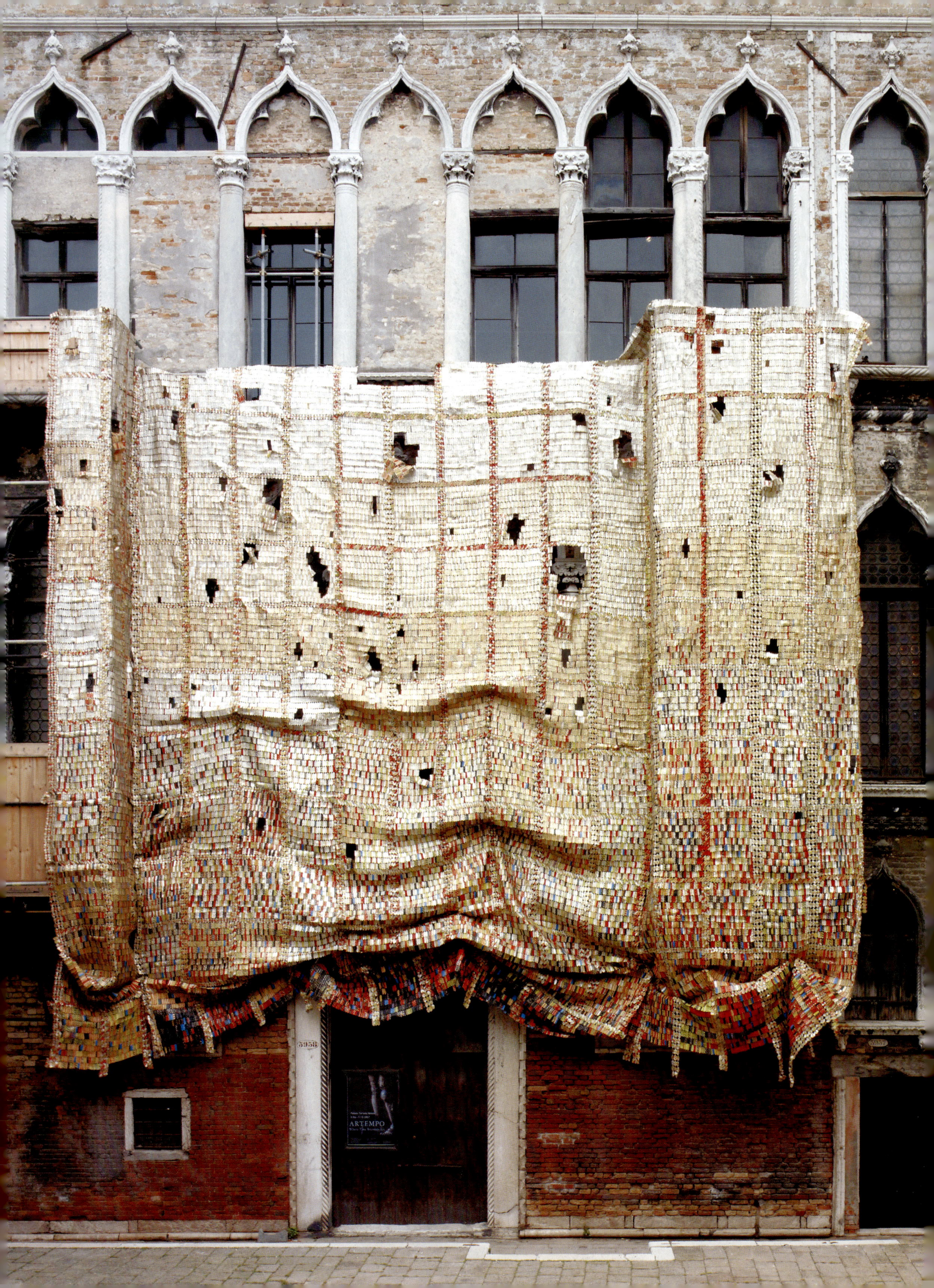
5958
ARTEMPO

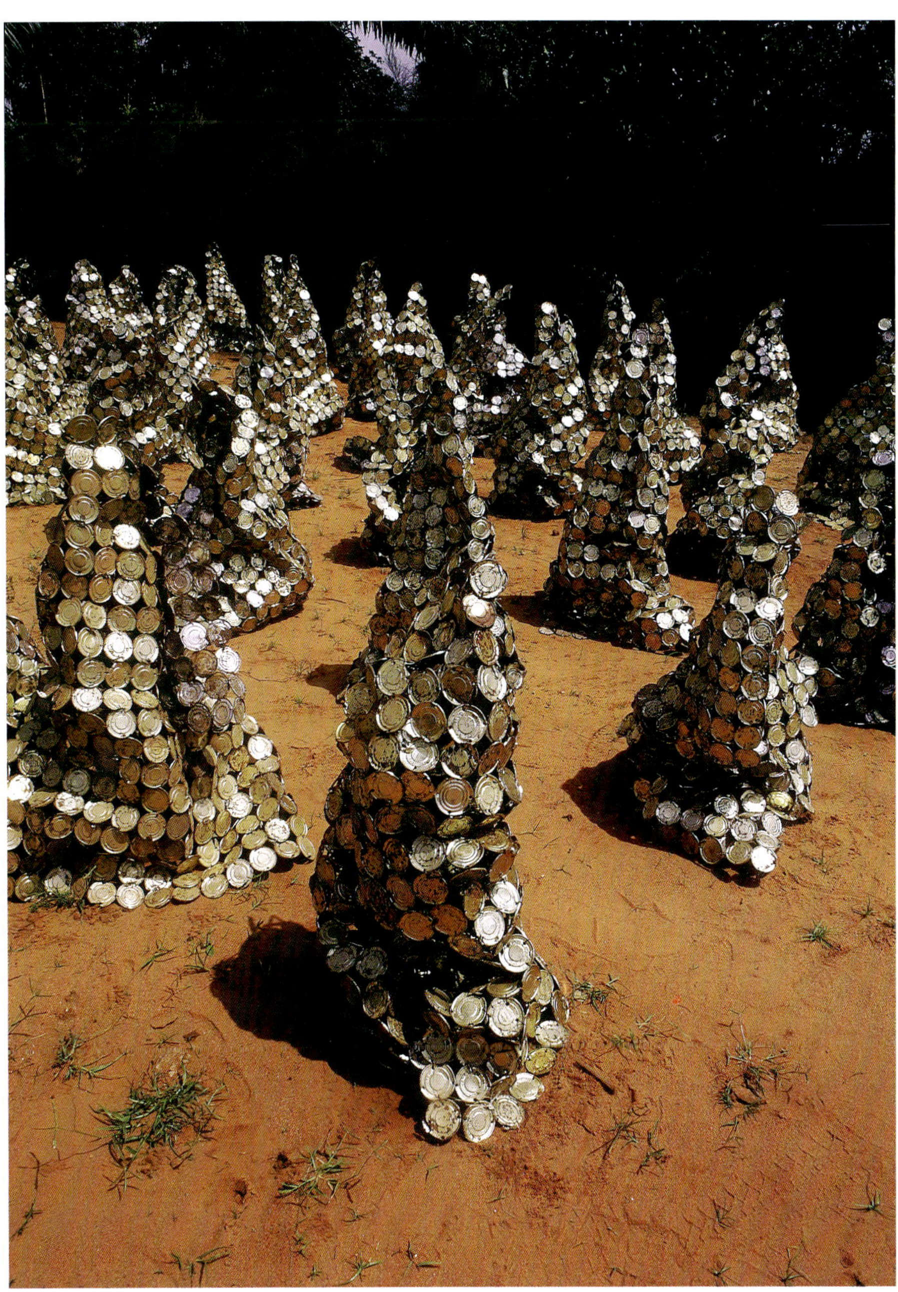

El Anatsui

OPPOSITE
Fresh and Fading Memories, 2007
Aluminum, copper wire, 358 x 236 inches
Installation view, *Artempo: Where Time Becomes Art,* Palazzo Fortuny, 52nd Venice Biennale, June 10–November 21, 2007
Private collection

ABOVE
Peak Project, 1999
Tin, copper, wire, installation dimensions variable, each sheet approximately 24 x 48 inches
Installation view, the artist's studio, Nsukka, Nigeria
Collection of the artist

I went to formal art school, an offshoot of Goldsmiths College in London. In my final year, the external examiner was a professor from Goldsmiths and the faculty was a mix of Europeans and a few Africans. Naturally most of us absorbed a lot of influence from the European tradition. We weren't exposed to local traditions, because the faculty weren't trained with that. I remember that in art history we didn't do anything about Africa. In my penultimate year, and final year, I used to go to the cultural center in the town where the university was situated. There I discovered that there was something known as art that belongs to the place, apart from what we were exposed to in school. When I made that discovery it really set my direction. I started to look more inward at the tradition of the place, in addition to what I learned about European art. I think that the situation made some of us richer, because a European art student wouldn't have known about such things. But I had it there, and I also had Europe brought to me. So I'm a product of these two traditions and many more.

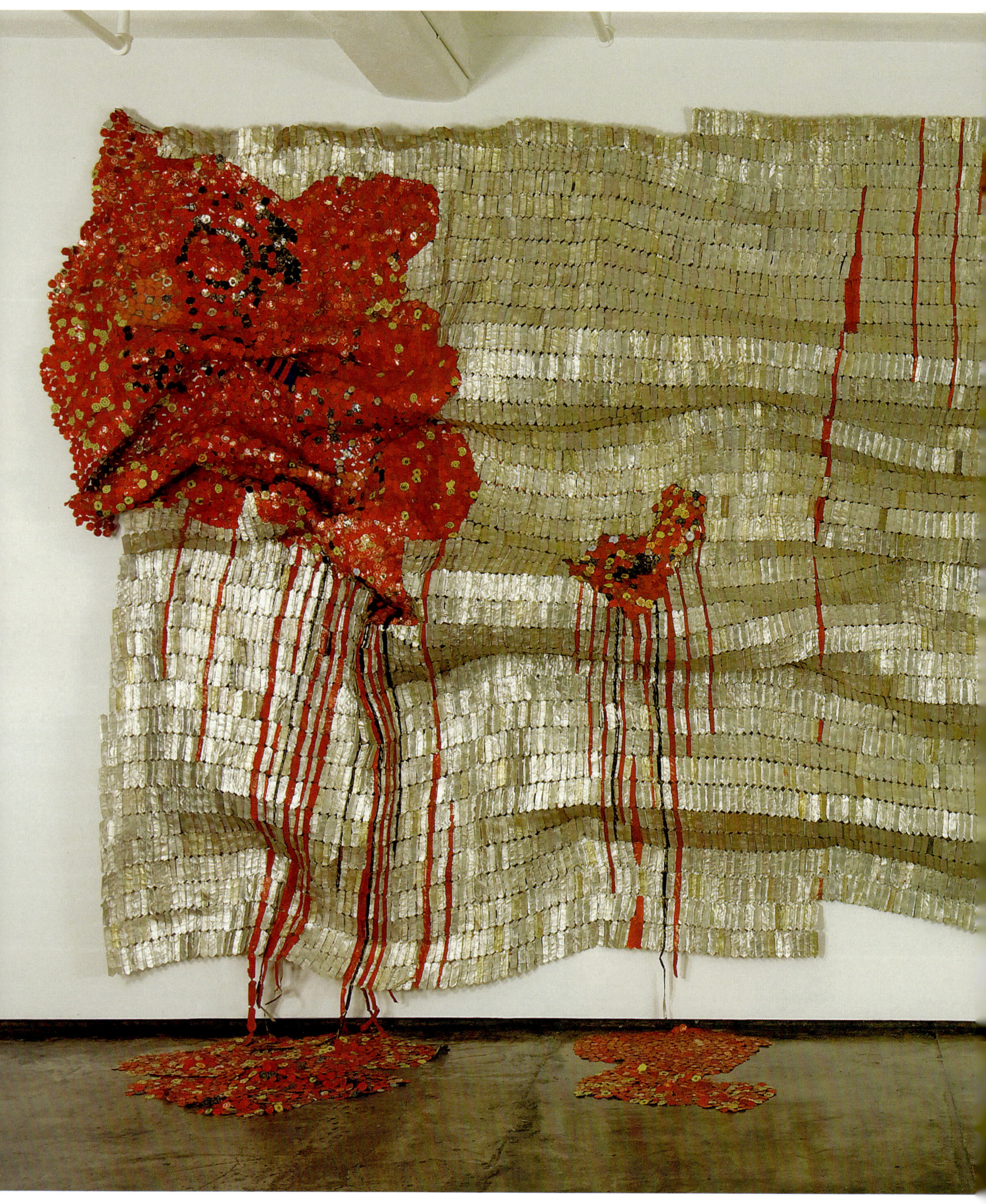

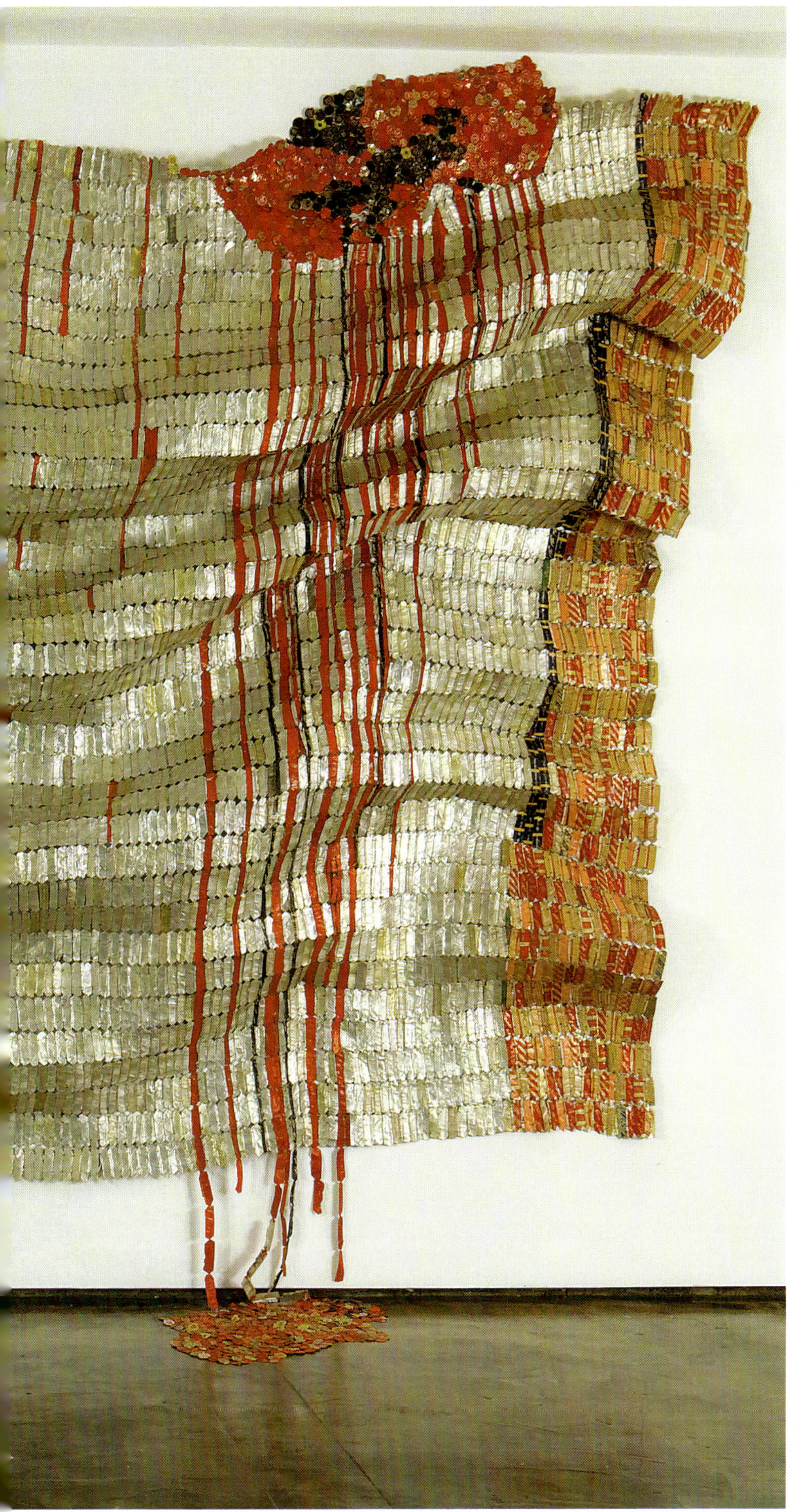

El Anatsui

Bleeding Takari, 2008
Aluminum and copper wire, 61 x 89½ inches
Collection of the Museum of Modern Art, New York, Gift of Donald L. Bryant, Jr. and Jerry Speyer, 201.2008

When I work I think I want, really, to create something that says or expresses things in ways that are not petty. Maybe that's how the monument mentality seems to come in. But as far as scale is concerned, scale is something else that I think is detected by the medium that I use and how it can effectively draw attention to itself. The first pieces that I did were moderate sized. I saw that if you have a scale that is petty, using discarded media, then the work is going to be petty—in fact, too petty for anybody to bother about trying to listen to. On a larger scale it becomes more effective. It's like the saying, "If you meet one ant, you're not going to notice an ant, but if you meet an army of them. . . ." So, the kinds of media that I use are like ants. One is not effective, but many are.

I don't think I'm concerned about beauty as a word. I do know that in most of our cultures—where I grew up—everybody would say, "Beauty is character. It's not a look." I tend to think of this as a very good way of defining beauty. Among the Igbo, or among my people, we don't regard beauty as something that belongs to the sense of sight only. It's a whole lot of things apart from that.

I don't know what tradition I place my work in. I don't think that's something that artists worry about. You would be closing yourself up if you placed yourself into a tradition. I think artists are meant to break tradition or to supply what tradition doesn't have. If there is something that I think art does, I think it awakens the spiritual. I *feel* it awaken. Standing before a really effective piece of work, you feel there's a spirit presence. You know there is presence other than the physical. And I think that is the value that I see art bring about—not just bringing out a statement.

Catherine Opie

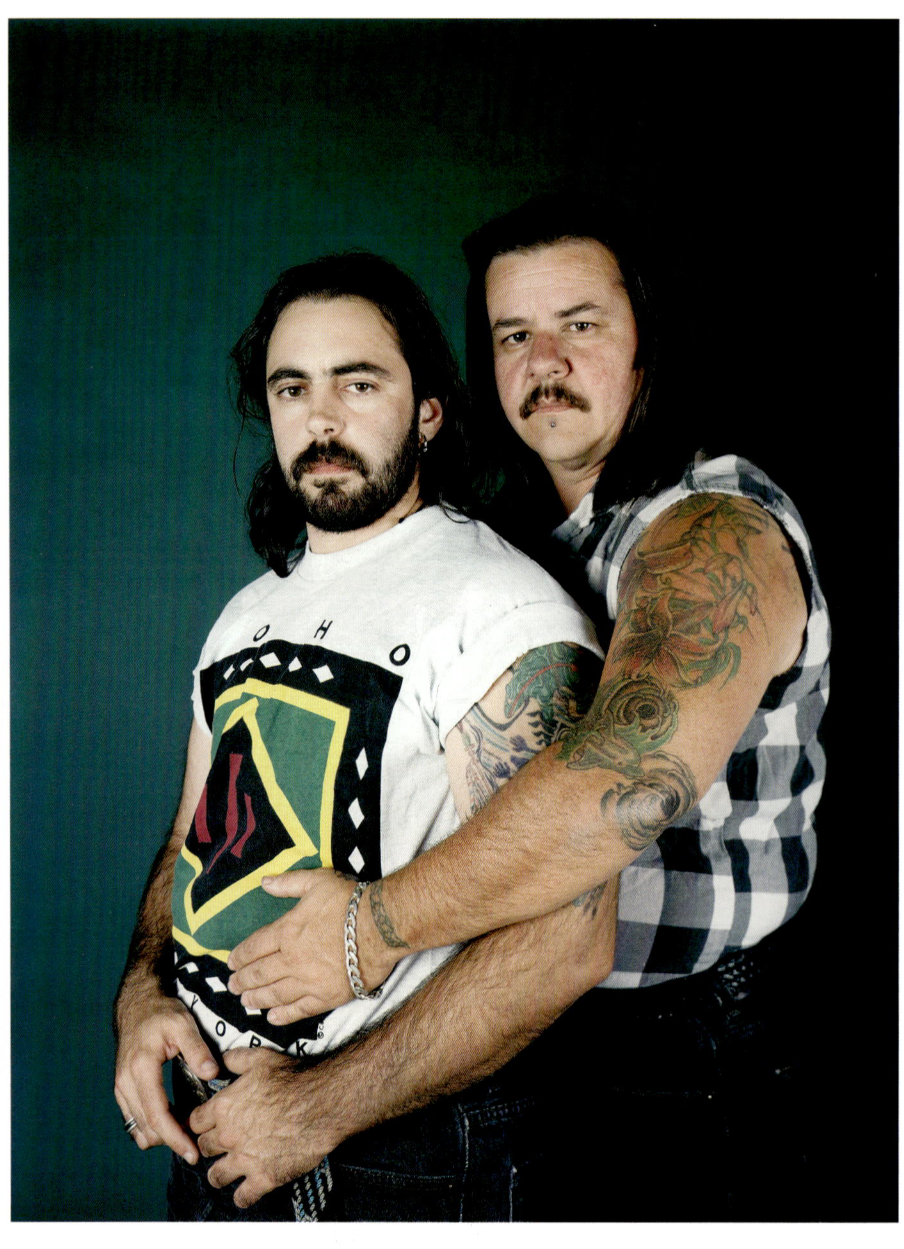

ABOVE
Mike and Sky, from *Portraits,* 1993
C-print, 20 x 16 inches
Edition of 8, 2 AP

OPPOSITE
Justin Bond, from *Portraits,* 1993
C-print, 20 x 16 inches
Edition of 8, 2 AP

I have vivid memories of going to the National Portrait Gallery. I was probably eight or nine. So often, we relate much easier to a visual world. I've always been a reader; I love fiction. That provides other kinds of images for me in my mind. But I think that I really felt very good about seeing those paintings, and that's one of the reasons why I've always been in love with a kind of rich light. And I think that's why people often call my work painting—because I'm using more tropes of lighting in relationship to painting than photography. I like faces to disappear in a shadow, which they do very easily in a painting. In a photograph, that's bad lighting. When I was printing all my work, it was very dark printed. I remember my teachers saying, "You know, you're printing a little heavy-handed." And I would just say, "Well, I like the way that looks."

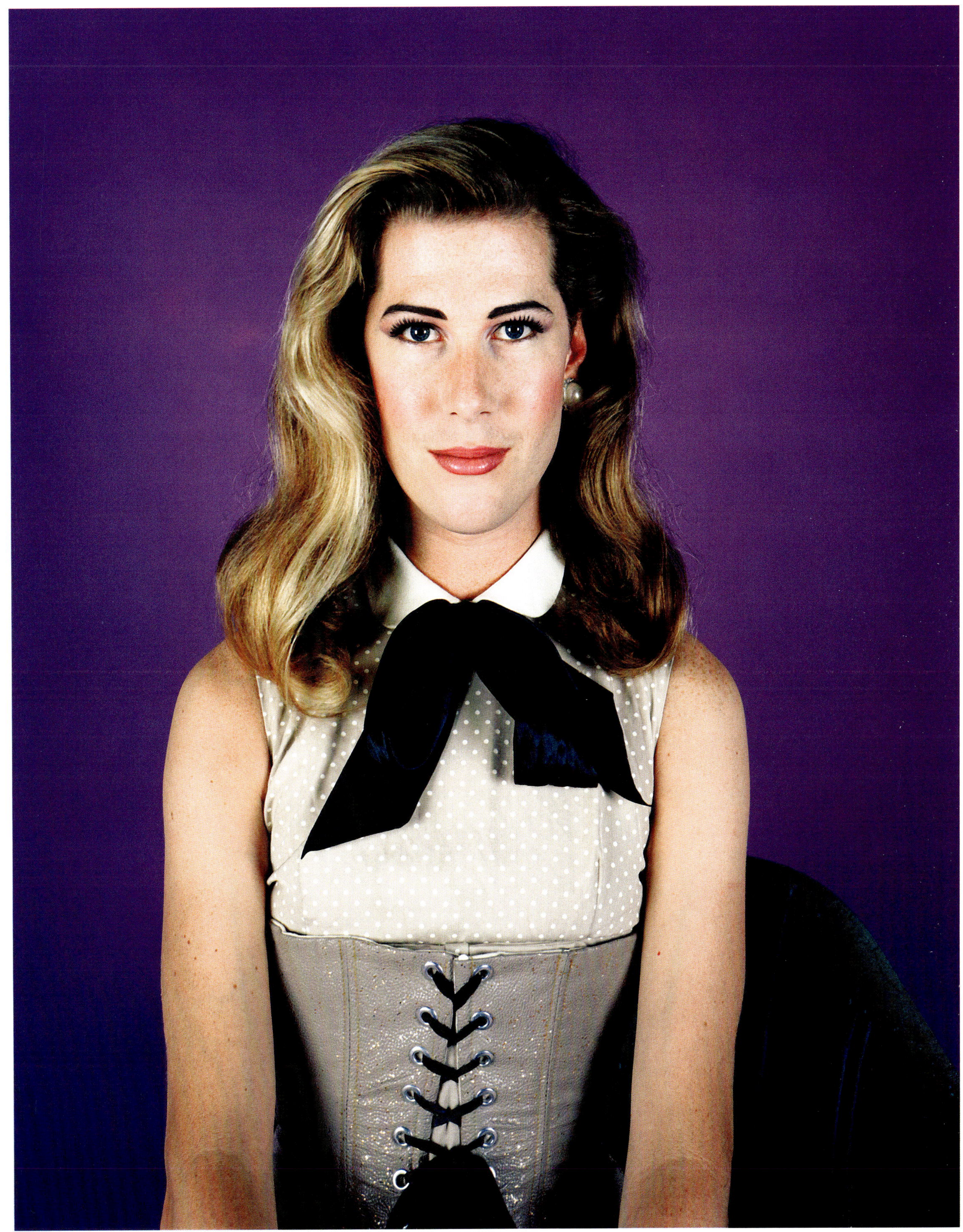

Catherine Opie

RIGHT
Norma & Eyenga, Minneapolis, Minnesota, from *Domestic,* 1998
C-print, 40 x 50 inches
Edition of 5, 2 AP

OPPOSITE, TOP
Miggi & Ilene, Los Angeles, California, from *Domestic,* 1995
C-print, 40 x 50 inches
Edition of 5, 2 AP

OPPOSITE, BOTTOM
Still Life #7, Bayside, New York, from *Domestic Still Lifes,* 1998
C-print, 30 x 40 inches
Edition of 5, 2 AP

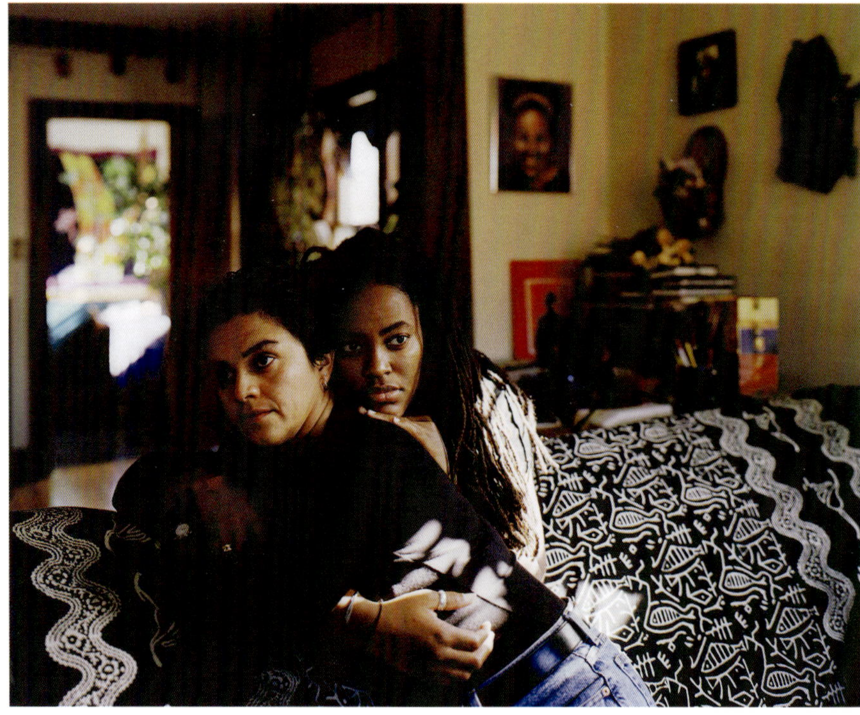

I picked up a camera when I was nine. I was interested in photography first through the sources that were at home. It was *Life Magazine*; it was *Look*; it was *National Geographic*. It was the notion that photography came out of a need to create a pictorial narrative in relation to life, and that you created this sense of document that also was history. When I went to San Francisco Art Institute and I was studying with Henry Wessel, Jr., Larry Sultan, and John Collier, Jr., it was directly out of the Szarkowski school of photography: looking at Winogrand, at Arbus; reading Szarkowski's book, *Looking At Photographs*; looking at that whole history of MoMA collecting from Steichen to Szarkowski. I was really interested, early on, in being a street photographer. I loved the images of Helen Levitt. I was amazed by what Robert Frank did—that photography worked best in relationship to pure observation. That was the core of it in relationship to its medium. But at the same time, the up-and-rising contemporary conversation in art in relationship to photography was the Pictures Generation—having Sherrie Levine begin to photograph Walker Evans and say that it was hers. Cindy Sherman. Richard Prince. That work was never really a part of my discourse at San Francisco Art Institute. When I went to CalArts it was challenging to have practiced and be fairly competent at a craft and feel that I absolutely didn't know anything that was happening on a contemporary level. I was studying with Allan Sekula and Catherine Lord. We weren't reading semiotics; postmodernism wasn't being discussed. We didn't all have *October* opened up, reading what Rosalind Krauss had to say. Within that two-year period there was an expectation for me to completely adopt and adapt that language in relationship to my practice. It was really difficult at first. I felt completely displaced in what a photograph could do. So I kept going out and making photographs of what I was observing. And I would bring them back in and I would talk about them in critique class and be questioned a lot. They were really hard questions to answer. Then I would go out and I would make more photographs instead of stopping work because I thought it was all bullshit, which is what a lot of my fellow students were doing. And I realized at a certain point, after working on the same thing for two years and trying to break up what they were saying to me and what I believed, that I could still create something in relationship to ideas of representation that felt like a document for me. But what I had to do at the same time was begin to critique the validity of it. Instead of it being real, which is what I came off of in terms of the street photography, it became representational. So there was a time when I just thought, "Oh, I just need to shift my language here. I can still do what I'm doing, but in terms of being a practicing contemporary artist I need to be able to shift certain ways that I construct things and look at them."

I started to go inside myself a little bit more in relationship to my own belief of what I was framing and portraying and representing for my audience versus trying to hold onto street photography and observation as being real. I had to fight that impulse of wanting it to exist just because it was important that it existed. And I think to a certain extent I still fight that a little bit. I still think that photography operates both in terms of the real and the not-real—that it is my construct. So the fight for me now is in relationship to PhotoShop. I don't take things out and I don't put things in.

It's really important for me that I can still find something valuable in relationship to the idea of an early observational photographer—that it can be found and I can wait for it. I can wait for light to change, and I can have a moment of meditation. I can allow that to happen. And that is my 'real' that still comes from the platform of being an observational photographer, which is defined in relationship to a documentary practice.

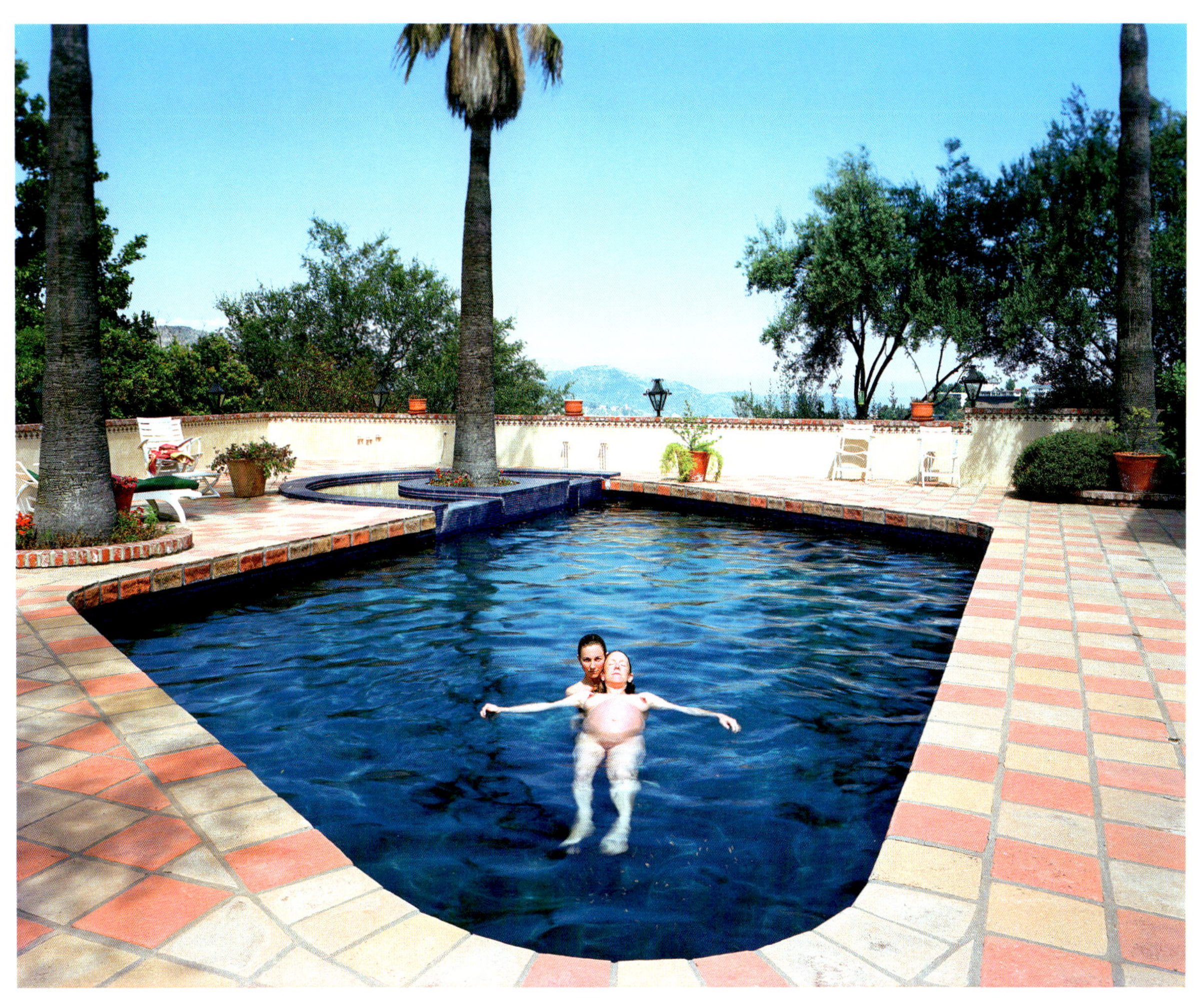

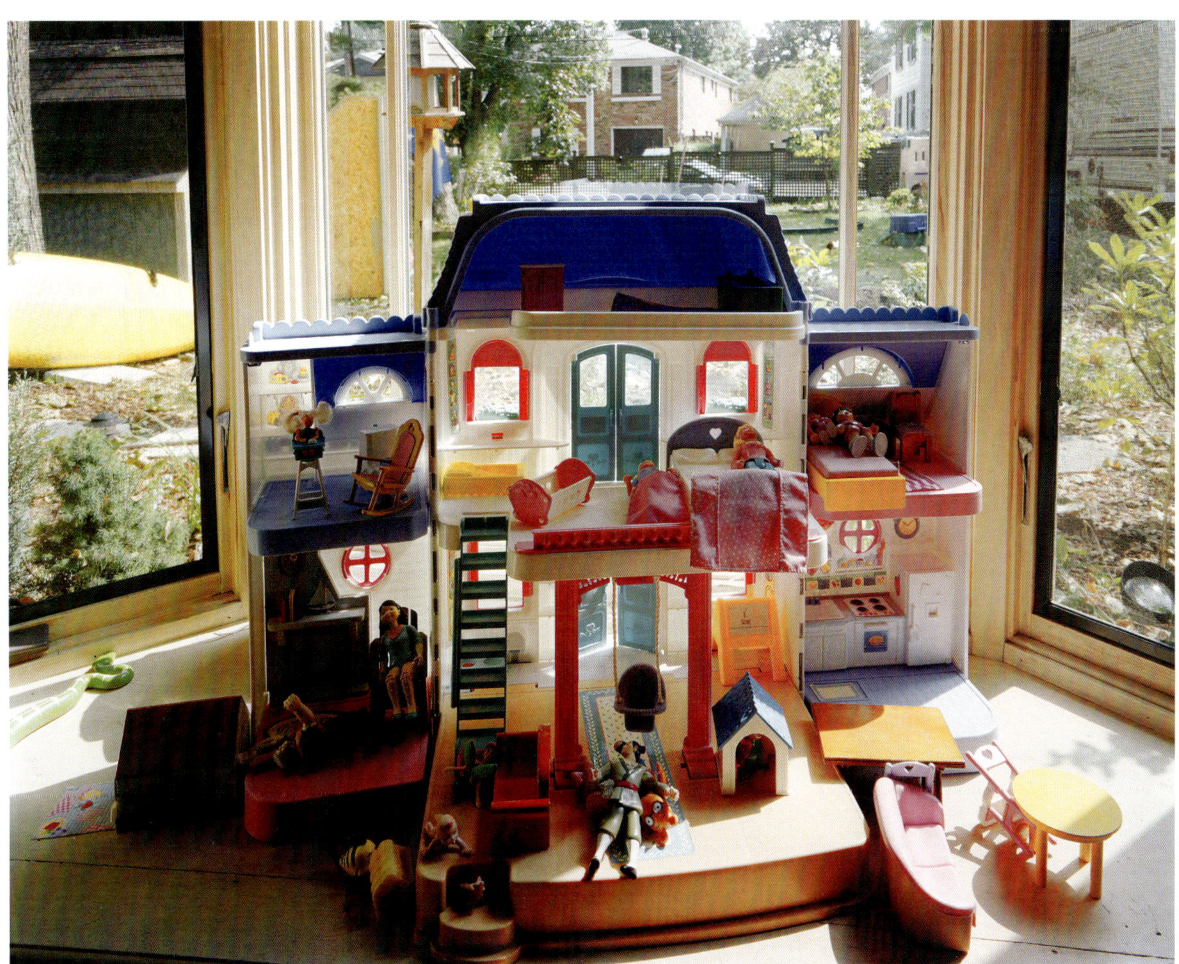

Catherine Opie

TOP
Untitled #9 (Wall Street),
from *American Cities,* 2001
Iris print, 16 x 41 inches
Edition of 5, 2 AP

BOTTOM
Untitled #5 (Wall Street),
from *American Cities,* 2001
Iris print, 16 x 41 inches
Edition of 5, 2 AP

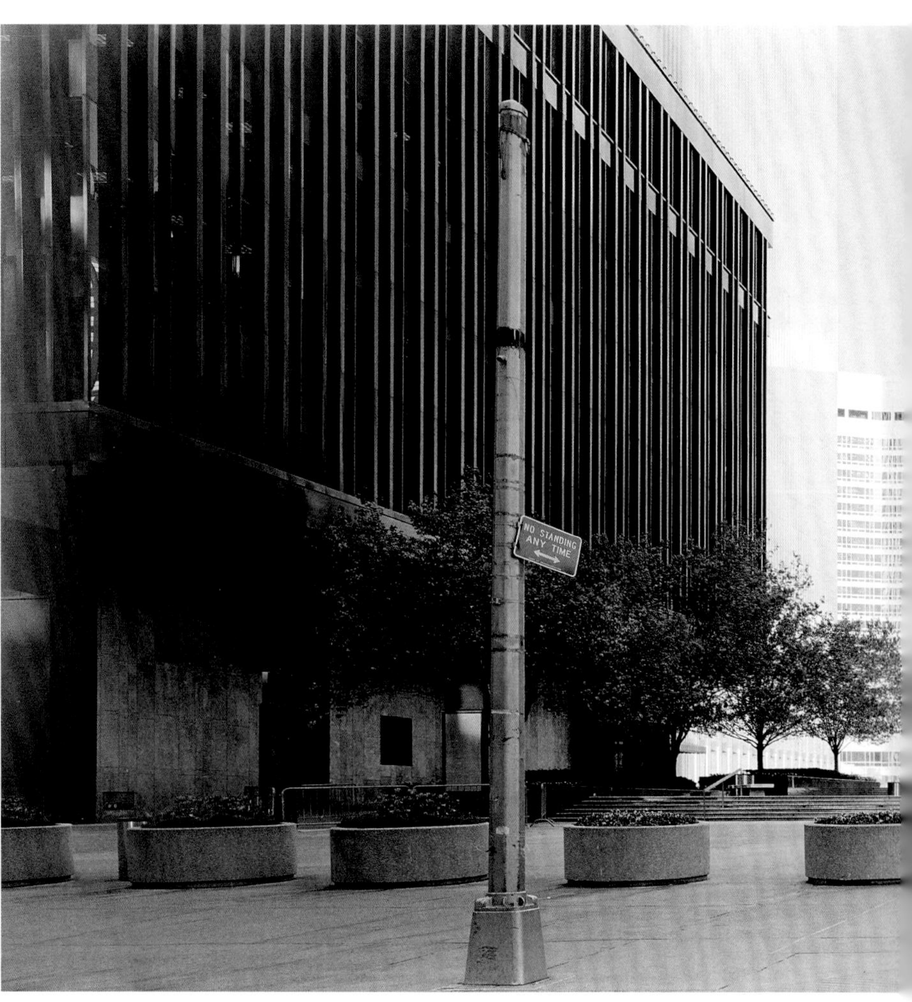

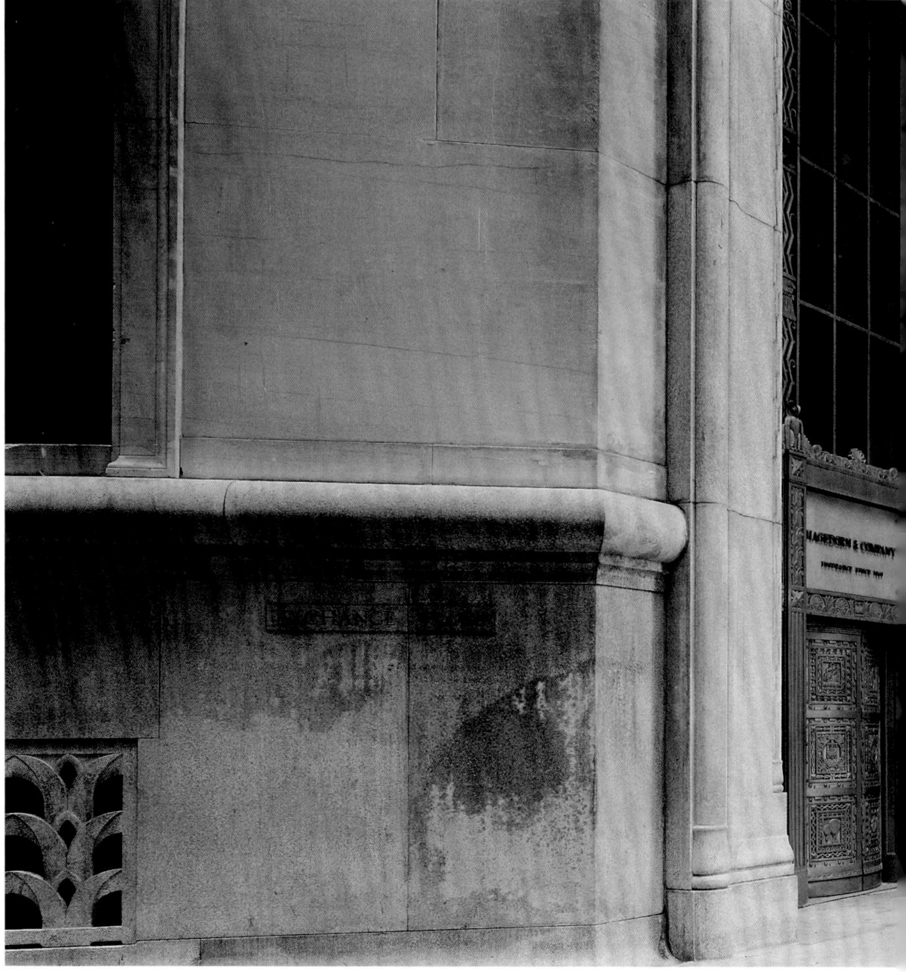

I am really interested in utopia—and also the 'dystopic'. I've read a lot of sci-fi novels that play with those ideas, and I'm a huge Octavia Butler fan. I'm interested in how she constructs ideas—not only of sexuality, but also of what is 'utopic' and 'dystopic'. In a way, it's the same kind of binary as normal and abnormal. Supposedly we construct those binaries to be able to create a model to live by. My 'utopic' notion is humanity: I'm utterly devoted and dedicated to being a humanitarian and trying to live my life in a way in which both my work and myself allow a kind of representation that creates kindness and a way to observe the world in relation to the way I think about it and view it. I have a hard time with mean photographs. There is already so much meanness and discouragement in this world. I'm not sure what it means to create representations of people that show them in their worst light. So I believe in creating representations that are sometimes tough but, at the same time, the core of humanitarian ideas exists within that. Even though there are some tough ideas in the work, it's still done in such a way that's not meant to ever be disturbing. So, my perfect world (which I'll never see because I don't believe that it exists) is about acts of kindness. It's about the fact that we have the ability not to have people starve. We have the ability not to go into war over religious ideology. We could become a sustainable country; we could stop global warming if we chose to. We just choose not to. And that's the 'dystopic' nature of humans. I could represent that, but I'm not interested in representing that. That's my *everyday*; that's the front-page newspaper. That's the Channel 4 News that I'm interested in creating a dialogue with in relationship to my time and what I observe. But I'm not interested in trying to make images that reflect what is so prevailing.

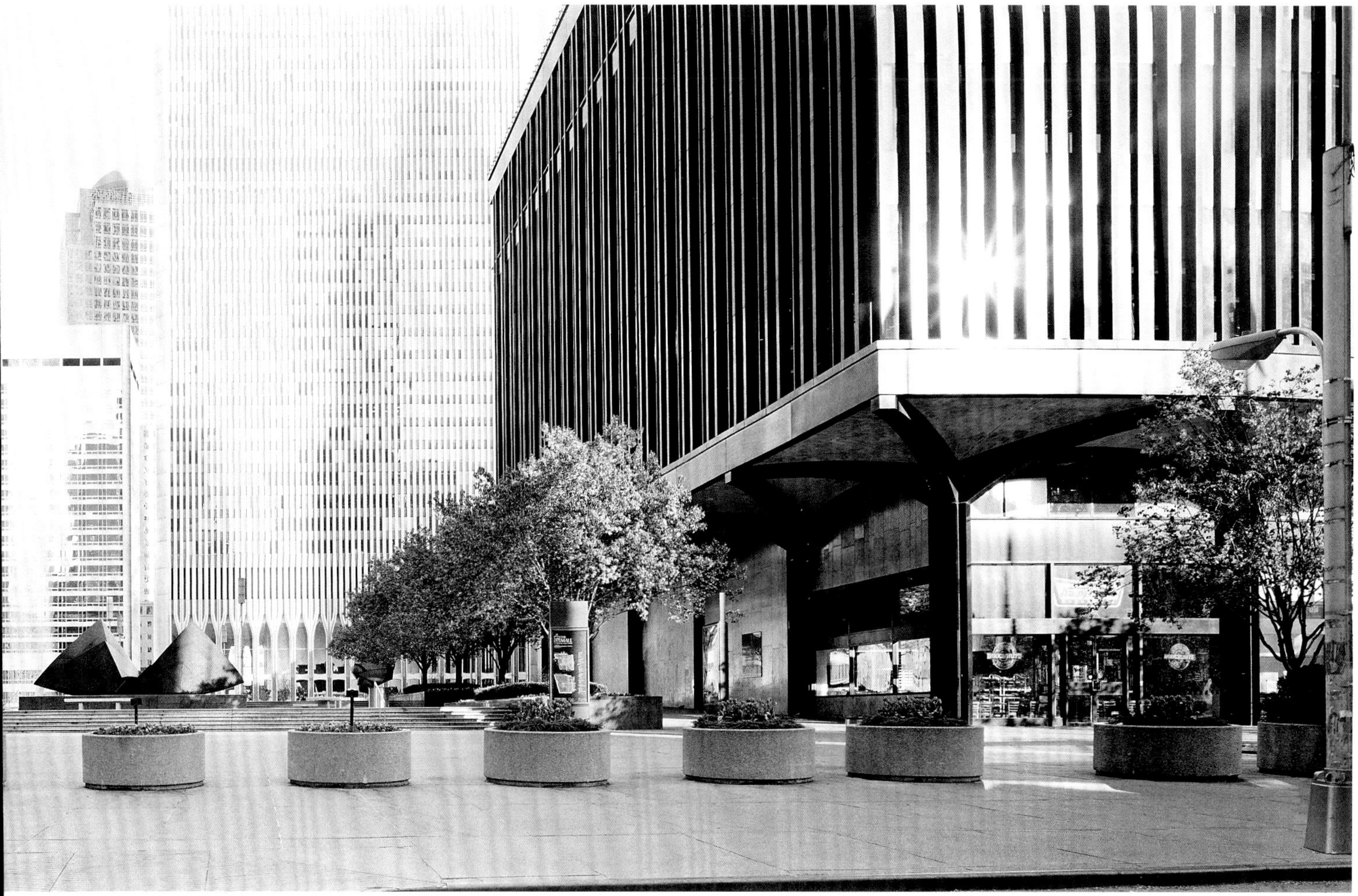

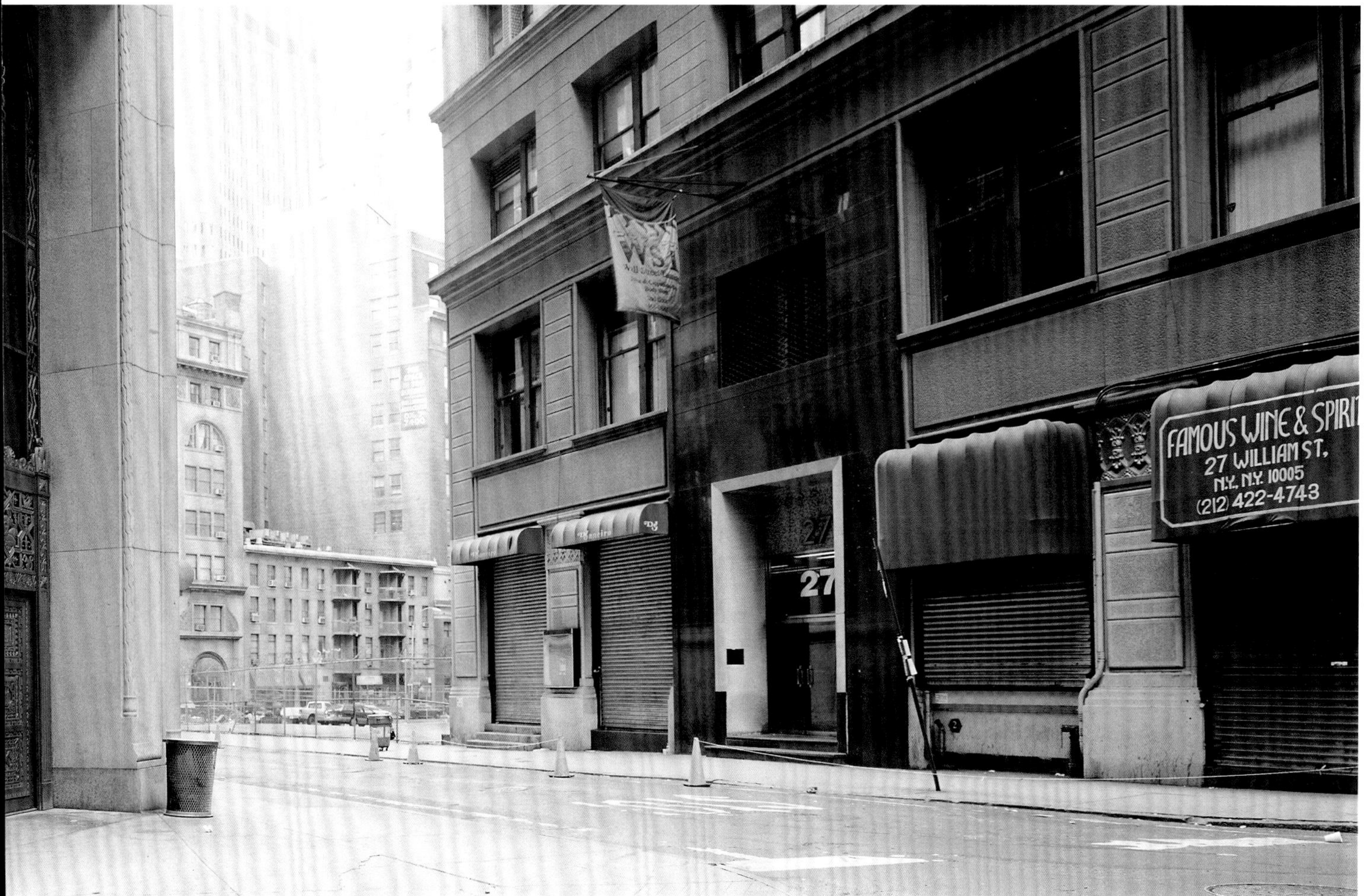

FAMOUS WINE & SPIRIT
27 WILLIAM ST.
N.Y., N.Y. 10005
(212) 422-4743
27

Right after 9/11, when I had finished *Wall Street* (2001), I was looking at exhibitions around Chelsea, and there was just one flower exhibition after another. The way that photography was changing radically within the art world was frustrating for me. If you made work that had street-photography language within it, you were thought of as a photojournalist, and 'documentary' as a language started getting wiped out. I was like, "Why aren't people observing anymore? What's wrong with this kind of observation?" I was compelled to pick up a camera and start photographing. I think it started with *In and Around Home* (2004–05), and I ended up photographing crowds of people. There are photographs in that body of work that are really important to me, that signified this shift of wanting to begin to photograph larger groups. I was back on the street with a camera in my hand, like I was in the early '80s in San Francisco, and I was looking at groups of people that had come together, to rally against sex offenders (*In Protest to Sex Offenders*, 2005) or to celebrate football (*Football Landscape #16*, 2009), and I realized that it was really important for me to no longer empty out the landscape, but to fulfill this other notion of creating documents of our time, in relationship to going out and observing—creating another way of looking at American landscape.

It's complicated to figure out how to weave together the ideas that I'm interested in—in relationship to looking at space and people and architecture—and create some kind of an external and internal narrative. I just try to do it with various bodies of work that allow reflection at the same time that they create potential for people to find commonality in relationship to the recognition of what the work is doing. The core that goes through all of the bodies of work is relationship to community. It's a perplexing question that I explore on multiple levels in different bodies of work.

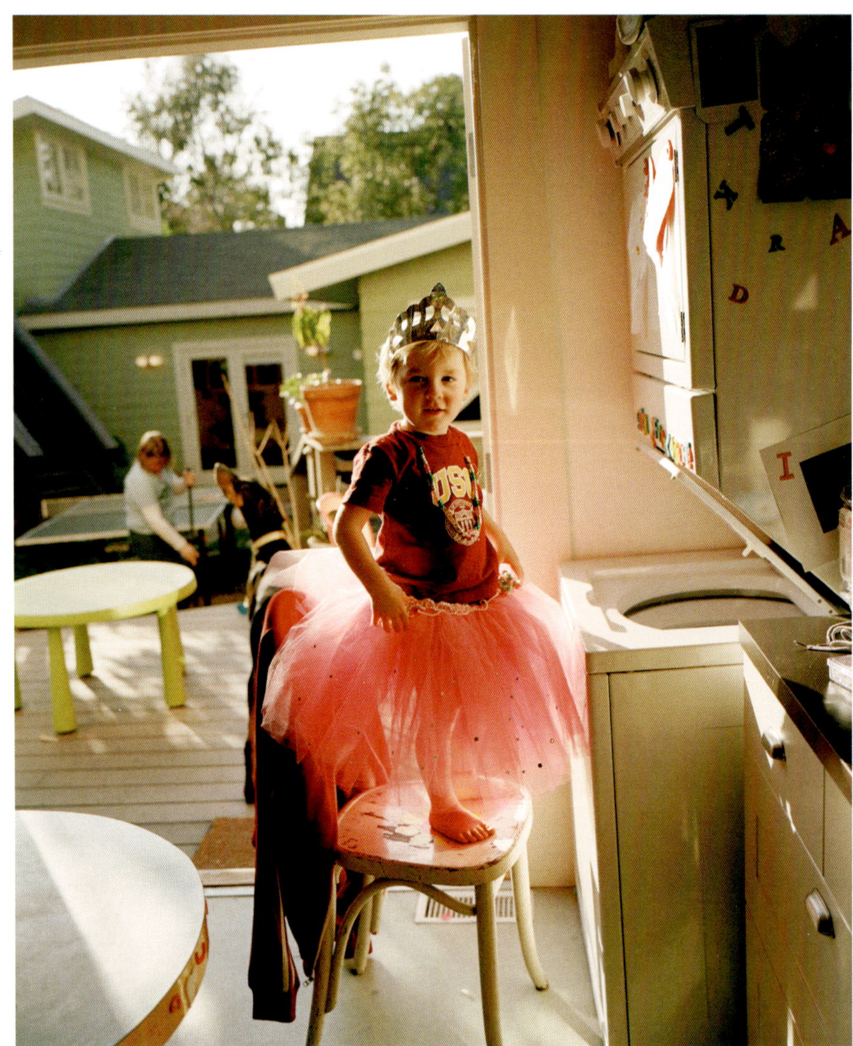

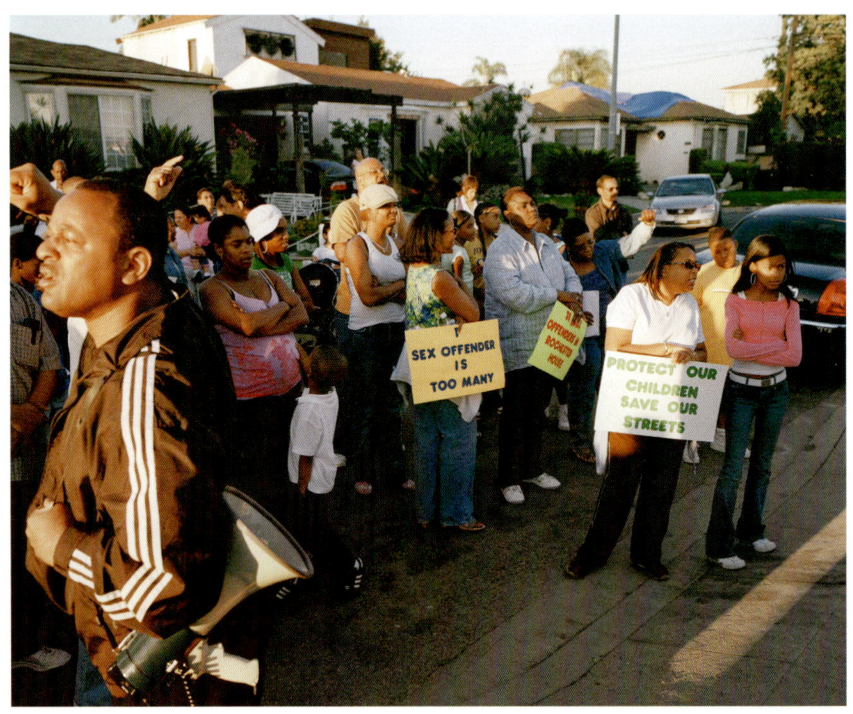

Catherine Opie

OPPOSITE, TOP
Oliver in a Tutu, from
In and Around Home, 2004
C-print, 24 x 20 inches
Edition of 5, 2 AP

OPPOSITE, BOTTOM
In Protest to Sex Offenders,
from *In and Around Home,* 2005
C-print, 16 x 20 inches
Edition of 5, 2 AP

RIGHT
Football Landscape #16
(Waianae vs. Leilehua, Waianae, HI),
from *High School Football,* 2009
C-print, 48 x 64 inches
Edition of 5, 2 AP

BELOW
Rusty, from *High School Football,* 2008
C-print, 30 x 22¼ inches
Edition of 5, 2 AP

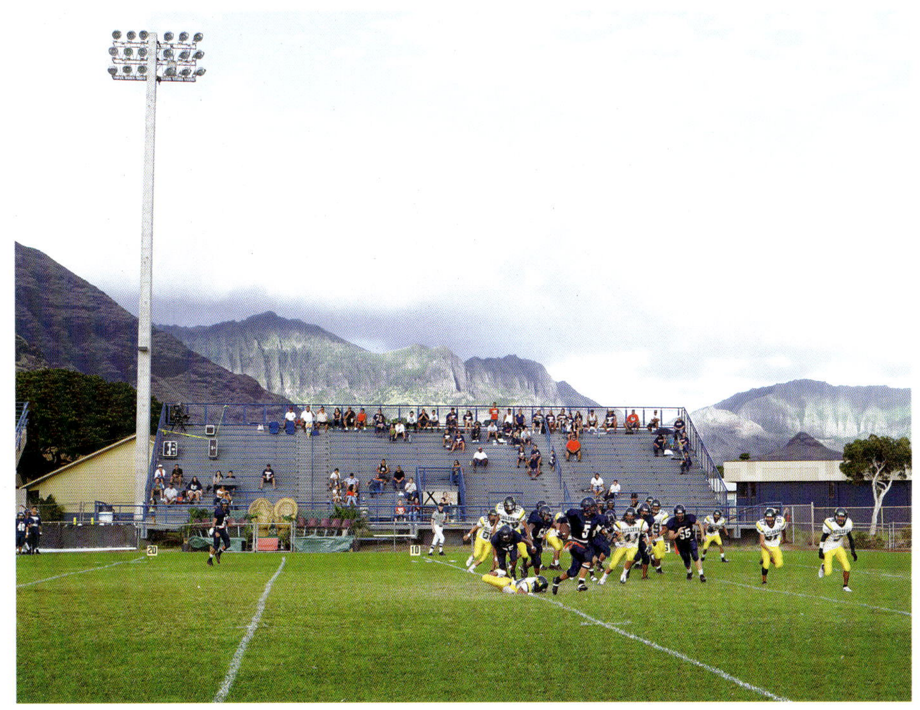

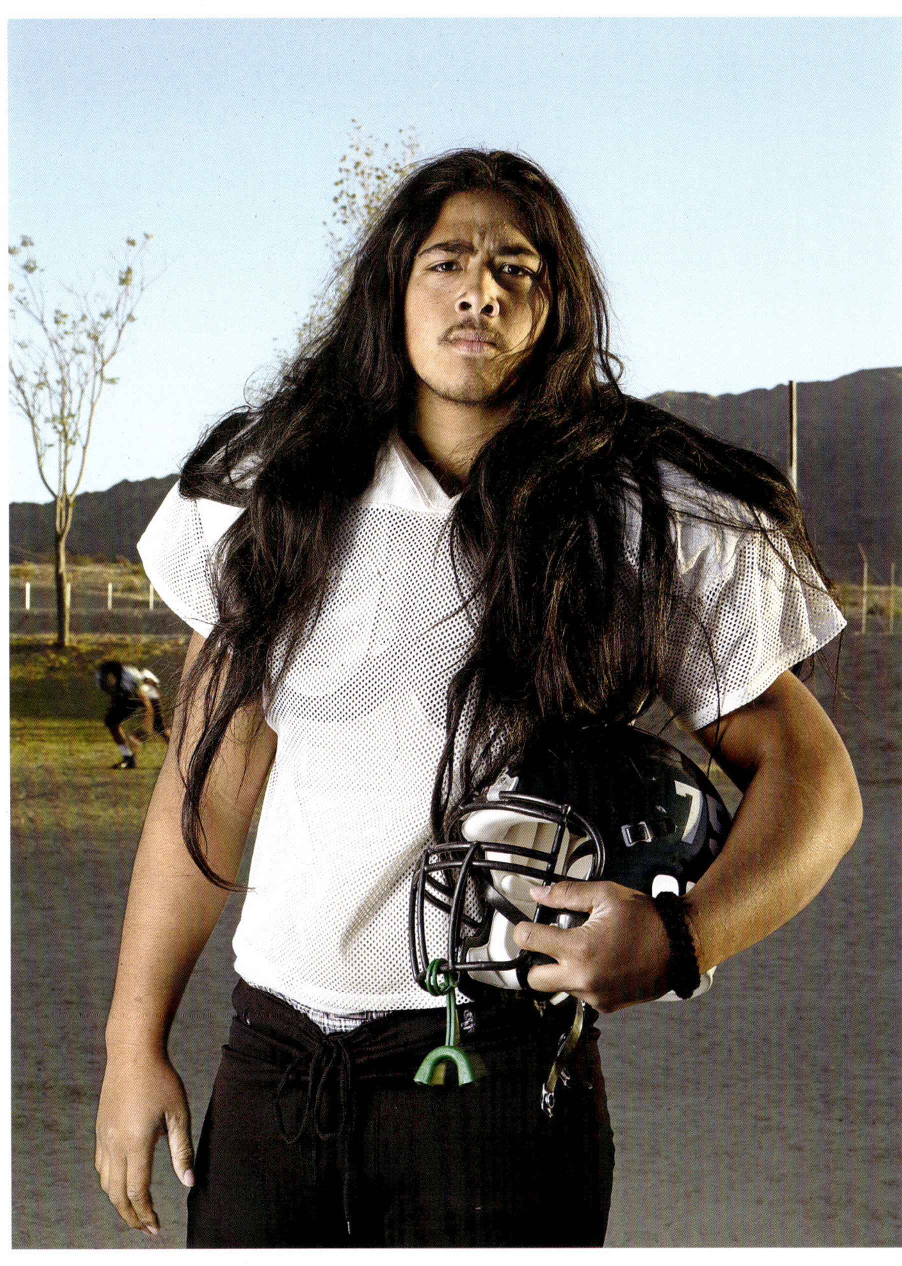

I decided that I wanted to create a portrait of our time in America, in relationship to the incredible opposition discourse. What I'm interested in is the notion of America being the great democracy (and I'm not *sure* that it's the great democracy). Within this notion, there are always binaries—normal-abnormal, 'utopic-dystopic', Republican-Democratic. I really wanted to make American landscapes in terms of identity—through Tea Party rallies, the Inauguration, Boy Scout jamborees, the Michigan Womyn's Music Festival. I became really aware of people taking space—exercising their freedom of speech. I was more interested in the way they occupied the landscape, whether or not I believed what was being spoken.

All of these things are always coming up in relation to the nightly news, and I'm fascinated with it as a construct. I love the nightly news; I have watched it since I was a kid. And that's probably because I was born in '61, and the nightly news was the constant of information: Vietnam and the civil rights movement. Those were the images that profoundly affected me—that formed me as a person—like the images of the Renaissance and paintings that I saw as a child in the art museums. And that's also probably, going deeper, the relationship to the notion of document or documentary in my work.

I'm fascinated with people's absolute belief systems. The permission they have taken in relationship to ideas of what it is to be a Christian is profound in my mind, in terms of the absolute hatred they profess. Religion comes up a lot, I think, in relationship to being queer. I have had signs held up to me saying, "God hates you; you will go to Hell." God hates me? I will go to Hell? What does that mean for you to be telling me that? I'm interested in the notion that religion is supposed to be the idea of a higher self. I am not sure why everybody is trying to define that his or her belief is the better belief system. I really struggle with this as a human being in relationship to a philosophical model of a system of belief in which people think they have it *right*, instead of everybody just saying, "Okay, you have your beliefs and maybe that's the way that you need for it to be constructed, but does it mean that I have to follow along?" I dig into the subjects of the work in an ongoing conversation in relation to the dilemmas that I have within my own mind. And I think that the clearest way to speak about it is that in a certain way the art for me is about the ability to create a conversation in terms of these disparate thoughts—these greater philosophical ideas.

Catherine Opie

BELOW
30 Minutes After the Inauguration,
from *Inauguration,* 2009
C-print, 16 x 20 inches
Edition of 25, 5 AP

OPPOSITE, ABOVE
Untitled #2 (Tea Party Rally), 2010
Inkjet print, 16 x 24 inches
Edition of 5, 2 AP

OPPOSITE, BELOW
Untitled #2 (Boy Scout Jamboree), 2010
Inkjet print, 18 x 24 inches
Edition of 5, 2 AP

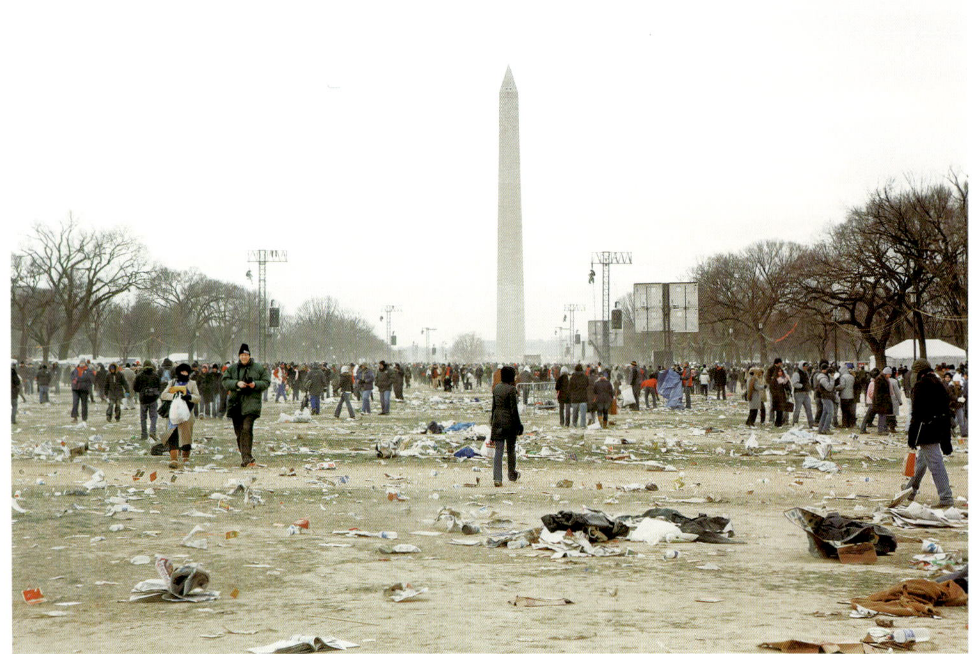

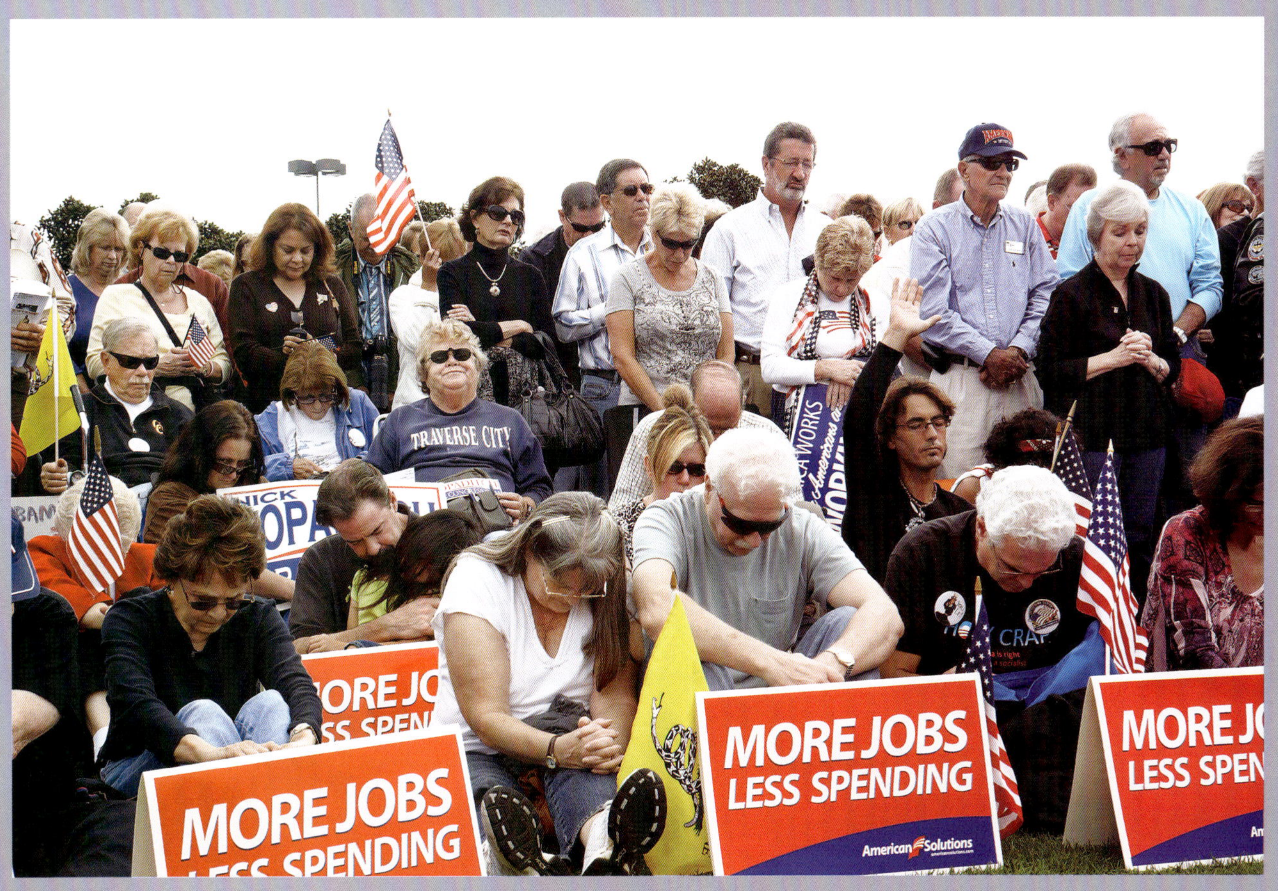
MORE JOBS
LESS SPENDING
MORE JOBS
LESS SPENDING
MORE JOBS
LESS SPENDING
American Solutions
TRAVERSE CITY

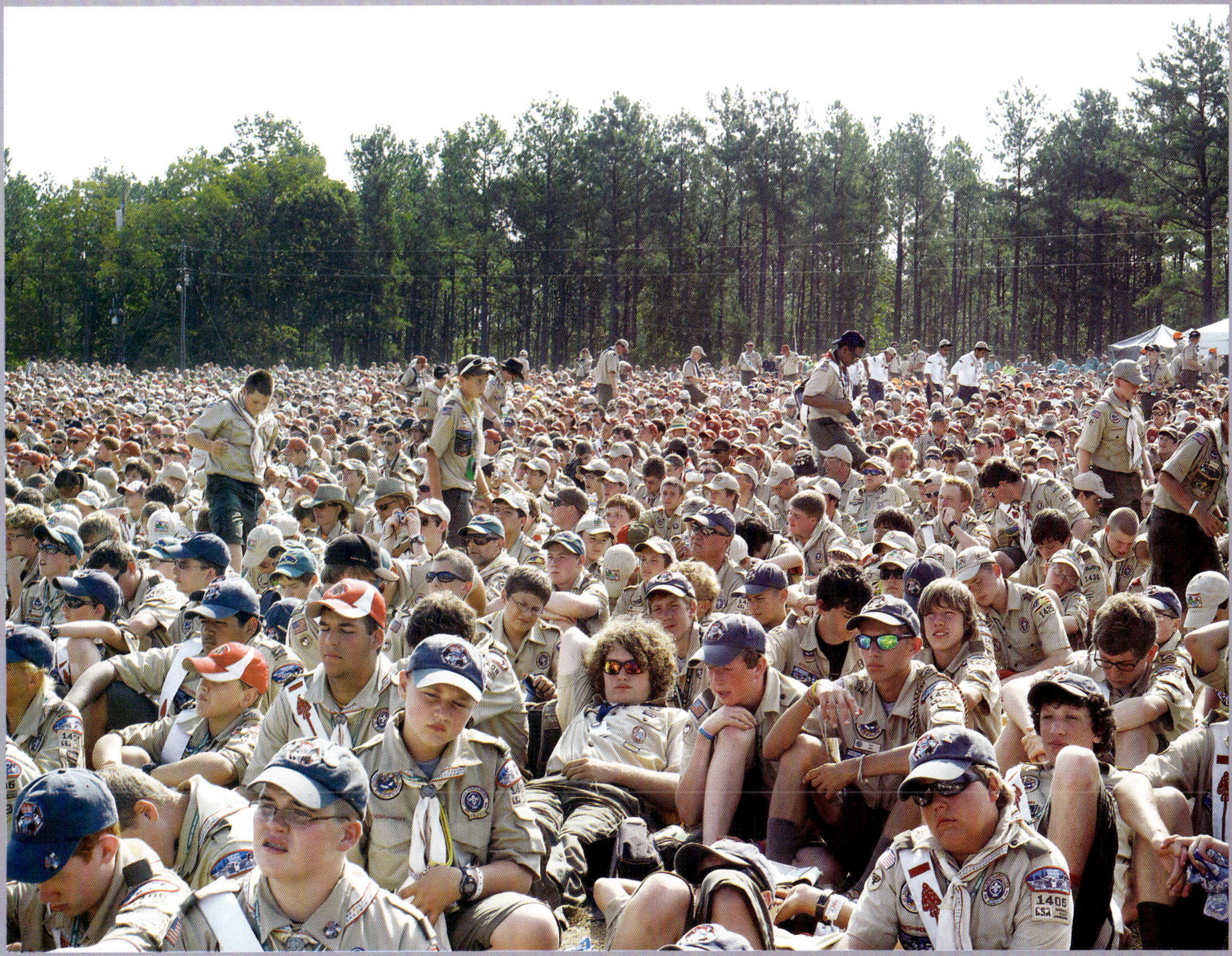

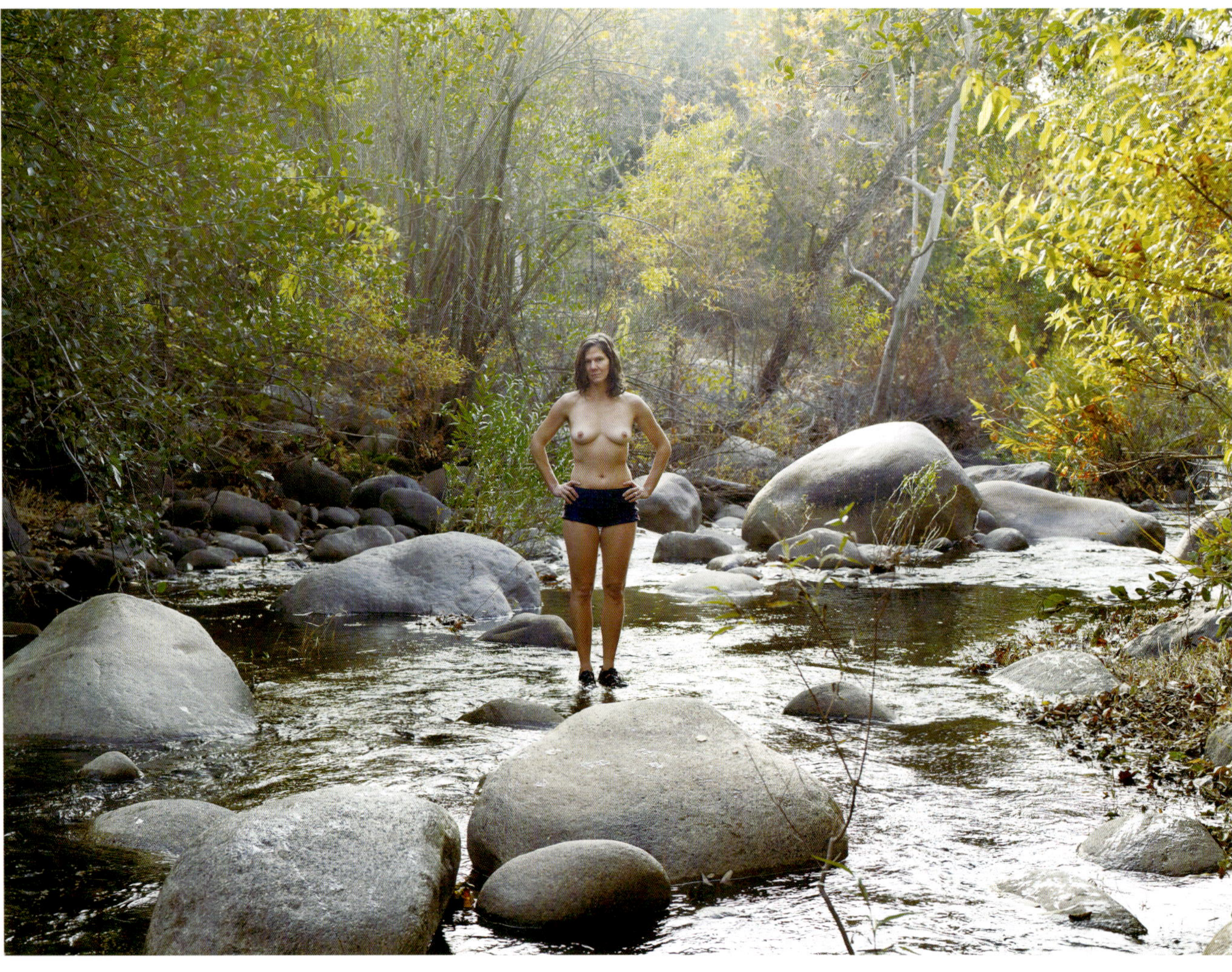

Catherine Opie

ABOVE
Julie, from *Girlfriends,* 2009
C-print, 37½ x 50 inches
Edition of 5, 2 AP

OPPOSITE, LEFT
Self-Portrait/Pervert, 1994
C-print, 40 x 30 inches
Edition of 8, 2 AP

OPPOSITE, RIGHT
Self-Portrait/Nursing, 2004
C-print, 40 x 32 inches
Edition of 8

I have a hard time with things that are formally messy. To the core, I have formal ideas of the way that things should look. And I think that also goes back to seeing those paintings early in my childhood. They just felt right to me. Everything was in its place. With the body of work where I was actually doing street photography and there's a messiness in some of those images, that's really hard for me. I'm much more comfortable when I have a lot of control in terms of framing. The space has to resonate just as carefully as what happens with formal issues. The shapes have to be right. If the shapes aren't right, or it's skewed a certain way or everybody's straight but a building is tilted, it drives me a little nutty on an aesthetic level. So I've always used the tropes of a formal language in constructing my images. It's what I'm comfortable with; it's what feels right to me. I think that often we innately learn things early on by looking, and that becomes our language. We can certainly change our language in terms of bodies of work that we're building, but I think that even though the work might change in terms of subject, the structure remains somewhat the same.

Some people who follow my career obviously know that I'm out within my sexuality. I am queer, and I have represented my own community in the work. But I don't think that that necessarily defines my ideas in terms of work. I don't think it defines them whatsoever. I think what actually defines my work is more in relationship to American identity than queer identity. I'm more interested in the absolute equality of producing images without the necessary attachment of it being radical *because* it's queer. It's more about absolute equality of representation versus trying to be radical. It's about inclusion, to a certain extent, and inclusion is a hard, odd word. A lot of people say,

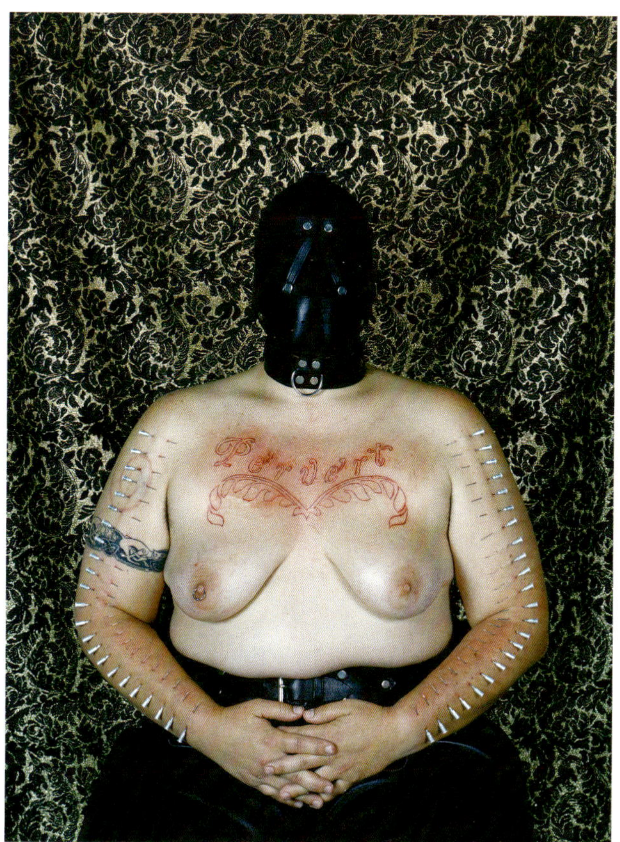

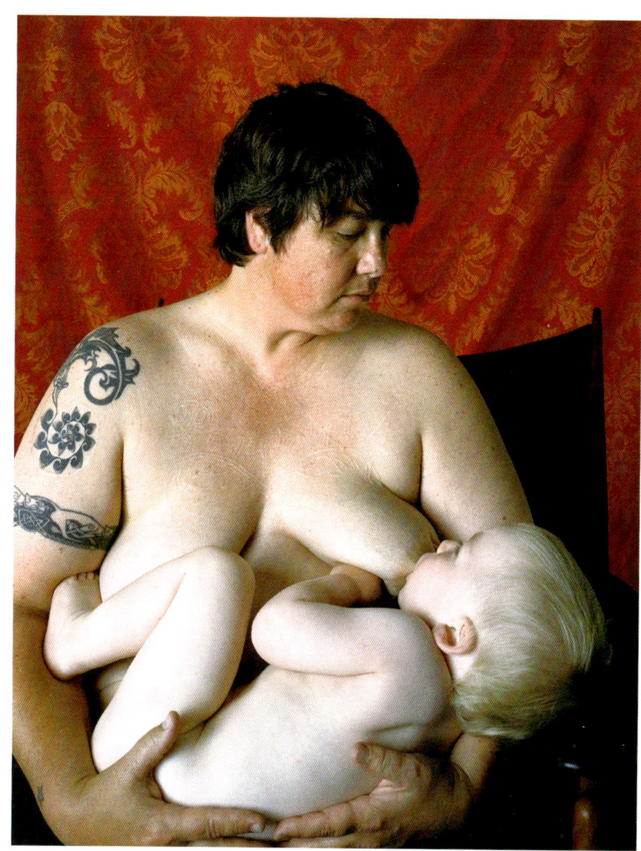

"Well—you want to be normal." What's normal? There is no normal. A lot of my work explores those notions and the convention of how tightly we define. The last body of work that I did is trying to ask those questions and break it up a little bit in terms of how tightly we think about our own community and where we belong. I just think it's interesting how people do want the work defined by the artist's sexuality.

Self-Portrait/Pervert (1994) and *Self-Portrait/Nursing* (2004). That was a ten-year span, between doing *Pervert* as a self-portrait and *Self-Portrait/Nursing*. People get so freaked out about those images—or those images bring up a lot of feelings or emotions. Somebody always is saying to me about *Self-Portrait/Pervert*, "Well, doesn't it hurt?" I'm like, "Yeah, it hurts." Part of it is painful. But at the same time there's a transcendence that happens within it. I like that the history is on the body. I think our bodies carry all kinds of history. *Self-Portrait/Pervert* was a bit more of an angry piece, right after the march on Washington—the gay and lesbian march on Washington in 1994. I came home and all of a sudden the queer community created a 'language of abnormal' ("Oh well, we're normal; they're abnormal") and started calling the leather community perverts. It was really shocking to me to have the language from my own community turned on me. So in a Hans Holbein, Henry the Eighth, way, I decided to just do this really bold self-portrait of myself as a warrior, and wear that on my body. And when you see *Self-Portrait/Nursing*, and you see the print of it, it really is beautiful—and all of that history is still on the body. But the history is now with me with Oliver.

I would never be closeted, and I would never *not* make the work that I've made, not in a million years. I'm proud that I've had a part of creating a visual history and discourse about my own life that's personal and political. But at the same time, it would be nice to have people look at the work in relationship to what is really before them, not these ideas that they've created as a definition of me as an artist.

Just look at what's before you, versus what you're putting on it because of past work. It's a hard thing right now: I get very frustrated that to a certain extent the queer identity never goes away. Not that I would ever want that to go away, but I also want work to be able to be talked about in relationship to a history of American genre painting. Guess what? It looks this way because I'm creating a conversation in relationship to that history. And if you only define it by portraits that were taken early on, then you're missing the whole point of how to expand the language. I'm more interested in this expansion versus that narrowing.

Catherine Opie

RIGHT
Untitled #4 (Surfers), 2003
C-print, 50 x 40 inches
Edition of 5, 2 AP

OPPOSITE
Untitled #9 (Icehouses), 2001
C-print, 50 x 40 inches
Edition of 5, 2 AP

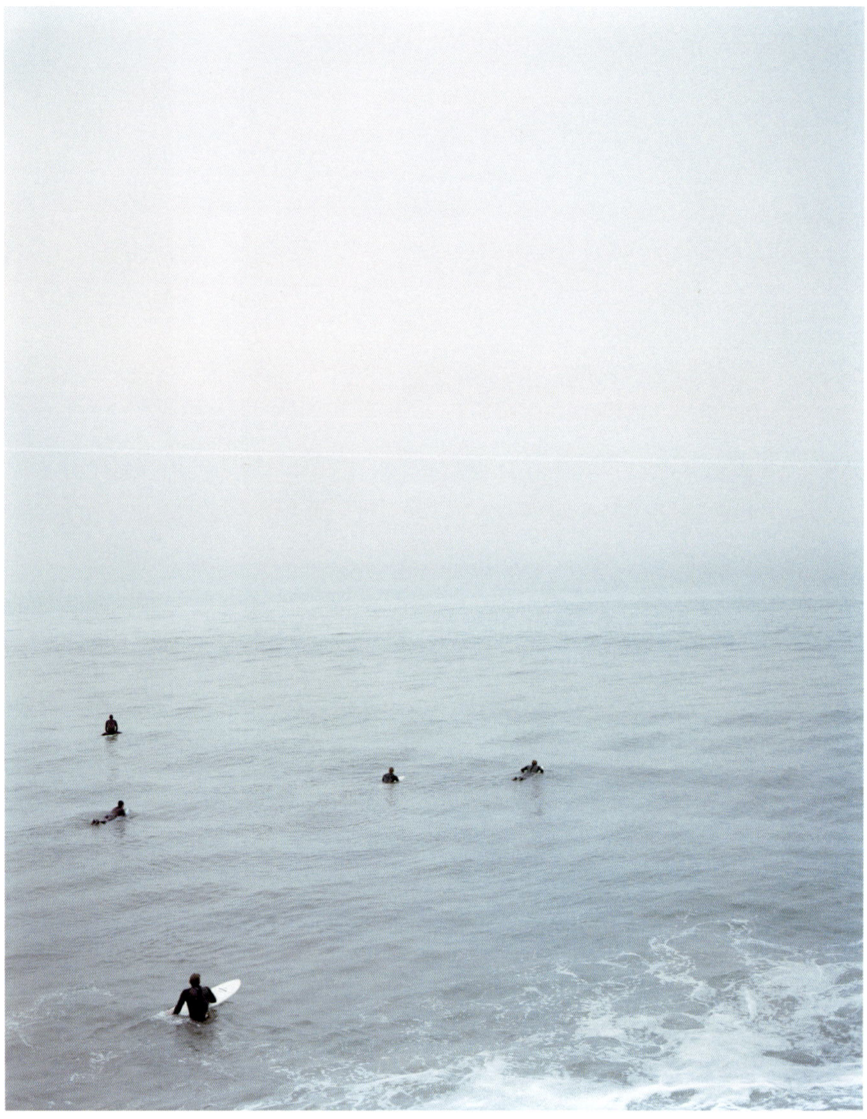

I don't think that *Surfers* (2003) would have existed if I hadn't made *Icehouses* (2001). There was a direct correlation that I was trying to bring to those bodies of work—the notion of a temporary community that exists on the water. One is frozen, the other is out in the Pacific Ocean, and both contain the metaphor of waiting. In *Surfers* I'm waiting for the perfect conditions where the waves are flat, it's between the sets, and the surfers are just floating, while in *Icehouses* the people in the ice-fishing houses are waiting in hope of catching a fish on that frozen landscape. I think that, as a society, we have forgotten how to wait. We have forgotten what boredom is. We have forgotten the idea of the expanse of time and the quietness that time can bring to us. My installation of these images across from one another at the Guggenheim Museum encapsulated the notion of temporary community but also that of a sublime landscape that is fractured but connected—ideas that I find really interesting to think about in terms of trying to construct bodies of work. How do you make an extended panorama that begins to be fractured in the same way that I think we are fractured as human beings? We're pulled this way and that—and if you can take time to go sit in an ice-fishing house or sit on a surfboard in between sets, there's almost a perfection of creating a moment of quietness for yourself. You're engaged in the world in a different way than looking down at your device and texting and all of those things that our world has changed. So I wanted to create metaphors of stop; wait; slow down; be active within that. And you can maybe even have an ethereal moment. I have always said that, even though my work often is very personal, there's never *not* politics within that. The two are completely merged in relationship with my identity. And even though I might be able to do the sublime or the quiet moment, there are also moments within that that are extremely political. There isn't ever a time in which those two things aren't being balanced out in my mind in relationship to creating representations of my time as an artist.

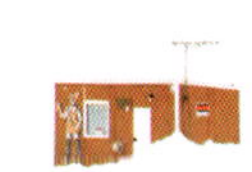

David Altmejd

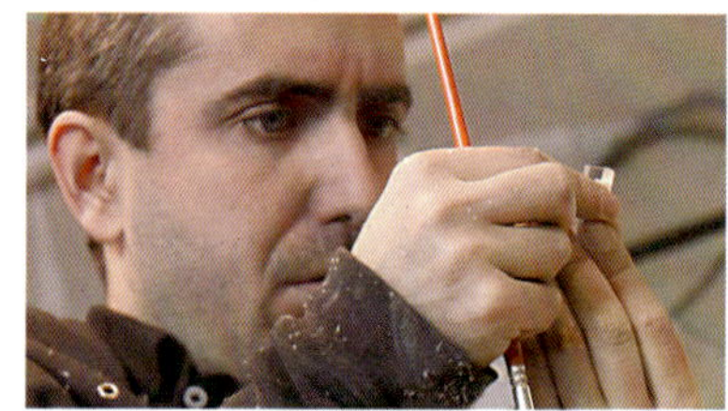

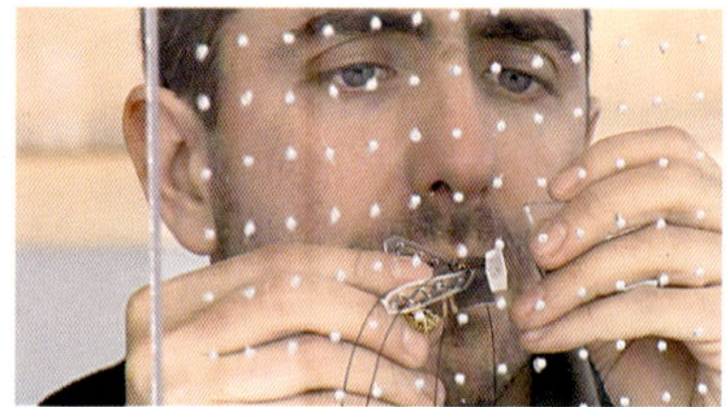

assume vivid astro focus

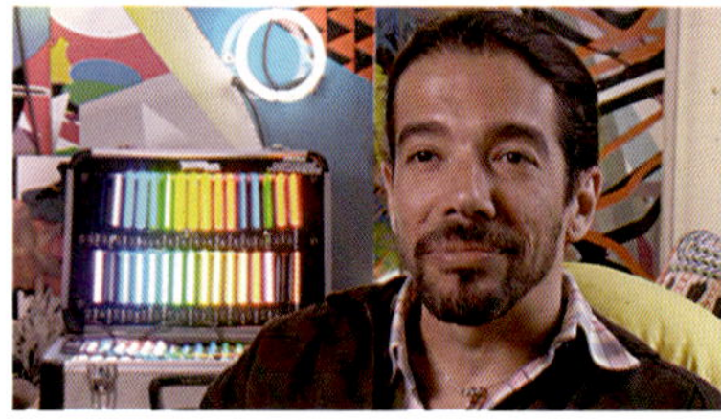

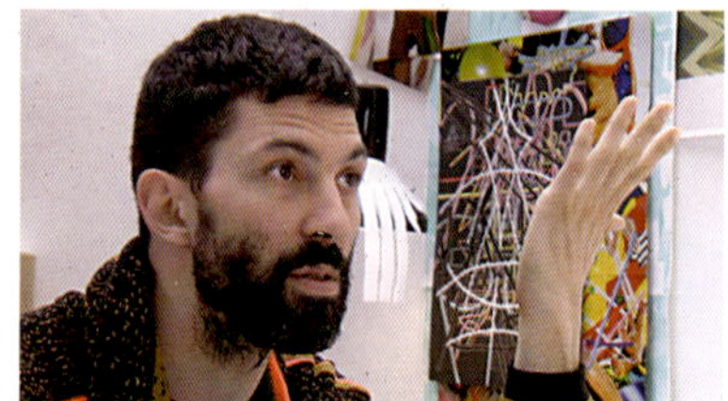

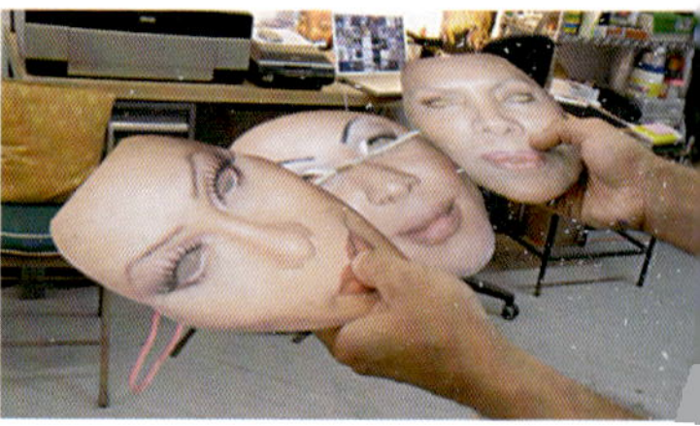

Lynda Benglis

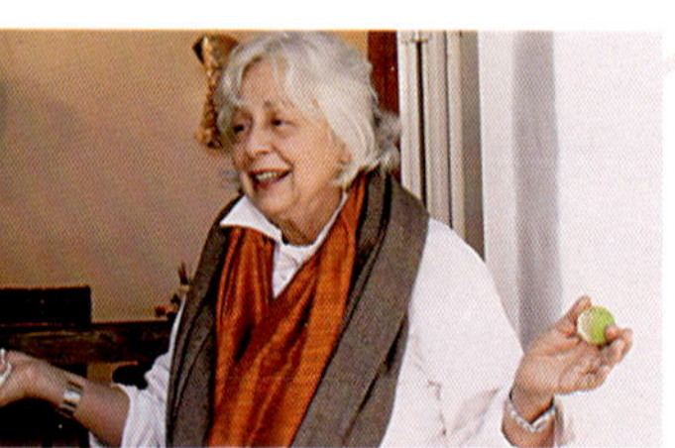

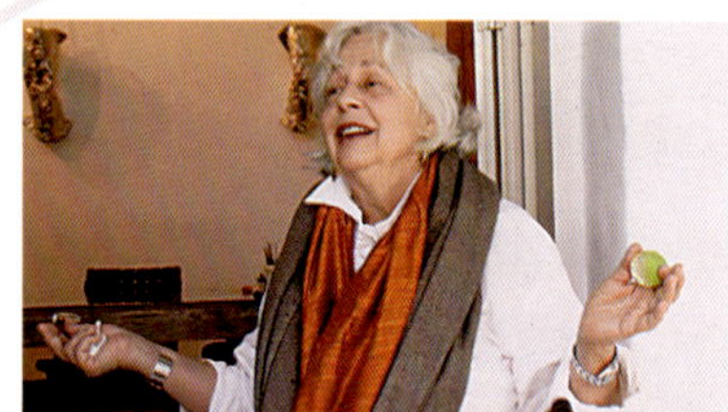

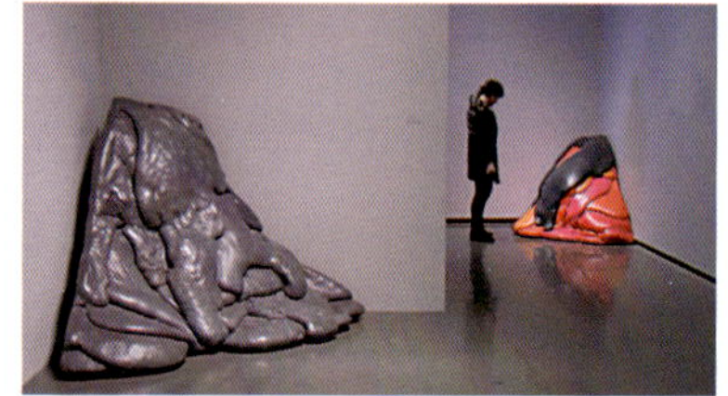

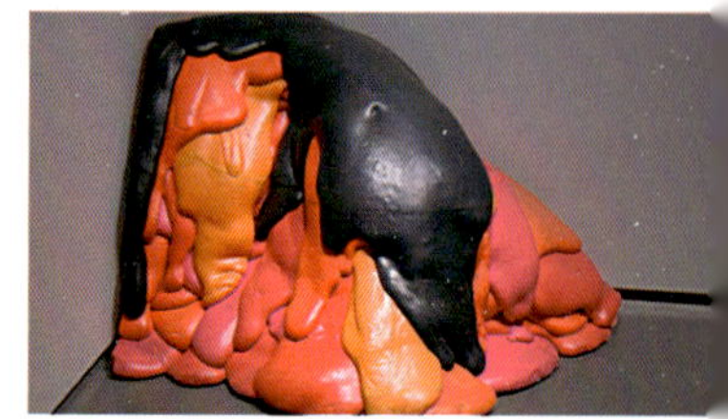

Tabaimo

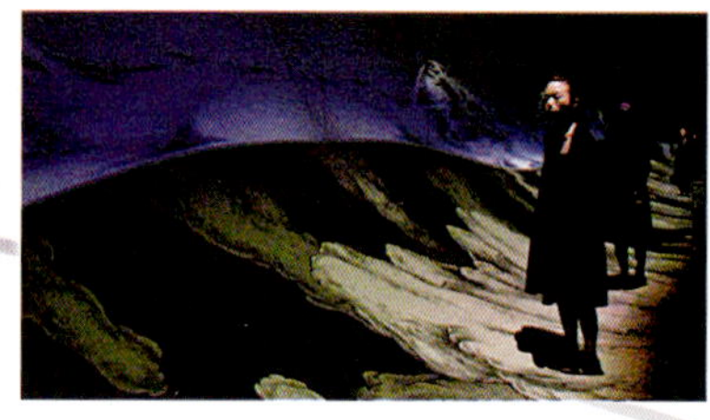

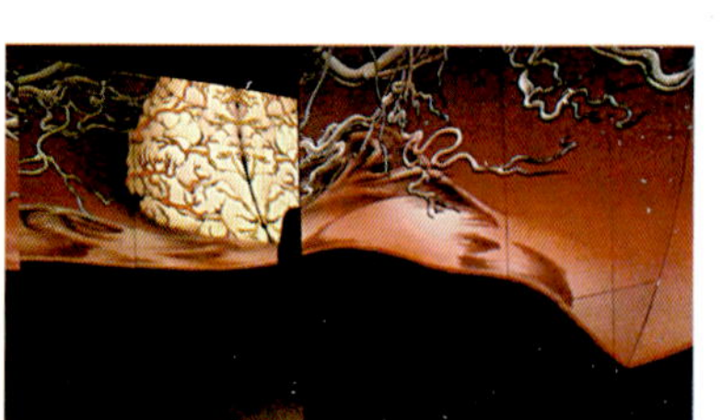

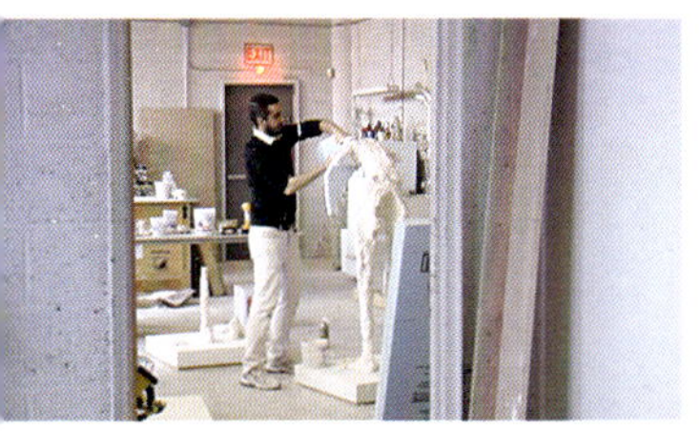
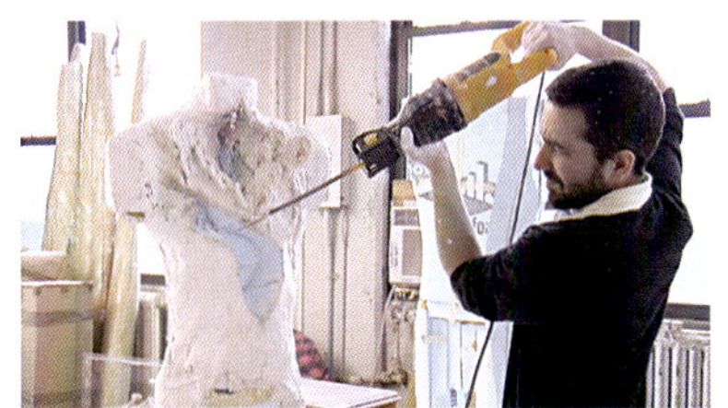
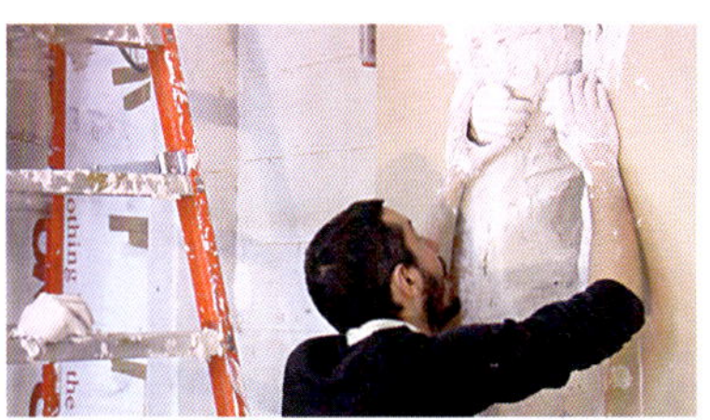
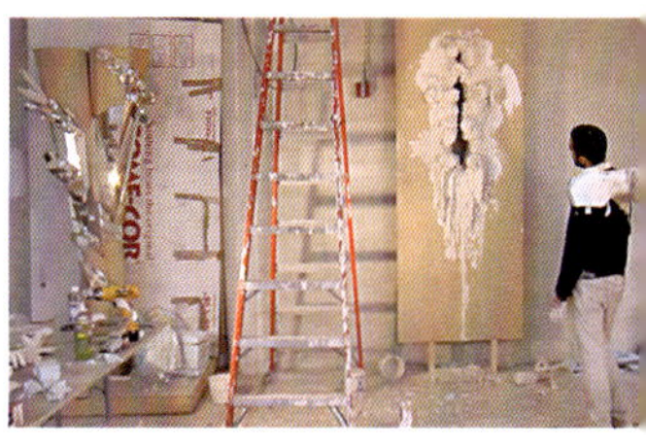
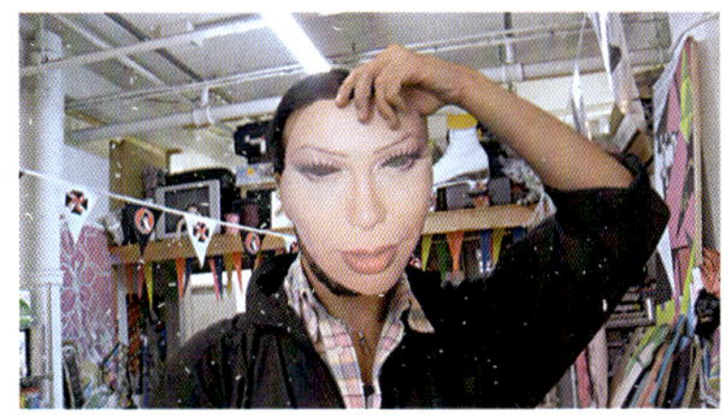
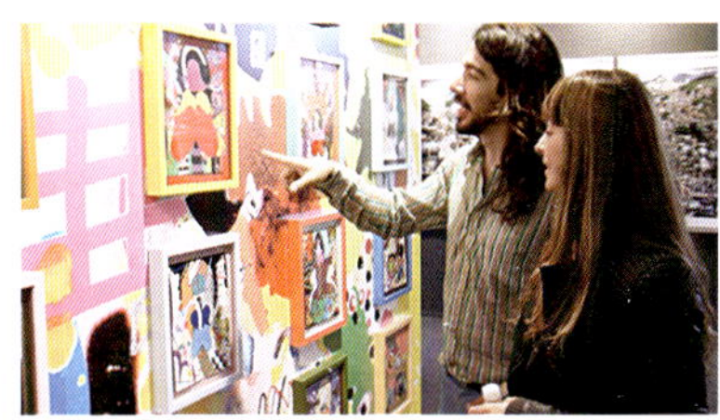
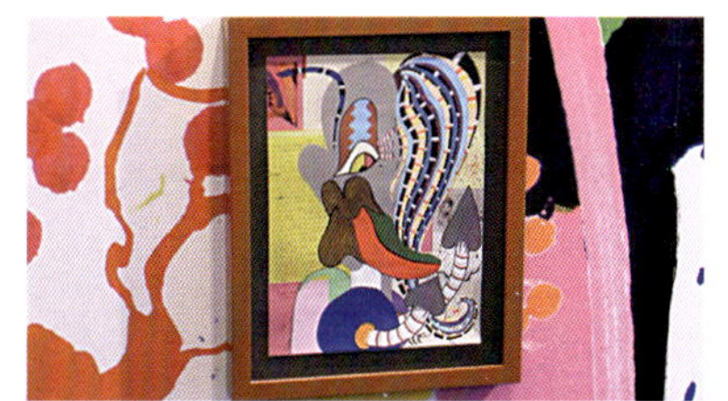

Boundaries

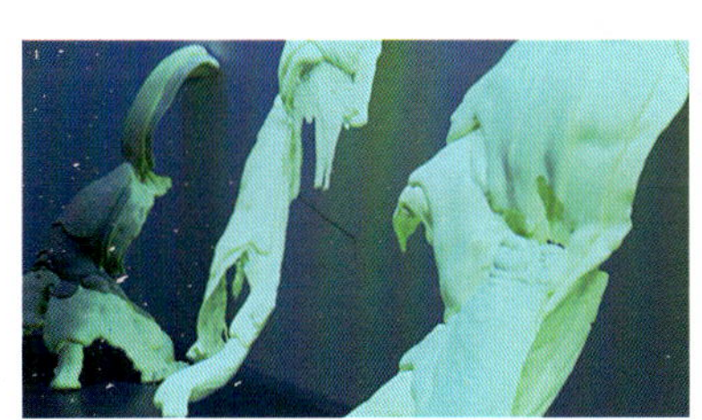
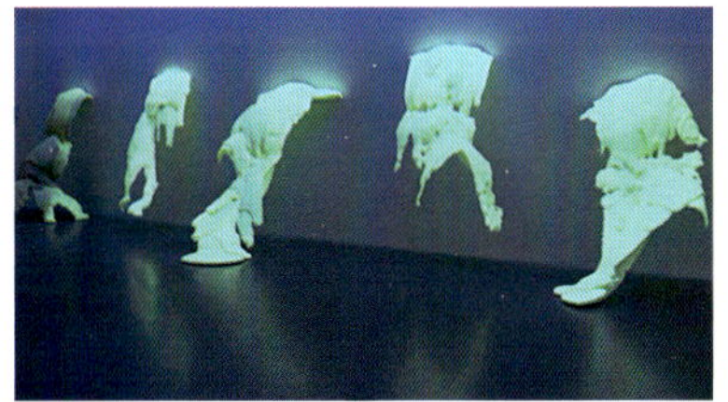
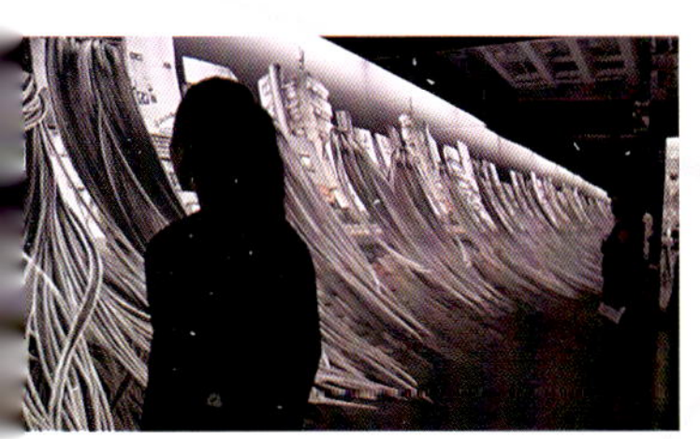
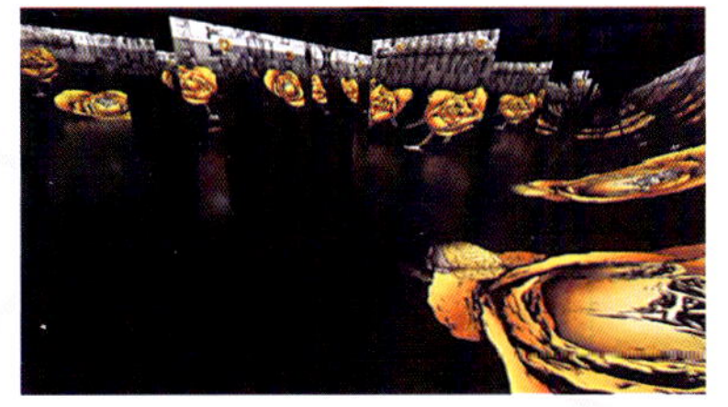
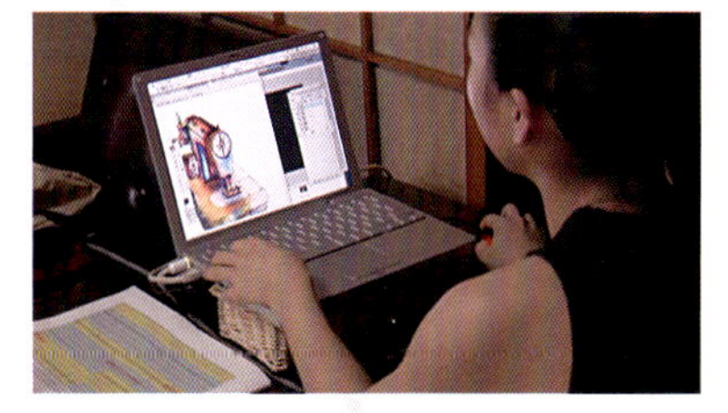
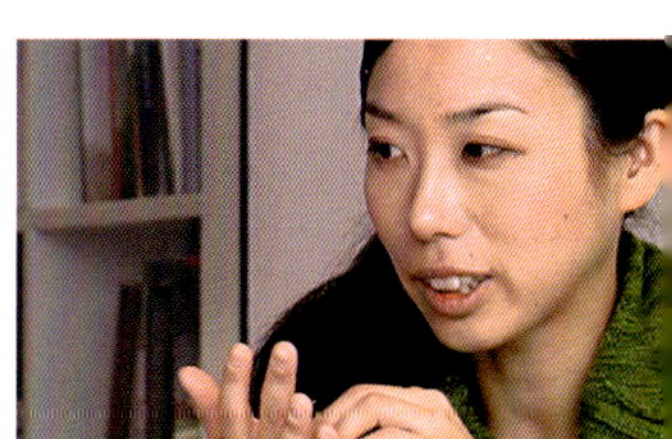

David Altmejd

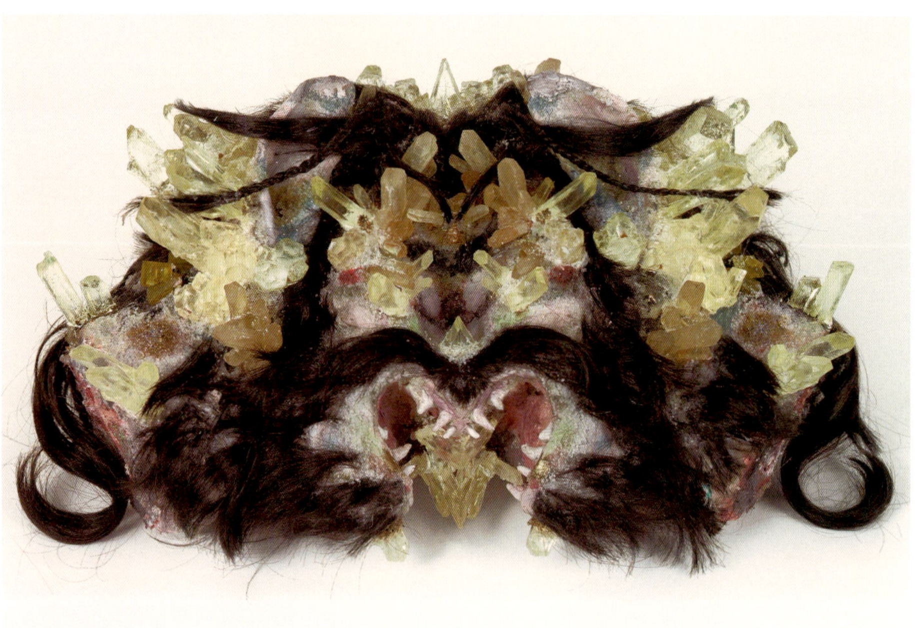

ABOVE
Untitled (Dark), 2001
Plaster, paint, synthetic hair, resin, glitter, 8 x 14 x 8 inches

OPPOSITE
Wood Clock, 2007
Wood, steel, mirror, epoxy clay, resin, paint, wire, artificial plants, taxidermy birds, shoes, crystals, fabric, glitter, 127 x 72 x 108 inches

I guess what I'm really interested in doing is making something exist in this world. When I was a kid, I didn't have so many resources. I didn't have access to a table saw when I was five years old, nor plaster, nor Plexiglas. All I had was paper and pencils. Now, I have other means. So, today, I don't do drawings because I have other materials that I find interesting. And I don't need to make sketches of the sculptures before I make them because I don't think that there's a lot of difference between putting ink on a piece of paper and gluing little pieces of crystal on Plexiglas. For me, they're similar things. When I make a drawing, I just put matter on paper and make it exist. And when I make sculpture I function the same way. Right away I just install materials in space.

I'm interested in science, the same way I'm interested in art, with a sort of child-like fascination with objects that grow, transform, and reshape themselves. I'm attracted to biology and living things. But I realized that science was not the right place for me because there was no intellectual rigor in the way I approached it. I was interested in coming up with new ideas and new perspectives. But you can't go through academia with that kind of attitude. You have to learn the language. And I realized very early in my studies in science that I wasn't interested in learning a language. I was really interested in *inventing* languages. So I figured out that art would be the perfect place for me because that's what's encouraged. To make something new and put it in the world, make it exist, and have people react to it—that's what I found fascinating.

For many reasons, I've always felt very different. My father comes from Eastern Europe. I'm Jewish, and I'm gay. Very early on, I wasn't very comfortable in my body because (it seems kind of silly to say) I was skinny. I was a late bloomer, always shortest in my class. So I always tried to be invisible as much as possible. When I started making sculpture I was able to exist through whatever object I wanted to make. And, actually, I found a way of existing much more intensely than I would have if I weren't an artist. I think I just found the balance: it's very satisfying to put my sculptures in the world.

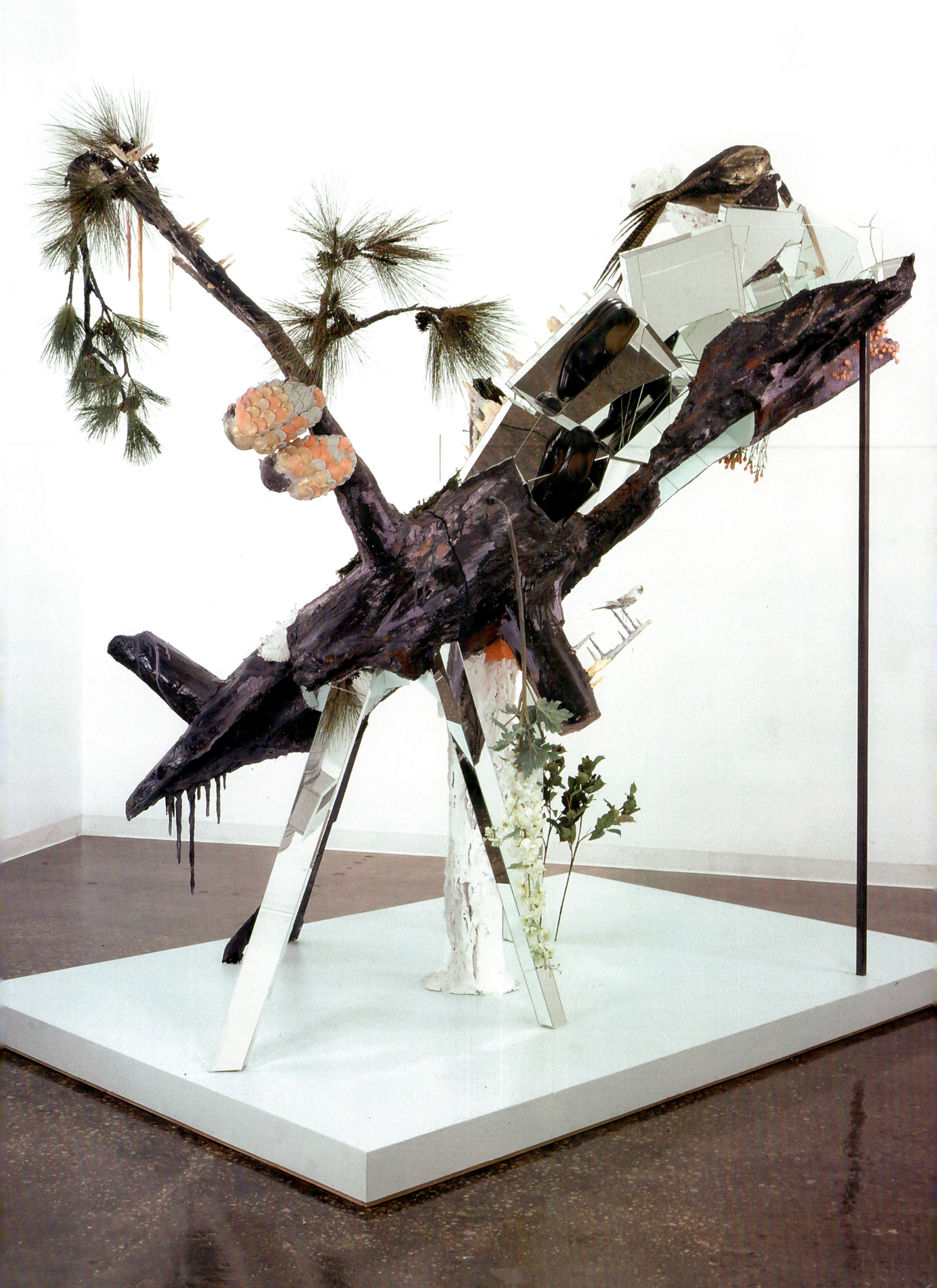

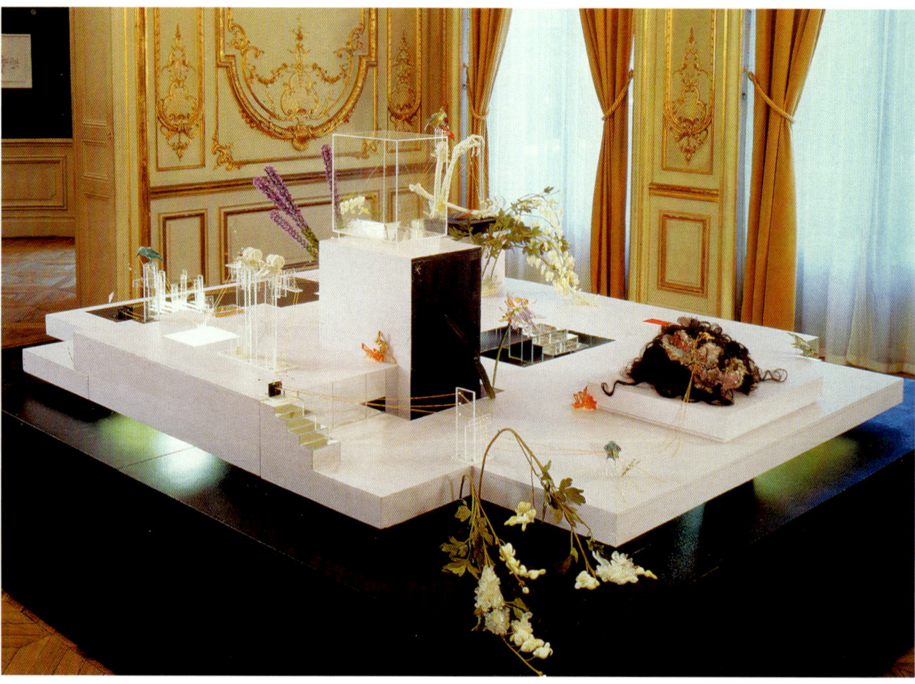

David Altmejd

ABOVE
Le dormeur du val, 2004
Wood, paint, plaster, resin, mirror, wire, glue, plastic, cloth, synthetic hair, jewelry, glitter, dimensions variable
Installation view of *Noctambule,* organized by D'Amelio Terras, New York at Fondation Dosne-Bibliothêque Thiers, Paris, June 24–July 10, 2004

OPPOSITE
The Swarm, 2011
Plexiglas, chain, metal wire, thread, acrylic paint, epoxy resin, epoxy clay, acrylic gel, granular medium, synthetic hair, plaster, foam, sand, quartz, pyrite, amethyst, assorted minerals, adhesive, wire, pins, needles, 102½ x 244 x 84½ inches

I like the idea that there's a logic of materials—that the work transforms itself, as if it has the power to generate its own material and build itself. So, for example, just to explain a little of that logic, the fact that in *The Swarm* (2011) the bee is made out of Plexiglas mostly comes from the fact that the box itself is made of Plexiglas. It's as if the box had given a little bit—as if somewhere in that simple minimalist Plexiglas box there had been a sort of mutation—and the Plexiglas had taken a different shape, which happened to be the shape of a bee, which happens to be generating gold chain. And the gold chain becomes something else, so that at the end, when you look at the piece, it seems like everything is coming from inside of it. The logic that was used to find a form comes from within the piece. I like the idea of losing myself into things and having a really intimate relationship with little objects like that so that at the end I can almost fetishize every cell of the bigger sculpture. Every square inch is precious and I have an intimate relationship with it. That's what's interesting.

I try to accumulate a lot of small figurative elements that are mostly referential—bees, insects, needles—to the point where the whole swarm is going to become a sort of abstract shape. Very often it's the other way around. The more you zoom in, the more abstract it becomes. But I want to start with the large abstract shape and, when you zoom in, you actually start recognizing things more and more.

I also want to give the impression that every little element that's present in the piece is generating the material that I end up using, as if that bee is generating gold chain, and I'm going to use it to build something else. For example, I'm going to use the gold chain generated by that bee to create something, like a geometric drawing in space.

The swarm of bees was the central element in *The Swarm.* That's all I wanted to do. But, as I installed it, I needed to hold the bees in space. It gave me a reason to attach other things. New things were growing around it, so it ended up being a really intricate piece that's diverse in terms of materials and references. But it only started as a swarm, and now it's just like one element that's lost amongst many inside that jungle. What I found really interesting to start with is that cloudlike shape that's very soft, floating in space. If you see pictures of swarms of bees or flocks of birds, they're really kind of light and soft. There's an interesting internal dynamic in them. They're like soft clouds, but at the same time they're aggressive. Every element has the potential to sting you. I found that combination of the softness of the abstract shape and the aggressive potential to be really nice.

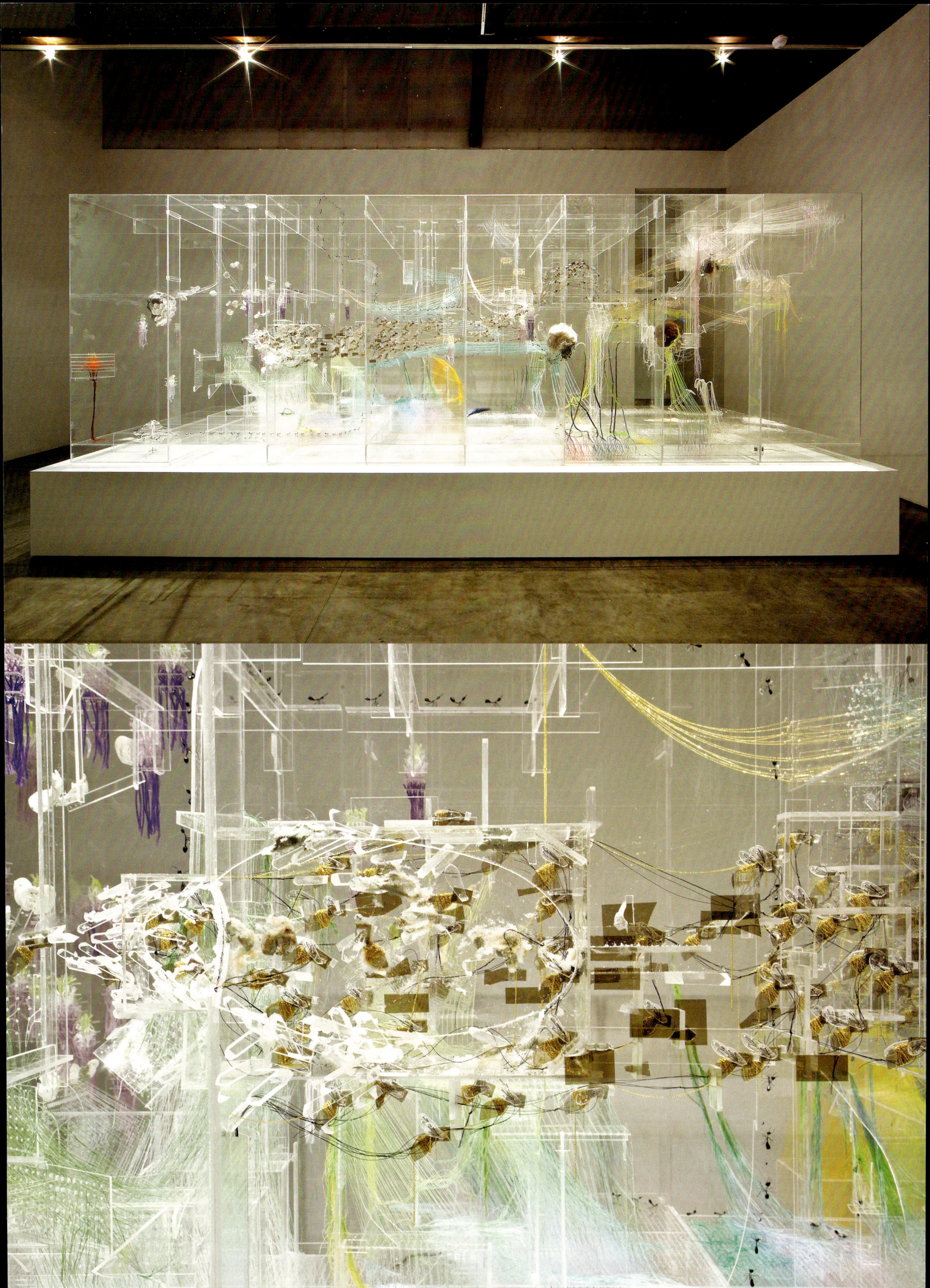

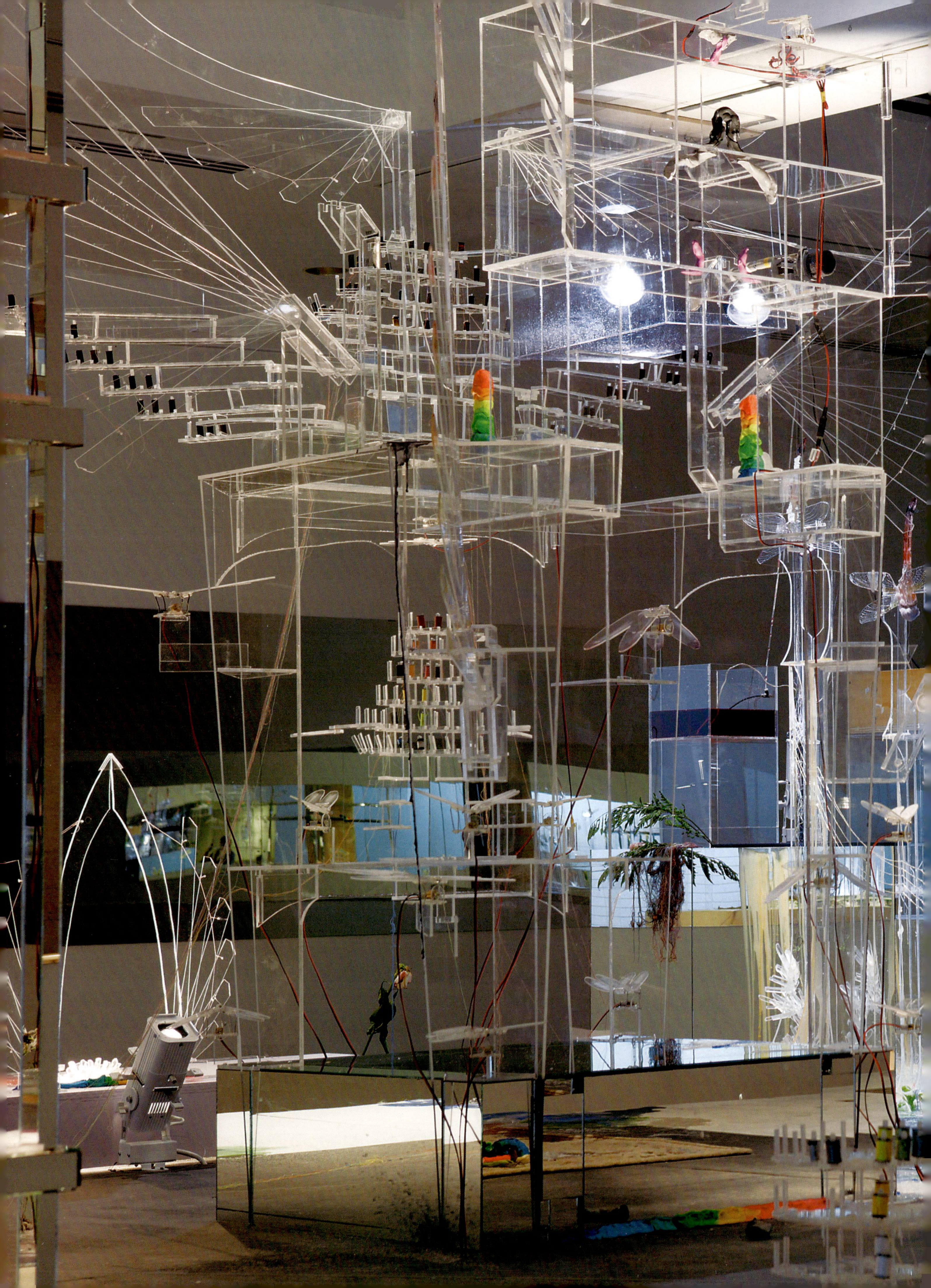

David Altmejd

Conte crépusculaire [Twilight Tale],
with performance detail, 2011
With composer-performer Pierre Lapointe
Galerie de l'UQAM, Montreal, Canada, May 4–7, 2011

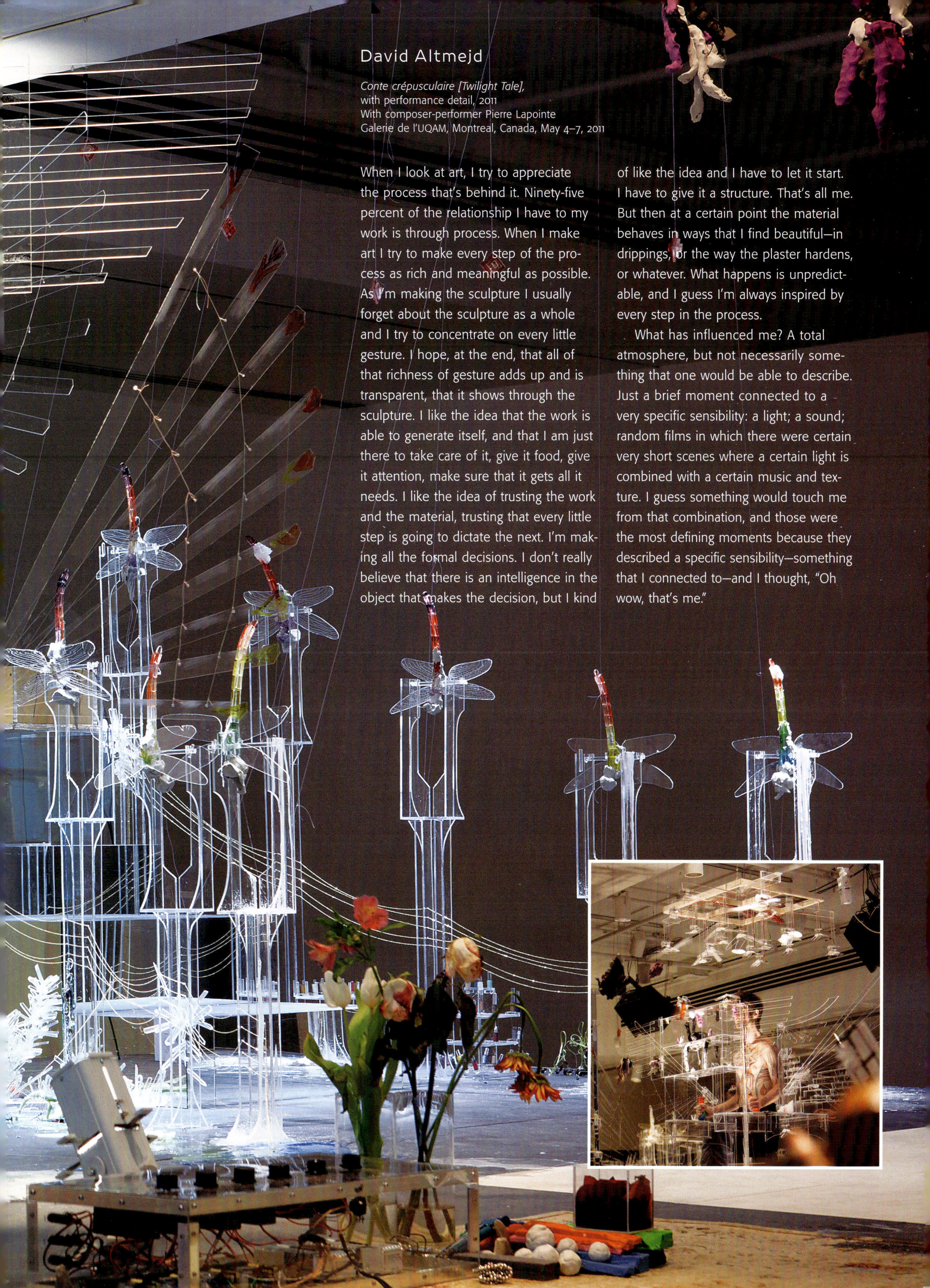

When I look at art, I try to appreciate the process that's behind it. Ninety-five percent of the relationship I have to my work is through process. When I make art I try to make every step of the process as rich and meaningful as possible. As I'm making the sculpture I usually forget about the sculpture as a whole and I try to concentrate on every little gesture. I hope, at the end, that all of that richness of gesture adds up and is transparent, that it shows through the sculpture. I like the idea that the work is able to generate itself, and that I am just there to take care of it, give it food, give it attention, make sure that it gets all it needs. I like the idea of trusting the work and the material, trusting that every little step is going to dictate the next. I'm making all the formal decisions. I don't really believe that there is an intelligence in the object that makes the decision, but I kind of like the idea and I have to let it start. I have to give it a structure. That's all me. But then at a certain point the material behaves in ways that I find beautiful—in drippings, or the way the plaster hardens, or whatever. What happens is unpredictable, and I guess I'm always inspired by every step in the process.

What has influenced me? A total atmosphere, but not necessarily something that one would be able to describe. Just a brief moment connected to a very specific sensibility: a light; a sound; random films in which there were certain very short scenes where a certain light is combined with a certain music and texture. I guess something would touch me from that combination, and those were the most defining moments because they described a specific sensibility—something that I connected to—and I thought, "Oh wow, that's me."

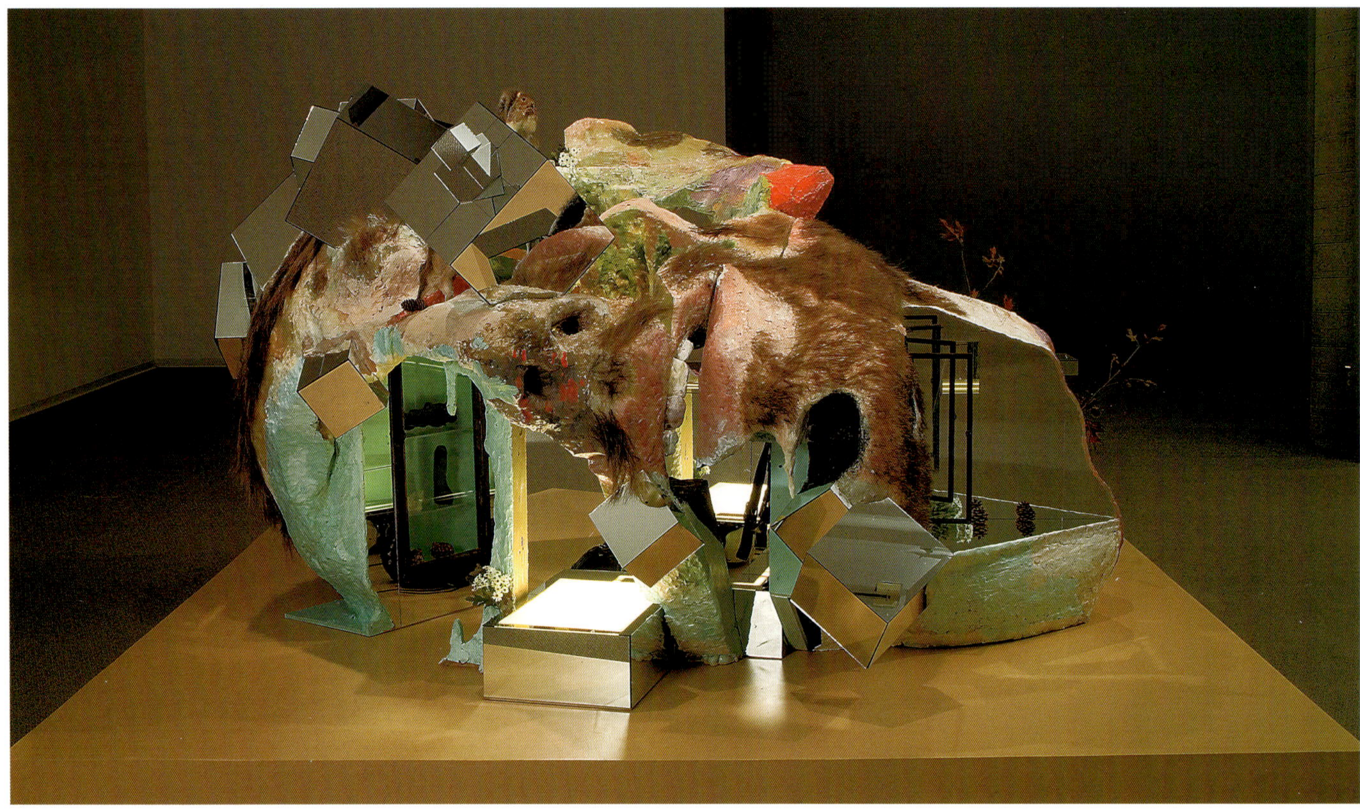

David Altmejd

ABOVE
The Hunter, 2006
Foam, epoxy clay, paint, horsehair, wood, glass, Plexiglas, mirror, artificial branches, leather hood, leather harness, taxidermy squirrels, lighting system, glitter, silicone, quartz, pyrite, hemimorphite, aragonite, 70 x 98½ x 98½ inches overall

OPPOSITE
The Vessel, 2011
Plexiglas, chain, plaster, wood, thread, wire, acrylic paint, epoxy resin, epoxy clay, acrylic gel, granular medium, quartz, pyrite, assorted minerals, adhesive, wire, pins, needles, 102½ x 244 x 86½ inches

The most defining constraint in sculpture making is dealing with the material. Yes, I come with my specific sensibility but, first, I have to deal with the material. Then, I try to inject my sensibility to give a certain flavor to the sculpture. That's how I make color choices. I see the importance of the choice of colors as changing everything inside the sculpture. I don't know why, but I'm extremely attracted to pastel colors. But they have to be dirty in some way. I like the combination of lavender and pink and maybe mint green, but there has to be some kind of dirty brown green just to infect the prettiness. Then, all of a sudden, I feel like I've found exactly the right balance. I work extremely intuitively, so I'm not focused on the production of meaning. But when I say that I use intuition, there's a difference between intuition and randomness. I don't think that those ideas are coming from just anywhere. I think that they're coming from a specific place in my head where there is probably already a certain knowledge and meaning. I try to build an object that's going to become complex enough, have enough layers, have enough references in energy, to start feeling like it's alive and even has the potential of developing its own intelligence and, therefore, the capacity of generating its own meaning. I'm not really interested in meaning as something that exists before the work. I'm interested in art as art-*making*—as the building of an object that will be able to generate meaning.

The new work is definitely about something very different. For example, *The Vessel* (2011): there's something almost religious about it, and it's really making a very strong reference to the body in its symmetrical shape. And the way it's radiating, it feels almost Catholic. So I can see it going in the direction of the idea of a center of energy and, then, a radiation of that energy and the body—something that wasn't as clear before in my work or in *The Swarm*. *The Vessel* looks a little bit like one organism, but *The Swarm*, because it's not symmetrical, becomes more like a landscape, less like a body, and is more difficult to experience. You can see it as a whole—as one large 'painting'—but it also encourages the viewer to experience the details, to zoom in.

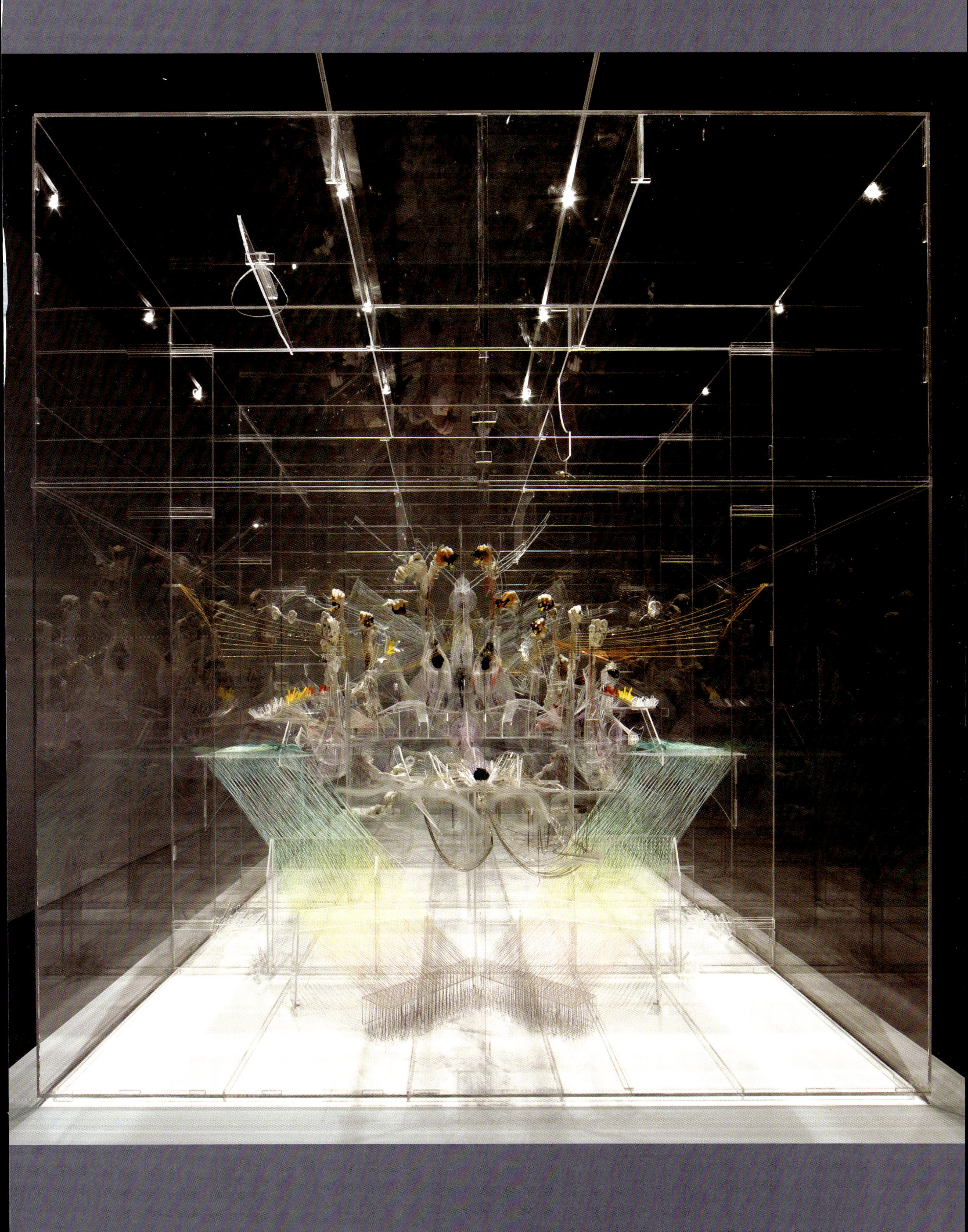

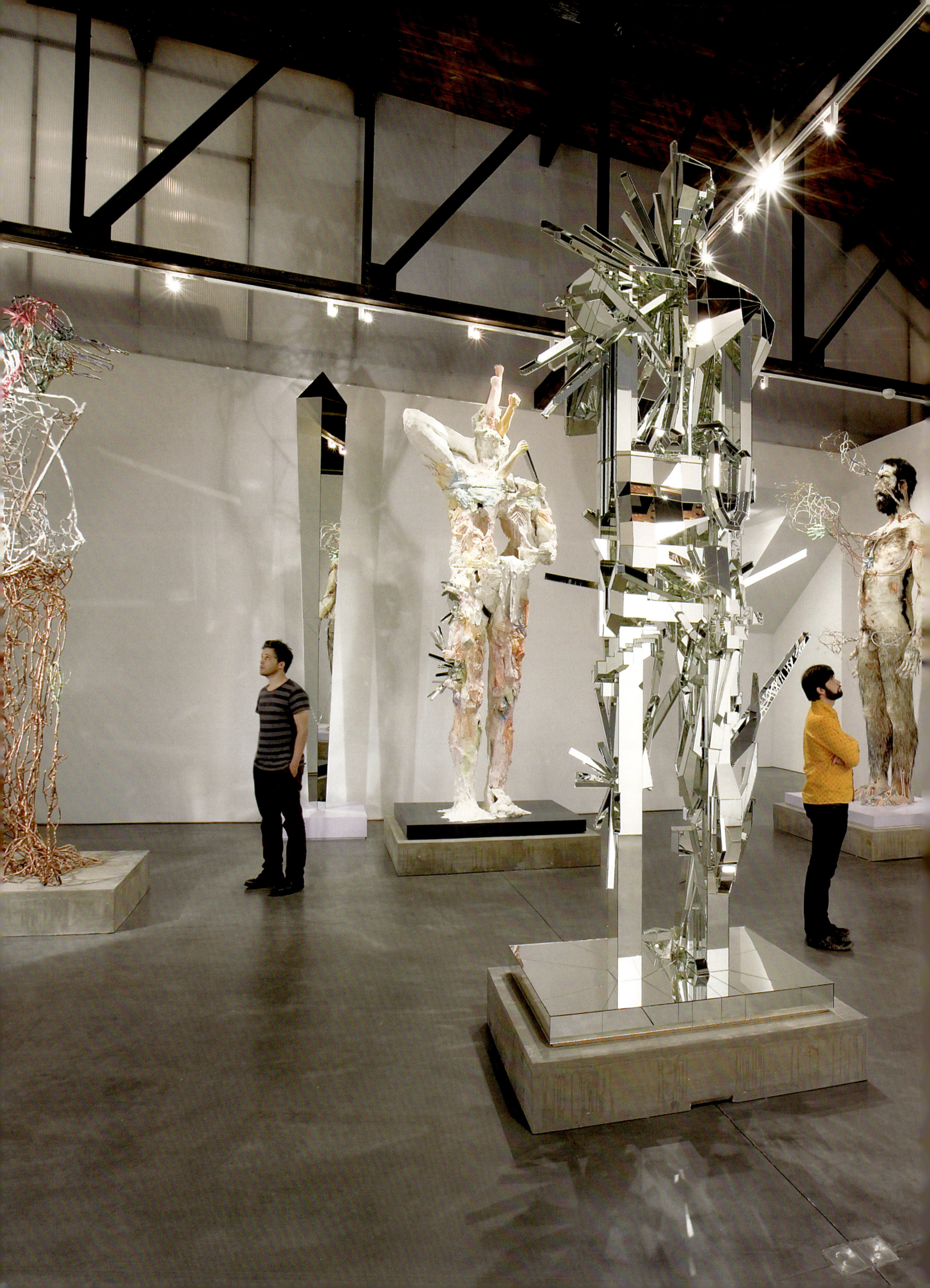

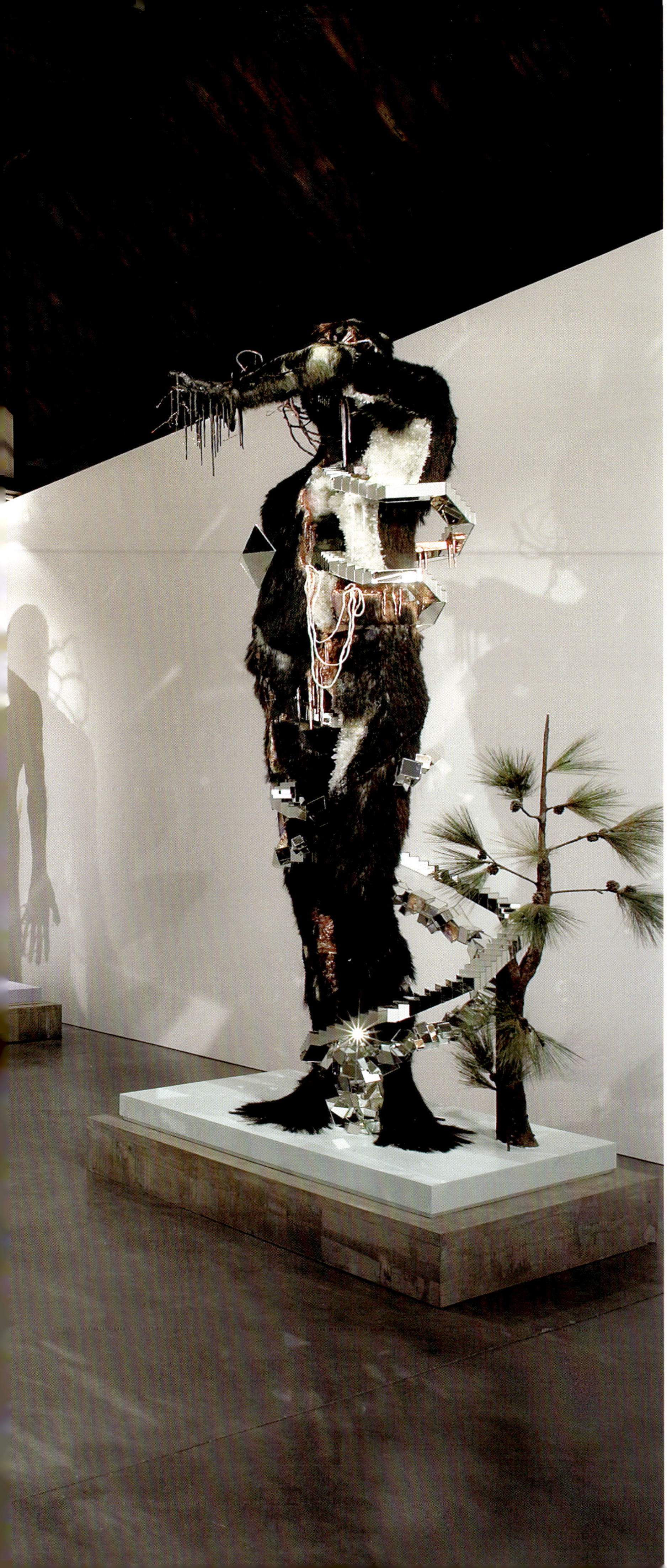

David Altmejd

LEFT
Installation view of *David Altmejd* at Andrea Rosen Gallery, New York, May 3–June 14, 2008

BELOW
YOU, detail, 2008
Plaster, wood, foam, paint, burlap, mirror, glue, 163 x 61 x 48 inches

When I was a young artist, when I started being so excited about the idea of making art and putting it in the world, I was obsessed with looking at art and looking at what everybody was doing. I wanted to know everything. I think that was because I was trying to position myself in that world. I wanted to be invisible as a person, but I didn't want my work to be invisible. It was very important to be able to do something that no one else was doing. It was very important also to decide what I was going to hate in art, and who my friends were going to be. Now I've reached a point where I've defined myself enough that I'm very satisfied with just drawing inspiration from my previous work. Every time I make a new piece, I get new ideas. I make new mistakes; I solve them. *The Vessel* and *The Swarm* are big enough to be considered (by me) like laboratories, inside of which I try things, combine materials in new ways, make mistakes, and come up with new ideas. And then I'll have a few years where I can draw from those pieces and make new ones. The work has developed enough complexity, layers, intelligence, and independence that it's able to transform itself. And the only reason I'm here is just to make sure that it's still alive, and that it's able to bloom the way it wants to bloom.

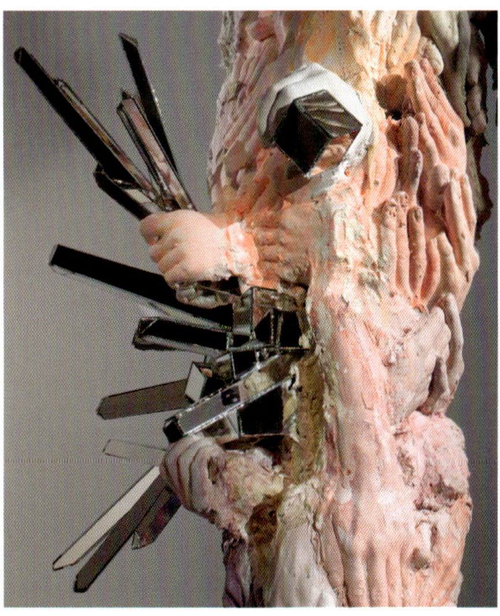

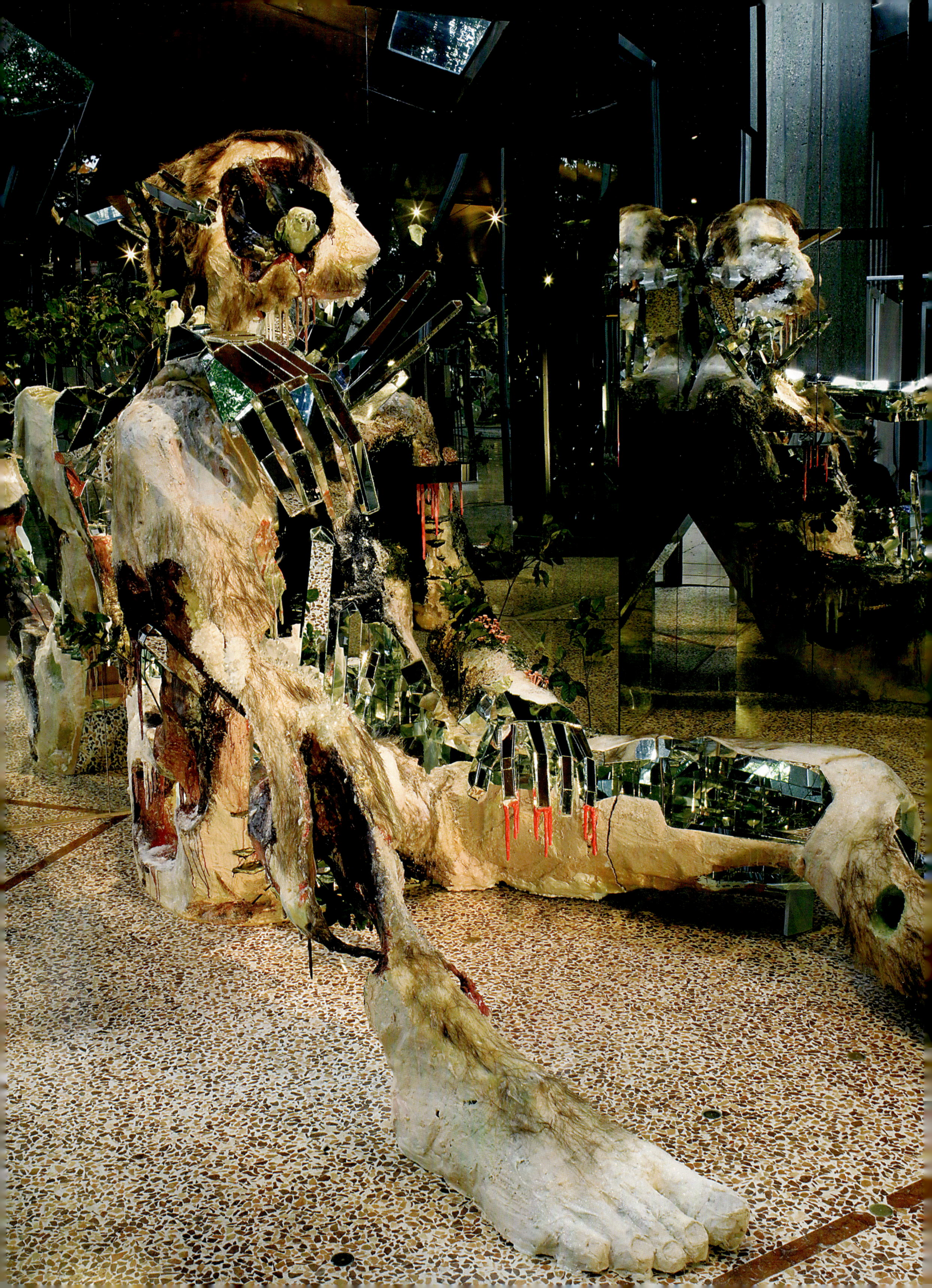

David Altmejd

OPPOSITE
The Giant 2, 2007
Foam, wood, glass, mirror, Plexiglas, resin, silicone, taxidermy birds and animals, synthetic plants, paint, pinecones, horsehair, burlap, chains, wire, feathers, quartz, pyrite, other minerals, jewelry, beads, glitter, 100 x 168 x 92 inches
Installation view of *David Altmejd: The Index,* Canadian Pavilion, 52nd Venice Biennale, June 10–November 21, 2007

RIGHT
The Index, detail, 2007
Steel, foam, wood, glass, mirror, Plexiglas, lighting system, silicone, resin, taxidermy birds and animals, synthetic plants, synthetic tree branches, bronze, fiberglass, paint, burlap, leather, pinecones, horsehair, synthetic hair, chains, wire, feathers, quartz, pyrite, other minerals, glass eyes, clothing, shoes, jewelry, beads, monofilament, glitter, 131 x 510½ x 363¼ inches
Installation view of *David Altmejd: The Index*, Canadian Pavilion, 52nd Venice Biennale, June 10–November 21, 2007

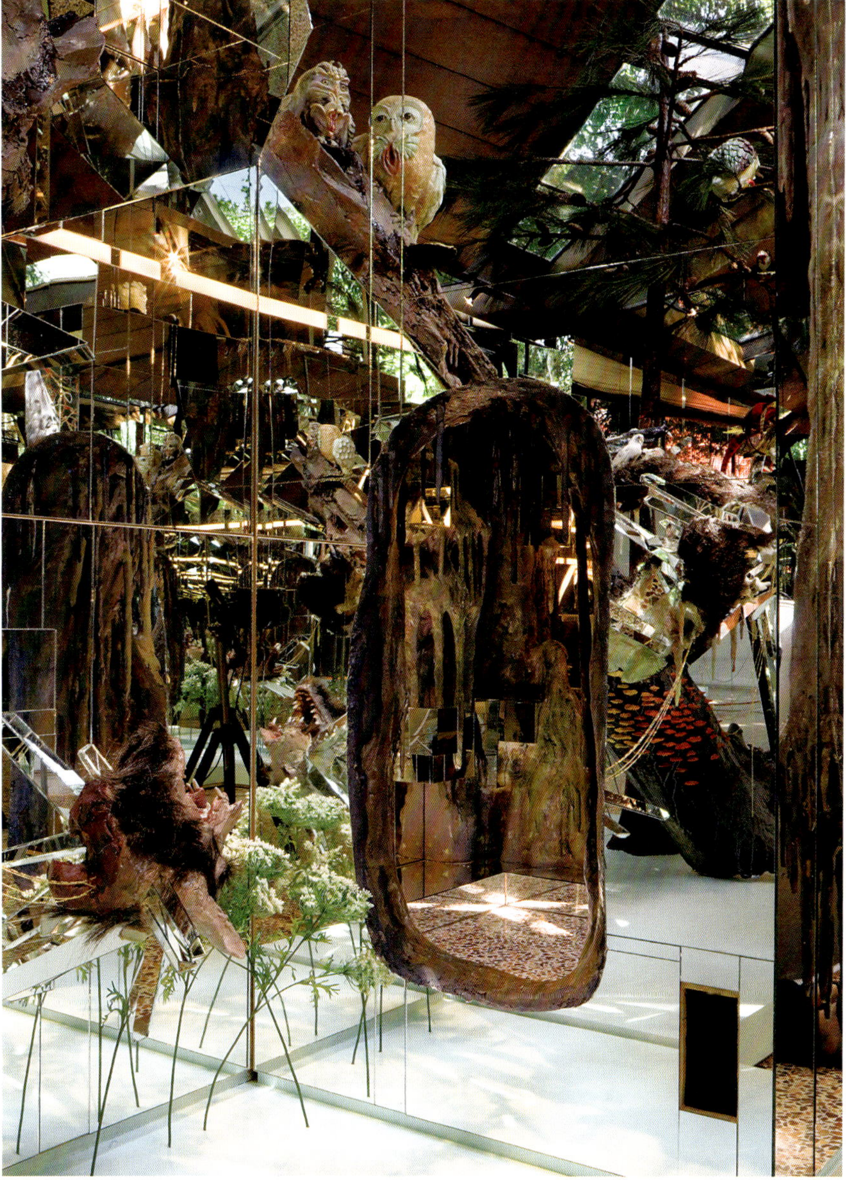

When I make a plaster figure, what's going to make it look like it's alive is not necessarily that it's going to represent a living figure. It's more because of the energy that comes from the making of it. So, when I put my hands on it or make a hole in it and drag plaster through it, it's really just to inject an energy into it. To make a hole and leave the imprints of my hand in an object is actually showing that I'm sculpting the object. I'm actually making the hole, building an object, going through it. I'm driving matter somewhere else. That's what makes it alive. So I like that contrast, which might potentially suggest death but actually makes the object more alive. The figures always have holes in them. But, I consider myself an absolute optimist, and I feel like these holes are what lets light and air through, what permits my hands to drag matter from one side to the other, from the back to the front. The holes become the source of *positiveness*. It's not negative; it's not morbid. It's the opposite. I love the holes. There's a flow when what's inside is potentially radiating outside. That's why there are ears, for example, all over some of my work. That's why I drill holes in the walls during an installation—in walls that are not considered pieces. For me, it's just a way of making energy travel through the space and creating a sort of balance. Thought, energy, spirit—lively energy—they're all coming from the same place and they all have the same role.

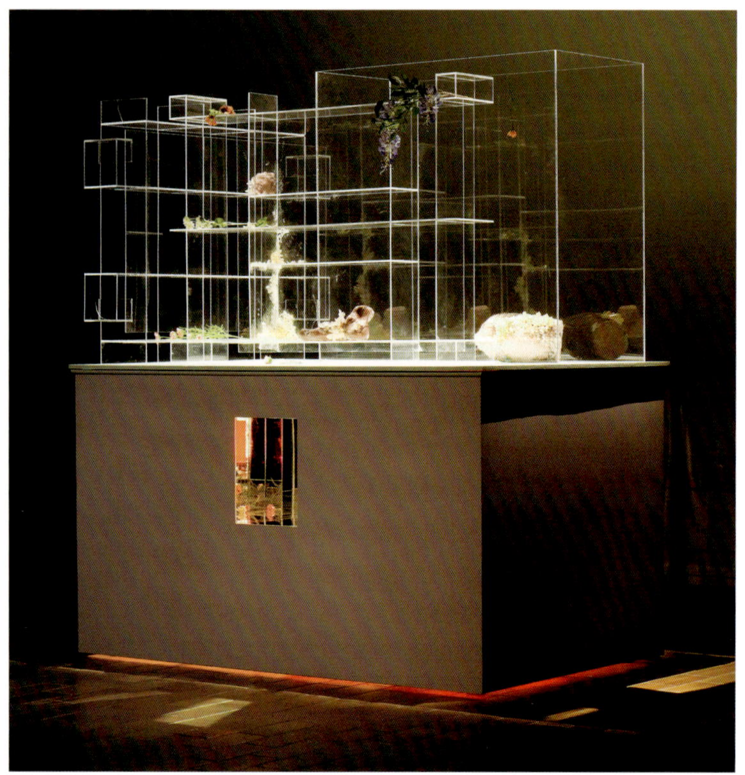

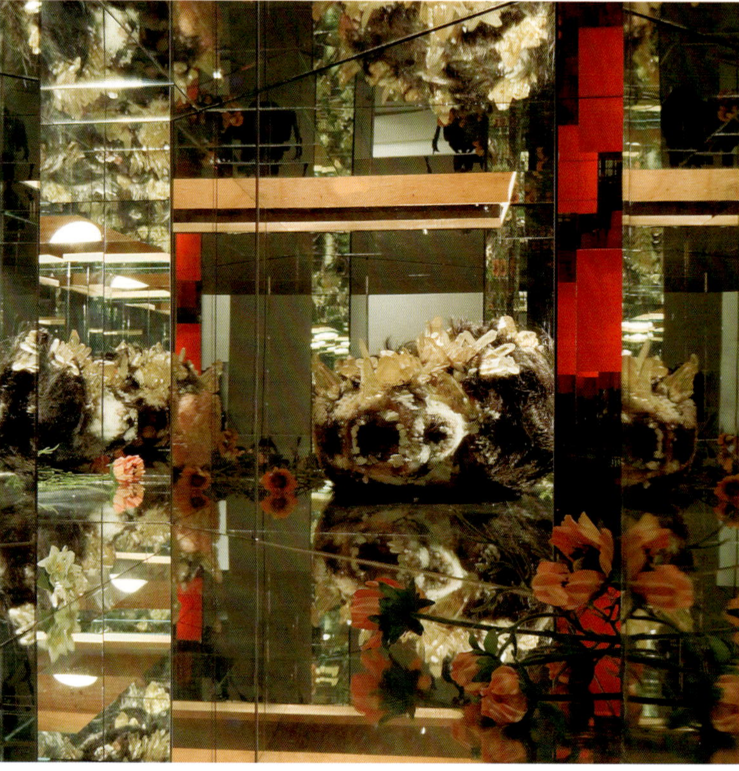

David Altmejd

ABOVE, LEFT AND RIGHT
Second Werewolf, 2000
Glass, mirror, wood, lighting system, acetate, Mylar, Plexiglas, foam, plaster, paint, epoxy clay, synthetic hair, quartz, rhinestones, silk flowers, 80¾ x 48¼ x 70½ inches

OPPOSITE
Installation view of *Colossi*
Vanhaerents Art Collection, Brussels, Belgium, April–June 2010 and April 2011–March 2012

Since I've been making sculpture I've always been obsessed with the idea of making it self-contained. So, as much as it can look like installation, it's never *really* installation. I've always made sure that there was a little element—like a little rock placed in the opposite corner—so that, in my mind, it wasn't installation. It was sculpture. Because everything was connected, it was possible to see it as one organism. It has always been very important for me to be able to see my work as organisms, however complex they are. Now, I think that I'm letting go of that constraint. But I was always a little anti-installation, probably because installation has always had the pretension to be cutting edge (whereas I found that it became the most academic thing). And I just thought that it was much more original to do plain sculpture.

I like the idea that my work is independent from me, and that I'm not trying to say anything specific. I just let it be whatever it is by itself. If someone hears the work say something that I never said, I can't really object to that. But I'm always surprised when people totally avoid the process aspect of the work. I don't know how criticism works, how art writing or art writers work. I imagine that when something is said about my work—when a really punchy sentence is written about it—it becomes material (as much as the work itself) that can be quoted or used by other writers. So it's almost as if talking about my work isn't really coming directly from the work. It's also coming from all those things that already have been said. So of course, talking about decaying werewolves (*Second Werewolf,* 2000) sounds really good—dynamic and kind of sensational. A lot of people just use that. It's in my work, but it was there years ago, for a brief moment.

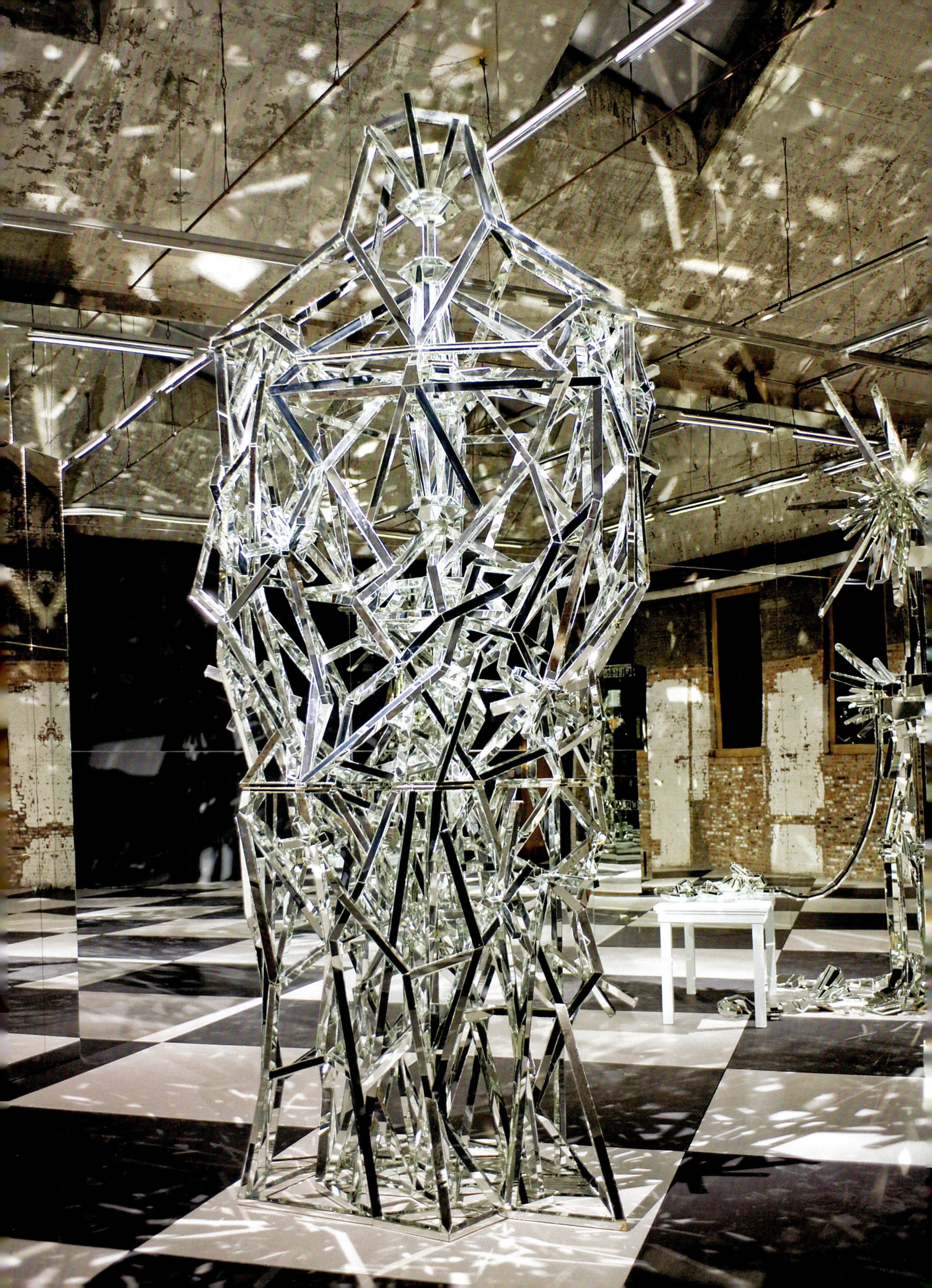

assume vivid astro focus

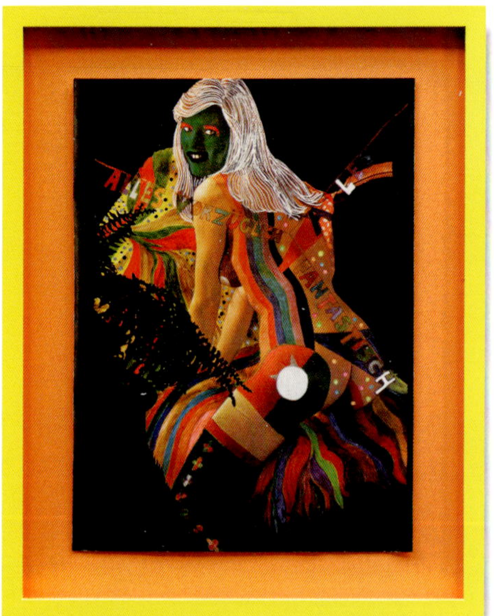

ABOVE
alles vorzuglich alles fantastisch (crawl girl 10), 2008
Marker and ink on paper,
14 x 11 inches

OPPOSITE
Walking on Thin Ice, 2002
Video, 5 min 51 sec
Featuring Carla Machado

The way we work? It's not like Eli's always doing one thing, and Christophe's doing something else. Sometimes it is the case, but it's not a specific pattern. People have this need to know—to track down—who is behind what. But, because we have a common interest in music, we think it's a bit like a band made up of different people playing different instruments. Whenever they play all the instruments together there is one sound. And that's actually the way we work. What really matters is the end result—a really overwhelming installation with a zillion things happening. Even though sometimes we like to do things on our own, we also like leaving the ego behind and merging with other people. That's something quite magical. So the core behind a project is Eli Sudbrack/Christophe Hamaide-Pierson and then we collaborate with other people because we are friends, or we like the work they do, or because it's relevant regarding a show we might work on. Then we invite those people or use work that they did in the past, and they become part of the installation. What matters is the result, and not who is behind it, even though it can be interesting if you start doing some research to know who made *this* thing and why, or how he did *that.*

The nature of collaboration is different from being hired to make something for somebody else, because you're not being told what to do. You are bringing your ideas to the table and they're part of a larger conversation. That doesn't mean there aren't times when people are saying, "Do this more; no, don't do that." But you're not obligated. Working collaboratively, everyone involved will have surprises. Things will happen that you wouldn't necessarily arrive at on your own. It just opens up a new door to the work.

At the beginning it was Eli working as an artist and calling himself assume vivid astro focus (avaf): Eli *aka* assume vivid astro focus. But he was also driven by the collaboration idea and so perhaps that's why he was not working under his own name. It became a bit confusing; people were always referring to assume vivid astro focus as *being* Eli. And when we started to work together full-time, a lot of people were still considering avaf as Eli, even though it was not the case any longer.

When Eli started assume vivid astro focus he created the name because he didn't want to be the focus of people's attention. And he also had a vision that other people could actually become assume vivid astro focus, too. From the beginning he wanted to be a collective—not only a collective working with other people but also a collective of people who have similar beliefs and are connected—not necessarily only through working together but through the Internet, let's say. We also wanted to have different pseudonyms, but we got sick of it. People just like labeling so much; they implant a lot of thoughts, prejudgment. And you just want to have something simple at some point. One goes through phases. At one point we said, "Let's kill avaf and come up with another name, another practice. Let's do something else."

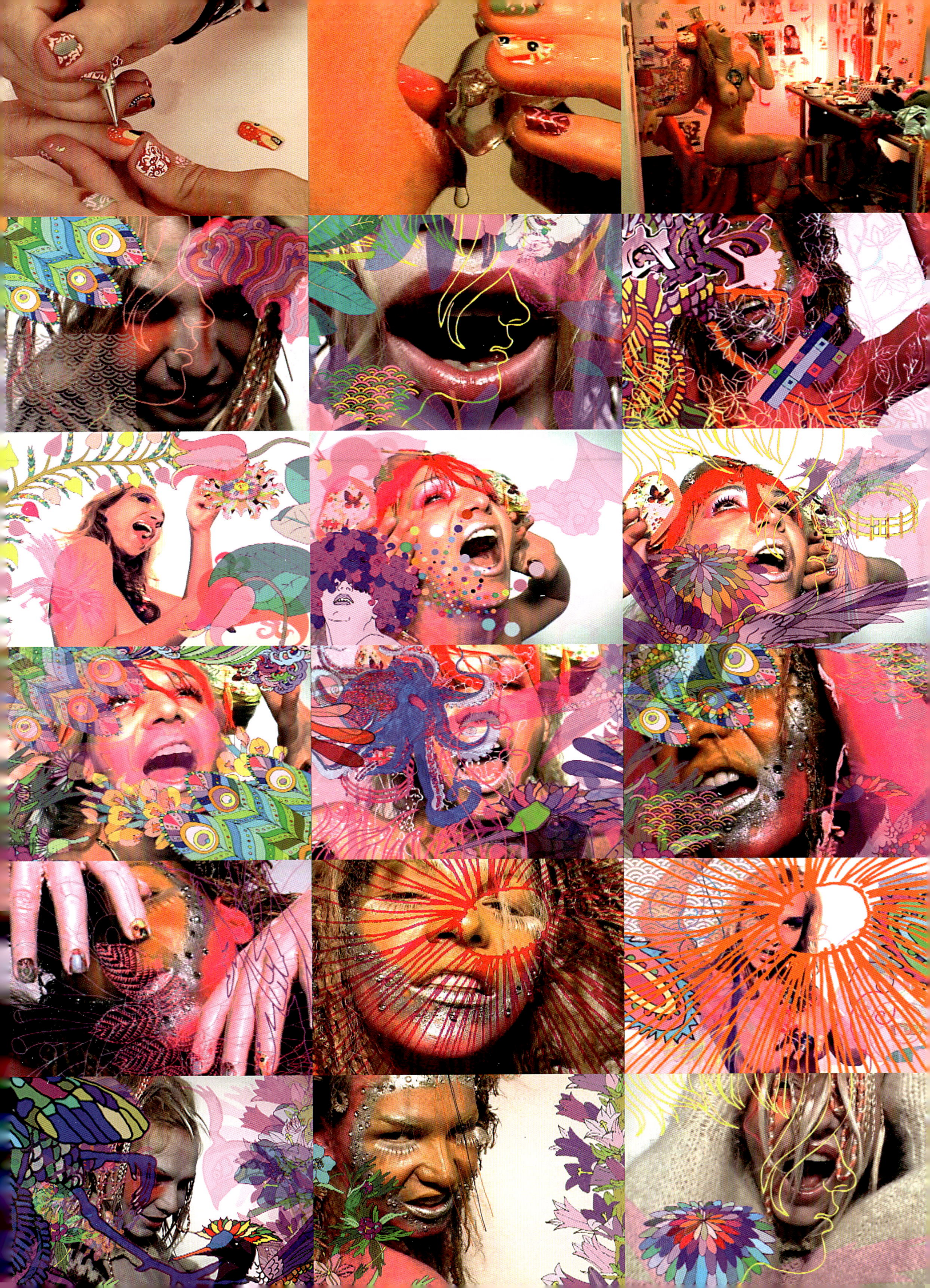

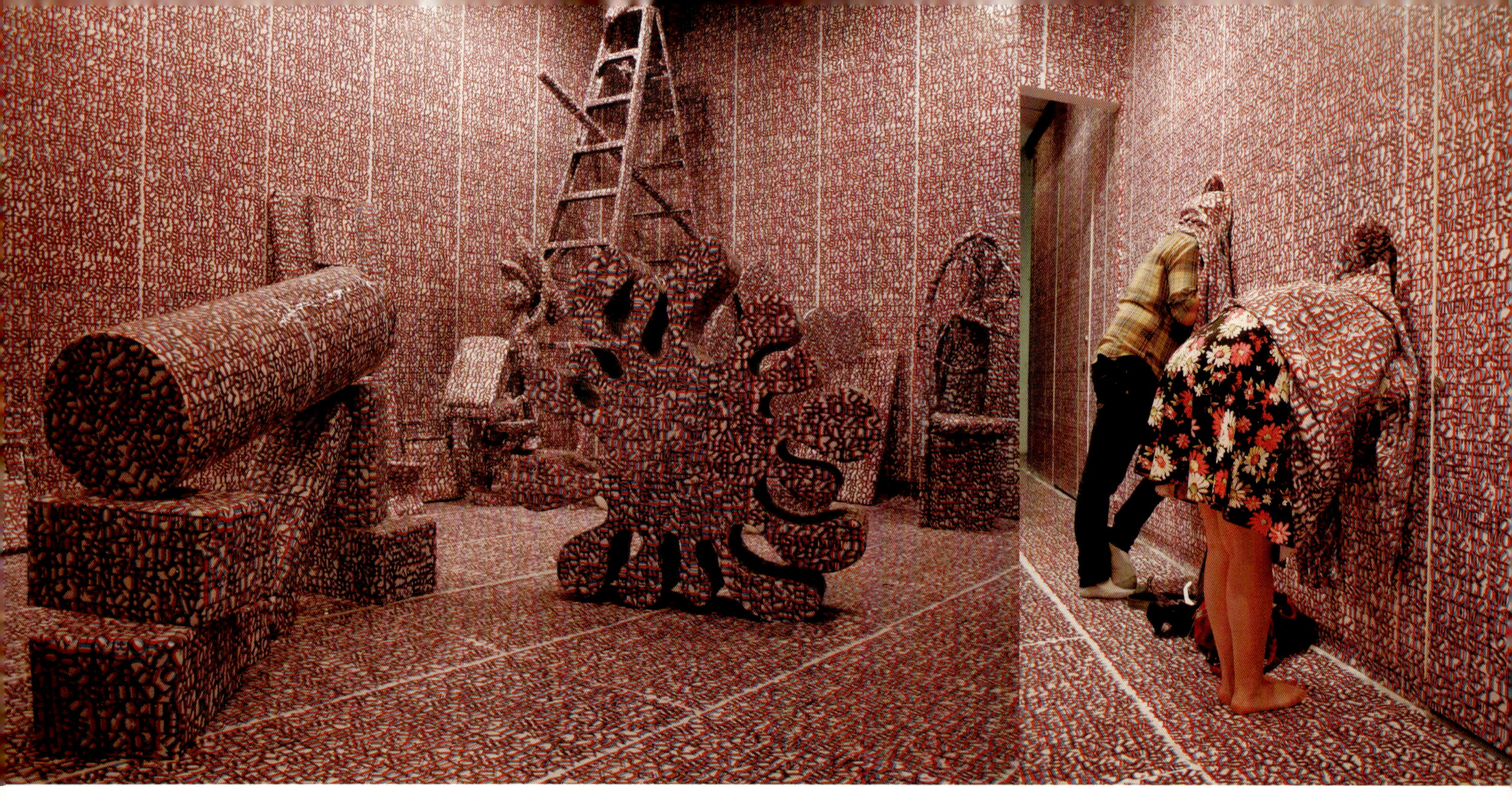

assume vivid astro focus

ABOVE AND OPPOSITE
a very anxious feeling, 2007
Mixed-media installation, dimensions variable
Performance program curated by Eric Schmalenberger and assume vivid astro focus
John Connelly Presents, New York

Avaf has a strong aesthetic, and sometimes you want to do something that is not related to it. It's not about betraying avaf; it's just because you want to do something else. Painters do paintings and eventually they will show them with other paintings, or not. We don't have this practice. Christophe doesn't make a neon sculpture just because he feels the need to make one. Usually, if he produces a piece, it's because there is a show and that piece is meant to be in it. We never produce one piece. It's always a whole bunch of pieces made together to be part of one installation. But then, of course, you can decontextualize. Even if we do a specific wallpaper for a given surface, the wallpaper—at the end—is a digital file. We're part of a digital era, so of course we're trying to develop the work accordingly. A collector is not buying the wallpaper that he's looking at on the wall. Once the show is over that wallpaper is destroyed. Whoever buys the wallpaper is buying a digital file on a DVD with a certificate of authenticity—a bit like buying video art on videotape—that doesn't exist physically until it is projected on the wall. It's the light beam and the projection on the wall that make a video piece. It's the same with the digital works we do.

Drawings are never just drawings in themselves. They're usually sketches for something else—for an installation or a wallpaper. But we wanted to start just drawing for the pleasure of it. We never have time to make more silent, more intimate work. We have so much stuff to do to create our immersive installations, but we also need to balance that with moments of more privacy in which we're actually creating our own installations for ourselves by making a drawing, immersing ourselves into that world—just drawing that moment. That's something we need to rescue. It's a conflict because of our belief in communal collective existence. But at the same time, one realizes that one also needs something that's more for oneself.

The starting point for our work is always a space. Funnily enough it goes back to Christophe's background, which is architecture. Every installation we've done so far is done specifically for the space we are given. We talk about ideas; then those ideas merge together and become specific. Sometimes we do research. Sometimes there are certain pieces that we just want to do, for instance a neon sculpture, regarding a club environment. Sometimes we want to do wallpaper. And then we start to build up and give birth to a piece. Performance is a very important part of our work. Sometimes there is an actual performance (or we've been collaborating with a performer like a musician). But there is also a performative *aspect* in the way we try to interact with the audience. The total work of art—that's what we aim for. We aim for hitting you in every single possible sensorial capability you have: ears, eyes. We haven't done any food, thoughts, or any taste experience yet. Maybe one day.

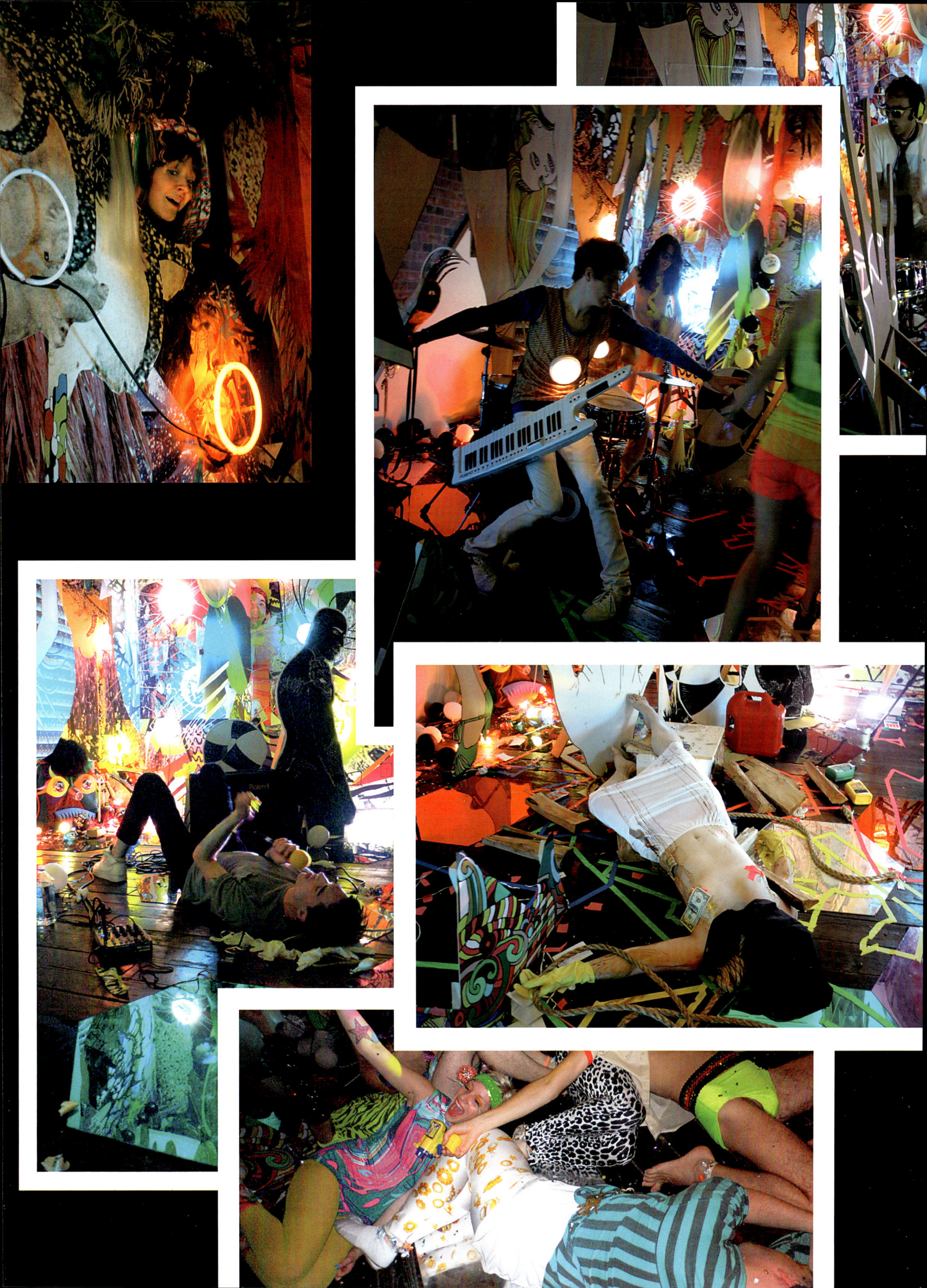
Roland

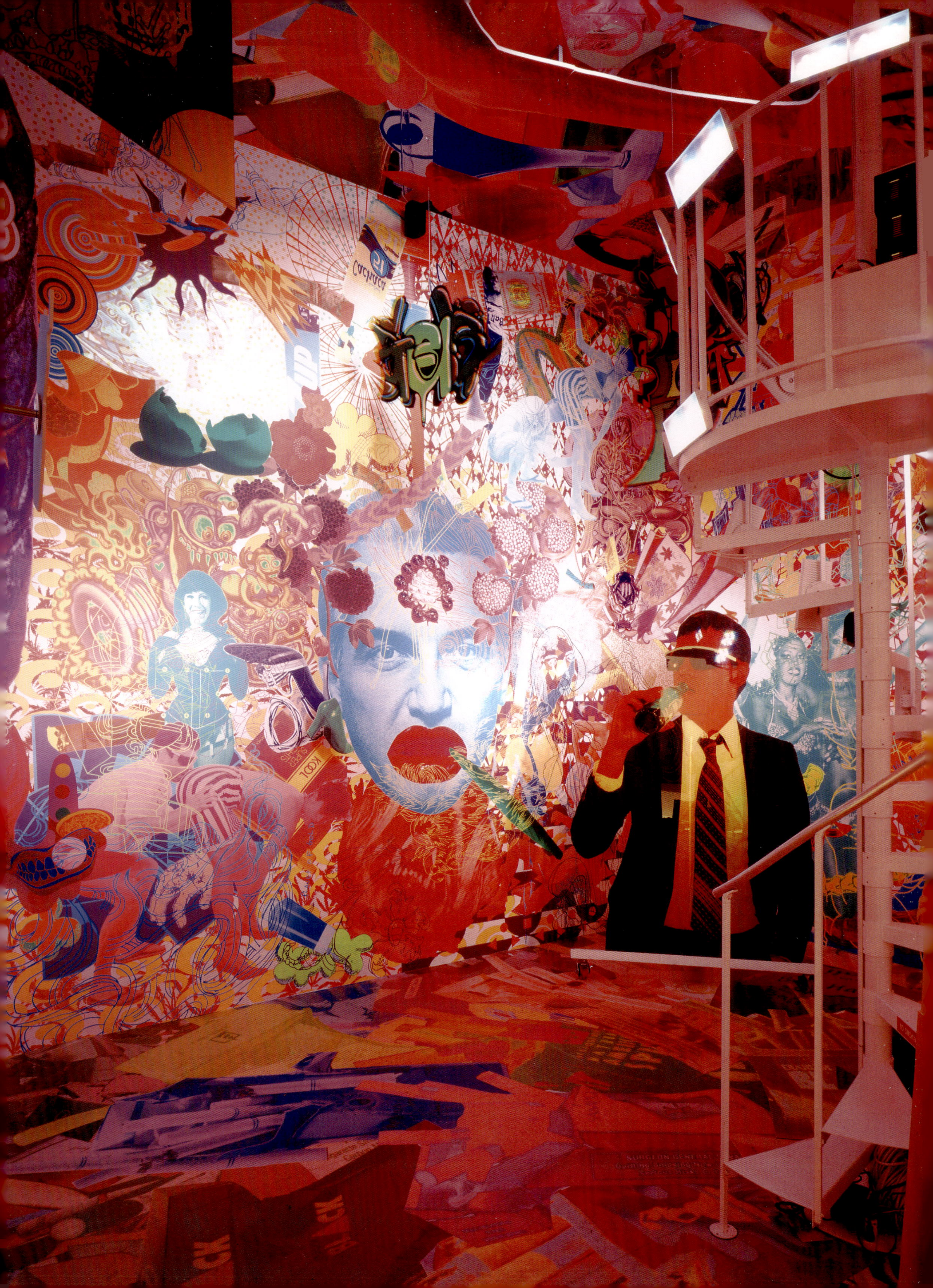

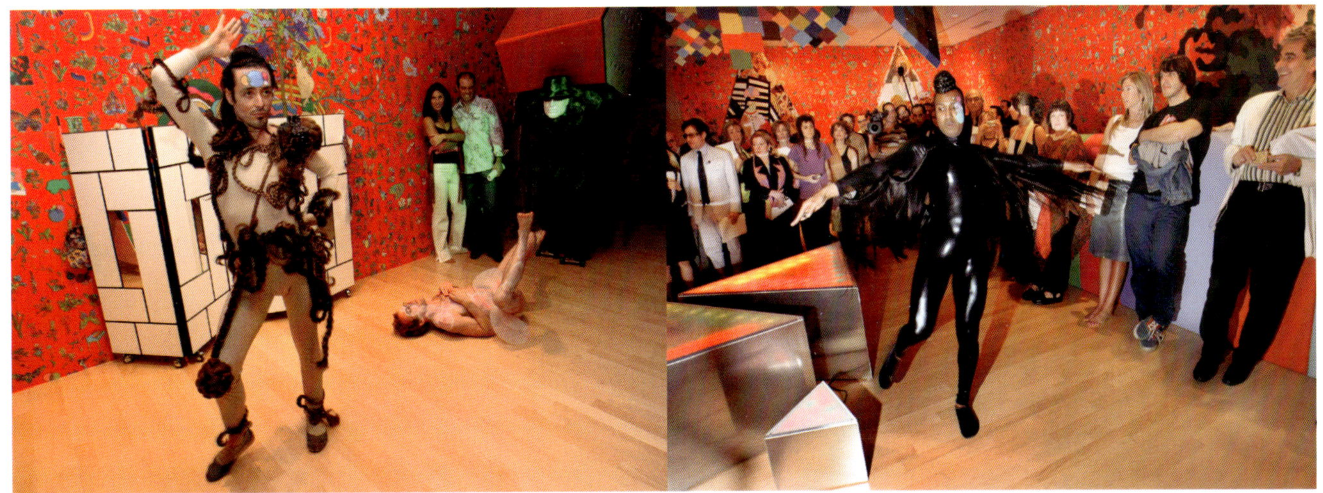

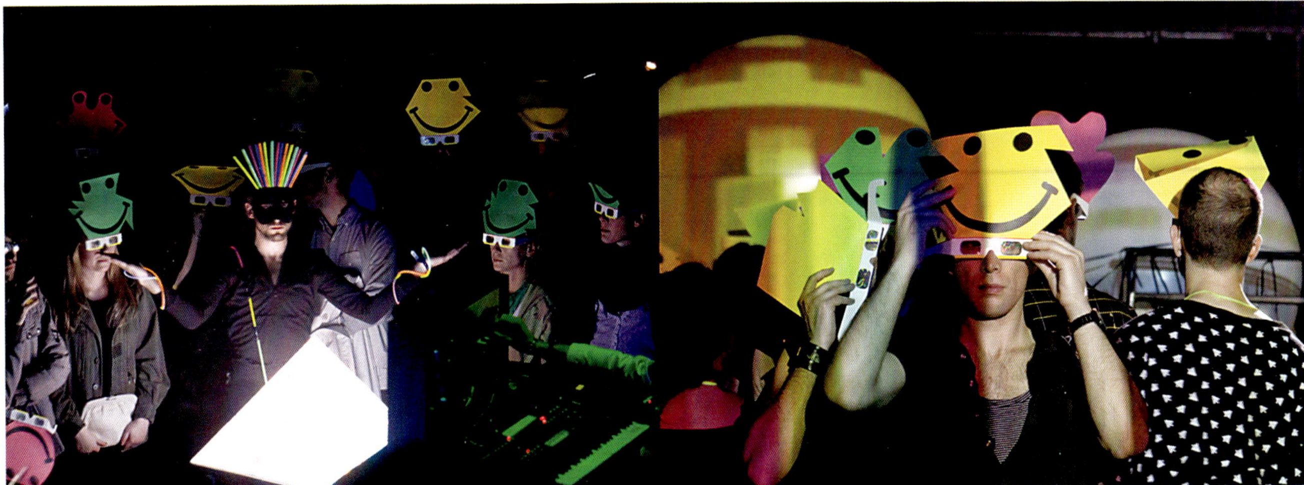

assume vivid astro focus

OPPOSITE
assume vivid astro focus VIII, 2004
Mixed-media installation, dimensions variable
2004 Whitney Biennial, Whitney Museum of American Art, New York

TOP
assume vivid astro focus XI, 2004
Mixed-media installation, dimensions variable
Opening night performances by Trajal Harrell Dance Style
Rosa and Carlos de la Cruz Collection, Key Biscayne

CENTER
Performance with Black Meteoric Star (aka Gavin Russom) as part of *Super#3–DFA Meets Dalbin,* 2008
Maison des Arts de Créteil, Paris
Organized by Dalbin, Paris

The whole mask thing is quite interesting. The first time avaf used a mask was for an installation at Rosa and Carlos de la Cruz's private collection (2004). We had the imagery that we were working on at the time for the Whitney Biennial (2004). We had made one installation, which was an homage to Los Super Elegantes, with whom we worked for a whole year. Eli didn't want to be recognized—didn't want to be pointed out as the artist. It was such a high-profile art event (it was quite intense), and he wanted to be left alone a little bit. So that was the idea of giving out masks. Then we started making masks for different shows.

We want people to concentrate on the work. We didn't used to show our faces, and it is still quite unusual for Eli to show his face to the camera. He doesn't want people to place a face on assume vivid astro focus. Whenever we make our installations, whenever we make our events, everybody in the room should be equal. That's one of the reasons we use masks. You're not one person; you're not *your* identity. You're actually a character, and you can free yourself to do whatever you want. So it's contradictory to expose one's face. That's always had the sense of spoiling what we're after. But, at the same time, when you give interviews wearing a mask, you detach yourself. Hiding behind a faceless character or a character that always changes its face can be fun but it's not necessarily truthful, honest, or intimate. And intimacy has always been something to be concerned about because that's the way to bring you in.

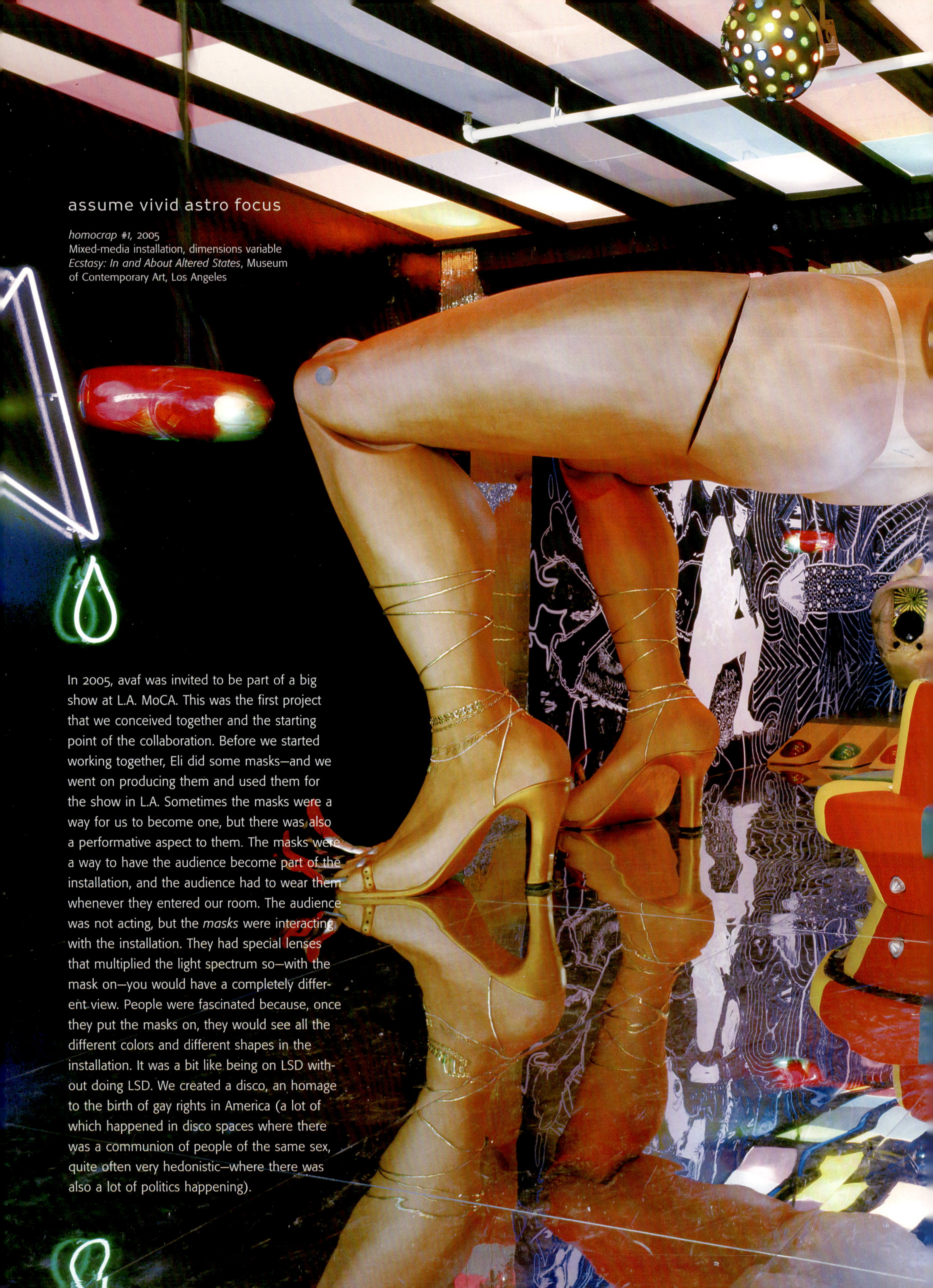

assume vivid astro focus

homocrap #1, 2005
Mixed-media installation, dimensions variable
Ecstasy: In and About Altered States, Museum of Contemporary Art, Los Angeles

In 2005, avaf was invited to be part of a big show at L.A. MoCA. This was the first project that we conceived together and the starting point of the collaboration. Before we started working together, Eli did some masks—and we went on producing them and used them for the show in L.A. Sometimes the masks were a way for us to become one, but there was also a performative aspect to them. The masks were a way to have the audience become part of the installation, and the audience had to wear them whenever they entered our room. The audience was not acting, but the *masks* were interacting with the installation. They had special lenses that multiplied the light spectrum so—with the mask on—you would have a completely different view. People were fascinated because, once they put the masks on, they would see all the different colors and different shapes in the installation. It was a bit like being on LSD without doing LSD. We created a disco, an homage to the birth of gay rights in America (a lot of which happened in disco spaces where there was a communion of people of the same sex, quite often very hedonistic—where there was also a lot of politics happening).

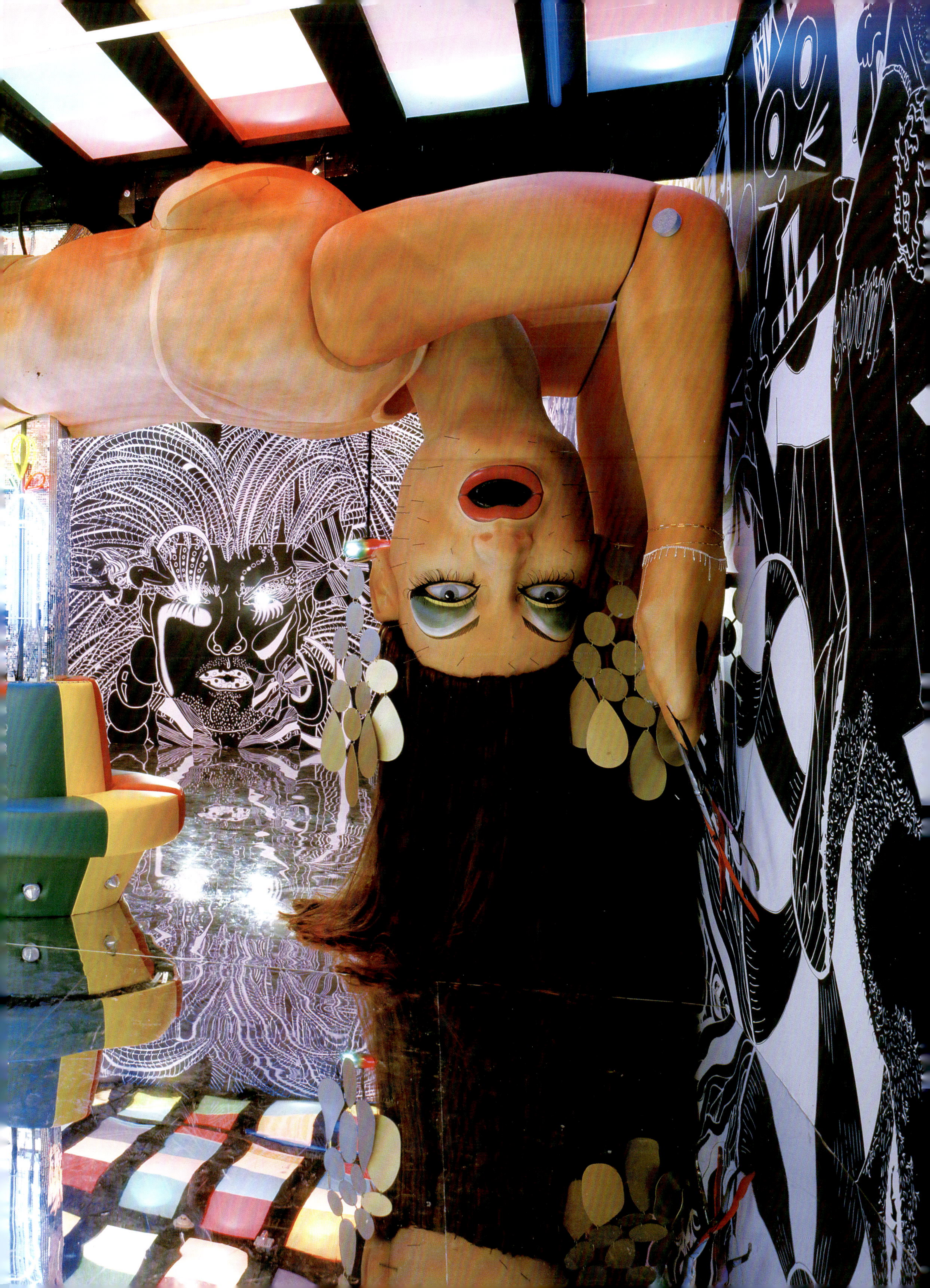

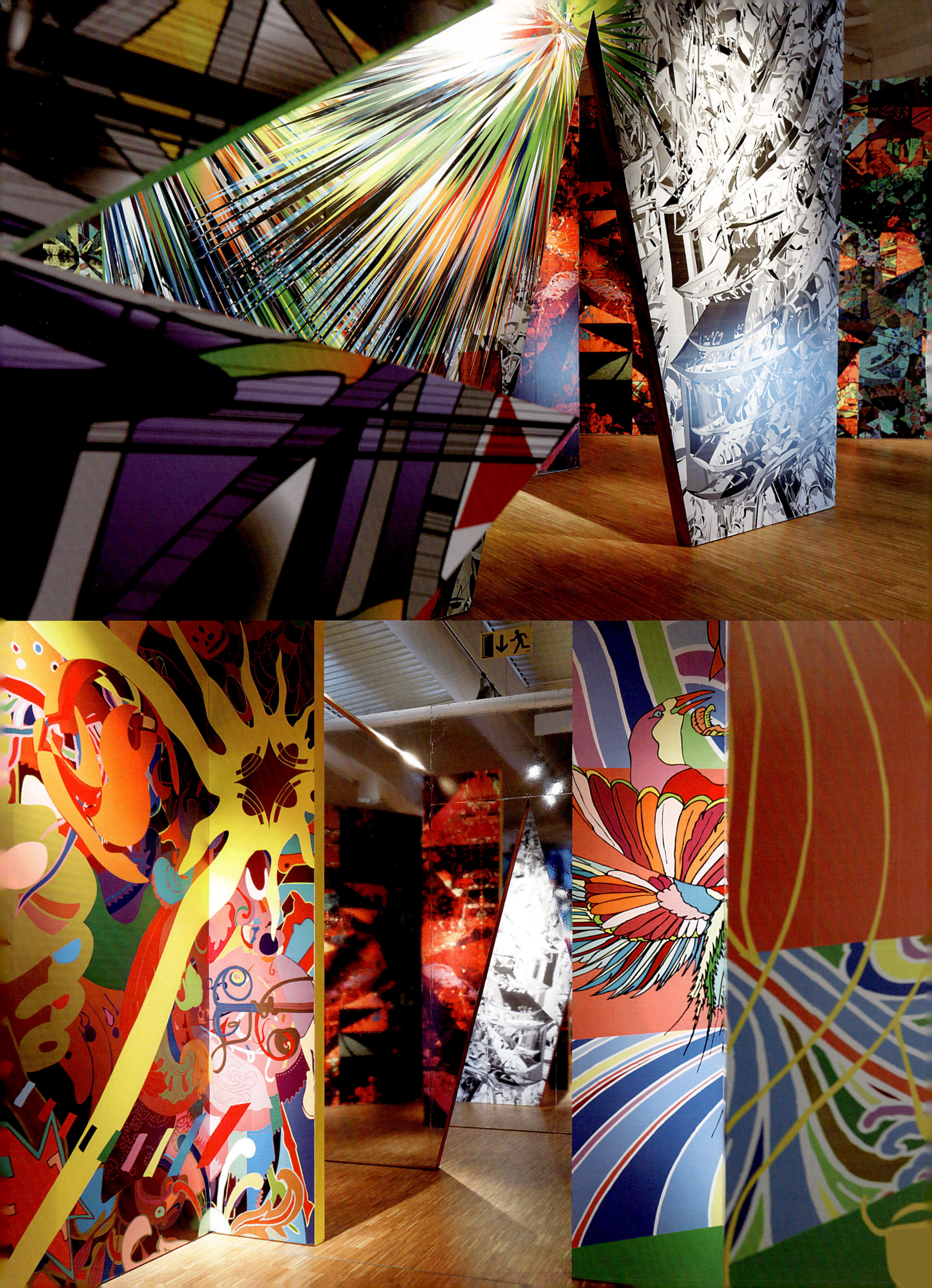

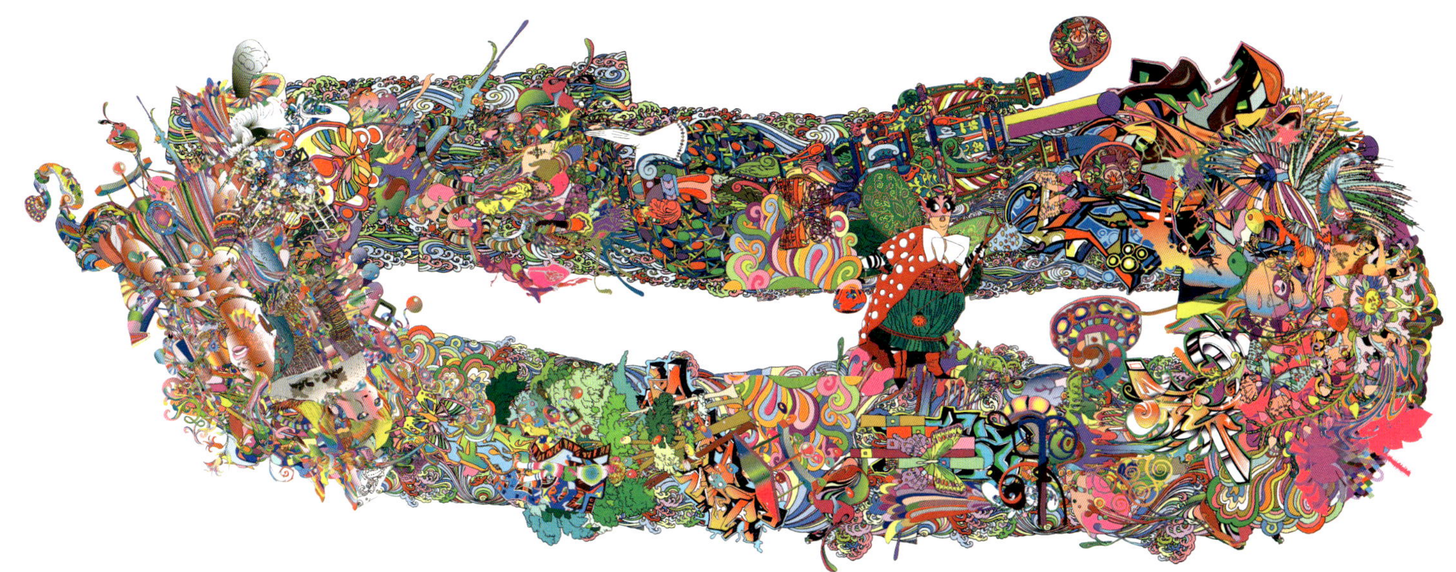

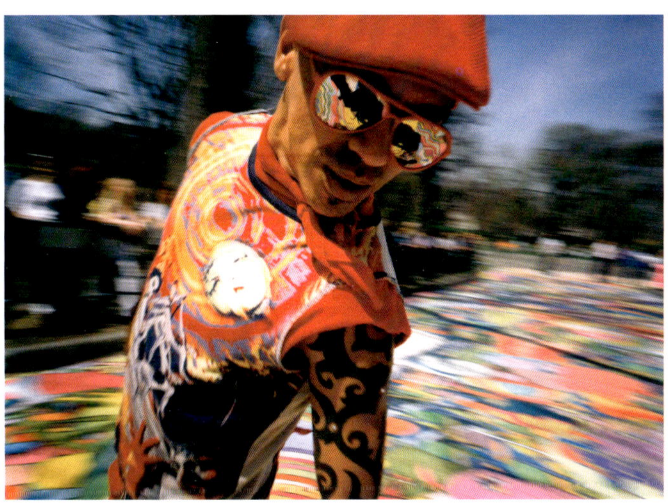

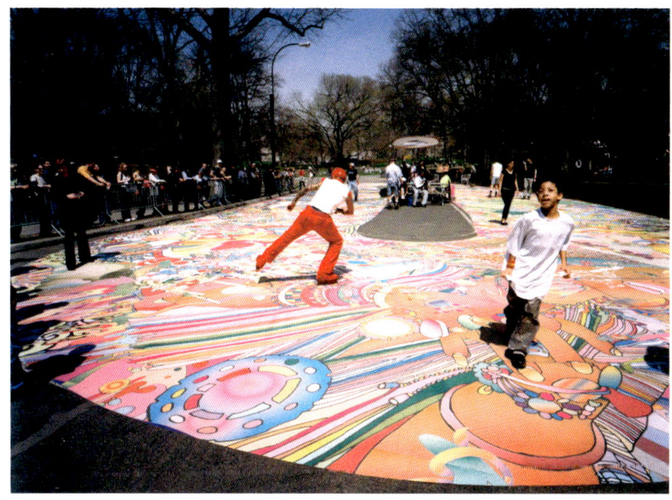

assume vivid astro focus

OPPOSITE, TOP AND BOTTOM
affektert veggmaleri akselererende faenksap, 2009
Mixed-media installation, dimensions variable
Retrospective of avaf wallpaper pieces displayed in labyrinth form, National Museum of Art, Architecture and Design, Oslo

TOP
Garden XI, 2004
Floor sticker, dimensions variable

CENTER, LEFT AND RIGHT
assume vivid astro focus IX, 2004
Floor sticker on dance skate rink; DJ booth designed by Rama Chorpash
In The Public Realm, Skate Circle, Central Park, New York
Public Art Fund in conjunction with the 2004 Whitney Biennial

Recently we've been appropriating and remixing our own work much more, rather than remixing other people's work. That process or action of making drawings of other people's drawings or appropriating a song was much more present in the early works. Nowadays, reconstructing our own work is actually very important for us. We're constantly remixing ourselves. With us, the thing is that there's never one lineage of thought. There are always many that contract and expand. They meet and then distance themselves from each other. So there's never just one way of doing something; there are always many ways. Sometimes it can be very referential and, then, maybe not. It's always sort of mixed, like a landscape—a representation of the things one is exposed to, not necessarily outer things but sometimes also things that come from inside, too.

For the show in Oslo in 2009, we decided to make a retrospective of our wallpaper pieces in a labyrinth form. The retrospective idea is always kind of funny because it's never going to be the same as when it was first shown. We wanted to create a different environment because most of them are made for the very first space where they were shown. The proportions of the Whitney Biennial wallpaper from 2004 replicate the walls at the Whitney. The sticker we made for Central Park in 2004 replicates the dimensions of the roller-skating rink it was made for. So there's always a memory of space in the wallpaper though, of course, you can't say that by looking at it. But for us, it's there. We know where it came from, what space it was originally made for. So whenever we do a retrospective, we're actually dealing with a new space, and we have to create a new way of displaying the work. So that's already a way of remixing it.

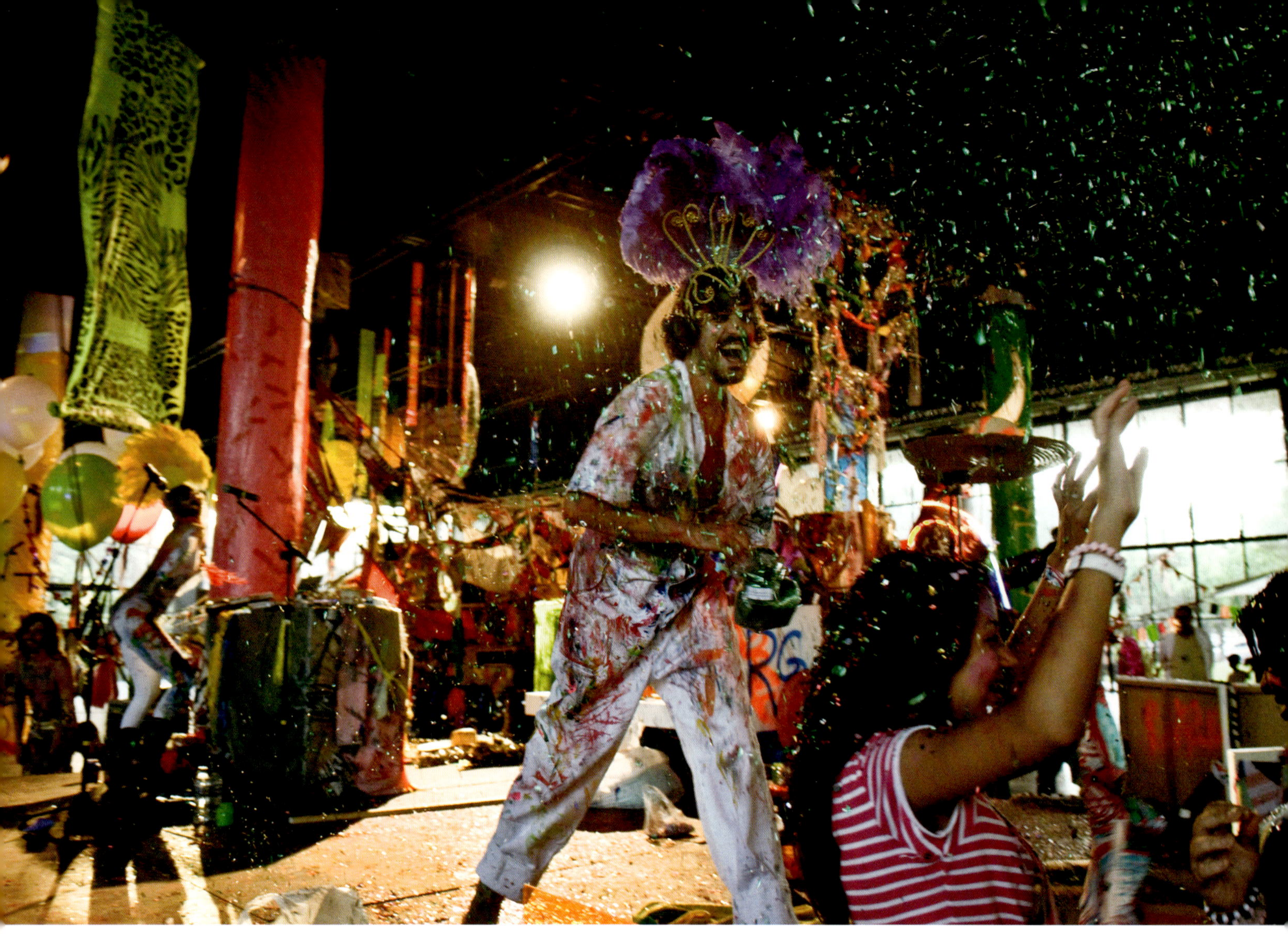

assume vivid astro focus

ABOVE AND OPPOSITE ABOVE
axé vatapá alegria feijão, 2008
Mixed-media installation and performance, dimensions variable
In Living Contact, 28th Bienal de São Paulo, Ibirapuera Park, São Paulo

OPPOSITE, LEFT AND RIGHT
Trava Cíclope, 2011
Color pigment on paper, 16 x 13 inches each

In 2008, we were invited to the São Paulo Bienal. They didn't want to show that much artist work that year so it was a bit controversial: most of the spaces in the Niemeyer building were completely empty. Only the last floor had some works of art. For the ground floor they invited different groups of artists to create something more performance-based. We proposed something like a work-in-progress installation with a performative aspect. We got a float, and we drove it all around São Paulo to bring it inside the space. During the week, we were collaborating with friends from São Paulo. We built a structure like a big blob—a massive thing that was growing and growing, day after day. We transformed the space with the float, and there were different actions happening during the week. We invited Gavin Russom, a musician friend from New York, to come for the very last day and he performed live on top of the float. It became a sort of rave with friends from São Paulo, who are not part of avaf and not working constantly with us—but people we relate to aesthetically. Since we were in São Paulo, and there was this work-in-progress concept behind what we proposed, it made sense that all of us should be together working on this one project.

We've been doing tranny drawings since we published our first book and started making dedication pages. Eli started to use the transgender image as a symbol of freedom, of being able to do what you want with your body to recreate your identity. So the tranny is an iconic figure among the things we do. It relates to the way we work. We're constantly recycling our work, reshaping what we do. Something has been done for one show, but then we reuse that thing in a completely different manner. So we also use the idea—the image—of the transsexual as a metaphor regarding the work. What is it about? It's about deconstructing your own identity. So we can completely apply this idea to what we do. We started making those drawings and sometimes filling them up with colors, like the ones kids play with. At some point those drawings were abstract shapes, then more formal shapes—figurative—and then we started making the figures look transsexual. We called them Cyclops trannies because they were tranny figures with just one big eye. We did a series of drawings inspired by the dedication drawings for the book, and then Eli decided to rip all the pages from our book and make drawings on the book pages for an art fair in São Paulo.

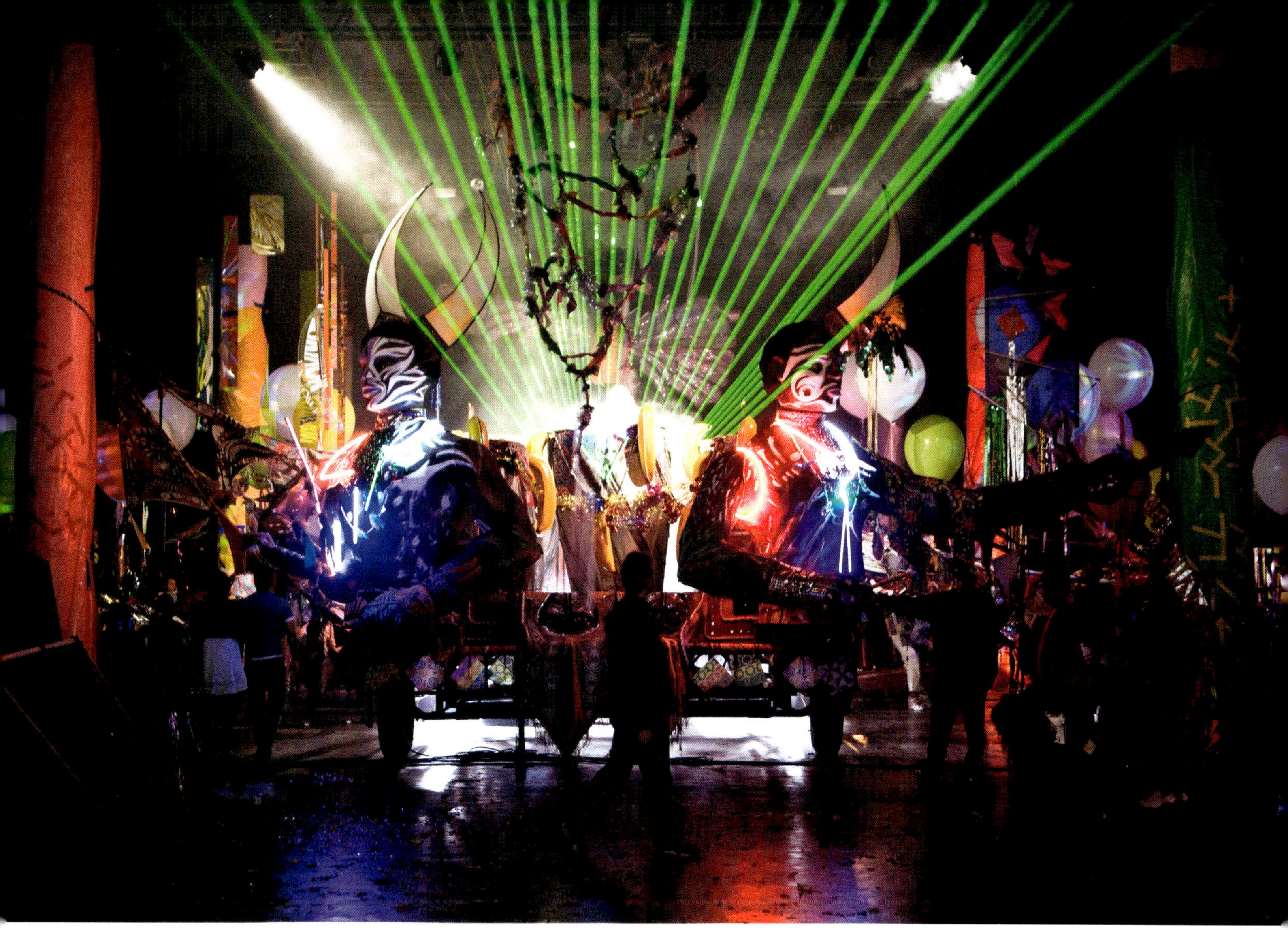

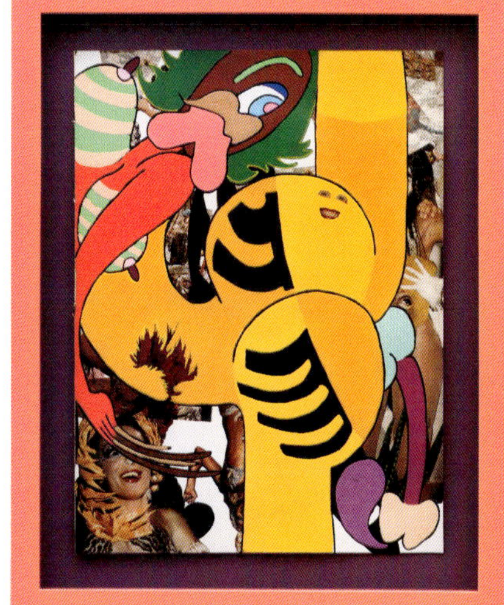

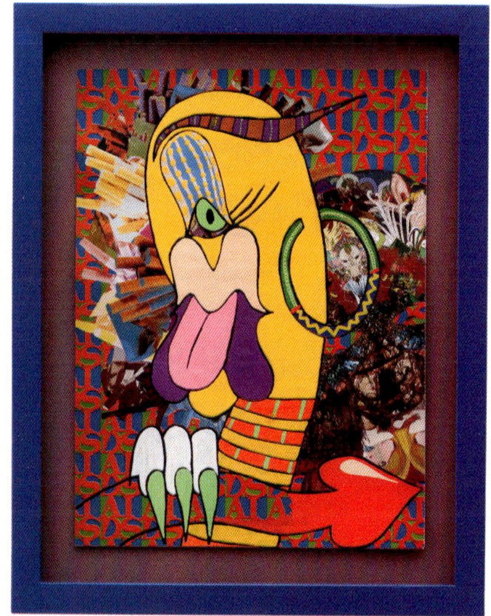

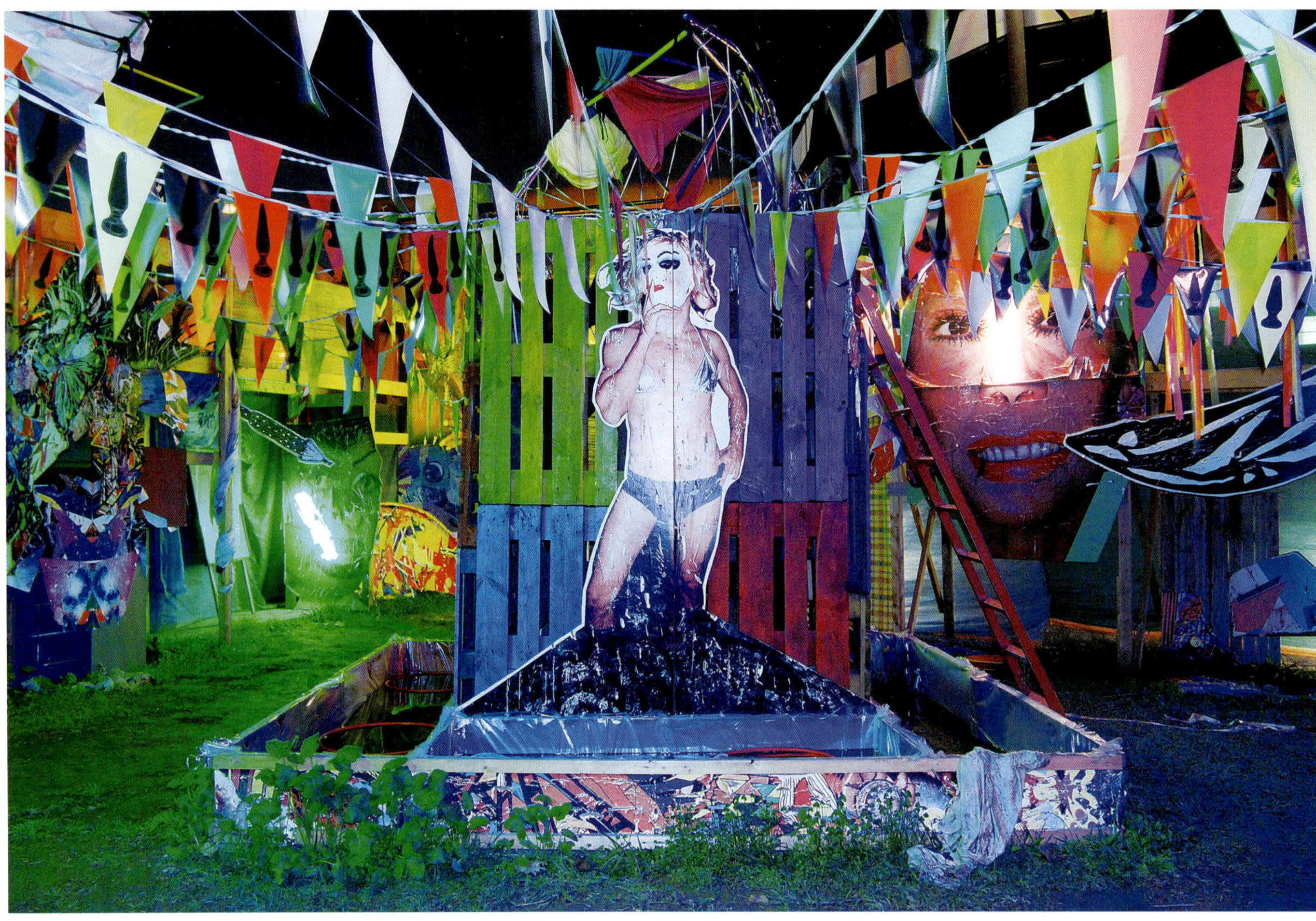

When we spent some time in New York, we were amazed and fascinated by all the construction sites—all the scaffolding. So for the Athens Biennale (2007) we created an environment that became a sort of hangout with scaffolding where people could climb. Not everybody understood that it was a structure made for people to play on, but that was the idea. For the Athens show, we were planning to use imagery of ourselves—like an element from wallpaper. So we were doing placards that we would mount on the structure we'd been building. And we don't know why, but there were some issues with the paste. We couldn't achieve a nice smooth finish. And so, one day before the opening, we slashed and completely destroyed our own installation. The only way to be pleased was by completely tearing down all the images—which was a bit ironic because, actually, the show was called *Destroy Athens*.

Demolition was also a core concept for *absolutely venomous accurately fallacious*, our 2008 demolition disco installation at Deitch Projects in Long Island City, New York. We were looking at a few different demolition sources. One of them was the symbol of the tranny as somebody who is demolishing her/his own body, creating a new identity, creating a new body. Transgender was also a big taboo issue—like a demolition of the status quo between the sexes—that we wanted to bring into the show. Demolition was also related to New York because a lot of the Long Island City and Brooklyn neighborhoods were being demolished at that point to give birth to big high-rises and real-estate exploitation. We were interested in the actual demolition sites—making a lot of installations in which we replicated the imagery of the woodstuds cheaply put together—and in the spontaneity of that sort of temporary construction that you usually put up just to bar people's access to something. The ceilings of the exhibition space in Long Island City were so high that it created a chapel effect. We covered all that space with the tranny images that we were working with at that point, mixing that with the other stuff that we had. And then, somehow, it was an homage to demolition.

assume vivid astro focus

ABOVE
afovi vevilosi aftistikon fantasioseon, 2007
Mixed-media installation, dimensions variable
Destroy Athens, 1st Athens Biennale, Technopolis, Gazi, Athens

OPPOSITE
absolutely venomous accurately fallacious (naturally delicious), 2008
Mixed-media installation, dimensions variable
Deitch Projects, Long Island City, New York

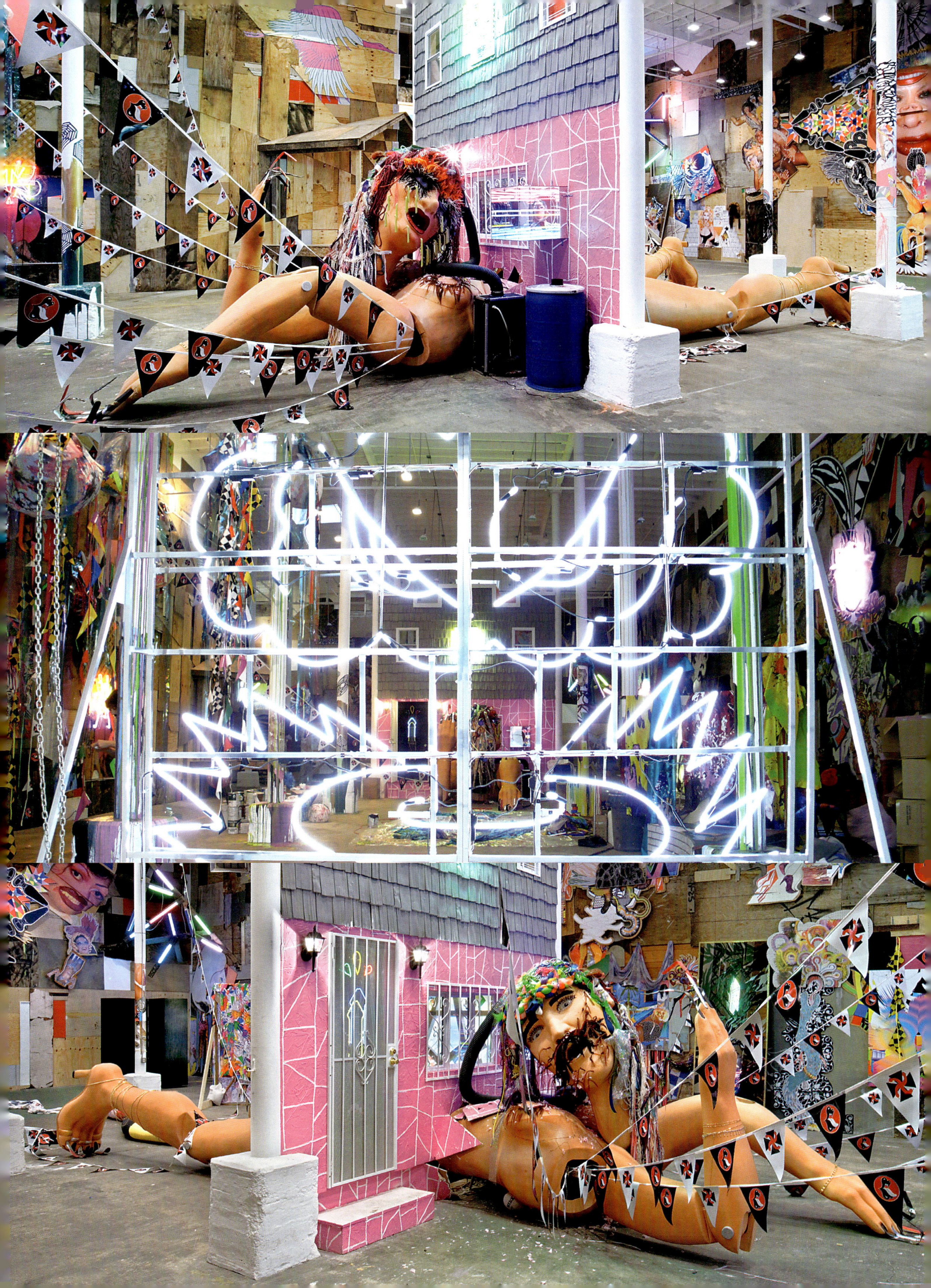

Lynda Benglis

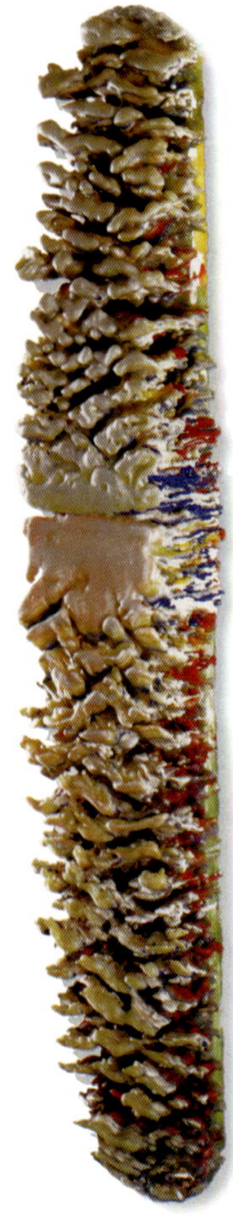

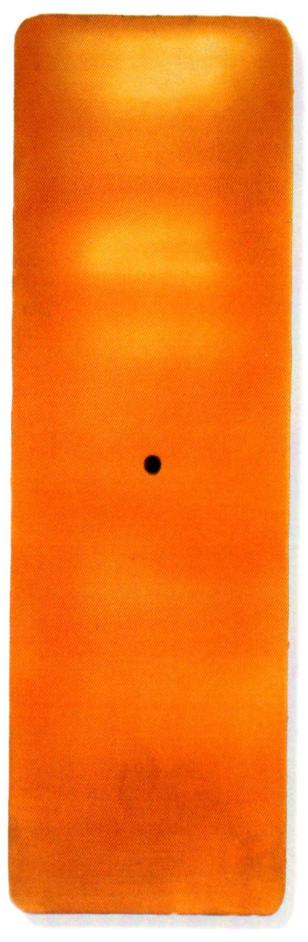

LEFT
Embryo II, 1967
Purified pigmented beeswax, damar resin on Masonite, 36 x 6 x 5 inches
Collection Museum of Modern Art, New York, gift of Agnes Gund

RIGHT
Untitled (Wax Piece), 1966
Purified pigmented beeswax and gesso on Masonite, 23 x 7 x 1 inches
Collection of Richard Tuttle

OPPOSITE
Contraband, 1969
Pigmented latex, 3 x 116¼ x 398¼ inches
Collection Whitney Museum of American Art, New York; purchased with funds from the Painting and Sculpture Committee and partial gift from John Cheim and Howard Read, 2008.14

I'm interested in a total gestalt that describes a form that may or may not exist and that moves into other forms or configurations—maybe as something, maybe as something else. It can be read in many different ways, through texture, through gesture, through the process.

In 1970 I had a show with Galerie Hans Müller in Germany. He took some of the puddle pieces, which were semi flexible polyurethane in bright colors on the floor, to the Basel Art Fair. At that time I was doing them in a small studio across from a school playground in Little Italy, on Baxter Street, near the police station. I occupied the top floor. I did many of the first wax paintings there and most of the latex paintings, except the really large ones. I cast these pieces on waxed linoleum, but when I showed them in galleries they were in situ on waxed floors. Two large pieces, *Contraband* (1969) and *Planet* (not illlustrated) were actually made for the Whitney Museum Anti-Illusion show (1969). I did not know they were going to call it Anti-Illusion. My idea when I saw the Whitney floor, which was a dark charcoal gray and still is, was that I would make these pieces and pop them up from the floor, *illusionistically,* using the bright color. In fact, I deliberately started using that color with the latex paintings from the beginning, and I understood that that was the only way I could make them distort the space. Carl Andre had already done a piece called *Lever* (1966) that was showing at the Jewish Museum, and I saw that piece. It was the only piece in the room, coming out of the corner, and I realized what an object or what something close to the floor could do to the space. So, when I was doing the wax paintings, I was thinking how I could do a painting that was relatively boundless in form and format. That's when I decided to switch from wax to latex rubber and pigment latex rubber. But with those paintings I also discovered the canned gas that made a marbleized kind of surface with many strokes of different colors. When I licked the flame onto that lozenge shape, it marbleized. And I understood then that that marbleized surface was not what I wanted with a contained format—but that I really wanted a format that was open-ended, and that the paint would have its own character.

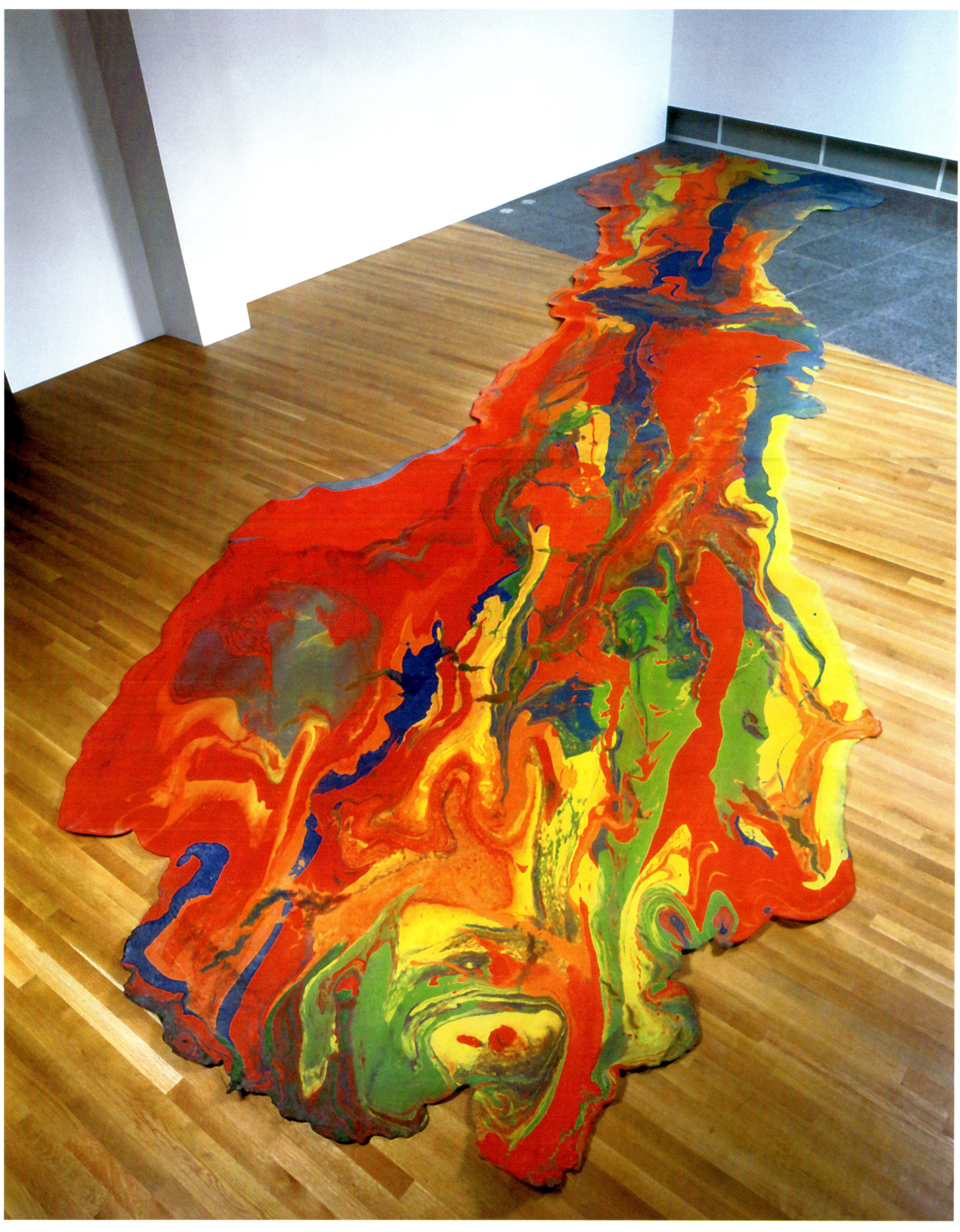

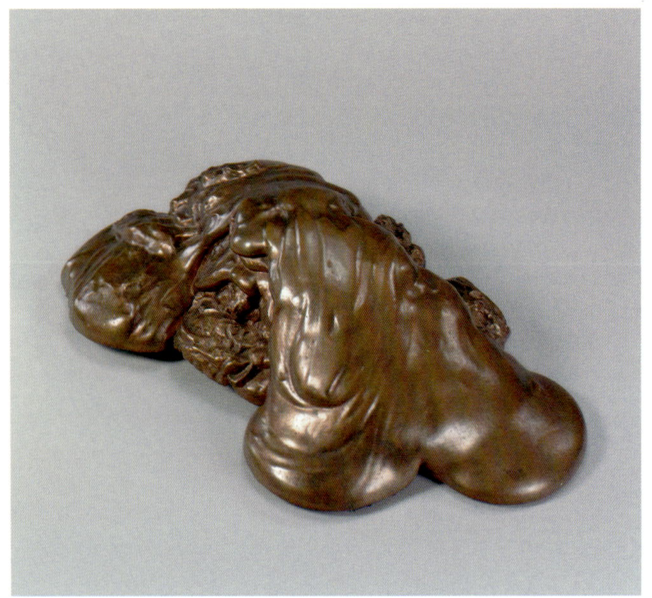

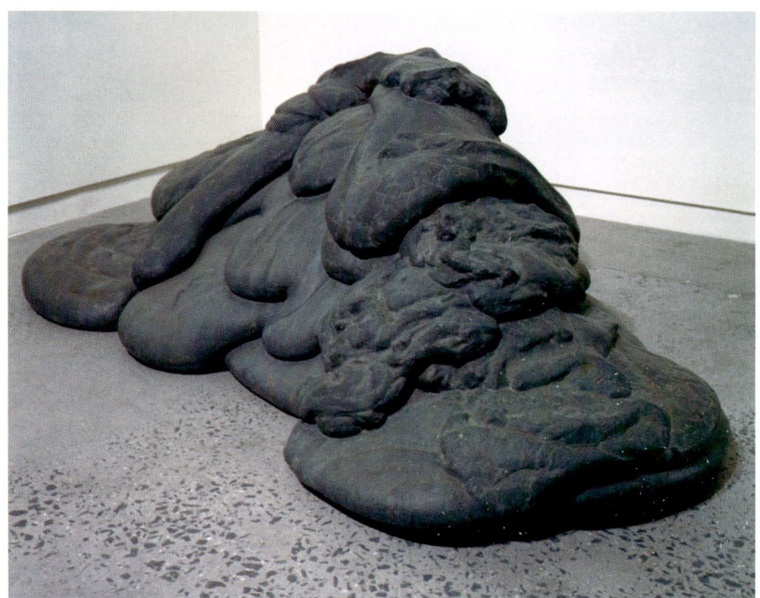

Lynda Benglis

LEFT
Come, 1969–74
Cast bronze, 13 x 49 x 30 inches

RIGHT
Eat Meat, 1973
Bronze, 24 x 80 x 54 inches

OPPOSITE
Wing, 1970
Cast aluminum, 67 x 59 x 60 inches

My early memories of making things? Mud pies—not that I was making mud pies but I think I was making mud mounds with pine needles. I remember even earlier, probably when I was between one and two, I began to play with what was on the ground, with a leaf and a stick and a mossy form. I think all children do that if they have the experience of growing up in nature, and they somehow find a way to imagine themselves being a part of it. At one point, maybe when I was six or seven, I did think I was doing not necessarily an artwork, but an invention. I was playing with string and I thought I was making a machine that had some kind of movement. I didn't know about Calder, but I was trying to balance some string and some objects on the string. I was trying to imagine something that worked in some way. Later, when I was growing up, I don't think I was so concerned with making anything.

Come (1969–74) was the first casting I did in bronze, and I called it *Come* because I had to travel from the L.A. area to New York to do it. *Eat Meat* (1973) was the second grouping I cast, and then I cast *Modern Art* (not illustrated). It was a sand casting. I just thought if the gods excreted, they would excrete this way: I have a gold patina on the bronze, and I did a silver patina on the aluminum. I showed all of these pieces and *Wing* (1970) at the Paula Cooper Gallery in 1970. I had no doubt that what I was doing was important for me, and I knew the pieces represented the way I felt. So I think I just didn't doubt myself, that's all. It was just a matter of being insistent on the fact that I should do them in this way. I would have risked anything, and I did. And I just felt very strongly, and still do, about whatever I decide to do because there are all kinds of reasons to do these things. I didn't question it. That's what's important. Brice Marden has referred to it as a *fact*: you make these *facts*. In other words, they're like statements of a reality that you feel in the context of the conversations that artists have with each other, with the world, and with their times.

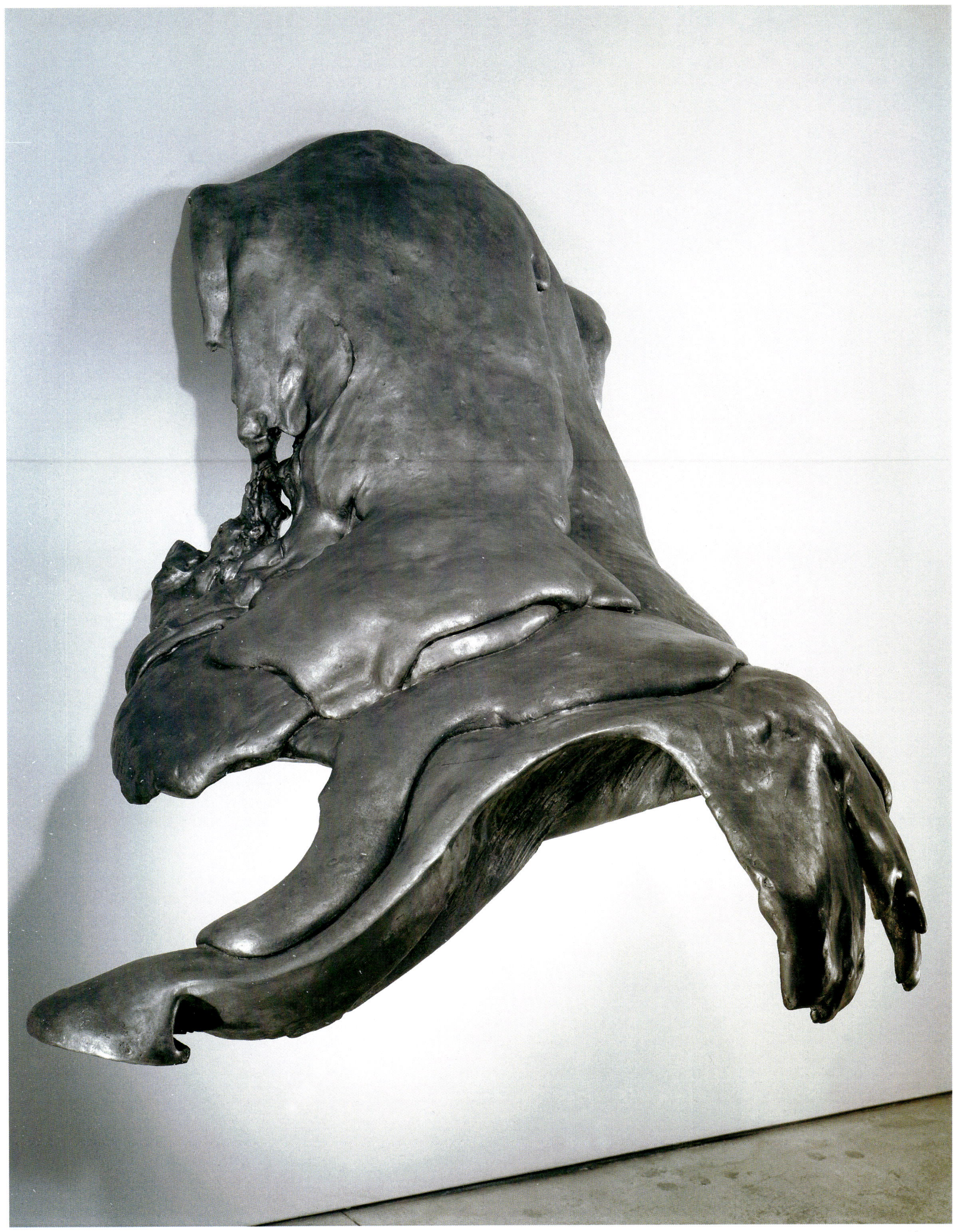

Lynda Benglis

Phantom, 1971
Polyurethane foam with phosphorescent pigments, 102 x 420 x 96 inches
Union Art Gallery, Kansas State University, Manhattan, Kansas

I think the phosphorescence in *Phantom* (1971) really had to do with growing up in Louisiana where there were fireflies and we had phosphorescence in the seaweed at night. Phosphorescence does exist in a natural way, and I was thinking about that when I did these works. I was also thinking about the idea of spirits and light and volumes, and about this thing that is illusionary, disappearing, and momentary, that disappears with the night or light, or

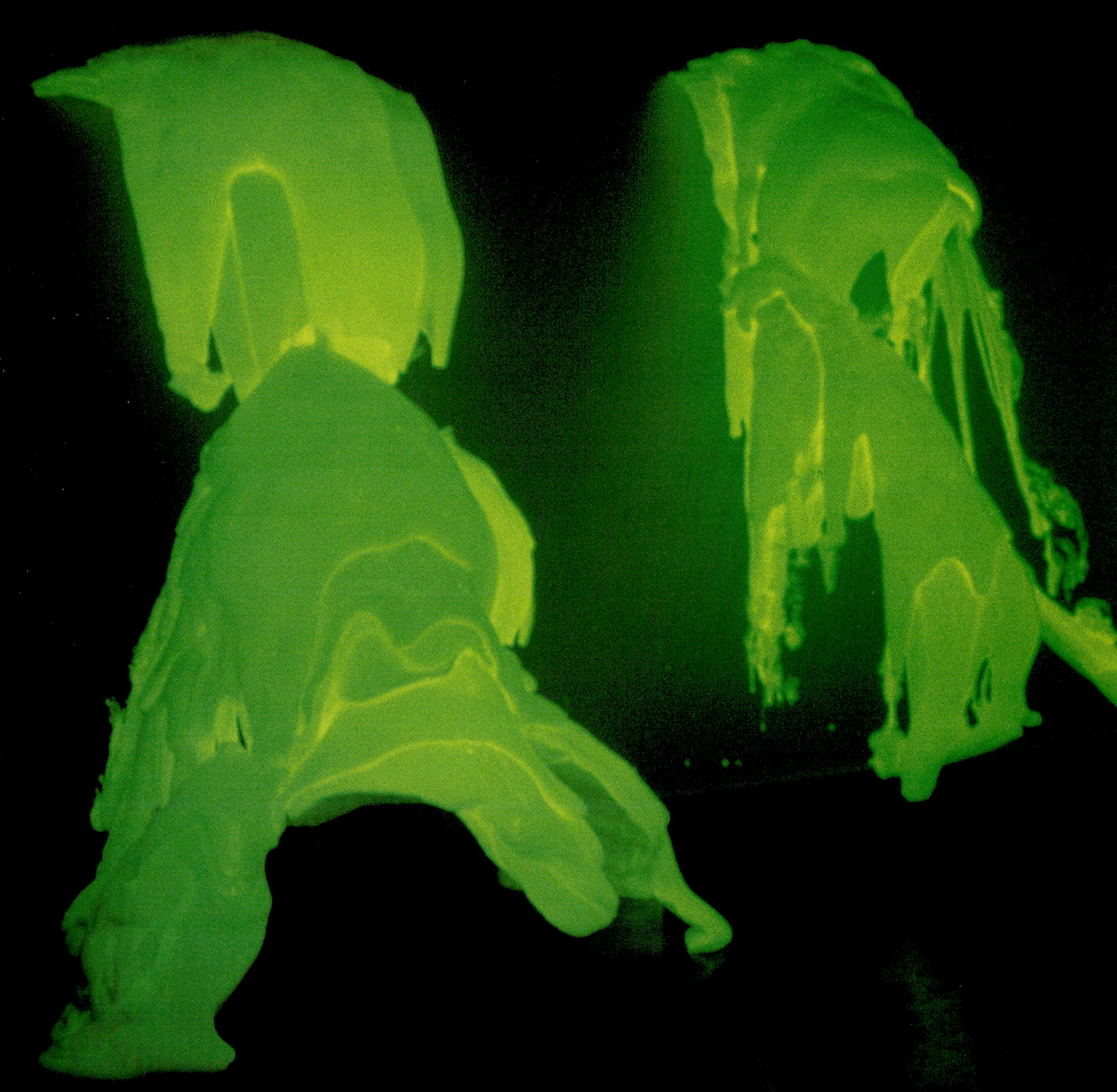

not. When I saw the pieces at the New Museum in 2011, lit with a black light, they reminded me for the first time of marble. Originally, in 1971, I had used vapor lighting, which was very intense and would bring out the green phosphorescence in them. And because of the vapor lighting from above, you could see the shadows of the flowing down of the material, very deep shadows, so what you knew because of the light was that they were rising in space and they were falling, too, at the same time. Your eyes were constantly adjusting to what was happening—down, up, down, up. They would be just dancing. And this is how I originally intended them to be seen. This was a phenomenon that was really very unusual: they were giving out something very magical. With the black lighting they did another thing. They became stone-like and frozen.

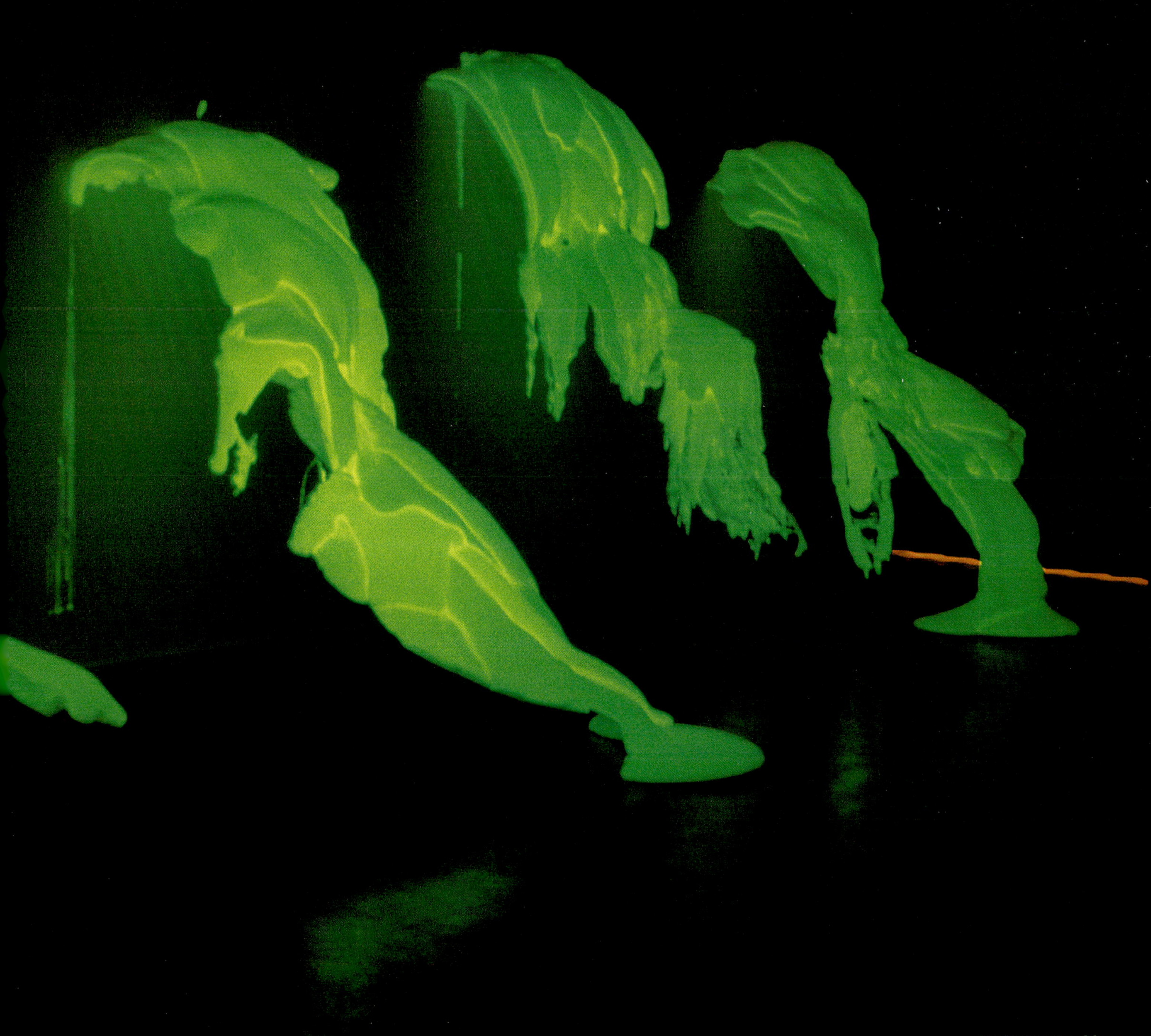

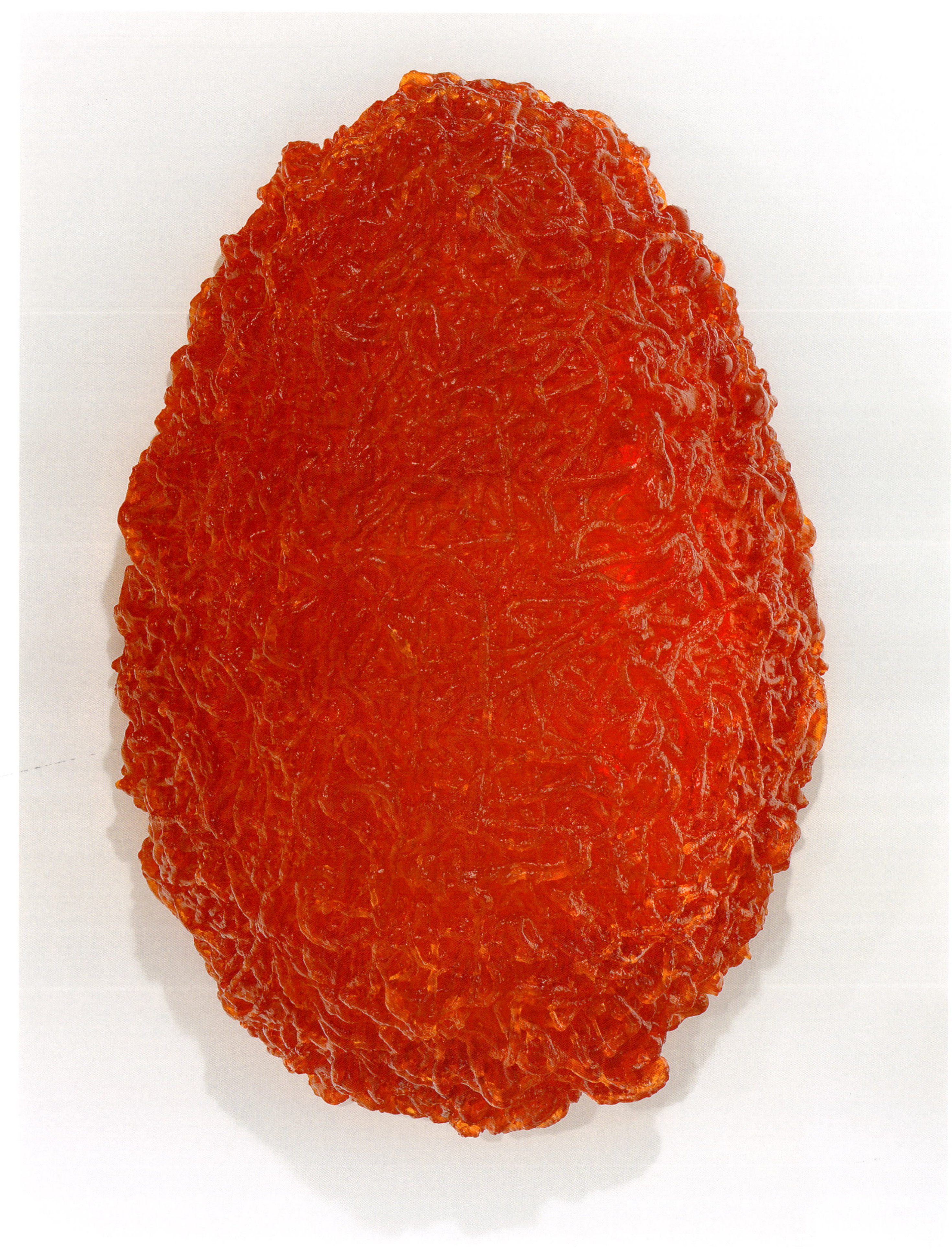

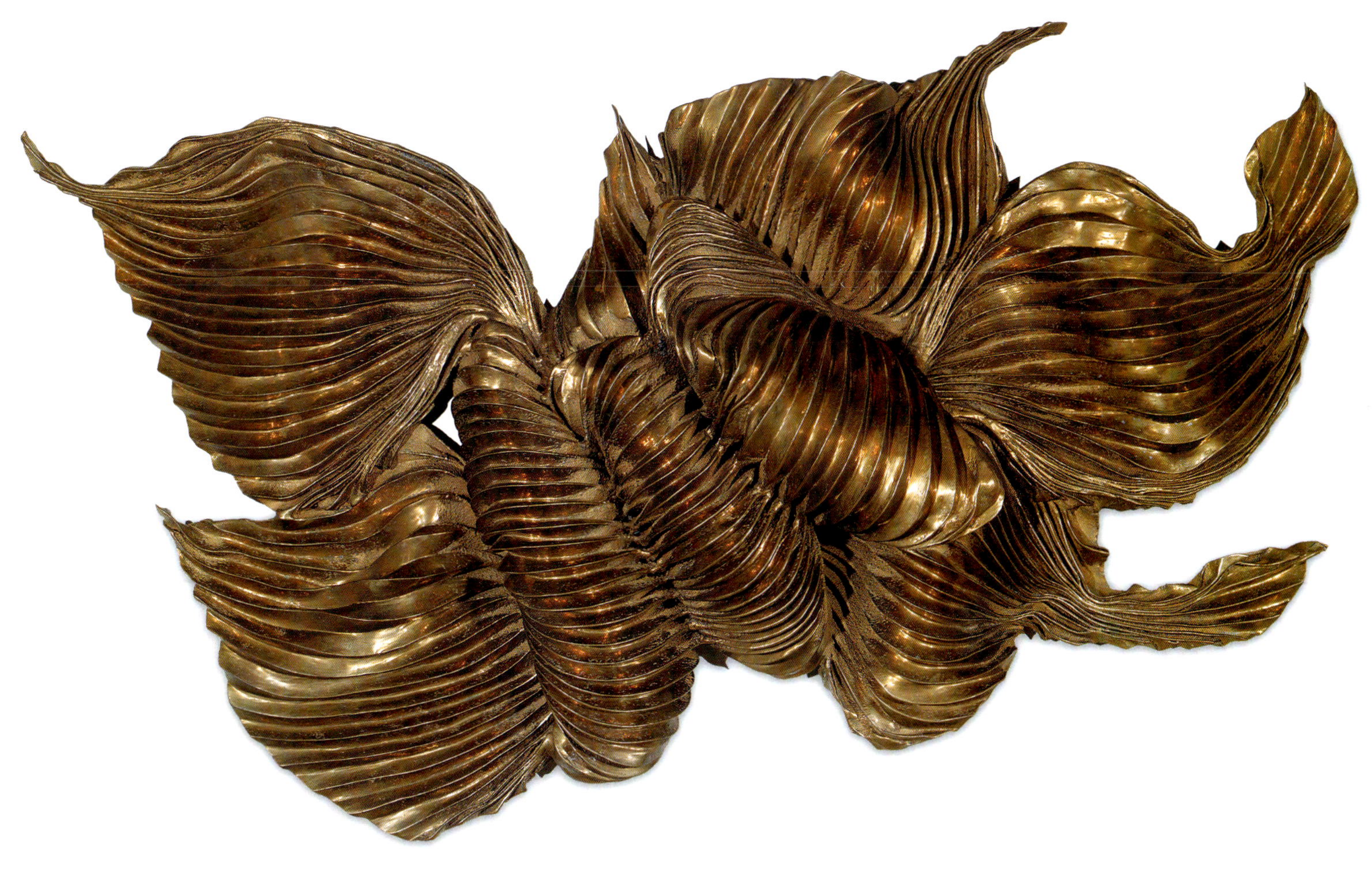

Lynda Benglis

OPPOSITE
Chiron, 2009
Cast tinted polyurethane,
51 x 35 x 17 inches

ABOVE
Raptor, 1995–96
Stainless steel, wire mesh, and
silicone bronze, 46 x 77 x 13 inches

I was always very aware of abstract work and the meaning of abstract work. I think you just are born with that understanding of how to communicate form, an innate feeling of structure that we have and we pay attention to or we don't. When we listen to sound or we see images, we either respond or we don't. And of course it depends on your state of reception as well. But in creating art, and in responding, you must have that purpose in mind. I kept developing the ideas, what is paint? what is form? what is painterliness? To me, it was painterly if a painting exploded off the canvas or exploded into form. It would be a liquid phenomenon. I thought, "Why can't you do something physically that involves your feelings and your proprioceptive responses? Why can't you do something that moves out into space and captures the feeling that you have internally of that freedom of line, that freedom of exuding exuberance, whether it's folded in or explodes out?"

The wall piece *Chiron* (2009) was drawn with a compressed urethane, but there were only a few colors that I could work in. One was clear, which sometimes reflected sort of purple because of the refractive index of the layering of the plastic. Certain plastics in the urethane had a kind of layering of refractive indexes and created an almost pearlescent feeling—that purple-y feeling that you get in *The Graces* (2003–05). But I could use orange, and the kind of smoky, black-gray charcoal, and the clear. And that's it. I tried to think about others, but essentially I felt the orange one was something that was more symbolic and more emotionally active than, say, the red cherry or the purple one. So I only went with the orange, and the black-gray, because of the quality of the color and the translucency and so forth.

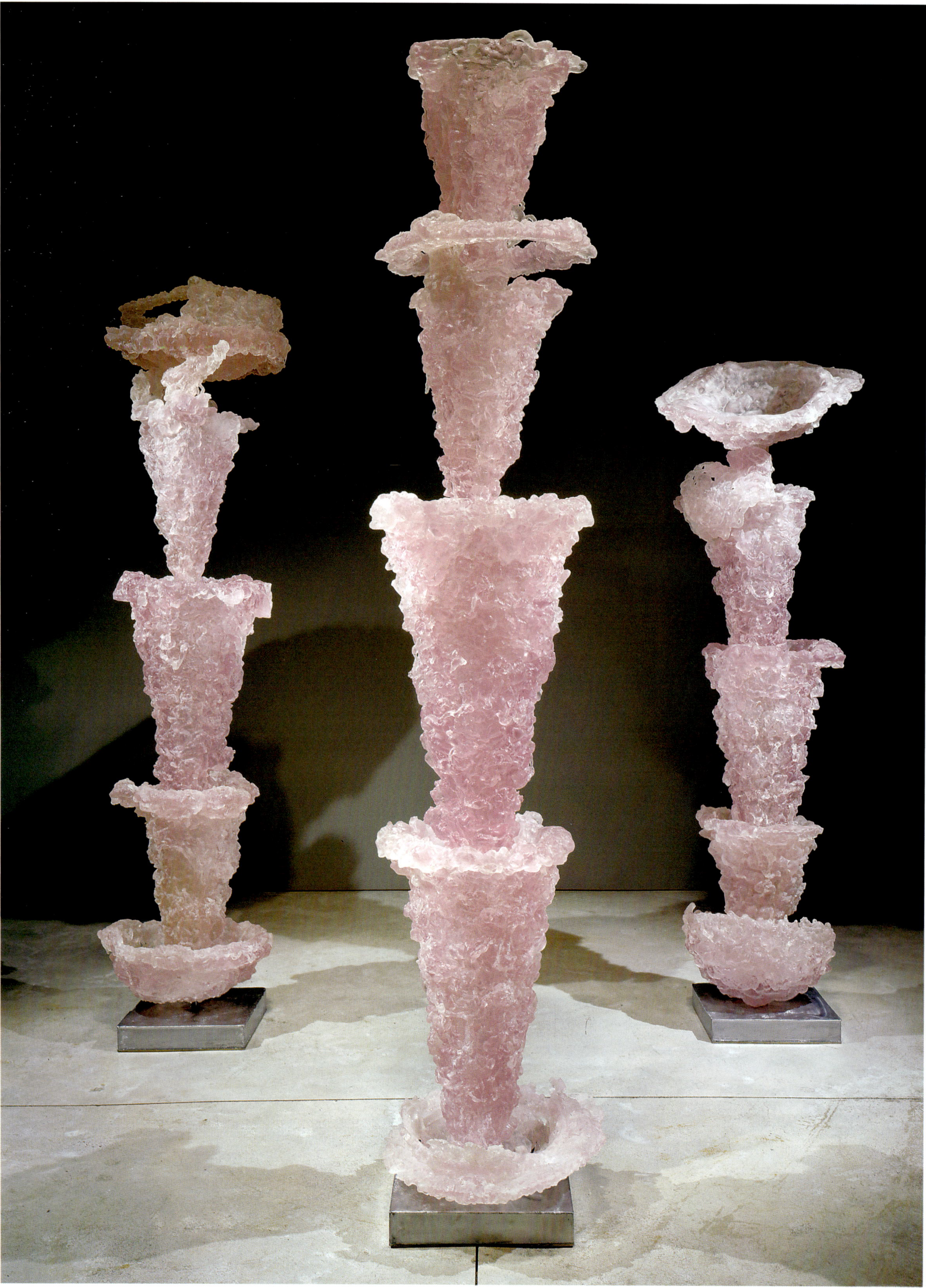

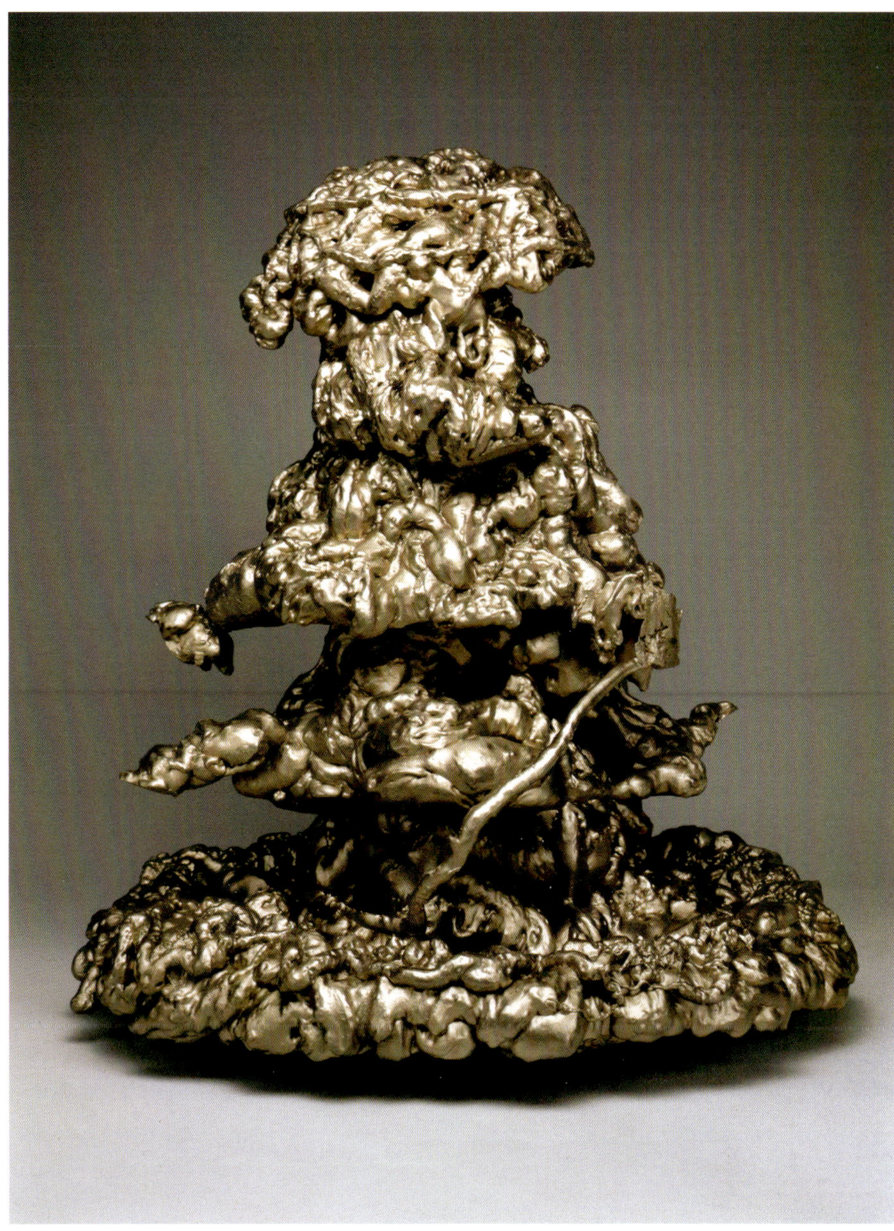

Lynda Benglis

OPPOSITE
The Graces, 2003–05
Cast polyurethane, lead, stainless steel
3 elements: 103 x 26 x 26 inches;
113 x 21 x 23 inches; 95 x 30 x 27 inches

RIGHT
Summer Dreams, 2003
Cast bronze, 30 x 27 x 25 inches

I've spent many winters in Easthampton, New York, looking out at the ice forms on the windows, and I've recorded them on my digital camera. When I discovered polyurethane plastic that looked like glass, I was very pleased that people thought it was glass castings. It had an illusion of ice, of frozen water, and I wanted *The Graces* (2003–05) to be a fountain (originally I designed them as a fountain). I don't quite know where my interest in fountains all began, but I think it was in the '70s that I had the idea because really what I was doing with urethane was a frozen kind of liquid form. And I thought that that liquid form could be extended with water and could be plumbed to that form. So I did a print—a lithograph—with the Landfall Press in Chicago. And then, later, when I submitted a proposal for the New Orleans World's Fair, I did win a fountain contest. I did a seventeen-and-a-half-foot cantilever in bronze with the liquid bronze umbrella-ing out. The water flow could be controlled at the foot, which was six feet in diameter, and the umbrella itself was about nine feet in diameter. I found, from the pours that I was doing at the same time whether at MIT, Milwaukee, or the Walker, that that was the most I could extend the form—seventeen-and-a-half feet. That's how the form visually hung together—and structurally, too—because I would pour across pours. So it could extend out both visually and structurally in that way and work. Anything larger would have not been human scale.

Lynda Benglis

BELOW

Zanzidae, 1979
Plastic, glass, and enamel on wire mesh, 60 x 70 x 8 inches

OPPOSITE, CLOCKWISE FROM TOP LEFT

Sparkle Knot V, 1972
Acrylic paint and sparkles on plaster, cotton bunting, and aluminum screen, 42 x 25 x 13 inches

Proto Knot, 1971
Acrylic paint and sparkles on plaster, cotton bunting, and aluminum screen, 29 x 20½ x 7 inches

Sparkle Knot IV, 1972
Acrylic paint and sparkles on plaster, cotton bunting, and aluminum screen, 29 x 20¾ x 9 inches

Psi, 1973
Enamel silver paint and sparkles on plaster, cotton bunting, and aluminum screen, 33 x 13 x 15 inches
Collection John Cheim

Making folded fan-like shapes brought me back to the time when I was a little girl, seven or eight years old. When I did the fans, it was a good way of creating reflective light in the gold that I was using. I was actually painting these forms, the surface, with an oil over the gesso and plastic and wire so that the actual light of the gold would be reflecting on the planes of very narrow depth, but would be self-reflecting, so it would emit a kind of light in the gold. The ceramics, for me, were about how to make gestures, an architecture of gestures, and how to make a painting physically—how to present it so that they're coming together and you have a kind of explosion or implosion of forms.

There's a *body* feeling about one's energy. Either it's a contained nutshell of a painting that becomes a kind of flowering of energy or a bursting of energy or a little bomb, or it explodes or implodes. A knot is sometimes an implosion, but a knot could also be an explosion of energy—so I have done both with the idea of that form. It's embryonic; it grows.

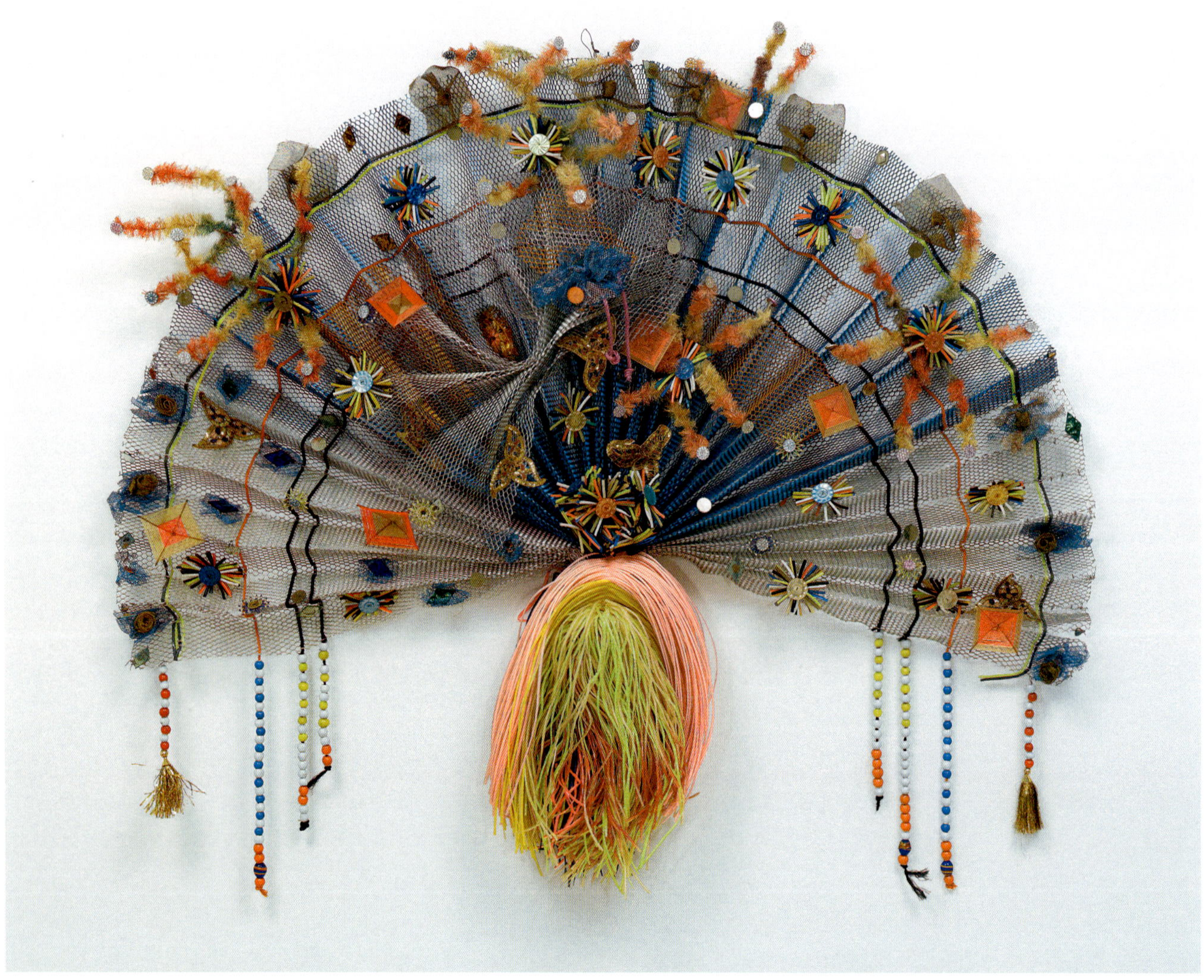

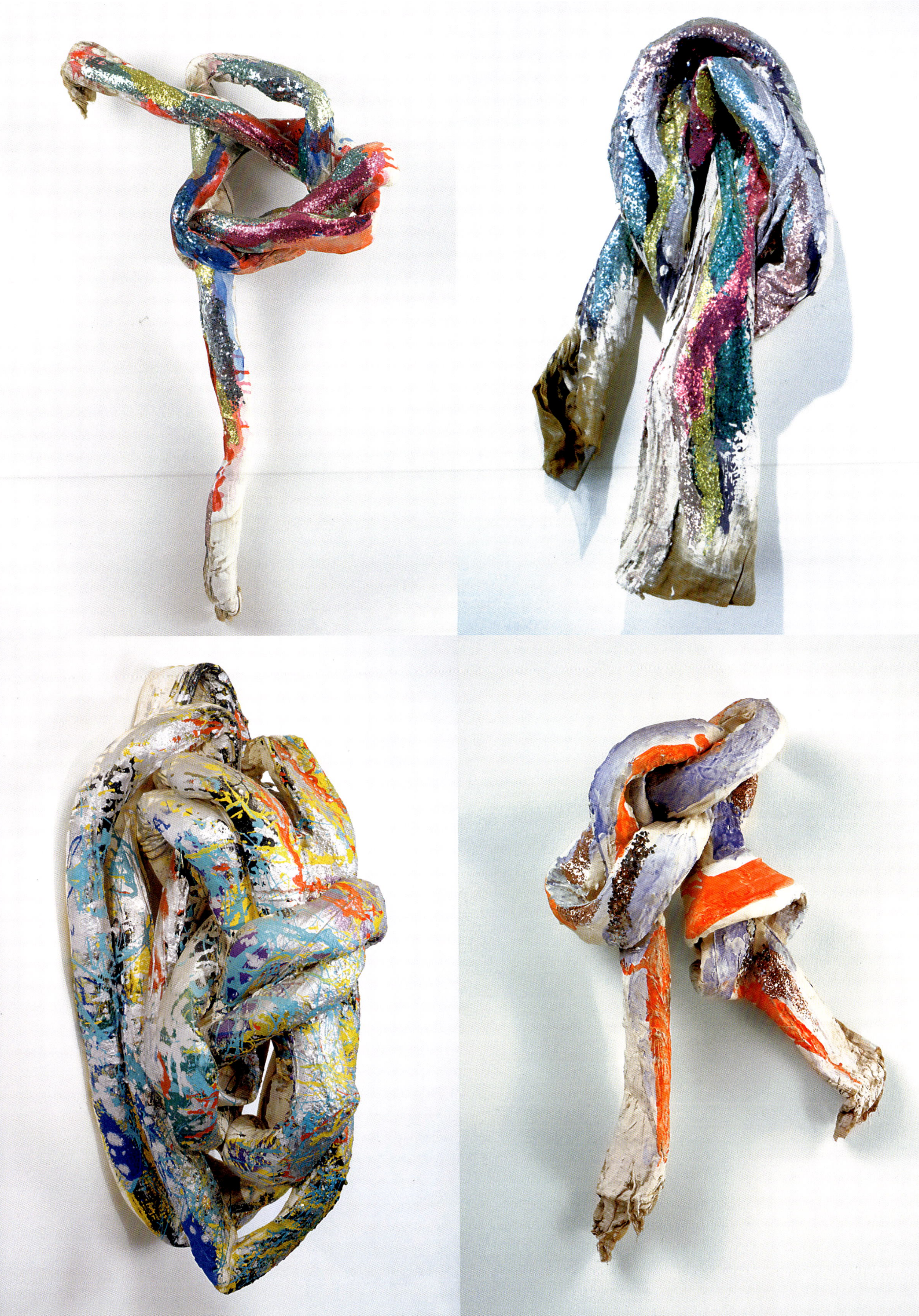

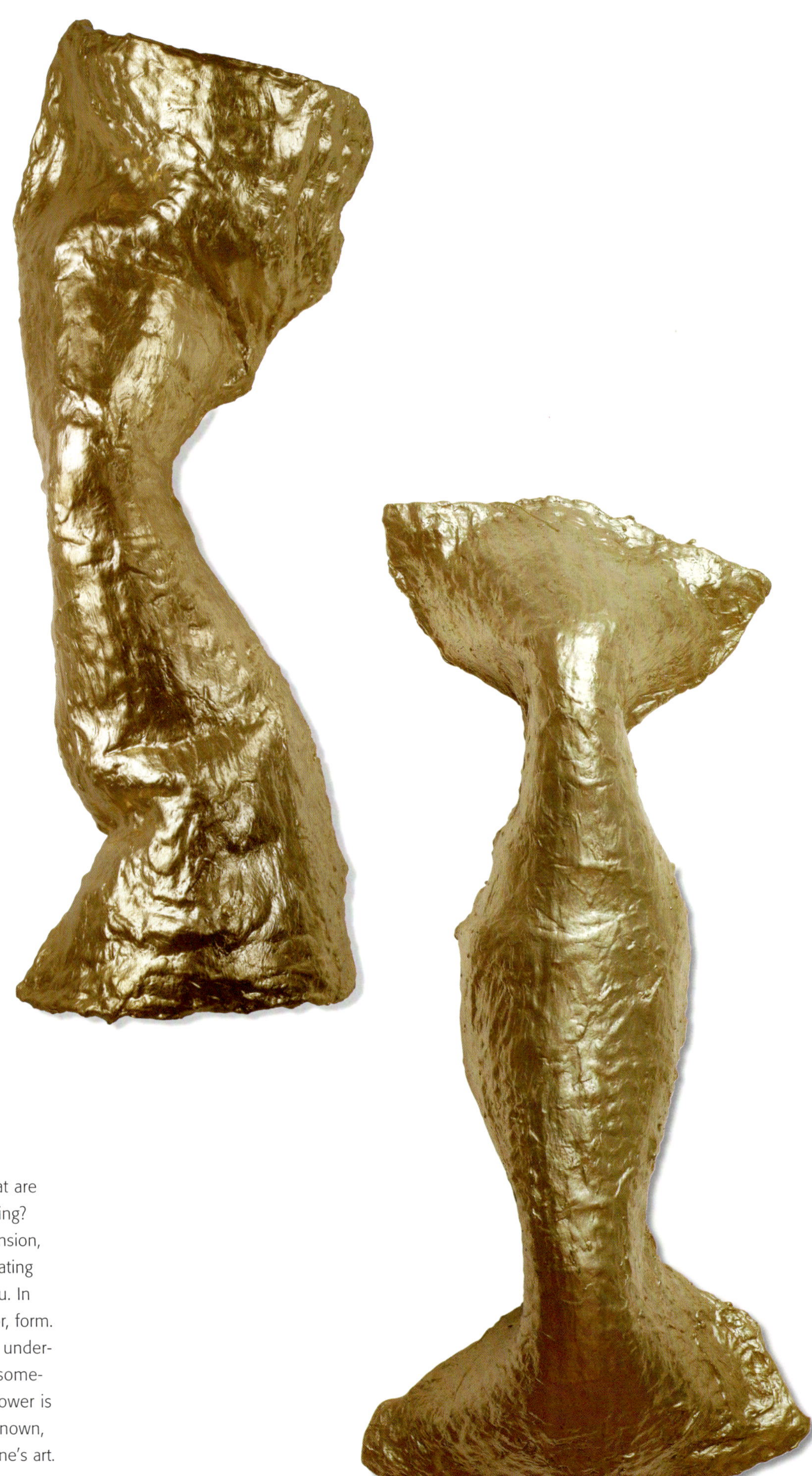

Lynda Benglis

ABOVE
Rhodos, 1978
Gold leaf, oil-based sizing and gesso on plaster, cotton bunting, and chicken wire, 55½ x 26 x 11 inches

RIGHT
Chicago Caryatids #4, 1979
Gold leaf, oil-based sizing and gesso on plaster, cotton bunting, and chicken wire, 45 x 16 x 9 inches

OPPOSITE
Medusa, 1999
Bronze, 25 x 25 x 12 inches

When you focus on something, what are you focusing on? What are you feeling? You're feeling the texture, the dimension, the gestalt. And you're freely associating everything. The image speaks to you. In what way? It's light. It's texture, color, form.

We look toward nature to try to understand form. And if we understand something, then we don't fear it. So if power is a kind of understanding of the unknown, then that's what one tries to do in one's art.

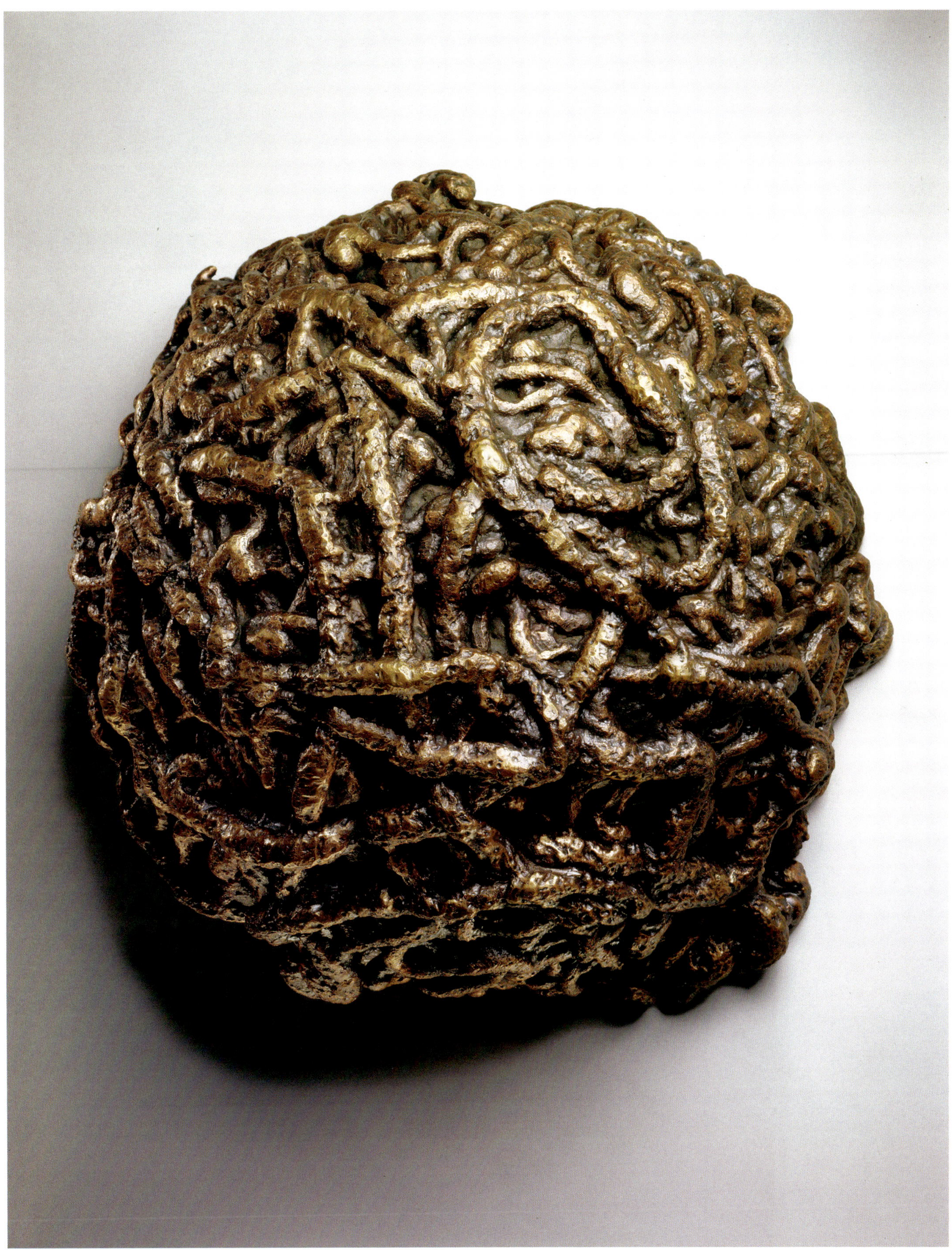

Tabaimo

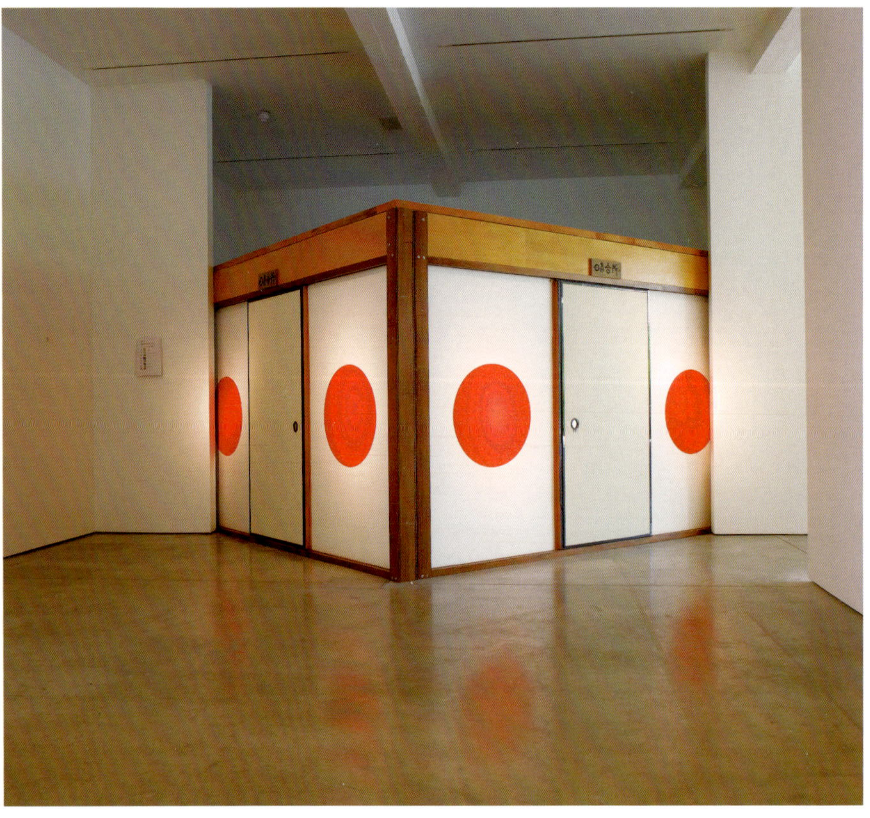

ABOVE AND OPPOSITE
Japanese Kitchen, 1999
Video installation, 5 min 10 sec
Tabaimo: Boundary Layer, Parasol unit foundation for contemporary art, London

The first video installation I ever made, *Japanese Kitchen* (1999), was my senior project at university. The work was meant to showcase everything I'd done there so that I'd have something to show for myself when I looked for a job. So I threw every technique I'd ever learned into making it and it just ended up turning into a video installation. At the time I didn't have the faintest idea that there was a whole category of contemporary art called video installation. All the people who appear—the salaryman, the housewife, the high-school student—have a clear calling card, so they look just like what anyone would imagine them to be. I used stereotypical characters so the viewer would be able understand the content even in the limited time of a short animation. If there's a person with glasses, a suit, and a necktie, everyone knows he's a salaryman. By using characters that don't need any explanation, I was able to concentrate on the content of the animation. When people watch *Japanese Kitchen* there are some who only see the dreadful part and some who only see the funny part. The perspective each person brings to it is a crucial factor in determining what impression they get. I also have a simultaneous sense of the funny and dreadful aspects but the piece's mode of expression keeps me at a distance. I've drawn the pictures voluptuously. They have a materiality, so that it seems that it would be possible to feel their temperature. But I can't actually feel their temperature and texture—though I can sense their possibility. It's as if the temperature and texture themselves have been removed to somewhere else. My inspiration was the situation of the housewife cooking and listening to TV—to a kind of talk-show type of news reporting. You might hear something painful or horrible, but ten seconds later you've already forgotten it. The most important thing is preparing the dinner. I wasn't trying to bring the awareness of suffering to life in the work. Rather, all that information is nothing more than a series of 'things'. I'm not expressing the suffering in my work.

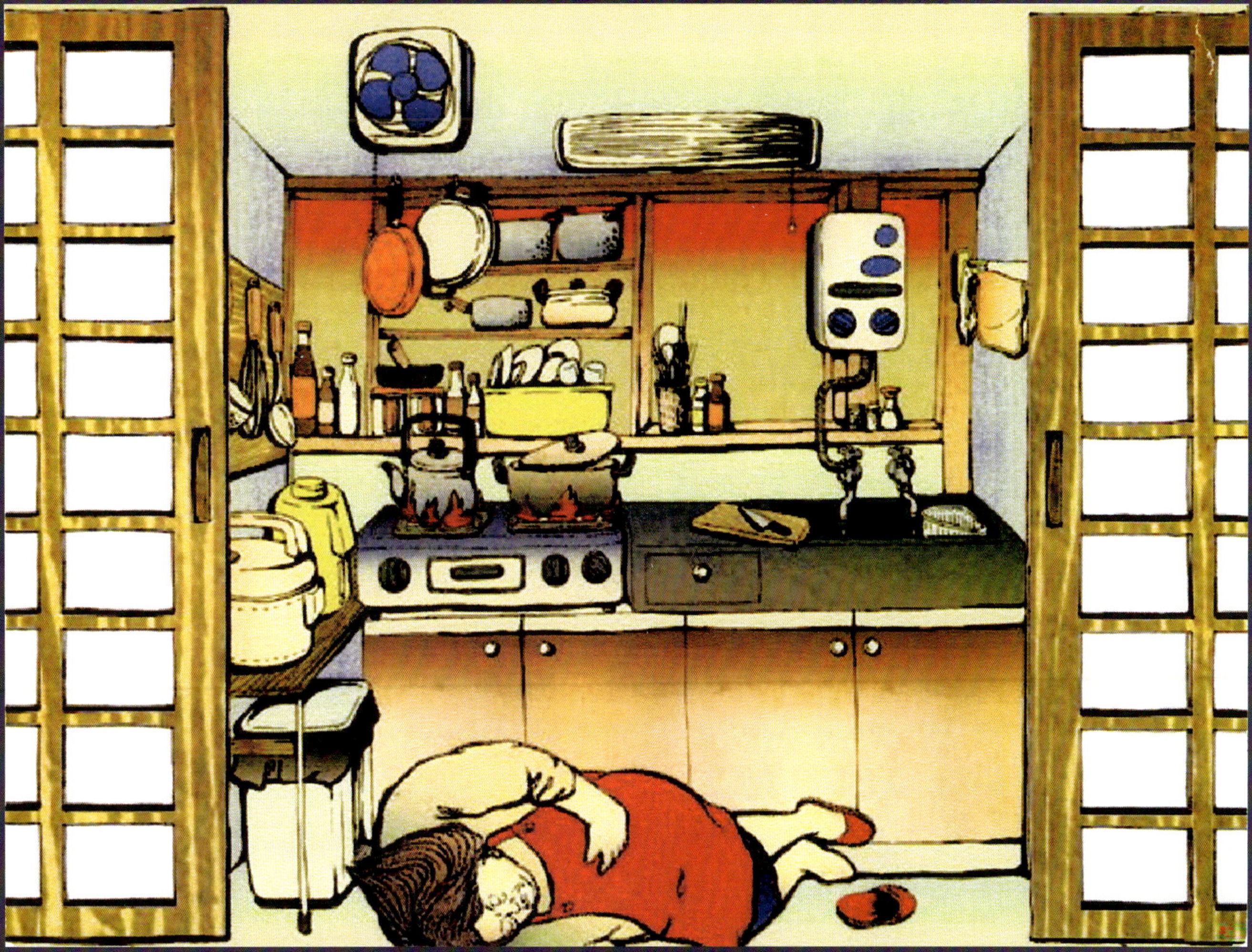

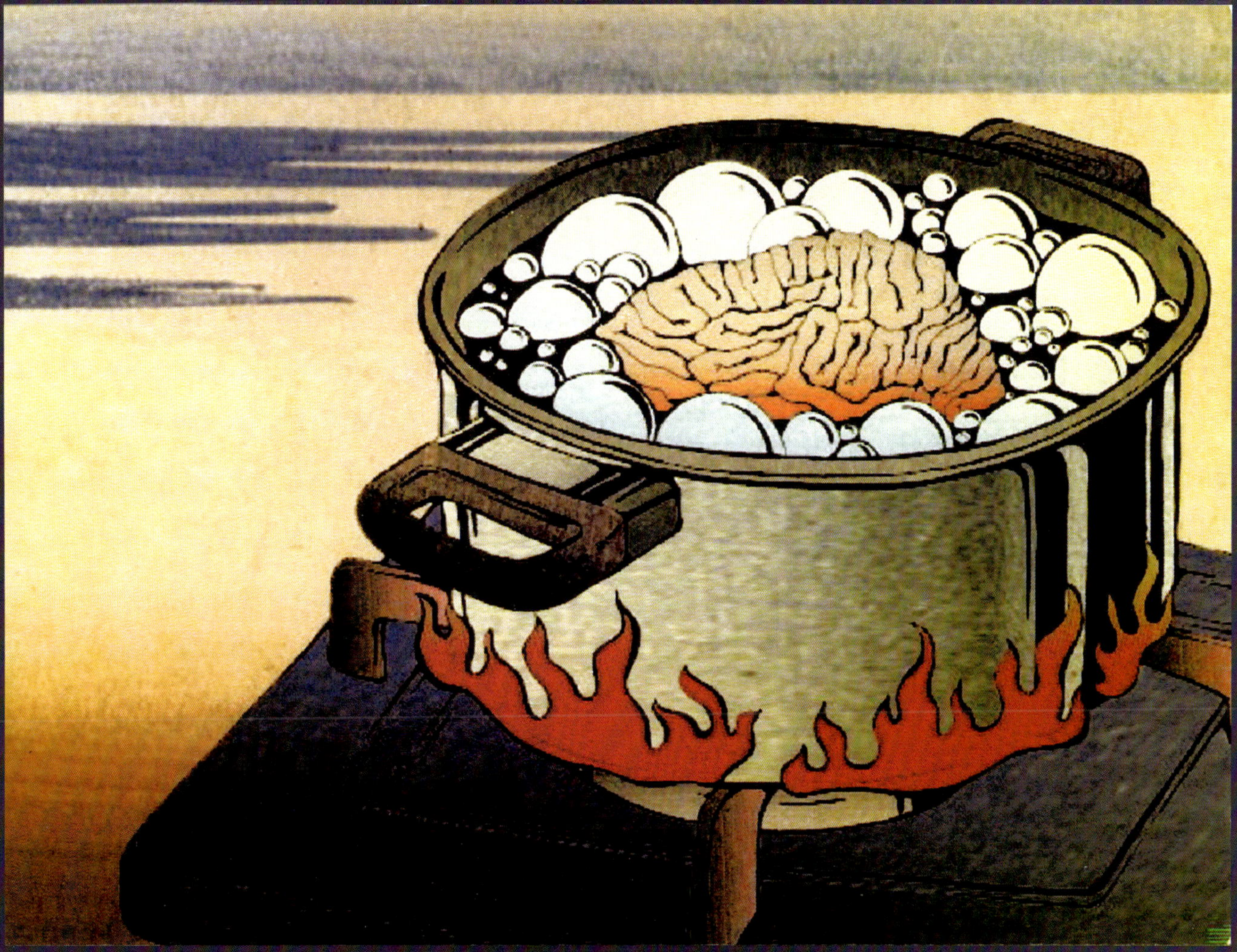

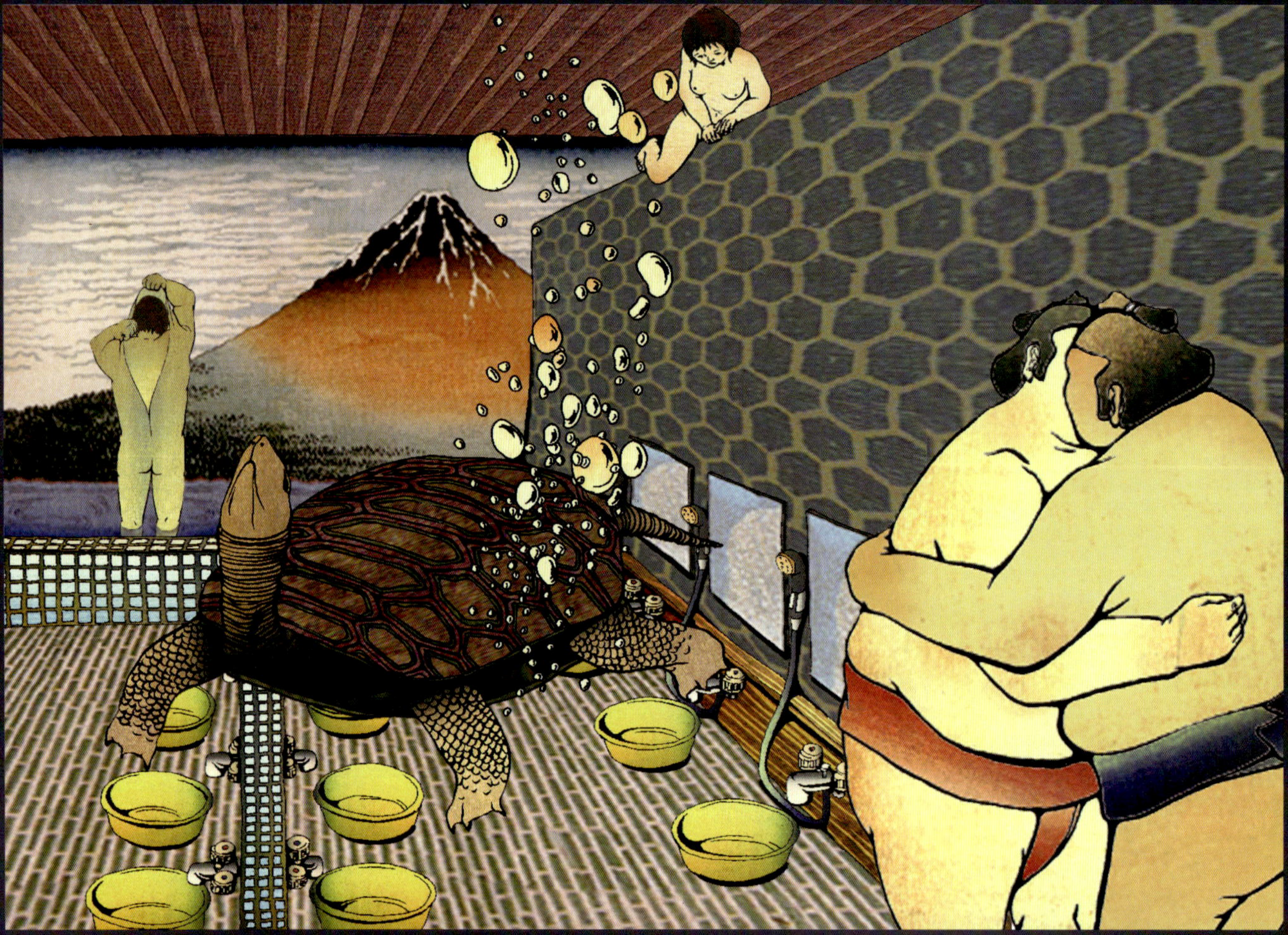

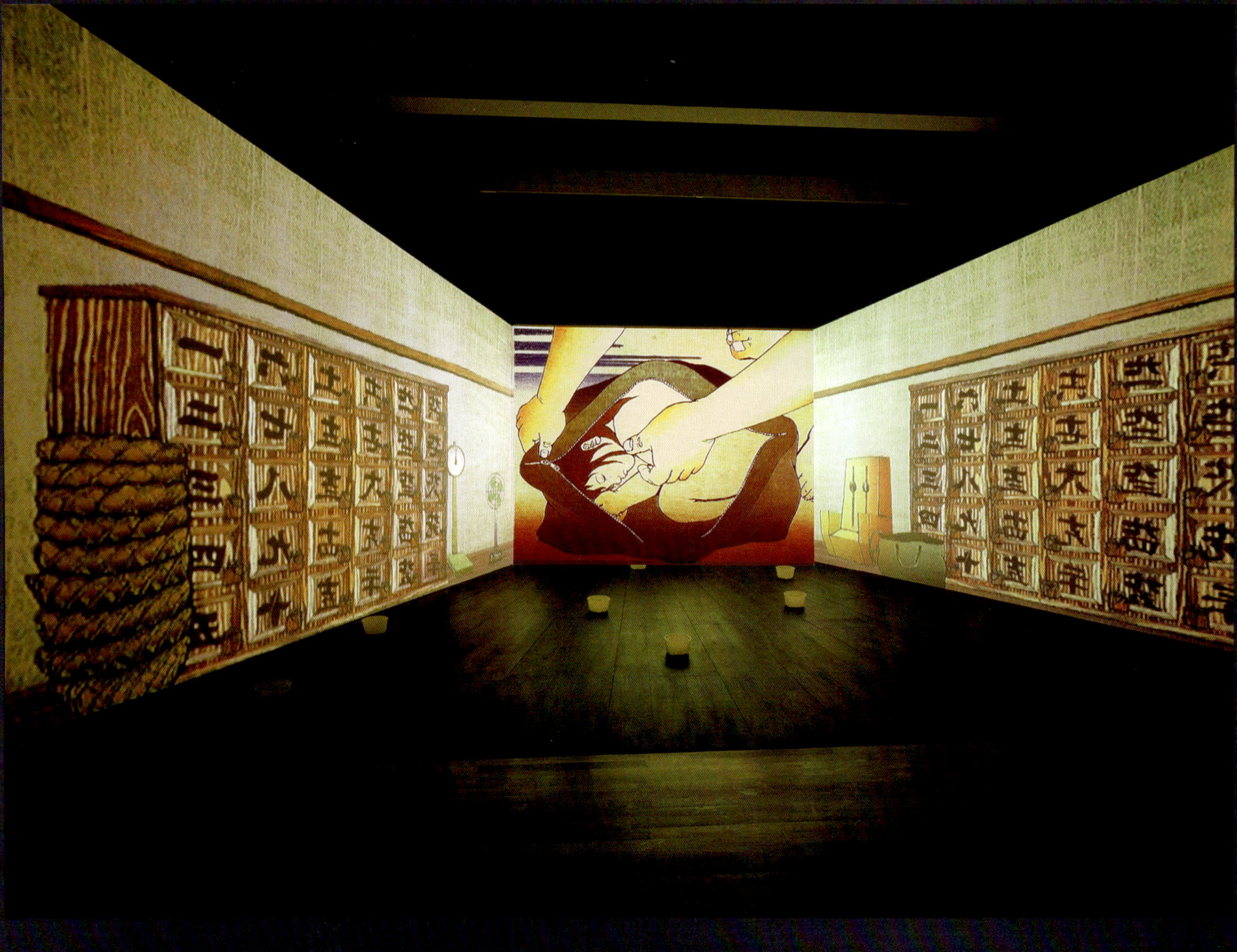

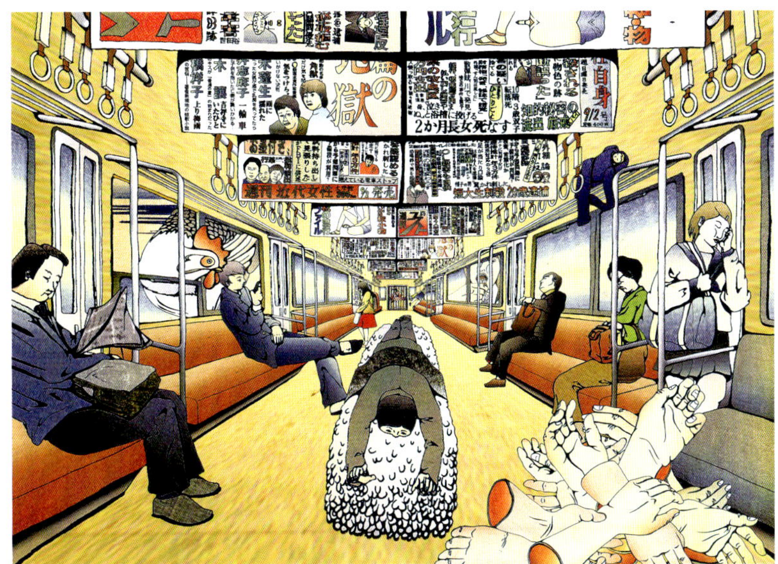

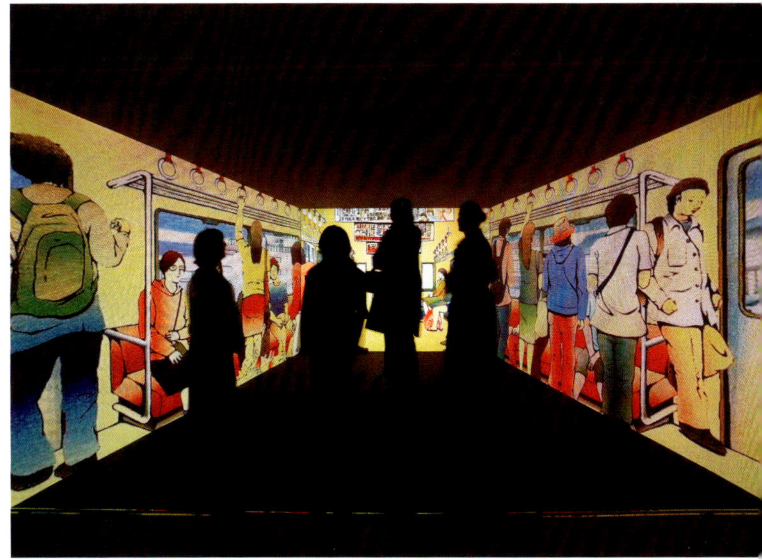

Tabaimo

OPPOSITE
Japanese Bathhouse-Gents, 2000
3-channel video installation with sound, 7 min 34 sec; 177 x 377 x 205 inches
James Cohan Gallery, New York

ABOVE
Japanese Commuter Train, 2001
Video installation, 8 min 3 sec
Fondation Cartier pour l'art contemporain, Paris

A lot of New Yorkers came to see my first exhibition of *Japanese Bathhouse-Gents* (2000) at the James Cohan Gallery in New York. While I was watching them from the side, I felt that they understood the work not because the work was able to make itself understood, but because they were viewing it from a basis they had in Japanese culture as it had penetrated there, in the United States. And when I watched the French people who'd come to see *Japanese Commuter Train* (2001), I felt something like empathy, which was different from the understanding of the New Yorkers. Japanese culture had penetrated France, too, but somehow it seemed less like they were trying to understand the work, and more like there was an element of common culture that enabled them to perceive that part of the work directly. The understanding in New York wasn't based on an underlying empathy. Understanding can be like establishing a context to accept something that's different in some way, and New York seemed to recognize a difference most strongly and accept it.

Japan's history of contemporary art is not so long. But for me there's something that comes before that. There are things that connect Japanese culture with art and contemporary art, things like novels, films, and maybe *ukiyo-e*, too. I think those things that have a tendency to be received in the West in unique ways form a history based on the strength of the relationships running through them. In countries where these things have penetrated and been understood to some degree, there is the possibility of deep understanding and empathy, just as Western art and contemporary art is understood by people with knowledge of the history of art in the West.

Tabaimo

guignorama, 2006
Video installation, 2 min 36 sec
YOROYORON: Tabaimo, Hara Museum of Contemporary Art, Tokyo

When I was doing the drafting for *guignorama* (2006)—or actually for *Ginyo-ru*, which was a work that came before *guignorama*, it was a period of enormous transition in my production. It was about a year after I had come back from England, and everything that I had believed in—the conviction that this is 'me' standing here—was gradually fading away. It left me floating aimlessly. *Guignorama* is a work from when my mode of production was changing as I tried to reexamine myself carefully and make this state of aimlessness my own. One thing about living in England that was different from Japan was that the news on TV was mostly world news, and the people I was living with were from places like Brazil and Colombia. We were living in the Jewish quarter so it was a completely different environment from Japan. In Japan (if you're just talking about Japan), you can pretty much see what's correct in a given situation, but in England there was a different way of arriving at what was correct in a house together with people from the other side of the world. Watching the world news, all the good and bad, it all depended from whose point of view you were looking. Then, when I came back to Japan, I found myself getting things wrong a lot. Unless you have an idea of where you stand and what world you're looking at, it's almost impossible to say what's correct. So I stopped being able to tell who could share my feelings and who I wanted that to be. I was honestly unable to settle on what was correct at a particular time for a particular person. In England, I had the experience of conversations going completely off track if I wasn't clear about where I was coming from. I had conversations that just didn't jell at all. I couldn't make the shift from the place where I was—the situation of being there and feeling what I was feeling—to make it part of a conversation. So it was as if the other person and I never really met. As a result I decided that I had to trust the world around me—the world that appeared before my eyes—and express it no matter how impossible a world it might be for someone else. It's not about stance or standpoint. Wherever I might be, I'm looking with these eyes, and whatever I'm feeling is a fact. It's correct. I changed my approach to production to accept what was correct for me, even though it might be incorrect for another person. There wasn't a correct answer anymore, like a mirror that would create an axis of objective understanding for anyone who looked at it. The only thing I could share with others was the fact of my own existence. So my work came to express the world that I was looking at, from a particular place.

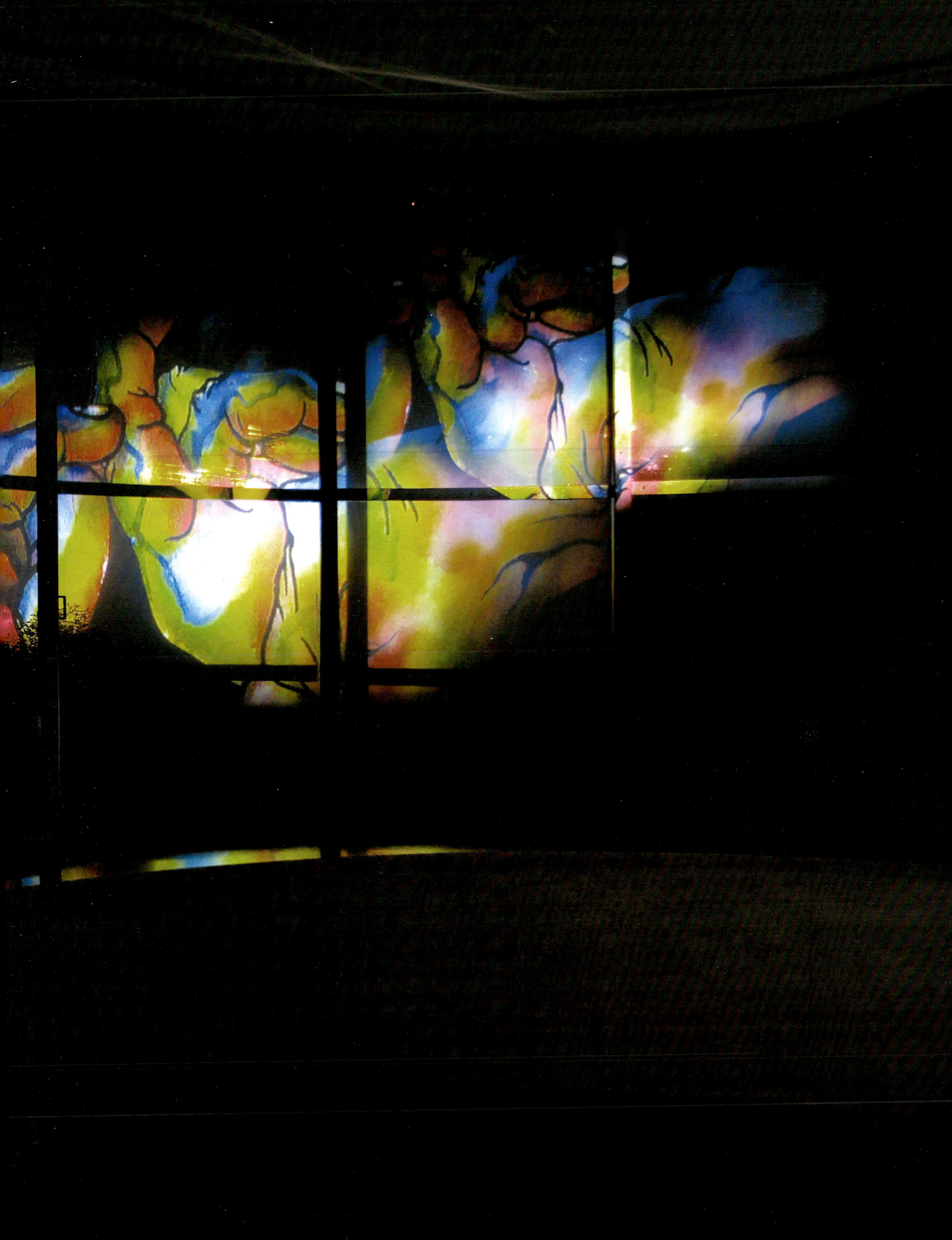

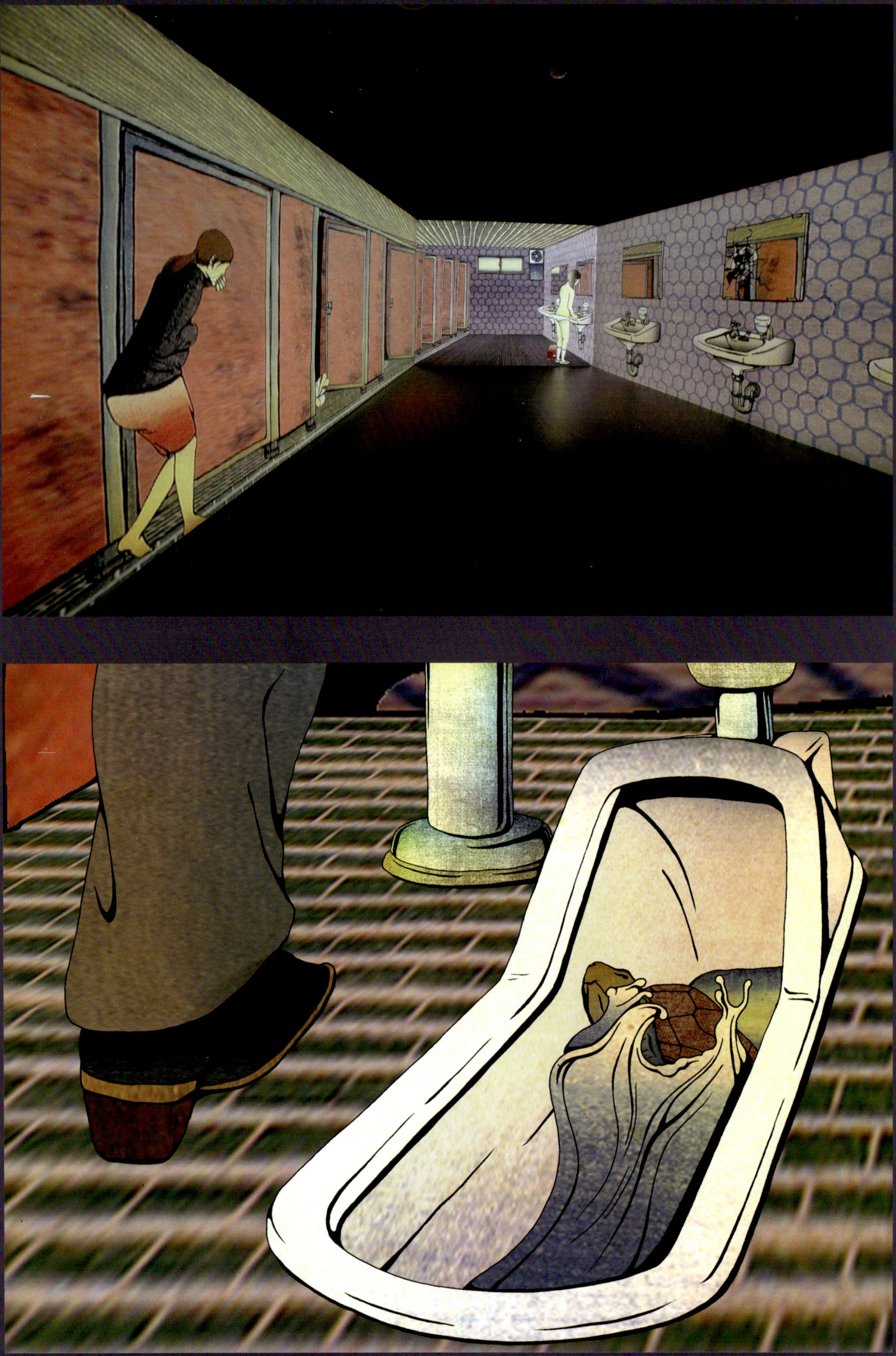

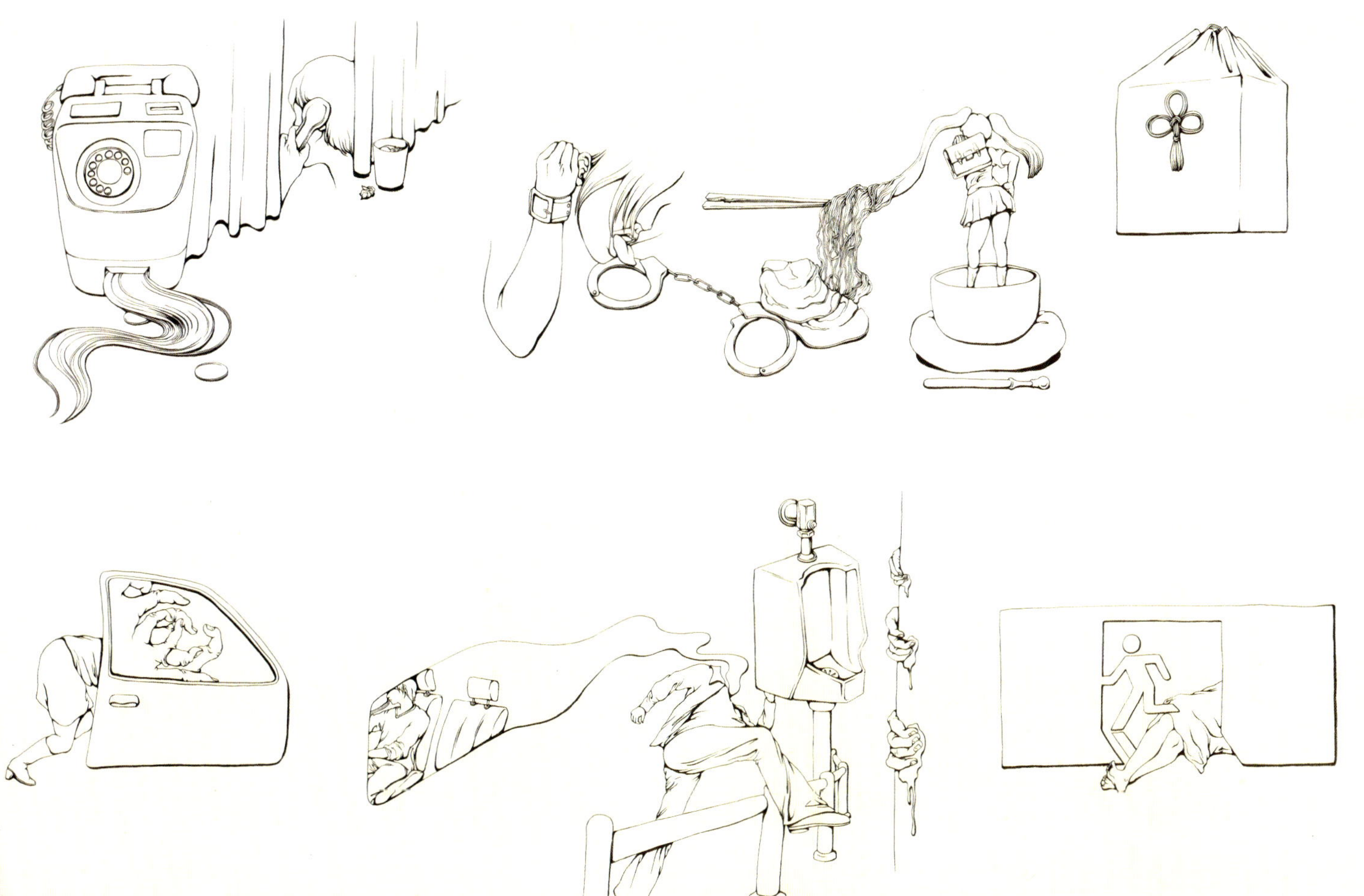

Tabaimo

OPPOSITE
public conVENience, 2006
Video installation, 6 min 5 sec
YOROYORON: Tabaimo, Hara Museum of Contemporary Art, Tokyo

ABOVE
akunin (024) and
akunin (025), 2006
Ink on Japanese paper,
13⅝ inches x 53½ inches each

Being able to read the story that I've arranged in the work isn't that important. I expect that people will pick out other stories besides that one. But storytelling is there: it's important for *public conVENience* (2006), and for *Japanese Kitchen,* but not so important for *guignorama.* As the creator, I think my task is to imbue the space, or the work, with the possibility of being made into something by the viewer. I see the work succeeding when the viewer engages with it actively—so I don't much endorse the idea of viewing things to try to discover the artist's message. Rather, I think that when the viewer takes on the work of discovering, or setting out to discover something, that will really bring the work together in an interesting way. I'm really happy when people can look at a work without being sidetracked by everyday ways of accounting for things. I want the viewer to think, "What does this work mean to me?" If the viewer thinks about this, then the work will become complete in a very positive way. I don't want my viewers to be affected by established or commonsensical ideas. I want them to be free from those ideas and then look at my work.

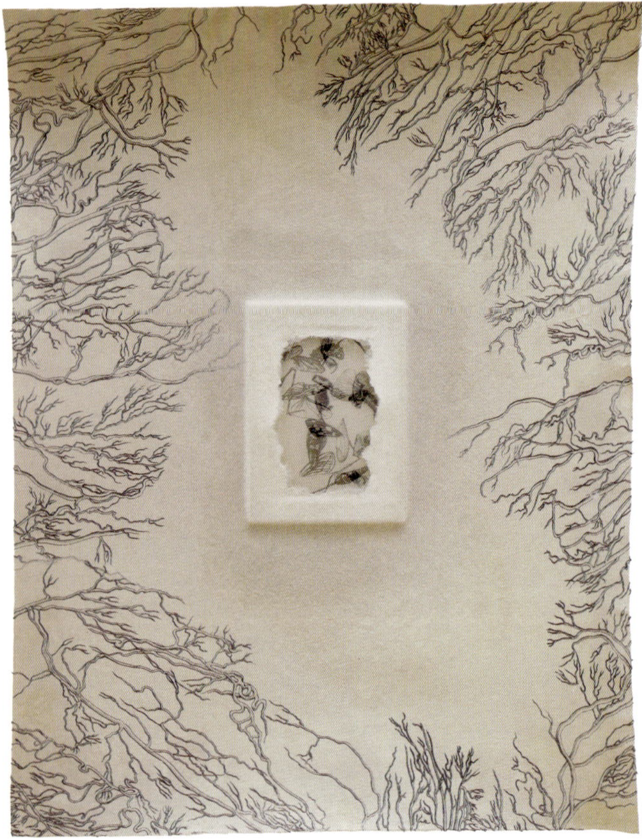

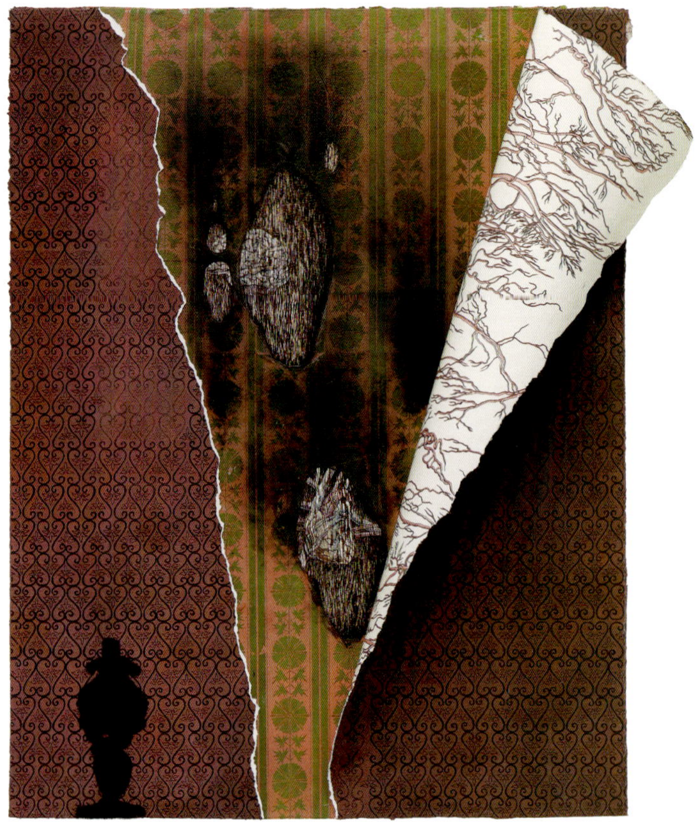

I haven't been particularly influenced by art. I've never been one to get fixated on something and search out every example of it. There's also a sense in which saying I've been influenced by this or that is embarrassing. I don't know whether it's a good idea to say so, but I feel I haven't seen very much in the way of art. I haven't been influenced much by Dada or anything like that. If there's one thing I think influences me before I've even started working on a project, it's manga—especially horror manga—and specifically two manga artists, Umezu Kazuo and Itō Junji. Apart from them I'm not aware of much influence from horror manga. As for films, there's Terayama Shōji's *Pastoral: To Die in the Country*, but I'm not aware of being influenced by Terayama Shōji's other films. As for people who've influenced me, Tanaami Keiichi has been my teacher ever since I was at university. He's a designer and an artist.

Tabaimo

LEFT
deep forest 1, 2009
Lithograph and flocking, 51¾ x 39½ x 2½ inches

RIGHT
wallpaper 04, 2009
Lithograph, screen print, flocking, and acrylic paint, 66 x 51¾ x 8 inches

OPPOSITE
yudangami, 2009
Video installation, 4 min 13 sec
Tabaimo: DANMEN, Yokohama Museum of Art

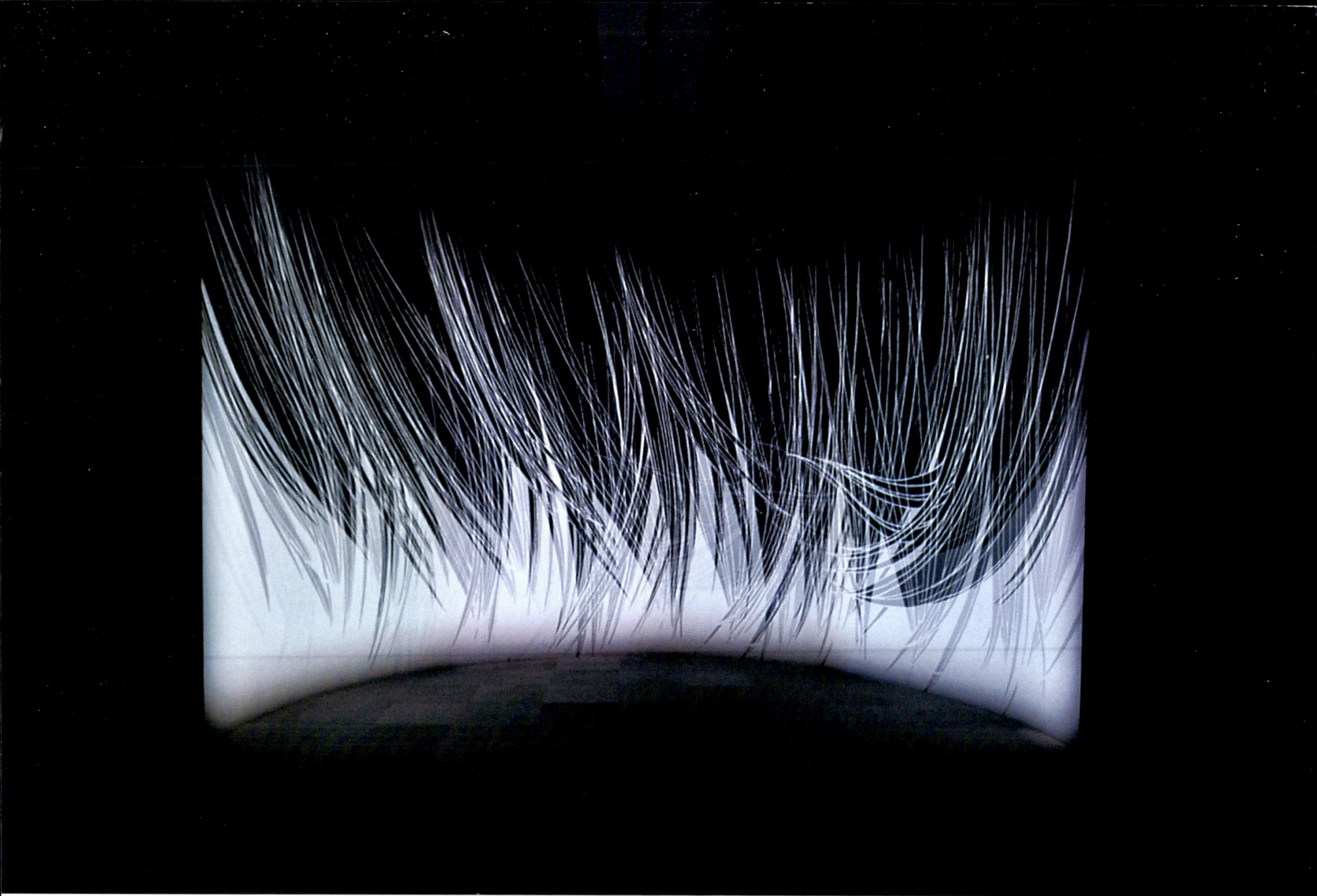

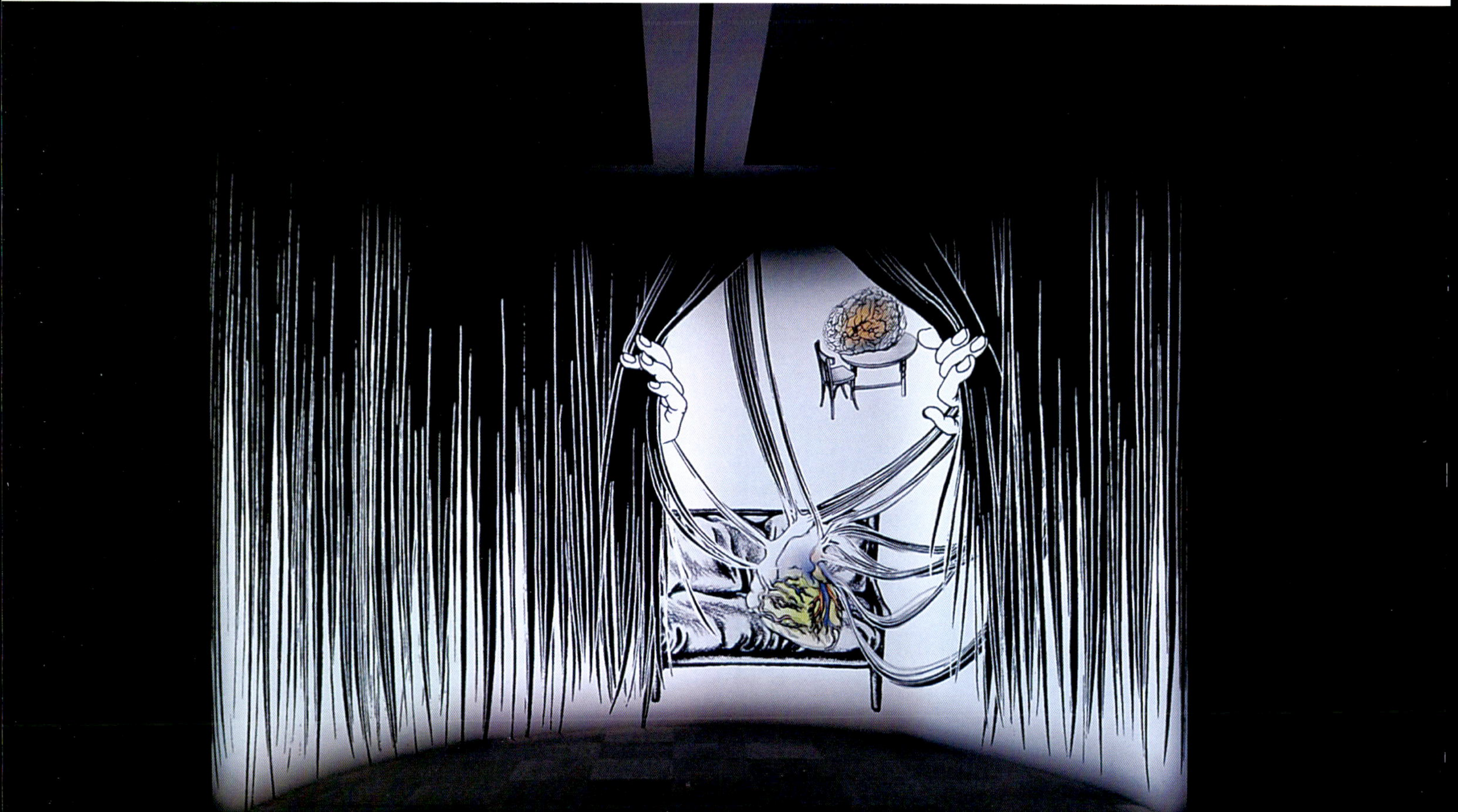

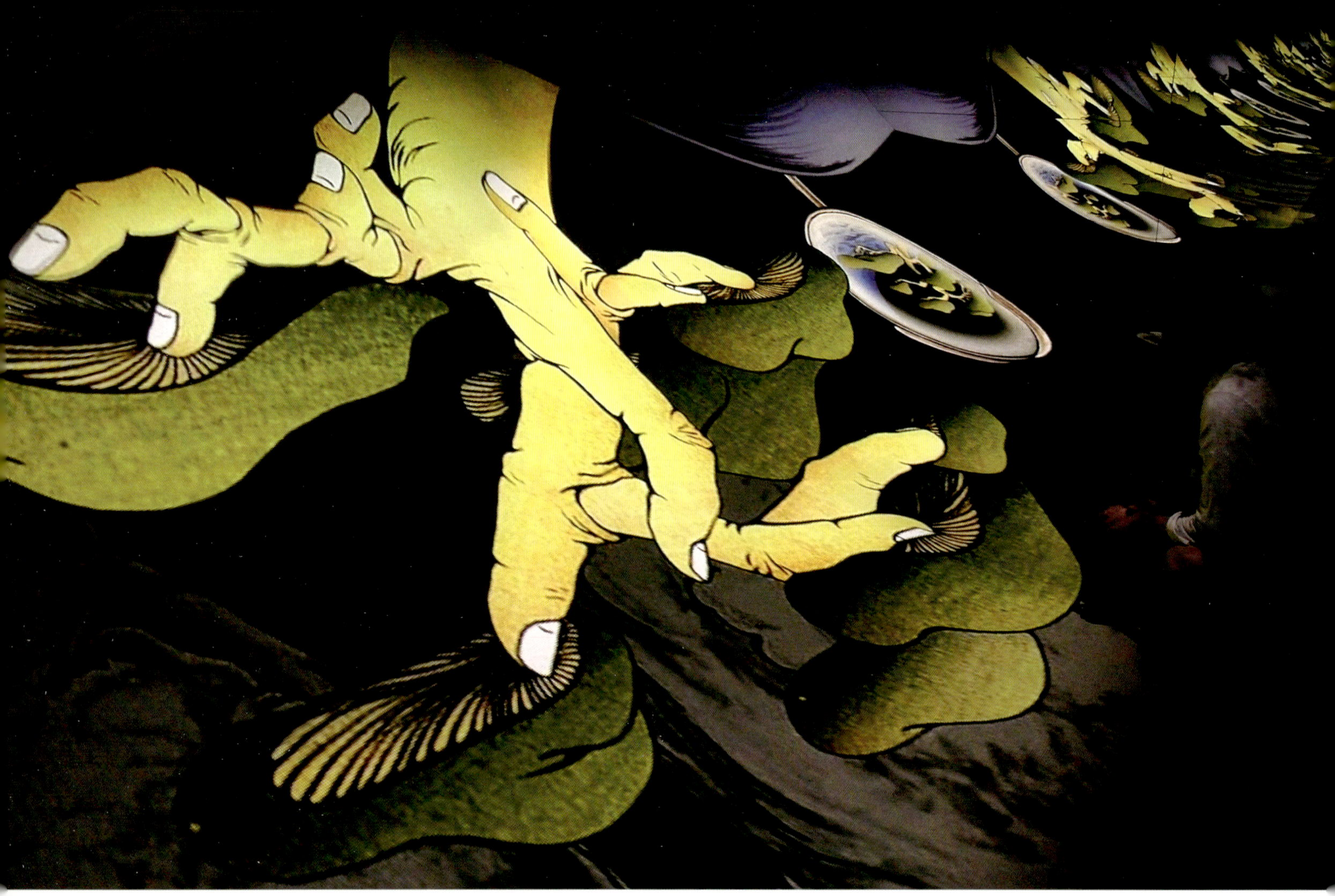

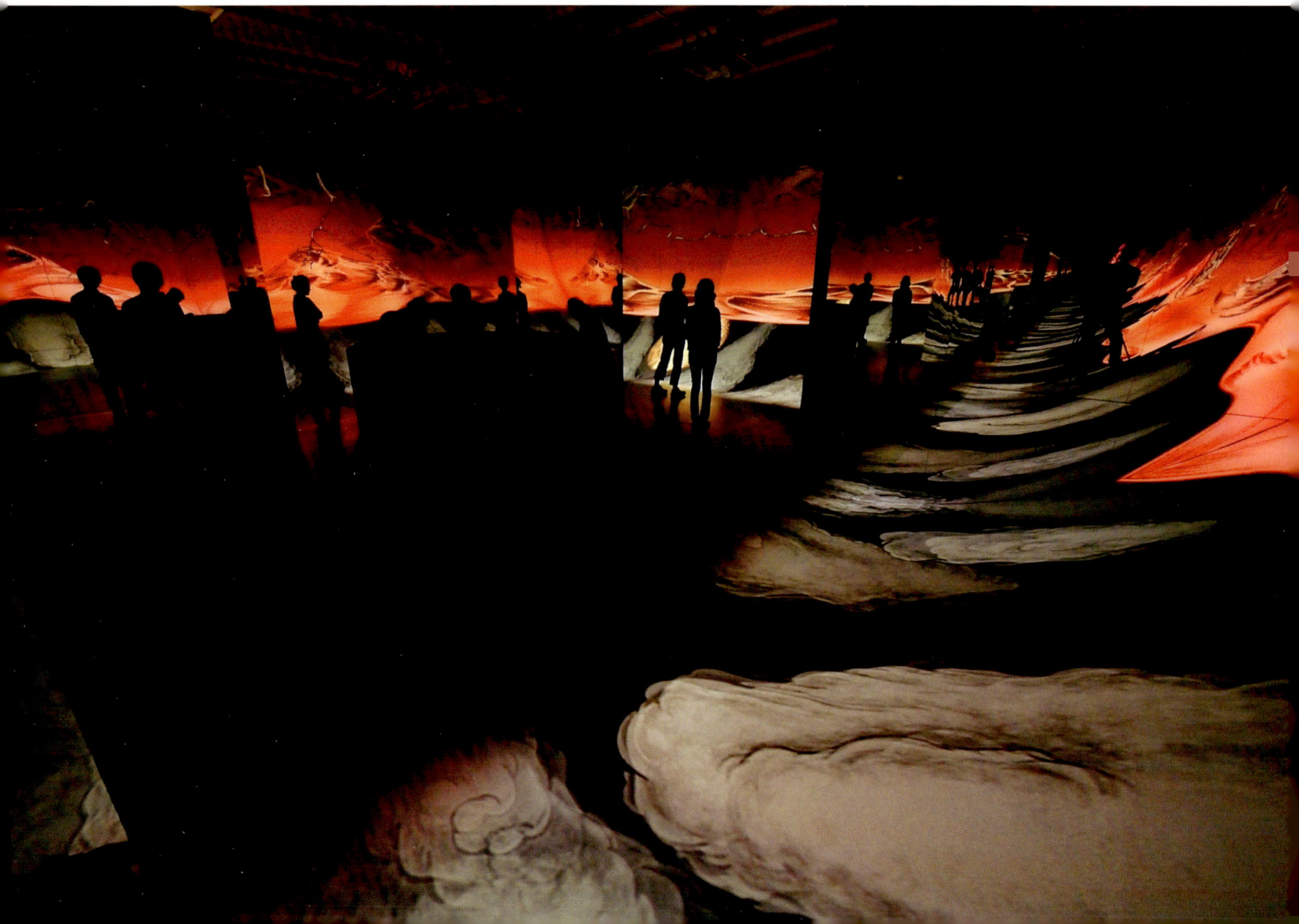

Tabaimo

OPPOSITE AND BELOW
teleco-soup, 2011
Video installation, 5 min 27 sec
Japanese Pavilion, 54th Venice Biennale,
June 11–November 27, 2011

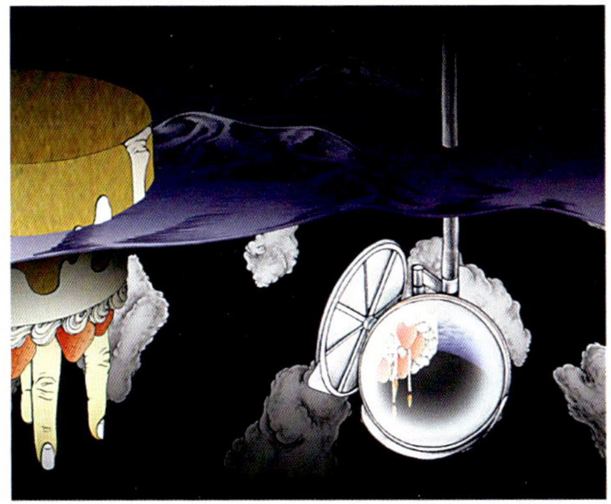

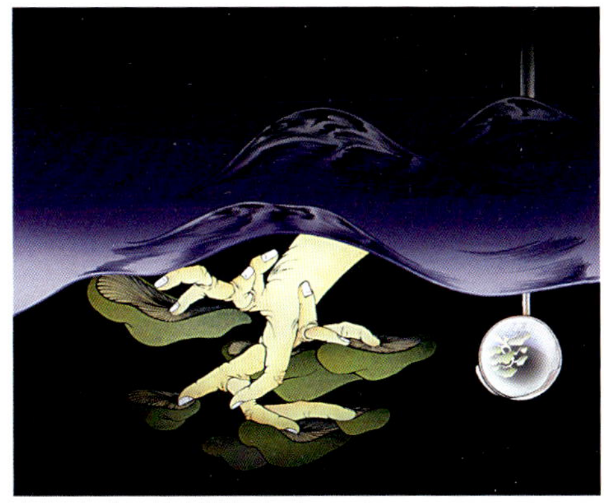

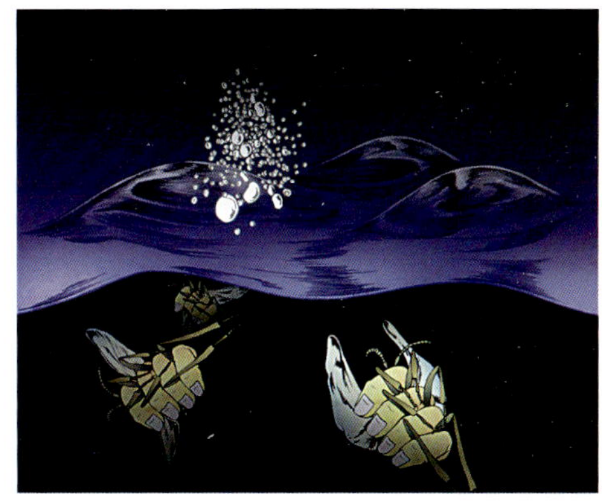

As soon as I heard that I'd been selected to exhibit at the Japanese Pavilion of the 2011 Venice Biennale, I went to have a preliminary look at the space. I found it was different from the spaces I'd used before—a very difficult space for an exhibition—and I realized that if I made this space into an enemy the whole thing would turn into a battle for me. So I decided I would make the space my ally in the project. When I got back to Japan I made a model, tried a few things out, and set about creating a work that the space would bring to life. There are four immovable walls sticking out into the middle of it. The walls aren't perpendicular to the outer walls, but form a trapezoidal shape. The placement of the walls, in fact, determined the structure of my work. The Pavilion has a hole in the ceiling and a hole in the floor. Rain falls through the roof. The concept is that, with the rain falling through, the building becomes one with nature. I decided to use the entire building as part of my work. One of the problems was that there's an area with pilotis (piers) supporting the building. When you look at the piloti area from outside, the space looks completely dead as though the air moving through it is stagnant. I wondered if there might be some way to assemble a work that would eliminate that impression so that, when you saw it, it would entice you into the Pavilion. I decided to make a structure that would draw people in. As I was putting the work together, I had the image in my mind of a Klein bottle [to understand what a Klein bottle is, imagine sewing two Möbius Loops together to create a single-sided bottle with no boundary. Its inside is its outside; it contains itself] and, in a sense, what I wanted to express was that shape. The idea solidified gradually as I incorporated the concept of the building itself. As you dug down deeper towards the inside, at some point you realized you were on the outside, and the things that you thought were physically small turned out to have been concealing things that were physically large. By utilizing the structure in my creative process, I was able to take all the detailed fragments of expression I had been drafting all along and make them into a dynamic expression. To explain what I mean, let's say I have a tree. The world I had been creating in my drawing up till then was the leaves and branches of that tree. But in this piece I feel I succeeded in representing the trunk.

So, rather than everything emerging from within me, I feel like I created this new work because I was given this *particular* space. Explaining the content is a bit difficult, but the title is *teleco-soup* (2011). The word *tereko* is used in the Kansai region in western Japan to mean 'topsy-turvy' or 'upside down'. I created a work where all kinds of things turn upside down or reverse order at some point—and so it became *teleco-soup*. I think the word 'soup' will remind everyone of a liquid that comes in a bowl but, at the same time, there's an association with the liquid that life emerges from, the primordial matter. So you have a very narrow association with soup, together with something linking it with the source of all life. I used the word 'soup' in the title to make people switch between these associations. Right at the start, when I began thinking about the concept for the work, I was inspired by a phrase from Zhuangzi, "The frog in the well knows nothing of the vast ocean." When I looked into it further I discovered that there are a lot of derivatives of the phrase in Japan, like, "The frog in the well knows nothing of the vast ocean, but knows the height of the sky," or "the blueness of sky." In Japan, there's a unique kind of sympathy for the sour-grapes aspect of it. Zhuangzi's original words suggest an image of someone really looking down on the frog, but another way of looking at it senses that there's something only the frog can know by being in the well. When I set to work on the piece I imagined myself as having turned into the frog. That's how I conceived and developed my images.

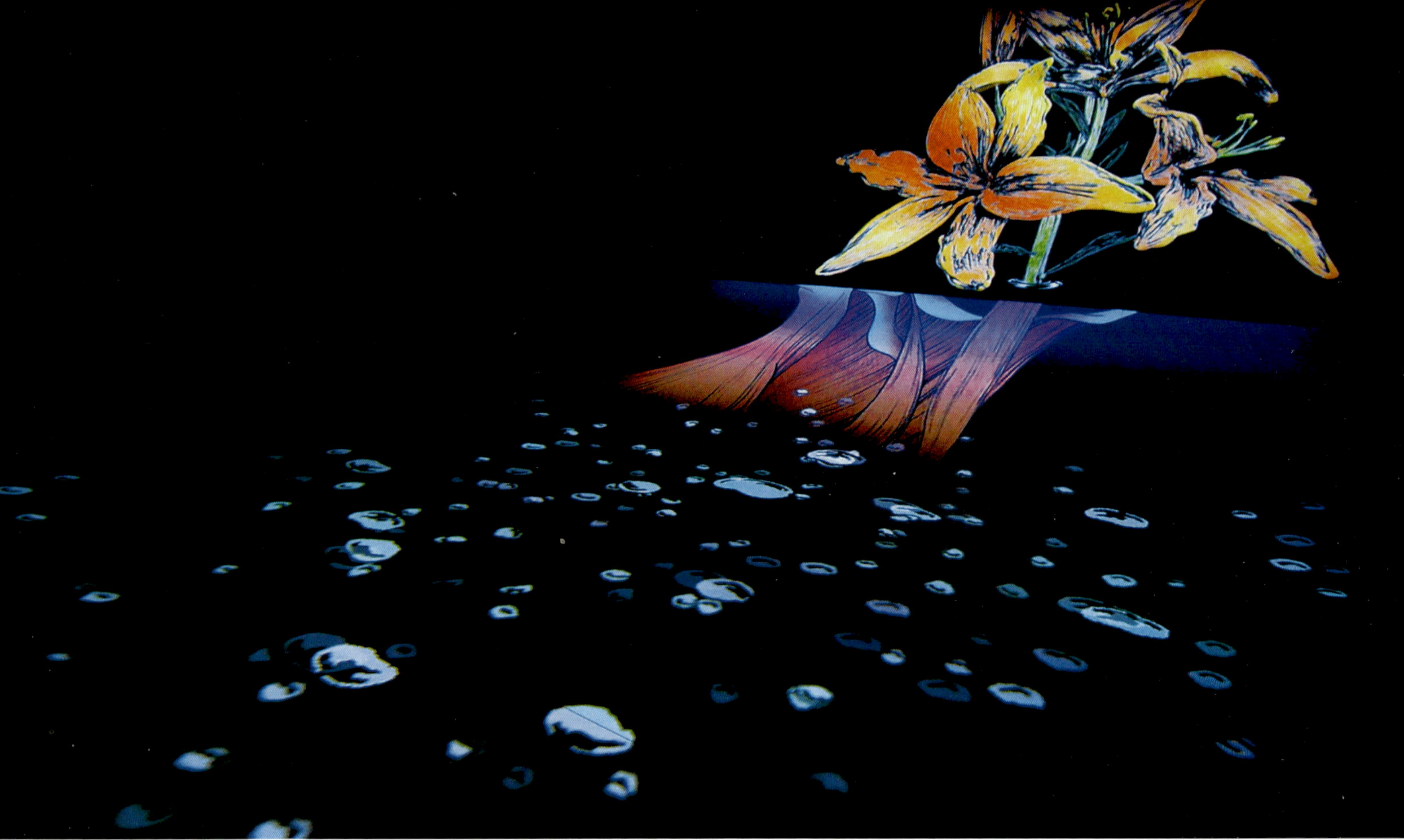

Tabaimo

ABOVE, LEFT AND RIGHT
BLOW, 2009
Video installation, 3 min 42 sec
Tabaimo: DANMEN, Yokohama Museum of Art

OPPOSITE, BELOW
midnight sea, 2006/2008
Video installation, 4 min 42 sec
YOROYORON: Tabaimo, Hara Museum of Contemporary Art, Tokyo

I'm someone who knows nothing about Western assumptions or common sense, so the frog's existence is very much my own. I'm not ashamed of myself for this though, and I don't believe it has a significant effect on my artistic production. I create from the place where I myself stand, and I think of that as a kind of method. I agree that the context of contemporary art in the West is probably important, but I create from within my own context and experiences. I don't set out to create from within the Western context and, if you try to interpret my work from that context it might lead you in a slightly different direction—which might in itself lead to an interesting interpretation. But I'm expressing the world I'm looking at, and I'm seeing the way I see it.

One thing that almost all of my recent works have in common is that—whether it's the place the viewer stands or something in the floor of the installation I've built—there's part of the work that shifts and sways and isn't firmly grounded, as if the floor collapses and falls away. Or there are bubbles coming up from below. I've been using a few varieties of this mode of expression, and it's an expression of how the place I'm standing is swaying or floating. The way I see it, my generation seems to stand on unstable ground.

I don't know about any critics who have misinterpreted my work but there is something I'd like to explain that might be misunderstood. Even in the course of this interview I talked about how I didn't understand the Western context and how I didn't intend to try to understand it better. This might be taken to mean that I'm rejecting the West, but it's more that I simply don't know it. And since I don't know about it and all of its valuable elements, it doesn't make any sense to talk about it as if I did. I am where I am, and although I can only speak as the person who is standing here now, difference itself is an interesting thing. Earlier I talked about Zhuangzi's frog in the well, but there's another saying of his about a "turtle who knows the vast ocean." If we are talking about the world of Western art, the turtle who knows the vast ocean knows the Western context. But if both the turtle and frog exist, and the turtle doesn't go into the well and the frog doesn't leave it, then the only way to realize a reconciliation between the two is through the kind of shift that I was talking about earlier. If the frog digs way down into the bottom of the well and the turtle keeps burrowing into the sand at the bottom of the ocean, I think they will arrive at a shared stratum. I'm aspiring to express that stratum, and if the turtle and frog meet halfway, then they may be able to make something in common. I believe art is the field where such a thing is possible.

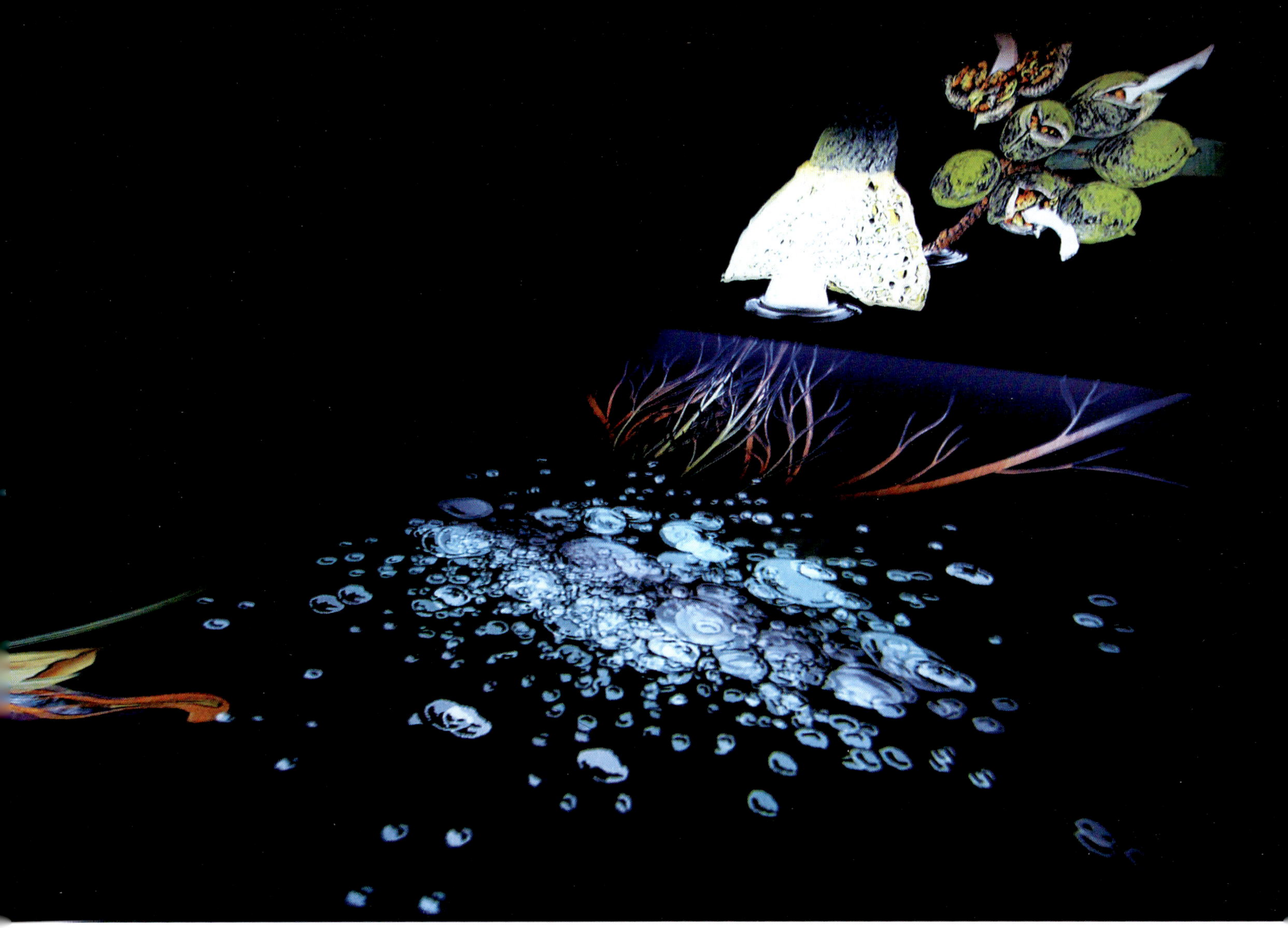

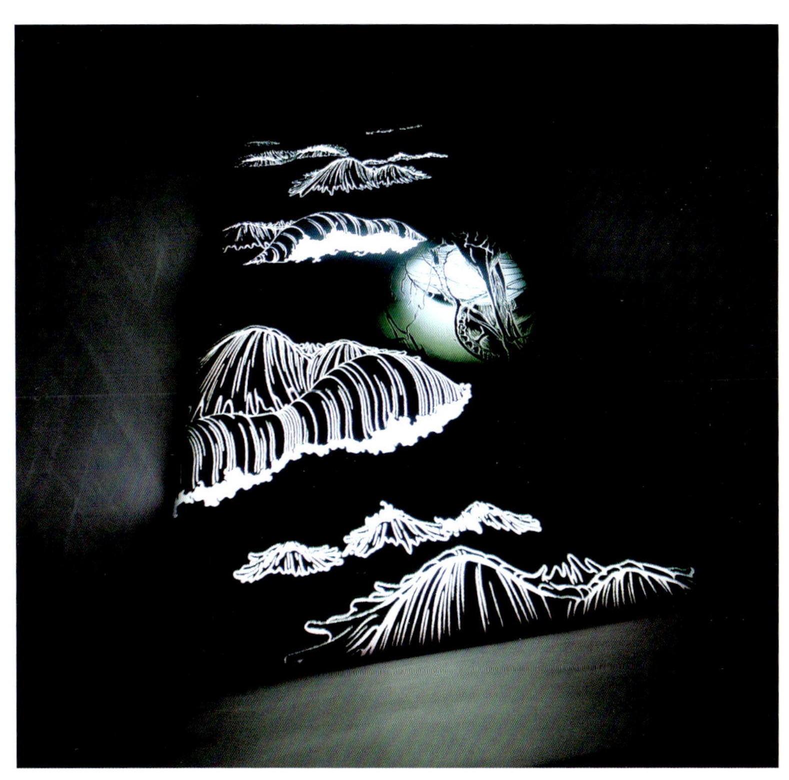

Marina Abramović

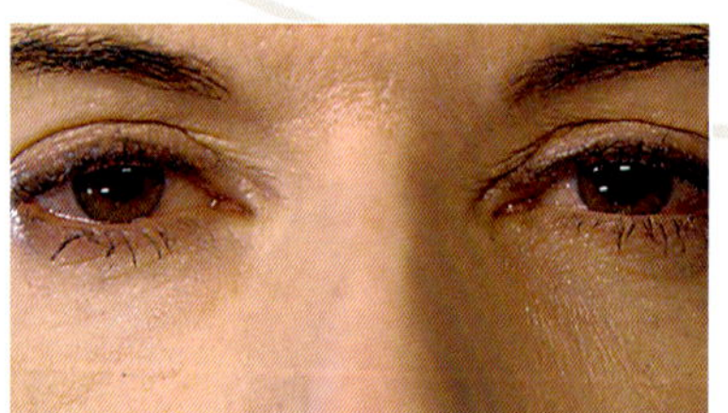
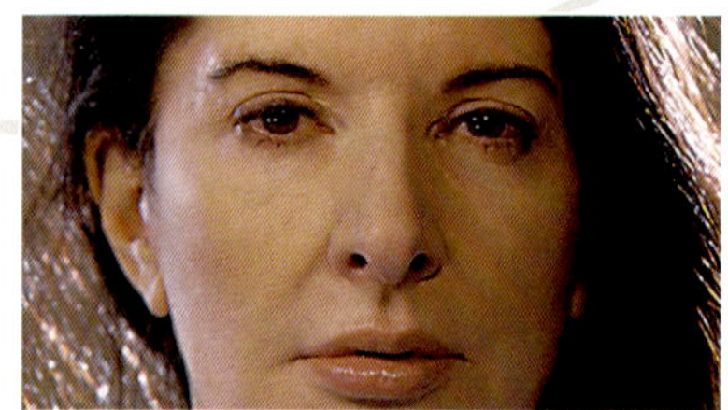
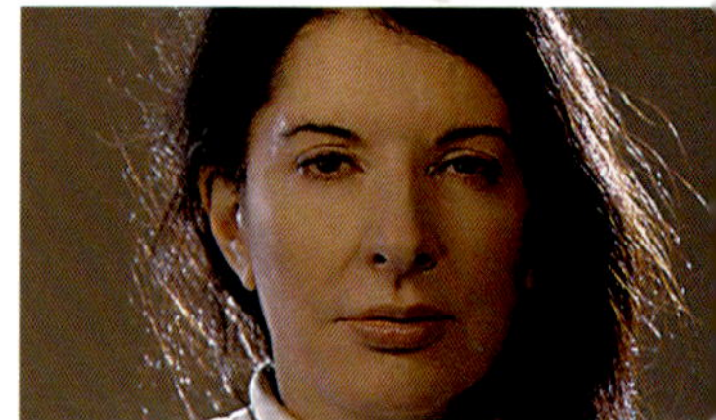

Glenn Ligon

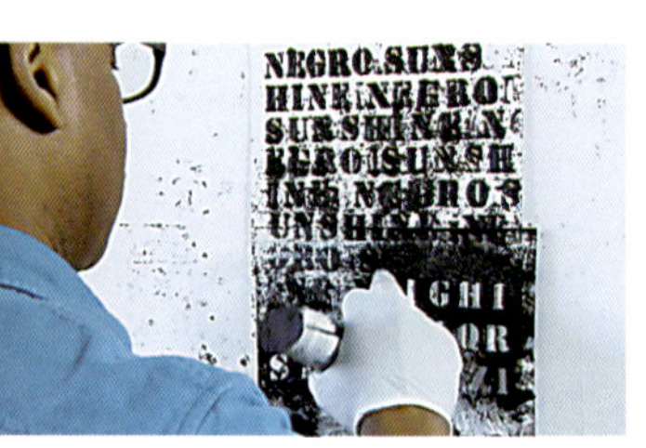

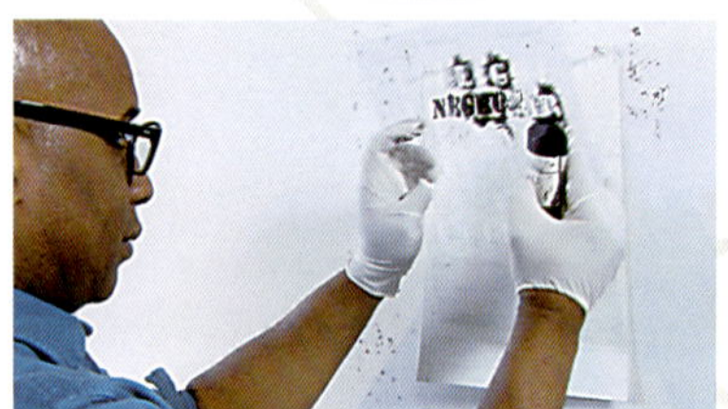
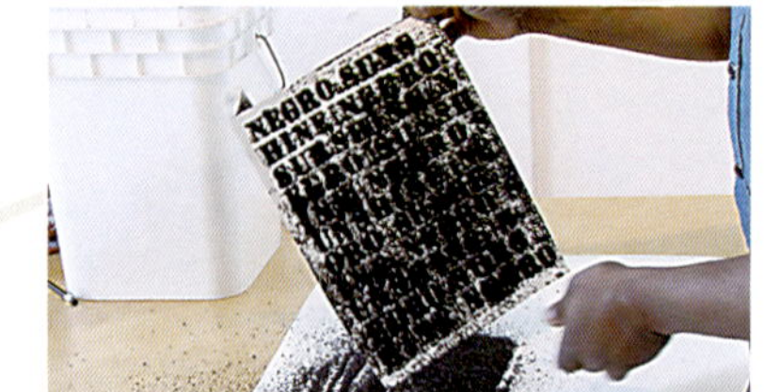
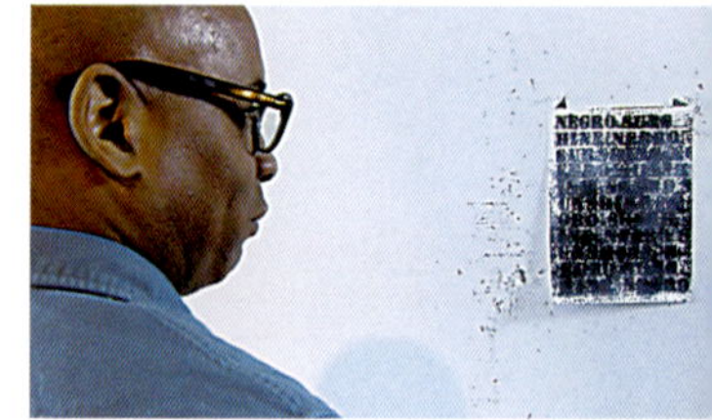

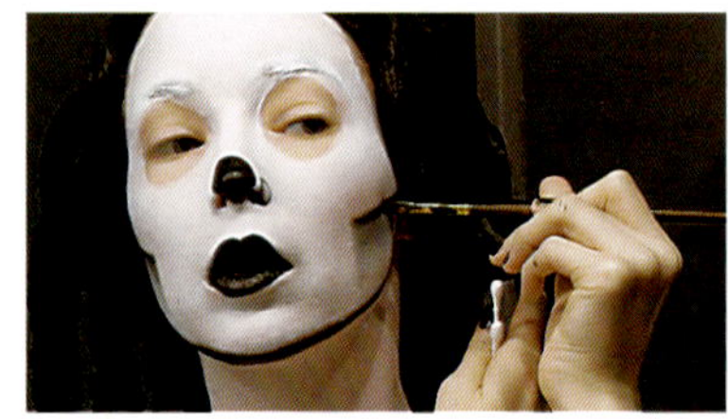
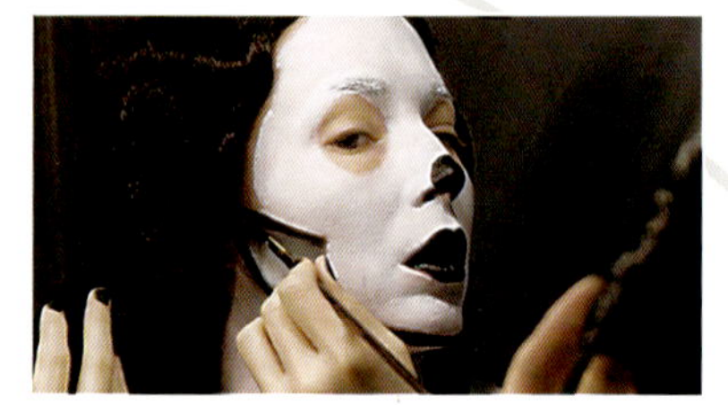
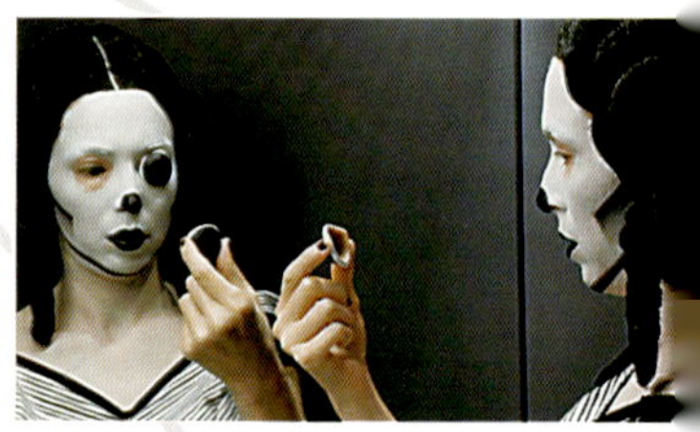

Mary Reid Kelley

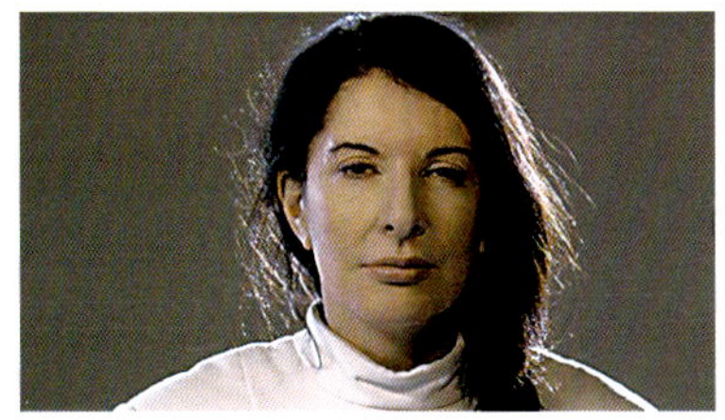
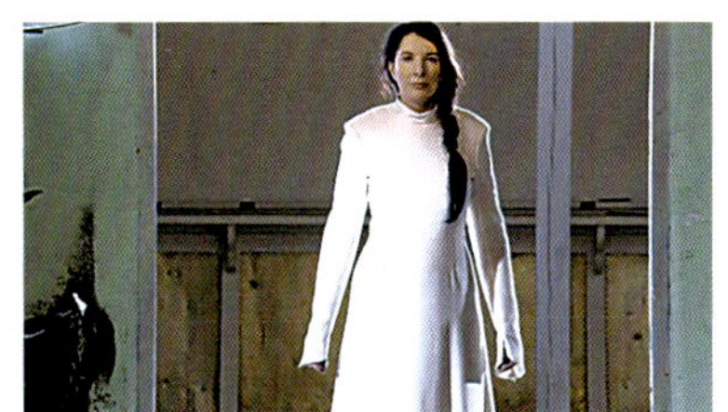
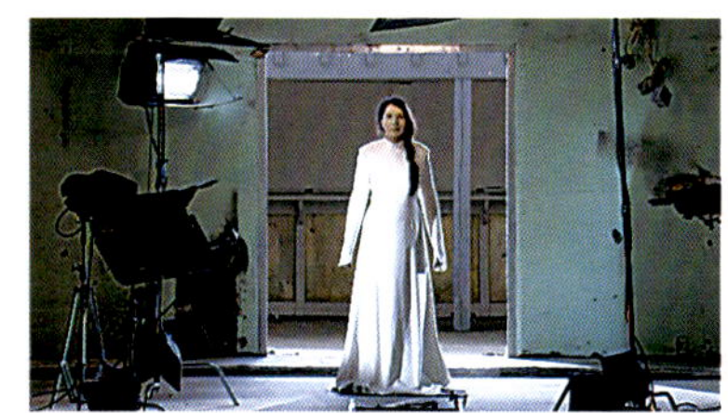

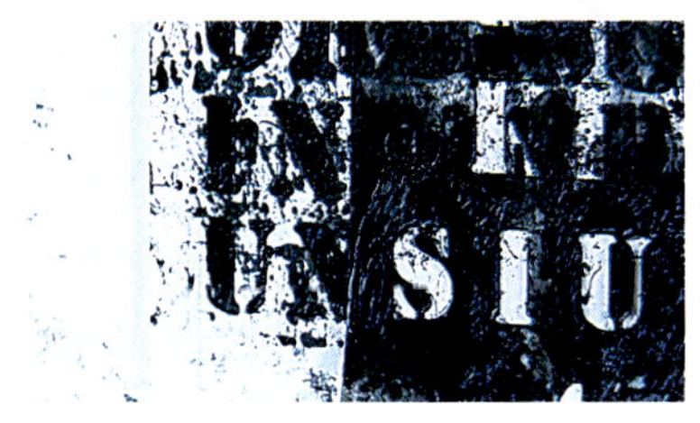
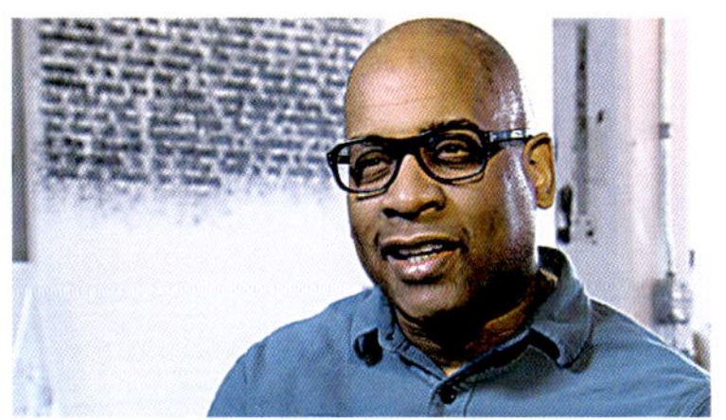

History

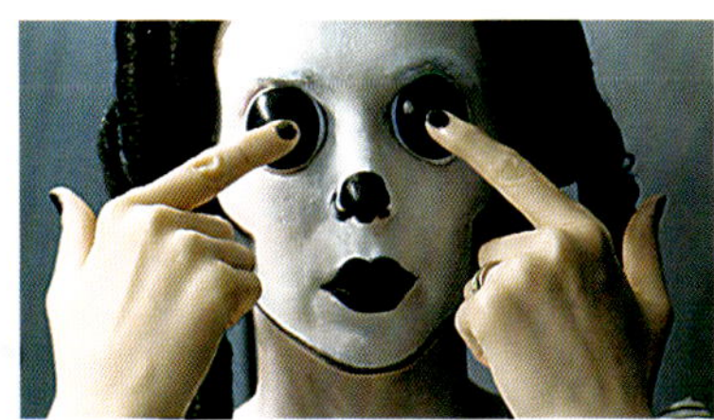
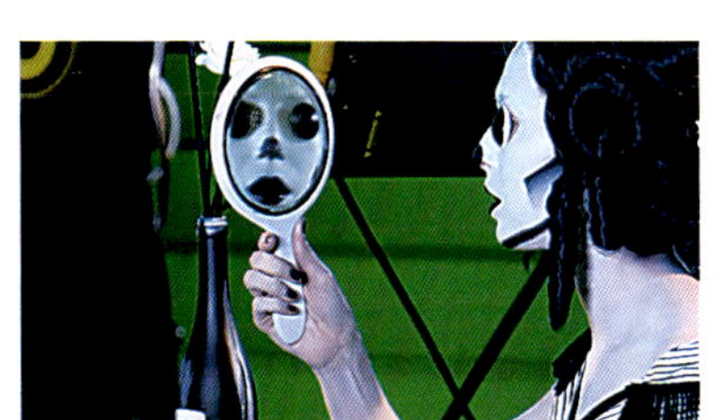
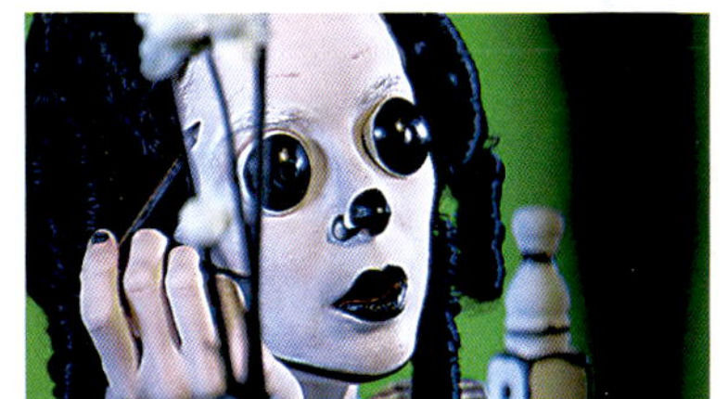

Marina Abramović

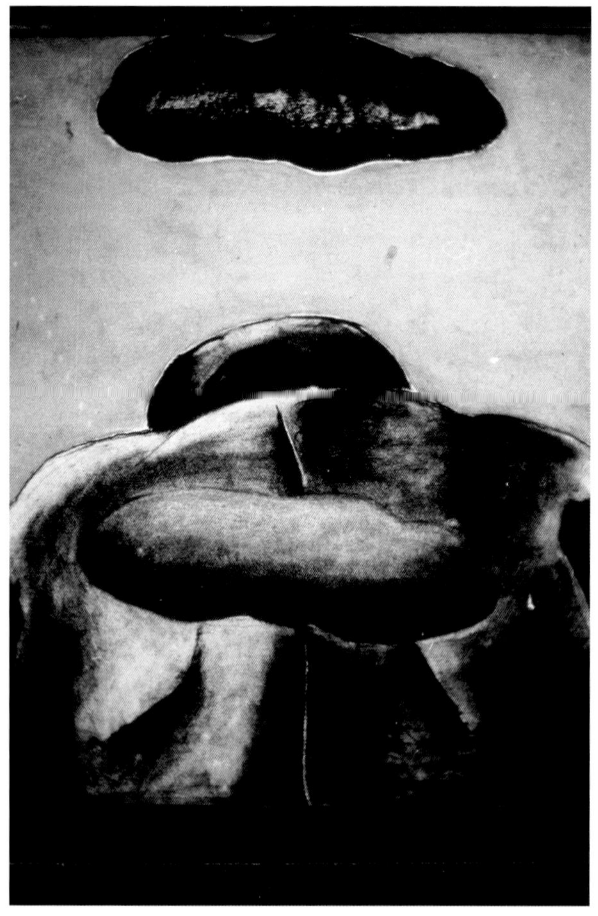

ABOVE
Cloud and its Projection, 1966
Painting

Marina Abramović and Ulay

OPPOSITE, TOP LEFT
Imponderabilia, 1977
Performance, 90 min
Galleria Comunale d'Arte
Moderna, Bologna

OPPOSITE, TOP RIGHT
Rest Energy, 1980
Performance, 4 min 10 sec
ROSC'80, Dublin

OPPOSITE, BOTTOM
Relation in Time, 1977
Performance, 17 hours
Studio G7, Bologna

When did I decide to be an artist? Ever since I can remember, I was always drawing. At age twelve I had my first exhibition, and I already considered myself an artist. I never wanted to be anything else. My first paintings were about my dreams. Sometimes I would wake up and reality would look like the dream, and the dream would look like the real thing. Later on, I remember, the dreams dissolved and I started being very interested in truck accidents. I was crazy about the Communists' big green trucks. I would go to the scenes of accidents, take photographs, and go back and paint them. Then I thought I would buy toy trucks and put them on the highways and wait for the trucks to smash them. Those little toys were always untouched by the big trucks, so I started painting the big trucks being smashed by the wonderful innocent little children's trucks. It was very metaphorical and poetical. Then I got into a new period altogether. I started painting the sky. I was crazy about clouds—all kinds of clouds. There were black holes. There were projections and shadows in the clouds, and it created a kind of mystical dimension (*Cloud and its Projection,* 1966). I remember a moment at the beginning of my twenties, lying on a grass field and looking into a plain blue sky. In the sky I saw twelve supersonic airplanes leaving completely sharp vapor trails, and the lines of the vapor trails dissolving into blue sky again. It was like a spiritual revelation for me. I stood up and wanted to go immediately to military headquarters and ask the generals if they could lend me twelve planes to make drawings in the sky. As my father was a general, they called him immediately to say, "Your daughter's completely crazy; get her out of here! Do you know how much it would cost to fly supersonic planes so that she can make drawings in the sky?" So, very early, I understood that there were certain things I couldn't do. But at the same time, I had a revelation in the moment of looking into the sky that, actually, I could use everything. I could use water, islands, fire, the earth, the air, and myself. And this was the moment when I somehow decided that it was completely ridiculous to go to the studio and make something two-dimensional when I could have the entire world. That's when I stopped painting.

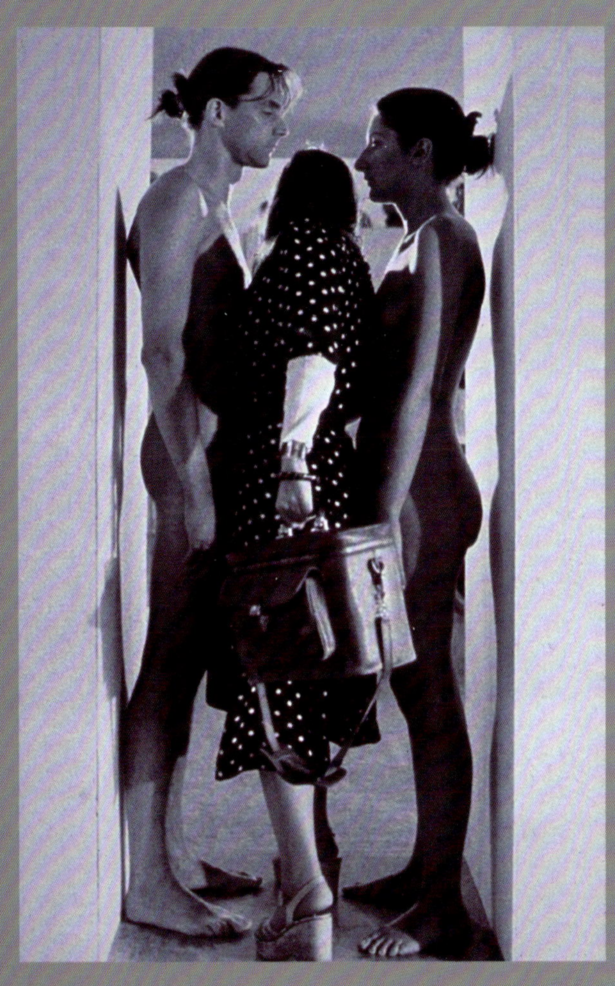

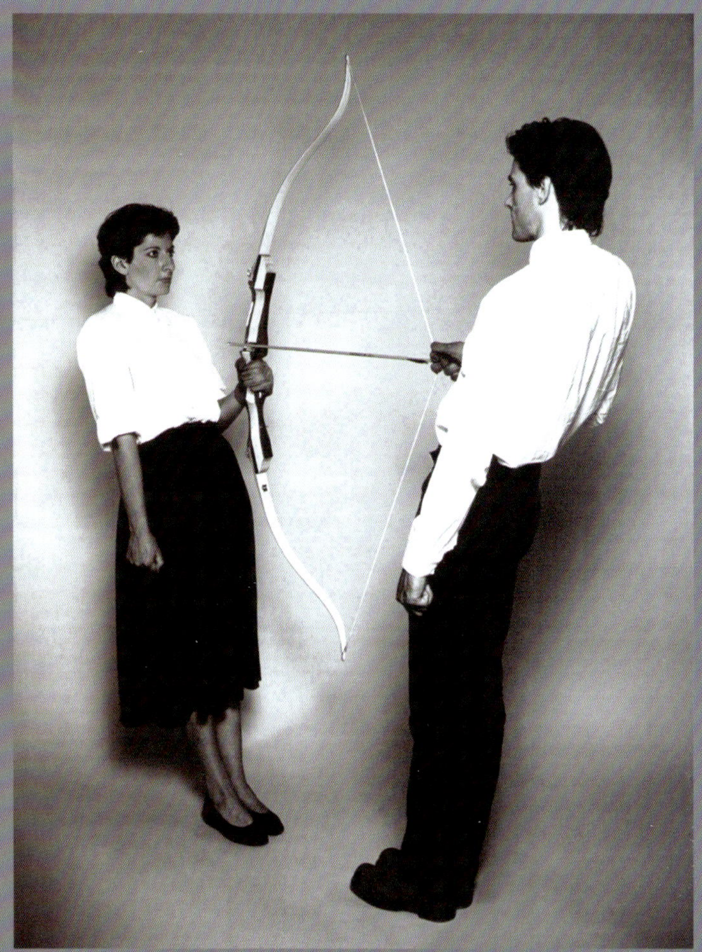

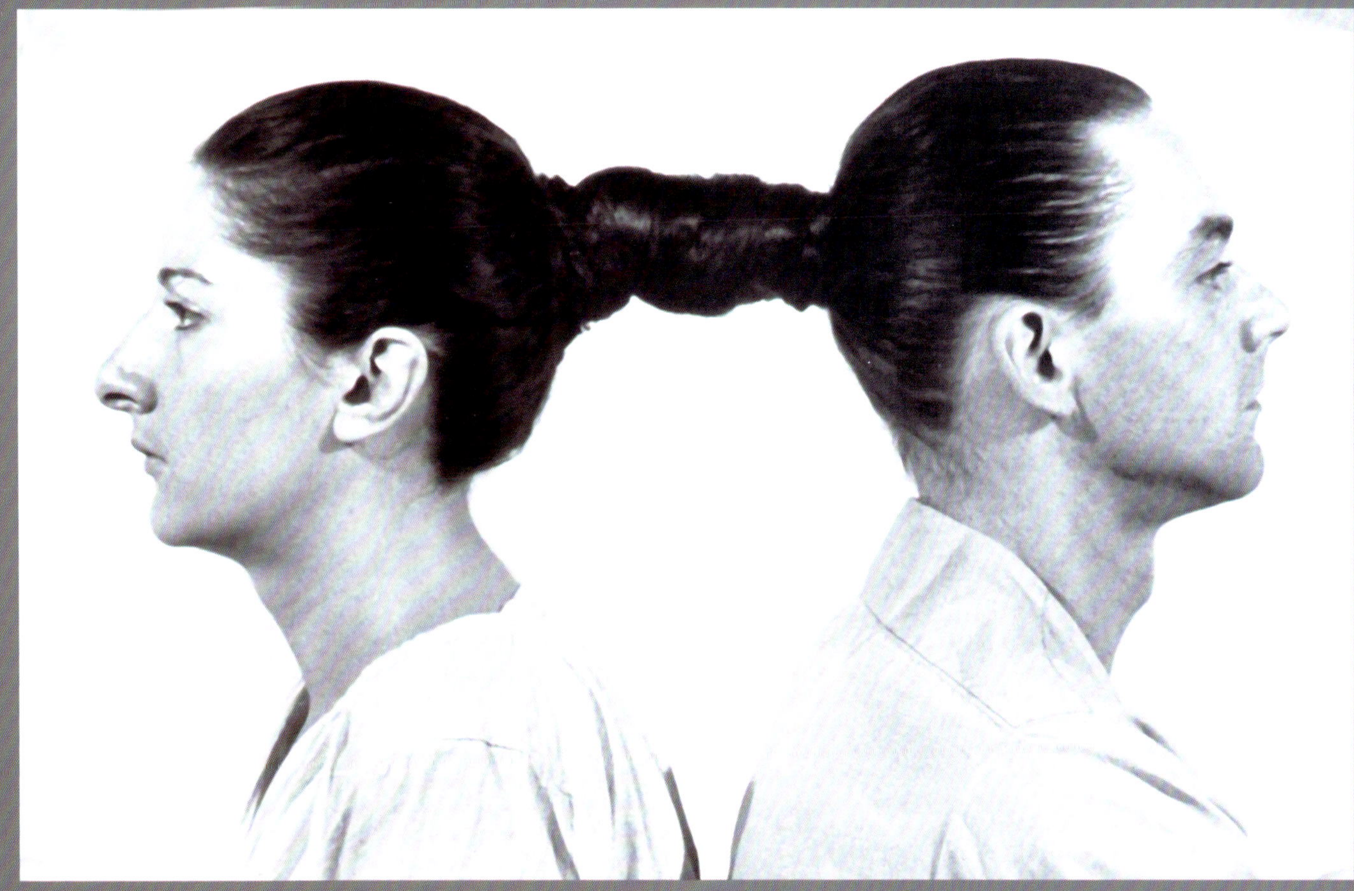

From that moment of revelation, my idea was to use sound to create environments where you had one impression through sound, but a completely different impression visually. My first idea was to put speakers with the sound of a bridge collapsing on the main bridge in Belgrade so that every three minutes the bridge would seem to be falling down, but visually it would not. To do such a project you would need to get permission from the mayor. So I went to the mayor's house and, again, the same thing happened: they forbade me to do it because the bridge could really fall down from the vibrations of that kind of sound. So I did it with the building where I was living. It was only for ten minutes because the inhabitants of the building ran out, thinking that everything was being bombed. That was kind of a big mess. I experimented more and more with sound. And then, somehow, I came to the point of *Rhythm 10* (1973), my first performance that used knives. The title, *Rhythm 10*, would suggest it was a sound piece: I had tape recorders and I was repeating certain actions, but it involved my body. And the moment I involved my body in the performance, I established an incredible energy dialogue with the public. It was so overwhelming that I could never come back to any other form of art.

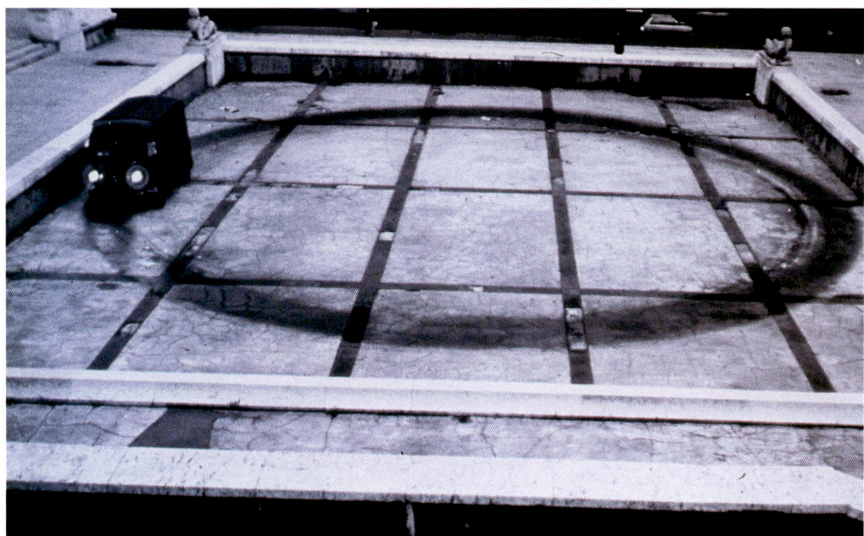

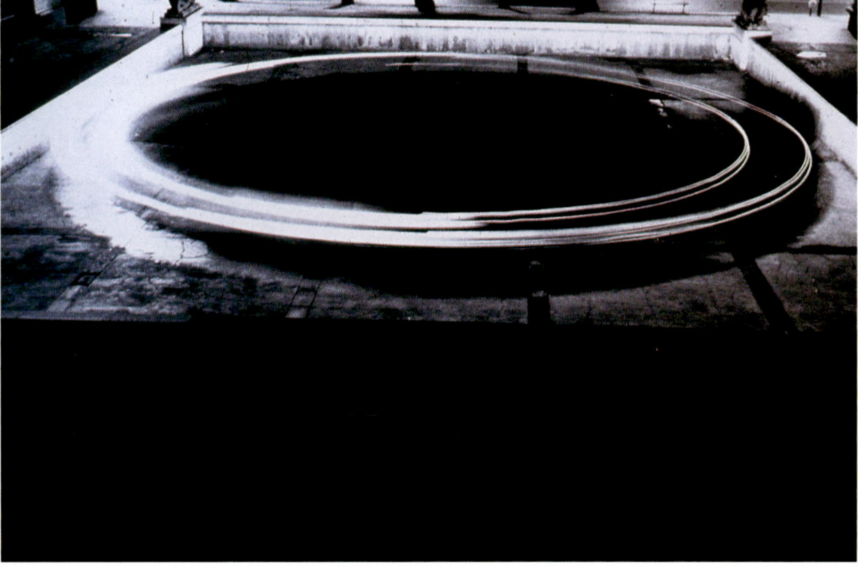

Marina Abramović

LEFT
Relation in Movement, 1977
Performance, 16 hours
10th Biennale de Paris

OPPOSITE, TOP
Rhythm 0, 1974
Performance, 6 hours
Studio Morra, Naples

OPPOSITE, CENTER
Rhythm 5, 1974
Performance, 90 min
Student Cultural Center, Belgrade

OPPOSITE, BOTTOM
Rhythm 10, 1973
Performance, 1 hour
Museo d'Arte Contemporanea,
Villa Borghese, Rome

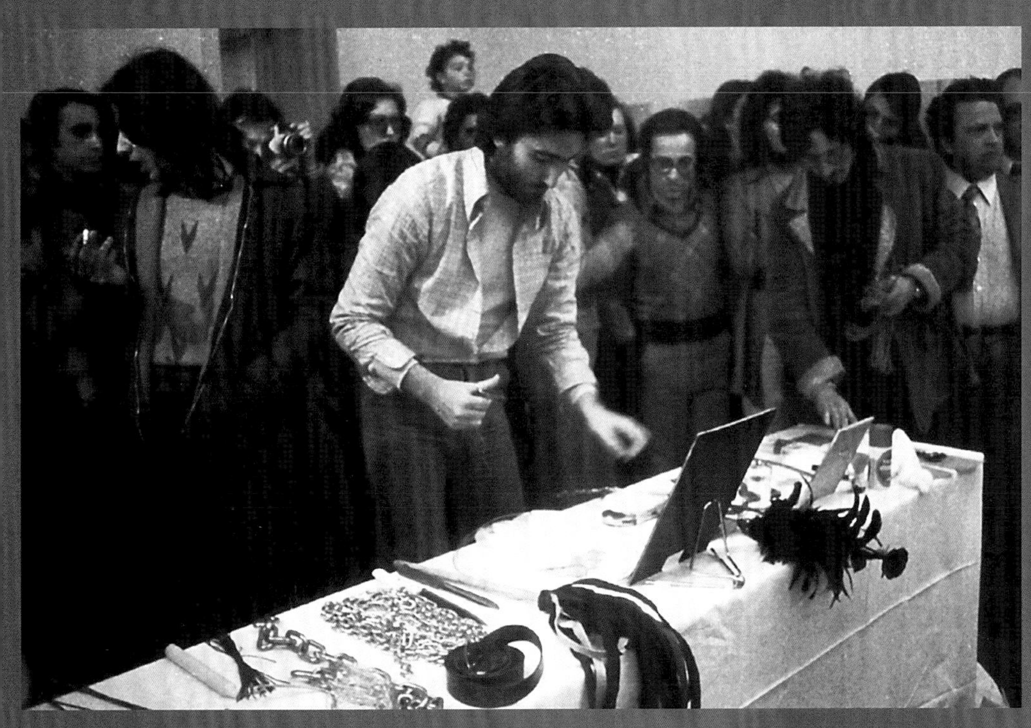
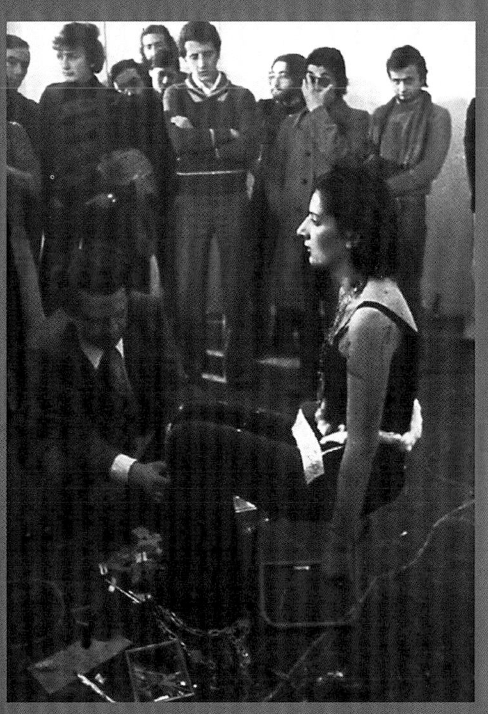
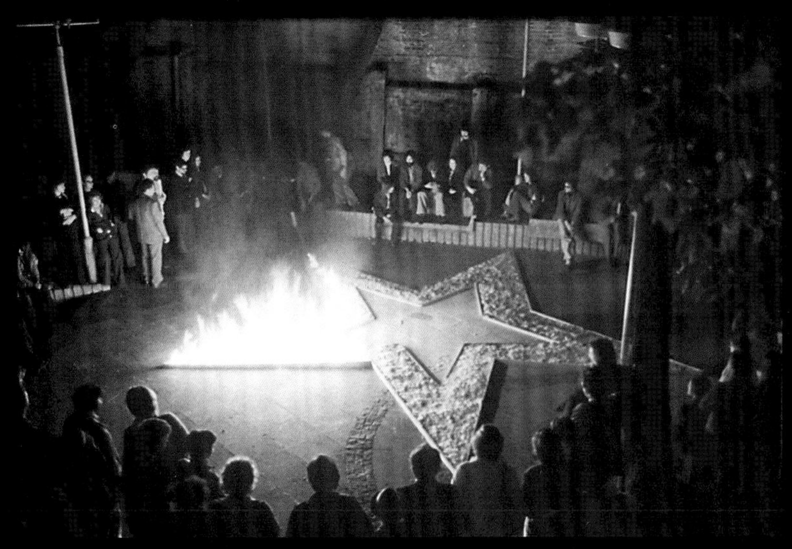
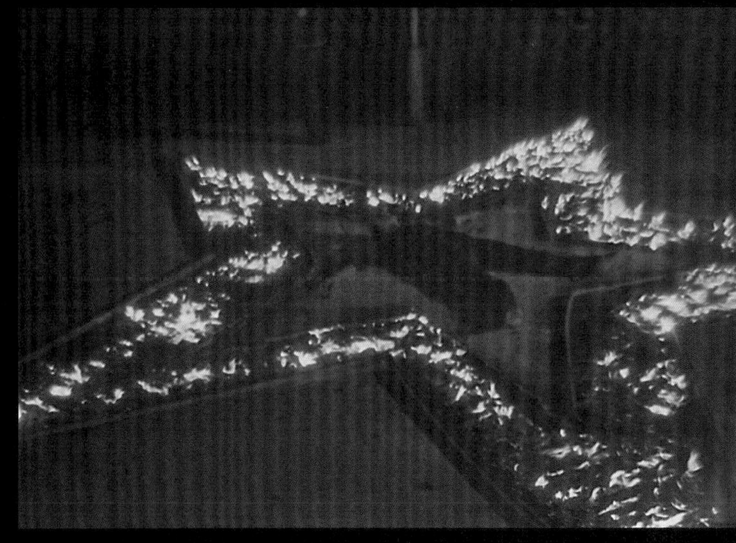
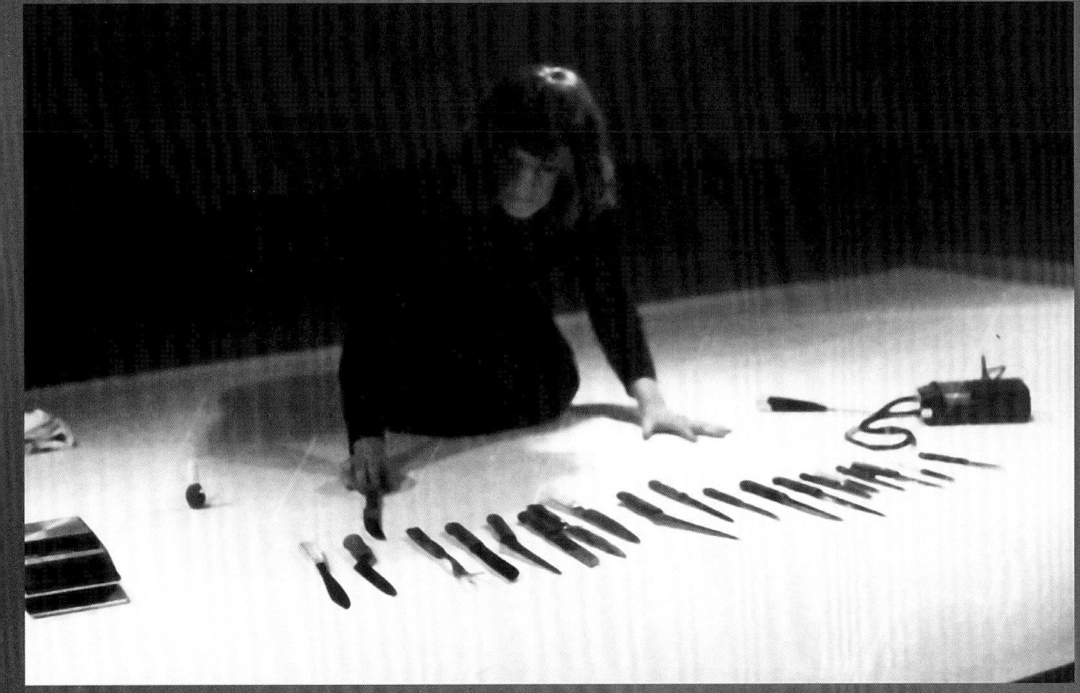
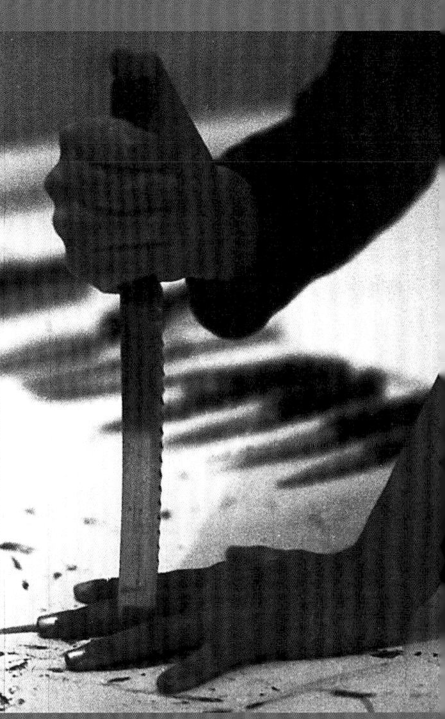

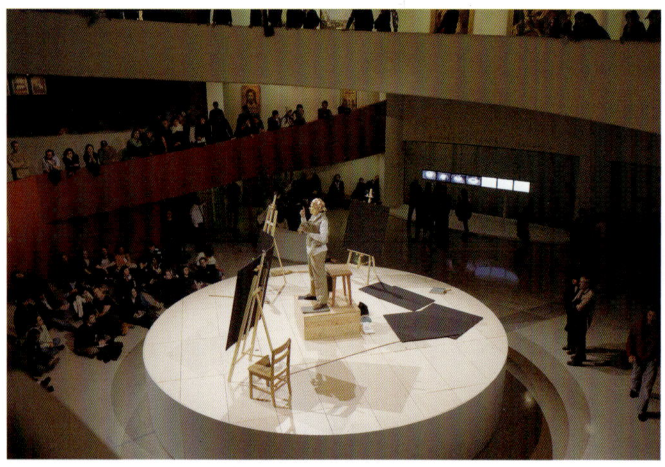

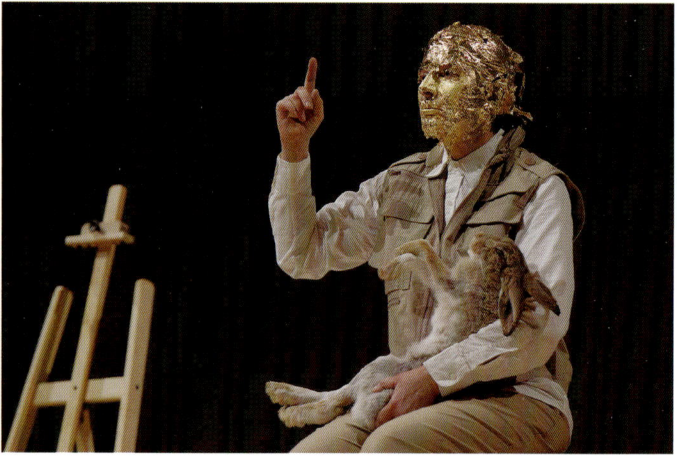

Marina Abramović

ABOVE
Seven Easy Pieces: Joseph Beuys's How to Explain Pictures to a Dead Hare (1965), 2005
Performance, 7 hours
Solomon R. Guggenheim Museum, New York

OPPOSITE
The House with the Ocean View, 2002
Performance, 12 days
Sean Kelly Gallery, New York

For me performance is a tool I use so that I can express myself. It is very important in the beginning of your career as an artist to find the best tool to express yourself—and I have to say that I was very lucky that it came so early, and so clearly, to me. One thing about performance that is extremely attractive to me is the immateriality of the immediate self. If you deal with painting you just have to have a nail on the wall. You hang the painting, and that's it. But performance is such an immaterial form of art. If you're not there to see it, you will miss it. Commentary or a video can never replace the live experience. So if you ask me, "What is performance art," my statement will be that it is a mental and physical construct that artists create in a specific time and place in front of an audience. The public and the performer create the piece. That kind of unity is very important to create the dynamic, balance, and chemistry. And then it's a good performance.

In my early performance work I didn't deal so much with time. I really embraced repetition—repeating a certain action over and over again—to come to an almost charismatic state of mind. The performances, in the beginning, were quite violent and very tough—running into the wall; cutting scars on my stomach; lying on ice; and beating myself to see how far physically I could go and actually transcend—transform—the painful experience into something else. The more performances I developed, the more I became interested in the mental state of peace. The extension of time became the important factor in my last three pieces—*House with the Ocean View* (2002), *Seven Easy Pieces* (2005), and *The Artist is Present* (2010; illustrated on pages 128–29). The last piece, which is the longest (six hundred hours), was actually what I understood—that the longer a performance gets the more transcendental and transformative it is to the performer doing it, but also to the public participating in it. So the long duration is actually the doorway to something else: how you can elevate the human spirit.

I've been asked so many times what kind of preparation I need when I'm doing a performance. I remember, especially, when I was doing *House with the Ocean View* that the night before I had lamb chops, chocolate mousse, and a glass of red wine. And then, the next morning, I just started. This was my preparation. You can prepare your body like an athlete, like an Olympic runner—whatever you want—but if you don't have the right state of mind you can't do it. It's really about state of mind. I could never do these long durational performances when I was in my twenties or thirties. I would not have had that kind of stamina. Now, physically, I'm older, but mentally I'm stronger—but I have to say that for the last performance I really did have to prepare myself. It took me almost one year—going to the Ayurveda clinic in India; cleansing the body; doing Yoga and breathing exercises; trying to eliminate lunch so that my body wouldn't create acids; training not to pee during the hours of sitting, and—most difficult—just to stay in the present. So the last performance was like training for the NASA program, for landing on some unknown planet, like the first woman walking on the moon. It was such a difficult thing, too. You know, I walked the Great Wall of China (*The Great Wall Walk*, 1988), and it took three months, but the public was not there so it was a totally different thing. But in *The Artist is Present*, in three months, it was life itself.

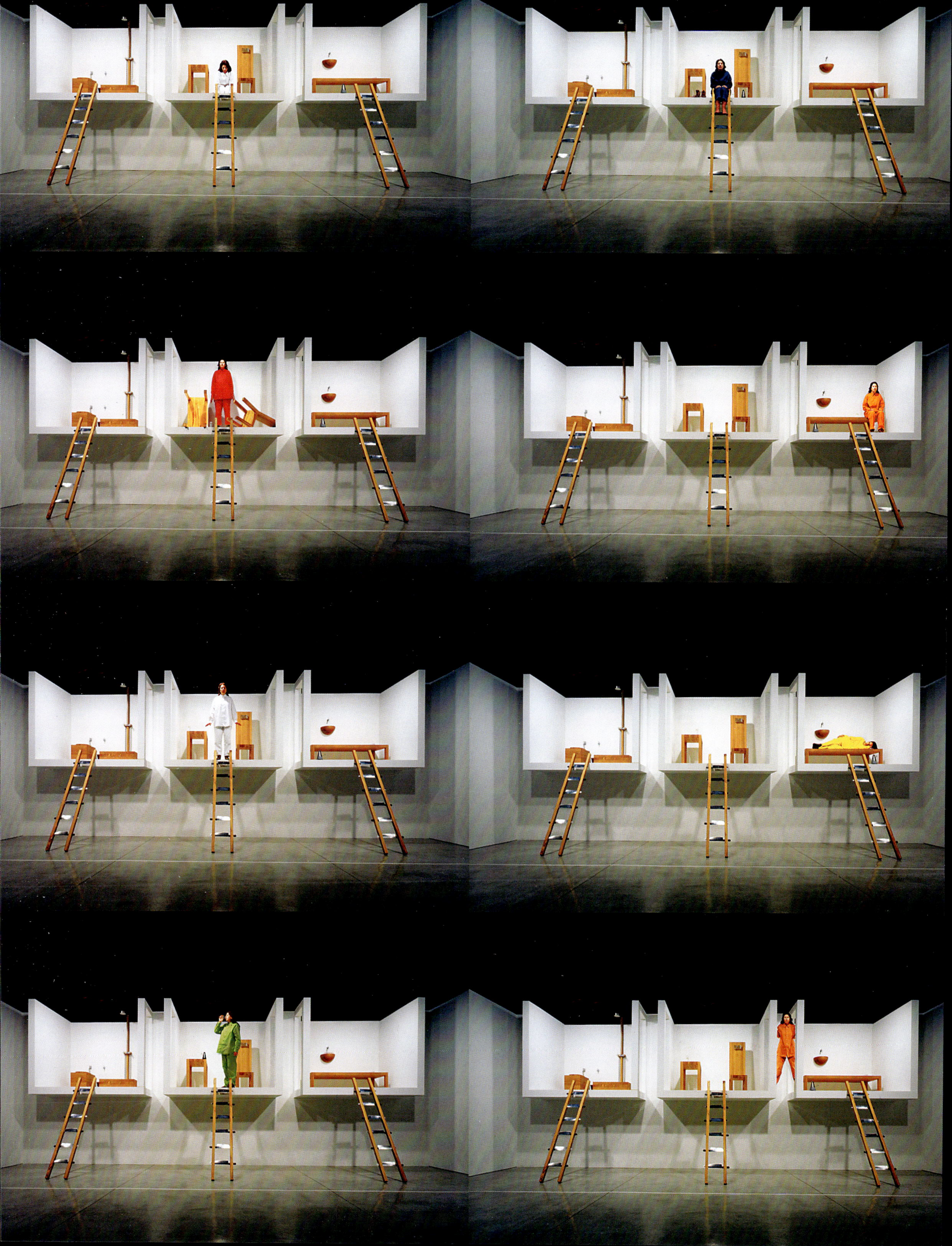

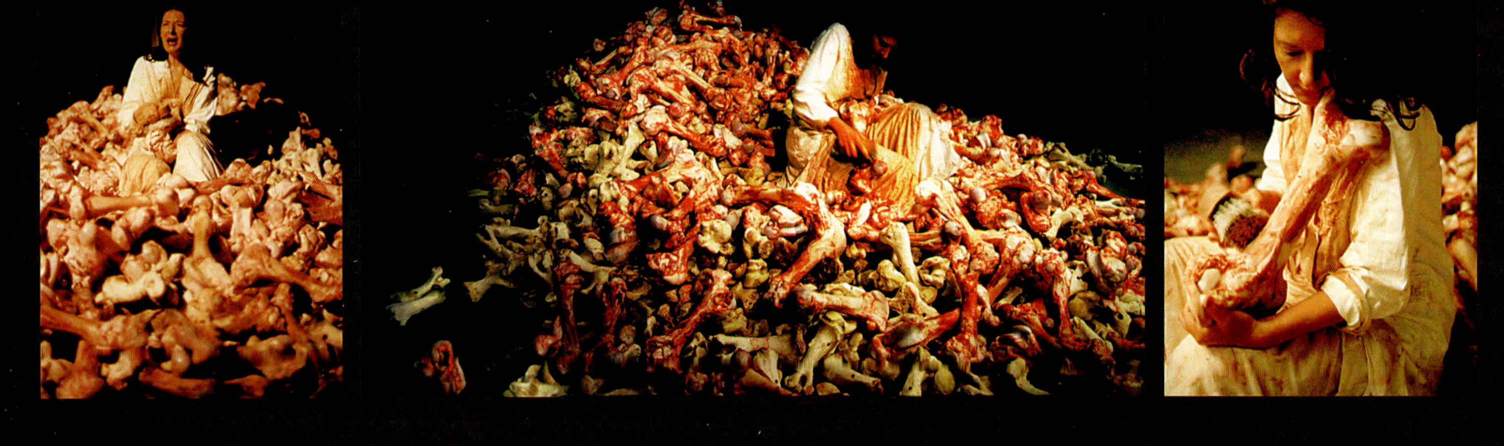
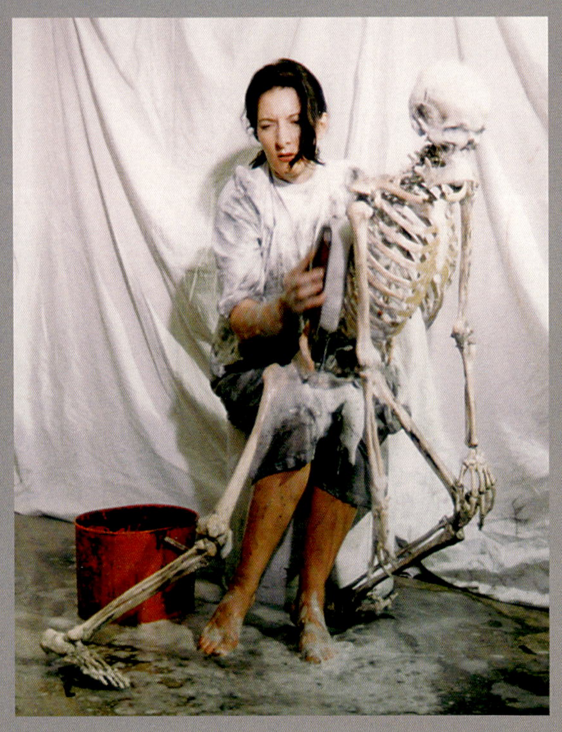
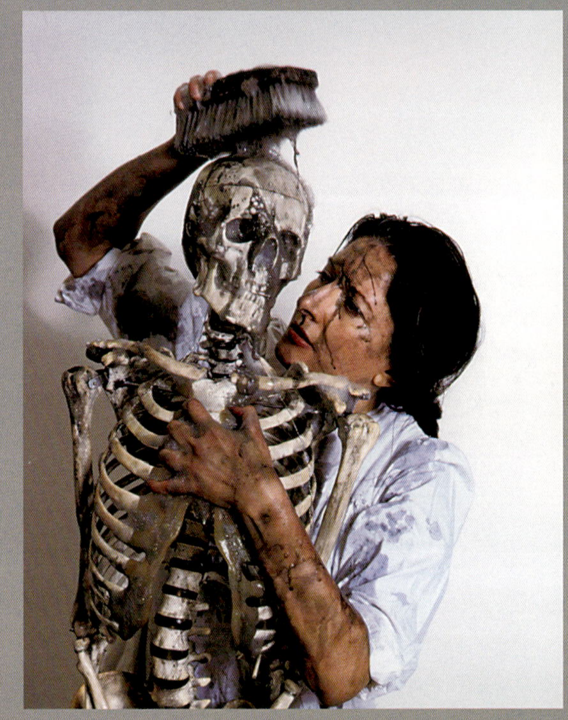
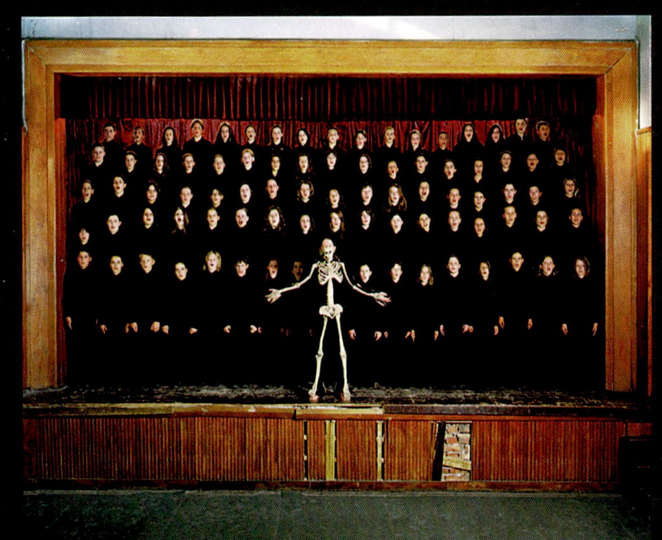
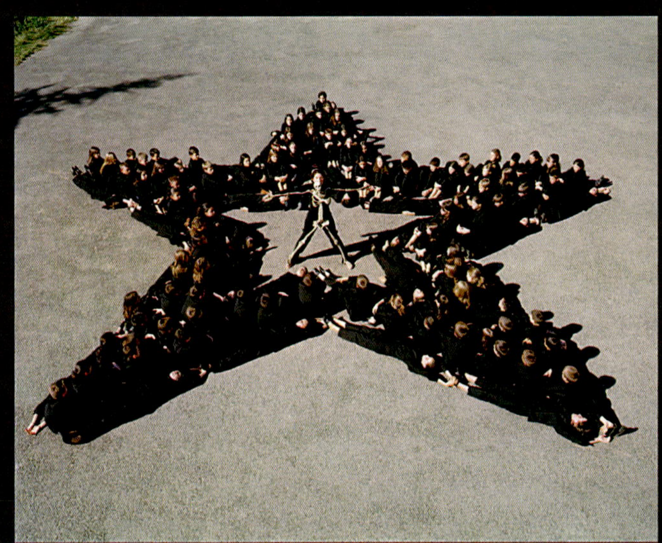

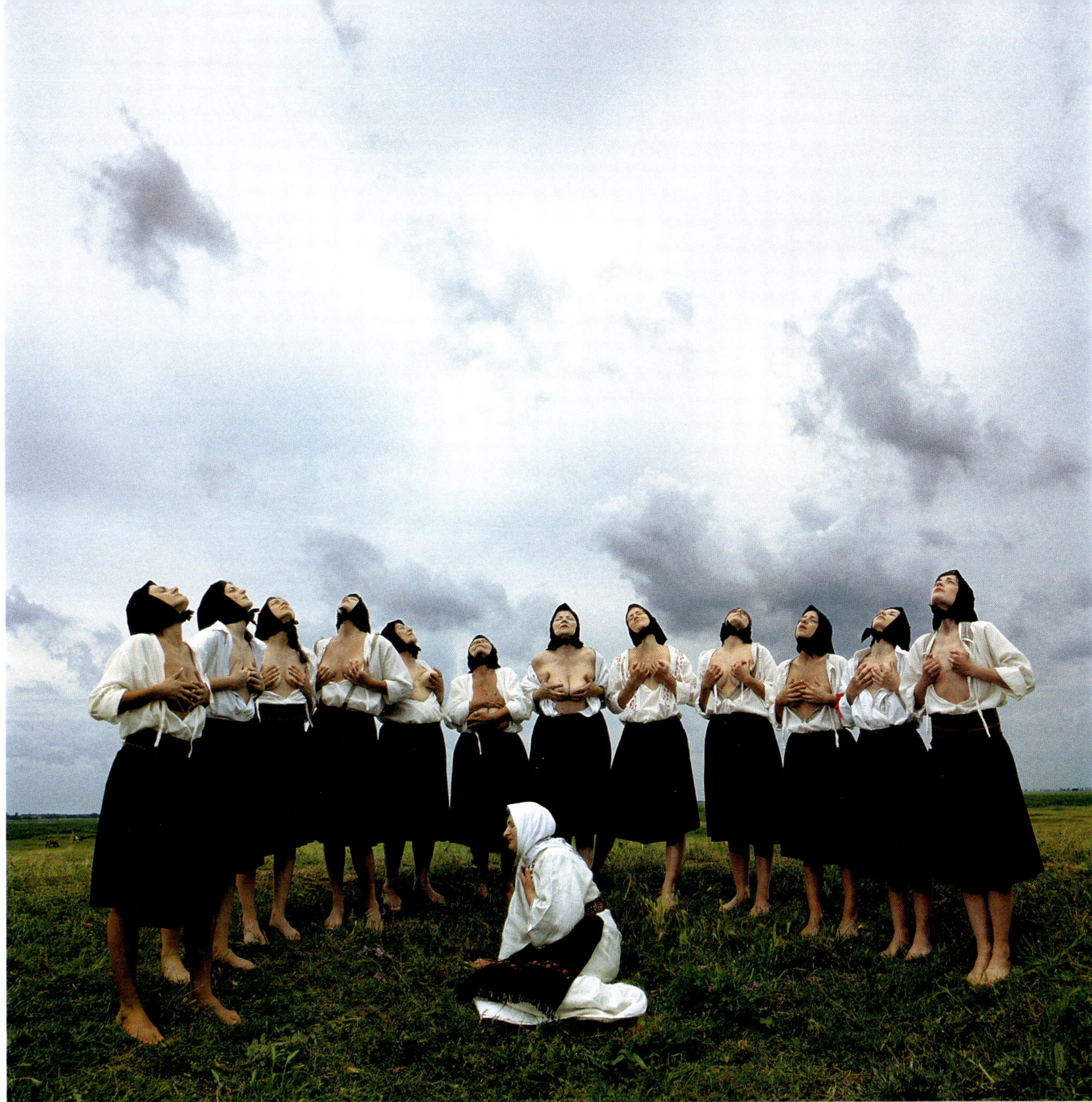

Marina Abramović

OPPOSITE, TOP
Balkan Baroque, 1997
Performance, 4 days, 6 hours
Three-channel video installation, 4 min 13 sec
47th Venice Biennale

OPPOSITE, CENTER
Cleaning the Mirror I, 1995
Performance for video, 3 hours
Oxford University

OPPOSITE, BOTTOM
Count on Us (Chorus), 2003
Five-channel video installation, 12 min

ABOVE
Women in the Rain (II), 2005
From the series, *Balkan Erotic Epic*
C-print

I had lots of issues as a child, and lots of fears. I was incredibly self-conscious; I couldn't even walk on the street if somebody was behind me and I heard their footsteps. I had lots of problems with my blood. I had to be in a hospital for almost one year when I was only six years old. So when I began to do performance I really wanted to overcome my fears and push my physical limits as far as I could go—to see that I had the power of mind over body. That was very important. And it was important, of course, to rebel against my circumstances—the family, social, and Communist background, and my old professors of art who believed in a type of art in which I didn't—and to think in different ways. Coming from former Yugoslavia and an 'interesting' family background, in which mother and father were Communist atheists, grandmother a religious fanatic, and grandfather a saint of the Orthodox Church, was a kind of unbeatable combination, full of contradictions, from which to grow as an artist. When I left Yugoslavia, I wanted to go as far as I could, so I completely embraced different cultures. Now, in the last ten or fifteen years, because I'm so far from my background I have a much bigger picture of it than I had when I was there. So I've started dealing with symbols from my culture and created a whole series of works like *Balkan Baroque* (1997), *Balkan Erotic Epic* (2005), and *Count On Us* (2003), which really address my background again.

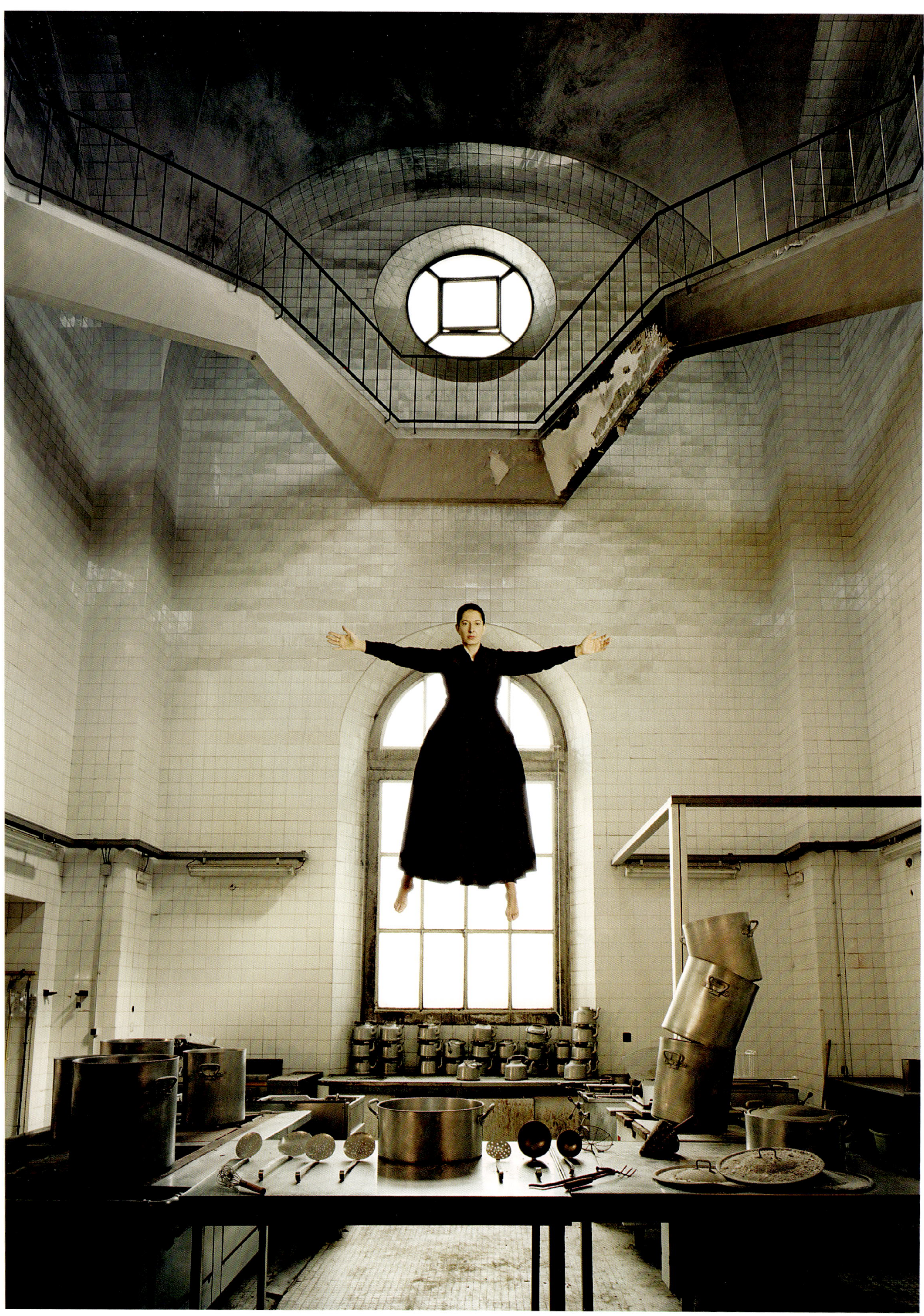

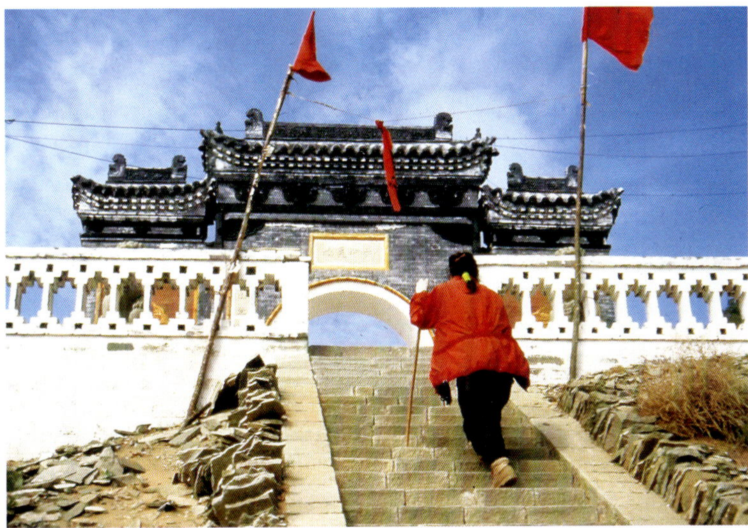

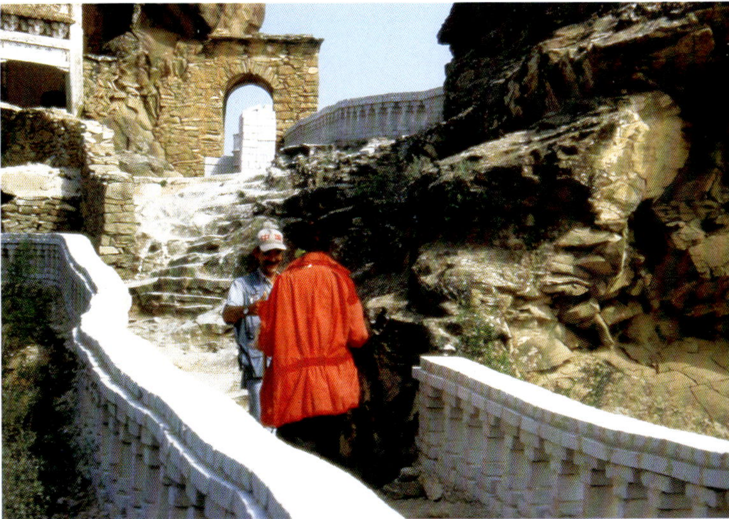

Marina Abramović

OPPOSITE
The Kitchen I, 2009
From the series, *The Kitchen—Homage to Saint Therese*
Color Lambda print

Marina Abramović and Ulay

ABOVE
The Great Wall Walk, 1988
Performance, 90 days
The Great Wall of China

Should my pieces be re-performed by others? As I open this subject, it's important to see which pieces I can or cannot permit to be performed. Now there is *Second Life*, and I am giving permission for all my pieces to be performed there because *Second Life* doesn't include a human presence. But if there is a human presence in any piece that has the potential of harming the performer, I will not give permission. But otherwise any piece, even if it's connected to me emotionally, can be performed by someone else. Take *The Great Wall Walk:* this was related to my whole history and a man I loved. It was personal, not only artistically but also on the private level. This was *my* story. If anybody does the piece again, it will be their story, but the bones of the piece will be the same: two people walking from the two ends of the Great Wall to meet in the middle and say goodbye. There will be a new story, but I will give permission for that. It's very important how you see the ego of an artist (mostly, artists suffer from too much of it). Ego can be like a mountain: when you have ego in front of your work you actually suffocate it. So I understand that this is important for me—to give permission to liberate my works from my ego. They can have their own life on their own, like children. And this is the attitude that I have about a theatre piece that Charles Atlas and I conceived in 1989. The idea is to give up control—to give up all the elements of a piece and let somebody else actually make a new mix (*The Biography Remix*, 2004). When I do my performances, I'm in complete control. But when it comes to whether the piece should have a next life, I have to give up control. And giving up control is one of the hardest things an artist can do in his lifetime.

So many times I've been asked how it came about that I made a theatre piece—because it's so different from performance. Performance people hated theatre, especially in the '70s, and theatre was a huge enemy—the black box with people sitting in the dark, where a knife was not a knife, blood was not blood, and everything's always fake. And then what happened was that I ended up playing my own life and art. It's a complete contradiction. I had finished walking the Great Wall of China and said goodbye to my partner, Ulay. It was one of the most painful moments of my life and I really didn't know where to turn. Spanish television was making very short (four-minute) biographies with different artists and filmmakers. And this sent to me Charles Atlas, a person I'd never met before. We were so different, from two different parts of the world. I was all about *minimal*—one thing at a time. Charlie was about *layers*—putting things together. What could we do with biography, in only four minutes? I said, "Maybe we can do one thing, like I'm washing my feet and that's my life. . . . Or I can have a head full of snakes and look into the camera, and talk about my life. . . ." I was waiting for Charlie to tell me what he was going to pick up. He looked at me and said, "All of it." In the end, it was really interesting because it was the most complicated thing I'd ever done and the most minimal he'd ever done. We met in the middle. A year or two later we came together again and said, "Why not actually stage this biography in a theatre context?" And that's how this biography was born. I took it as a kind of model, and every five, six, seven years I ask another director to direct my 'life' to see what he will do with this material. The only thing we never change is the beginning with the very apocalyptic image that Charles Atlas conceived: I'm hanging on a cross, holding two snakes in my hands, and under me there are dogs eating bones (eating my past or future, whatever you want to say). And then a singer comes onto the scene and sings about life and beyond. Then the biography starts. Now I'm doing the new version (*The Life and Death of Marina Abramović*, 2011), in which I add my own funeral. Robert Wilson is going to stage it.

Marina Abramović

BELOW
The Biography Remix, 2004
Performance
Directed by Michale Laub
The Romaeuropa Festival, Rome

OPPOSITE
The Life and Death of Marina Abramović, 2011
Performance
Directed by Robert Wilson
Manchester International Festival

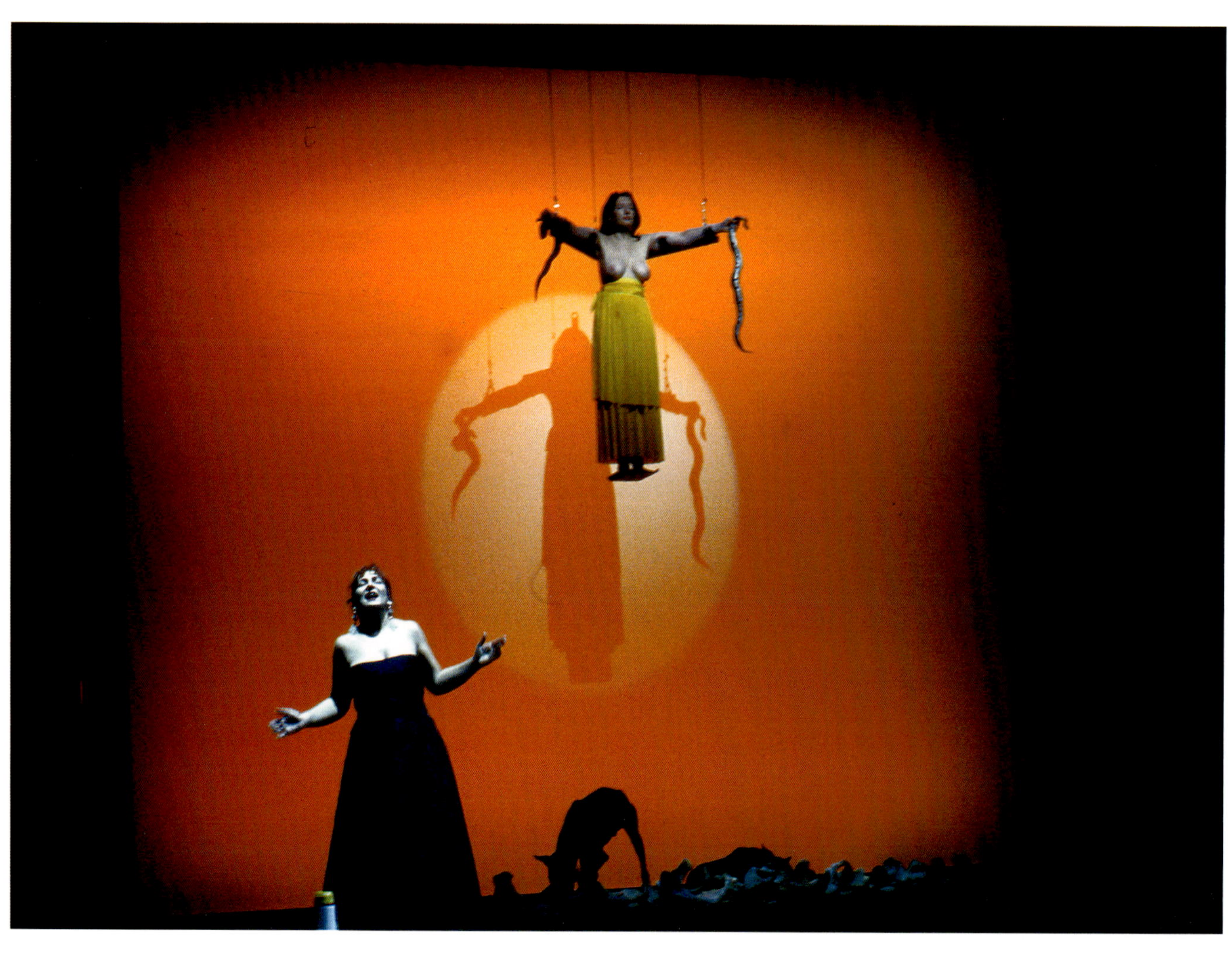

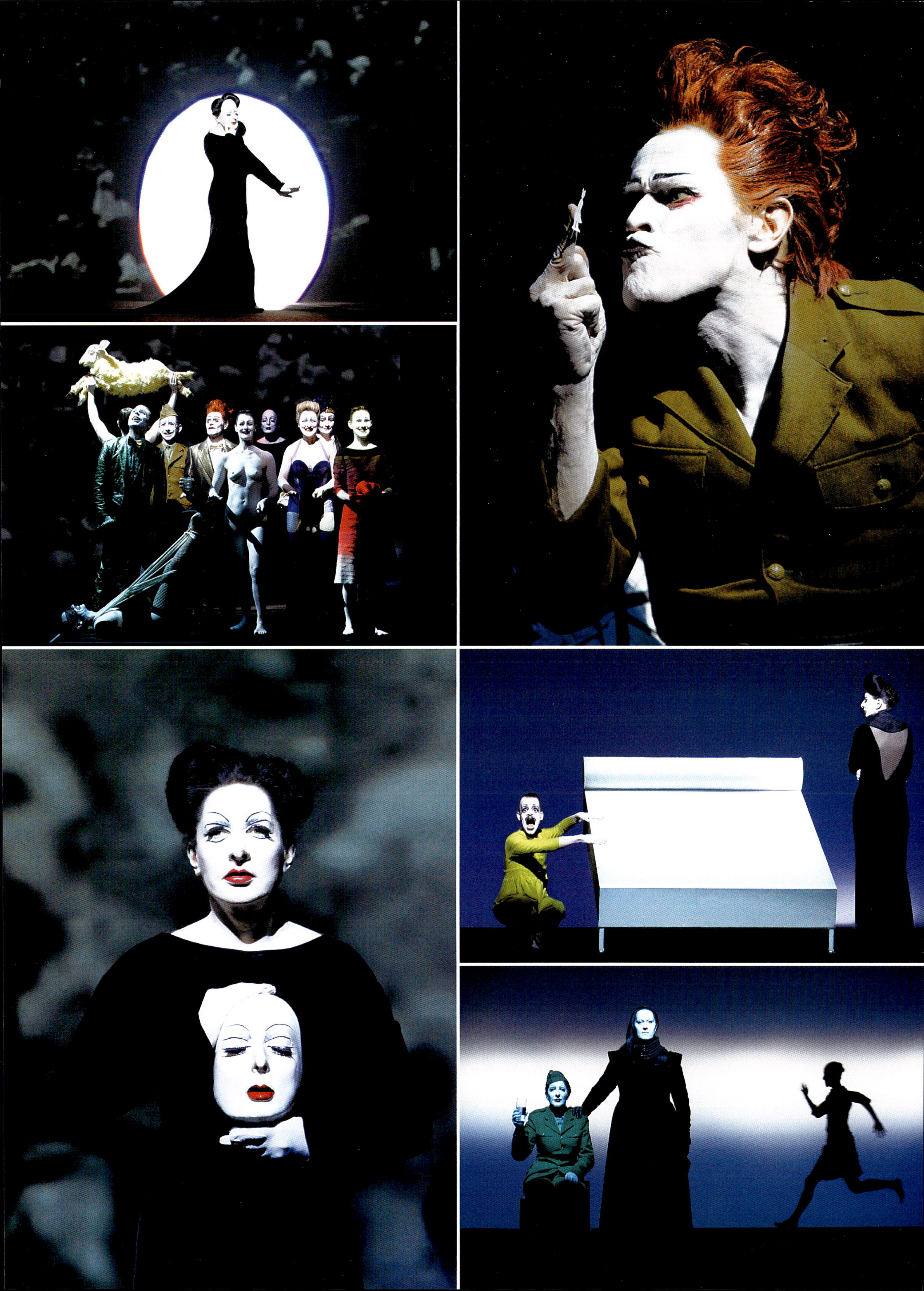

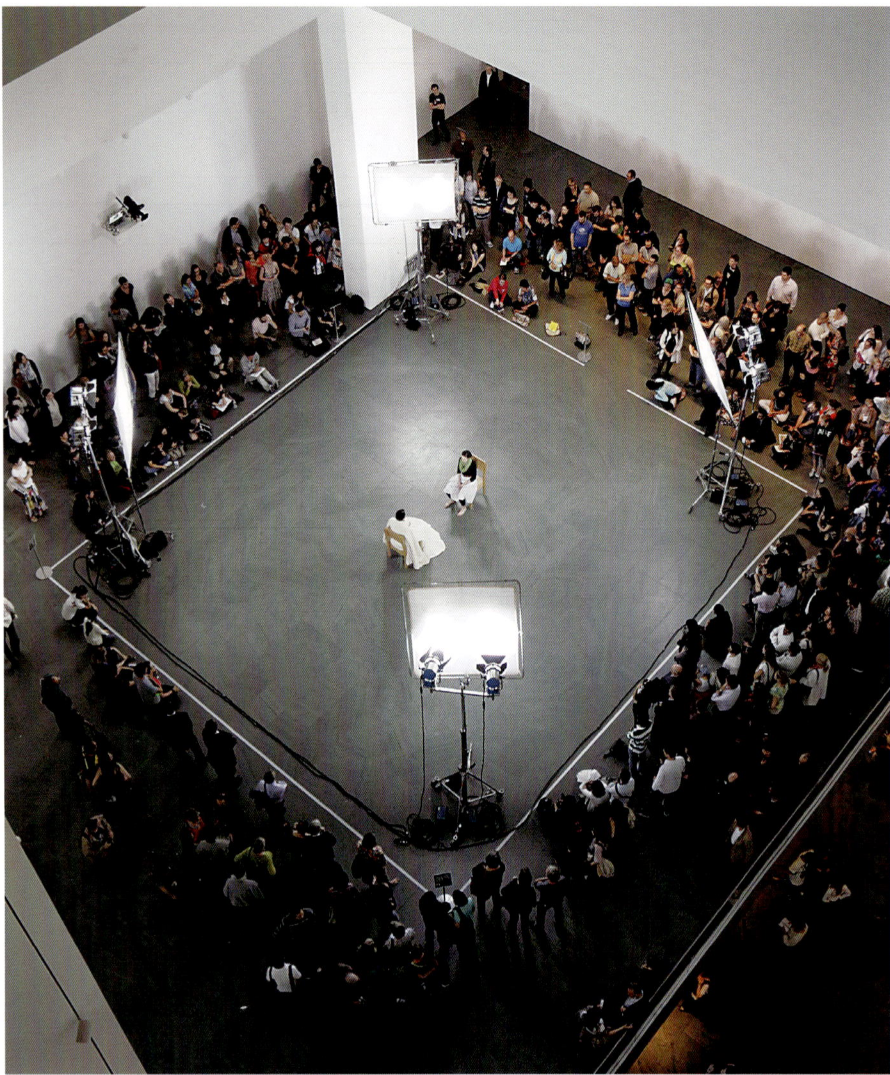
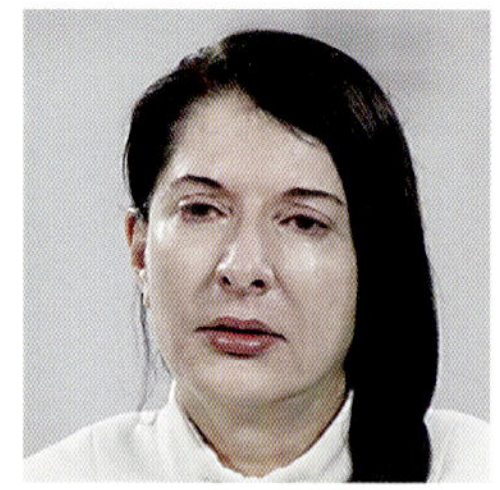
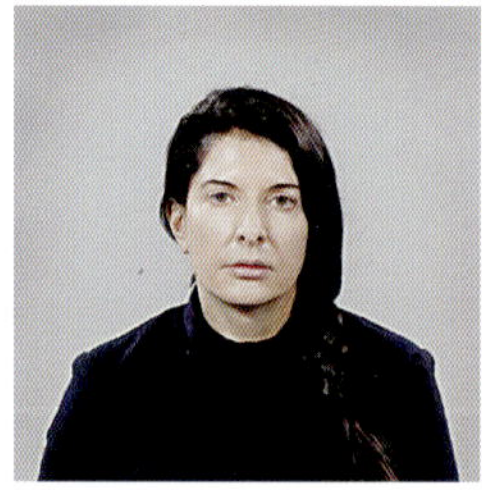
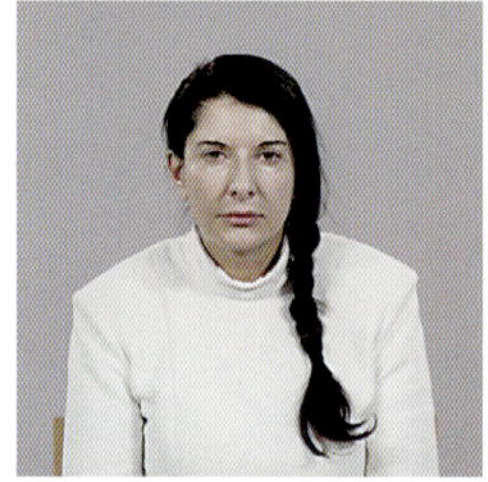
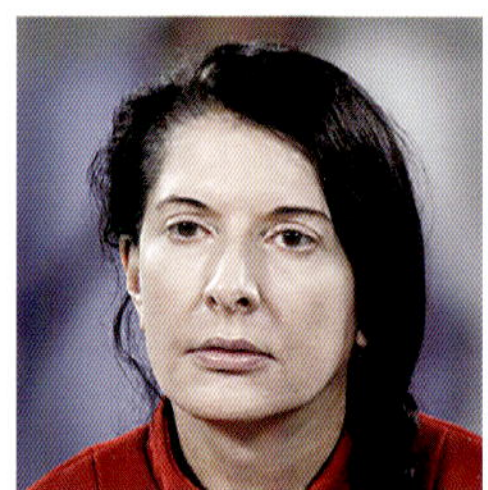

Marina Abramović

ABOVE AND OPPOSITE
The Artist Is Present, 2010
Performance, 3 months
The Museum of Modern Art, New York

What is my function on this earth, anyway? What is the role of an artist? In many ways I sacrificed my entire life to be an artist. No family; no children. Being an artist is a huge responsibility. I don't think it's just about being in the studio, creating the work and not caring what's going on around you and in the world. In my case, somehow, I created three groups of work. I call the first "artist body," and it's just very simple. It's me performing in front of an audience. The second is "public body"—creating objects (I call them 'transitory' because they're not sculptures) and circumstances, which the public can actually perform and experience for themselves. The third would be "student body"—my function as a teacher. You come to a point in your life when you really have to transfer knowledge unconditionally to a younger generation of artists—and not only transfer knowledge, but also help them in their development. If, when I make my performances or any kind of event, I see only my generation coming, I know that I am doing very badly. But if ninety percent of the audience is a younger generation, I know that my life and my work are a living form of art, and it's going well. Art has to be so many different things. It has to have many layers of meaning. If art is only political, it's just one layer—one day you're dealing with one piece of news and the next day it is old. Like an old newspaper, you just throw it away and the art has no meaning anymore. So you have to have a new arc, and a new political and spiritual element. And you have to be disturbing, ask questions, and predict the future. And all these layers can be in one piece. If you have the layers, then the piece of art can have many lives. The whole idea is how you can have many lives in the performance, too.

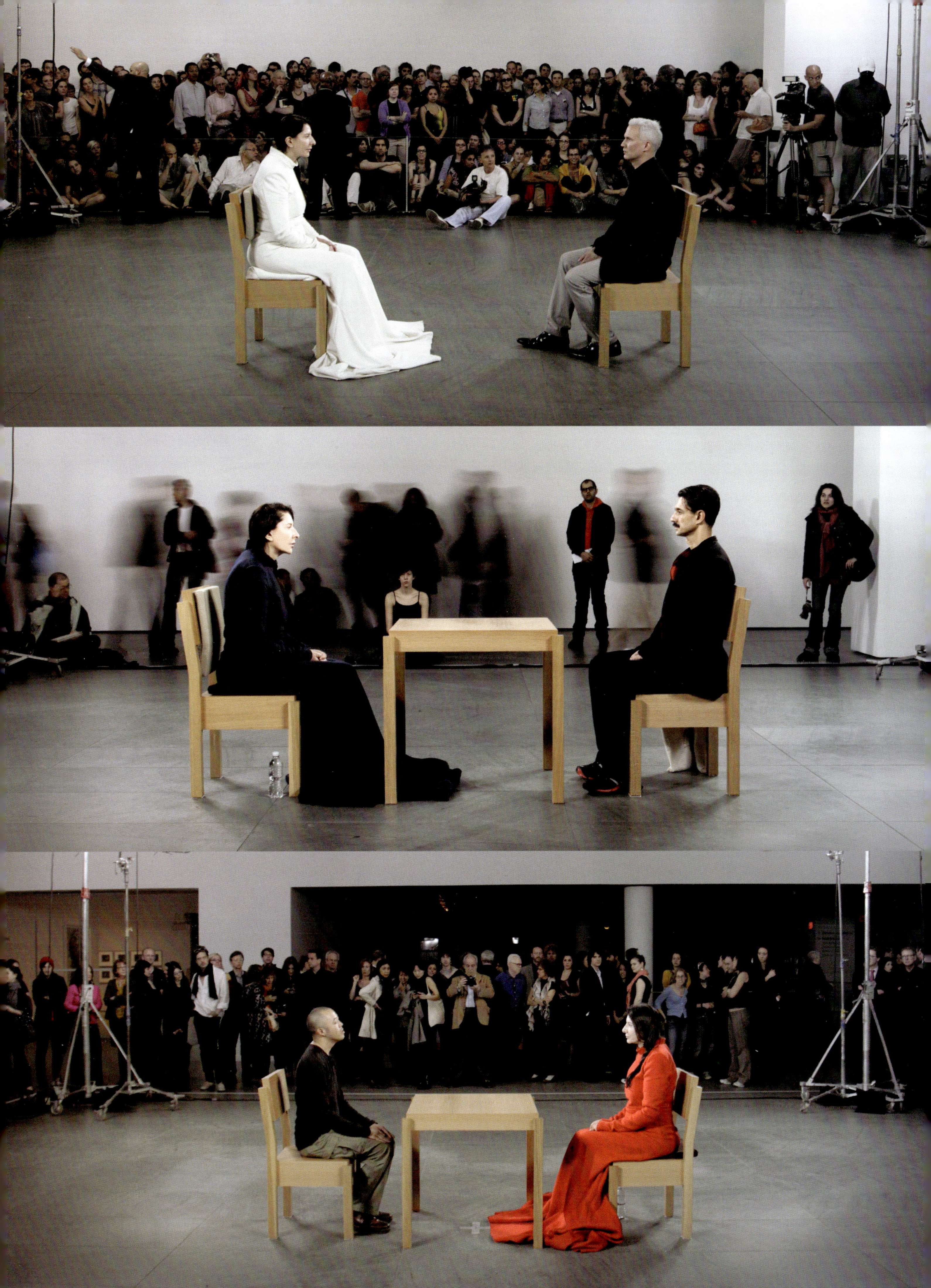

Glenn Ligon

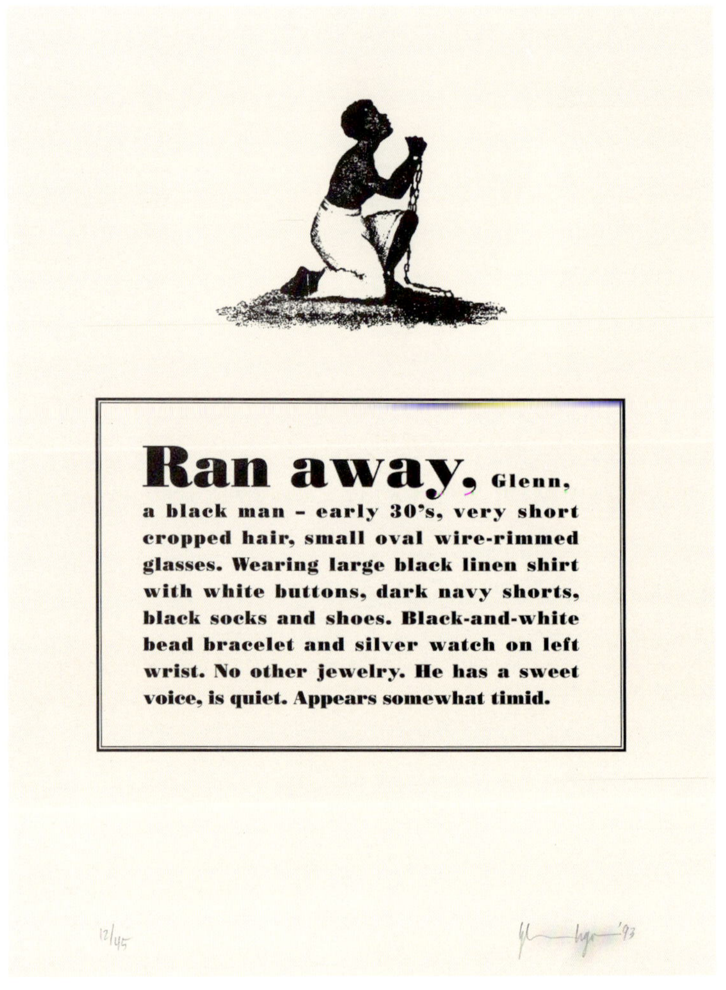

ABOVE
Runaways, detail, 1993
Suite of 10 lithographs, 16 x 12 inches each
Edition of 45, 10 AP

OPPOSITE
Endless Column/Nu Nile (Yellow), 1985
Synthetic polymer, ink, and graphite on paper, 22 1/8 x 15 1/4 inches
Collection of the artist

The artists that I was interested in when I first started working were Willem de Kooning, Franz Kline, Jackson Pollock—that whole generation of Abstract Expressionists. I wanted to be an Abstract Expressionist. That's what my paintings looked like when I was in high school and college. Later on I became interested in people who had a different kind of content in their work—Jasper Johns, Rauschenberg—people who brought letters, numbers, and images into the work. Then I became interested in conceptual artists—Joseph Kosuth, Barbara Kruger, Jenny Holzer—people who were interested in the social context in which art operates, or in its political context. So all of those things melted together in my head and produced the trajectory of the artworks that I make now. At a certain moment I decided that being an Abstract Expressionist wasn't quite going to do it, and that produced a kind of crisis in the studio. I decided to incorporate the things that I was thinking about, the things I was reading, into the work directly. And when I first started doing that, I was just going to use my handwriting. After a while I decided, "No, I'm interested in what other people have to say. I'm not interested in telling my own stories." So the work became more about quotation—using texts from various literary sources—making letters with stencils in order to have a little bit of distance from the source material or from the notion of handwriting and self-expression. There's nothing wrong with self-expression. It just has its limits. The things that I was interested in were already in the world so they didn't need me to create them again. They just needed to be brought into the work. And, you know, I'm starting to make work at a moment when appropriation is in the air, when artists are using the stuff of the world—newspaper articles, magazine photos—trying to think about how this stuff has any relationship to the art world. My interest was a little bit different than that because I'm making paintings. They're not directly based on media images.

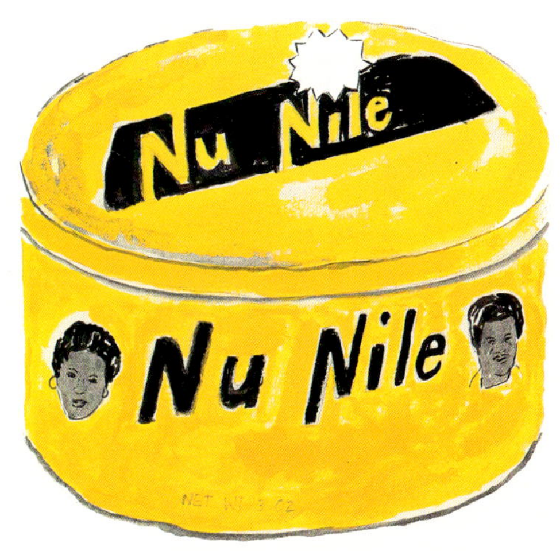
Nu Nile
Nu Nile

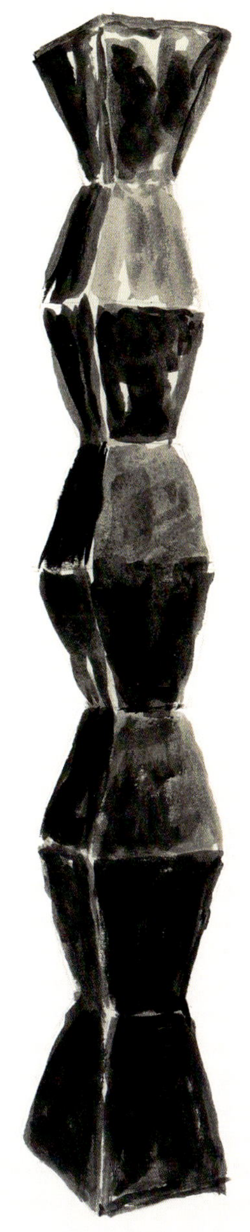

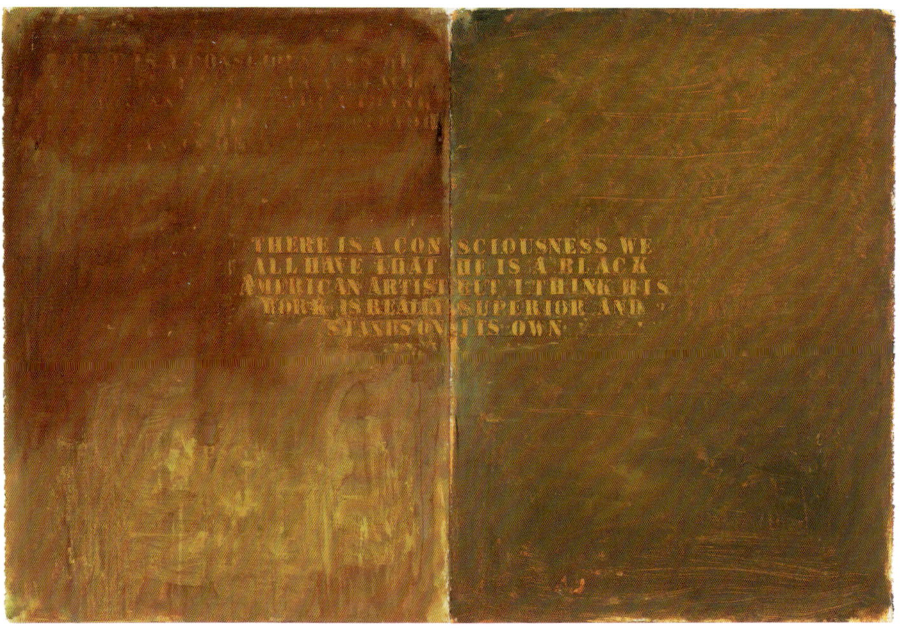

Glenn Ligon

ABOVE
Untitled (There Is a Consciousness We All Have . . .), 1988
Oil, synthetic polymer, oil stick, and graphite on two sheets of paper, 30 x 44¾ inches overall
Collection of the Museum of Modern Art, New York, gift of Jan Christiaan Braun in honor of Agnes Gund

OPPOSITE, LEFT
Untitled (I'm Turning Into a Specter Before Your Very Eyes and I'm Going to Haunt You), 1992
Oil stick, gesso, and graphite on canvas, 80⅛ x 32⅛ x 2 inches
Collection of the Philadelphia Museum of Art, purchased with the Adele Haas Turner and Beatrice Pastorius Turner Memorial Fund, 1992

OPPOSITE, RIGHT
Untitled (I Feel Most Colored When I Am Thrown Against a Sharp White Background), 1990
Oil, oil stick, gesso, and graphite on wood, 80 x 30 inches
Collection of Eileen Harris-Norton

The first text paintings I made were single sentences by Zora Neale Hurston, a writer of the Harlem Renaissance. I was using plastic letter stencils and oil crayons—using single sentences, quotes from her essays—to make paintings. I thought I wanted to have very clean edges on those letters. But if you make letters using oil paint and plastic letter stencils, they aren't clean. Oil paint wants to spread out. If you're using stencils you're trying to make something with a sharp boundary. But oil crayons want to break out of those boundaries. They're messy; they don't keep their shape. For about six months I tried to figure out how to make these oil crayons make nice neat letters. Then I realized that the fact that they didn't make nice neat letters was actually much more interesting, and that the act of writing these sentences over and over again and the oil stick spreading out, smearing, smudging, and transforming these letters into abstraction was what the paintings were about. But it took six months to figure that out. At some moment, I realized that the thing that I was struggling against was the thing that the painting was about. It was about the messiness of the letters, the fact that they changed. If you're making a painting with letters and those letters are from a sentence from an essay, and the letters sit on that canvas very neatly, they're not so different than the book that you got them from. The fact that the letters that I was using became very messy, smudgy, almost abstractions, meant to me that I was taking that text and making it do something else—almost teasing out of it some other meanings. That happens not only through the transition from legible to illegible text, but also through the way that the lines are broken at the edge of the canvas. In a painting that has a text that repeats from top to bottom, you know what it says at the top (and even though it's harder to read at the bottom you still know what it says). That the ghost of that meaning is still there at the bottom, and that you bring that knowledge of what you've read to this very abstract thing, was all interesting to me. If you make a text painting, it wants to be read. If you make a text painting that becomes difficult to read, it creates tension in the viewer. He or she wants to read it, but can't. I find that difficulty productive. Often, the texts weren't easy; they were about difficult things. And so the way the paintings were made had to reflect that difficulty.

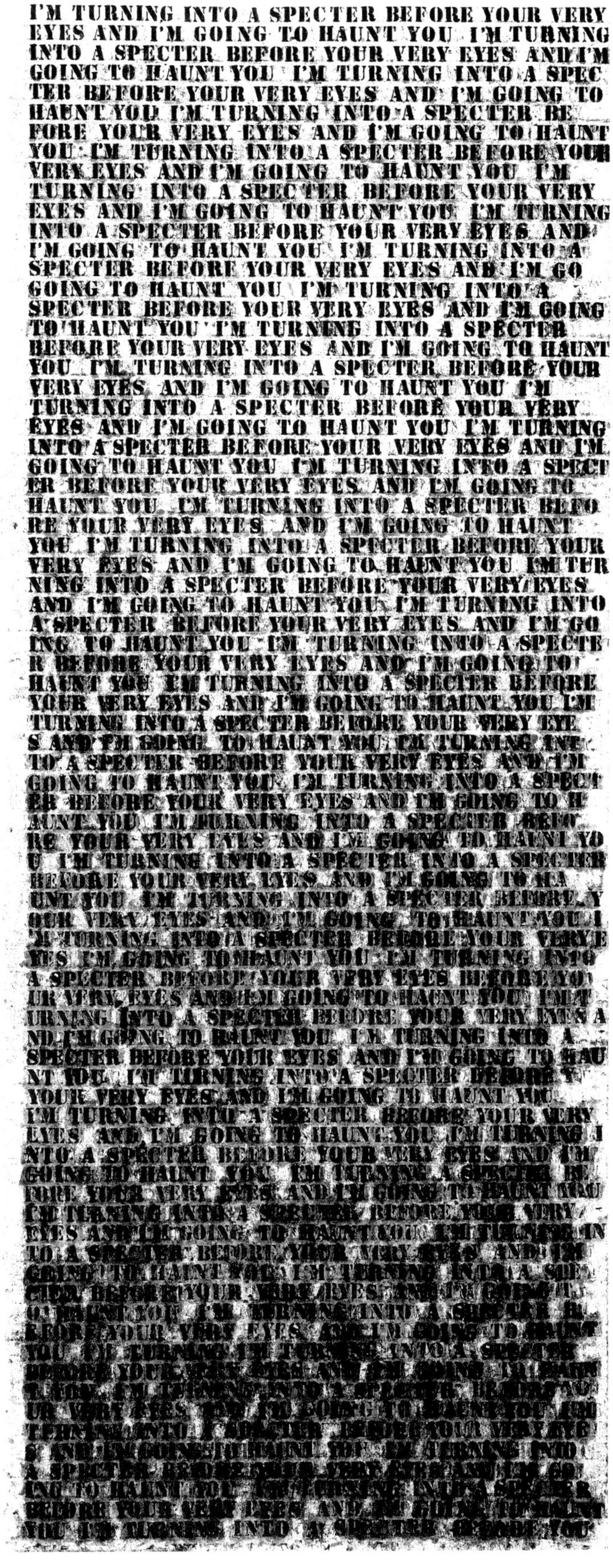

I'M TURNING INTO A SPECTER BEFORE YOUR VERY
EYES AND I'M GOING TO HAUNT YOU I'M TURNING
INTO A SPECTER BEFORE YOUR VERY EYES AND I'M
GOING TO HAUNT YOU I'M TURNING INTO A SPEC
TER BEFORE YOUR VERY EYES AND I'M GOING TO
HAUNT YOU I'M TURNING INTO A SPECTER BE
FORE YOUR VERY EYES AND I'M GOING TO HAUNT
YOU I'M TURNING INTO A SPECTER BEFORE YOUR
VERY EYES AND I'M GOING TO HAUNT YOU I'M
TURNING INTO A SPECTER BEFORE YOUR VERY
EYES AND I'M GOING TO HAUNT YOU I'M TURNING
INTO A SPECTER BEFORE YOUR VERY EYES AND
I'M GOING TO HAUNT YOU I'M TURNING INTO A
SPECTER BEFORE YOUR VERY EYES AND I'M GO
GOING TO HAUNT YOU I'M TURNING INTO A
SPECTER BEFORE YOUR VERY EYES AND I'M GOING
TO HAUNT YOU I'M TURNING INTO A SPECTER
BEFORE YOUR VERY EYES AND I'M GOING TO HAUNT
YOU I'M TURNING INTO A SPECTER BEFORE YOUR
VERY EYES AND I'M GOING TO HAUNT YOU I'M
TURNING INTO A SPECTER BEFORE YOUR VERY
EYES AND I'M GOING TO HAUNT YOU I'M TURNING
INTO A SPECTER BEFORE YOUR VERY EYES AND I'M
GOING TO HAUNT YOU I'M TURNING INTO A SPECT
ER BEFORE YOUR VERY EYES AND I'M GOING TO
HAUNT YOU I'M TURNING INTO A SPECTER BEFO
RE YOUR VERY EYES AND I'M GOING TO HAUNT
YOU I'M TURNING INTO A SPECTER BEFORE YOUR
VERY EYES AND I'M GOING TO HAUNT YOU I'M TUR
NING INTO A SPECTER BEFORE YOUR VERY EYES
AND I'M GOING TO HAUNT YOU I'M TURNING INTO
A SPECTER BEFORE YOUR VERY EYES AND I'M GO
ING TO HAUNT YOU I'M TURNING INTO A SPECTE
R BEFORE YOUR VERY EYES AND I'M GOING TO
HAUNT YOU I'M TURNING INTO A SPECTER BEFORE
YOUR VERY EYES AND I'M GOING TO HAUNT YOU I'M
TURNING INTO A SPECTER BEFORE YOUR VERY EYE
S AND I'M GOING TO HAUNT YOU I'M TURNING INT
O A SPECTER BEFORE YOUR VERY EYES AND I'M
GOING TO HAUNT YOU I'M TURNING INTO A SPECT
ER BEFORE YOUR VERY EYES AND I'M GOING TO H
AUNT YOU I'M TURNING INTO A SPECTER BEFO
RE YOUR VERY EYES AND I'M GOING TO HAUNT YO
U I'M TURNING INTO A SPECTER INTO A SPECTER
BEFORE YOUR VERY EYES AND I'M GOING TO HA
UNT YOU I'M TURNING INTO A SPECTER BEFORE Y
OUR VERY EYES AND I'M GOING TO HAUNT YOU I

I FEEL MOST COLORED WHEN I AM THROWN
AGAINST A SHARP WHITE BACKGROUND. I
FEEL MOST COLORED WHEN I AM THROWN
AGAINST A SHARP WHITE BACKGROUND.
I FEEL MOST COLORED WHEN I AM THROWN
AGAINST A SHARP WHITE BACKGROUND. I
FEEL MOST COLORED WHEN I AM THROWN
AGAINST A SHARP WHITE BACKGROUND. I
FEEL MOST COLORED WHEN I AM THROWN A
GAINST A SHARP WHITE BACKGROUND. I
FEEL MOST COLORED WHEN I AM THROWN A
GAINST A SHARP WHITE BACKGROUND. I FEEL
MOST COLORED WHEN I AM THROWN AGAINST
A SHARP WHITE BACKGROUND. I FEEL MOST
COLORED WHEN I AM THROWN AGAINST A
SHARP WHITE BACKGROUND. I FEEL MOST
COLORED WHEN I AM THROWN AGAINST A
SHARP WHITE BACKGROUND. I FEEL MOST CO
LORED WHEN I AM THROWN AGAINST A SHARP
WHITE BACKGROUND. I FEEL MOST COLORED
WHEN I AM THROWN AGAINST A SHARP WHITE
BACKGROUND. I FEEL MOST COLORED WHEN
I AM THROWN AGAINST A SHARP WHITE BACK
GROUND. I FEEL MOST COLORED WHEN I
AM THROWN AGAINST A SHARP WHITE BACK
GROUND. I FEEL MOST COLORED WHEN I AM
THROWN AGAINST A SHARP WHITE BACKGRO
UND. I FEEL MOST COLORED WHEN I AM
THROWN AGAINST A SHARP WHITE BACKGROU
ND. I FEEL MOST COLORED WHEN I AM THROW
N AGAINST A SHARP WHITE BACKGROUND. I
FEEL MOST COLORED WHEN I AM THROWN

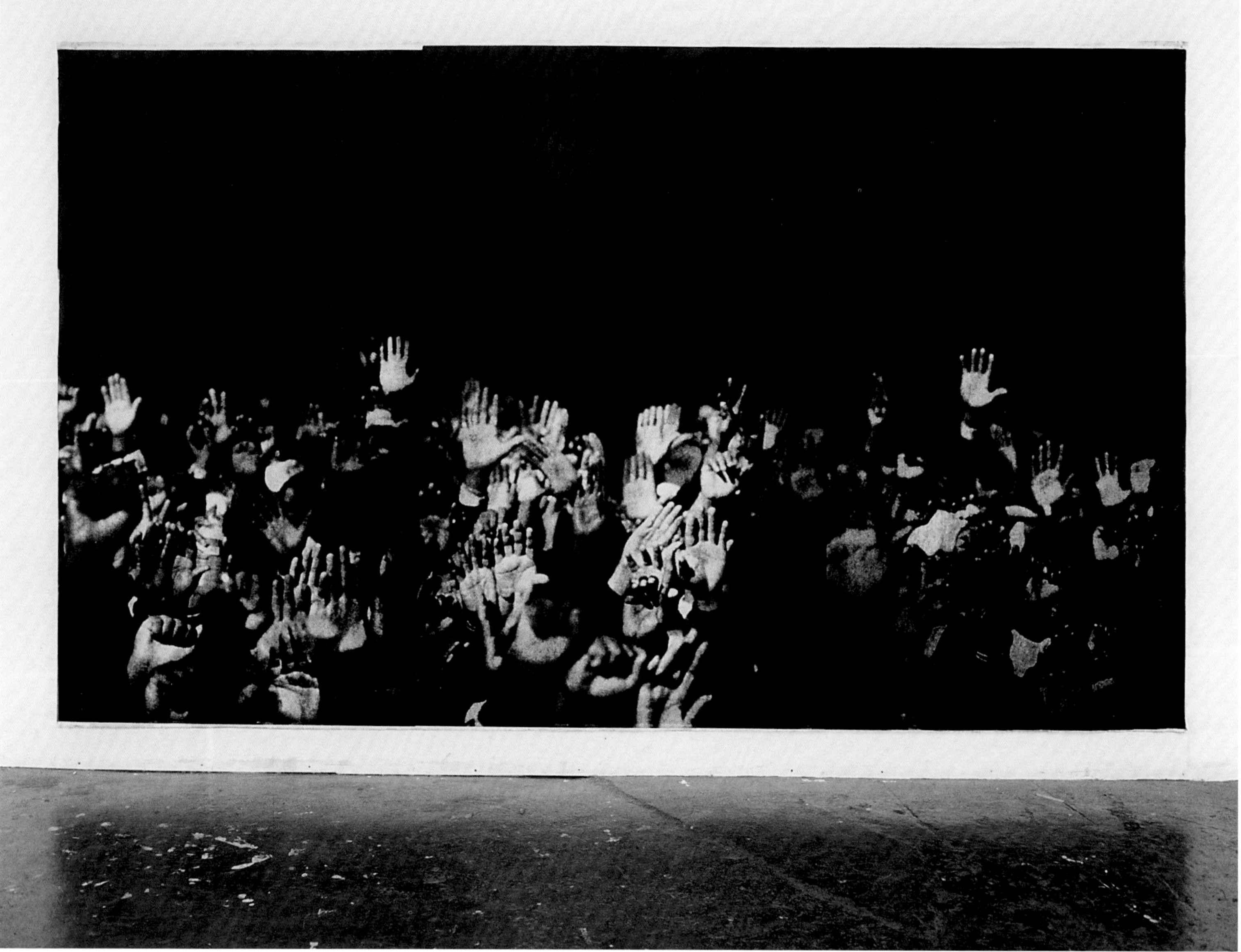

Glenn Ligon

ABOVE
Hands, 1996
Silkscreen ink and gesso on unstretched canvas, 82 x 144 inches
Collection of Eileen Harris Norton

OPPOSITE
Ice Cube's Eyes, 1995
Silkscreen ink on canvas punching bag, 51 x 14 x 15 inches
Private collection

Paintings are hard work. I don't love making paintings. But I think artists make things because they can't really do anything else. So often, when I'm struggling on a canvas and it's not working out and I've been working for months, I think, "Why am I doing this?" It's not love, but it's that artworks are ideas. And art and ideas take a long time to be born—a long time to gestate. So I guess what I'm committed to is not love of painting, but love of the idea of making ideas. That's what an artist does—sit around all day thinking about things and making things that are about ideas. I'd rather be doing that than anything else. The struggle's always about what you want to say versus the means you have to say it with—or your abilities or skills or the technical limitations of the medium you're working in. So there's always the ideal painting in your head, and you never quite get to that. You make something: it's almost there; it's not quite right. You make something else: it's almost there; it's not quite right. Eventually that is the process, and you just keep going with that. That sort of dissatisfaction—the desire to say something better, to make an image or a text work better in a painting, to say more than you've said before, to go out on limbs, to be adventurous, to not bore yourself—is what keeps you going. That's the struggle.

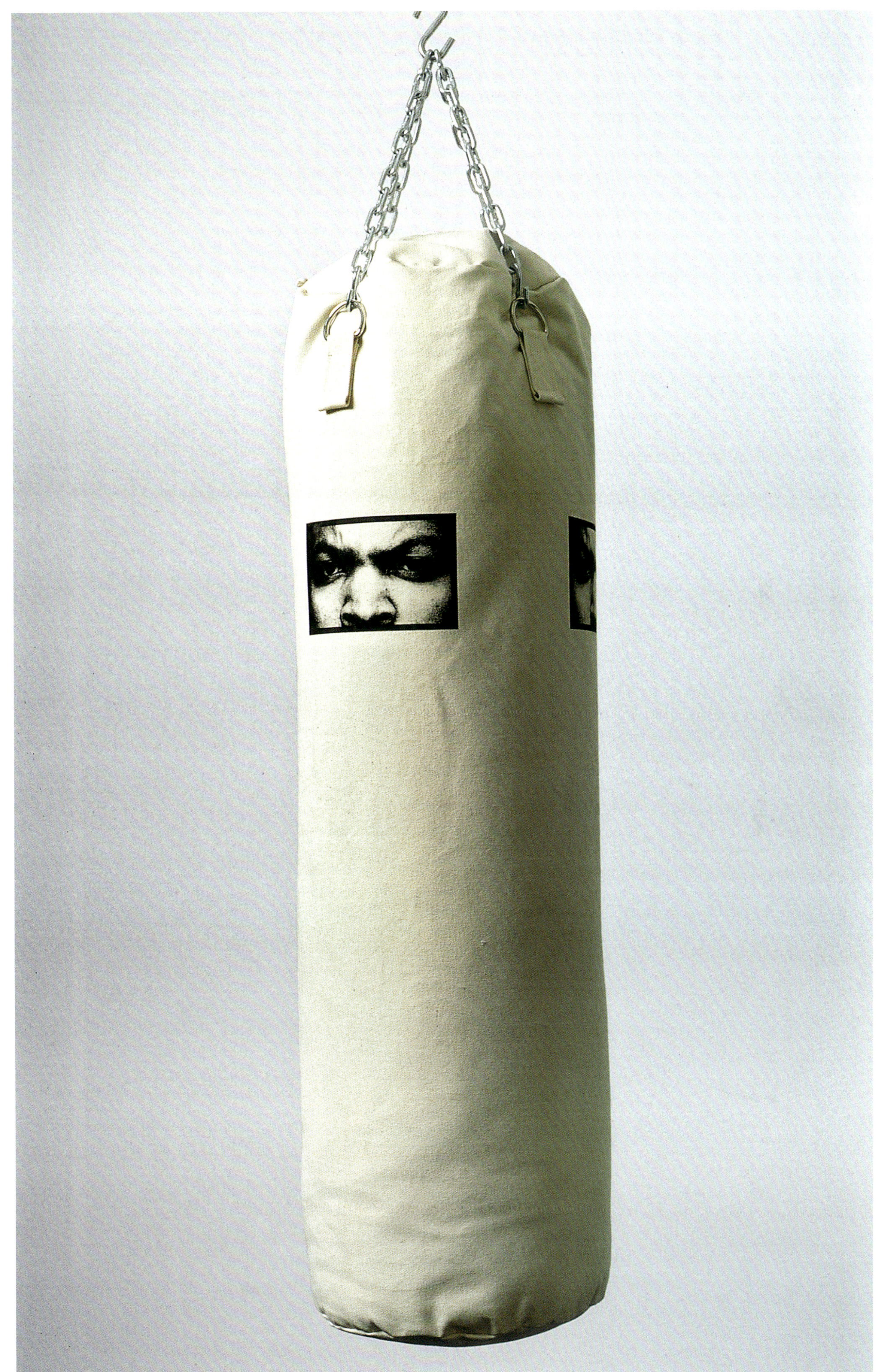

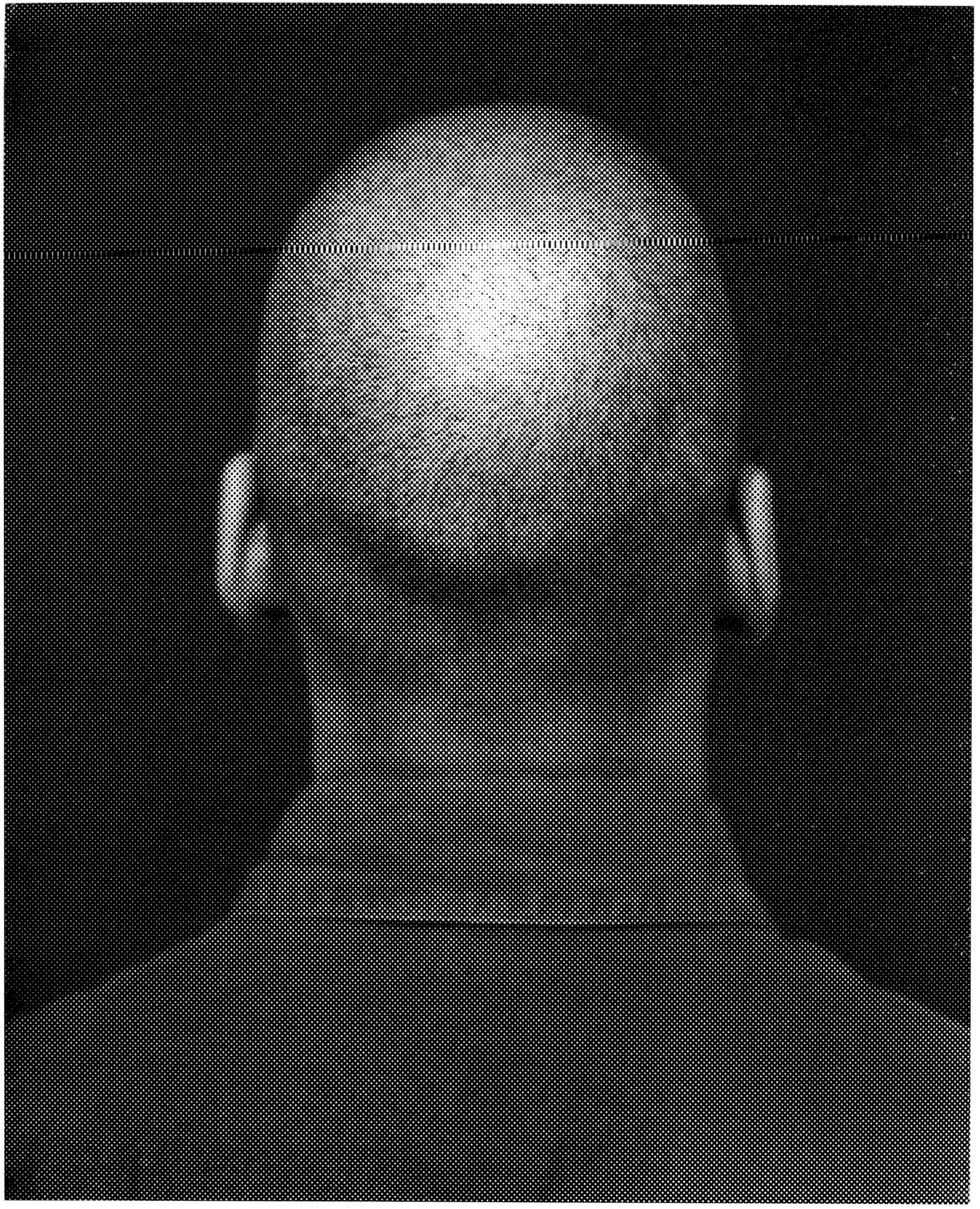

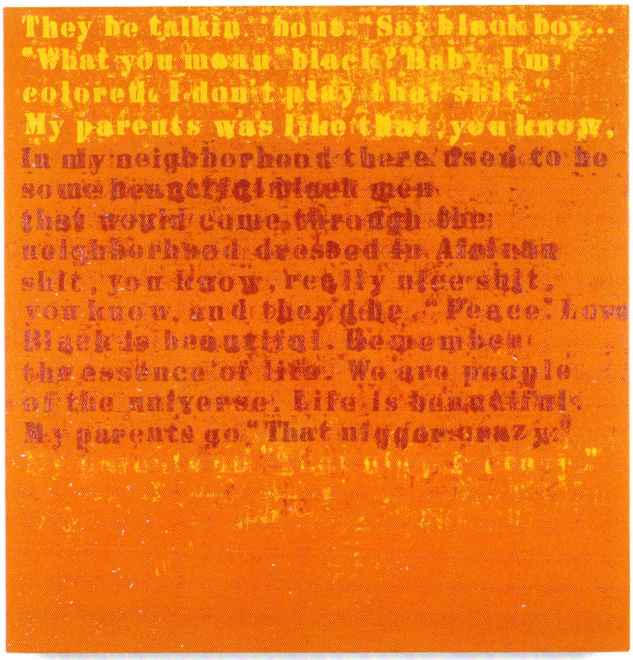

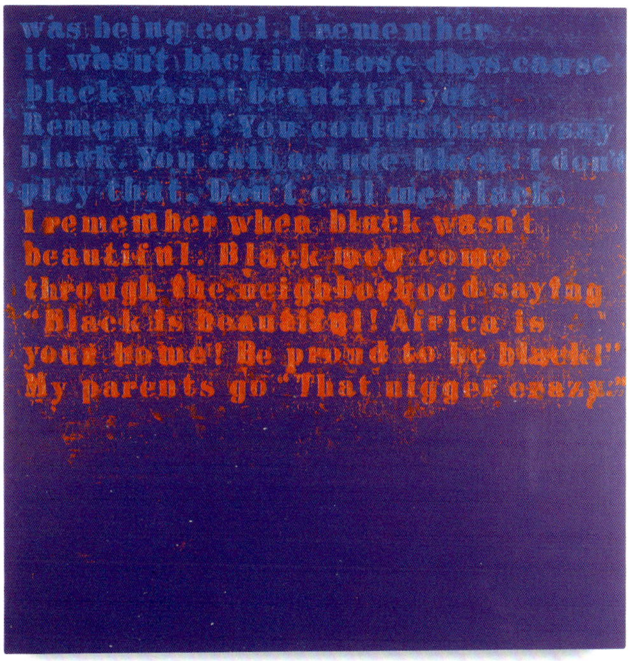

Glenn Ligon

OPPOSITE
Self-Portrait, 1996
Silkscreen ink and gesso on canvas,
48 x 40 inches
Collection of the artist

LEFT
In My Neighborhood #1, 2004
Oil and acrylic on canvas, 32 x 32 inches

RIGHT
When Black Wasn't Beautiful #1, 2004
Oil and acrylic on canvas, 30 x 30 inches
Collection of Susan Hancock

Artworks operate on different levels. When you go to a museum and look at a Renaissance painting, for example, you look at a painting that's about a story. For many people, that story is not present. But there are levels on which you understand that painting because it depicts a scene, or it's beautiful. But it's richer if you know the story that it's based on. And I think the same with my paintings. One can approach a painting simply as an object that has a certain kind of beauty or as an object that has a text in it, that has different levels of legibility so it's a struggle to read. If one knows that the text in the painting is from an essay, then that opens up the painting in a certain way. It gives it a different level of meaning. But I don't think that the paintings are about everyone knowing everything at the same moment. I think they're like any artwork. It's a discovery. The things that I looked at when I was sixteen, when I was walking around museums on my own, read very differently to me now that I'm fifty. My appreciation is different because I know the stories behind them. But I don't think that's crucial. Things become richer if you know more, but it's not like they're 'un-rich' if you don't.

Some of the key works in the Whitney show (2011) are the text paintings that take single sentences from essays by Zora Neale Hurston, Ralph Ellison, and Walt Whitman and repeat those sentences down door-sized panels. Those were the paintings that started the whole trajectory of using text in my work. The Richard Pryor paintings are key for me because they allowed me to reintroduce color. If you use jokes by a comedian like Richard Pryor they need to be jokes in color. So the paintings had to have color in them. But they allowed me to go back to my Abstract Expressionist days, too, when I made paintings that were very colorful. Paint is a very sensual material. It's lovely to work with and lovely to look at. De Kooning said it was invented to depict flesh. I don't depict flesh in my paintings, but I use it to depict text, to depict words. It's also inefficient. We're used to images, magazines, and newspapers. We're used to seeing text printed. We're not used to seeing text made out of paint. And there's a kind of slowness and inefficiency about rendering text in paint that's interesting to me. It slows your reading down, and it slows the viewer down. We're in a world that's very fast, so things that slow you for a minute—that give you pause, I think—are good.

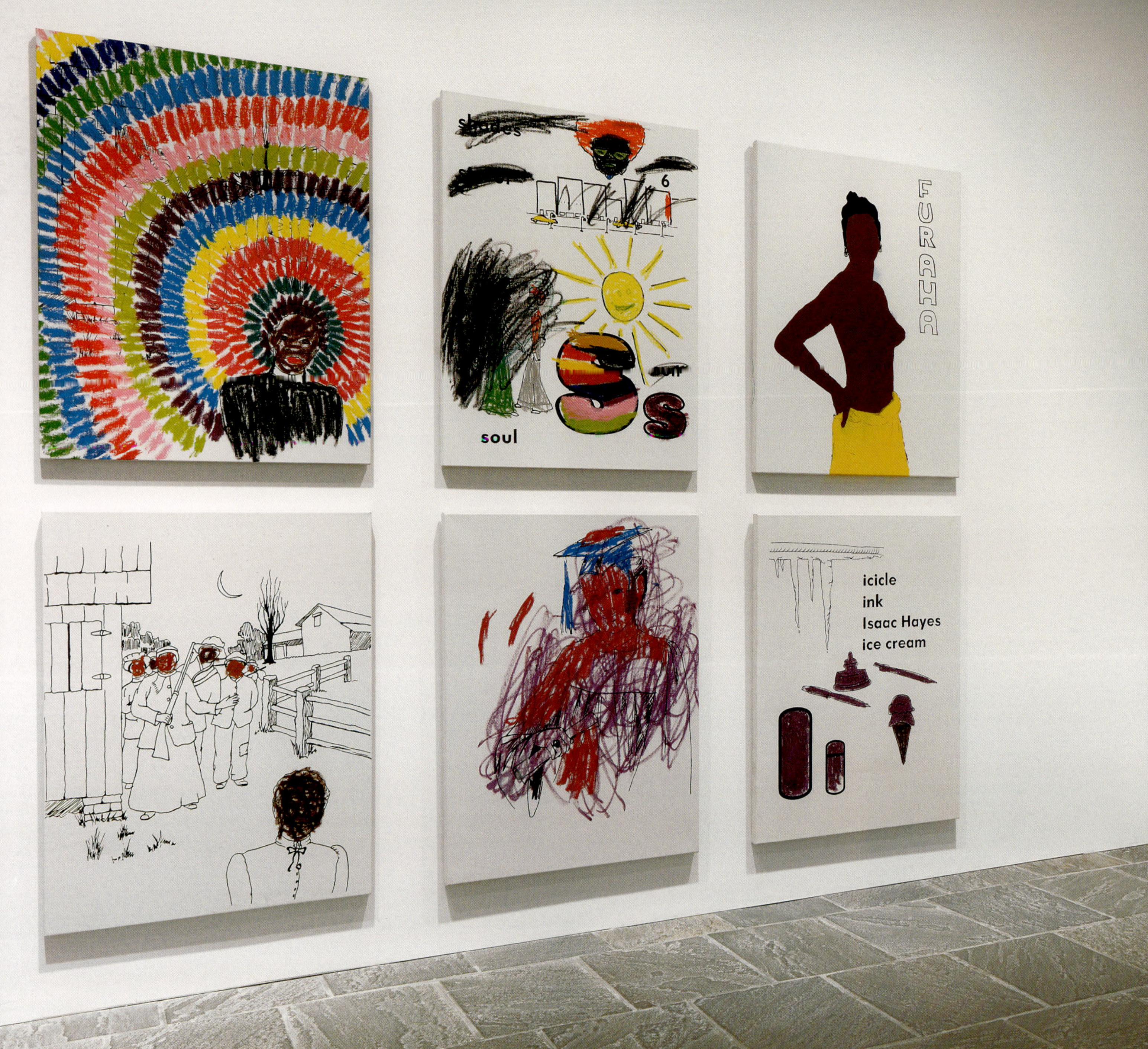

Glenn Ligon

ABOVE
Iinstallation view of *Glenn Ligon: AMERICA,* Whitney Museum of American Art, March 10–June 5, 2011

OPPOSITE, TOP
Boys with Basketball, Harriet Tubman, Salimu, Letter B #3, 2001
Oil crayon and silkscreen on paper, 23 x 16½ inches
Collection of Gregory R. Miller, New York

OPPOSITE, BOTTOM
Malcolm X (Version 1) #1, 2000
Vinyl-based paint, silkscreen ink, and gesso on canvas, 96 x 72 inches
Collection of Michael and Lise Evans

The Coloring Book paintings were done by finding kids who wanted to color. Kids always want to color. I just gave them images that I had found in an archive of 1960s' and 1970s' Afrocentric coloring books. Educators were trying to figure out how to teach black history, and they created coloring books that had images that any coloring book would have—boys playing basketball, a girl swinging on a tire. And juxtaposed with those images are images of people like Frederick Douglass, Harriet Tubman, or Martin Luther King. When I found these coloring books and realized the political agendas behind them I became very interested in them. And when I had them given to very young kids (three, four, five years old) to color, I realized very quickly that their relationship to those images was much more distant than I imagined. Images are just images. They colored them in because they liked the image—or they didn't color them in because they didn't like the image. So even though I tried to impart some of the sense of what these images meant, it really wasn't about that for them. But, then, seeing the way the

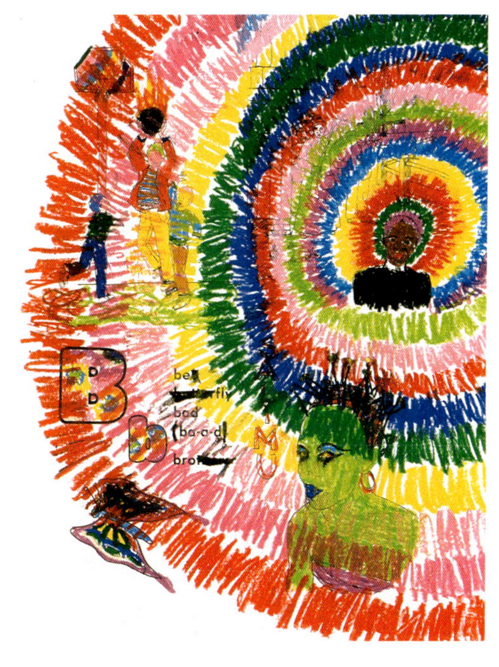

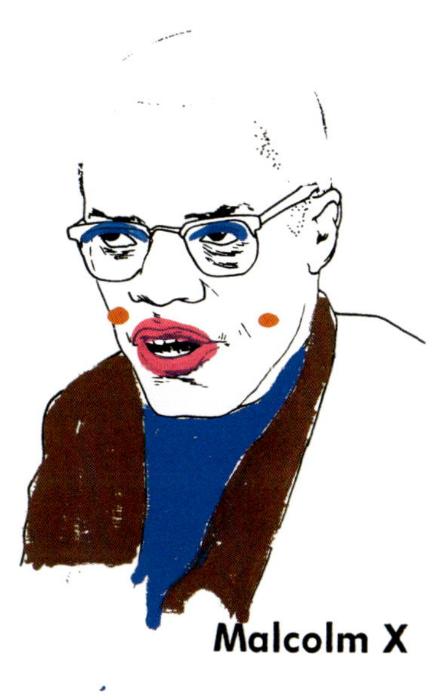

kids colored on these images (for example, there is an image of Malcolm X with lipstick and eye shadow and blush), I realized that the kids' use of these images had nothing to do with the political intent of the images. And that was what was interesting to me. That disconnect between what the kids imagined those images to be and what I as an adult bring to an image of, say, Malcolm X, was what the work was about. So I collected the kids' drawings and made paintings that were based on them. When they were first shown, one room had the kids' drawings and the other room had my paintings based on the drawings. Kids don't do bad drawings. There's no such thing as bad kids' drawings. That was a revelation to me. I thought this was going to be an easy project. I'd just project the drawings onto big canvases and draw them out; it'd be easy. And then I realized that I really had to learn how to draw to make these paintings. I really had to inhabit the way a kid would hold a crayon or paint a painting. Picasso said he had to spend his whole lifetime to learn to draw like a child. And I now know what he meant; it's hard. But it was very instructive for me. In the vocabulary of my work, because so much of my work is about quotation, I'm using texts from other people. This was an extension of that project. In some ways I commissioned my own source material in that I had these kids' drawings to *copy*, quote-unquote. The kids' drawings became paintings that I made, but in some ways they were still the kids' drawings. So it was about a kind of collision between the two things.

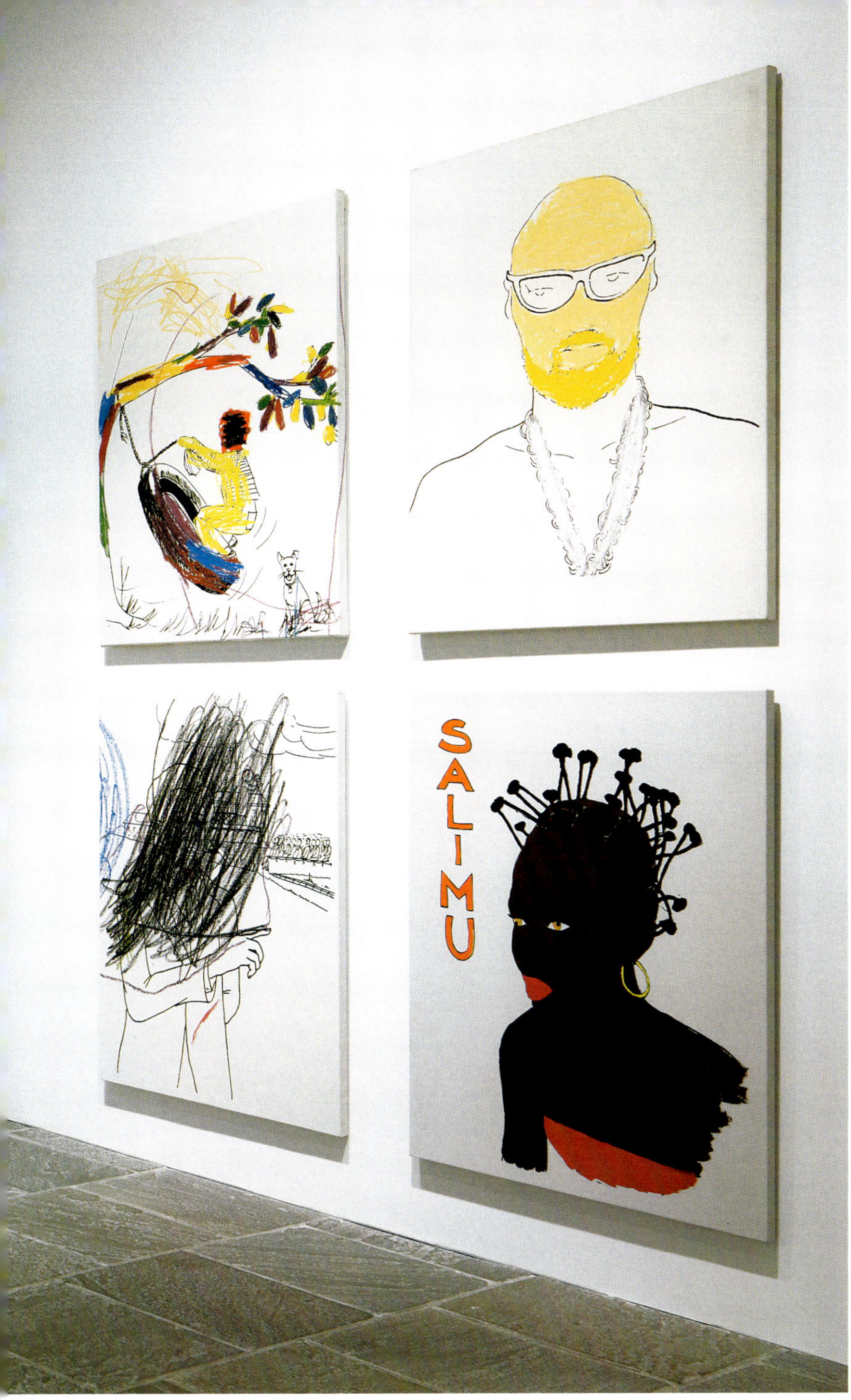

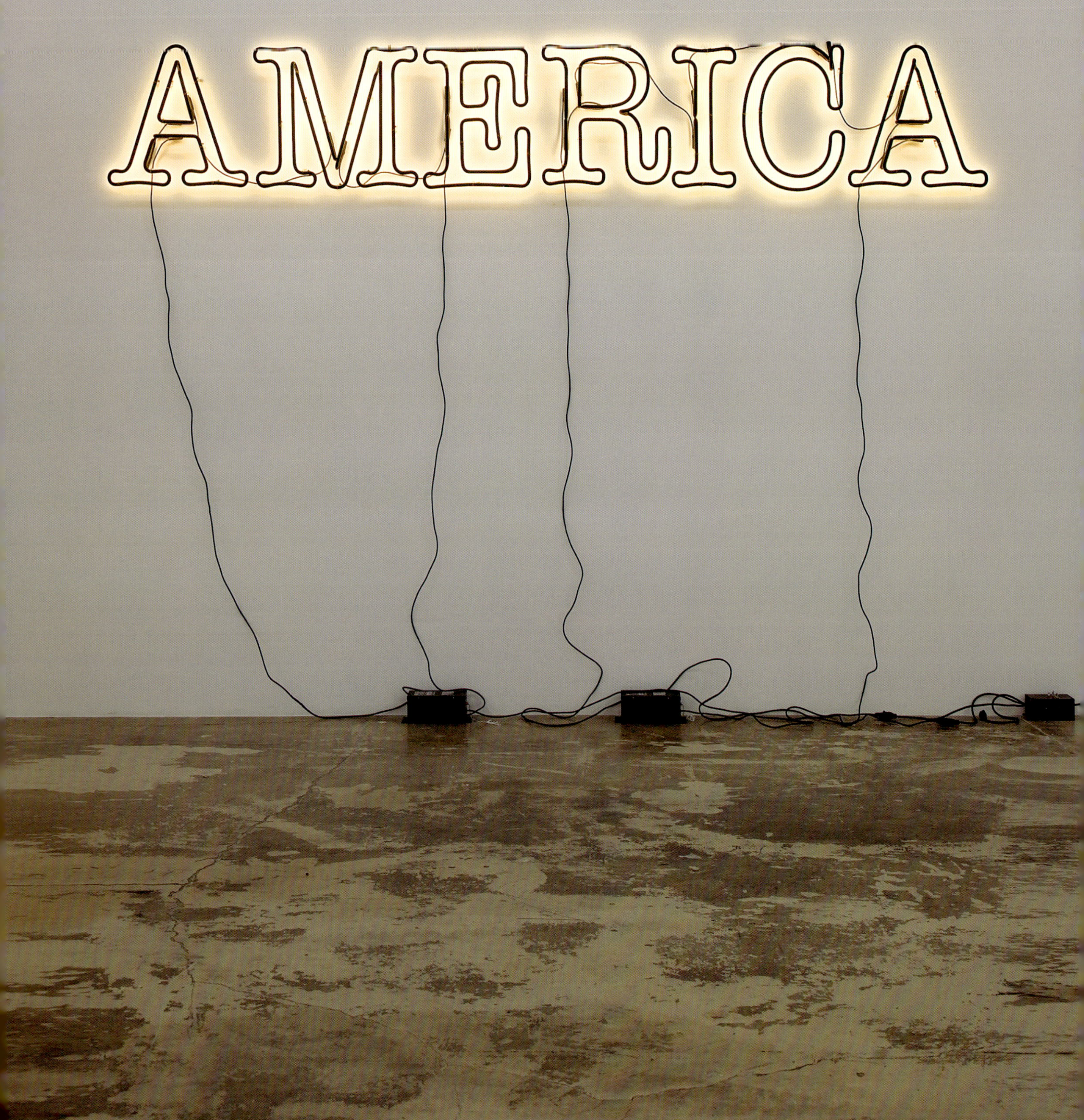
AMERICA

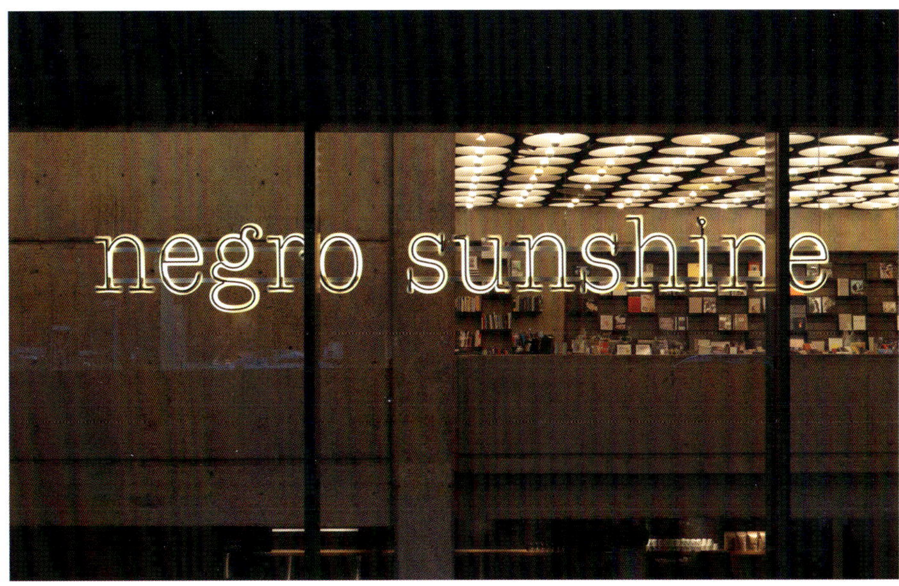

Glenn Ligon

OPPOSITE
Untitled (America), 2008
Neon and paint, 24 x 168 inches
Rubell Family Collection

ABOVE
Warm Broad Glow II, 2011
Neon, paint, and powder-coated aluminum, 29 x 242 inches
Glenn Ligon: AMERICA, installation view at Whitney Museum of American Art, March 10–June 5, 2011

I first started doing neons because there's a neon shop in my building. One day I walked inside. Up to that point I'd been making paintings using black text on white background. So, just as a joke, I said, "Is there such a thing as black neon?" And the owner of the shop said, "That's against the laws of physics. Black is the absence of light." But we started talking about it and I realized one could take a neon tube and simply paint it black on the front. It would read as a black letter or a line, but it would also read as neon because there would be light coming from behind. And once I realized that was possible, it became the connection between my painting and the neons using text. Lots of artists have neons (Bruce Nauman, in particular, comes to mind). So there were precedents. But for me, it was really about finding the connection between the work I was already doing and neon. Until we had that discussion about black light, that hadn't happened. The first neon was based on a little fragment of a Gertrude Stein novel called *Three Lives*, and it was about fourteen feet long. It was kind of thrilling to see it the first time. It was one of the biggest things I'd ever made and incredibly ephemeral because neon tubes are fragile and light. So much of my painting was about encrusted surface—very heavy, dense surfaces—and here was this thing that was emitting light and looked light. It was quite a nice segue into another mode of working.

I was interested in Gertrude Stein because she is interested in American history—trying to describe what America means, which is one of my projects, too. But I'm also interested in Stein because of her repetition of language, because of the deliberate way that she breaks the language. So when I first read *Three Lives*, I just read it to *read*. I hadn't read much of Stein before and I thought this might be a good starting place. It had some narrative that I could jump into. And then I saw that phrase, "negro sunshine," and the coupling of *negro* with *sunshine*—the idea of the blackness of a people as an opposition to the lightness of the sun—was funny to me (black being cultural, not literal blackness or darkness). There are always funny things like that in Stein that stop you in your tracks a little bit. And those two words stopped me in my tracks. But I realized that they would make two great words to use in neon—a neon painted black on the front, *negro,* but also *sunshine* being the light that comes out of the back of those words. The light that shines against the wall is the sunshine. So I could play with that—make that word sculptural in some ways—but also make it about light. And it seemed to me that kind of play was akin to Stein, to things that were happening in the novel. I found the descriptions of the characters riveting at points. And, particularly, that word *negro* in conjunction with the word *sunshine*, I found fascinating.

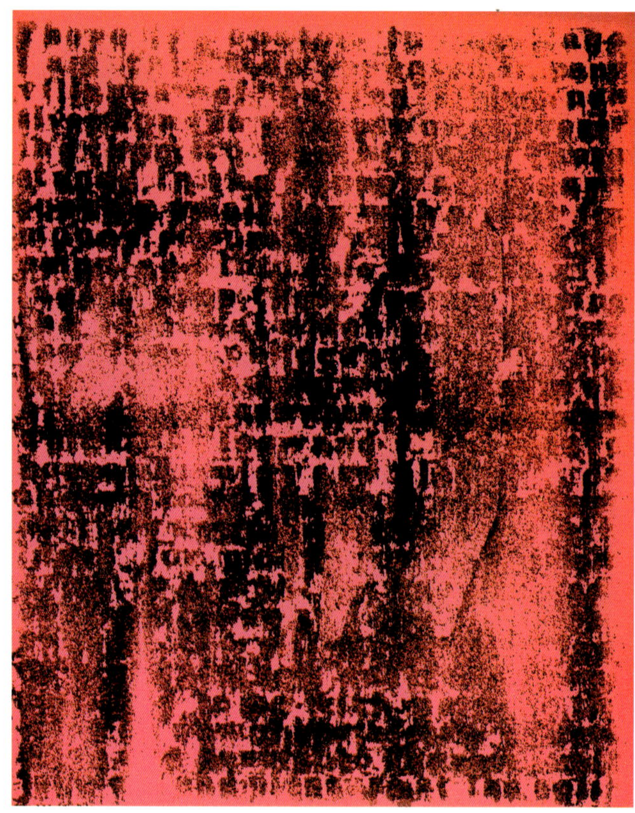

Glenn Ligon

LEFT
Figure #20, 2009
Acrylic, silkscreen, and coal dust on canvas, 60 x 48 inches

RIGHT
Figure #21, 2009
Acrylic, silkscreen, and coal dust on canvas, 60 x 48 inches

OPPOSITE
Palindrome #1, 2007
Neon, 8 x 105 inches

I started using quotation to get away from the autobiographical. If one uses a quote from somebody else, it is autobiographical because you've used it. It becomes part of who you are: "Glenn Ligon makes paintings using other people's texts." It's a way of connecting to the world, but it's also a way of talking about things that mean something to me. So text, even as quotation, *is* autobiographical but it's autobiography filtered through other people's writings, images, or thoughts. My work is always about quotation, so if there are things that are shocking or transgressive in the work they come from a source that is already in the world. In a way, I think the work is about pointing back to those things. So it's not about me. It's about a body of knowledge and ideas, already out in the world, maybe 'under-known', that I'm bringing into another field by using a quotation. Often my work has been thought about as an expression of my identity. And I think, while the work in some cases might touch on the notion of identity in general, it's never about my identity. As I said, my work is always quotation. So if it's about identity, it's about American identity. The work starts from me because that's where any artist's work starts, but is quickly about other things. It's quickly about the way one is placed in the culture, in society. It's not about *me*. It's about *we*.

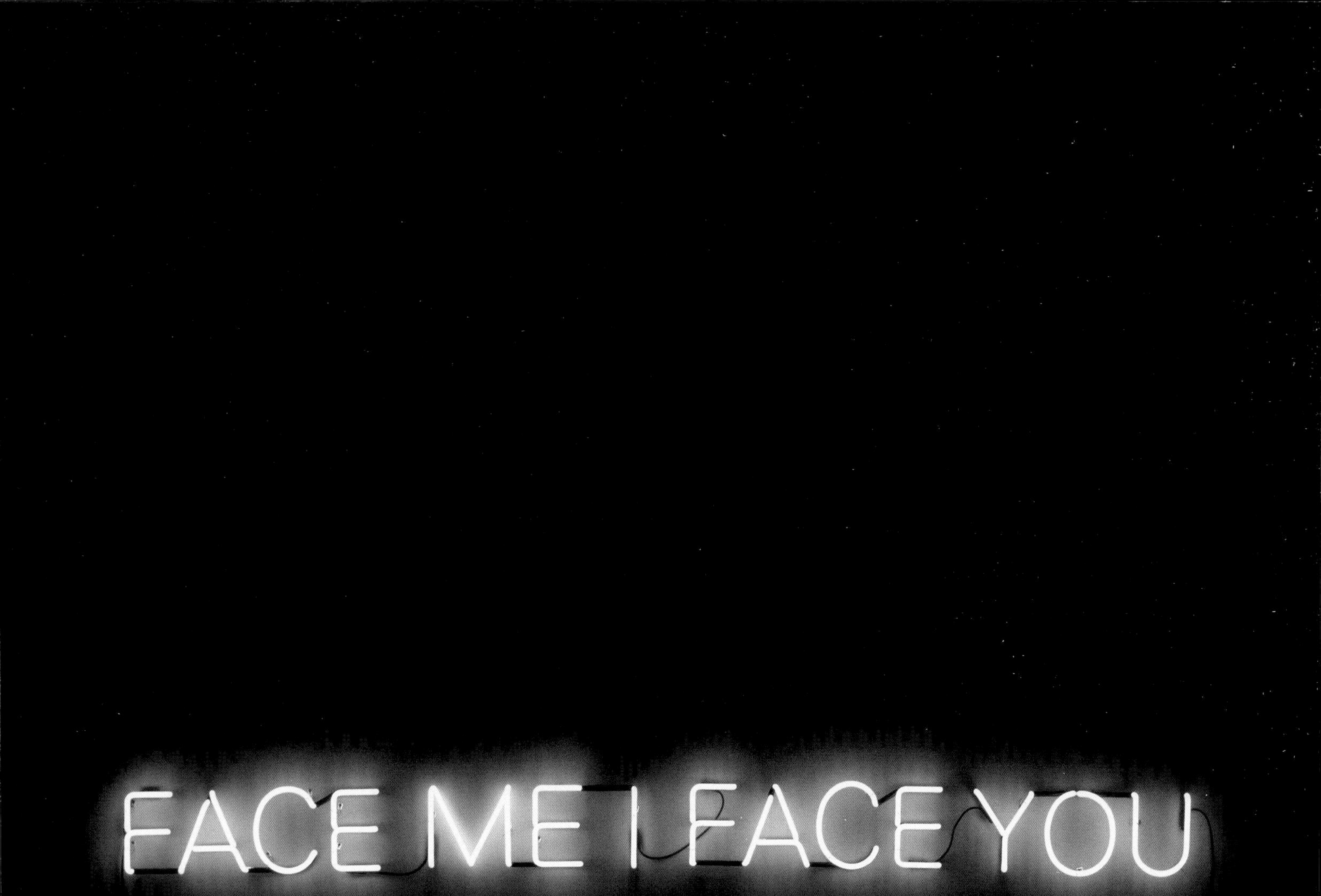

FACE ME I FACE YOU

Mary Reid Kelley

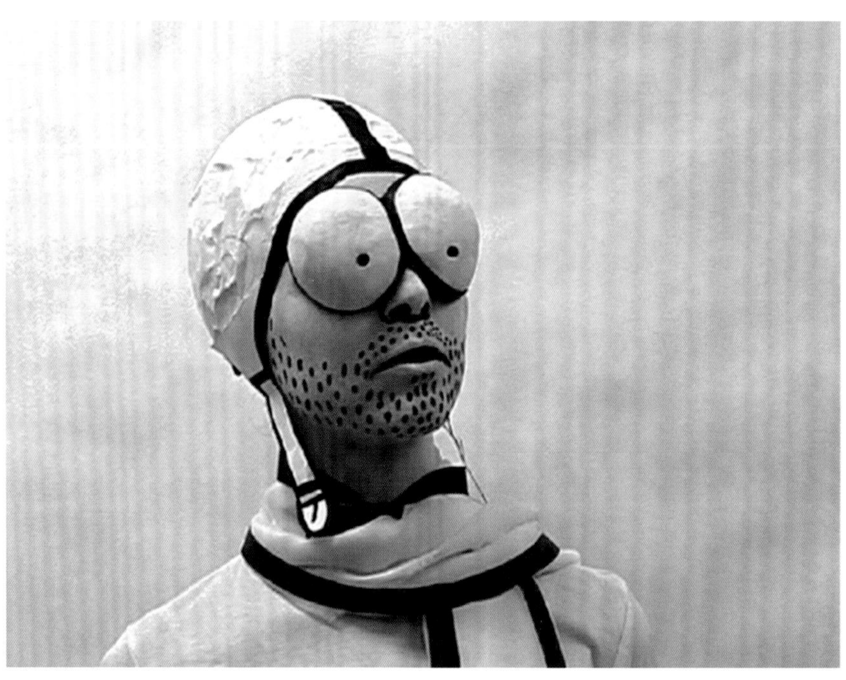

ABOVE
Camel Toe, video still, 2008
Video, 1 min 25 sec

OPPOSITE, TOP
Spit, Spit, Spit, Spit, Spit, 2008
Graphite on paper, 9¾ x 10 inches

OPPOSITE, BOTTOM
Mergy, Bergy, Fergy, 2008
Graphite on paper, 9¾ x 9¾ inches

Generally, I call my works videos, but I also call them films because they have a beginning, middle, and end. They also function as texts. And, in a way, I think of them very much as moving paintings. I don't have a very clear narrative of how it happened but, starting off as a painter, I guess I just got more and more drawn to highly interpretive and layered spheres of language. I was very engaged with visual artists like Jenny Holzer and Kara Walker, who work with language. I felt like there was so much text and accumulating language in my work that finally it just seemed like a good idea to make it time-based. Either I was going to make paintings that were just giant blocks of text or I could do what I really wanted to do—to spend time writing. But also I started thinking more about the kinds of visual works that I was drawn to, which—even though they were static—were cumulative and narrative, or had some sort of text component. One of the things that I love about encountering paintings—even a static painting, a Titian or any sort of painting that you can imagine—is looking at them over time and coming back and viewing them again. So when I make video works, I love the idea of people coming back to them and seeing them over and over. That's why I've decided to keep them short—fifteen minutes, ten minutes, seven minutes. I'd love for people to watch them again the way you can go back to a beloved image or a painting and always get something new. That's probably one of the most salient connections between being a painter and now working in this medium.

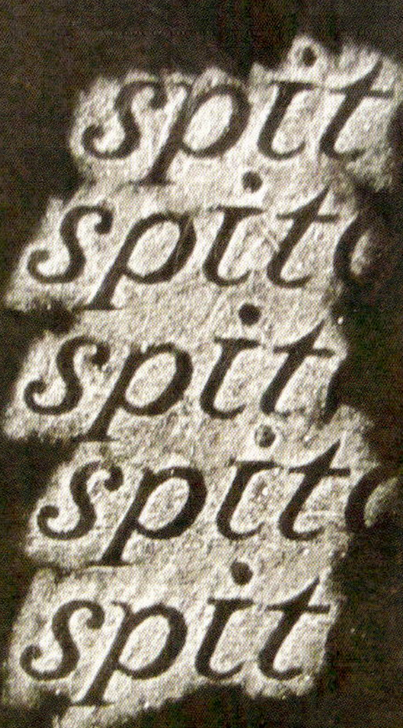
spit
spit
spit
spit
spit
MRK 08

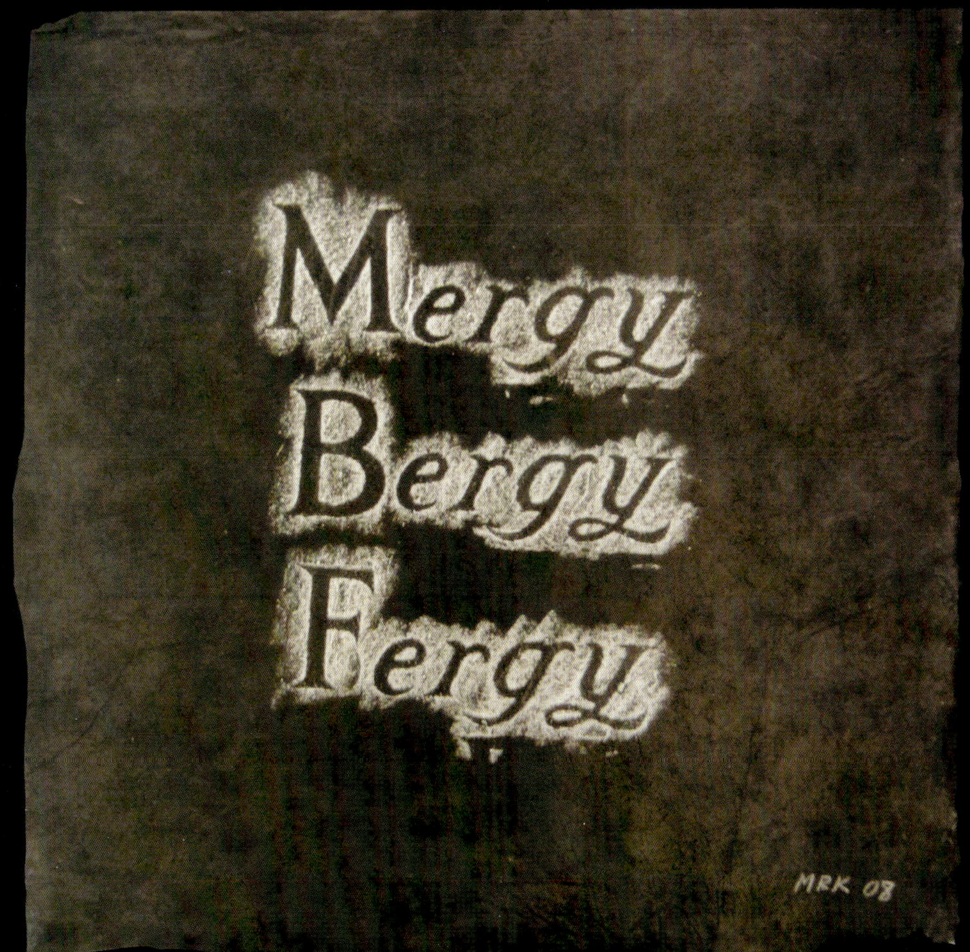
Mergy
Bergy
Fergy
MRK 08

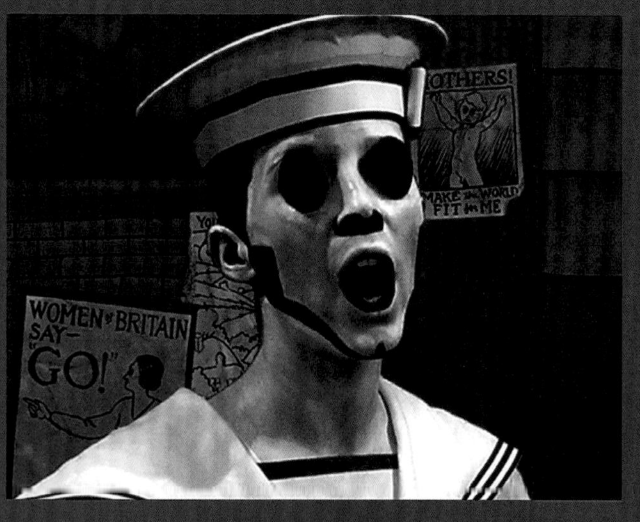

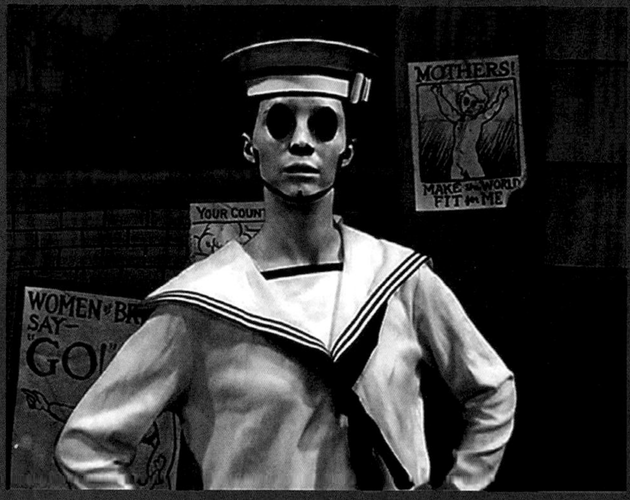

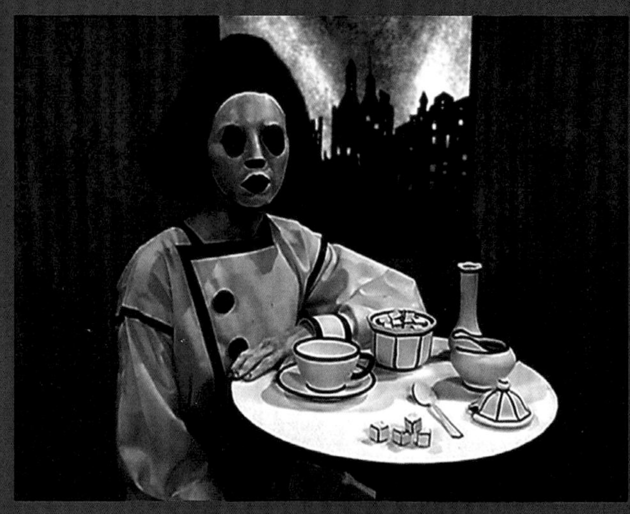

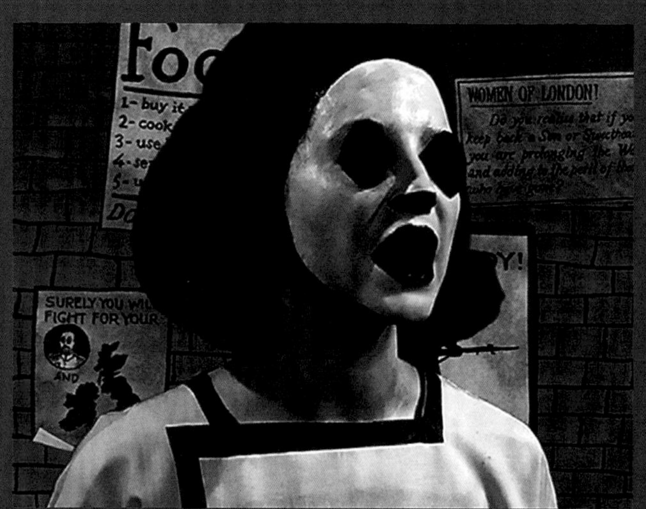

OR GIVE IT TO
ME, BECAUSE
I'HN GHGGHN
FHW ET.

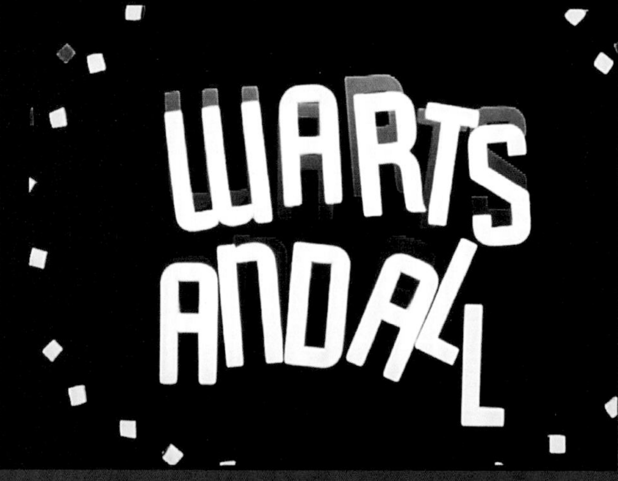

END
VIRTUOUS
SLOP!

THAT'A
CAPITAL

Mary Reid Kelley

OPPOSITE
Sadie, The Saddest Sadist, video stills, 2009
Video, 7 min 23 sec

RIGHT
The Queen's English, video still, 2008
Video, 4 min 20 sec

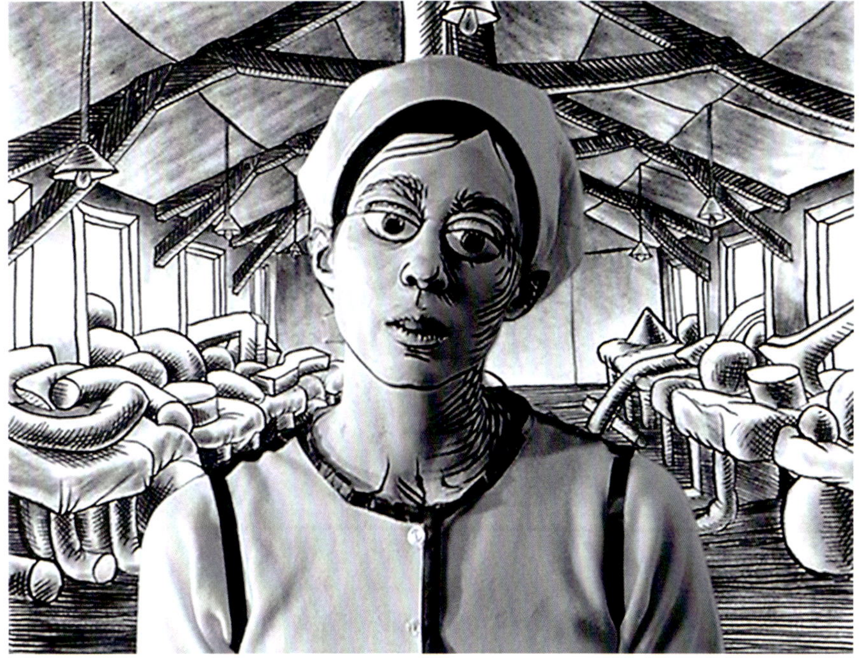

The artists that I have a strong gravitational pull towards are women who were working in the '60s and the '70s, particularly Adrian Piper, Hannah Wilke, and others—like Carolee Schneemann. They combine text and image and use themselves in the work. Their work is cumulative but, of course, it's also discrete. You can appreciate their works as texts or pictures, but you can also read their bodies of work over time.

Storytelling in my work? It's definitely narrative, although not much happens. I'm interested in the characters' internal monologues and reasoning. And as the videos follow the trajectory of the characters, they're justifying to themselves what they're doing. But I think what interests me most is the cumulative layers of interpretation. Even though I love all the data, all the minutiae—the costumes, the details, the detritus, and the photographs—I really just love the interpretation. You have this sphere of action where there's an event, say, a battle or a Tahrir Square—something like that. You're in this sphere of action. And then it eventually widens to a sphere of interpretation. The farther away in time you get from the events, the farther you get into the sphere of interpretation. That's where my interest lies. In terms of why I was so particularly drawn to the First World War, I think it was partly an issue of opportunity. I just fell into an amazing pile of fascinating data at Yale. I never thought of myself as a writer. I never sat down to try to do it. I would do it just in play, or on the spur of the moment. So I didn't actually try to write until I got engaged with the First World War, and I've only been writing as part of the work for the last couple years. But I've always liked wordplay and poems, and it's always been an interest of my family (we used to sing together and make up rhymes together). I really like how words and phrases tend to connect together and how they don't have an independent, separate meaning—or don't necessarily have a pure meaning. My dad is a notorious punster. Puns are usually not welcome, but I love that aspect of puns—how an unexpected pun will elicit a groan or a roll of the eyes. It's almost like we're horrified by a sudden presence in our midst of something gumming up the works of our conversation. I often think it is much more difficult to stop playing with words and actually say something and use them to communicate. But I also think words just *want* to play, and it is more difficult to keep them from playing with each other than it is to actually think of wordplays, puns, and rhymes. The first time I used wordplay extensively in the work was in *The Queen's English* (2008). And in that video, the character (a nurse) is observing the death of a soldier. I had been reading a lot of First World War memoirs and poetry. The people who were writing then were forced to develop new metaphors, new language, to describe what had happened because the old metaphors didn't ring true anymore. People were dying in ways that were unprecedented (one of the great poems by Wilfred Owen describes men dying from nerve gas). This was a brand-new way of killing people. There was no poetic precedent telling him how to aestheticize this death. He had to invent a new way. There's a lot of euphemism in talk about death. It's difficult to just say exactly what happens. So in *The Queen's English* there are a lot of euphemisms, and they start tearing apart the nurse's speech. The viewer can't really tell what's happening with the view obscured by euphemisms.

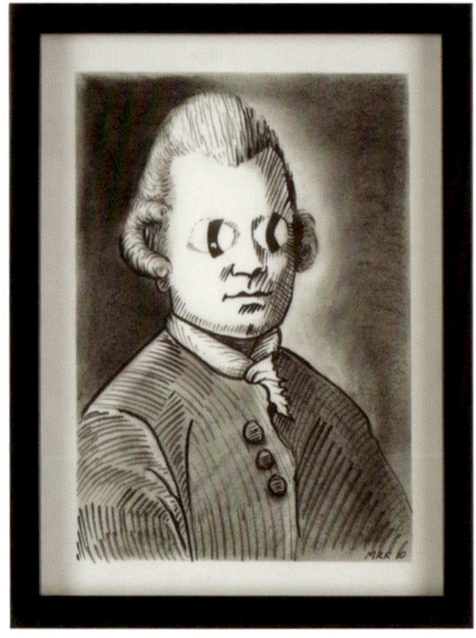

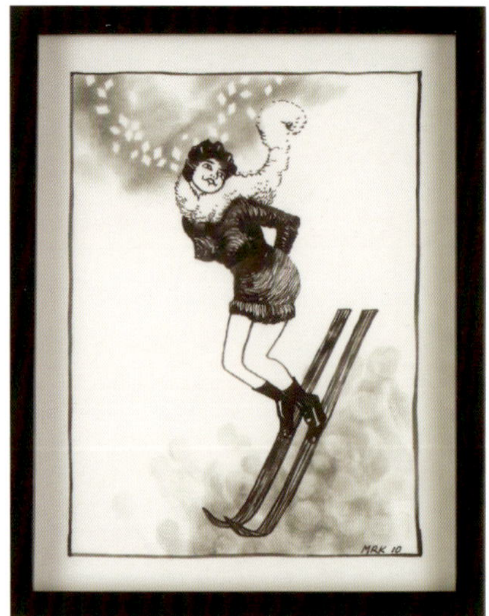

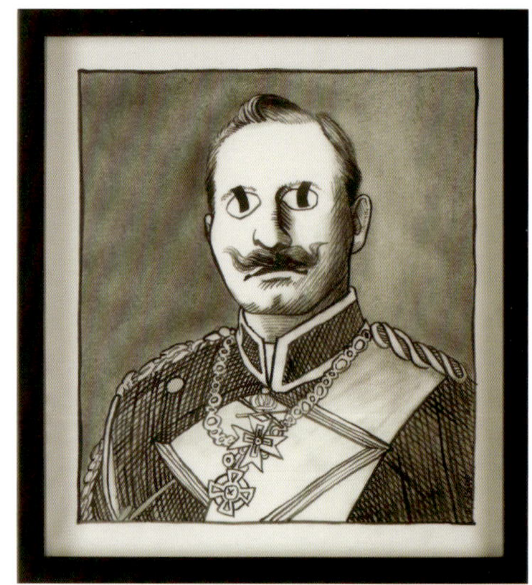

Mary Reid Kelley

ABOVE, LEFT TO RIGHT
Lessing, 2010
Ski Girl, 2010
Kaiser, 2010
Ink and graphite on vellum,
8½ x 11 inches each

OPPOSITE
You Make Me Iliad, video stills, 2010
HD video with sound, 14 min 49 sec

Puns are something that you start doing compulsively. You turn a corner where you have played with language too much, and then it becomes a struggle to actually say what you mean. We all struggle to say what we mean, but I think punning really illuminates the paradox of how constantly we're living in language. We're dependent on it but yet we're not in control of it. Our meanings are always sneaking out the back door and coming in the front door to surprise us. So I'm very attached to puns and wordplay. When I started doing it in the First World War pieces I had conceptualized it: these puns were absurd and very dark—and particularly appropriate to the First World War and its long farce of death and destruction. But I think that puns are much more widely applicable and have much more to say about our eternal condition of being strangers within language.

The title of the new film is *The Syphilis of Sisyphus* (2011). I was struggling for a while after finishing *You Make Me Iliad* (2010), thinking I'd like to do something from a different time period, and I was fishing around in this suspended state for so long that it's difficult for me to remember what came first. But even during that time I kept a running list of wordplays, just random things and, before I had decided what the new film was about, had started writing jokes. So many jokes are pun-based, so it's just a matter of wording them—finding a pun or wordplay and then constructing a joke to fit. I think I had written something down about the myth of Sisyphus, and then the phrase 'syphilis of Sisyphus', and I ended up coming back to it a while later and thinking that it could be a title for something. I was drawn to the nineteenth century, and then I started looking at the medical history of syphilis. What I love most about the research is the history of ideas and intellectual history. Medical history is a part of that—the way people thought about disease and how it evolved from a medieval faith-based idea where the medical is very much united with people's religious beliefs. But the nineteenth century, particularly in Paris with the Paris School of Medicine, was really when medicine probably first became a science. People were willing to drop some of the older metaphors about the body and illness. Becoming a doctor or a medical student meant spending time with people who were sick rather than memorizing Hippocrates.

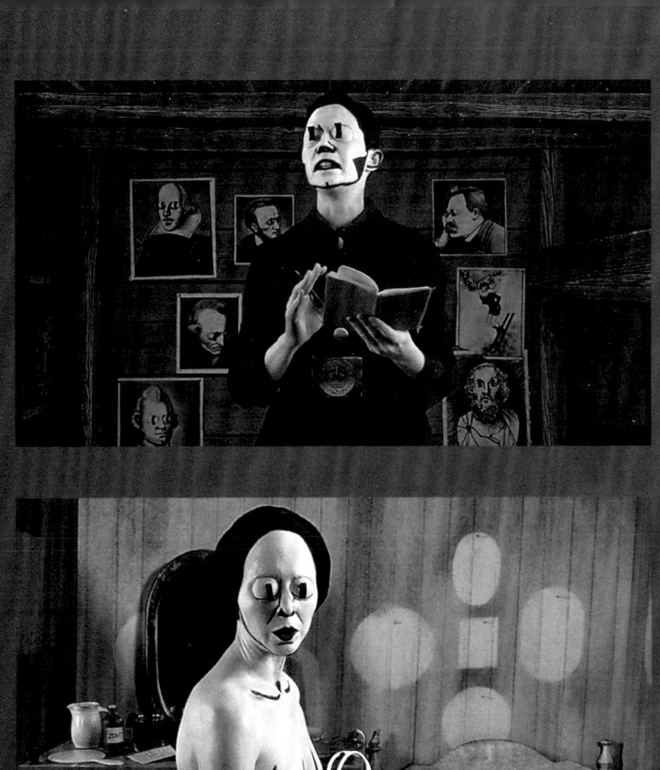

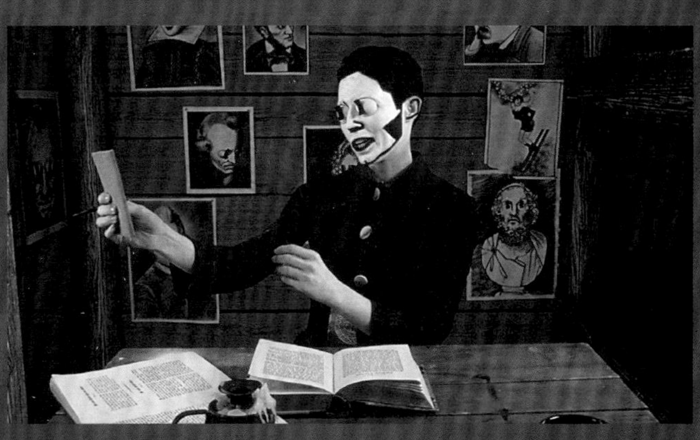

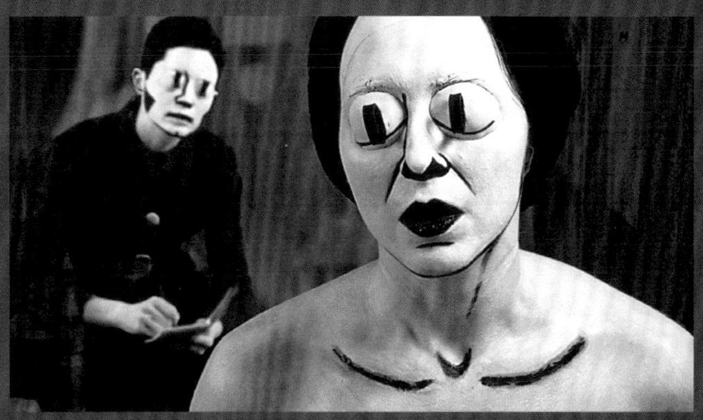

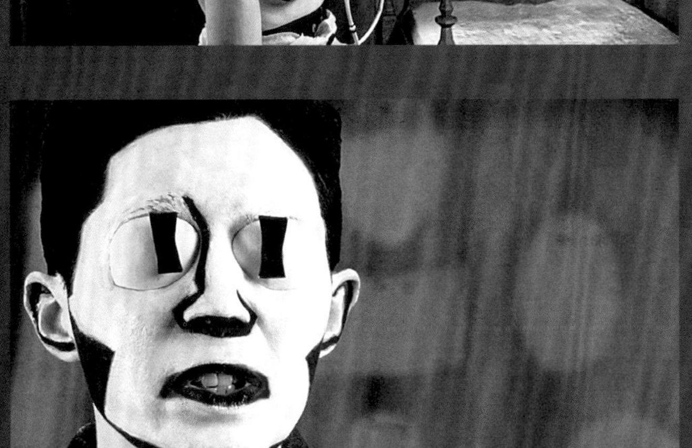

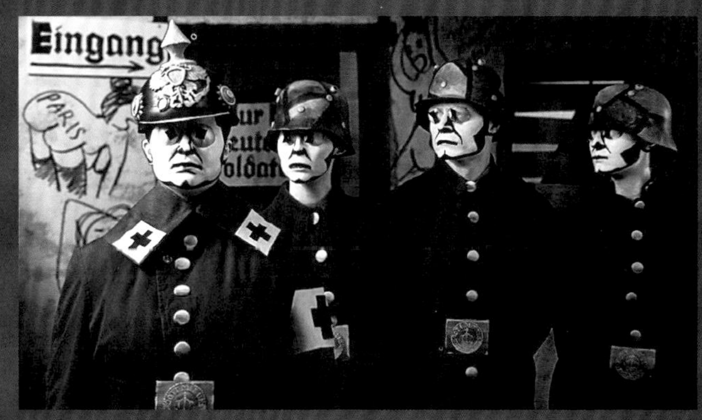
Eingang
PARIS

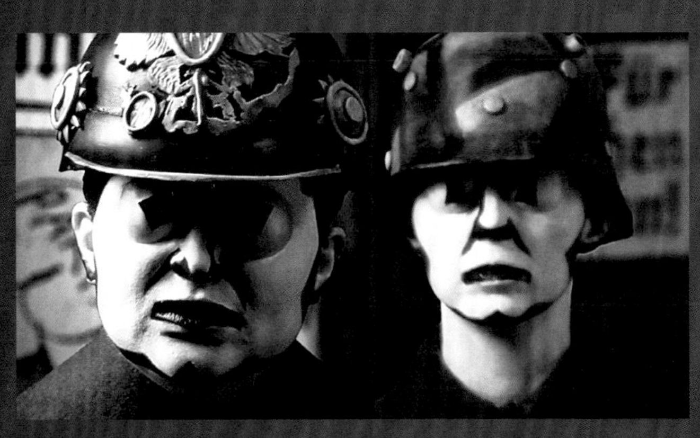

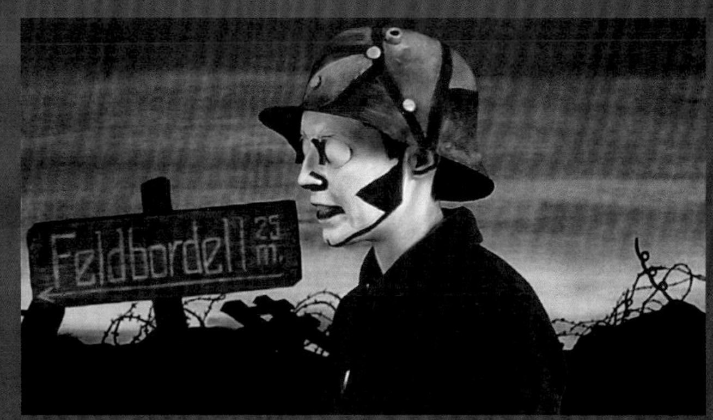
Feldbordell 25 m.

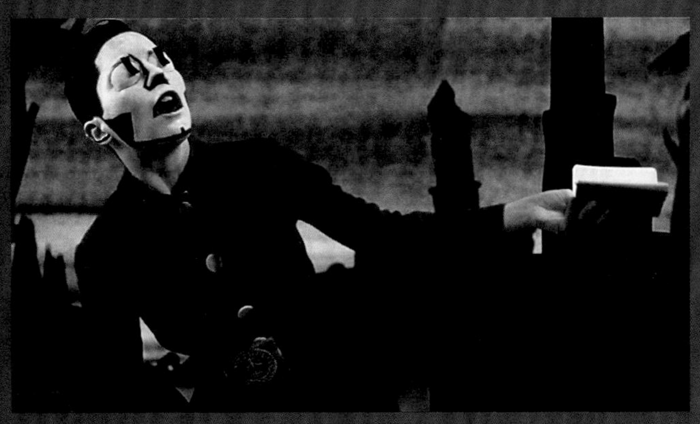

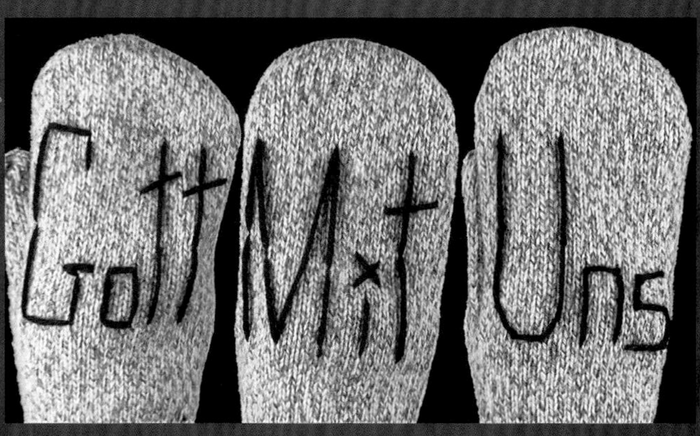
Gott Mit Uns

Mary Reid Kelley with Patrick Kelley

The Syphilis of Sisyphus, video stills, 2012
HD video, 11 min 2 sec
Support provided by the Curtis R. Priem Experimental Media and Performing Arts Center (EMPAC)

One of the reasons that the work is going backwards in time from the early twentieth century to the mid-nineteenth century is that when I was doing research for First World War-related things, especially with poetry, it was the poetry that drew me backwards. The poets writing at that time were very engaged with the poets of the previous generation, who were in turn engaged with previous generations. So I think it's really the literature that draws you backwards through this accumulation. I was also confused by the terms 'Romanticism' and 'Enlightenment', so I wanted to look more closely at what those things meant. In choosing a different

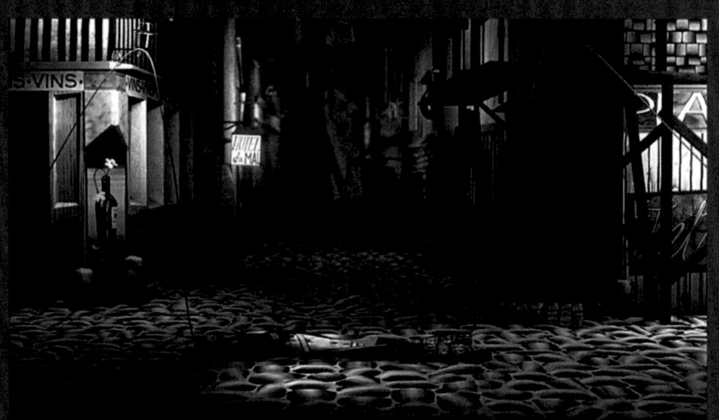

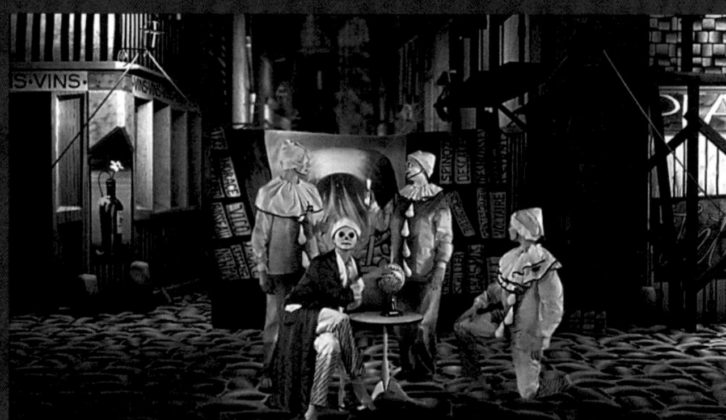

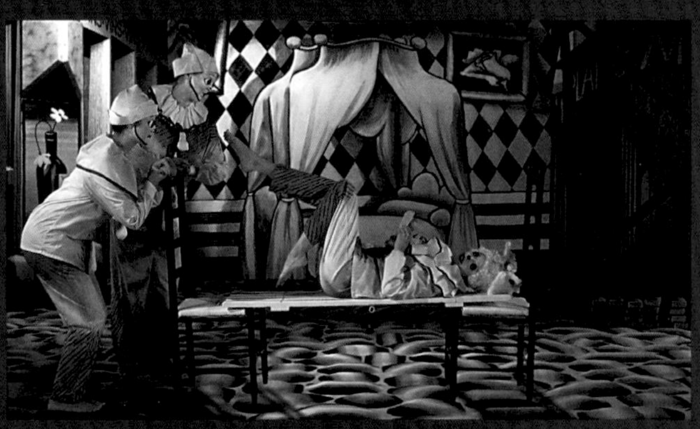

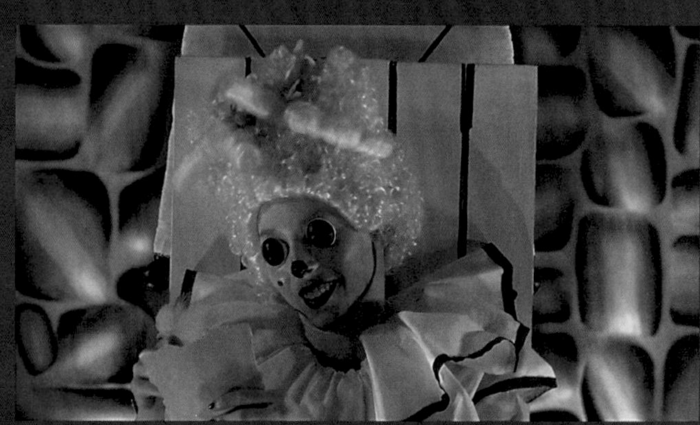

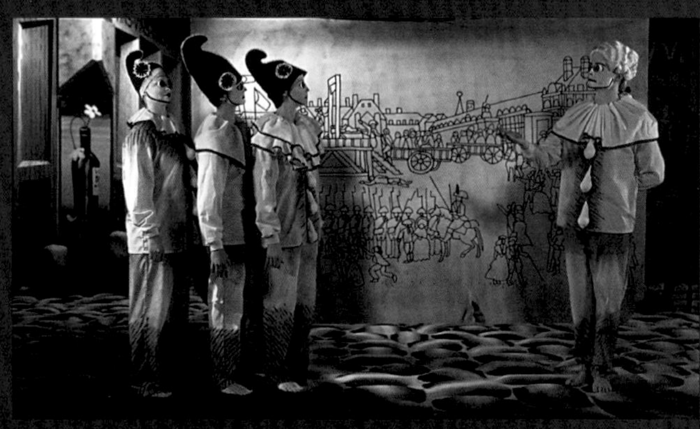

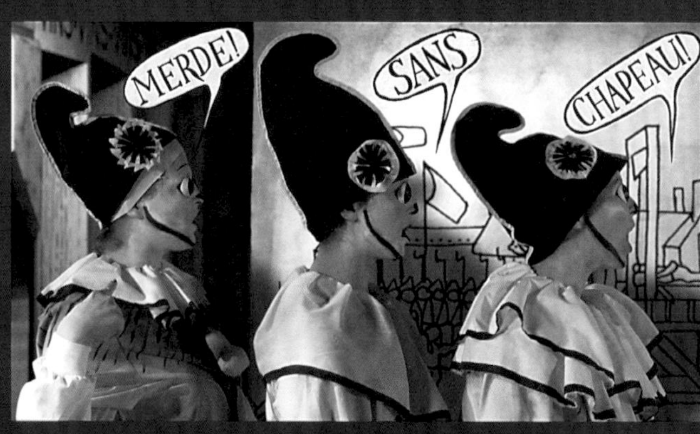

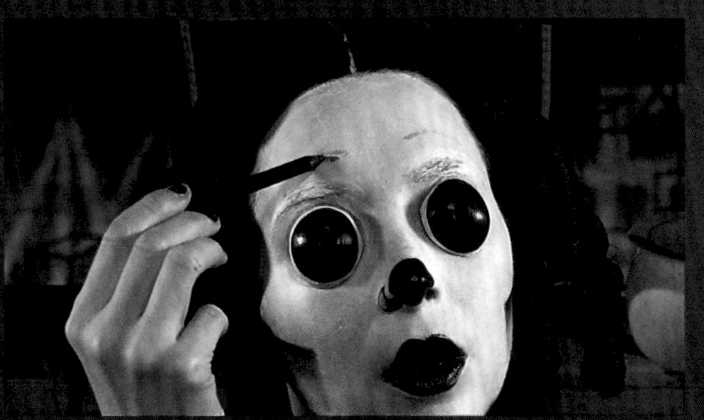

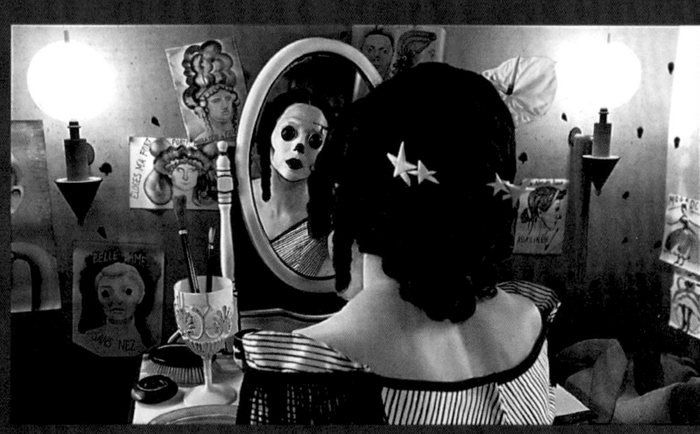

time period from the First World War I also had to find something that had the element of farce to it, the element of being drawn into the abyss in an absurd way. That's why nineteenth-century Paris was so interesting. Starting with the French Revolution, the French had a wave of successive revolutions—kick out the king, bring the king back, bring the king's cousin back, bring the nephew of Napoleon I back. By the time we get to the 1850s, it had just become an extended humiliation. They couldn't do anything—couldn't make it work. That is what is interesting to me about that time period and what might resonate today—the idea of events being out of control.

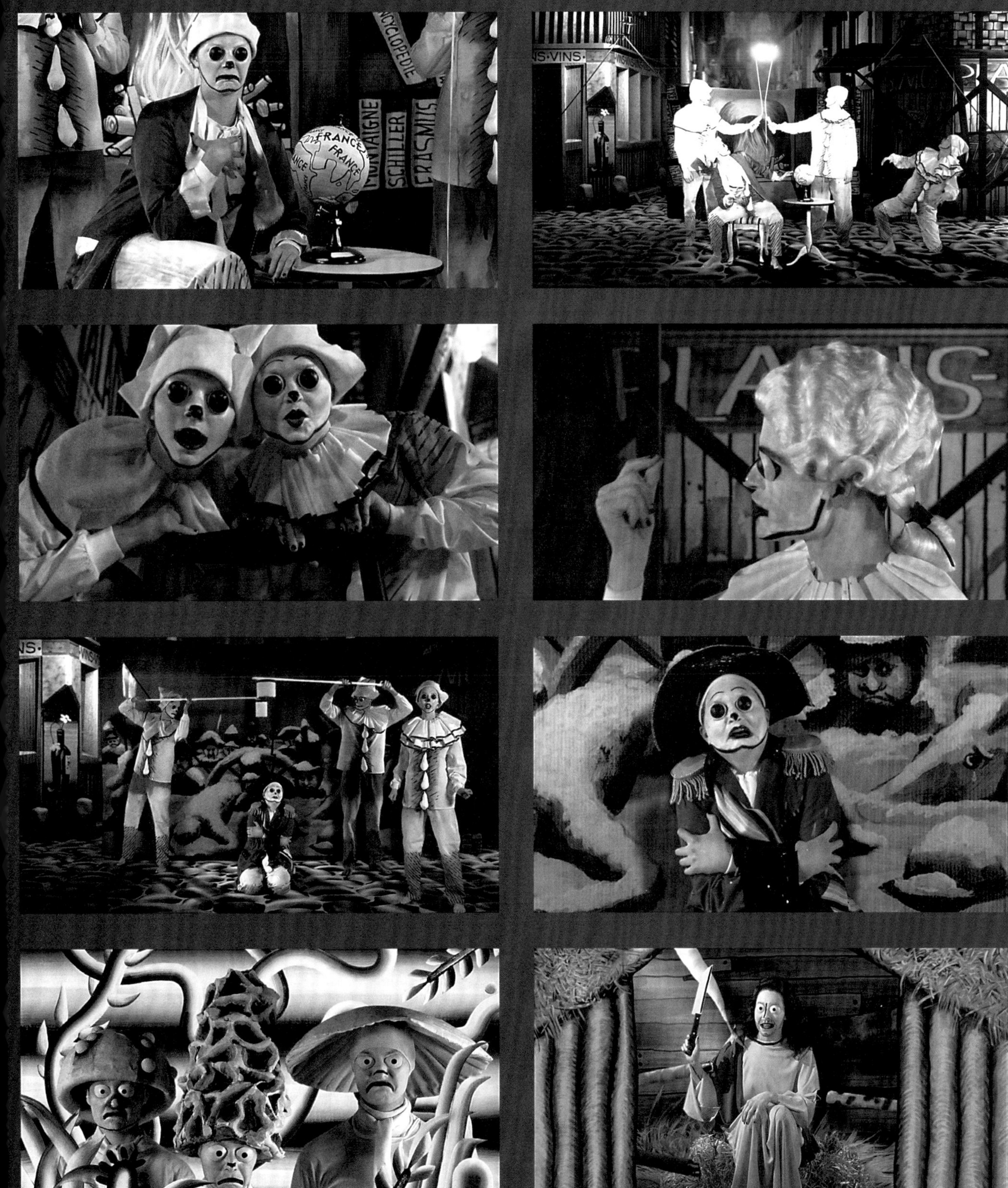

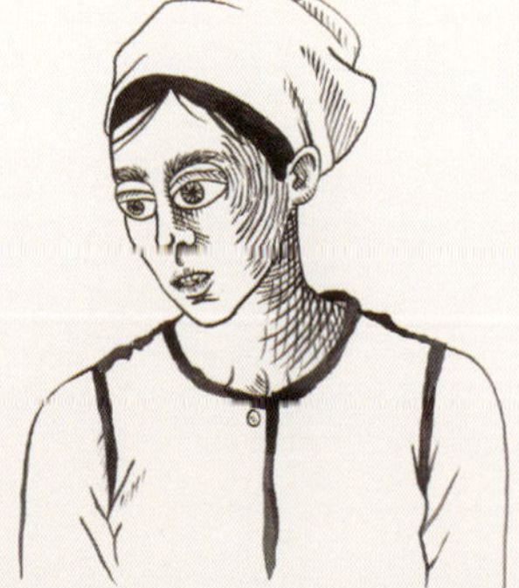
MRK 10

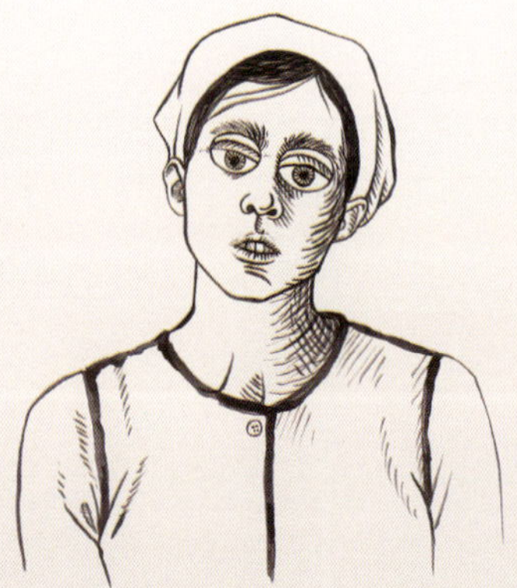
MRK 10

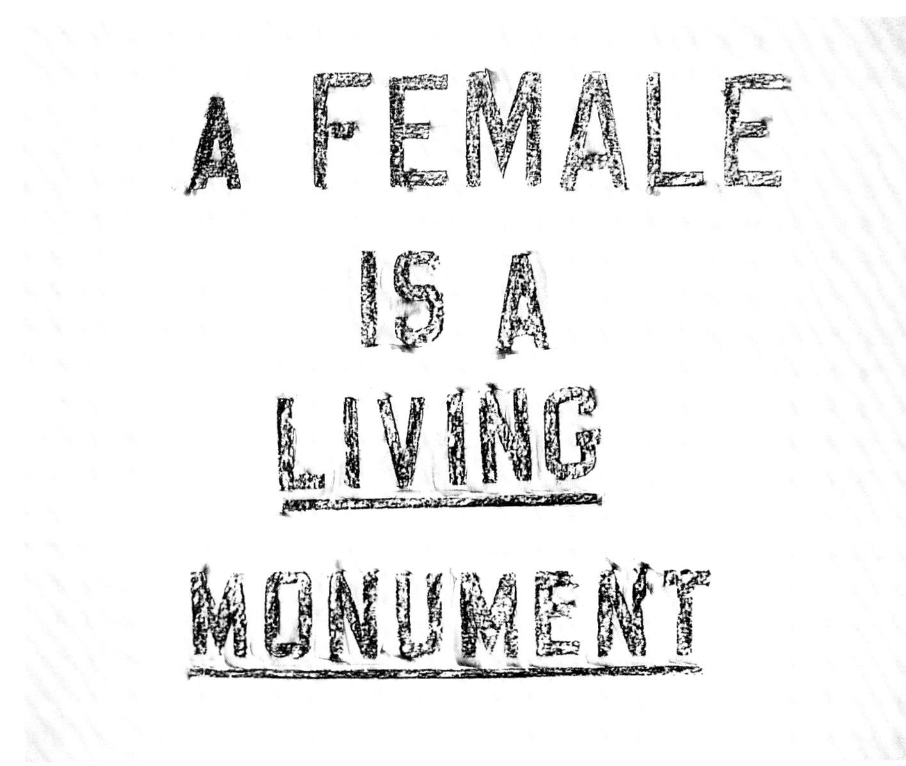

Mary Reid Kelley

OPPOSITE
Untitled (The Queen's English), 2009
Watercolor on paper, 9 x 12 inches each

ABOVE
A Female Is a Living Monument, 2008
Pencil on paper, 18½ x 20½ inches

I was always aware of history as almost a professionalized realm, something dignified that you learned from. It was not till later that I started thinking that you could play with it and just because you read something in a history book, that that was the only interpretation. There are many, many more layers. People are possessive about history. They always want something from it. So—what do I want from history? I do love reading about it, and all the small details of it. I've thought so much in *The Syphilis of Sisyphus* about how important style is to history—and I hadn't really thought about that before. But you can't separate politics from aesthetics, especially in history. People want conflicting things from history: they want it to be true, reliable, to come from a position of authority, and they want it to be literal. But it's also important that history be used to make metaphors. The reason that I'm interested in history now is to try to imagine it, but also to imagine some sort of artistic language for it—to give it some sort of artistic context.

It troubles me that politically and historically so much of the burden of events falls disproportionately on women, or that a lot of conflicts are fought on the backs or bodies of women. Women and the roles of women, globally and historically, have been consistent interests for me. But women have been stuck so far behind—and what they have had to say is so far lost—that my interest is in going back and trying to imagine them, artistically. I'm not trying to glamorize, redeem, or fetishize their trauma. But it's a question of worth. What is their experience worth? Is it possible to make art from that experience? Is it a strong enough experience? For a lot of people the answer is no. It's a dual insult and problem. There's the primary problem of being left out of the historical record. And then there's the problem that artistic avenues for dealing with the experience were blocked. The first insult compounds the second because there are so few documents of women's experiences. So, in terms of my role, it's almost as if the only way that to reconstitute that experience is through art, through imagination. And that's what I'm trying to do.

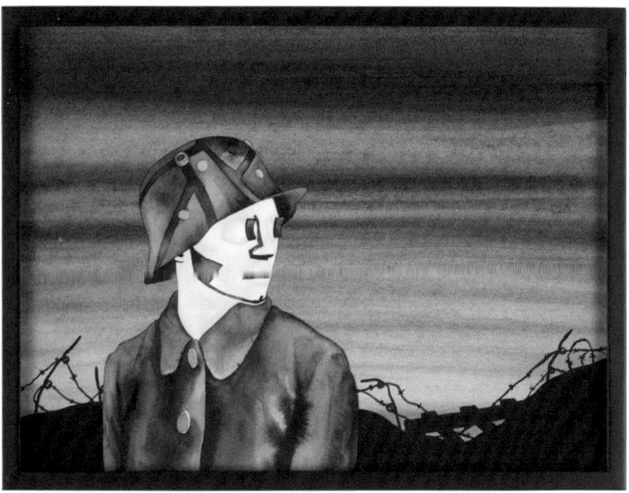

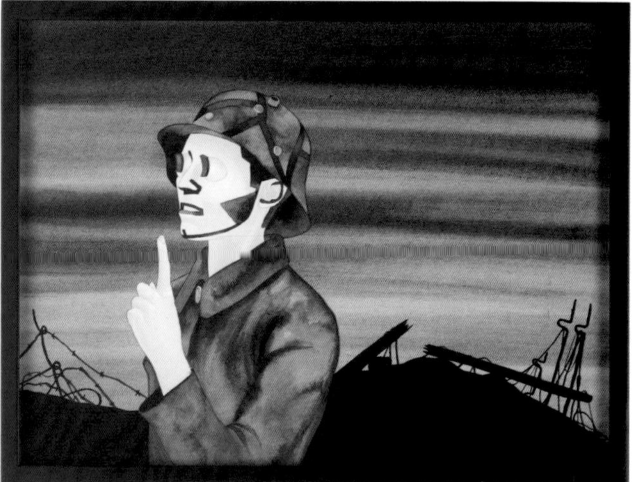

Mary Reid Kelley

ABOVE
Soldier in Helmet 1, 2010
Soldier in Helmet 2, 2010
Ink, acrylic, and charcoal on paper,
10 x 14 inches each

OPPOSITE, TOP
Sisyphus (Chiffonniers Vins), 2011
Collage, watercolor on paper,
16 x 20 inches

OPPOSITE, BOTTOM
Marie Antoinette Saltimbanque, 2011
Collage, watercolor, and acrylic on paper,
18½ x 15⅝ inches

A lot of the work that I am drawn to is in black-and-white. And there are two reasons that, so far, most of my work has been in black-and-white. One is because the restrictions and the limitations that are placed on the work are important and I think that I just don't think in color. I love looking at color. Many people are brilliant with color and that's just how they approach everything. I'm not like that. Black-and-white allows me to do what I'm really interested in visually. It would be so much more difficult in color. It would take another several steps because it would be much more of a technological puzzle and problem. Even though the work is time-based, it has an overriding allegiance to works on paper, and that includes both printed word and graphic imagery. The black-and-white of the videos hearkens to two things—comics and print media—and also to early film. The connection with early film is most definite in *You Make Me Iliad,* which is based on German (Weimar) cinema. I think there's also an interesting connection with text. Black-and-white could imply some degree of certainty about where you stand. And I think it goes along with the idea of extended polemic or political speech, which—in *The Syphilis of Sisyphus*—conflates the aesthetic and the artistic with the political. Even though Sisyphus is talking about beauty and nature and she's applying her cosmetics, her speech sounds political. It sounds like ranting.

When I think about what I want for the work, it's a language experience. When you're listening, the brain is constantly anticipating what's about to happen—usually, correctly. And that's why we can communicate with each other. What I'm trying to make happen in the text, first, and then in the film is that what is being set up linguistically is not what's delivered. So the character and his or her desires are being turned inside out at the moment that they speak of them. It's mainly a linguistic effect that I'm looking for, like the real-time betrayal *of* language *by* language—or the betrayal of a person by language, or a person giving something away that he or she doesn't intend to give away. In some ways, the characters are always blind in a crucial way. There's something that they can't see. These characters are blind to what they're doing and giving it away at the same time.

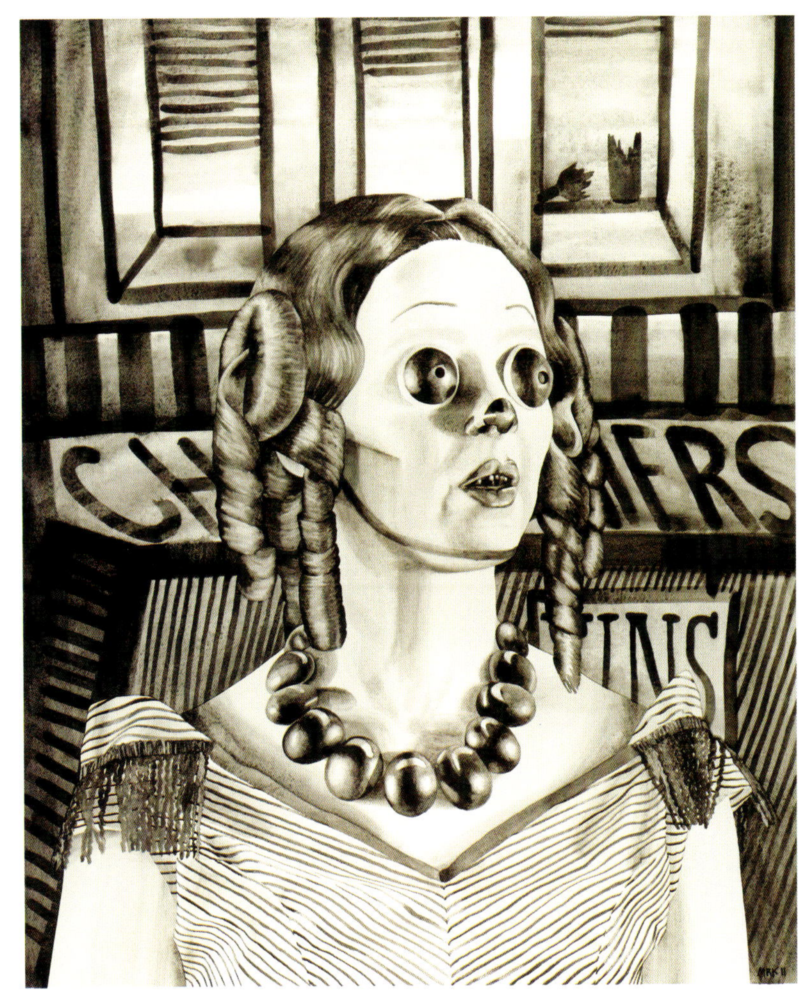
CH
ERS
INS
MRK 11

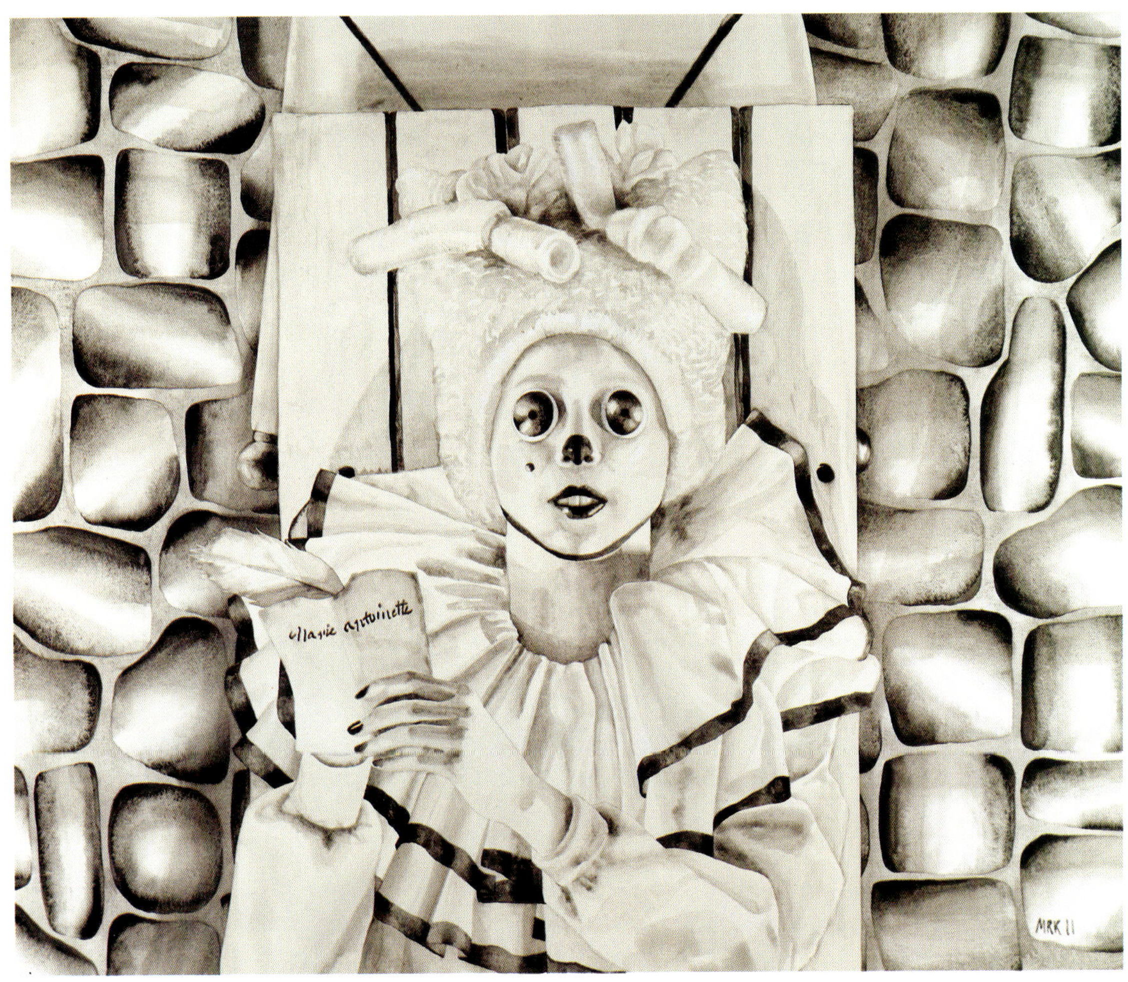
Marie antoinette
MRK 11

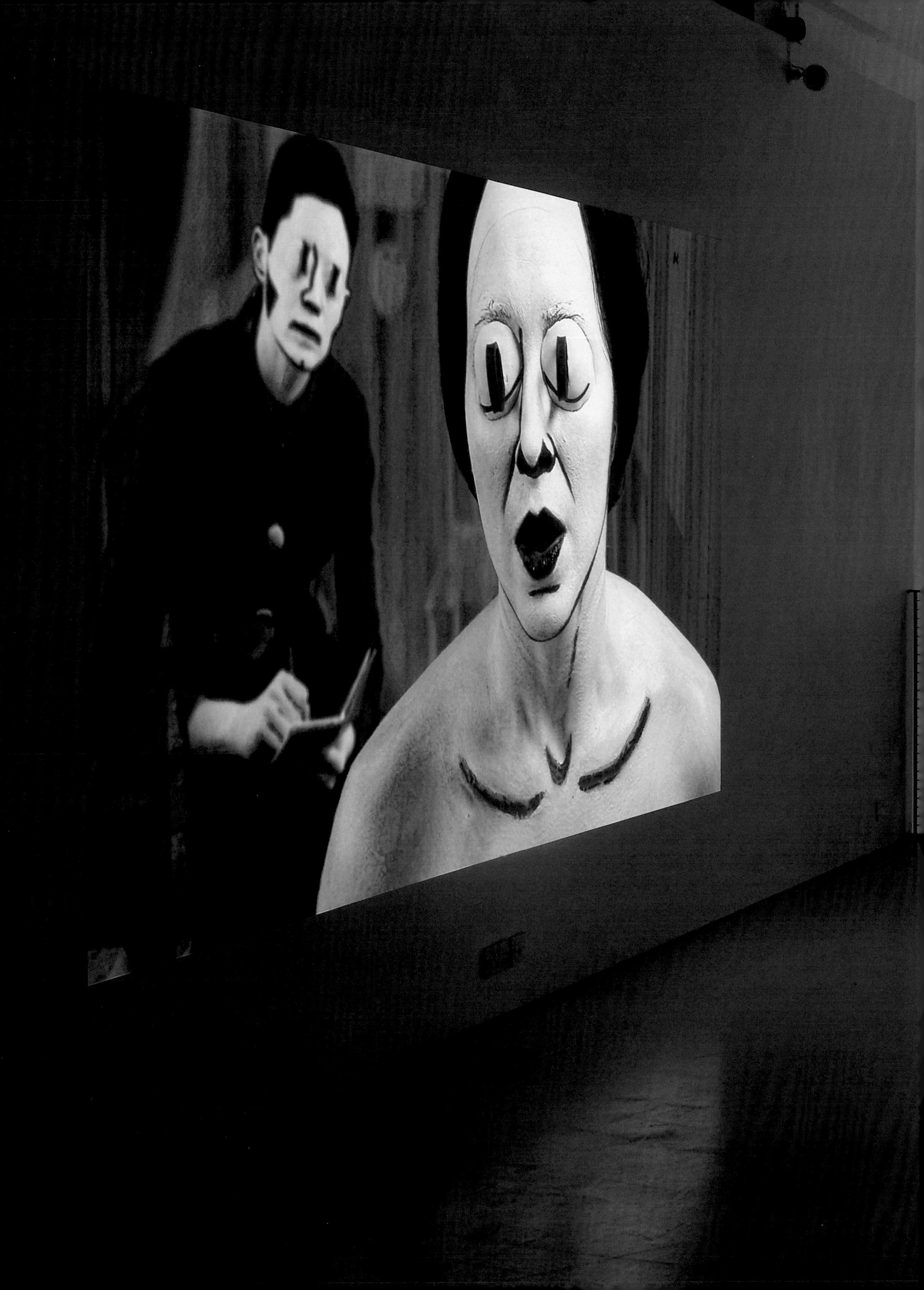

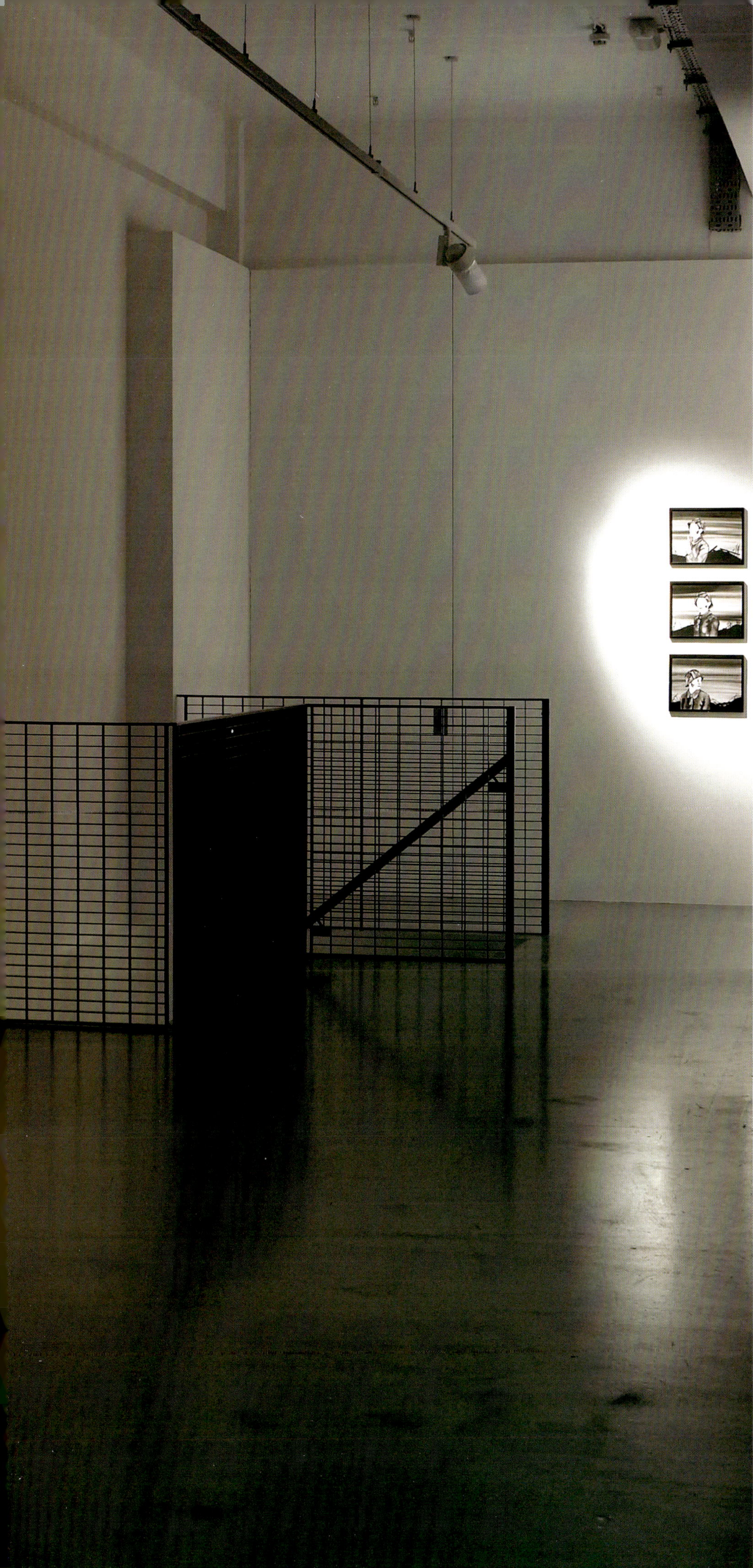

Mary Reid Kelley

You Make Me Iliad, 2010
Installation view at Pilar Corrias,
September 10–October 6, 2010

The thing that I just love about puns is that puns happen in the brain of the viewer. So I could say a pun and, frequently, it could just go by. It takes the other person to recognize it, kind of like the question, "If a tree falls in the forest and nobody is there to hear it, does it fall?" If a pun is said and nobody realizes that it's said, it just didn't happen. So a big part of the work is made in the brain of the viewer—and that's why you don't pull a goofy face when you deliver your funny line. Let the audience or the viewer construct the element of the humor. The viewer does the work of the wordplay. If you think about the way Shakespeare wrote his plays, he wrote for everybody. Some things were quite highbrow, some things anybody could get, and some jokes we're just figuring out now because they don't make sense anymore, being so coded in the language of the times. In my work, a lot of the puns are just straight linguistic inversion. Like 'Britannia rules the waves', 'Britannia waives the rules'. And then, some references are more artsy or more geared to people who read too much *ArtForum*. I like to have the possibility that you don't need to be super-well-read. It's not an elite thing. It's like a cubist perspective, like words that are seen from two different angles.

I do all of the writing, all of the research. But it's when the films actually start to be made that Pat, my husband, really starts contributing. He's holding the camera. Although we go back and forth quite a bit, I've got a very definite idea of what I want for some shots—and for some shots I don't. What we do is my choice. And then, once we're on the way, Pat is always enthusiastic to just pick up whatever is happening and run with it, with me. It's sometimes a struggle to get people to realize how important what he does is. He gives the work form. We never would have started doing this if he hadn't been there and picked up a camera.

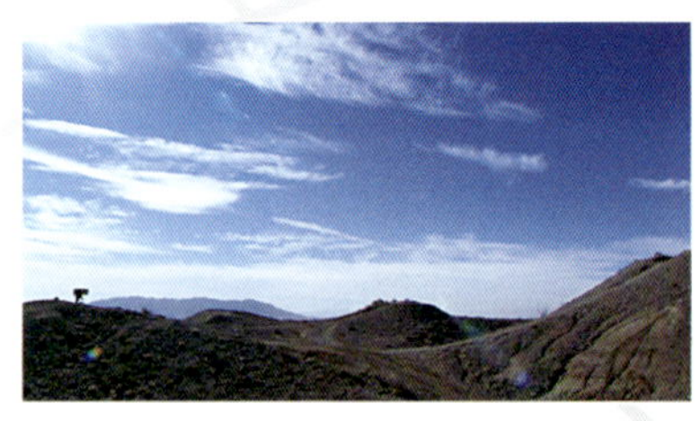
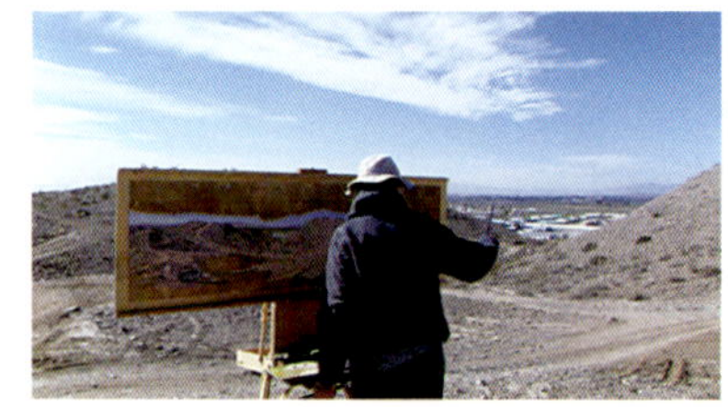
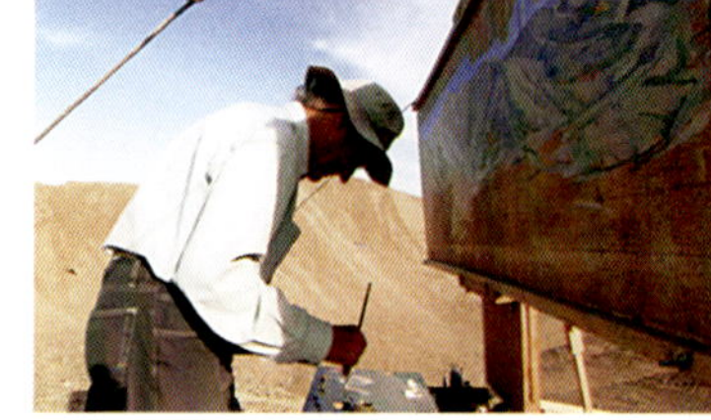

Rackstraw Downes

Robert Mangold

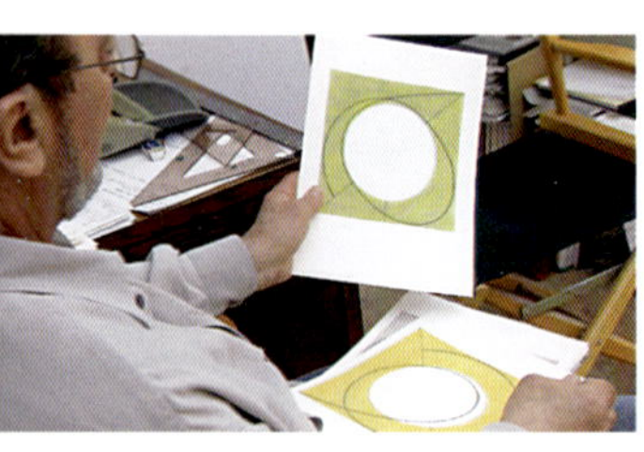
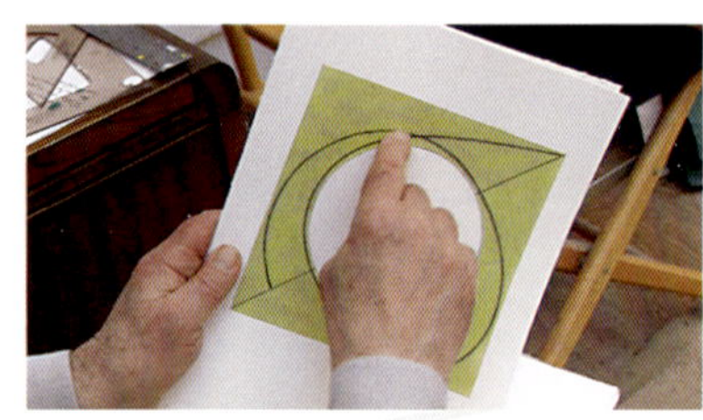
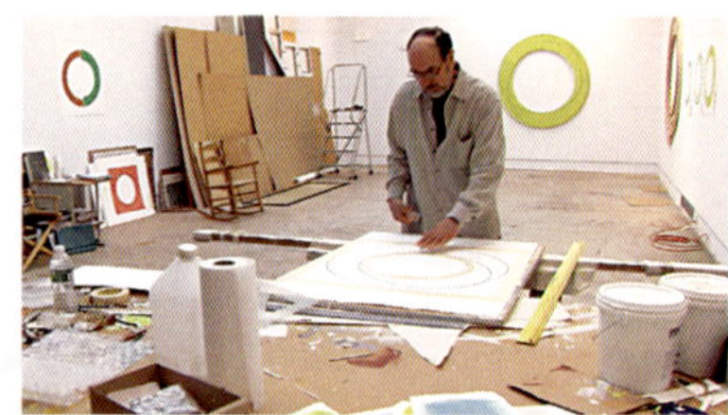
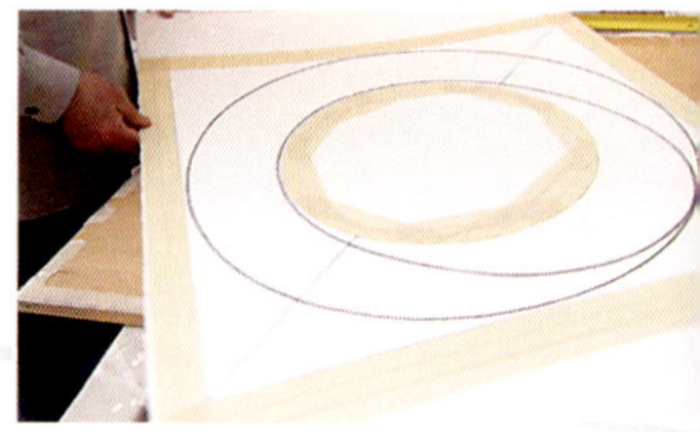

Sarah Sze

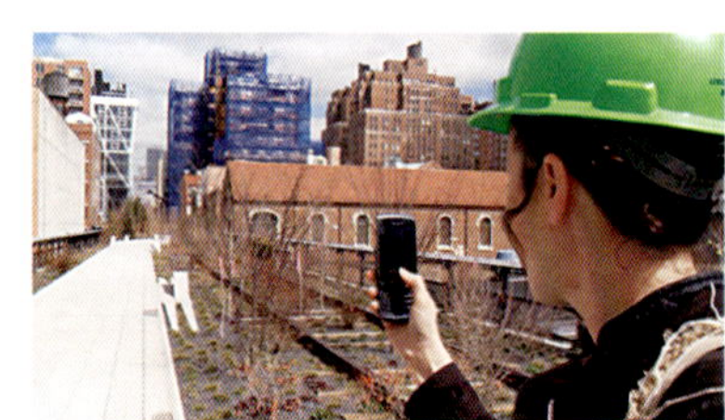
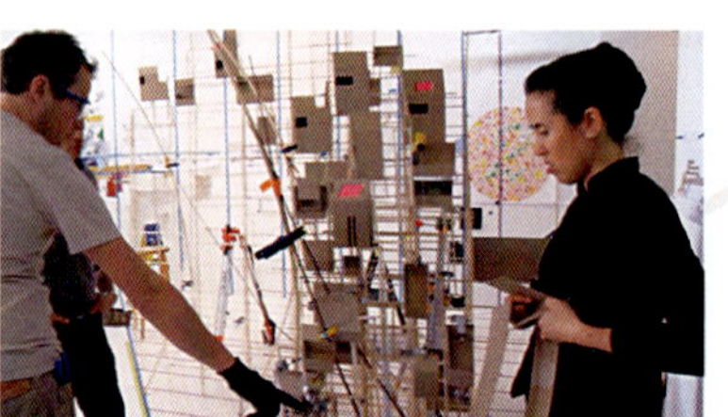

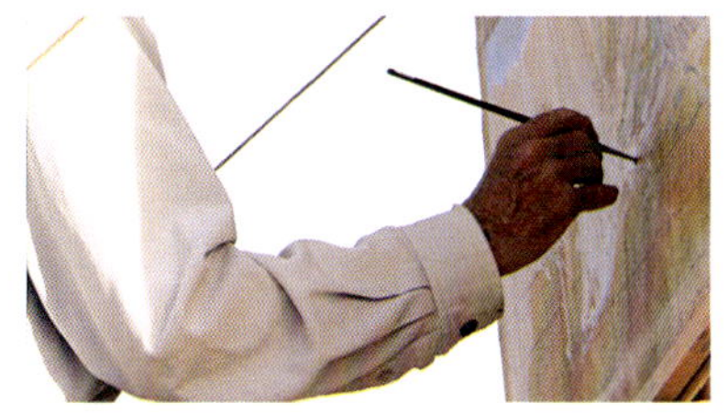
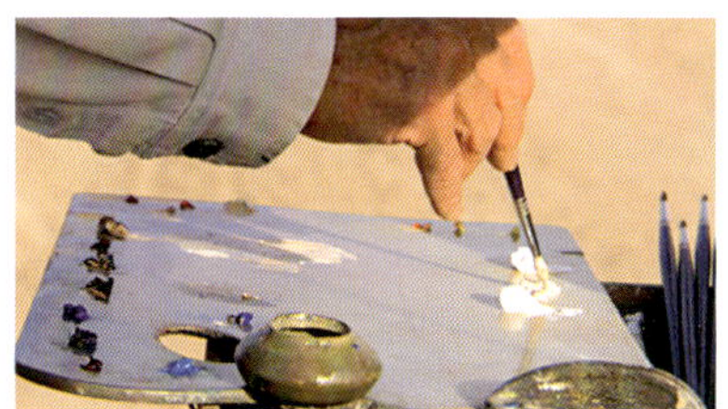
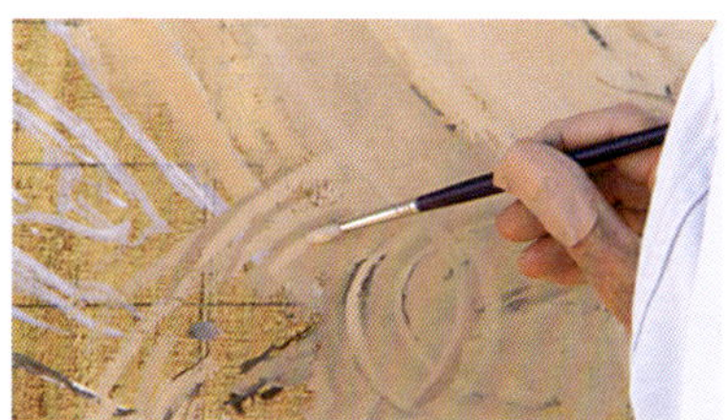

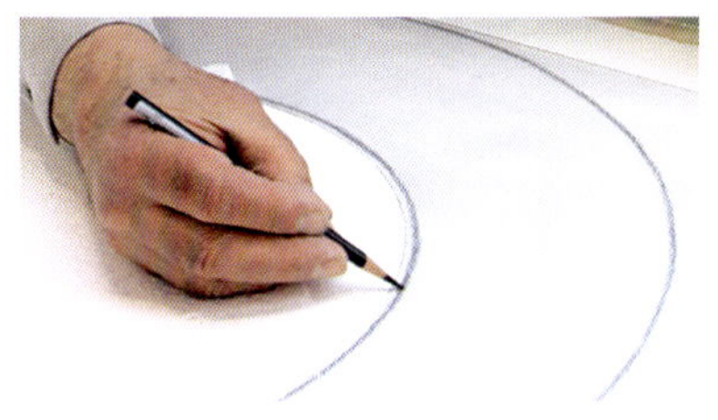
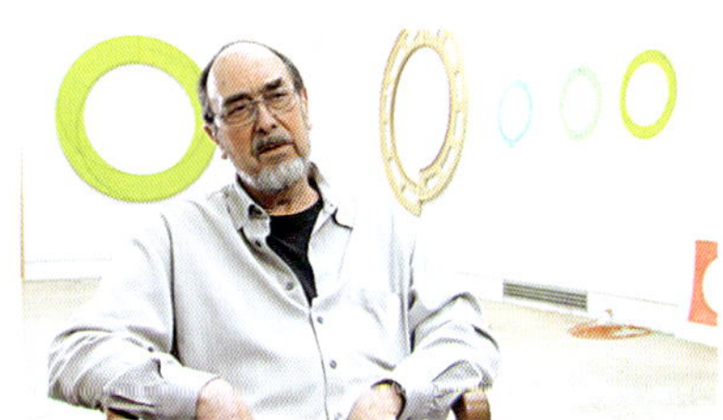

Balance

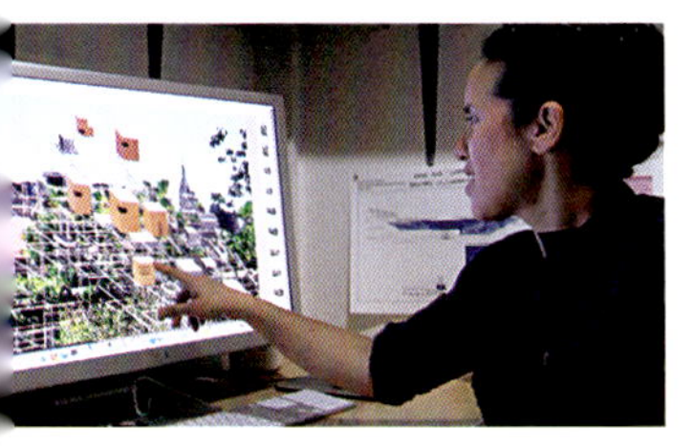
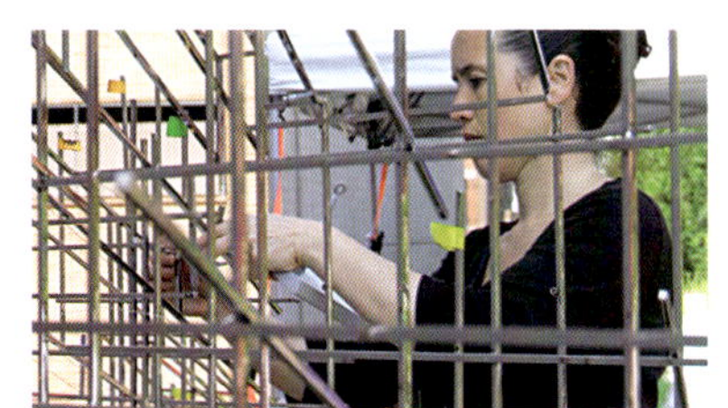
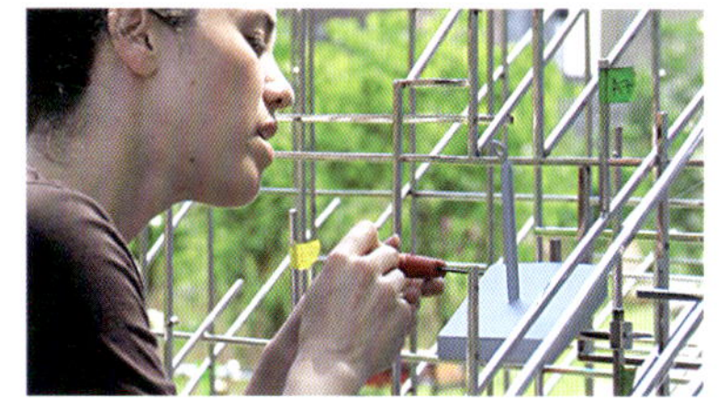
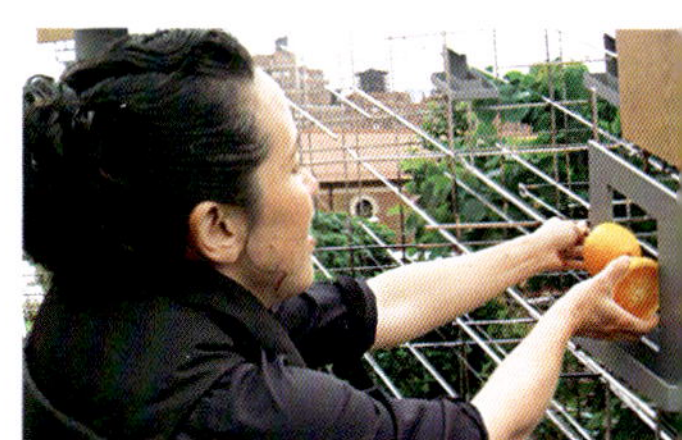

Rackstraw Downes

I think that when you're walking around looking for somewhere to paint, or just going about your business and see something you want to paint, it is because there is already something in the trajectory of your work that is saying, "Hey, pay attention to me. I'm ready now, I'm next; I'm the next thing to try." One year in Maine I was painting in the woods and fields and making all these green paintings. I went to pick up a friend at the airport in Augusta and I drove across the Memorial Bridge. I suddenly realized that Augusta is red brick and blue sky, blue water for the river, and a yellow parking lot that they were bulldozing down. Not a touch of green in it. And I said, "This is fantastic, I'm going to paint this." I didn't want to paint an urban scene or go to cityscape painting. I'd done enough landscape painting. I wanted those colors. And that's what I mean by an inner need—that you're doing something and you're beginning to wear low on it. Your energy's dying down, and you want to try something else. And you don't even know you're looking for it until you see it.

RIGHT
Dunham's Farm Pond, 1972
Oil on canvas, 16 7/8 x 21 inches
Private collection, New York

OPPOSITE, ABOVE
The Mouth of the Passagassawakeag at Belfast, ME, Seen from the Frozen Foods Plant, 1989
Oil on two-part canvas, 36 3/8 x 84 1/4 inches
Private collection

OPPOSITE, BELOW
The Pulaski Skyway Crossing the Hackensack River, 2007
Oil on canvas, 24 x 66 1/2 inches

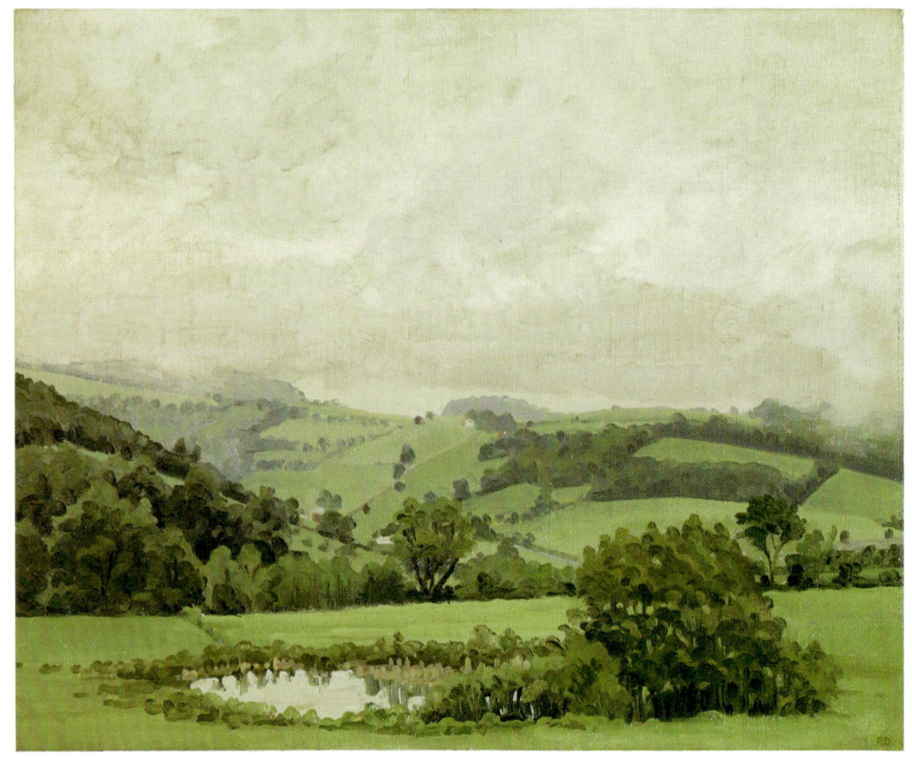

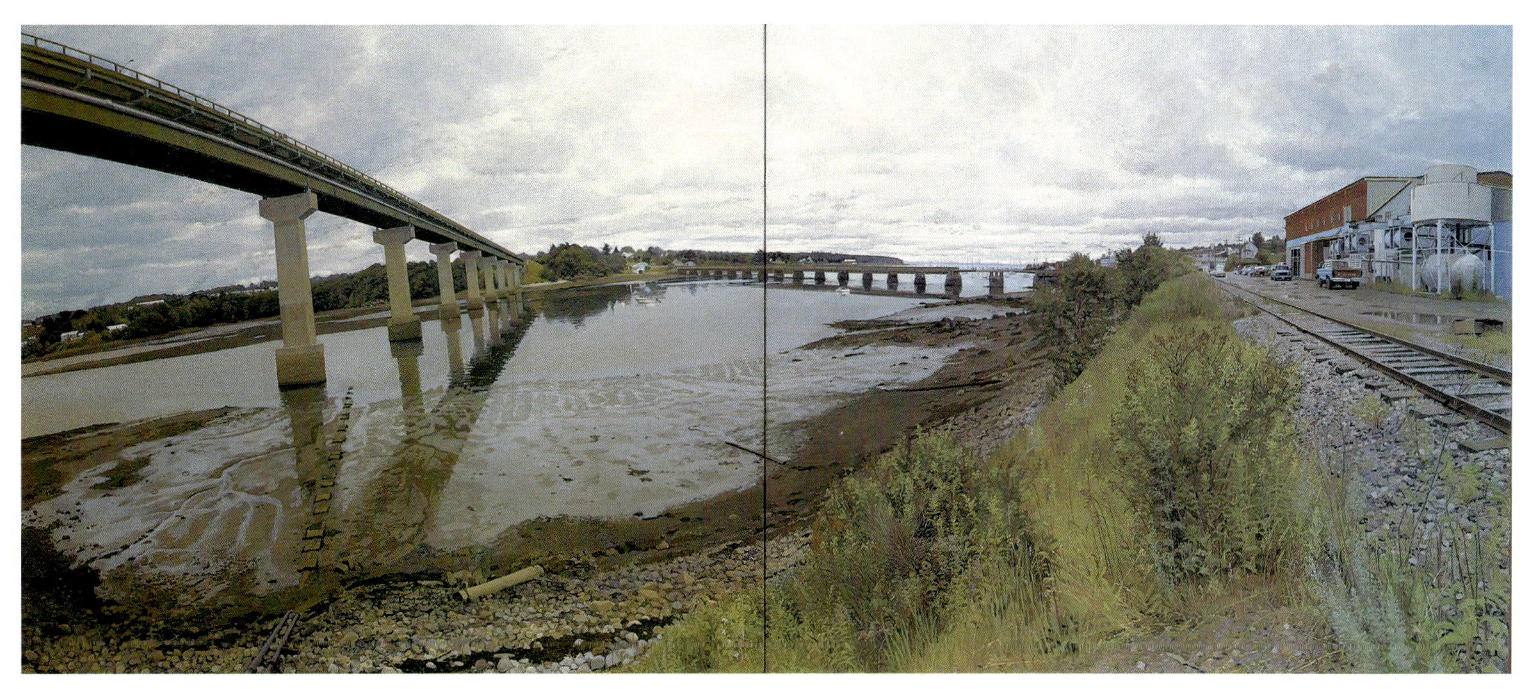

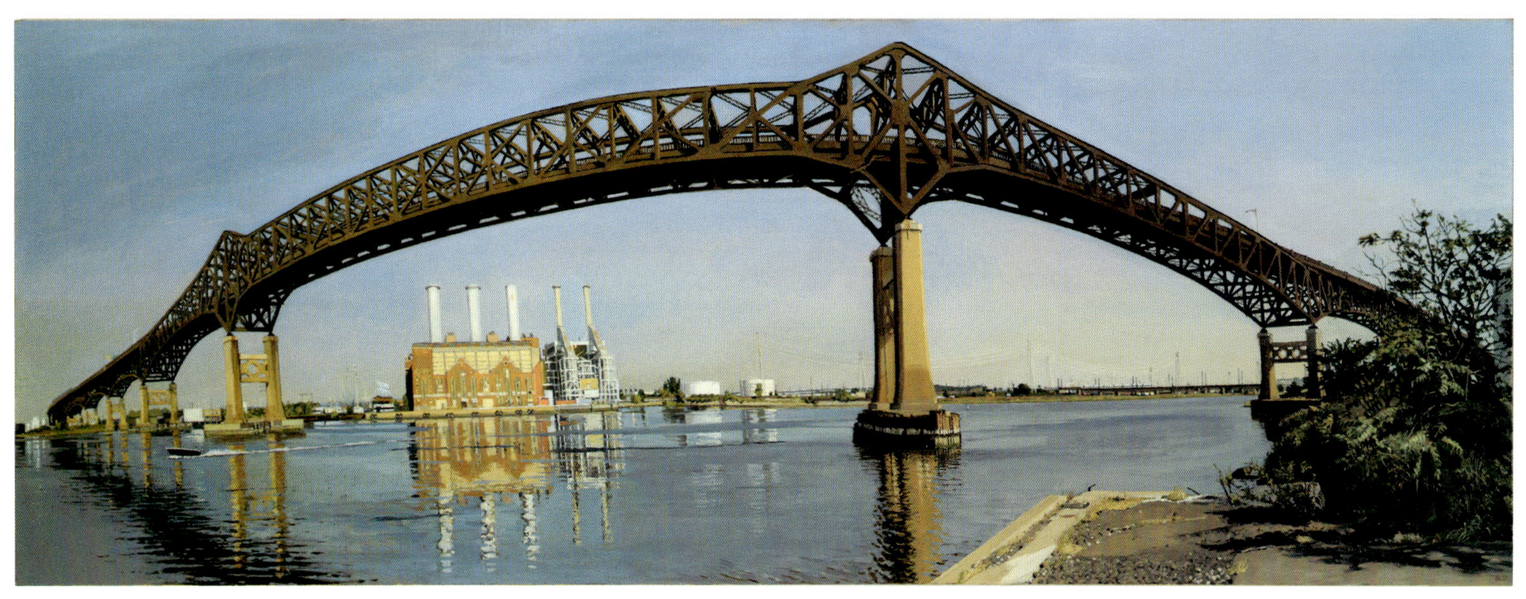

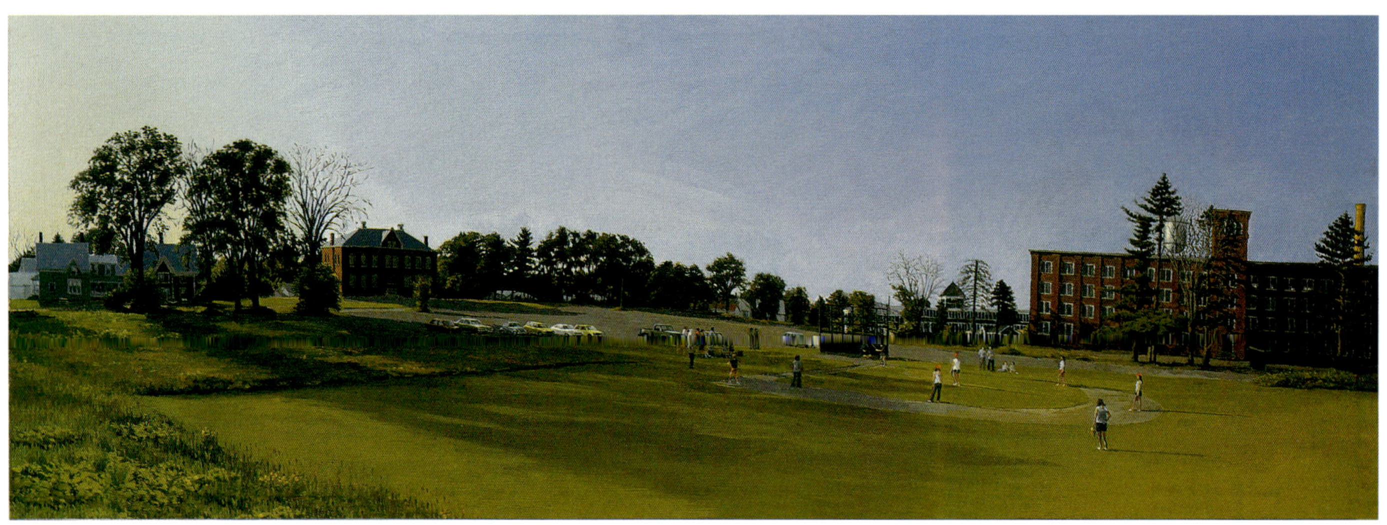

Rackstraw Downes

ABOVE
Softball Practice, Skowhegan, 1975
Oil on canvas, 13¾ x 40⅝ inches
Private collection, New York

OPPOSITE, ABOVE
Ventilation Tower with Estivating Snow Plows, 1988
Oil on canvas, 38¼ x 50¼ inches
Collection of Arthur Goldstein, Upper Saddle River, New Jersey

OPPOSITE, BELOW
Demolition and Excavation on the Site of the Equitable Life Assurance Society's New Tower at 7th Avenue and 52nd Street, 1983
Oil on canvas, 32 x 36 inches
Collection AXA Equitable, New York

You're exploring as you paint. What is the structure? What is the interest here? What *will be* the interest here? You go to a place and you are attracted to it for reason A, but once you start painting, reason A disappears. It has nothing to do with it anymore. Let's say it was some factory workers having a good time in the evening, playing softball. And it's mothers' night off and so it's the girls' team tonight. And you say, "This is kind of nice. I like this. . . ." Let's say that's the reason you start. And then everything else becomes important. How long should the shadows of this tree be in the late afternoon? How do you get the scale of these buildings around here to work with the scale of the figures? All these other considerations come in, and that initial idea is completely lost and forgotten. And you're involved with the softness of light on the tall grass and the way it changes when it gets to the mown area of the grass. Why is it doing that, and how do you express that in the movement of your brush? All these other things become important to you and that old theme, that 'literary' theme that first attracted to you the site, is finished. It's gone.

Perspective is not what I'm interested in, that's for sure. No. I am empirical in that sense. I went out into the landscape in Maine and started working just as though I were an abstract painter. I didn't start out with the idea that your vanishing point is here and your flanking trees are here and here. I began to find that things that perspective told me didn't seem to be true to my eyes. I'm not sure what is true to my eyes. I'm not sure it's something that I can really ascertain or write down or say in definitive terms. But I know that everything changes as you make the minutest movement as you turn your head, and still more when you turn your shoulders. And so one thing I do often is make marks on the ground where my feet are, especially working in the city with urban forms. Because those urban forms sometimes get very disturbing if you get some building that's not in the right position or somehow the wrong size. It seems more disturbing because there are sixteen windows on the twelfth story and there are sixteen windows on the second story. So they've got to be the same even if that building seems to taper as it goes off into the sky. The fact that you have these problems is, of course, the reason that makes you want to go out and do it again. It's always alive. I don't want solutions. That would not be interesting to me. The process itself is an unsolved problem and always will be.

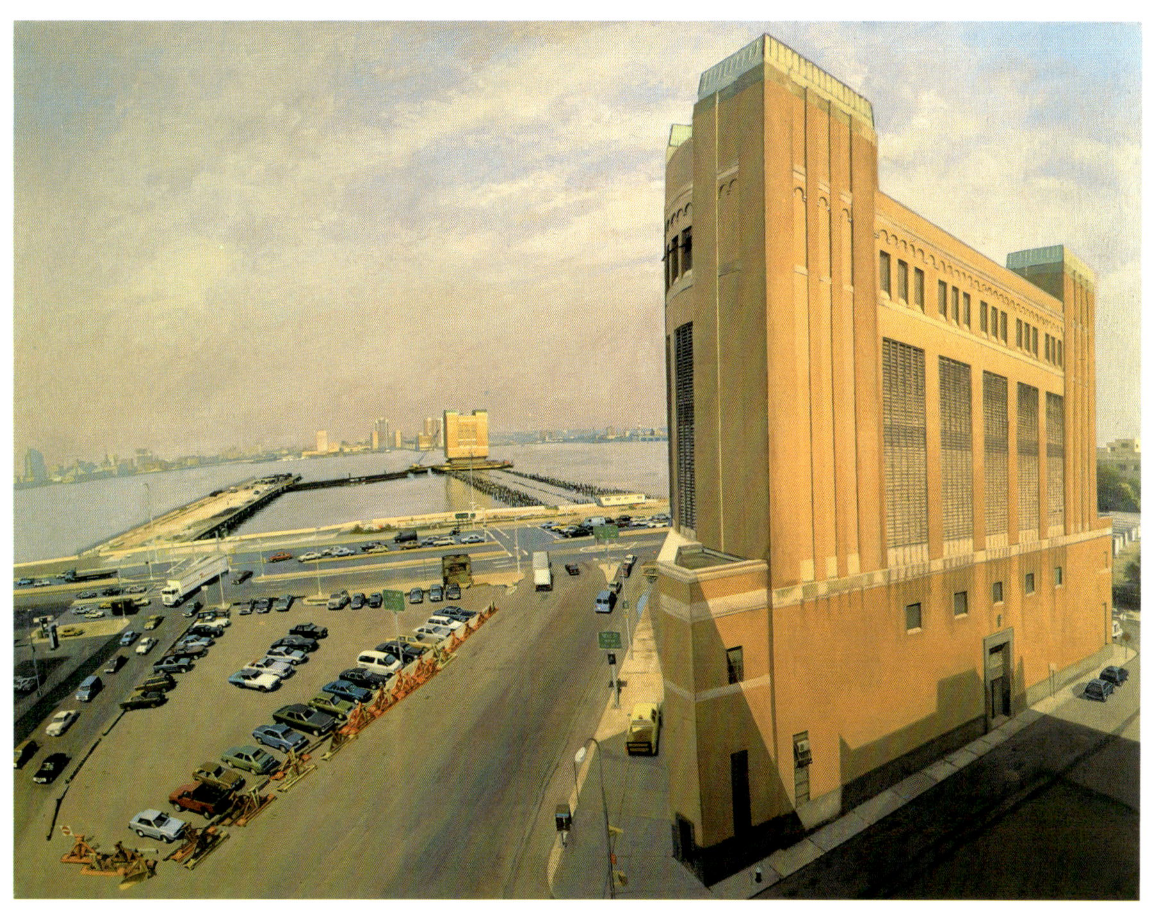

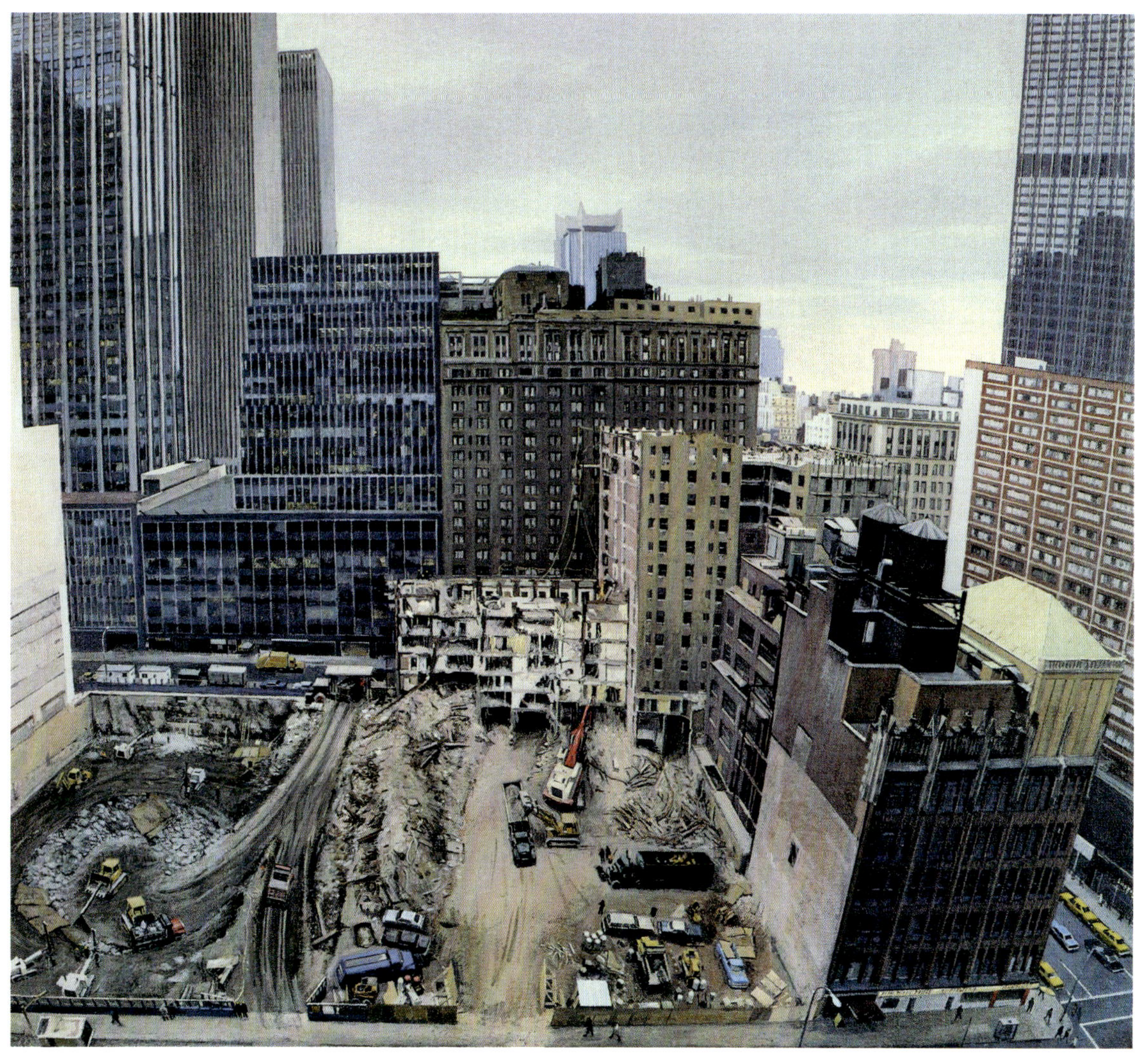

Rackstraw Downes

TOP
P. H. Robinson Generating Station, Dickinson, TX: Eight Ibis Feeding with an Egret, 1991
Oil on canvas, 16 x 108 inches
Collection of the Museum of Fine Arts, Houston, Museum purchase with funds provided by Houston Lighting and Power Supply

BOTTOM
U. S. Scrap Metal Gets Shipped for Reprocessing in Southeast Asia, Jersey City, 1994
Oil on canvas, 16 x 120¼ inches
Private collection, New York

The grid? Let me tell you what it isn't about. When I was in art school I remember Jack Tworkov going into Richard Serra's studio. He was painting de Kooning-esque abstractions in those days. And he said that one idea to structure your painting is to divide it into six rectangles and put something—some painting event—in each rectangle. My grid isn't about that at all. I make the painting or drawing, and then I decide that it has worked out certain aspects of proportion—how big things ought to be and where they should be in the painting—and I want to hang onto that. That's useful work that I've done. It's settled certain things about the painting. So I stretch the grid over it with red threads rather than draw lines over it. Red tends to show up very well on any color. I use that grid so that I can transfer that drawing or small oil painting onto the final canvas that I'm going to use. It's very hard to take a large canvas out into the landscape, and it's hard when the canvas is big to get started in finding where to put your major masses and shapes, and so on. So that work on the small scale gets you

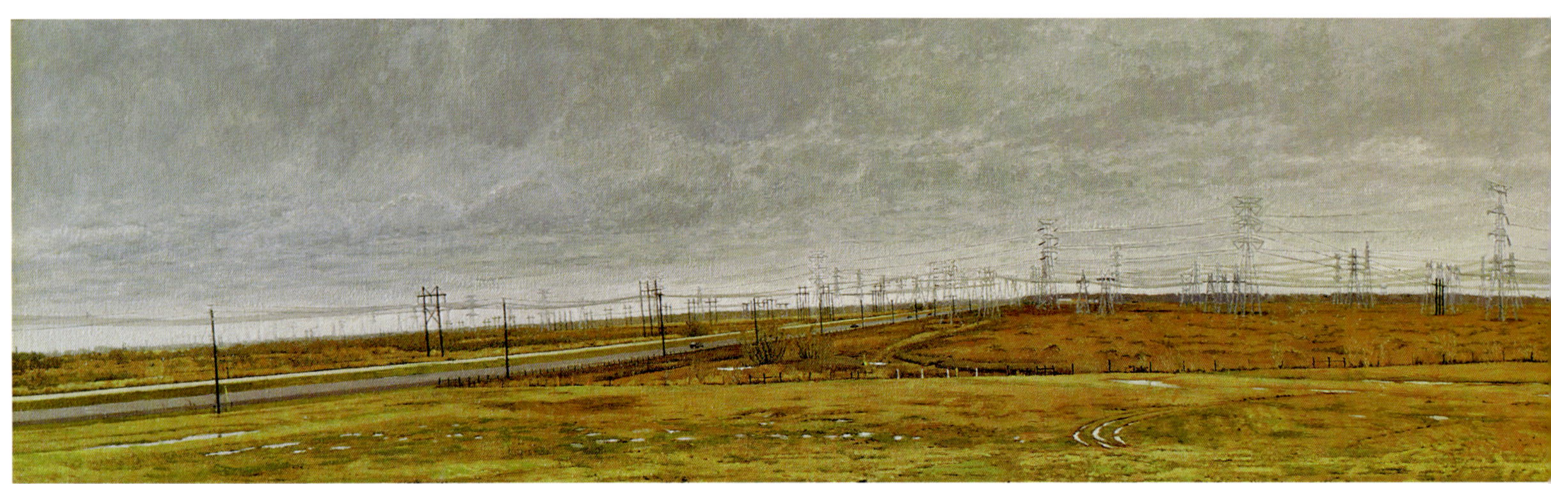

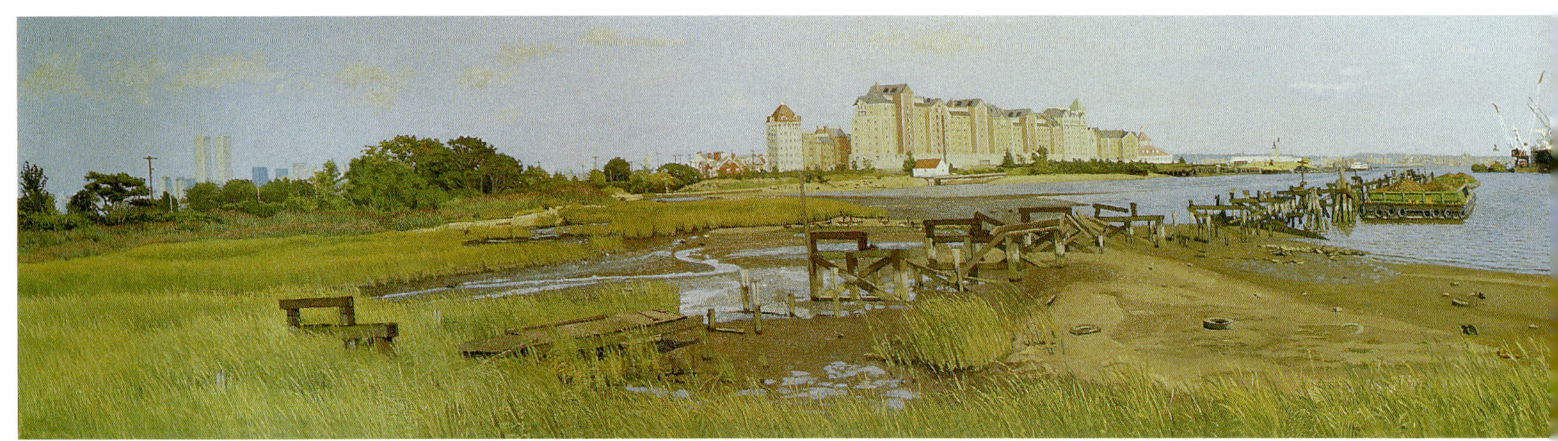

started. It never stays quite like that as the painting proceeds, but it does give you a place to start. And so that's what the grid is there for. It's entirely utilitarian. It has no significance of any kind at all.

I'm not a manifesto artist. I'm not saying art ought to look like this or, now we've gotten to this point in history, art has got to be X, Y, or Z. I'm not at all interested in that. When I came into art school we all wanted to fling paint around like de Kooning, or build up a rectangle into something like a Mondrian square. Al Held, who was my teacher, whom I greatly revered, used to say that each shape has a personality. And I think to myself, "Yes, it does in your painting, but Josef Albers used a square precisely to get *rid* of the personality of shape so that he could see the interaction of color only." I think that there are ways you go about making paintings that make them feel contemporary that you're not even aware of. Paul Valéry said just the opposite. He said that the traditional part of your painting is the part you're not aware of, the part you just receive without realizing you've received it. That's a terribly interesting topic.

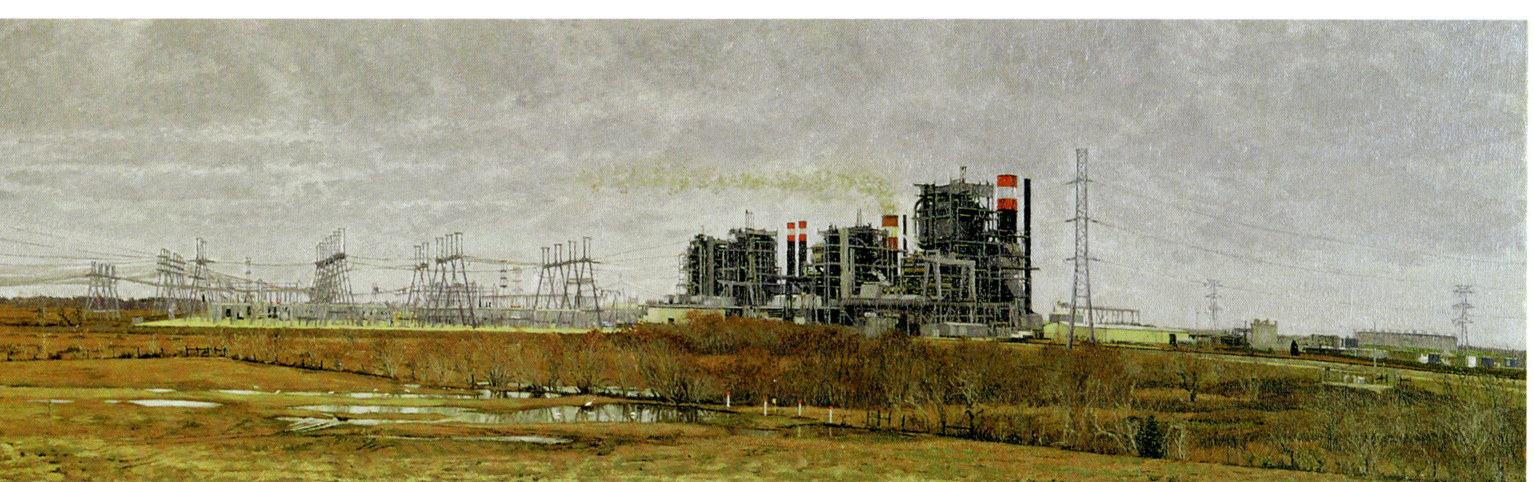

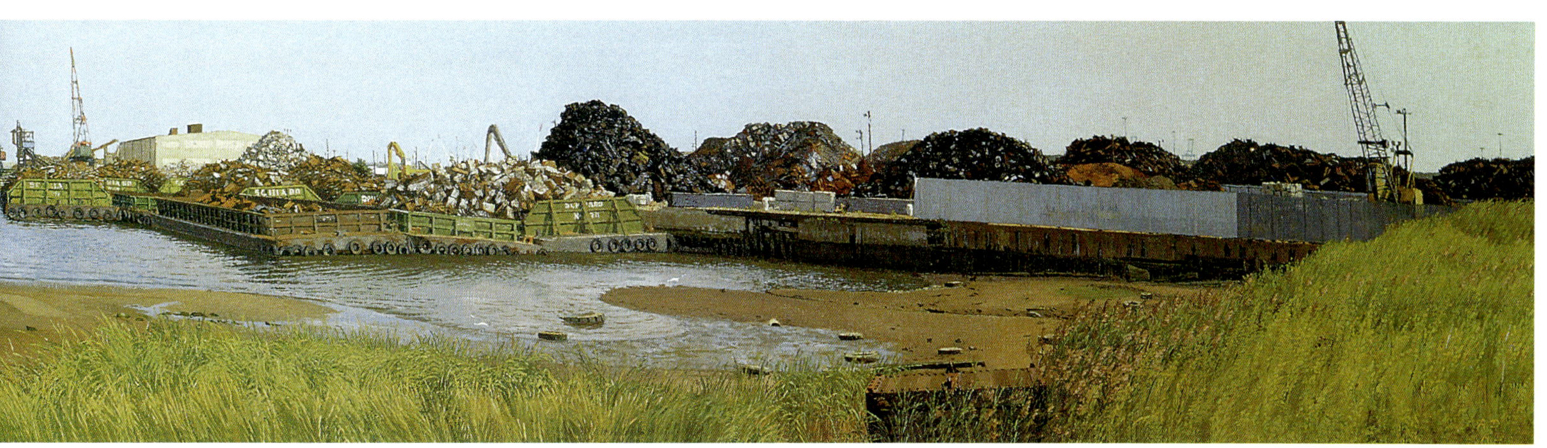

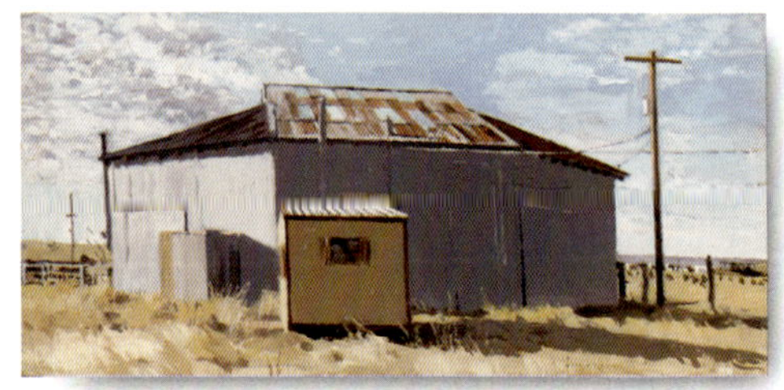

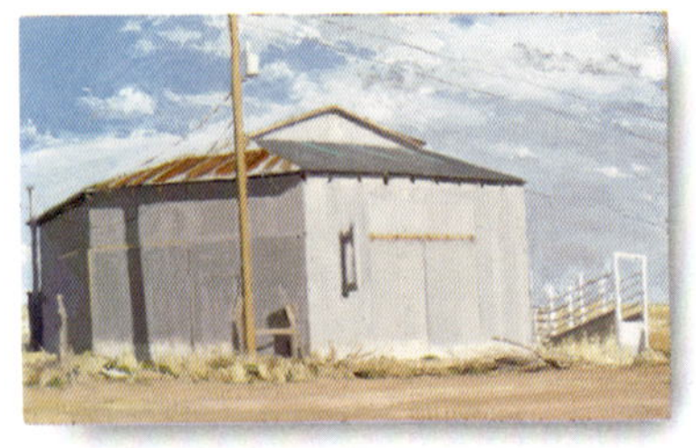

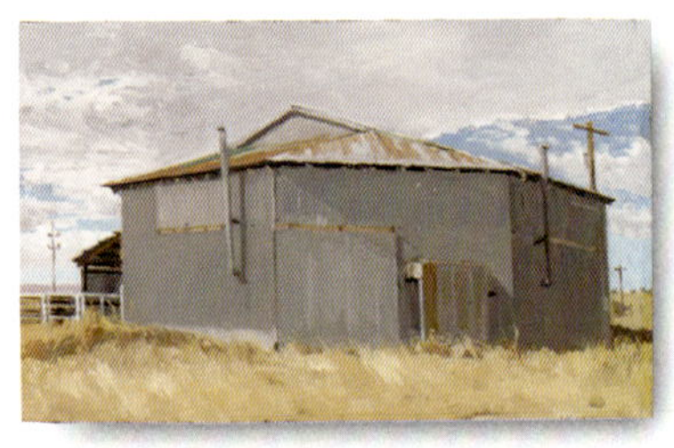

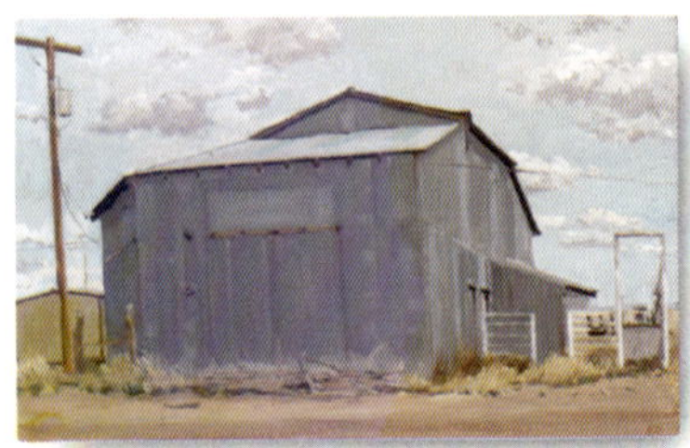

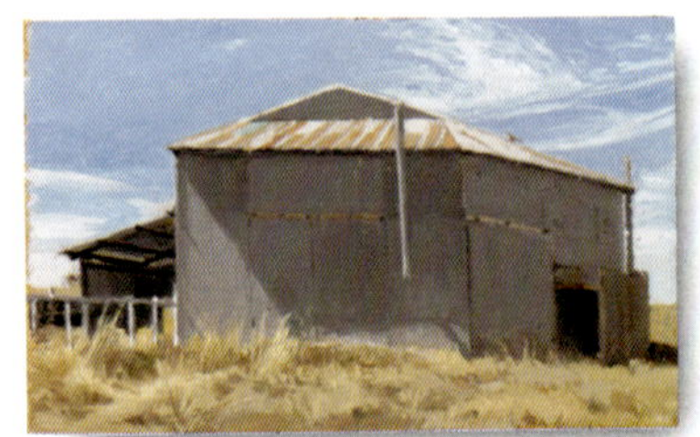

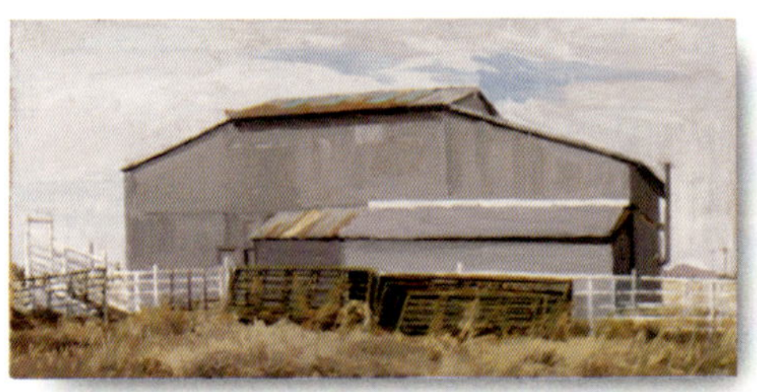

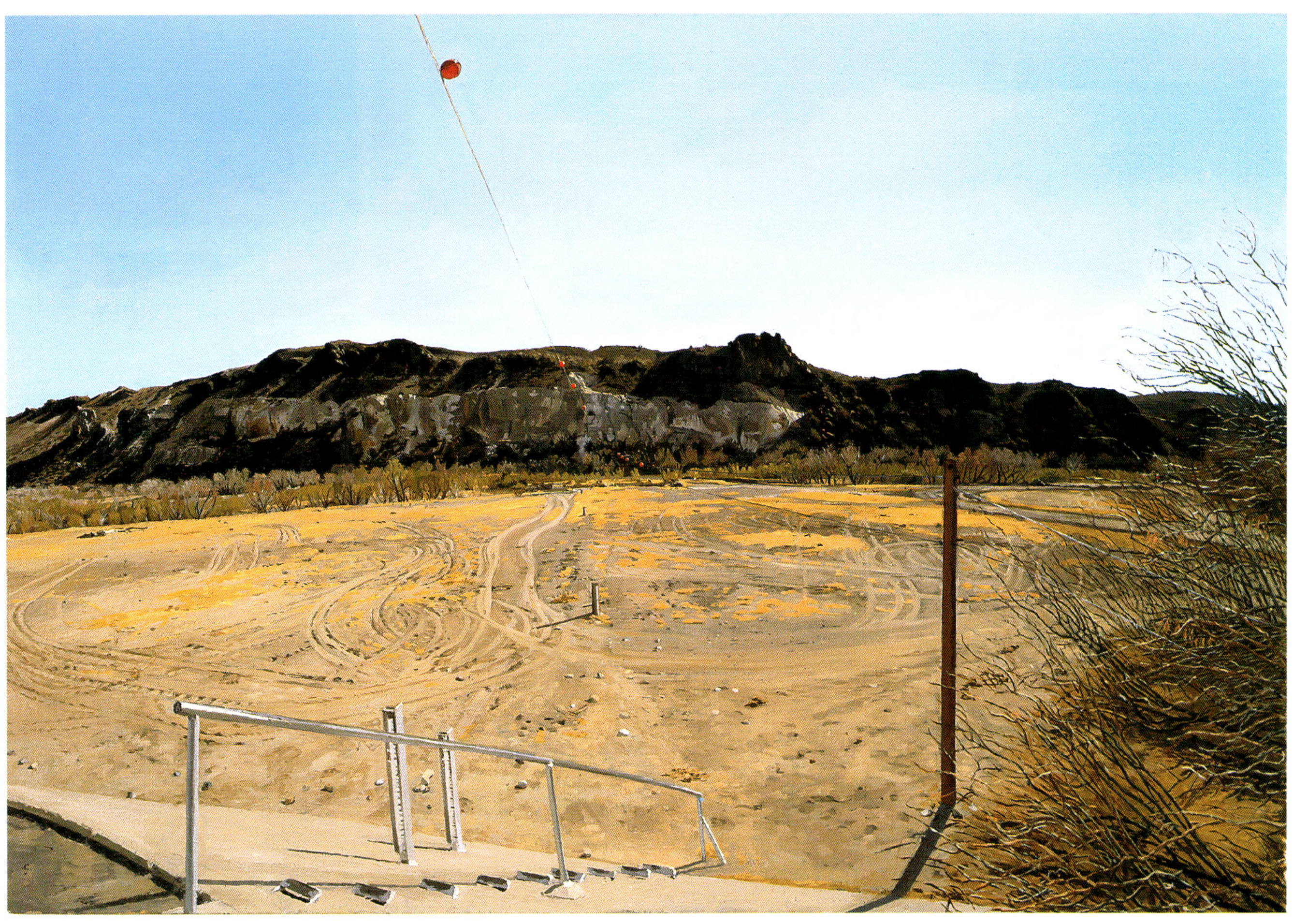

Rackstraw Downes

ABOVE
Water-Flow Monitoring Installations on the Rio Grande Near Presidio, TX (5 parts: part 2, *Facing South, The Flood-Plain from East of the Gauge Shelter,* 10 A.M.), 2002–03
Oil on canvas, 28½ x 48 inches
Collection of the artist

OPPOSITE
Circumambulation Clockwise of the Six-Sided Bull Barn, Marfa, TX, 2007
Oil on canvas, six panels,
37 x 37 inches overall
Collection of Ellen Phelan and Joel Shapiro, New York

I first came out to Marfa because of the mountains. I had been painting for many years in New Jersey, and on the Texas coast near Galveston, High Island, and Beaumont. All flat as could be. And I'd been working in these flatscapes for a good many years. I think I was just very interested in the mountains. I've seen magnificent mountains, and these weren't magnificent and I liked that. I didn't want a magnificent mountain. I don't like mountain rhetoric. You know, "Isn't it grand?" I thought to myself, "Can you paint a modern mountain—a mountain that's cool?" So I came to Marfa. In the meantime I had been painting in the World Trade Center, and I came out here and painted Donald Judd's buildings instead of the mountains. I didn't touch the mountains. Then I came down to Presidio and I immediately responded to the Sandhills. There's something about those Sandhills. They're not classic mountains at all; they're very odd. But you've got the up and down business. And you've got height and depth. Looking down and looking up are really interesting painting ideas and they're very different from painting flatscape or painting on the level ground.

I was astonished at the drama of the light that was so intense as it moved around those forms. They're sort of monochromatic, a yellowish gray kind of color. The shadows were first on one side and then on the other in the late afternoon, opposite from the morning, totally different, totally changed. Those mountains became very interesting to me, when I saw those changes happening in front of my eyes—a change from yellowish gray to almost pitch black, almost as dark as I could make it, taking out my ultramarines and my burnt umbers and mixing them together to get the blackest black—the deepest black.

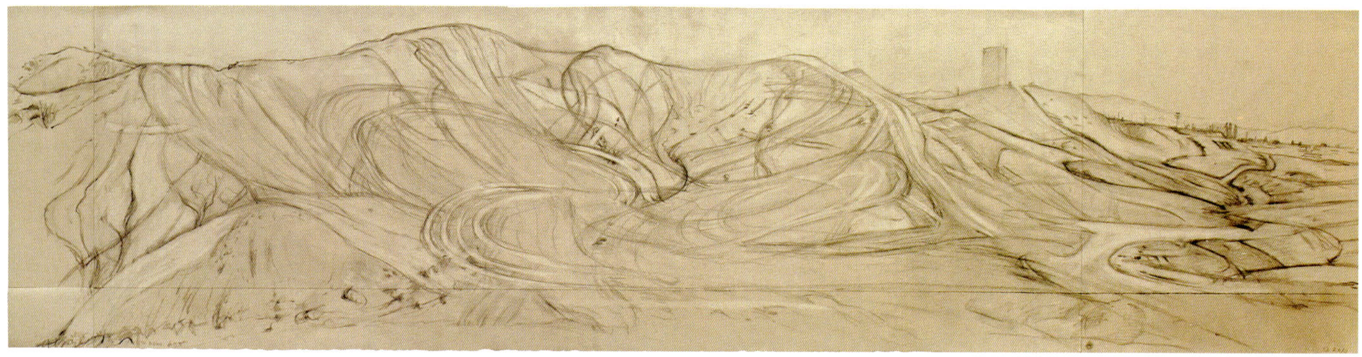

Rackstraw Downes

ABOVE
The Sandhills, Presidio, Looking Northeast, 2010
Graphite on tan paper, 14½ x 46 inches

OPPOSITE
At the Confluence of Two Ditches Bordering a Field with Four Radio Towers, 1995
Oil on canvas, 46 x 48 inches
Private collection

The first time I tried it I felt it was going to be a terribly boring painting. It seemed like there were just endless folds and creases in those mountains. I got halfway into the painting and said, "No, I'm not interested in this," and put it away. Several years later I pulled some of these things out and I thought, "Darn it, this is rather interesting, especially with that cell tower in it. That kind of takes the romance out of it. It's a little vinegar to cut the romantic oil. I think I'll give it a try."

I want to keep my emotions out of it. My emotion should be the emotion of respect—almost reverence—for form. I go over that little shadow, over and over again, till I get that shape. It has a character, some kind of little curlicue where that rock sticks up. You've got to get that curlicue, and you're not satisfied till you get it. That's the fascinating world—that's my world—when I'm working on those paintings, in that business of trying to actually get it. Finally you say, "Yes, that does have character." But it's not the character that I see when I look out there. So I scrape it off and try again. There's a rapport between my image and that real thing out there. They understand one another; they answer to one another. Sometimes you pull back and say, "I can't get it today." So you move to another part of the painting and work over there. Sometimes you never get it. Sometimes you get something else that you didn't exactly mean. And sometimes you feel you got as close as you could ever get. And that is the answer right there: that's the picture.

I started out as an abstract painter. You made the shape that you wanted to make, or thought you wanted to make. And you kept painting on it until it looked right, without regard for anything else except this desire in your own head or heart. I'm not willing necessarily to detach the head and the heart. But when I started painting from representation, the issue really was to put a little tripwire in front of me so I couldn't just make what I wanted to make. I would make something that's out there and make something *like* that. It was a way of introducing variety or change or something else into the painting. I found it unbelievably intriguing and I've stuck more or less with that for forty years now. And I find that changing the stuff that's out there keeps reinvigorating you. That's how you reinvent yourself, to some extent. Raffaele Frumenti, one of my favorite writers on painting, said that the landscape artist seems to have to move to a new location in order to reinvent himself. And I think there's some truth there. Not altogether true, but some truth.

Landscape painting? I think that the image interferes with and intrudes on the painting process. Or you invite it to intrude on the painting process when you paint an image. For many people the painting process is pre-established, partly, by learning from the past. And there are those artists who believe so passionately in the appearance of 'museum' paintings that they will do anything to get that appearance. And then you can go about using the process to *represent* an object. Whereas I think there's another idea, based in American abstract painting of the '40s and '50s, which is that you paint directly. You put paint down straightaway on the canvas and what you look at is the paint. You're not really looking to see; you look at the paint, and it's got to be alive. And then in order to make it evolve, or make more it varied, you introduce the image because the image makes certain demands on you when you put that paint down. But, finally, it's a blob of paint.

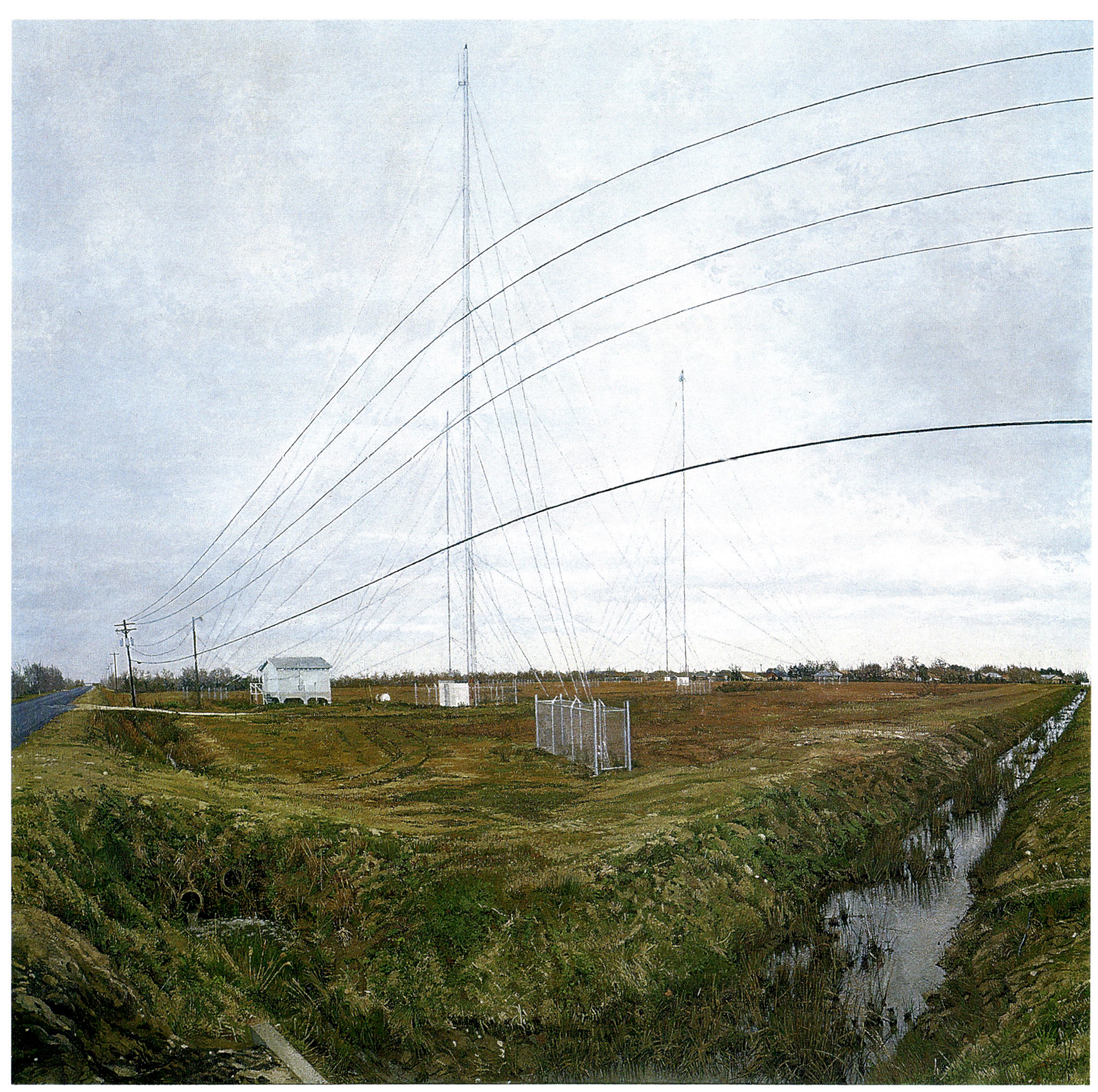

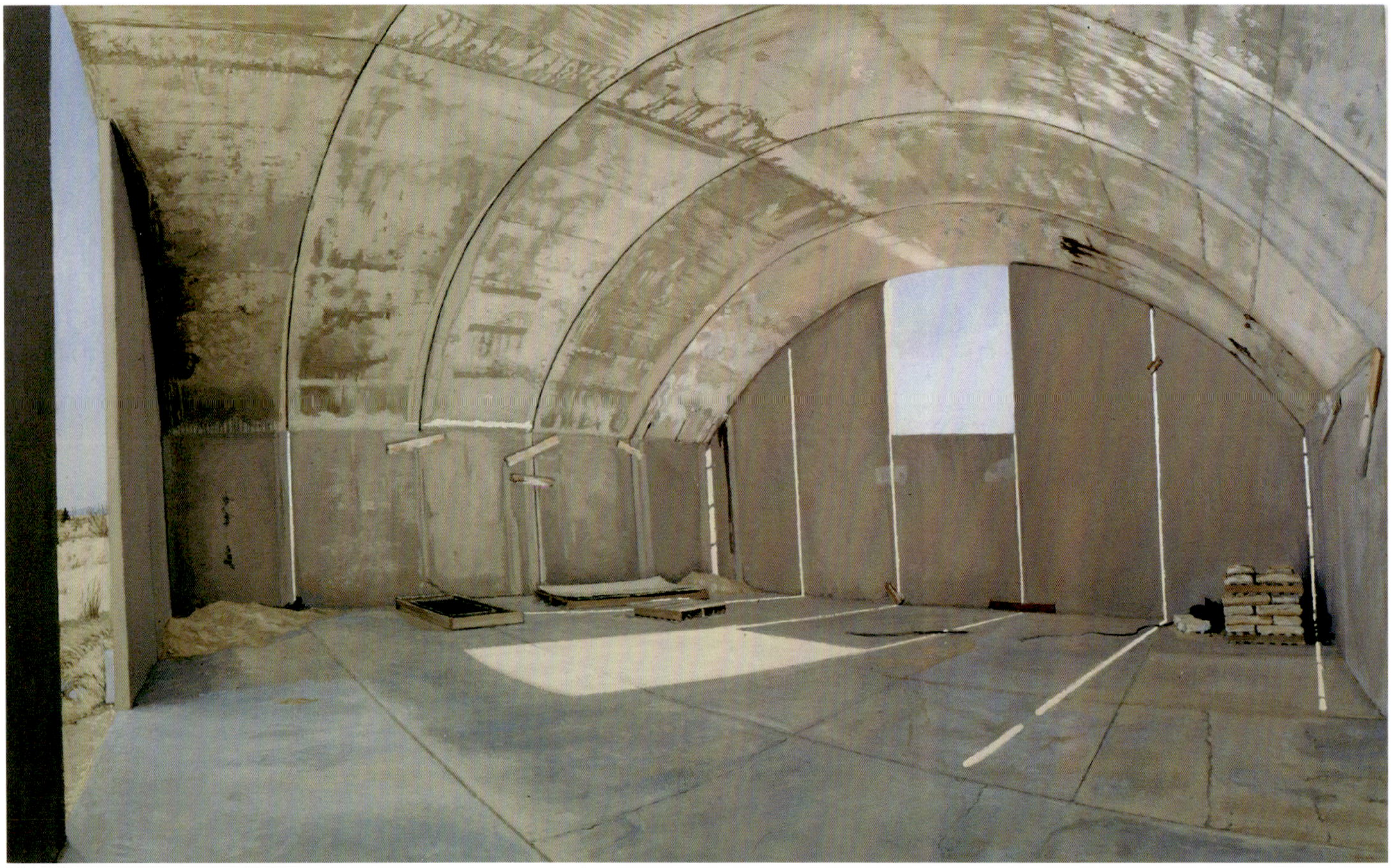

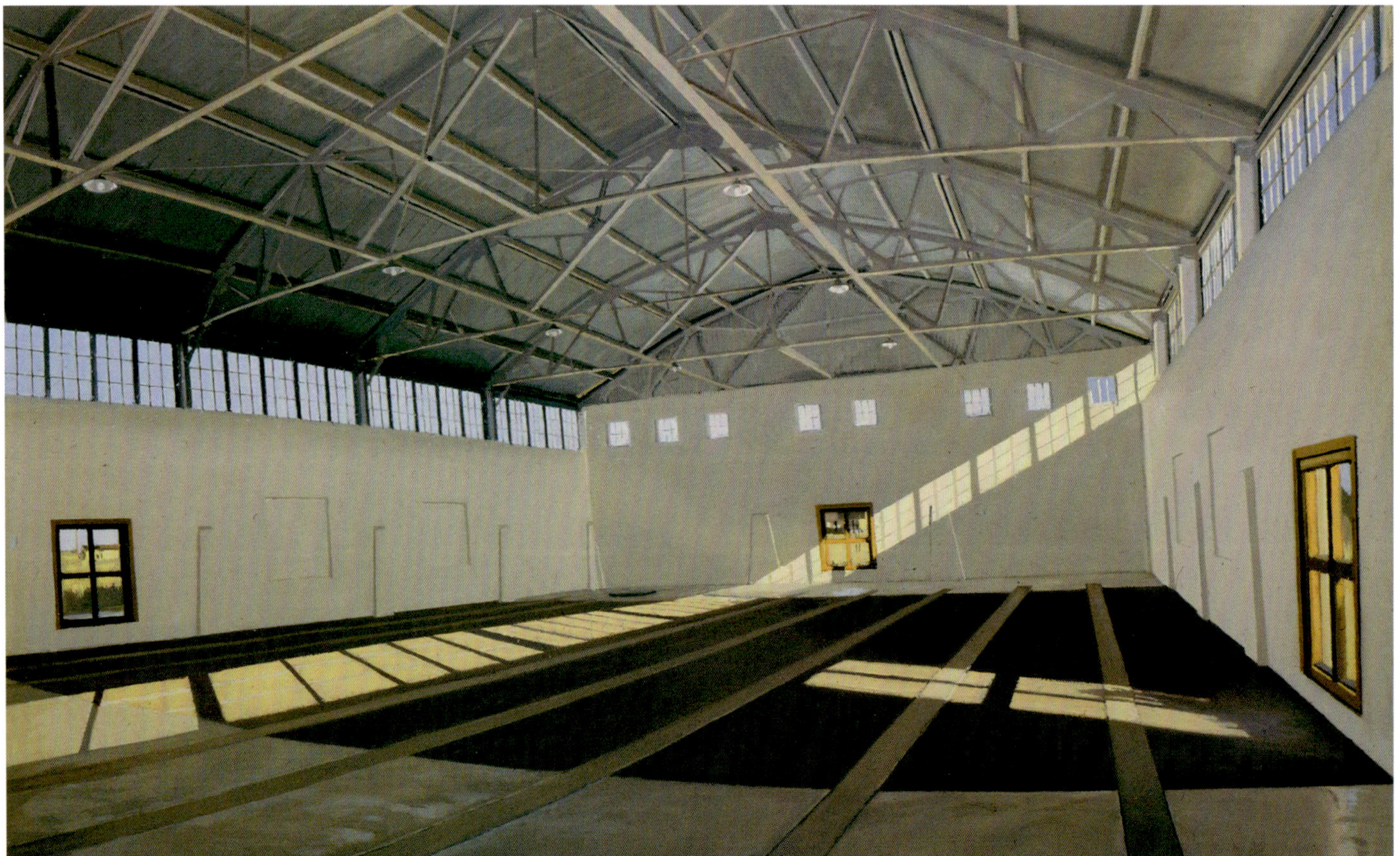

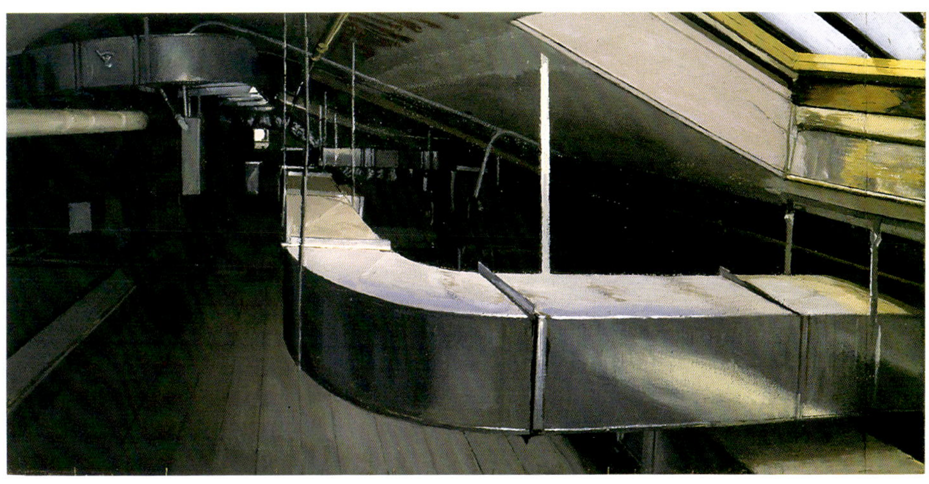

Rackstraw Downes

ABOVE
Snug Harbor, Metal Duct Work in G Attic (4 parts: part 4), 2001
Oil on canvas, 15¼ x 35½ inches
Collection of the artist

OPPOSITE, ABOVE
Chinati, East Concrete Building Interior, 1998
Oil on canvas, 27 x 45¼ inches
Collection of I. B. Wilson, Houston

OPPOSITE, BELOW
The Arena, Chinati, 9 A.M., Looking North, 1999
Oil on canvas, 30⅛ x 48¼ inches
Collection of Mr. and Mrs. Walter C. Wilson

I don't think of myself as a landscape painter. In the popular envisioning of that term, a landscape consists of a painting with a field and a pond and a tree and a mountain in the distance. It's a sort of recipe. And I hope very much that my paintings don't look like recipe paintings. So I like to say I paint my environment —my surroundings—because that gives you the idea that it is a physical thing that surrounds you. It takes it immediately away from the flat-plane image of the world, which comes from looking at flat paintings on a flat wall. So when you say, "That's a picturesque view over there," you mean it's a view like a picture. It's already flattened out in your head. That's another reason why I don't paint from photography. I don't want that work done for me—and a lens does do some of that. It organizes it. Somebody working with a camera can move much faster than I can, can see all kinds of things that I don't see—which is wonderful. It's a beautiful art. But it's not what I'm doing. 'Surroundings' implies that the landscape does really curve around you. If you're standing on a high hill and you look at a straight road in the foreground of your painting, down below, it'll tend to curve up and the horizon will curve down. Photography does challenge me (and nineteenth-century panoramic photography is very interesting to me). But I'd rather not use it; I'd rather not use the term 'realism'. It's very hard to say why a culture accepts one delineation of the world and not another as being realistic. Why do the Japanese see things in that special kind of perspective? Why do they see things isometrically and we see them with a vanishing point? Why do we see objects in the horizontal plane diminish as they go away from us, but objects in the vertical plane parallel and not diminishing? It's very odd. Take Saenredam, the great Dutch painter of interiors, whose work I love. Once when I was on my way to India, I took an enormous detour in order to see one painting by Saenredam—the biggest painting that he ever made. The ceilings, domes, and vaults of his churches are enormous. They're out of proportion in terms of height to the base of the painting, and that's because he observed this parallel quality, even in very high churches. So this thing up here is far away from us and it seems too big. That interests me very much. There is no solution to the representation of the world. There can't be a solution. As soon as you take a three-dimensional world, in which there is movement, and place it on a two-dimensional surface, you move into the world of metaphor, inevitably. And perspective is an attempt to standardize the metaphor of the depiction of space. And so the idea that there could be such a thing as *real* realism, *final* realism, that this is how to do it, seems to me to be nonsense.

Rackstraw Downes

BELOW
Henry Hudson Bridge, P.M., 2004
Graphite on blue paper, 25⅛ x 21 inches

OPPOSITE
Henry Hudson Bridge Substructure, P.M., 2006
Oil on canvas, 39 x 32 inches

Seeing is culturally taught and the art of representation is culturally taught. It's quite interesting. I have a Japanese friend, who came to my studio last year, and she looked at a drawing and she used the word 'crazy', as a good word about art. "Oh no, that's too crazy!" And I think it was that there was this enormous festoon of lines, and it was impossible to see really what it constructed as a solid mass. So I think that there are cultural requirements. We say an image has got to do this or it's got to do that, or it's unsatisfactory. I used to play a game with a landscape painter who used to spend some time in Maine with me. Sometimes we'd go out painting together in the landscape. As we drove down the highway, we'd play this game: How do you mix that bush over there? How do you mix that mountain over there? How do you mix the surface of the road here? And we'd come up with totally different answers. And I remember discussing the road, a tarred road, with Alex Katz. He'd say, "Well you could go towards purple or you could go towards the gray or you could go towards. . . ." There were numerous options there. And perhaps another artist would have seen yet more.

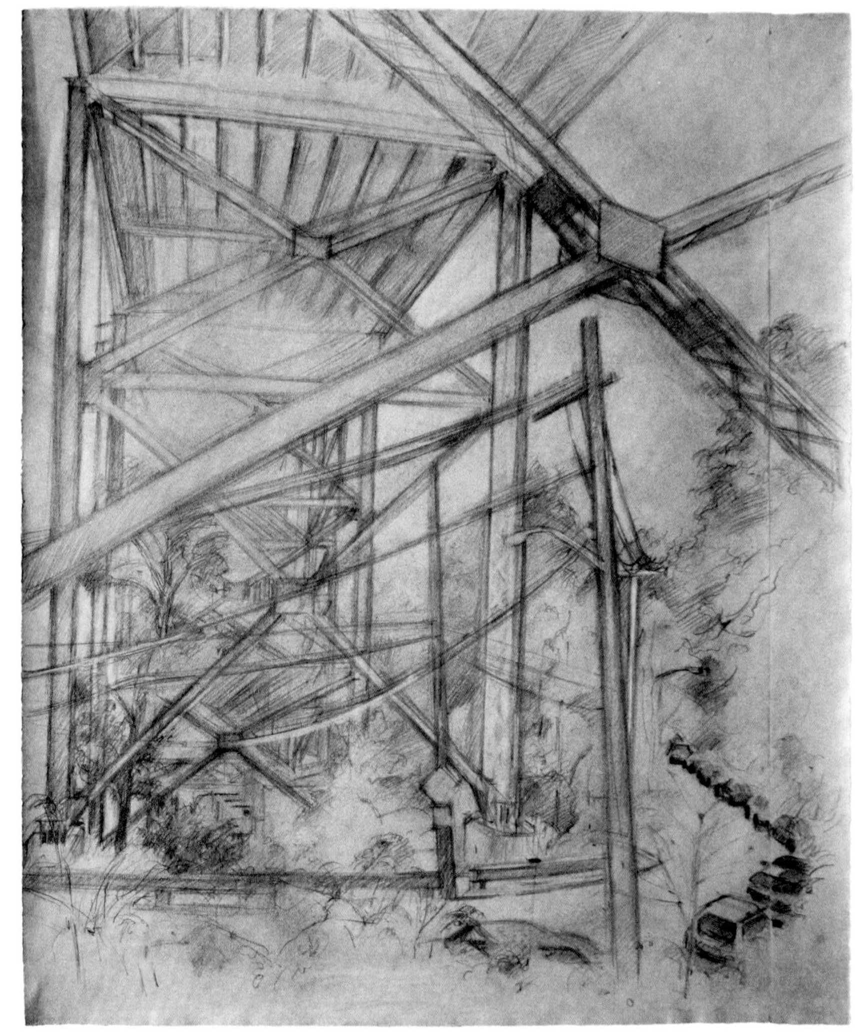

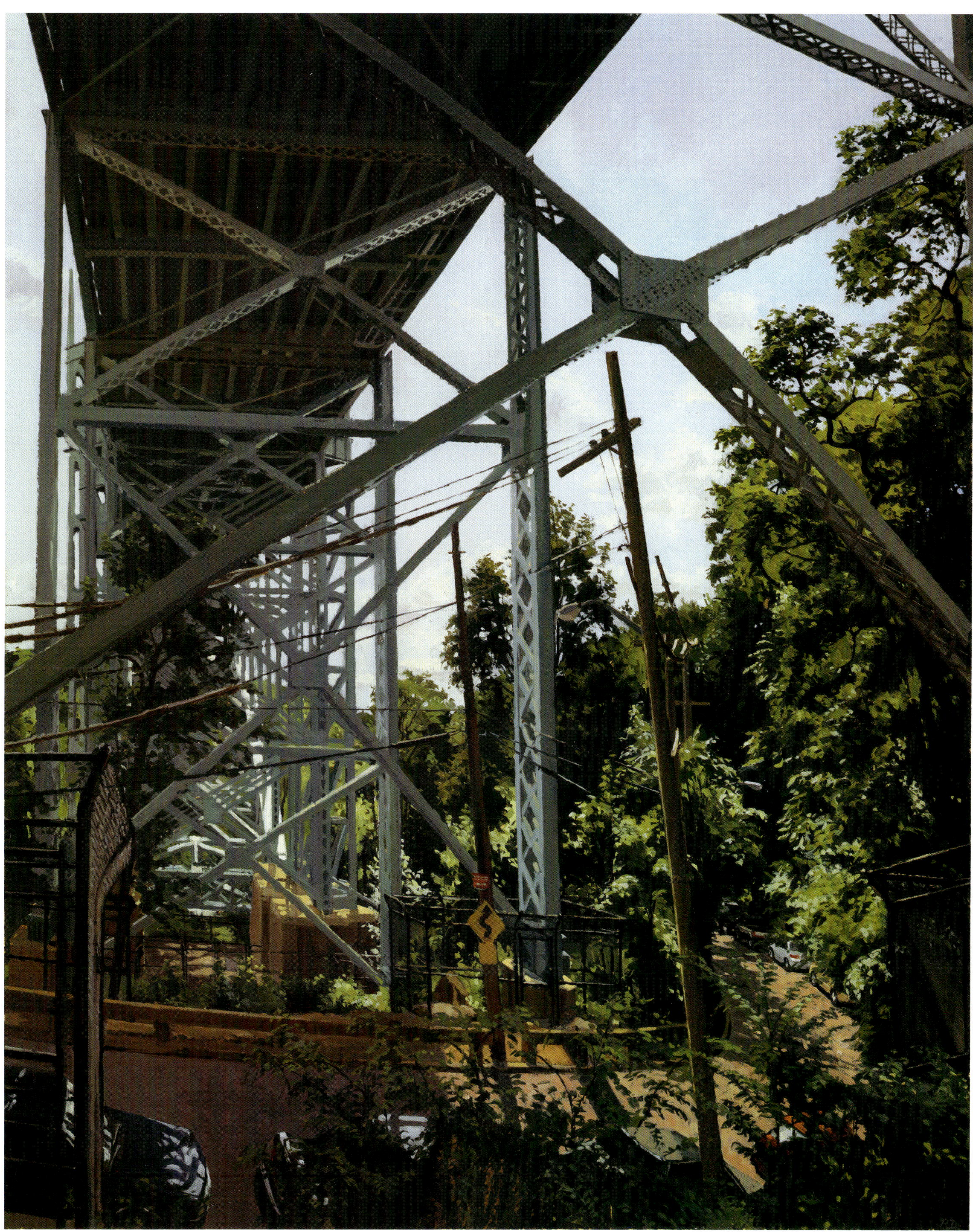

Robert Mangold

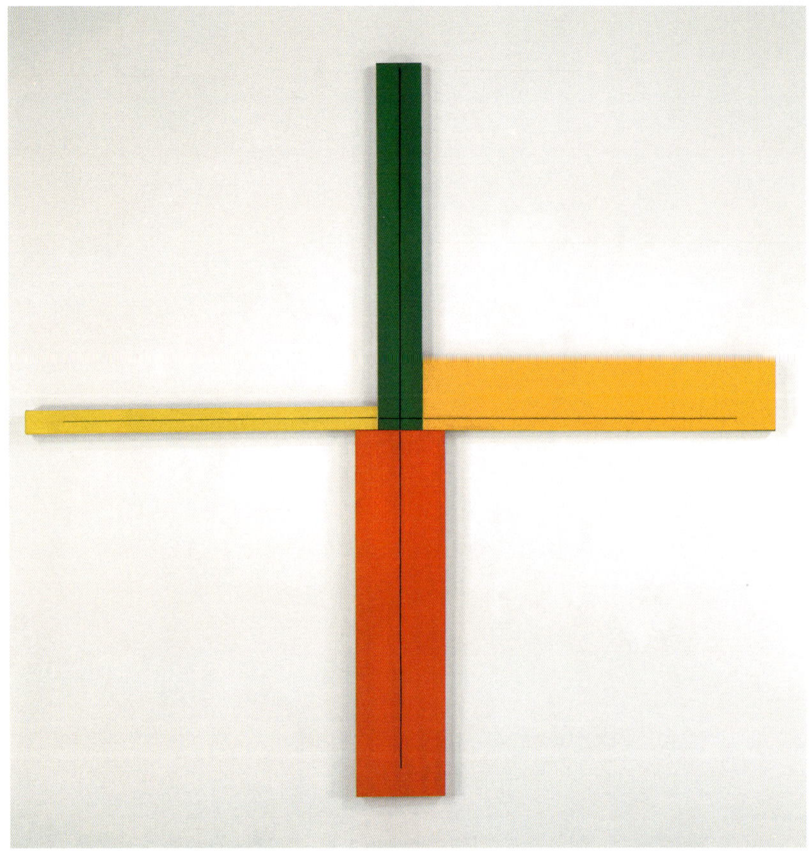

ABOVE
Four Color + Painting, 1983
Acrylic and black pencil on canvas, 96 x 102 inches
Private collection

OPPOSITE
Three Color Frame Painting, 1985–86
Acrylic and black pencil on canvas, 91 x 80⅛ inches
Private collection

My big moment in my early years was when I was a student, in the late 1950s. A group of us went to the Carnegie International, and I saw Abstract Expressionist painting for the first time. I was doing normal student work, and I suddenly saw potential in abstract art just for pure directness and for the scale and physicality of it. It wasn't abstract in nature. It wasn't the controlled-design kind of space of Kandinsky (not that there's anything wrong with Kandinsky). It was totally different—this very direct *affront* that you had to deal with and relate to. I don't even know if I liked it when I saw it, but it was something that I had to understand. I knew it had power that no other painting that I had seen up to that point did. That was a life-changing thing. I went back to art school and tried to paint paintings with little bits of this and little bits of that. A little bit of a Sam Francis over here and a little bit of something else there. The affront was a challenge. There was a sense that these works were presenting you with a visual weight that was very different. It's not that it was better than anything else, but it was very different than anything else I'd experienced—whether it was a Rothko or a Kline. The great de Kooning, *Gotham News*, was in that show and Alberto Burri and Tàpies had large paintings in that show. And in a sense they melted a little bit into it. I saw the relationships of all of it, and I was thrilled. So it was going back, trying to do that, and realizing I couldn't just start trying to do that, but that, at least, I had to understand the roots of Surrealism and how it got there.

The first Pop Art shows were very powerful influences on everybody. And it was in trying to come to terms with this kind of art that Barnett Newman was particularly important to me. It was something about the kind of architectural space he created, the sense of the zip in relation to the frame, the sense of *you* in relation to the zip. It is not surprising that there are photos of people standing in front of his paintings. The idea of physically being in relation to the painting was very important. This was what I wanted to do. So he was probably the most important of those artists for me.

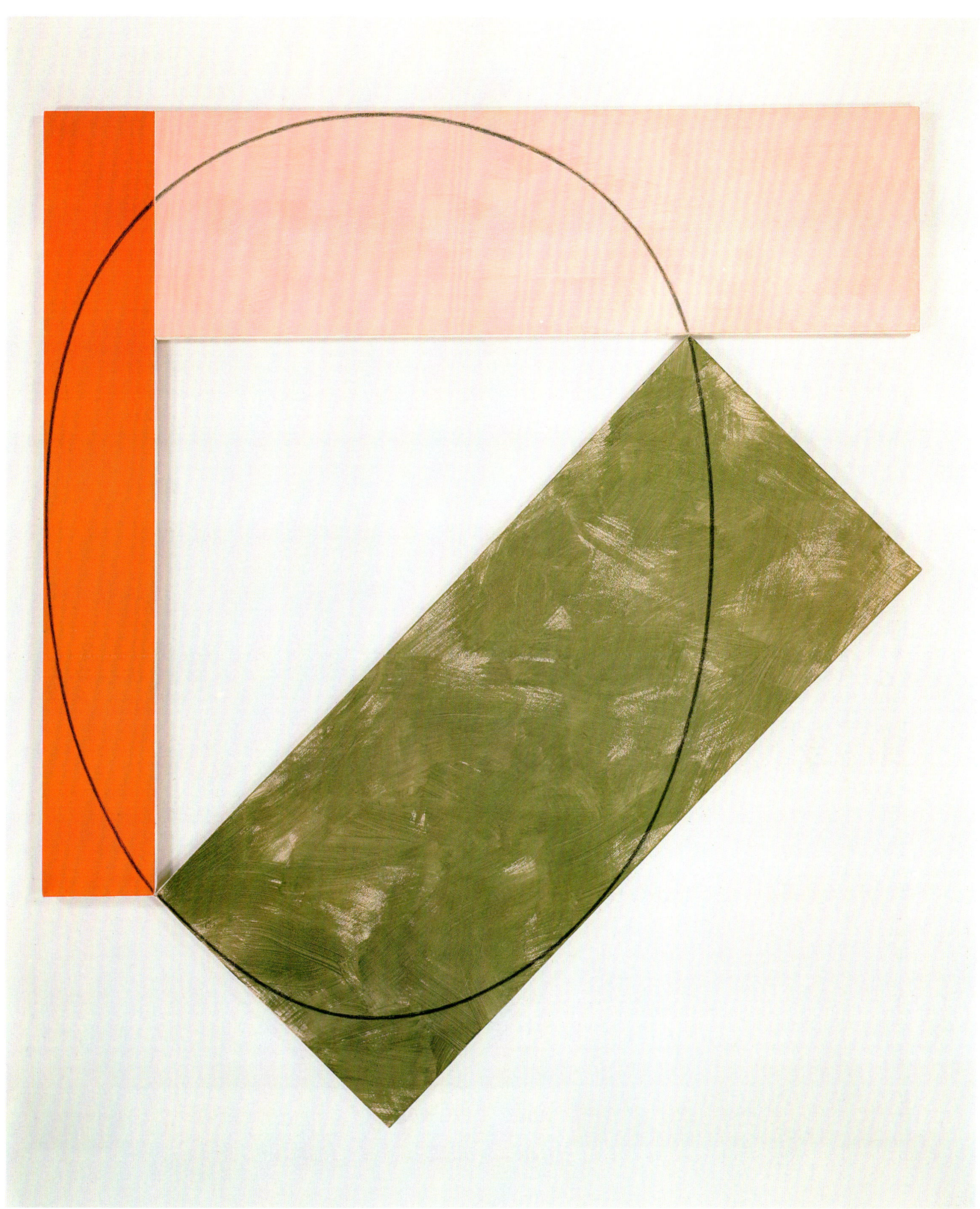

Robert Mangold

BELOW
Red Wall, 1965
Oil on Masonite, 96½ x 96½ inches
Collection Tate Modern, London

OPPOSITE
Yellow Wall (Section 1 & 2), 1964
Oil and acrylic on plywood and metal,
8 x 8 feet overall; 8 x 4 feet, each panel
Collection National Gallery of Art, Washington, D.C.

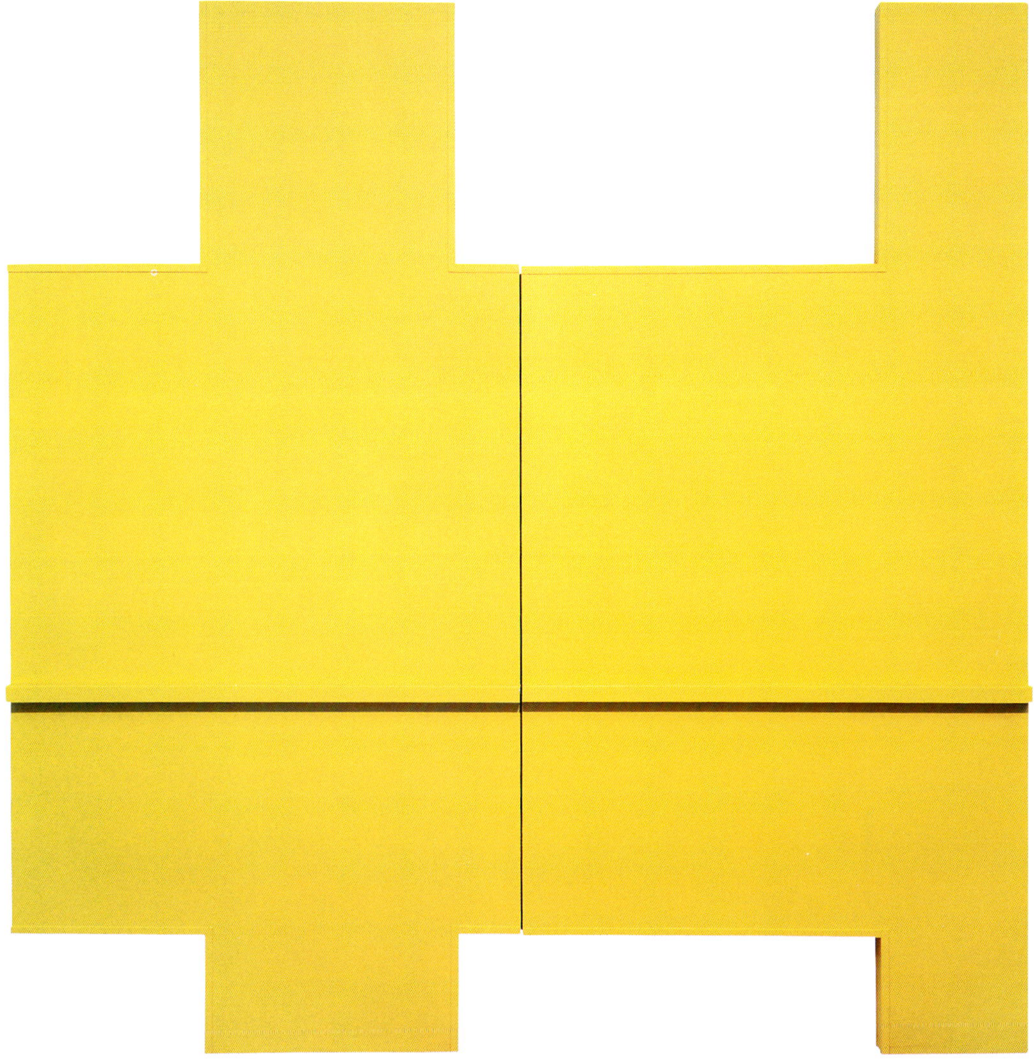

As a young artist I was very connected to what was going on in New York. A number of people—without communicating to each other—had decided that it was a time to start over. What were the elements of paintings? What made a painting a painting? And this was a time of great movement towards sculpture. Everybody was abandoning painting. At one point I had a piece in my studio that was very three-dimensional. And, then, I had a piece that was totally flat on the wall. And it became very clear that the flat piece was the one I was really interested in. It was all part of what later became Minimalism—a seemingly simple single idea exposed in a raw way for people to experience. It was refreshing, and it got rid of a lot of stuff that needed getting rid of so that you could start things over. Maybe all generations feel like they're starting over. But this was a period when it was certainly true—a great period for the expanding idea of simplified form expressing complex ideas.

The thing that began to fascinate me about painting was that it didn't deal with time in the sense that almost every other medium does. You could take a picture of a painting and you'd have it all there. That sounds silly. Obviously you don't really have everything there when you take a picture, but the idea was that painting was one view. Plunk. You get in front of it; you look at it; you've seen it. That doesn't mean you don't stand there and look at it longer, but the point is that it's all there at once. And I thought that, rather than being a detriment, that was a real asset. There was something powerful about that moment of being all there with it and having a relationship in a direct way. Sculpture you can walk around. You can do different things in relation to it before you have to come to an opinion. Painting doesn't give you any of that time. It plants itself in front of you and says, "Here I am." You either turn your back on it or you get involved in it. I like that. It's a strength, not a weakness.

I moved to New York City in the summer of '61. I was in love with New York at that point. And one of the things that I became aware of is that—whether you ride the bus or a cab or subway—you see everything in bits and pieces, in parts. You'd see buildings and gaps between buildings, going by. I became very interested in this idea of pieces of architecture that were both solid and atmospheric—and that a form, one way, could be a gap between buildings, and in another way it could be a building. It was this sense of atmosphere that changed one to the other. So I made *Walls* and *Areas*. One was the color of red brick and the other of yellow brick. From that period I went to works that concentrated on the curve, the curved edge, the curved circle part.

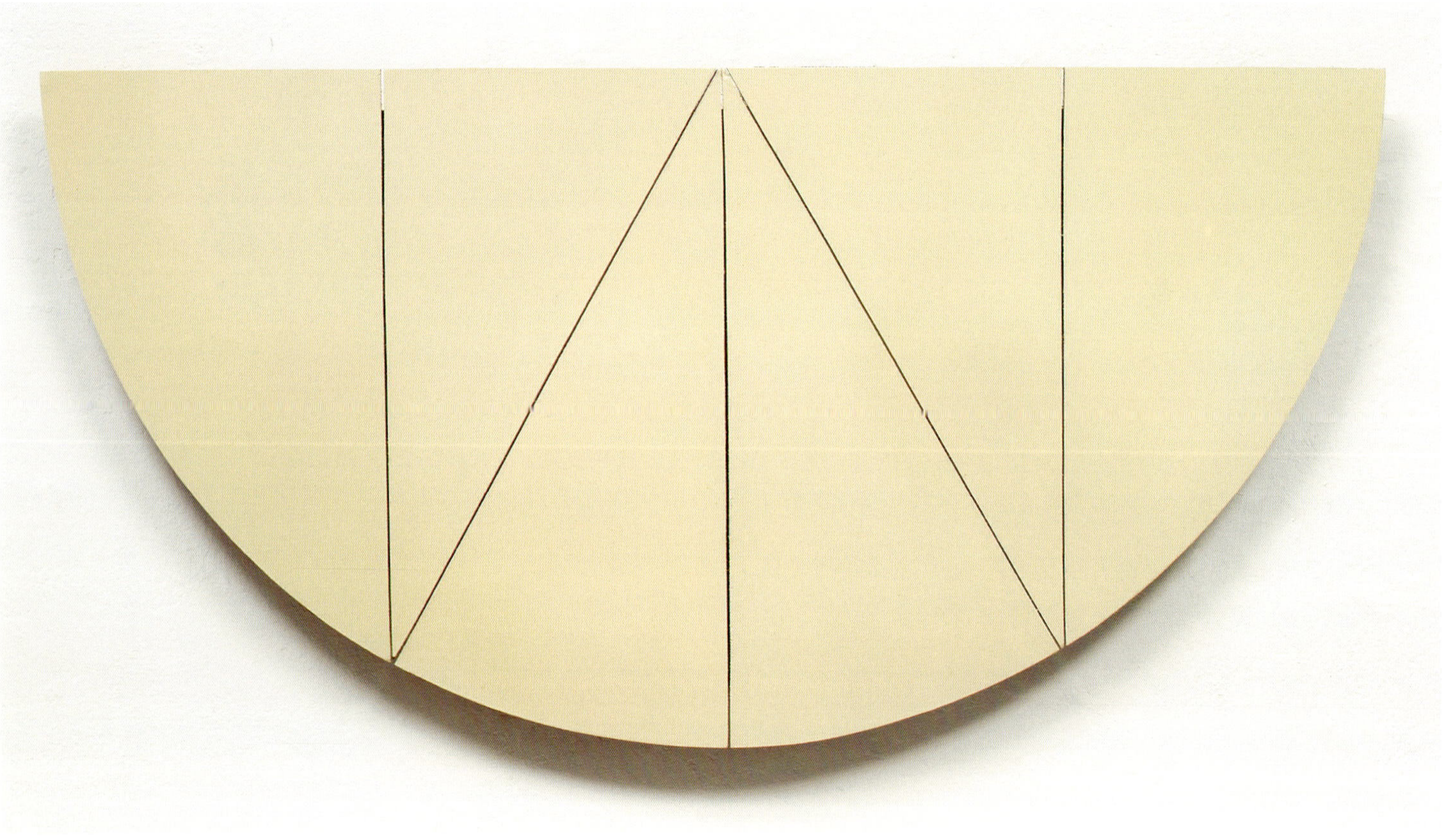

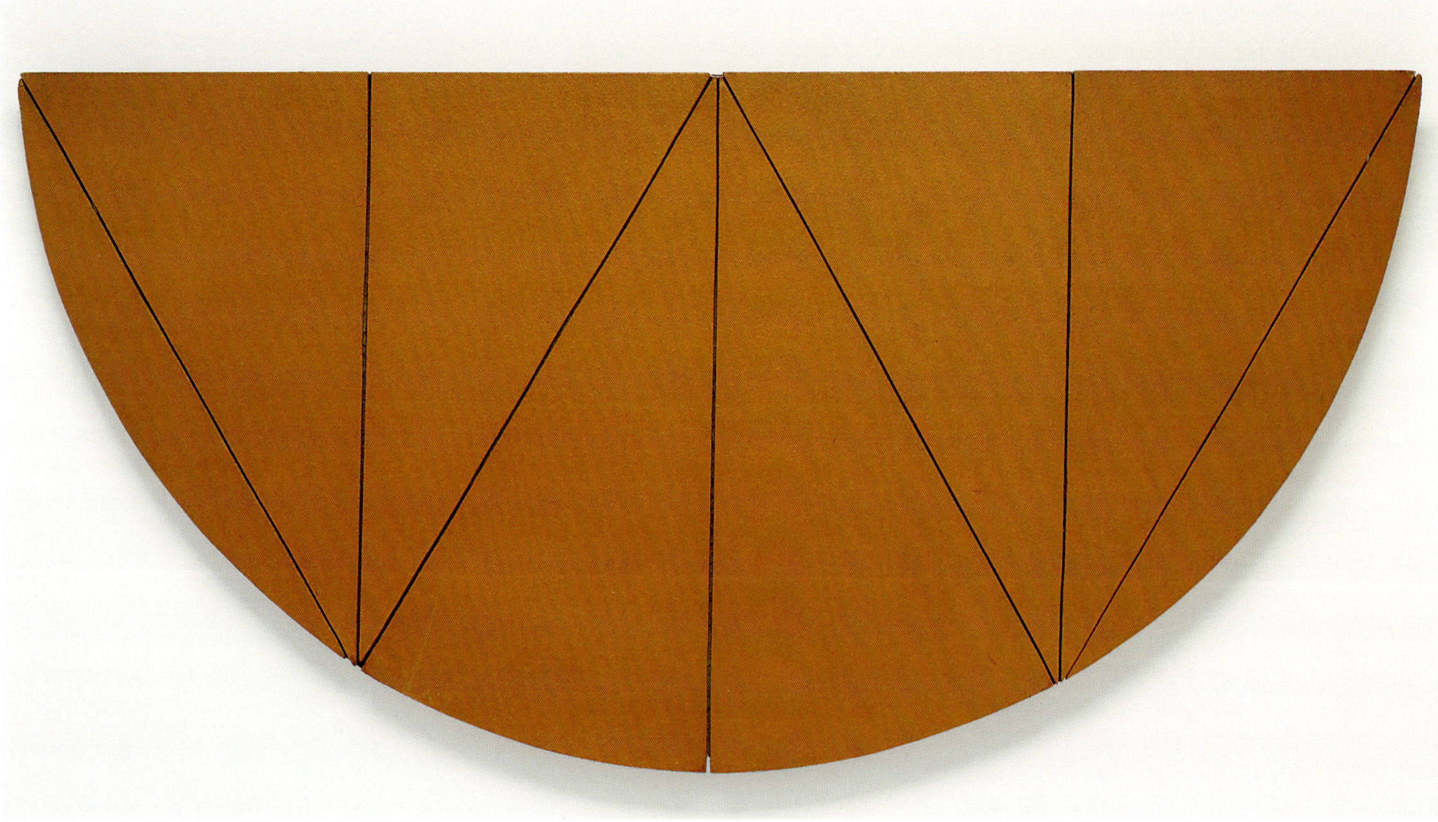

Robert Mangold

OPPOSITE, TOP
½ Manila Curved Area (Trisected), 1967
Oil and black pencil on Masonite, 12 x 24 inches
Private collection

OPPOSITE, BOTTOM
Untitled ½ Curved Arc W Series (first model), 1968
Acrylic and black pencil on Masonite, 12 x 24 inches
Private collection

RIGHT
V Series: Central Section (Vertical), 1968
Acrylic and black pencil on Masonite, 48 x 48 inches
Private collection

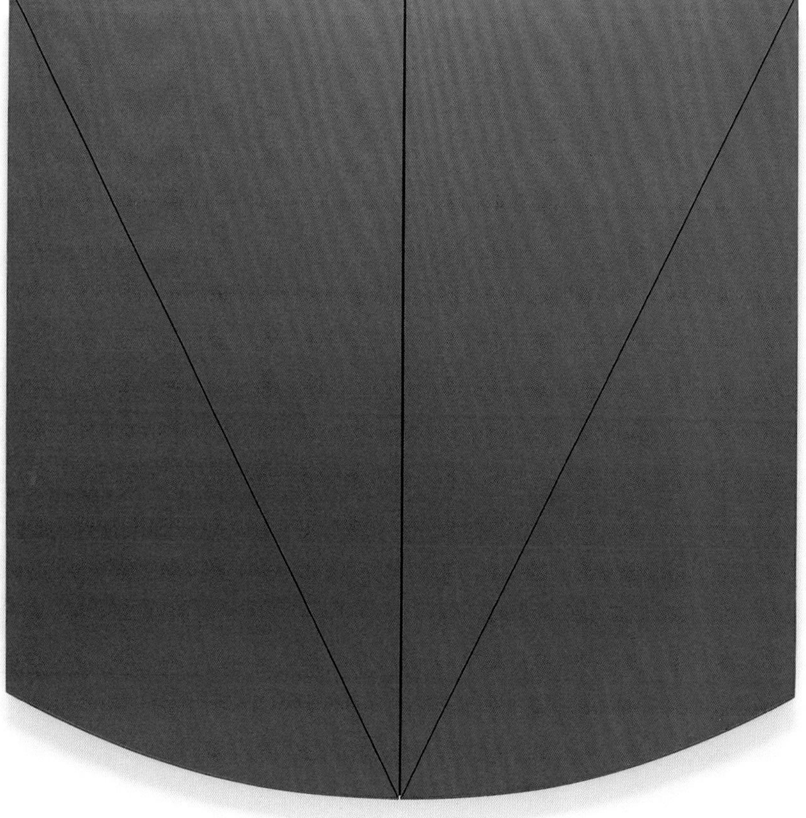

I spent a summer in the country. Looking out across the hills, I would see the same ideas of atmosphere and form, except that they were mountains and sky. And so I tried to do some little studies that were hills and sky. They weren't very good; they became scenic. But what came out of that was the idea that if I didn't use an organic mountain curve and instead used a compass curve for the bottom edge of these forms, it would become something totally different and interesting. So first I started doing parts of circles and curved areas of one circle in sprayed oil. Then I switched to acrylic and was rolling the acrylic on. Then I started doing the *Frame* paintings and things in the '80s where I was actually using brushed surfaces. I wanted more activation into the areas of color. And I went from there and back. Today I still use a roller for all of my paintings, really, and I use pastel for the studies. The pastel allows for a kind of transparency, like watercolor. I use paint in a thinner way so it's a little more translucent. But it all has to do with certain attitudes about painting that have changed over the years. It's kind of hard to simplify this into a running thread, but at a certain point I wanted to look *into* the paintings. I wanted the paintings to have an inner life. It had to do with why I thought painting was unique and why I thought painting was important. We can go back to Brancusi—those wonderful pictures of Brancusi in his studio, where the pieces and his chair and his bed and stools and everything all become one. It's all like a Brancusi world, but it only could be done by a sculptor. Sculpture is physical. Sculpture is like the chair I'm sitting in; sculpture is like the table. And the thing that intrigued me and that I had set out to investigate was that painting was not. Painting is physical; it's heavy. I know; I take paintings up and down from the wall. But on another level they're really not physical. There is a kind of transience to their existence. They're unlike the chair I sit in. They're unlike the floor. They have a very specific identity—an in-between status. A painting is an in-between object. It's not a window. It doesn't open on to anything. Its status is not of a physical world in the way that sculpture is. It's a make-believe world. And one of the reasons I went into thinning the paint and making the paint more transparent was that I wanted the forms in the painting to have an interior. I wanted them to open a little bit. I wanted atmosphere, or incident, or something, so that it wasn't like a plank or a side of a wall. That transition in my work was like going from where I wanted it like a wall to where I no longer wanted it like a wall.

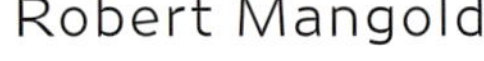

Robert Mangold

BELOW
Split Ring Image, 2008
Pastel and black pencil on paper,
31½ x 29½ inches

OPPOSITE, CLOCKWISE FROM TOP LEFT

Study Attic Series XIV, 1991
Acrylic and black pencil on paper,
30¼ x 22¼ inches
Colby College Museum of Art
Gift of the Alex Katz Foundation

Study Attic Series VIII, 1990
Acrylic and black pencil on paper,
30 x 24¾ inches
Colby College Museum of Art
Gift of the Alex Katz Foundation

X Within X, 1980
Collage, acrylic, and pencil on paper,
10½ x 9¼ inches
Collection Chinati Foundation

Study Attic Series XII, 1991
Acrylic and black pencil on paper,
30¼ x 22¼ inches
Colby College Museum of Art
Gift of the Alex Katz Foundation

I have a sense of physicality. The fact that the lines are drawn makes you think of someone's arm doing that. I like the paintings big because I like you to be able to relate to them in body size. The drawings are fine but they're pointing to the idea of the final work, which will be physically larger. If the *Ring* paintings are small, you look at them in a very different way than if they're your size. You're relating to them in a human scale when their boundaries are roughly the size of your arms outstretched. It gives you a sense of connection to the arm as compass.

I do a lot of drawings. Little thumbnails. From these I choose certain ones that I'm going to make into paintings. So I do a lot of works on paper, building up to the idea of a work on canvas. I want to see how something's going to look. If it presents me with a visual structure that's a little off from what I've done in the past, then that gets my curiosity. Each time I do one it presents a slightly different situation. I build up the library of structures so that I can get down to the four or five that interest me the most. There's no way to do them all, but I do them all on paper so they exist. Then it gives me some way to make decisions. I do pages and pages of drawings. They're really all tryouts. In some cases, one idea follows another and in some cases it doesn't.

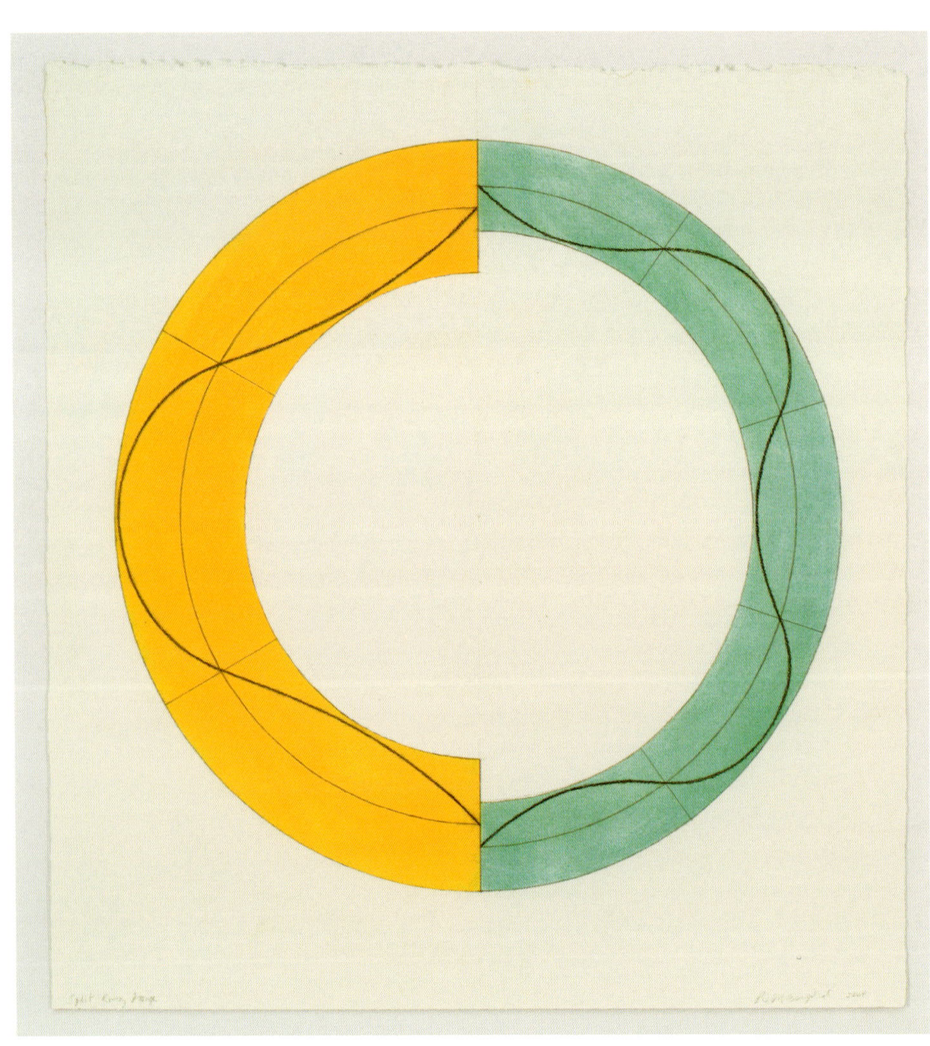

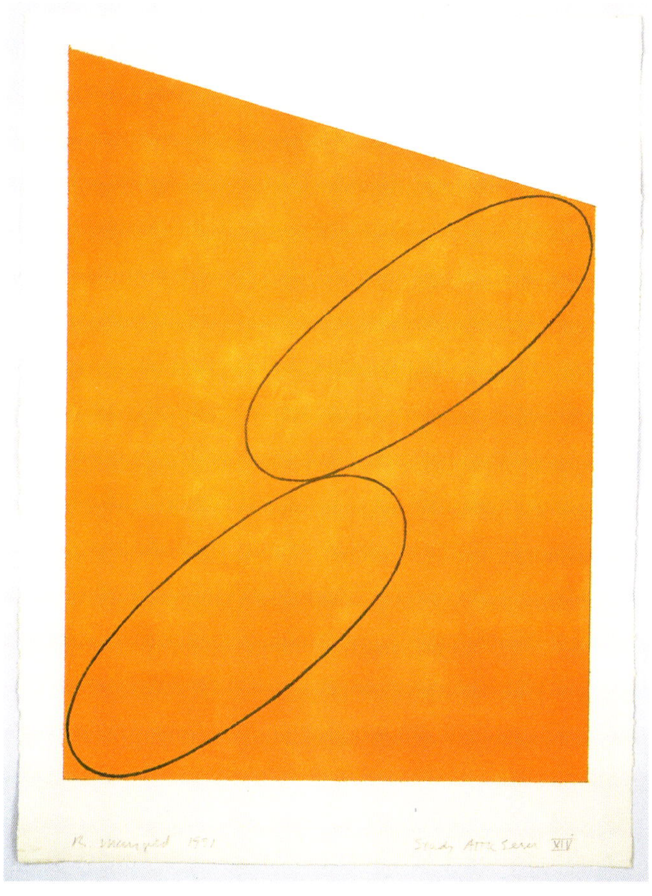

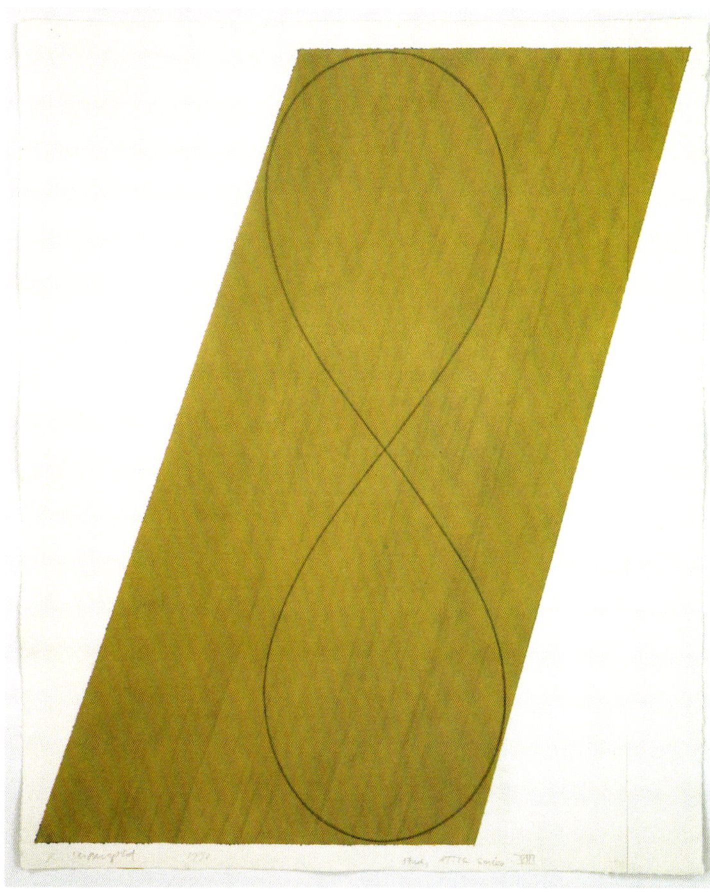

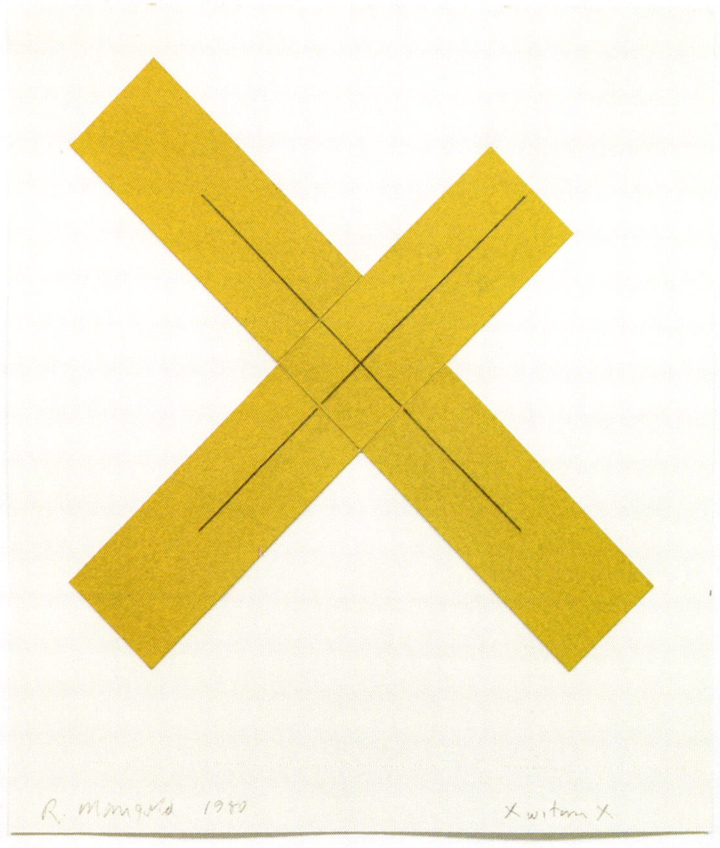

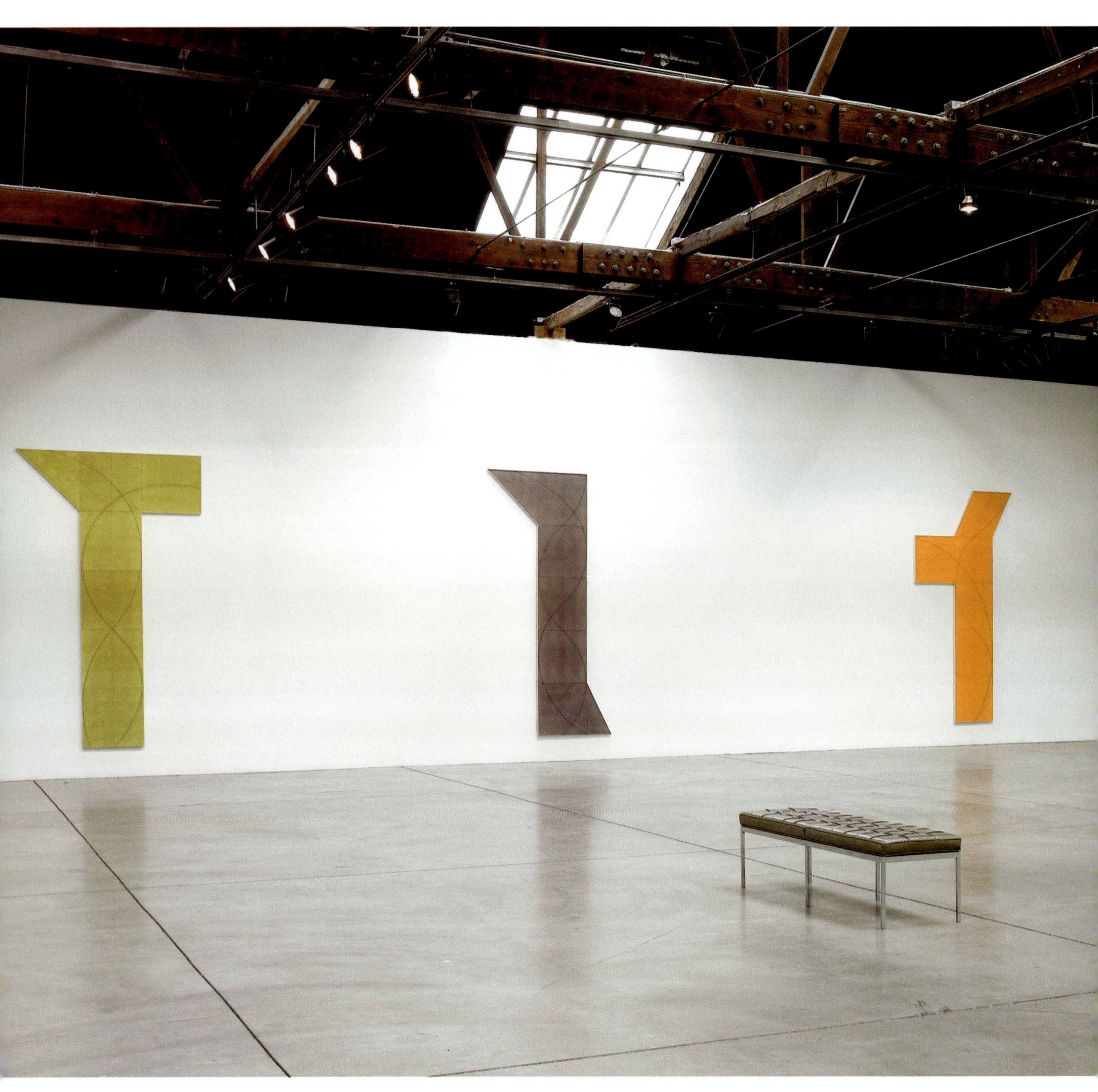

Robert Mangold

Robert Mangold: Column Structure Paintings, 2007
Installation view, Pace Gallery, New York

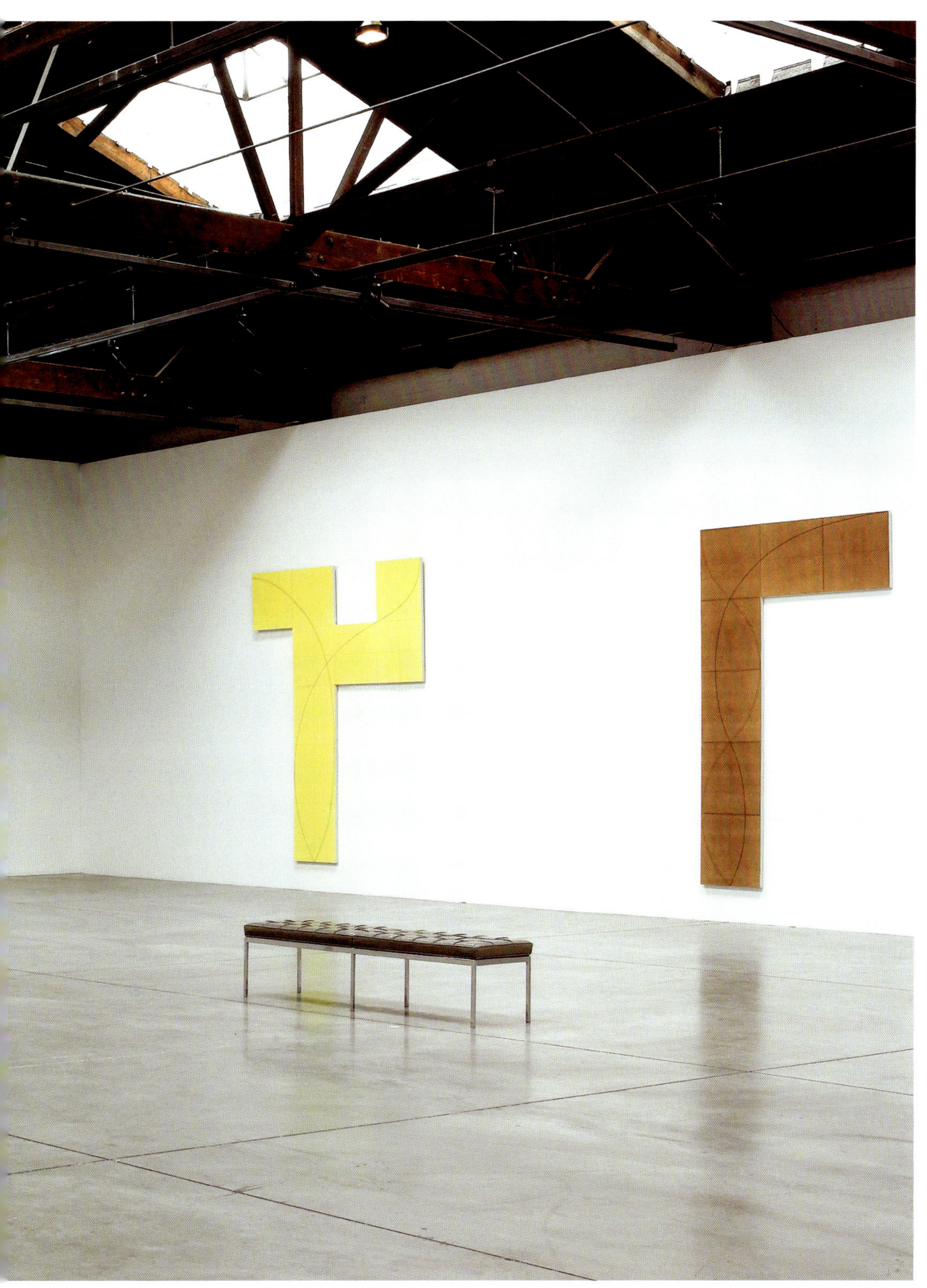

The *Column* paintings? Arthur Danto swears that they had to do with 9/11. No, they didn't. I was thinking about this long before 9/11. But when I had two of them on the wall, there was an undeniable sense that it was strange to be doing two columns. Barnett Newman comes into the picture again. I got an invitation to the Barnett Newman show in Philadelphia, and on the card there was this vertical piece of his. Almost all of my work had been horizontally left-to-right reading art. And I suddenly thought it would be really interesting to work on a vertical painting that you couldn't read that way. Again, it's my idea of thwarting the viewer. You can't read a vertical painting from left to right. So then how do you read it? Do you go up and down? It was something I wanted to deal with. I thought of Brancusi and his endless towers. The idea was that I was going to do paintings that were sealed on the side. The sides became containers for them. But the sense was that, in the mind, they could continue up and they could continue down—that you could imagine this grid going on, or not. So it was a different kind of space—a totally different way of reading. And it was the first time that I was using a grid. I was doing curves that went from one grid to the next to the next. It became very engaging for me for a while, dealing with this. And actually I'm still working off that if you think of the *Rings* as being two connected columns. Only now I've brought the two vertical lines going up, you have them bent into a wheel.

Robert Mangold

RIGHT
Four Color Frame Painting #4, 1984
Acrylic and black pencil on
canvas, 10 x 7 feet
The Nelson-Atkins Museum of Art, Kansas City
Purchase acquired through the generosity of
the William T. Kemper Foundation–Commerce
Bank, Trustee, 2001.14.A-D

OPPOSITE, TOP TO BOTTOM

Blue/Black Five Panel Zone Painting, 1998
Acrylic and black pencil on canvas,
90 x 330 inches
Collection Museum of Modern Art, New York

Orange/Gray Four Panel Zone Painting, 1998
Acrylic and black pencil on canvas,
75 x 220 inches

Yellow/Black Zone Painting IV, 1996
Acrylic and black pencil on canvas,
90 x 198¼ inches
Private collection

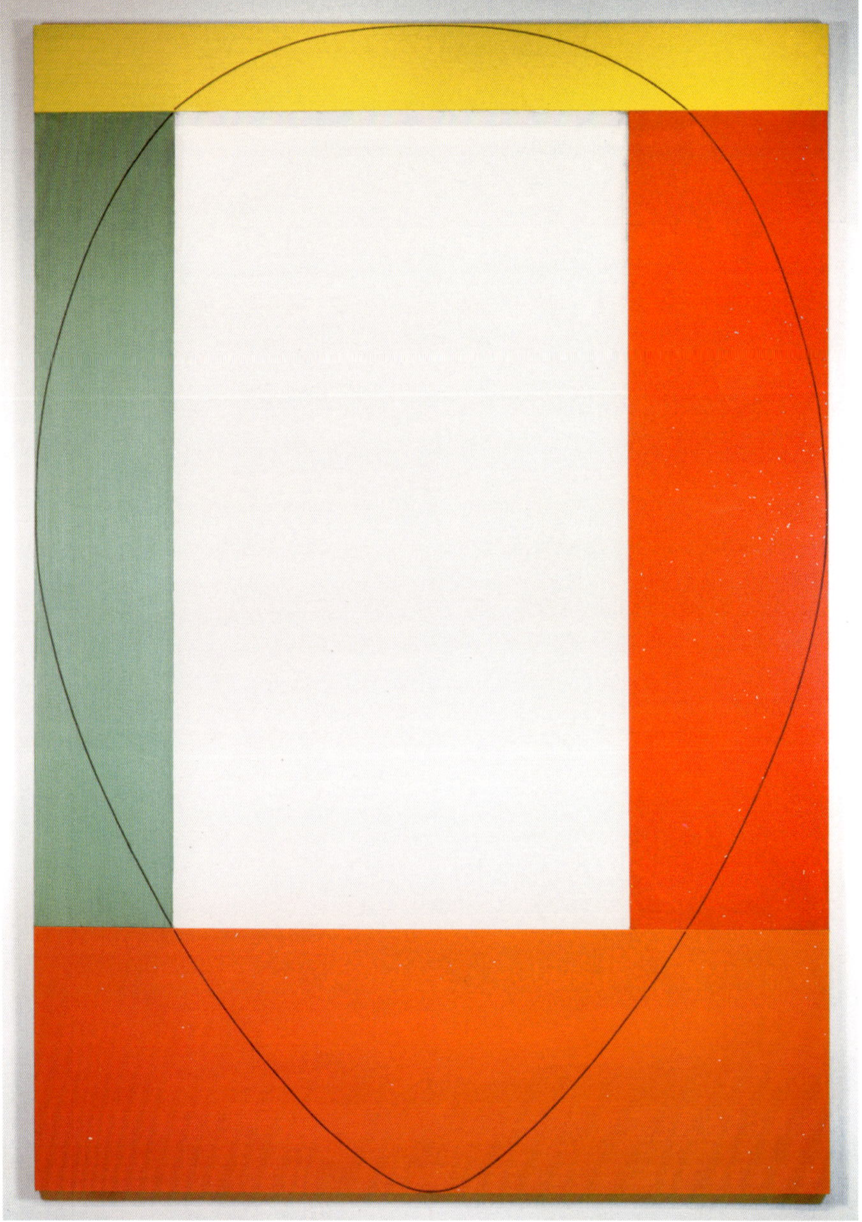

I've done a lot of paintings where the center is absent. I have no idea why. It's in a lot of my work. It keeps coming back in one form or another. The idea of a painting with a big emptiness in the center is a subject that I like. The center as void is really interesting. And I like setting up problems for the viewer. How do you visually deal with what would be a frame or a ring for what's usually in the center? How do you deal with the idea that that would be missing? In the *Zone* paintings, it was the idea of what was missing that intrigued me. And when I did *Circles Within A Square* and *Squares Within a Circle* (not illustrated), everything was always aligned to the edge. There's a connection to the edge that maybe has to do with the fact that shape has always been so important to me. Maybe edge is more important than in a lot of people's work. And by picking away the center, that even forces that viewing a step further. It's like the main course isn't there, and you're sitting down and having to deal with everything around what would normally be the main course.

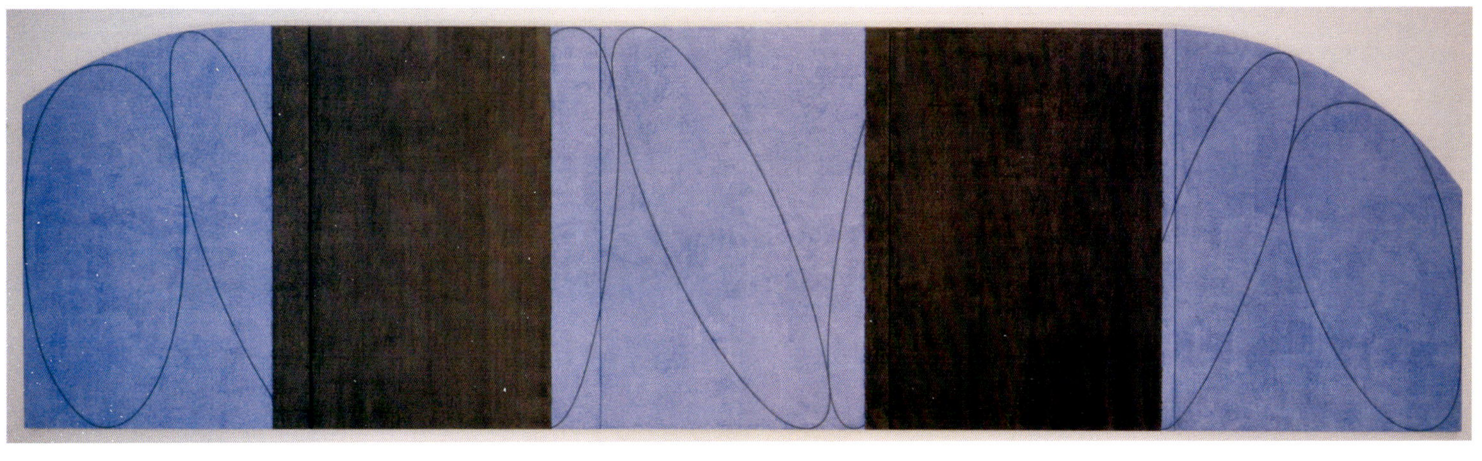

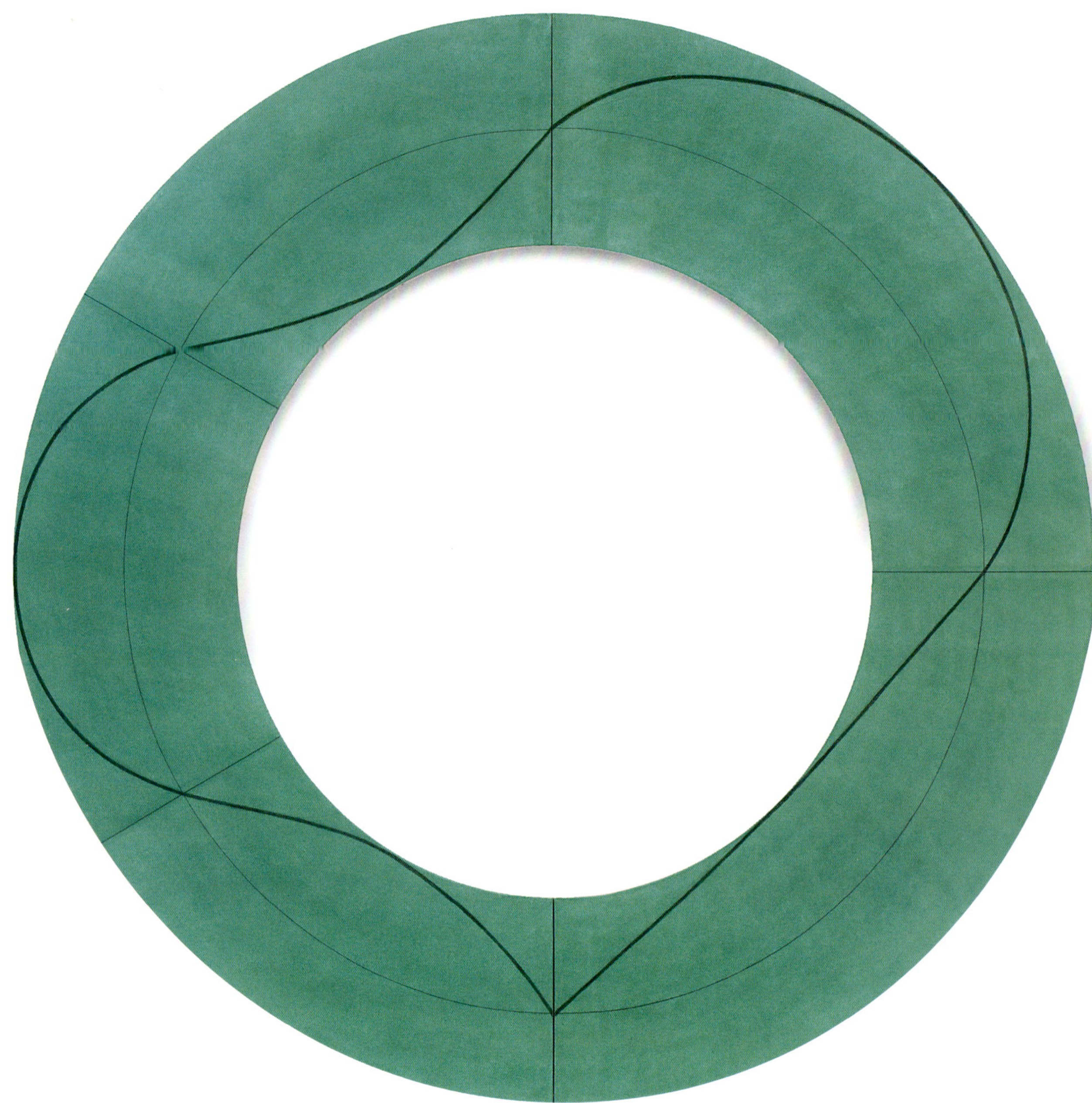

Robert Mangold

ABOVE
Ring Image C, 2008
Acrylic, graphite, and black pencil on canvas, 96 inches diameter
Private collection

OPPOSITE
Split Ring Image 1, 2009
Acrylic, graphite, and black pencil on canvas, 96 inches diameter
Private collection

Whenever I do new paintings, I think of connections—with my own work of the past and sometimes with other people's work that I never thought a great deal about. There are always cultural connections in the work. I don't paint from subject matter. I live in the country, and I see wonderful sunlight and great cloud formations and all kinds of stuff—but I'm never aware of any of that coming into my art in any direct way, ever. So rather than my influence coming from nature, it comes from culture. In the early days, it was a culture of the sides of trucks and buildings and Lower Manhattan hallways and subways. The other part comes from the history of art and the culture of our times. I'll tell you a funny story just to show you a culture connection, and I almost hesitate to tell this story because too much could be made of it. When I was young, I used to go to the movies with my mother. You'd have the previews, the main feature, and the newsreel. There was a newsreel sign-off that had a very powerful effect on me (I've remembered it for all these years). It was a camera facing sideways, and the camera would slowly turn towards you. And then the circle would get bigger and bigger and bigger until it covered the whole screen. Actually, it was a double circle—one circle, two lenses. And it's remarkable that that

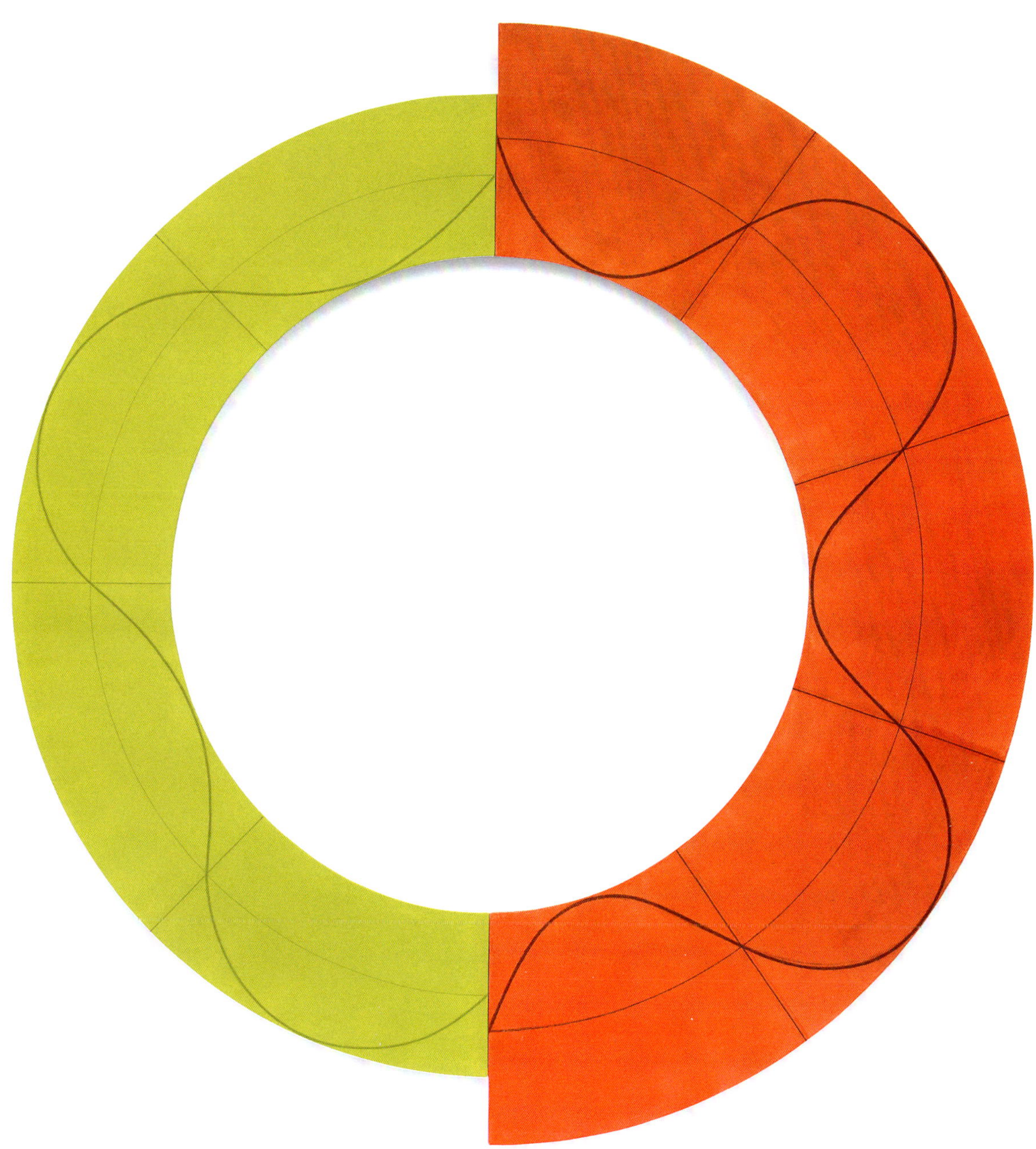

image in the movie theater had such a powerful effect on me. Not that I'm doing paintings of that, but that there was something in that form that I had a very strong response to when I was ten years old. There's nowhere to go with that, but it's just a little sidebar that I thought was amazing. When I actually did find it (it was called *The Eyes and Ears of the World*), I downloaded it onto my computer and looked at it. It still gives me chills.

Maybe at first look it seems as though my paintings are just formal ideas—a linear idea for making *this* form fit in *that* form or making *this* complete *that*. I think I have an extremely strong formal interest. But I also have this thwarting of the formal element. I'm always implying that maybe this doesn't fit, or maybe it's not complete. Or what the heck happened to the center of those paintings? Sometimes I think I'm just juggling formal things around. But then there are other times when I argue with myself about it.

A lot of people see spiritual connections in the work, which I don't mind. I think I'm probably a romantic artist. And I think romanticism by nature implies something beyond a formal idea. I'm absolutely not a religious person, but I like the idea of different contents and certainly don't deny the idea that emotion plays in painting. I can remember seeing contemporary paintings that I thought were really great and being in a hurry to get into my studio while that was still fresh in my mind—while that intensity, that emotional high, was still there—so that I could look at my painting and say, "Is there any of that in there?" There is an unknown element that you're striving for, that goes beyond. Otherwise any one of my little diagrams in a notebook could be a picture. What I'm looking for is something that takes a step beyond that. I don't even know how to define what that step is except that somehow it opens something and sets something off that makes me want to do and see it done.

Sarah Sze

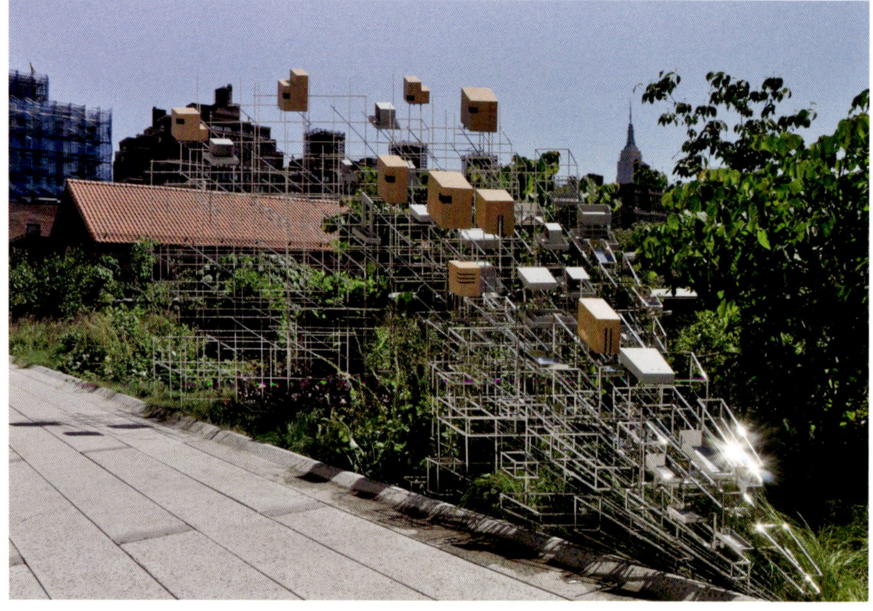

ABOVE
Still Life with Landscape (Model for a Habitat), 2011
Stainless steel and wood, 9 x 22 x 21 feet overall
Commissioned by the High Line

OPPOSITE
Untitled (Studio), 1996
Mixed media, dimensions variable
Installed at the artist's studio for the School of Visual Arts Graduate Program, New York
Collection of the artist, New York

I was asked to do an artwork on the High Line, an abandoned elevated train track in Manhattan that was made into a park—a sort of promenade. The piece that I conceived is a habitat and an observation site where you can see the birds, butterflies, and insects that survive on the High Line in this intense metropolis. I did tons of research, working with the Cornell Lab of Ornithology, which does incredible urban wildlife projects. It was helpful to talk with the scientists about how my idea would work—which birds would come, which might not—and the bare-bones logistics and amazing facts about the wildlife that exists in urban areas all through the United States. One of the Lab's goals is to get people to observe nature for ten minutes at a time (ten minutes of observation is an incredibly long time for most people to look at something). This idea of slowing down and observing is central to the visual arts, too.

The High Line frames the city views, with different areas to stop and look. Just going up one level from the street creates an interesting peacefulness. You get up there, and there's only one thing you can do. You just walk. Subtle things happen; your sense of sound changes. You're on the West Side of Manhattan, so there is an incredible wind that comes in suddenly. The light is different at different times of day. As you walk the High Line you encounter openings (as the walkway meets the cross streets)—and closings (as it's enclosed by building walls). Scale, and how to deal with it, is crucial when you're working outdoors, especially in Manhattan. The spectacle of space and the scale of information are so high that size is crucial. But one of the things that I'm interested in is to take a public piece and have it feel intimate. I want it to feel human-scale all of a sudden. Looking from far away, you have a vast feeling of space—and then, when you get to my piece, you feel slightly enclosed, embraced by the piece itself, slightly nested, which plays on the idea of the habitat. One thing essential to my piece is that it's an experiment. We're dealing with nature, and we don't know what's going to happen (will the birds nest there, or not?), so there's a flexibility built into the project. And that's interesting in terms of my whole body of work, which has a mutable quality and often *feels* like an experiment. A lot of it has the rawness of the studio or laboratory—where things could happen, fall apart, or grow—as if you're entering at a live moment in a process.

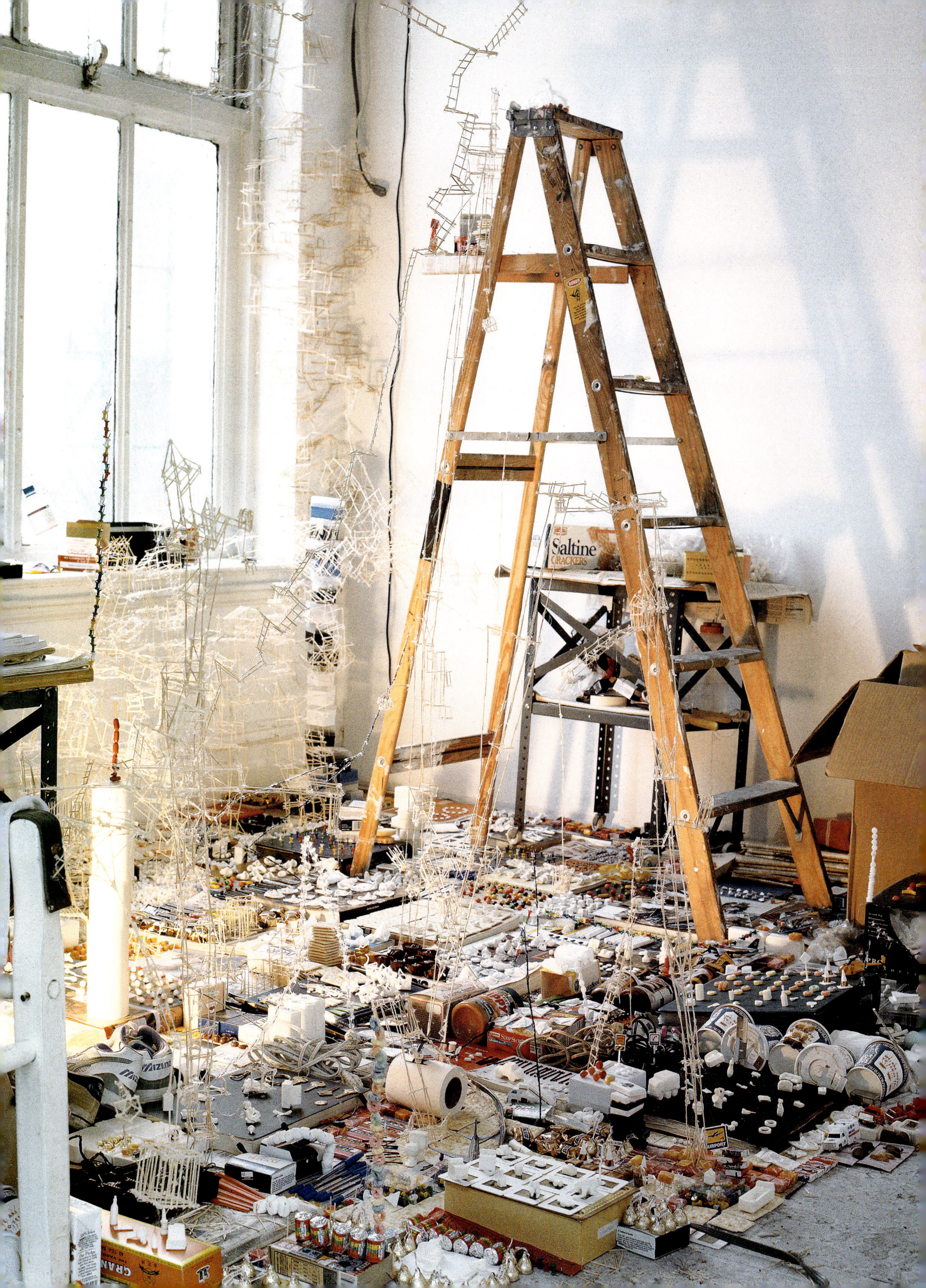
Saltine
CRACKERS
AIRPORT

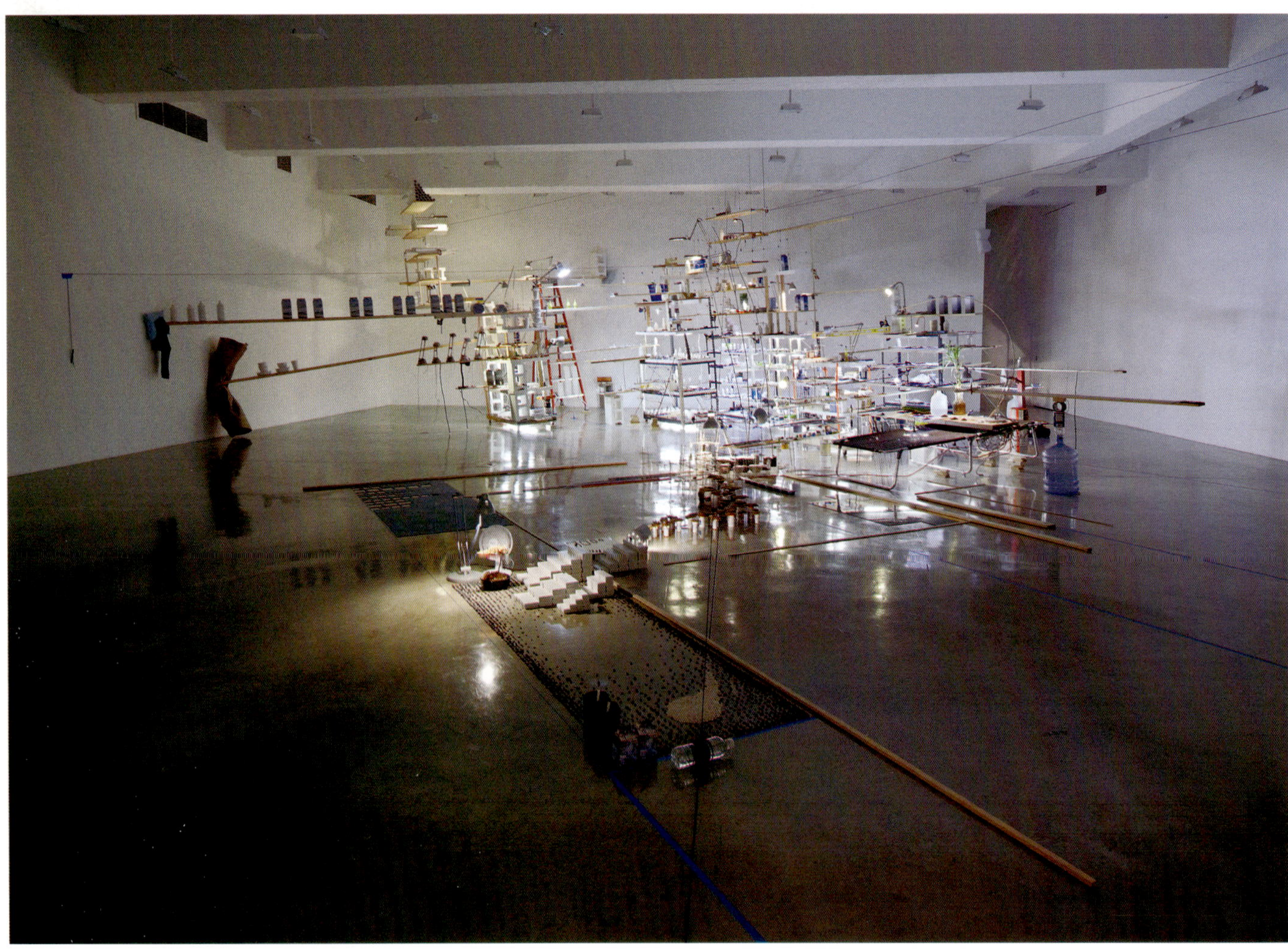

Sarah Sze

ABOVE AND OPPOSITE
The Uncountables (Encyclopedia), 2010
Mixed media, metal shelves, wood shelves, lights, plastic bottles, milk cartons, 179 x 547 x 498 inches
Tanya Bonakdar Gallery, New York

One of the important things about *The Uncountables (Encyclopedia)* (2010) is how you move through and into it. In both locations where it was installed, the entrance framed the piece so that it was on a tilt, and the first thing that happened is that your regular sense of space was slightly disoriented. And then, when you walked up to the piece, you didn't know which direction to go in. Immediately, there was a choice. Usually people went to the left. But, as you turn left, the entire piece shifts and breaks apart. And then it becomes a very clear walkway, so you walk very quickly into the piece. With installation, there's often a decision about entering an artwork: there's a carpet or a curtain—and *then* you're walking into it. But I wanted to create a piece where you found yourself in the middle and you didn't even realize how you'd gotten there. When you're there, you focus down on the smaller objects and your whole sense of scale shifts. I was interested in the impossibility of having to create a system where you can document and explain all information, in the decisions about what goes into the system and what doesn't, and the idea of it being quickly outdated. I was thinking about how we organize information—how we name it, and how we lay it out. I started with having shelves almost as a frame for objects—and with the idea of creating a place we recognize but which sits between many recognizable locations, like a library, storage space, or supermarket, where we try to make decisions or find information physically in space. The question is how do you orient yourself in those locations? I make things shift constantly as you're moving through the piece. So you'll be in a section where you find things that look like jewelry. But when it starts to look too much like jewelry I'll switch it to a shoe store. And if it looks too much like a shoe store I'll make it look like a morgue. I'm constantly 'changing the volume' in terms of scale, balance, and subject matter so that your idea of discovery is being tripped up every time you locate yourself.

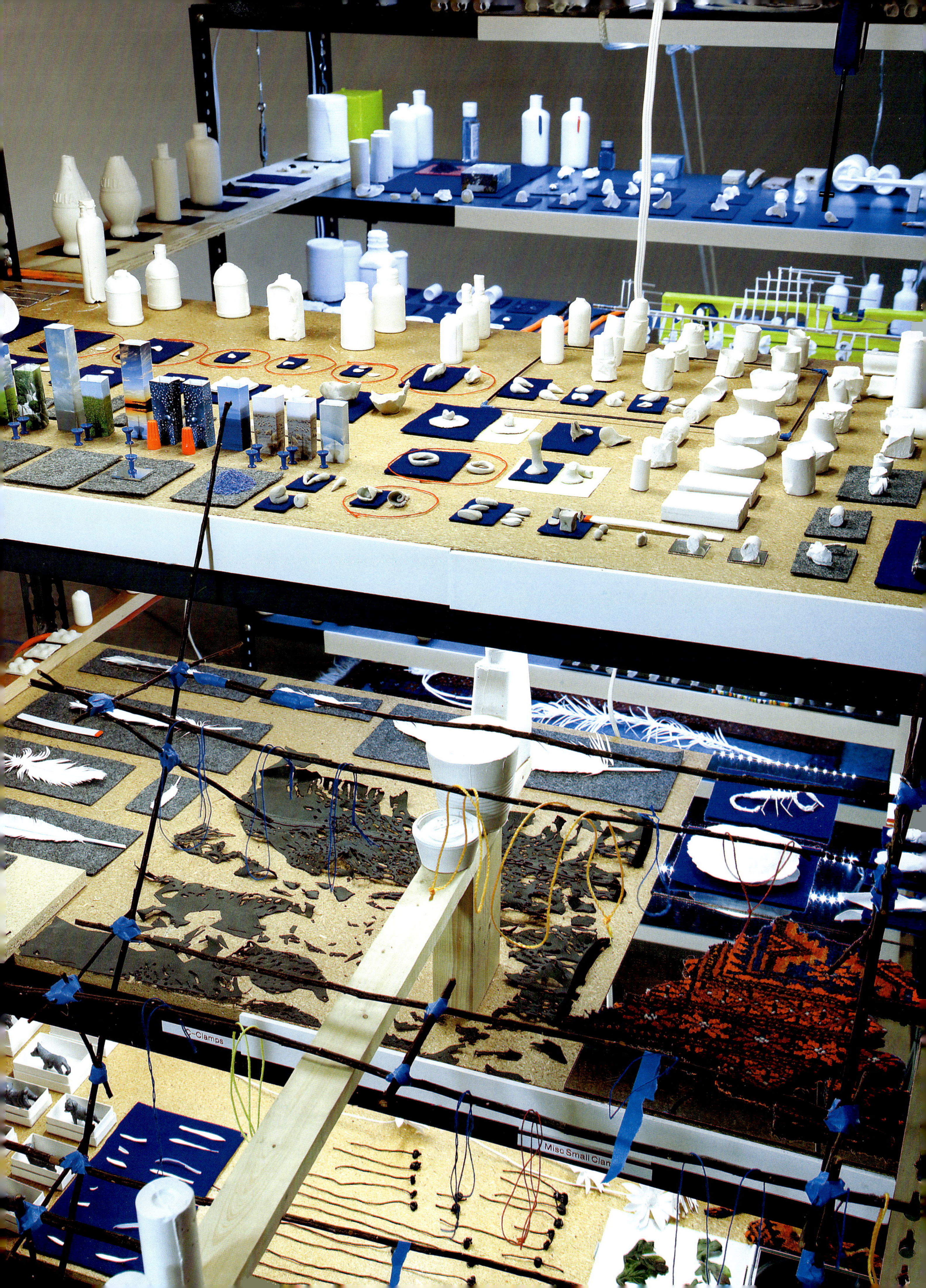
C-Clamps
Misc Small

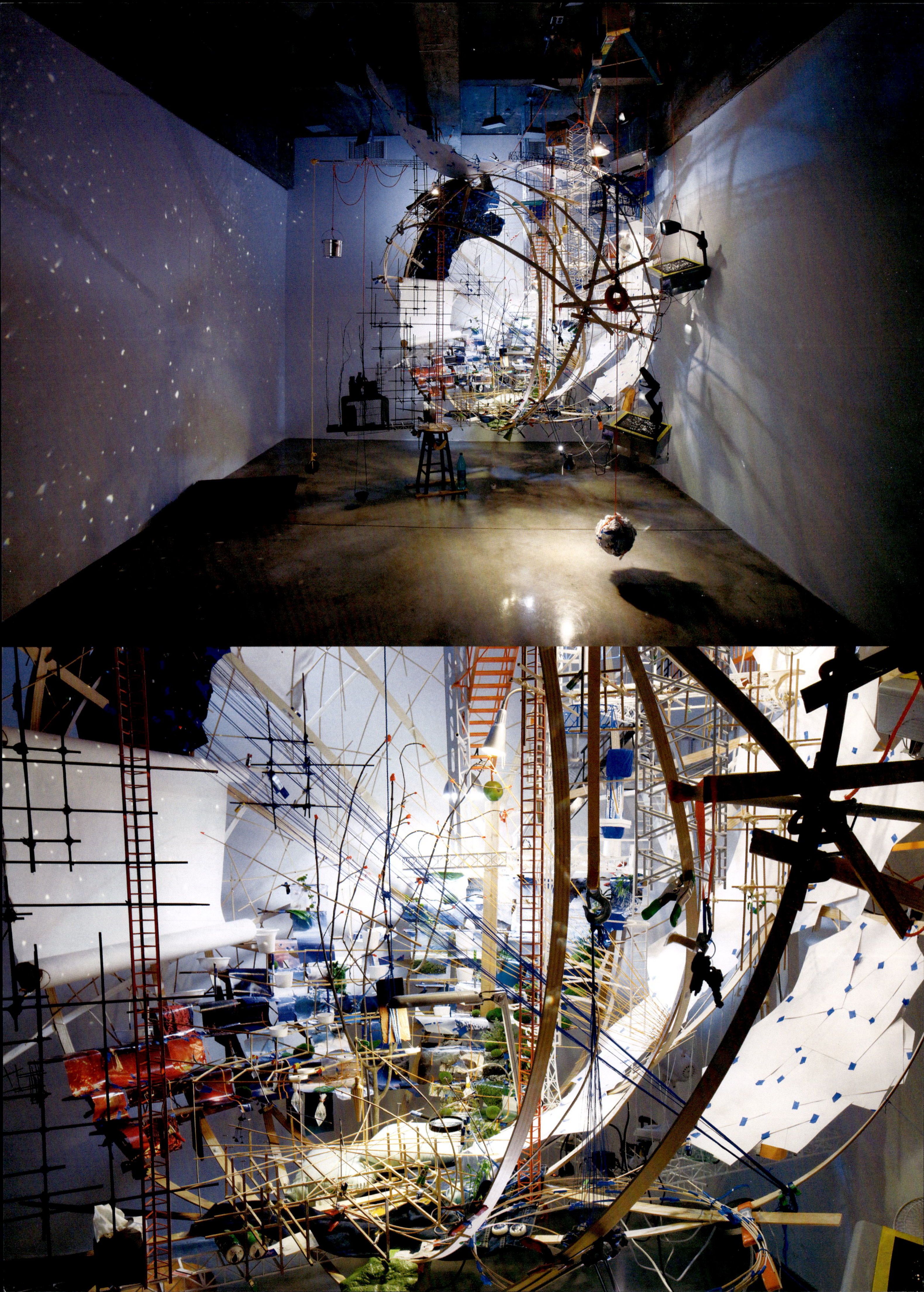

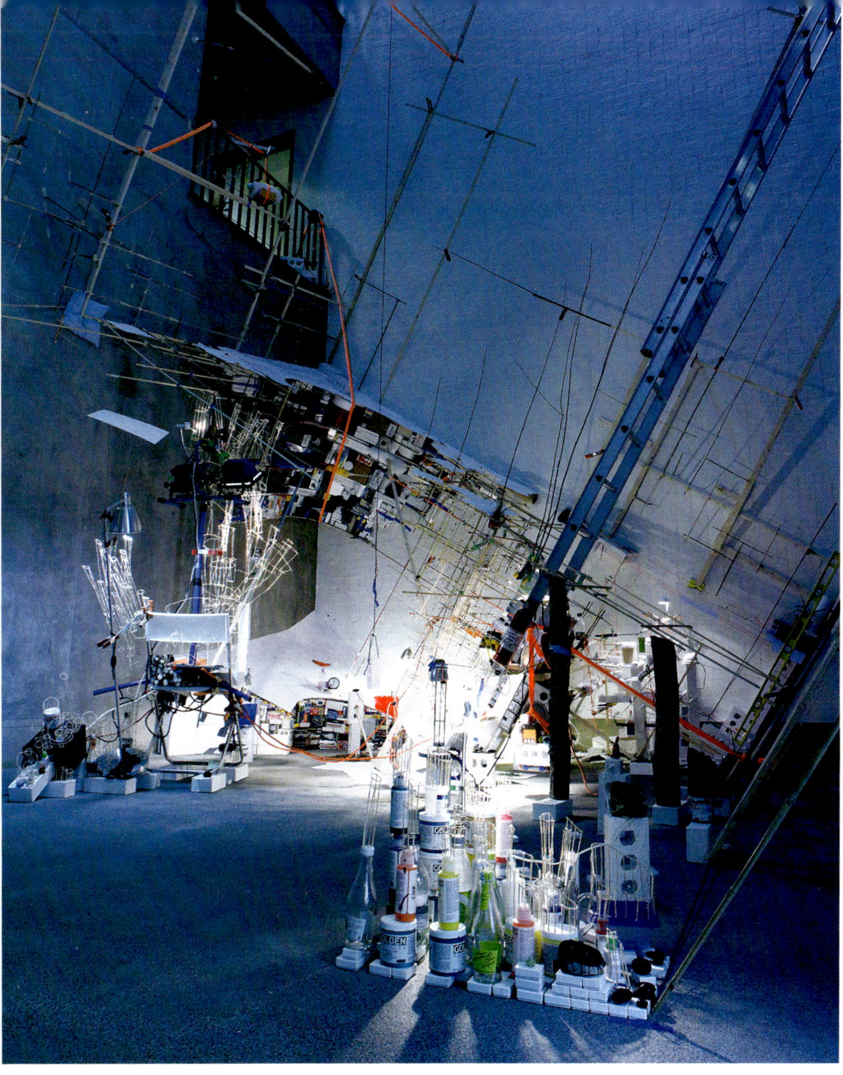

Sarah Sze

OPPOSITE, TOP AND BOTTOM
360 (Portable Planetarium), 2010
Mixed media, wood, paper, string, jeans, rocks, 162 x 136 x 185 inches
Tanya Bonakdar Gallery, New York
Collection National Gallery of Canada, Ottawa

ABOVE
Just Now Dangled Still, 2008
Mixed media, dimensions variable
Liverpool Biennial, Liverpool
Commissioned by the Liverpool Biennial International 08

360 (Portable Planetarium) (2010) was at Tanya Bonakdar Gallery in New York at the same time as *Encyclopedia*. So the whole show was about the idea that you would go to different locations in the gallery and have entirely different experiences. But the *Planetarium* piece is similar to the *Encyclopedia* piece—in that a planetarium is also an impossible project that attempts to imagine our universe and locate us in vast space. The idea was to build a planetarium of ambitious potential but to make it very rickety and pieced together, as if it was falling apart or half constructed and would probably fail or have to be re-envisioned.

Arthur Danto brought up an idea that interests me. He talked about how my work was more like a scientific model than an architectural one because there's constant running into failure. The *Encyclopedia* piece was a good example. Originally, in the studio, I realized the most interesting vantage point is when you're on the angle, not straight on. When we brought it to the gallery, I had tilted it that way. But when I reinstalled the entire piece, I thought, "There's not enough movement here; there's not enough disorientation. It doesn't have the feeling of teetering." So we took the entire piece apart, got the exact angle, on site, and entirely rebuilt it.

I don't think so much about balance in the work, as about teetering—about locating an edge where meaning, scale, and balance are teetering—so that even the structure of the pieces seems to be in a state of flux that's never still. So if you think you've located the end of the piece, then you discover there's another section. It's the idea of complexity where there is no center that's stable. What I'm really thinking about is how to make a piece feel like it has a life so that, when you experience it, you think about its making, its demise, and you feel when you come to it that it's actually a moment in time and that you experience it 'live'.

Sarah Sze

RIGHT
Day, 2005
Offset lithography, silkscreen
Image: 38¼ x 71¼ inches
Sheet: 39 x 71¾ inches
Edition of 27, 8 AP

BELOW
Night, 2005
Offset lithography, silkscreen
Image: 38¼ x 71¼ inches
Sheet: 39 x 71¾ inches
Edition of 27, 8 AP

OPPOSITE
Seamless, 1999
Mixed media, dimensions variable
The Carnegie International 1999–2000,
Carnegie Museum of Art, Pittsburgh
Collection Edwin C. Cohen

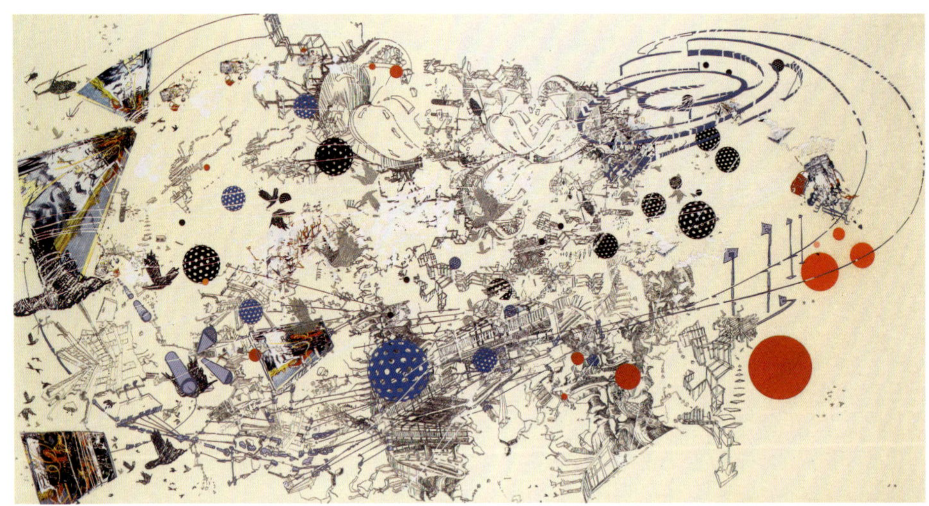

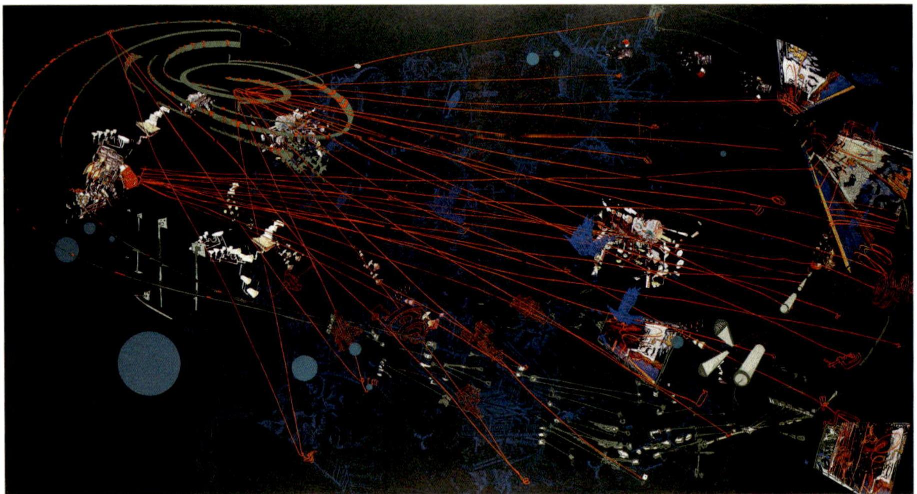

At the very core of my work, I'm thinking about the edge between life and art, and trying to have the viewer move in and out of that all the time. So I juxtapose something that's very familiar with something that's very unfamiliar, and even want to blur your experience of seeing the work in the real world. So, for example, by seeing that piece on the High Line you start to see birds elsewhere. And by seeing the *Encyclopedia* piece, you start to think more about how information is organized in a library, store, or storage space. I am thinking about how I experience the world personally, but also how we experience the world, space, and information culturally. My father is an architect, so I grew up around models and plans, with his 'eye', looking at construction sites—and always talking about buildings and cities. So that's definitely part of how I learned how to see the world. My husband is a scientist. And, actually, there are a lot of similarities in his laboratory and in my studio. We talk about failure. Every week there's failure versus a success in the laboratory—and the same thing in the studio. I studied architecture as an undergraduate, and then I switched to art. For me, the freedom of art was crucial. I don't think I'm practical enough to be an architect. So I became an artist, which was very impractical.

I'm trying to think about how three-dimensional and two-dimensional space are represented and about what you can do with a drawing that you can't do with a sculpture, and vice versa. I'm always pondering what's essential to one medium, and when I started doing sculpture I immediately thought, "Okay, this is because I was a painter and an architect in the beginning." I'm trying to make things that sit 'in between', and so I think a lot about perspective—isometric perspective versus one-point perspective—and how the two meet, where they don't, and how you can play with them. The thing that's interesting about isometric perspective is that parallel lines stay the same in space. This is what traditionally was used in Asian drawing, as opposed to one-point perspective. It's becoming popular now because you need to use isometric perspective for 3-D modeling (when you turn a corner, parallel lines have to stay parallel). When you look at 3-D space in films and TV, there's a different way of reading it, and sometimes you can see that it's kind of awkward. But we're actually trained to read space more in an isometric model. This is one of the ideas that actually spawned the High Line piece and a lot of my drawings. So I'm just playing with seeing in two and three dimensions—playing with them in sculpture where they're not usually used, and in drawing.

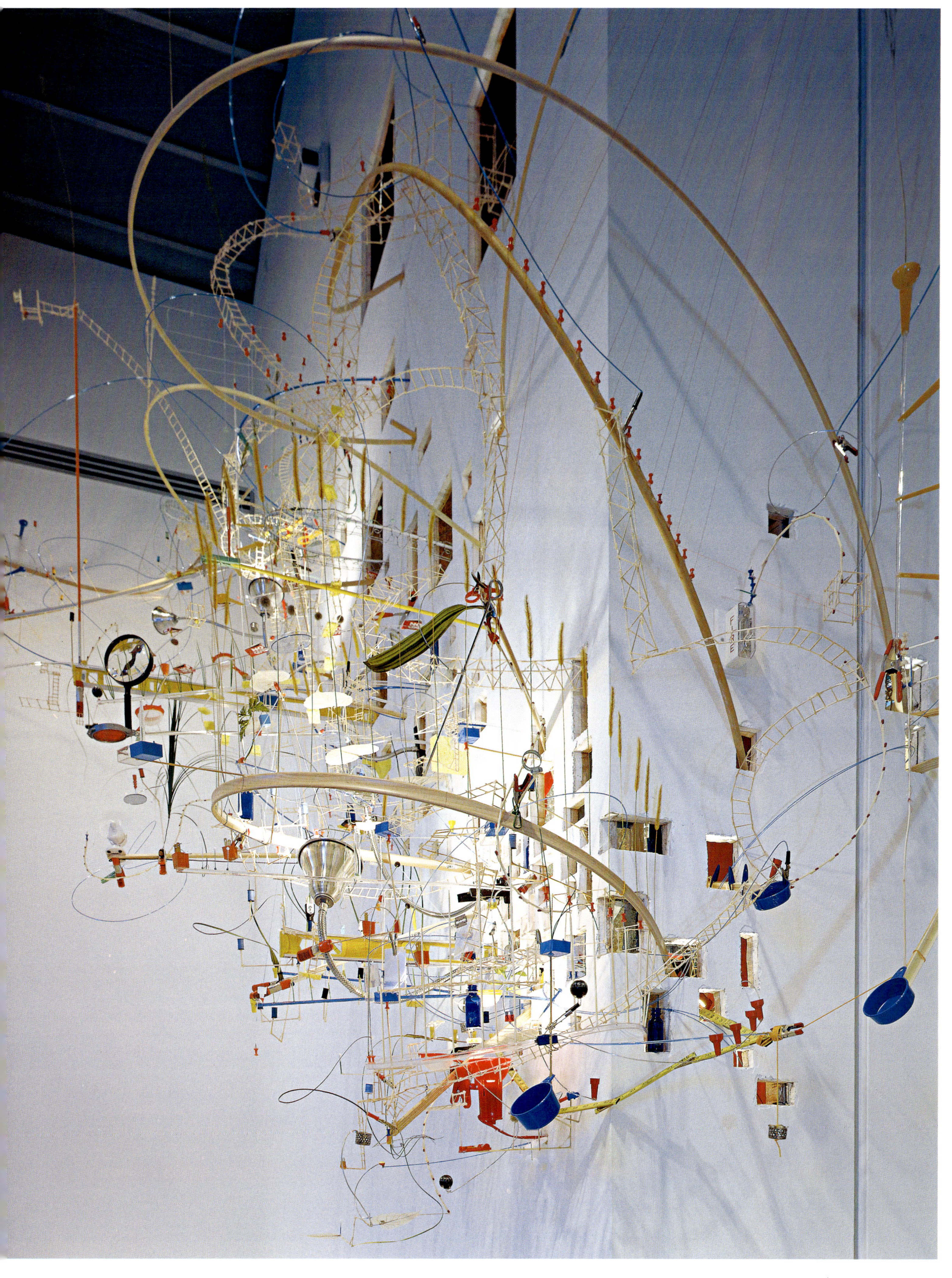

Sarah Sze

RIGHT AND OPPOSITE
Things Fall Apart, 2001
Mixed media, dimensions variable
010101: Art in Technological Times,
San Francisco Museum of Modern Art
Collection of San Francisco Museum
of Modern Art

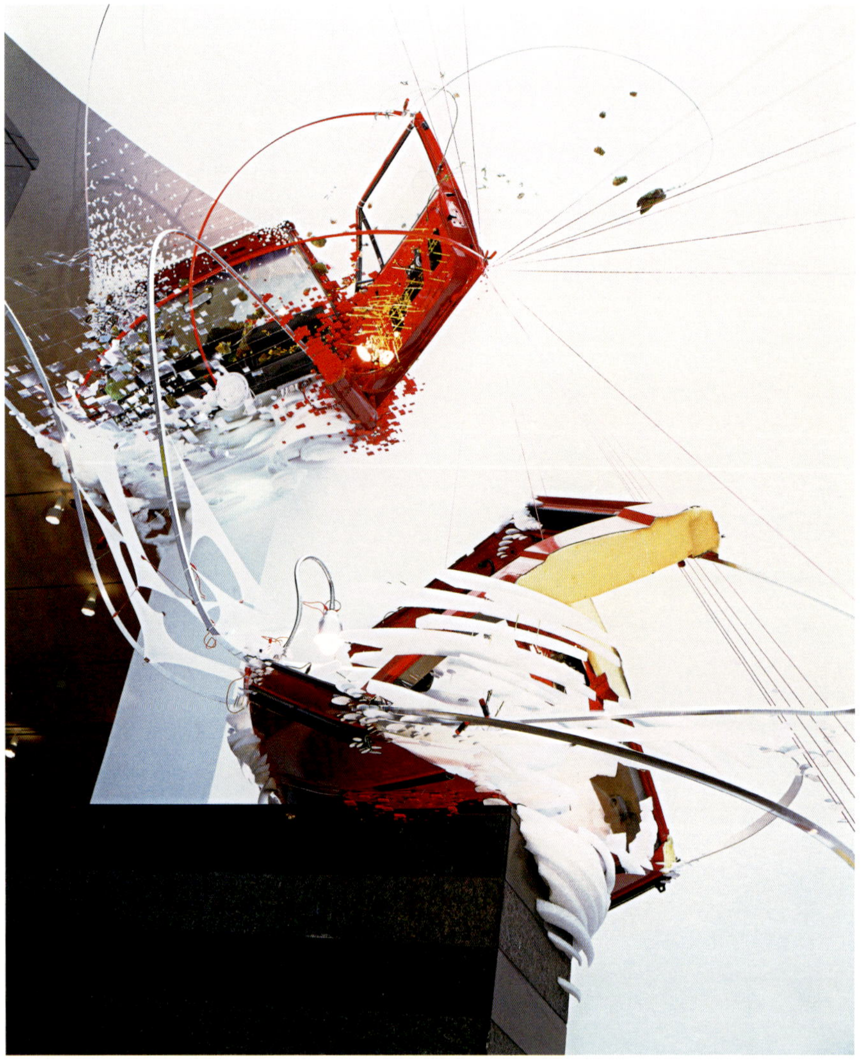

Part of being an artist is giving oneself permission to make choices and not judge them. The hardest thing is to be able to trust an action when it might be completely absurd—but to trust that the outcome actually might be fruitful. It might not be, and then you have to have the resilience to pick yourself up again and try something else. But you also have to have a way of cutting off the cerebral judging of what you're doing so that you can actually see results and respond to them. The work *makes* the work: you have to keep working through it even when it's failing—so that you can make progress.

I am interested in dance and choreography —the choreographic experience of the viewer through space, how you speed up and slow down, become aware of and lose the sense of your body in relation to the work. And I'm interested in time as narrative. You can think of my work as a kind of narrative of movement through space. What I love about traditional Japanese gardens and landscaping is the way of choreographing space so that you feel as if you're wandering in a natural way. Experiences of discovery are presented in the way a path will turn, curve, and step, but you feel that they have the freshness of being in a direct relationship to nature. There's framing where you look and where you have to step. You look down to watch your feet, and when you look up there'll be something framed in the landscape far away. You just sort of see it, whether or not you recognize that it's framed. The idea of even having you look down and then look up again is filmic, in that you're looking through space and frames. That's also why I photograph my work a lot because I know in advance where those locations are going to be, where everything clicks into place suddenly for the viewer.

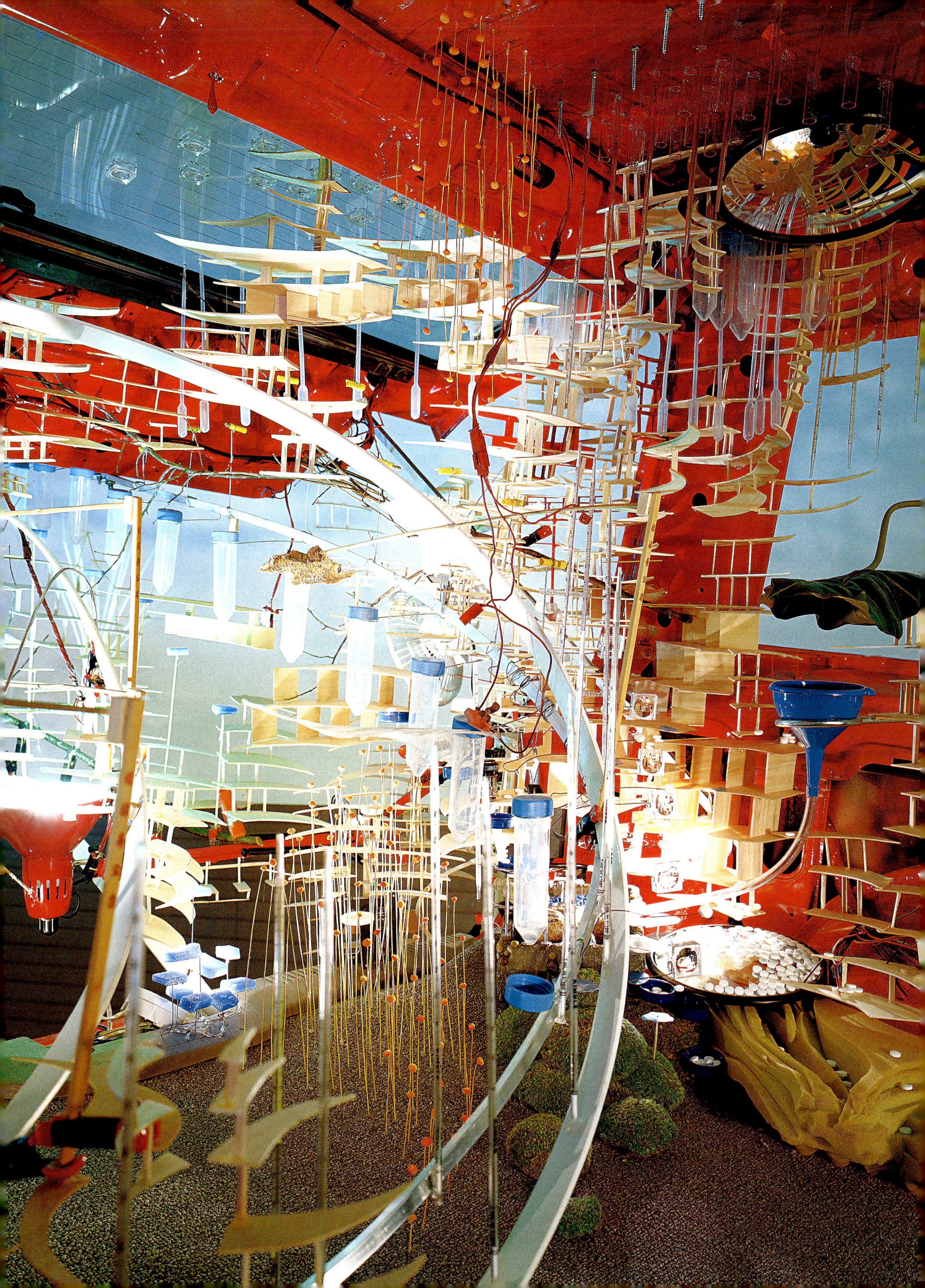

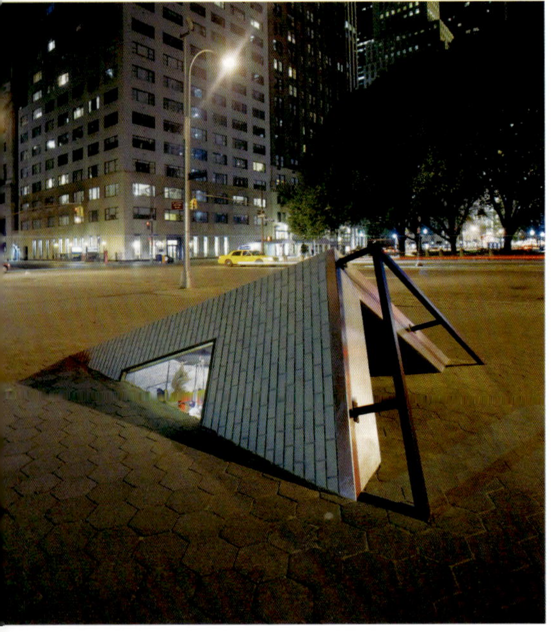

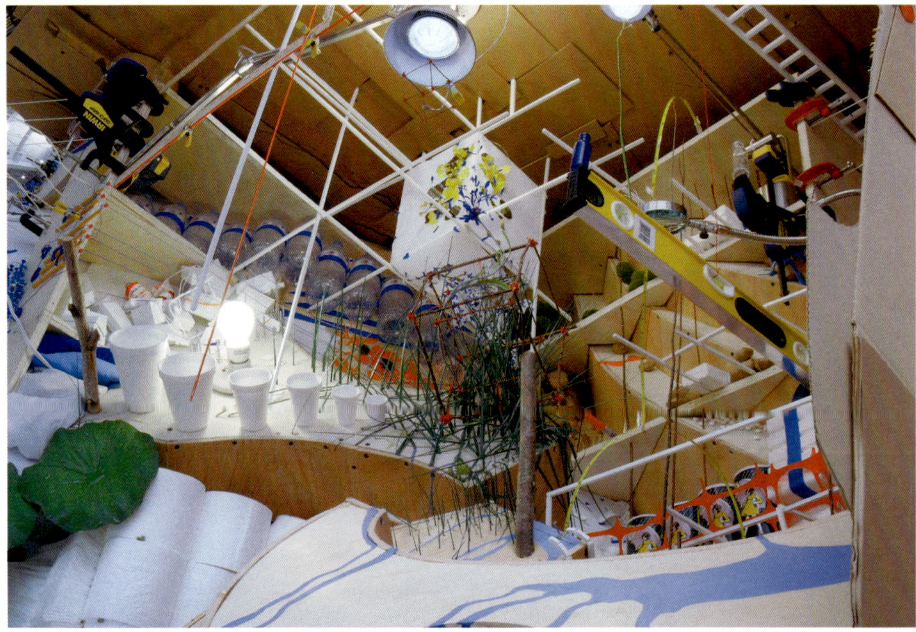

Sarah Sze

ABOVE, LEFT AND RIGHT
Corner Plot, 2006
Mixed media, 189 x 202 x 154 inches footprint, depth of 4 feet
Corner Plot, Doris C. Freedman Plaza, New York
Commission for the Public Art Fund, New York
Collection of the artist, New York

OPPOSITE
Hidden Relief, 2001
Mixed media, dimensions variable
Asia Society, New York
Collection of Nancy and Stanley Singer

Living in Japan was a profound experience because it showed me how aesthetics and art, and the way that they can be integrated into life, could be entirely different in another culture. To see that shift in the way people look at beauty, the handmade and the machine-made, and value those things, makes you reconsider how your own culture does this as well. Most artists are addicted to looking as much as they are to making art. From a very young age, I was making art. I was always thought of as the artist in the house, the artist in whatever class I was in. It was only when I tried to stop making art, and had a profound sense of loss and disorientation, that I knew that looking at art had been such a sustenance for me and began to realize that looking and making are married so closely. That's when I really started to become an artist, knowing that I wouldn't be able *not* to. But I think my work became interesting when it began to relate more to thinking about experiences I had in the world that were completely unrelated to art.

If there is a misconception about my work it's that it's made out of trash. It's something that I'm actually very precise about. I never use trash. I want to give you something generic, so I do not want the materials to have a history. Another misconception is interesting because it's about language. If you look at the writing about my work, it almost always starts with a list. People want to know what *things* are in the work. So they want to name each thing and have a list: *da-ta-da-ta-da*. And it's funny, because that list gets reproduced so much that there'll be Q-tips listed for a piece, but there are no Q-tips in it. Your real experience of the work has nothing to do with those individual materials, so there's a strange gap in the way the work is described or written about. More interesting to me is that the experience of the work is much more abstract than that. It is much more about experience than it is about naming.

My work has a lot to do with formal qualities—color, light, edge, texture, weight, and gravity. All of these things are as essential as any particular object. Improvisation is crucial. I want the work to be an experience of something live and to have the viewer see decisions happening on site the way you see a sports event, or live jazz, and know that it's never going to happen again. That feeling of something happening in the moment is crucial. So a lot of the works give the feeling of going into a studio—and this allows for a sense of intimacy with the work in the way that a studio visit can be more interesting than a museum show.

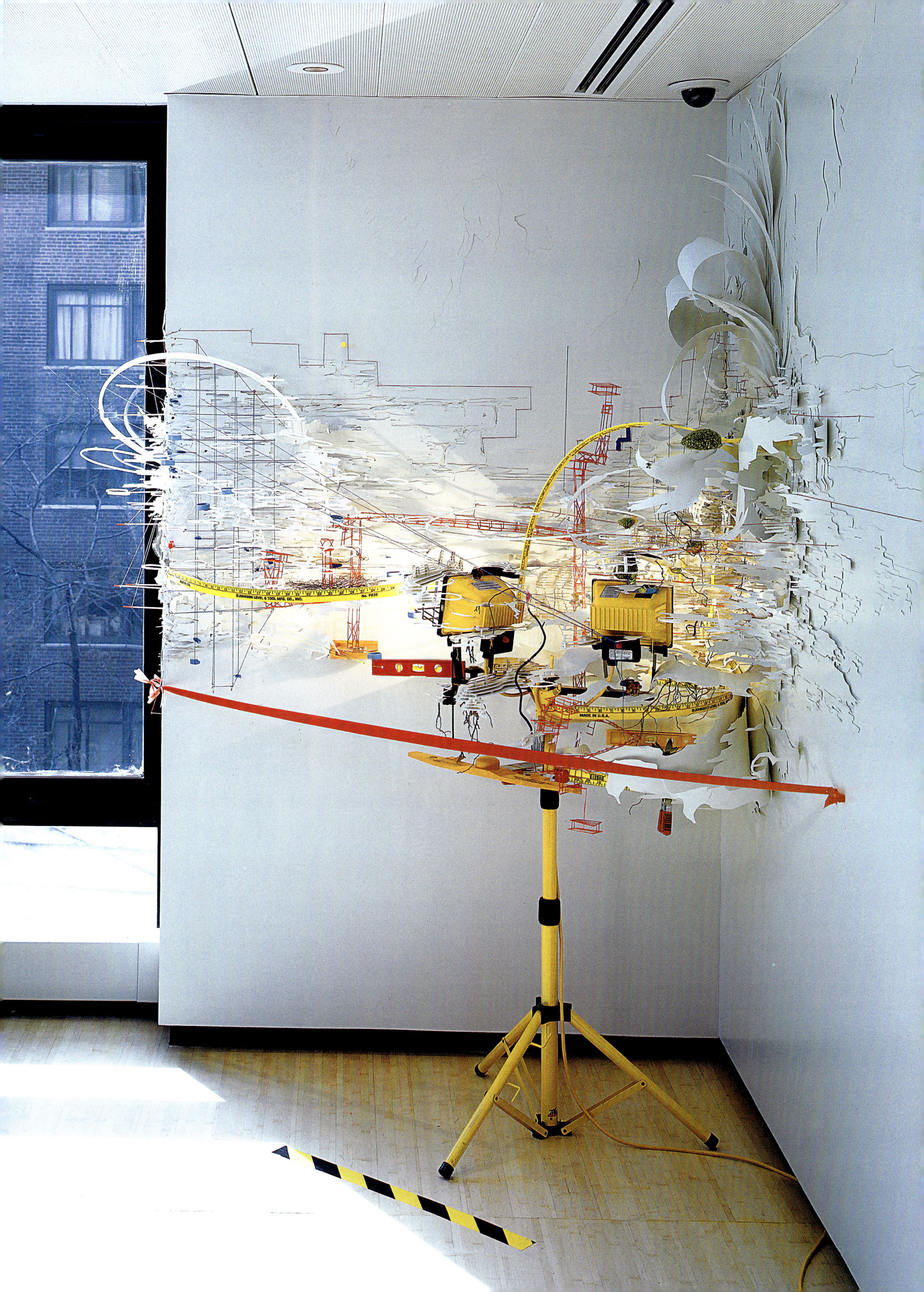
JOHNSON LEVEL & TOOL MFG. CO., INC.
No. P236
MADE IN U.S.A.

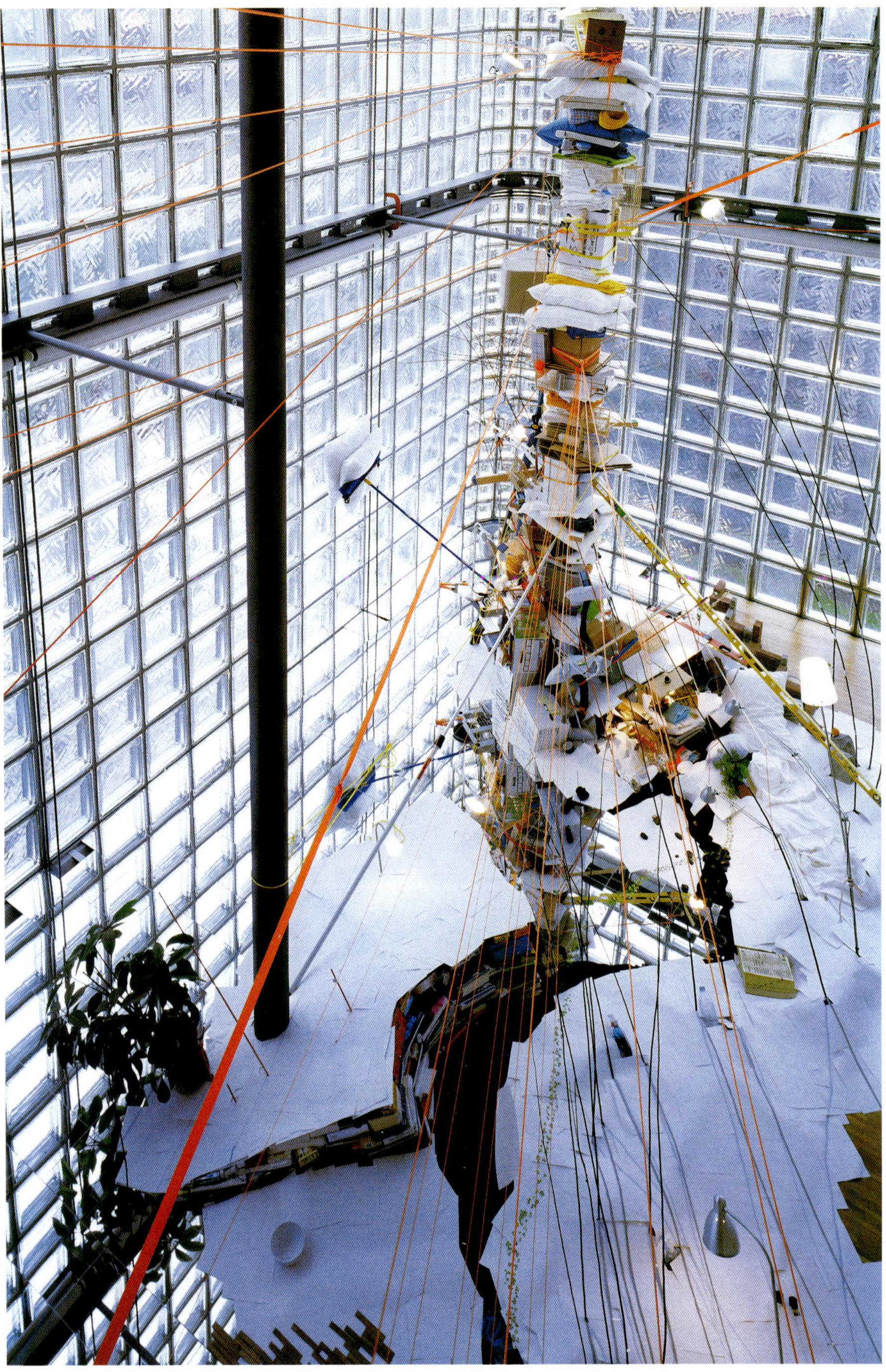

Untitled (Tokyo) (2008) is small-scale, but very large in length and very small in width. It's about the idea of using spaces that go unnoticed or unoccupied and about the viewer having a really strong experience of discovery in an unexpected place. A museum is completely designed around gallery spaces, so it's always a nice opportunity to put a piece in a corner or a hallway or near the ventilation equipment by the window. It feels like a remnant of something that happened. I think about how we see things, whether it's recognizing, triggering a memory, discovering, or investigating. I always want to create an experience of recognition and I think that comes to an idea about intimacy and the public. Almost always in my work there's a location that feels strangely intimate and you're surprised by a kind of intimacy in the experience of the work.

What's spontaneous is always most interesting for the artist and for the viewer. That's my own experience as an artist. You can spend a lot of time conceptualizing and thinking but it's in the making and the process where, after all that planning, something spontaneous occurs that you had no idea was going to happen. And when that happens, it's interesting.

Sarah Sze

ABOVE
Untitled (Tokyo), 2008
Mixed media, dimensions variable
Sarah Sze, Maison Hermès 8F Le Forum, Tokyo

OPPOSITE
The Art of Losing, 2004
Mixed media, dimensions variable
The Encounters in the 21st Century, 21st Century Museum of Contemporary Art, Kanazawa
Collection of 21st Century Museum of Contemporary Art, Kanazawa

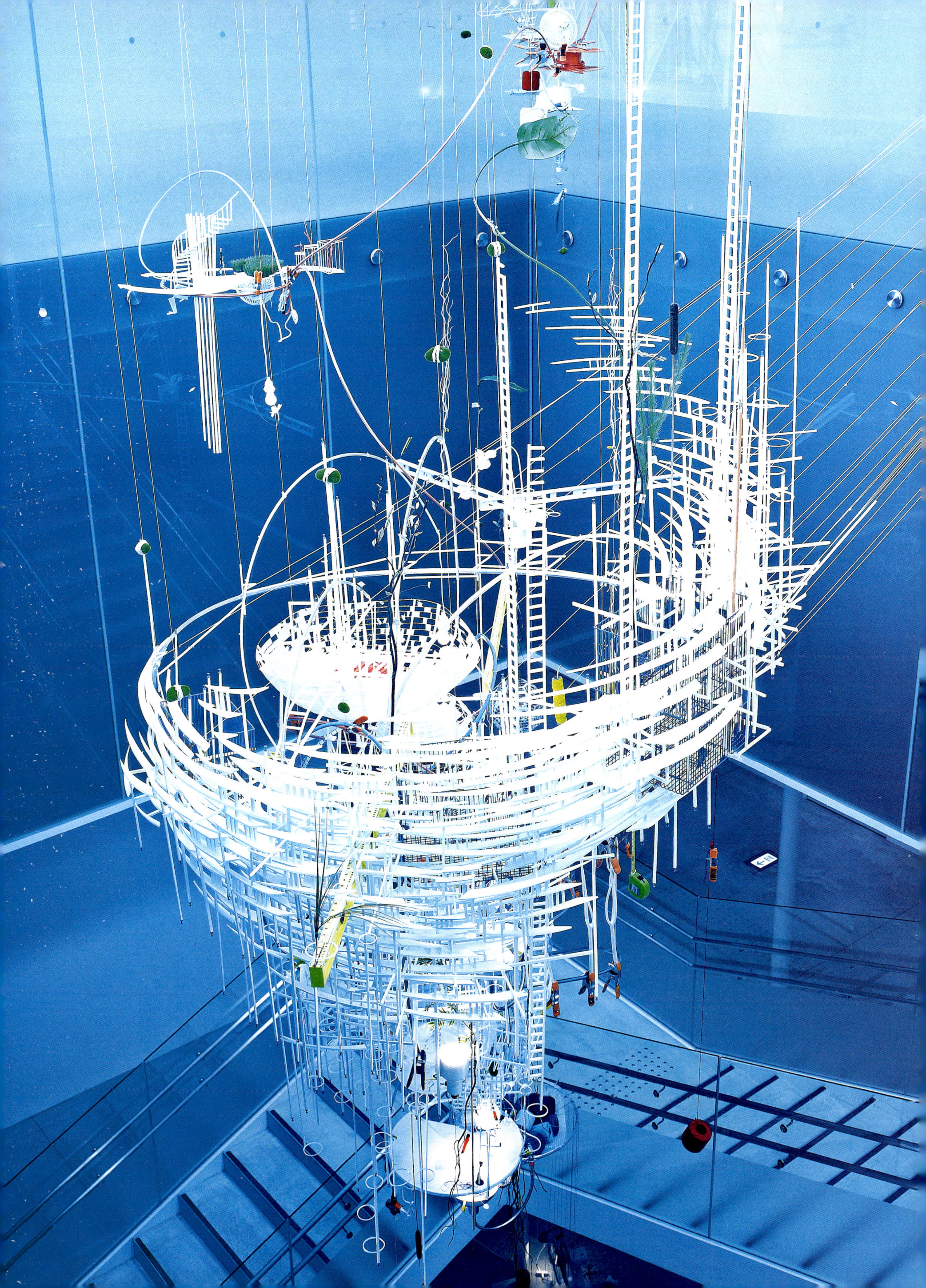

Biographies of the Artists

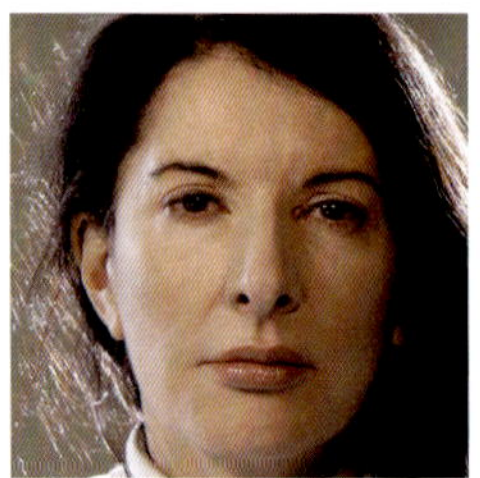

Marina Abramović

Marina Abramović was born in Belgrade, Yugoslavia in 1946. A pioneer of performance as a visual art form, Abramović has used her body as both subject and medium of her performances to test her physical, mental, and emotional limits—often pushing beyond them and even risking her life—in a quest for heightened consciousness, transcendence, and self-transformation. Characterized by endurance and pain—and by repetitive behavior, actions of long duration, and intense public interactions and energy dialogues—her work has engaged, fascinated, and sometimes repelled live audiences. The universal themes of life and death are recurring motifs, often enhanced by the use of symbolic visual elements or props such as crystals, bones, knives, tables, and pentagrams. While the sources of some works lie in her personal history (the circumstances of her childhood and family life under Communist rule in the former Yugoslavia), others lie in more recent and contemporary events, such as the wars in her homeland and other parts of the world. Marina Abramović attended the Academy of Fine Arts in Belgrade (1965–70) and the Academy of Fine Arts in Zagreb, Yugoslavia (1970–72). She received an honorary doctorate from the Art Institute of Chicago (2004). She has also received many other honors, including a Golden Lion at the 47th Venice Biennale (1997); a Bessie (2003); and awards from the International Association of Art Critics (2003, 2007). Abramović has had major exhibitions and performances at the Garage Art Center, Moscow (2011); Manchester International Festival (2011); Museum of Modern Art, New York (2010); Solomon R. Guggenheim Museum (2005); Whitney Biennial (2004); Hirshhorn Museum and Sculpture Garden (2001); Irish Museum of Modern Art (2001); Documenta (1977, 1982, 1992); and the Venice Biennale (1976, 1997, 2009). Marina Abramović lives and works in New York City.

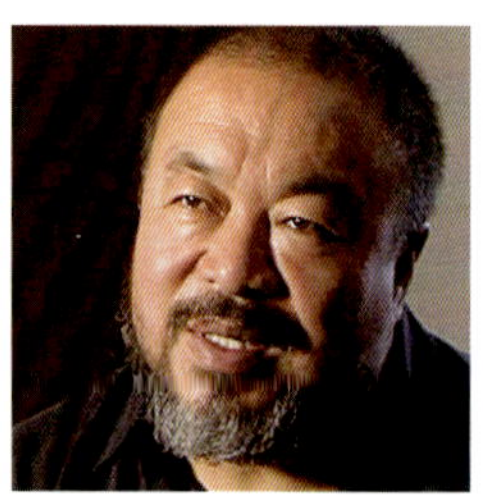

Ai Weiwei

Ai Weiwei was born in Beijing, China in 1957. An outspoken human rights activist, Ai was arrested by Chinese authorities in April 2011 and held incommunicado for three months. Upon his release, he was prohibited from traveling abroad, engaging in public speech, and was subjected to continued government surveillance. Ai's position as a provocateur and dissident artist informs the tenor and reception of much of his recent work. He infuses his sculptures, photographs, and public artworks with political conviction and personal poetry, often making use of recognizable and historic Chinese art forms in critical examinations of a host of contemporary Chinese political and social issues. In his sculptural works he often uses reclaimed materials—ancient pottery and wood from destroyed temples—in a conceptual gesture that connects tradition with contemporary social concerns. He also employs sarcasm, juxtaposition, and repetition to reinvigorate the potency and symbolism of traditional images and to reframe the familiar with minimal means. A writer and curator, Ai extends his practice across multiple disciplines and through social media to communicate with a global public and to engage fellow artists with projects on a massive scale. Ai Weiwei attended the Beijing Film Academy and the Parsons School of Design in New York. He has received an honorary doctorate from the Faculty of Politics and Social Science, University of Ghent, Belgium (2010), as well as many awards, including the Skowhegan Medal (2011) and the Chinese Contemporary Art Award (2008). His work has appeared in major exhibitions at Kunsthaus Bregenz (2011); the Victoria & Albert Museum, London (2011); Asia Society Museum, New York (2011); Tate Modern, London (2010); São Paulo Bienal (2010); Haus der Kunst, Munich (2009); Mori Art Museum, Tokyo (2009); and Documenta XII (2007). Ai Weiwei lives and works in Beijing, China.

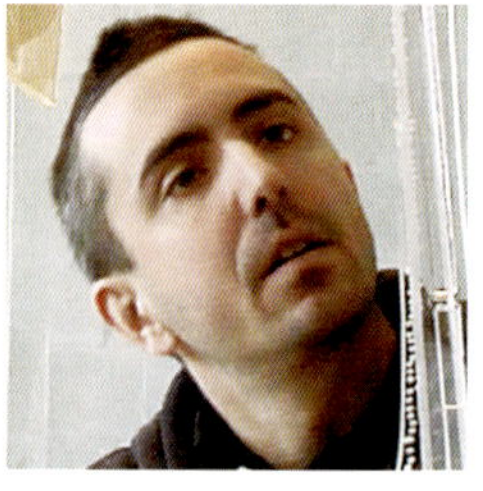

David Altmejd

David Altmejd was born in Montreal, Canada in 1974. With an almost childlike fascination for objects that grow, transform, and reshape themselves, Altmejd creates sculptures, suffused with ornament, that blur distinctions between interior and exterior, surface and structure, representation and abstraction. Meaning, for Altmejd, does not exist in advance of the work in process. His interest lies in the *making*—the building of an object that will generate meaning. Using armatures in the forms of giants and angels that convey both human and supernatural energies, he abandons standard narrative conventions in favor of an exploration of materials, processes, and structures. In diorama-like tableaux, Altmejd pairs objects laden with symbolism—crystals, gold chain, bondage gear, and taxidermy birds and animals—with virtuosic applications of materials such as plaster, glitter, thread, minerals, mirrors, and Plexiglas. In dazzling displays of 'active' sculpting—holes and passages *pushed* through forms to *drive* matter "somewhere else"—Altmejd's work expresses the intense flow of energy traveling through space and teeters between investigations of sexuality, decay, spirituality, death, and—always—life. David Altmejd received a BFA from the Université du Québec à Montréal (1998) and an MFA from Columbia University (2001). His work has appeared in major exhibitions at the Brant Foundation Art Study Center (2011); Vanhaerents Art Collection, Brussels (2010); National Gallery of Canada, Ottawa (2010); New Museum (2010); Solomon R. Guggenheim Museum (2010); P.S. 1 Contemporary Art Center (2009); Museum of Contemporary Art, Los Angeles (2009); Liverpool Biennial (2008); Fundació La Caixa Museum, Barcelona (2007); Venice Biennale (2007); and the Whitney Biennial (2004), among others. David Altmejd lives and works in New York City.

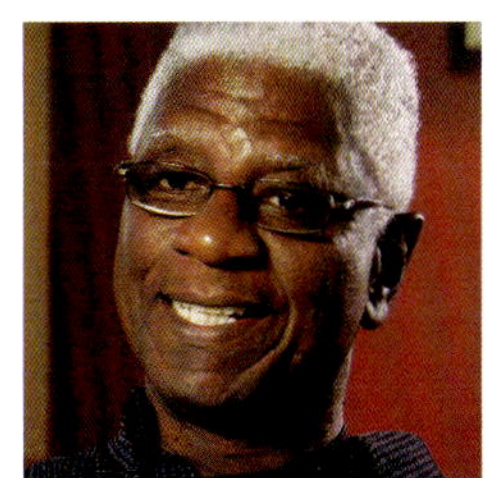

El Anatsui

El Anatsui was born in Anyanko, Ghana in 1944. Many of Anatsui's sculptures are mutable in form, conceived to be so free and flexible that they can be shaped in any way and altered in appearance for each installation. Working with wood, clay, metal, and—most recently—the discarded metal caps of liquor bottles, Anatsui breaks with sculpture's traditional adherence to forms of fixed shape while visually referencing the history of abstraction in African and European art. The colorful and densely patterned fields of the works assembled from discarded liquor-bottle caps also trace a broader story of colonial and post-colonial economic and cultural exchange in Africa, told in the history of cast-off materials. The sculptures in wood and ceramics introduce ideas about the function of objects (their destruction, transformation, and regeneration) in everyday life, and the role of language in deciphering visual symbols. El Anatsui received a BA from the College of Art, University of Science and Technology, Kumasi, Ghana (1969) and since 1975 has taught at the University of Nigeria, Nsukka. His works are in the public collections of the Metropolitan Museum of Art, New York; Museum of Modern Art, New York; Los Angeles County Museum of Art; Indianapolis Museum of Art; British Museum, London; and Centre Pompidou, Paris, among many others. Major exhibitions of his work have appeared at the Sterling and Francine Clark Art Institute, Williamstown (2011); Royal Ontario Museum, Toronto (2010); National Museum of Ethnology, Osaka (2010); Rice University Art Gallery, Houston (2010); Venice Biennale (2007); and the Biennale of African Art, Senegal (2006). El Anatsui lives and works in Nsukka, Nigeria.

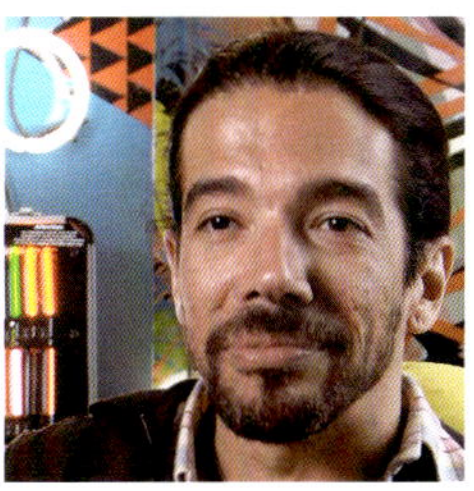

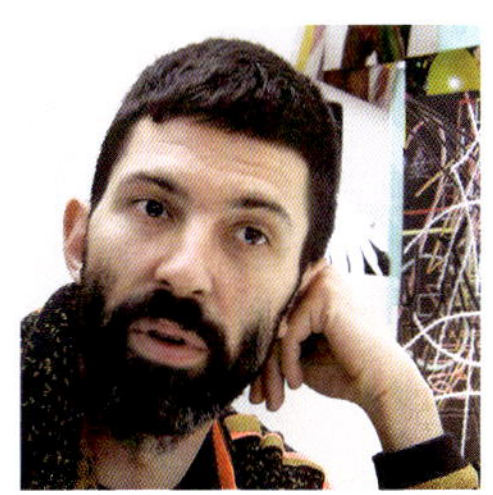

assume vivid astro focus

The collective assume vivid astro focus (avaf) was formed in New York City in 2001. Its principal members are Eli Sudbrack (born in Rio de Janeiro, Brazil in 1968) and Christophe Hamaide-Pierson (born in Paris, France in 1973). Avaf fuses drawing, sculpture, video, and performance into carnavalesque installations in which gender, politics, and cultural codes float freely. A study in visual adaptation and modification, avaf's work recycles and transforms imagery from one project to the next—often in the form of densely patterned wallpapers and graphic signage. Personal expression and a lust for life feature prominently in projects simultaneously rooted in the politics of free speech, civil rights, and the dissolution of rigid classifications of class, gender, and national identity. In frequent collaborations with musicians, designers, dancers, and other artists, avaf challenges conventional assumptions about authorship and the role of the artist's persona in contemporary society and the art world. Avaf has received awards from the Rema Hort Mann Foundation (2002) and the Public Art Fund (2007). Its work has appeared in major exhibitions at Centro De Arte Contemporaneo, Murcia (2010); the New Museum (2010); National Museum of Art, Architecture and Design, Oslo (2009); Yerba Buena Center for the Arts, San Francisco (2009); São Paulo Bienal (2008); ENEL Contemporanea, Rome (2008); Museum of Modern Art, New York (2008); Museo Reina Sofia, Madrid (2007); Museum of Contemporary Art (MOT), Tokyo (2007); Museum of Contemporary Art, Chicago (2007); Kunsthalle Wien Project Space, Vienna (2006); Museum of Contemporary Art, Los Angeles (2005); Indianapolis Museum of Art (2005); Tate Liverpool (2005); the Public Art Fund (2004); and the Whitney Biennial (2004). Eli Sudbrack lives and works in New York City and São Paulo; Christophe Hamaide-Pierson lives and works in Paris.

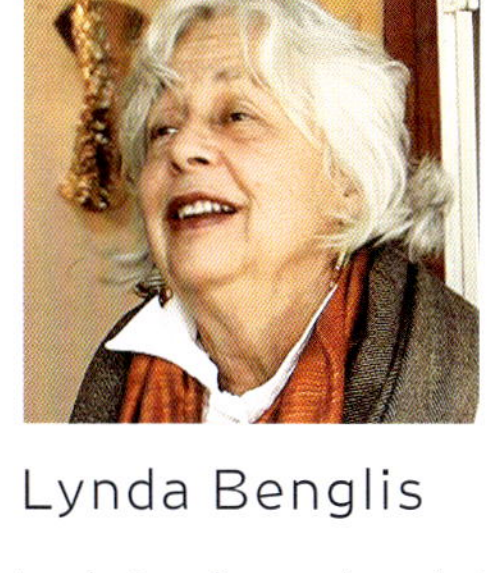

Lynda Benglis

Lynda Benglis was born in Lake Charles, Louisiana in 1941. A pioneer of a form of abstraction in which each work is the result of materials in action—poured latex and foam, cinched metal, dripped wax—Benglis has created sculptures that eschew minimalist reserve in favor of bold colors, sensual lines, and lyrical references to the human body. But her invention of new forms with unorthodox techniques also displays a reverence for cultural references that trace back to antiquity. Often working in series of knots, fans, lumps, and fountains, Benglis chooses unexpected materials, such as glitter, gold leaf, lead, and polyurethane. In more recent works, she explores diverse cultural heritages (Indian architecture, Greek statuary, Chinese ceramics), translating ancient techniques and symbols for use in contemporary contexts. In her early adoption of video, Benglis introduced feminist, biographical, and burlesque content to structuralist narratives. Lynda Benglis received a BFA from Newcomb College (1964) and an honorary doctorate from the Kansas City Art Institute (2000). She has received many awards, including a Guggenheim Fellowship (1975) and grants from the National Endowment for the Arts (1979, 1990). Her works are in the public collections of the Albright-Knox Art Gallery; Dallas Museum of Art; Los Angeles County Museum of Art; Solomon R. Guggenheim Museum; Museum of Contemporary Art, Los Angeles; Museum of Modern Art, New York; National Gallery of Art, Washington, DC; Philadelphia Museum of Art; San Francisco Museum of Modern Art; Tate Modern; Walker Art Center; and the Whitney Museum of American Art, among many others. Lynda Benglis lives, works, and travels between New York City; Santa Fe; Kastelorizo, Greece; and Ahmedabad, India.

Rackstraw Downes

Rackstraw Downes was born in Kent, England in 1939. Often described as a realist painter, Downes prefers not to use that term. He views the act of seeing and the art of representation as culturally taught, with different cultures accepting different delineations of the world as realistic. He does not think of himself as a landscape painter, but as a painter of his surroundings—his environment. Often painted in a panoramic format, Downes's images evince careful attention to details as well as to broad expanses of their surroundings. Created *plein air* in locations as diverse as metropolitan New York, rural Maine, and coastal and inland Texas, and without resorting to the use of photography, his compositions feature horizons that bend according to the way the eye naturally perceives. Downes often works in series, examining single scenes from multiple angles, over time, and in the process reveals changing qualities of light and shadow as well as changes in his own point of view. Rackstraw Downes earned a BA from Cambridge University (1961) and a BFA and MFA from Yale University (1964). He has received numerous awards, including a John D. and Catherine T. MacArthur Foundation Fellowship (2009); John Simon Guggenheim Memorial Fellowship (1988); and National Endowment for the Arts Grant (1980). He was inducted into the American Academy and Institute of Arts and Letters (1999). His works are in the public collections of the Metropolitan Museum of Art; Museum of Modern Art, New York; Whitney Museum of American Art; National Gallery of Art, Washington, DC; Museum of Fine Arts, Boston; Museum of Fine Arts, Houston; and the Art Institute of Chicago, among many others. Rackstraw Downes lives in New York City and Presidio, Texas.

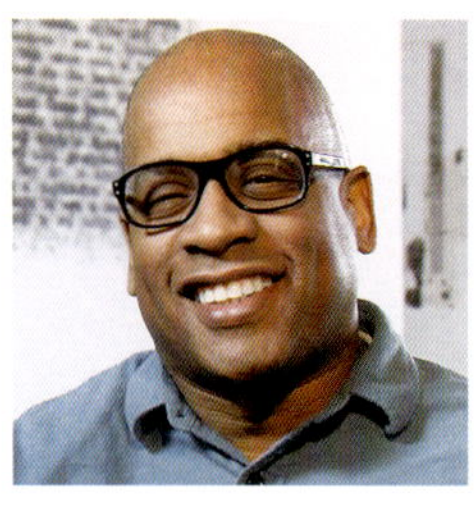

Glenn Ligon

Glenn Ligon was born in the Bronx, New York, in 1960. Ligon's paintings and sculptures examine cultural and social identity through found sources—literature, Afrocentric coloring books, photographs—to reveal the ways in which the history of slavery, the civil rights movement, and sexual politics inform our understanding of American society. Ligon appropriates texts from a variety of literary writers including Walt Whitman, Zora Neal Hurston, Gertrude Stein, James Baldwin, and Ralph Ellison, as well from more popular sources such as the comedian Richard Pryor. In Ligon's paintings, the instability of his medium—oil crayon used with letter stencils—transforms the texts he quotes, making them abstract, difficult to read, and layered in meaning, much like the subject matter that he appropriates. In other works that feature silkscreen, neon, and photography, Ligon threads his own image and autobiography into symbols that speak to collective experiences. "It's not about me," he says. "It's about *we*." Glenn Ligon received a BA from Wesleyan University (1982) and attended the Whitney Museum Independent Study Program (1985). He has received numerous awards, including the United States Artists Fellowship (2010); Joyce Alexander Wein Artist Prize from the Studio Museum in Harlem (2009); Skowhegan Medal for Painting (2006); John Simon Guggenheim Memorial Foundation Fellowship (2003); Joan Mitchell Foundation Grant (1998); and Visual Artist Fellowships from the National Endowment for the Arts (1989, 1991). His works are in the public collections of the Los Angeles County Museum of Art; Museum of Contemporary Art, Chicago; Museum of Modern Art, New York; Philadelphia Museum of Art; San Francisco Museum of Modern Art; Solomon R. Guggenheim Museum, Tate Modern; Walker Art Center; and the Whitney Museum of American Art, New York, among others. Glenn Ligon lives and works in New York City.

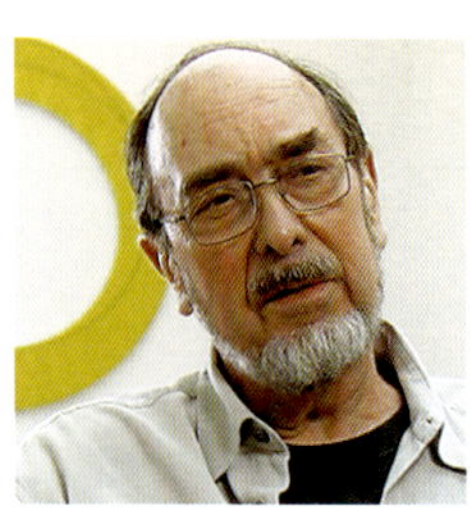

Robert Mangold

Robert Mangold was born in North Tonawanda, New York in 1937. With classical restraint, Mangold translates the most basic of formal elements—shape, line, and color—into paintings, prints, and drawings whose simplicity of form expresses complex ideas. He renders the surface of each canvas with subtle color modulations and sinewy, hand-drawn graphite lines. While his focus on formal considerations may seem paramount, he also delights in thwarting those considerations—setting up problems for the viewer. Over the course of years and in multiple series of shaped canvases that explore variations on rings, columns, trapezoids, arches, and crosses, he has also provoked viewers to consider the idea of paintings without centers. In addition to works on paper, and canvases whose physicality relates to the scale of the human body, Mangold has also worked in stained glass for architectural projects. Robert Mangold received a BFA and MFA from Yale University (1963). He has been inducted into the National Academy (2005) and American Academy of Arts and Letters (2001), and has received many awards including the Jawlensky-Preis der Stadt Wiesbaden Award (1998); the Skowhegan Medal for Painting (1993); and a National Endowment for the Arts Grant (1967). His work has appeared in major exhibitions at Documenta (1972, 1977, 1982); the Whitney Biennial (1979, 1983, 1985, 2004); and the Venice Biennale (1993). His works are in the public collections of the Art Institute of Chicago; J. Paul Getty Trust; Solomon R. Guggenheim Museum; Hirshhorn Museum and Sculpture Garden; Museum of Contemporary Art, Los Angeles; Museum of Modern Art, New York; National Gallery of Art, Washington, D.C.; and Whitney Museum of American Art, among many others. Robert Mangold lives and works in Washingtonville, New York.

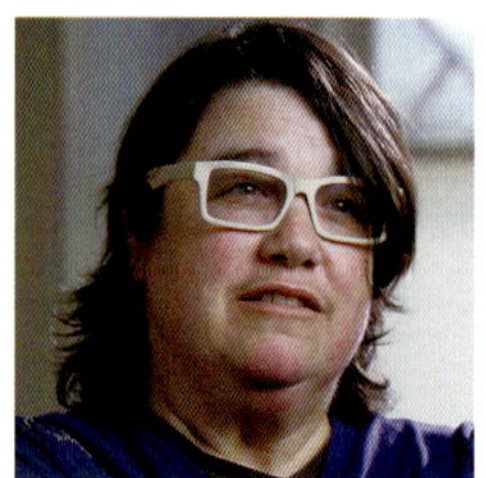

Catherine Opie

Catherine Opie was born in Sandusky, Ohio in 1961. Opie investigates the ways in which photographs both document and give voice to social phenomena in America today, registering people's attitudes and relationships to themselves and others, and the ways in which they occupy the landscape. At the core of her investigations are perplexing questions about relationships to community, which she explores on multiple levels across all her bodies of work. Working between conceptual and documentary approaches to image making, Opie examines familiar genres—portraiture, landscape, and studio photography—in surprising uses of serial images, unexpected compositions, and the pursuit of radically different subject matters in parallel. Many of her works capture the expression of individual identity through groups (couples, teams, crowds) and reveal an undercurrent of her own biography vis-à-vis her subjects. Whether documenting political movements, queer subcultures, or urban transformation, Opie's images of contemporary life comprise a portrait of our time in America, which she often considers in relation to a discourse of opposition. Her work resonates with formal ideas that convey the importance of "the way things should look," evidence of the influence of her early exposure to the history of art and painting. Catherine Opie received a BFA from the San Francisco Art Institute (1985), an MFA from CalArts (1988), and since 2001 has taught at the University of California, Los Angeles. She has received many awards, including the President's Award for Lifetime Achievement from the Women's Caucus for Art (2009); United States Artists Fellowship (2006); Larry Aldrich Award (2004); and the CalArts Alpert Award in the Arts (2003). Her work has appeared in major exhibitions at the Institute of Contemporary Art, Boston (2011); Los Angeles County Museum of Art (2010); Guggenheim Museum, New York (2008); MCA Chicago (2006); and the Walker Art Center, Minneapolis (2002). Catherine Opie lives and works in Los Angeles, California.

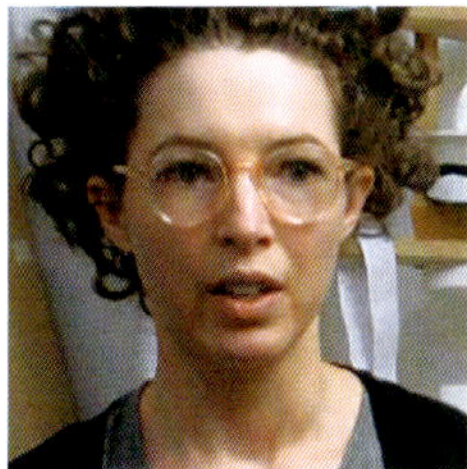

Mary Reid Kelley

Mary Reid Kelley was born in Greenville, South Carolina in 1979. In videos and drawings filled with punning wordplay, Reid Kelley presents her take on the clash between utopian ideologies and the realities of women's lives in the struggle for liberation and through political strife, wars, and other historical events. Performing scripted narratives in rhyming verse, the artist—with her husband Patrick Kelley and various family members—explores historical periods through fictitious characters such as nurses, soldiers, prostitutes, and *saltimbanques.* Adopting a stark black-and-white palette while synthesizing art-historical styles such as Cubism and German Expressionism, Reid Kelley playfully jumbles historical periods such as World War I and France's Second Empire to trace the ways in which present concerns are rooted in the past. Mary Reid Kelley earned a BA from St. Olaf College (2001) and an MFA from Yale University (2009). She has received awards from the American Academy in Rome (2011); the Rema Hort Mann Foundation (2009); and the College Art Association (2008). Major exhibitions include Salt Lake Art Center (2011); SITE Santa Fe (2010); Institute of Contemporary Art, Philadelphia (2010); ZKM Museum of Contemporary Art, Karlsruhe, Germany (2010); and the Rochester Art Center (2007). Her work is in the public collections of the Goetz Collection, Munich; Yale University Art Gallery; and the University of Michigan Museum of Art, Ann Arbor. Mary Reid Kelley lives and works in Saratoga Springs, New York.

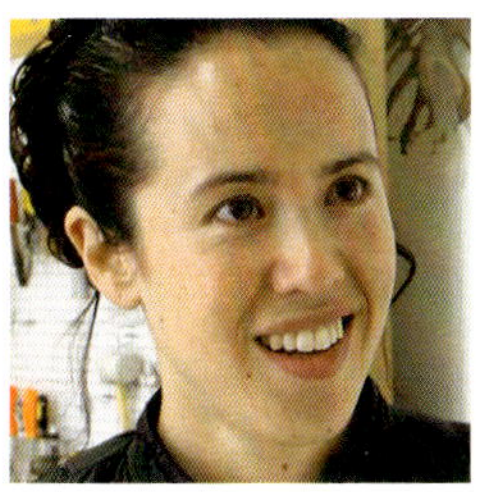

Sarah Sze

Sarah Sze was born in Boston, Massachusetts in 1969. Sze builds her installations and intricate sculptures from the minutiae of everyday life, imbuing mundane materials, marks, and processes with surprising significance. Combining domestic detritus and office supplies into fantastical miniatures, she builds her works, fractal-like, on an architectural scale. Often incorporating electric lights and fans, water systems, and houseplants, Sze's installations balance whimsy with ecological themes of interconnectivity and sustainability. Whether adapting to a venue or altering the urban fabric, Sze's patchwork compositions seem to mirror the improvisational quality of cities, labor, and everyday life. On the edge between life and art, her work is alive with a mutable quality—as if anything could happen, or not. Sarah Sze received a BA from Yale University (1991) and an MFA from the School of Visual Arts (1997). She has received many awards, including a Radcliffe Institute Fellowship (2005); John D. and Catherine T. MacArthur Foundation Fellowship (2003); Louis Comfort Tiffany Award (1999); and the Rema Hort Mann Foundation Award (1997). Major exhibitions of her work have appeared at the Asia Society Museum, New York (2011); 10th Biennale de Lyon (2010); BALTIC Centre for Contemporary Art (2009); Malmö Konsthall (2006); Whitney Museum of Amerian Art (2003); Walker Art Center (2002); São Paulo Bienal (2002); Museum of Contemporary Art, Chicago (1999), and Fondation Cartier pour l'art contemporain, Paris (1999), the Carnegie International (1999), and the 48th Venice Biennale (1999). Sarah Sze lives and works in New York City.

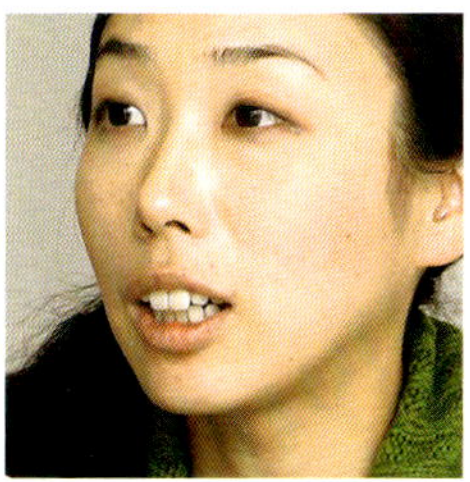

Tabaimo

Tabaimo was born in Hyogo, Japan in 1975. Tabaimo's drawings and video installations probe the unsettling themes of isolation, contagion, and instability that seem to lurk beneath daily existence in contemporary Japan. She draws aesthetic inspiration for her animated videos from a combination of Japanese art forms—ukiyo-e woodcuts, manga, and anime—while she often sets her layered, surrealistic narratives in domestic interiors and communal spaces such as public restrooms, commuter trains, and bathhouses. Tabaimo populates her work with uncanny characters that, either through mutation or as victims of inexplicable violence, become fragmented in their relationships to the environment and their own identity. Installed in theatrical, stage-like settings, her work is attuned to the architecture and the viewers within it. Tabaimo graduated from Kyoto University of Art and Design (1999). Her work has appeared in major exhibitions at the Venice Biennale (2011, 2007); Parasol unit foundation for contemporary art, London (2010, 2007); Yokohama Museum of Art, Tokyo (2010); National Museum of Art, Osaka (2010); Philadelphia Museum of Art (2010); Moderna Museet, Stockholm (2009); Museum of Contemporary Art, Los Angeles (2007); Fondation Cartier pour l'art contemporain, Paris (2006); Hara Museum of Contemporary Art, Tokyo (2006, 2003); Israel Museum, Jerusalem (2005); National Gallery of Victoria, Melbourne (2004); Walker Art Center, Minneapolis (2003); and the São Paulo Bienal (2002). Tabaimo lives and works in Nagano, Japan.

List of Illustrations

Marina Abramović

Marina Abramović and Ulay

Ai Weiwei

David Altmejd

El Anatsui

assume vivid astro focus

Lynda Benglis

Rackstraw Downes

Glenn Ligon

Robert Mangold

Catherine Opie

Mary Reid Kelley

Sarah Sze

Tabaimo

Photographic Credits and Copyrights

CHANGE: pp. 16–27 © Ai Weiwei; p. 16, courtesy Three Shadows Photography Art Centre and Chambers Fine Art; pp. 17–19, 23, courtesy the artist; pp. 20–21, courtesy Haus der Kunst; p. 22, courtesy Tate Modern; pp. 24–25, courtesy Mary Boone Gallery, New York; pp. 26–27, courtesy AW Asia; pp. 28–35, 38–41 © El Anatsui, courtesy the artist and Jack Shainman Gallery, New York; p. 30 (top), photo by Kelechi Amadi-Obi; p. 30 (bottom), photo by Andy Keate; pp. 31–32, photos by Jerry L. Thompson; p. 33, photo by Noel Brown; pp. 36–37, photos by Nash Baker, © Nash Baker; p. 39, photo by Martin Barlow; pp. 42–55, © Catherine Opie, courtesy Regen Projects, Los Angeles.

BOUNDARIES: pp. 58–71, © David Altmejd; pp. 58–59, 61, 64–70, courtesy Andrea Rosen Gallery, New York; pp. 58, 61, 65, photos by Jessica Eckert; p. 59, photo by Jason Mandella; p. 60, photo by Bertrand Huet, courtesy D'Amelio Terras, New York, and Andrea Rosen Gallery, New York; pp. 62–63, photos by David Jacques, courtesy Galerie de l'UQAM, Montreal; p. 64, photo by Denis Farley; pp. 66–67, photo by Tom Powel; pp. 67 (right)–69, photos by Ellen Page Wilson; p. 70, photos by Wayne Baerwaldt and M.N. Hutchinson; p. 71, photo by Joost Vanhaerents, courtesy Vanhaerents Art Collection, Brussels; pp. 72–85 , © assume vivid astro focus; p. 72, photo by Hans-Georg Gaul, courtesy Peres Projects, Los Angeles/Berlin; p. 73, courtesy the artists; pp. 74–75, photos by Joanne Kim, courtesy John Connelly Presents, New York; p. 76, photo by Mauro Restiffe, courtesy Whitney Museum of American Art, New York, and Peres Projects, Los Angeles/Berlin; p. 77 (top), photos by CM Guerrero and assume vivid astro focus, courtesy Rosa de la Cruz; p. 77 (bottom), photos by Yves Malenfer, courtesy Dalbin, Paris and Galerie Hussenot, Paris; pp. 78–79, photo by Josh White, courtesy MoCA, Los Angeles, and Peres Projects, Los Angeles/Berlin; p. 80, photos by Andreas Harvik, courtesy National Museum of Art, Architecture and Design, Oslo; p. 81 (top), courtesy the artists; p. 81 (bottom), photos by Eric Weiss, courtesy Public Art Fund; pp. 82–83 (top), photos by Edouard Fraipont, courtesy Fundação Bienal de São Paulo; p. 83 (bottom), photos by Edouard Fraipont, courtesy Casa Triângulo; p. 84, photo by Vassilis Polychronakis, courtesy Athens Biennale, Athens, and Peres Projects, Los Angeles/Berlin; p. 85, photos by Tom Powel Imaging, courtesy Deitch Projects, New York; pp. 86–99, © Lynda Benglis / Licensed by VAGA, New York, courtesy Cheim & Read, New York; pp. 100–113, © Tabaimo; pp. 100–107, 109–113, courtesy Gallery Koyanagi, Tokyo and James Cohan Gallery, New York; p. 100 photo by Stephen White; p. 103 (right), photo by Patrick Gries; pp. 104–106 (top), 113 (bottom), photos by Hirotaka Yonekura; p. 108, photos by Singapore Tyler Print Institute, courtesy Singapore Tyler Print Institute, Gallery Koyanagi, Tokyo and James Cohan Gallery, New York; p. 109, 112–113 (top), photos by Yasushi Kishimoto; p. 110, photos by Ufer! Art Documentary.

HISTORY: pp. 116–129, © Marina Abramović; pp. 116–119, 127–129, courtesy the Marina Abramović Archives; pp. 120–126, courtesy the Marina Abramović Archives and Sean Kelly Gallery, New York; p. 120, photos by Kathryn Carr; pp. 121–122 (top), photos by Attillio Maranzano; pp. 128–129, photos by Marco Anelli (for the Museum of Modern Art, New York); pp. 130–131, 133–143, © Glenn Ligon, courtesy Regen Projects, Los Angeles; pp. 130, 133 (right)–136, 137 (right), photos by Dennis Cowley; pp. 131, 138–139, photos by Ronald Amstutz; p. 132, © MoMA licensed by SCALA / Art Resource, NY, © Glenn Ligon, courtesy Regen Projects, Los Angeles; p. 137 (left), photo by Joshua White; p. 139 (top), photo by Adam Reich; p. 139 (bottom), photo by Dan Dennehy; p. 142, photos by Fredrik Nilsen; pp. 144–157, © Mary Reid Kelley; pp. 144–145, 147, courtesy the artist; pp. 146, 150–153, 155, courtesy the artist and Fredericks & Freiser, New York; pp. 148–149, 154, 156–157, courtesy the artist and Pilar Corrias, London.

BALANCE: pp. 160–173, © Rackstraw Downes, courtesy Betty Cuningham Gallery; p. 161 (top), photo by Ani Rivera; pp. 161 (bottom), 166, 173, photos by Christopher Burke; pp. 162, 167, 170–171, photos by Nicholas Walster; pp. 163–165 (top), photos by Zindman/Fremont; p. 165 (bottom), photo by Affordable Photo; pp. 168, 172, photos by Philip Ennik/Betty Cuningham Gallery; p. 169, photo by Benjamin Dimmitt; pp. 174–187, © 2012 Robert Mangold, member Artist Rights Society (ARS), New York, courtesy The Pace Gallery, New York; pp. 174–176, 185, photos by Ellen Page Wilson; p. 177, photo by Bill Jacobson; p. 178 (top), photo by Joerg Lohse; pp. 178 (bottom), 181 (top–bottom left), 187, photos by G. R. Christmas; pp. 180, 181 (bottom right), 186, photos by Kerry Ryan McFate; pp. 182–183, photo by Ellen Labenski; pp. 188–201, © Sarah Sze, courtesy the artist and Tanya Bonakdar Gallery, New York; pp. 189, 195–197, 199, 201, photos by Frank Oudeman; pp. 190–192, 198, photos by Tom Powel; p. 193, photo by Adatabase; p. 200, photo by Keizo Kioku.

PRODUCTION STILLS: pp. 12–13, 56–57, 114–115, 158–159, © Art21, Inc.

ENDPAPERS: Glenn Ligon. *Stranger #41*, detail, 2007–09. Oil stick, gesso, and graphite on canvas, 96 x 72 inches. Collection of the artist. Photo by Ronald Amstutz, © Glenn Ligon, courtesy Regen Projects, Los Angeles.

TITLE PAGE: El Anatsui. *Bleeding Takari*, detail, 2008. Aluminum and copper wire, 61 x 89½ inches. Collection of the Museum of Modern Art, New York, Gift of Donald L. Bryant, Jr. and Jerry Speyer, 201.2008.

TABLE OF CONTENTS: Sarah Sze. *Hidden Relief*, 2001. Mixed media, dimensions variable. *Hidden Relief*, Asia Society, New York. Collection of Nancy and Stanley Singer. Photo by Frank Oudeman, © Sarah Sze, courtesy the artist and Tanya Bonakdar Gallery, New York.

Editor: Marybeth Sollins
Associate Curator: Wesley Miller
Designer: Russell Hassell

Printed in the United States by The Studley Press, Dalton, Massachusetts

Library of Congress Control Number: 2011940000
ISBN: 978-0-615-54566-0

art21

Art21, Inc.
286 Spring Street
New York, NY 10013
www.art21.org